Landschaftsverband Rheinland

Guides and papers of the
Rheinisches Freilichtmuseum and the
Landesmuseum für Volkskunde
at Kommern
No. 61

Brave New World

Rhinelanders Conquer America

The Journal of Johannes Herbergs

Edited by
Dieter Pesch

Martina Galunder-Verlag

Martina
Galunder
Verlag

©: Landschaftsverband Rheinland
Rheinisches Freilichtmuseum and
Landesmuseum für Volkskunde in Kommern, 2001
Published by: Martina Galunder-Verlag
Translated by: Angelika and David Orpin
Typesetting and Layout: Dieter Pesch, RFM
Printed by: Martina Galunder-Verlag

Printed in Germany
ISBN 3-931251-92-6

The exhibition is
under the patronage of the
Premier of the
State of North-Rhine-Westphalia

Wolfgang Clement

This project was generously supported by

 Kulturstiftung der Länder, Berlin

 Nordrhein-Westfalen-Stiftung Naturschutz, Heimat-/Kulturpflege

Förderverein Rheinisches Freilichtmuseum Kommern e.V.

 WestLB

 Arbeitsamt Euskirchen

 Infokom, LVR

Stadt Mechernich

 Kreis Euskirchen

Firma Naue Sealing, Kempen

Forstamt Essen

Table of Contents

Organizers of the Project
"Brave New World –
Rhinelanders Conquer America"

Project Manager
Dieter Pesch

Research – Exhibition Concept
Peter Mesenhöller
Kornelia Panek
Dieter Pesch
Markus Schmitz
Sabine Thomas-Ziegler

Administration
Toni Berger
Silke Brohm
ClaudiaNickel
Andrea Retterath
Inge Ruschin

Construction Manager
Norbert Dresken

Construction Team
Reiner Blindert
Werner Engel
Alexander Gramlich
Reiner Hilger
Karl-Heinz Hucklenbroich
Achim Kauschke
Markus Klein
Stefan Knebel
Andrea Kruth
Edgar Lauterbach
Daniel Linden
Gerd Linden
Herbert Linden
Jörg Linden
Stefan Meurer
Ester Müller
Jürgen Pick
Guido Schmitz
Heinz-Josef Schmitz
Helmut Schmitz
Mathias Windgassen
Hendrik van Atteveld
Antonia Zimmermann
Johannes Zingsheim

Restoration
Johannes Lückenbach
Peter Weiß
Oliver Zahn

Electrical Engineering
Andreas Bellgardt
Bodo Schlinke

Video Production, Photography, Graphics
Klaus Dittert
Michael Faber

Press and Public Relations, Marketing
Inken Bößert
Martina Krause
Bernhard Meier

EDV – Internet Café
Claus Cepok
Rolf Aust
Jürgen Bachem
Rene Coellen
Gerhard Düren
Elisabeth Felser
Hans-Georg Göhring
Christian Hermann
Peter Hönow
Michael Kemper
Manuela Ketterer
Heike Krause
Markus Müller
Ute Pantenburg
Maike Reutter
Rolf Robens
Ralph Rybak
Jörg Salvador
Erich Schmickler
Hubert Schöler
Frank Transfeld
Ulrich Trapp

Secretariat
Lisa Jenniges
Bernadette Müller

Driver
Alfons Kesternich

Cleaners
Katharina Runde
Irene Fähnrich

Preface

Arise! Ronsdorf, arise!
Since today, as the day the Lord hath made thee,
The sky is smiling so brightly upon thee,
So take thy drum and beat it strongly.
Arise! Ronsdorf, arise!

Petrus Wülffing, Ronsdorffs Music=Schul,
Mülheim on the Rhine, vol. 2, 1763. p. 221.

The energy-filled spirit of optimism that character-
izes the hymn written by the preacher Peter Wülffing seems to have inspired the newcomer to Ronsdorf, Johannes Herbergs, when he decided to sail
to Philadelphia together with his cousin Peter Heinrich Strepers to secure the family's overseas estate.

A similar spirit of optimism was probably felt by
the thirteen families on their departure from Krefeld in 1683 when, following William Penn's advertisement, they went to establish the first German settlement on the North American continent:
Germantown.

The members of the thirteen families from the
Lower Rhine were pioneers who were to explore
the possibilities and conditions for living in an unknown country. They prepared the way for relatives, friends and fellow countrymen who were
impatiently waiting for positive news. From 1684
on, emigration from the Lower Rhine continued,
as becomes apparent from the manifold writings
of Franz Daniel Pastorius, the first "Burgomaster"
of Germantown.

Although emigrants from the Rhineland played an
important part in the settlement of North America,
the publications by historians of the Rhineland
rarely deal with the topic. Except for local studies
on Krefeld and some town monographs that only
cursorily touch on the subject of emigration, the
"Forschungsstelle Rheinländer in aller Welt", led
by Joseph Scheben, was the first to embark on

systematic research into emigration from the Rhineland in the late 1930s and early 1940s and also
made contact with American researchers.

Frequently and unjustly, Scheben has been called
an academic accomplice of the Nazis. The latter
certainly intended to use the contacts to Germans
abroad as a means of propaganda for their own
ends. However, unlike many other representatives
of the humanities at the time, Scheben did not allow
himself to be used for the Nazis' propaganda. His
1939 publication "Untersuchungen zur Methode
und Technik der deutschamerikanischen Wande-
rungsforschung" ("Studies on methods and tech-
niques for research in German-American migration") bears witness to the first transatlantic scientific study, which is a source of inspiration for an assessment of emigration from the Rhineland in the
nineteenth century. Scheben was employed by the
Rhine Province. When the Landschaftsverband
Rheinland was established in 1953 as its successor, Scheben's research unit was not revived.

For five years now, staff at the Rheinisches Freilichtmuseum have been engaged in an ambitious
project: the documentation of emigration from the
Rhineland to North America. Although the initial
plan had been for a publication and an exhibition
spanning the entire period of emigration – from its
beginnings until the present day – in view of the
wealth of material found both in the Rhineland and
in the United States it soon became obvious that a
treatment of the topic, especially from an interdisci-
plinary perspective involving historians, ethno-
graphers, scholars in American, linguistic, religious
and legal studies, could only be realized in stages.

As a first step, through cooperation between German and American researchers the period of early
emigration from the Rhineland could be documented with the study of a family from the Lower Rhine.
It spans the period from the establishment of the

Province of Pennsylvania to the Declaration of Independence of the United States of America.

This period is certainly the most important both for the Rhineland and for the building of the Province of Pennsylvania. For the contacts of the first pioneers who were instrumental in preparing the ground for other emigrants reached far beyond the Rhineland. Mostly, information followed religious ties. Without the mediation by Mennonite families who had emigrated from the Mönchengladbach and Krefeld areas in 1683, the huge influx of their brethren in faith from Switzerland, Alsace and the area of the former Palatinate from the early 1700s on would certainly not have set in to such a degree.

For the region of modern-day North Rhine, however, the early emigration period is not one of mass emigration. That only followed in the nineteenth century when a large number of guides to emigration were published on the Lower Rhine and in the Berg country to draw attention to the pitfalls of the voyage and the confidence tricks played on newcomers in America – mostly by fellow Germans. Emigration societies were founded in which potential emigrants made contact with trustworthy individuals who generally had been to the United States themselves already. Mass emigration from the Rhineland to America began in the 1820s and 1830s and gradually waned again toward 1900 when the slogan "from rags to riches" lost credibility.

During the preparations for the exhibition, the project received a great deal of information from private individuals on family members who had emigrated. Numerous letters dating from the nineteenth century were sent in where, in most cases, only a few years after their departure emigrants could tell their relatives at home how they had made good in America. Often they enclosed an Eagle, the most valuable American gold coin at the time, to prove their new wealth.

My sincere thanks go to the political representatives and the senior officials of the Landschaftsverband for enabling the unit in Kommern to document the emigration from the Rhineland. When the idea was born, it was impossible to foresee the immense wealth of material we would find in state archives, but even more in individual families. The contacts to historical societies throughout the Rhineland which – mostly out of local interest – were involved in research on emigration from the Rhineland showed that the Rhineland, unlike other regions in Germany which have been active in migration research for many years, has some catching up to do. In view of the strong interest in the topic expressed by the people of the Rhineland even before the exhibition actually opened, continuing the documentation to cover emigration in the nineteenth century seems imperative.

I want to thank all those who have contributed to the project in any way, the numerous people in Germany and in America who helped with the academic work, the people who lent exhibits, but most of all my colleagues in Kommern whom, over several years, I inundated with work to a degree that was, at times, unbearable. To name but a few among many, I would like to thank Toni Berger, administrative manager, and Norbert Dresken, construction manager, who patiently bore the main burden in setting up the exhibition and who, together with their staff, contributed many ideas on how to stage it. I also thank Kornelia Panek and Markus Schmitz who in various ways undertook difficult research for this publication both in Germany and the United States and significantly contributed to the editing of the commentary to the journal and to the layout.

Dieter Pesch
Kommern, March 2001

Introduction

At an auction in 1997, a diary of a journey from the Rhineland to North America was discovered and made available by the buyer, a private person, to the Rheinisches Freilichtmuseum Kommern. At that time, preparations for the exhibition "Schöne Neue Welt – Rheinländer erobern Amerika (Brave New World – Rhinelanders Conquer America)" were already in full swing. At the very first reading, the scholars at the museum realized that a very important source text on emigration from the Rhineland had come into their hands.

In 1764, Johannes Herbergs, who had come to Ronsdorf from Waldniel on the Lower Rhine, and Peter Heinrich Strepers, a native of Kaldenkirchen[1], embarked on a journey to Pennsylvania in order to recover the overseas inheritance of their grandfather which had come into other hands. This was a property of 5,000 acres which Jan Strepers, merchant and innkeeper at Kaldenkirchen, had bought on March 10, 1682, from the Rotterdam merchant Benjamin Furley, a representative of the Proprietor of the province of Pennsylvania William

Fig. 2 Francis Place (1677-1728), William Penn. Colored pencil, approx. 1695. HSP.

Penn, for the sum of £100 Sterling. Meticulous businessman that he was, Johannes Herbergs painstakingly noted down all of the preparations for and the course of the journey, all income and expenses as well as the legal disputes with the new owners of Strepers' properties in his journal.

Johannes Herbergs seems to have been the driving force behind the undertaking. All in all, he crossed the Atlantic four times in order to bring to a good end what he deemed a just family cause, although he was related to the Strepers family by marriage only. Born in 1717, he had married Adelgunde Sieben, a granddaughter of Jan Strepers. Peter Heinrich was a direct descendant of Jan Strepers. He was baptized on September 7, 1736, at the Reformed Church at Kaldenkirchen. The fact that he was Jan Strepers' great-grandson was of great importance for the claims he was to make to the inheritance in Pennsylvania[2].

Before setting out for Pennsylvania, Peter Heinrich Strepers and his cousin Johannes Herbergs, almost twenty years his senior, called on their relations on the Lower Rhine to enlist their participation in the travel expenses as well as in the legal costs

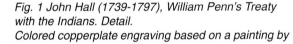

Fig. 1 John Hall (1739-1797), William Penn's Treaty with the Indians. Detail.
Colored copperplate engraving based on a painting by Benjamin West (1738-1820), London 1775. RFM.

they were bound to incur. The bookkeeping section of the diary (pp. 148-175) shows who actually contributed money. Strangely enough, none of the direct descendants were willing to support the undertaking. Hollender, Mickenschreiber, Königs, Moll, Laufs and Dürselen are the names of male and female cousins who were indirect descendants. They were merchants, mostly dealing in textiles, who maintained contacts to the Netherlands and England and used them to help the travelers.

But the diary not only tells the story of Johannes Herbergs and Peter Heinrich Strepers. It also sheds light on the first organized emigration from the Rhineland to the New World, the exodus of what were called the thirteen Krefeld emigrant families who in 1683 left their home country mainly for religious reasons. They were Quakers, Mennonites or members of the Reformed faith sympathizing with these, who trusted the Proprietor of the province of Pennsylvania who, in his Charter of Privileges[3], guaranteed freedom of religion.

Not all of the thirteen emigrants, in which number only the male heads of families are included (altogether the group numbered at least thirty-three people[4]), originally came from Krefeld. Their or their fathers' home was the Lower Rhine region with the towns of Mönchengladbach, Rheydt, Rheindahlen, Wickrath, Wickrathberg, Kempen, Dülken, Kaldenkirchen etc. From the 1620s onward, the Mennonites had been exposed to increasing religious prosecution in the Duchy of Jülich. They were either expelled from the country or only allowed to practice their faith under the most difficult conditions and on payment of protection money. Many of them sought to hide under the cover of the established churches by having their children baptized as Reformed Protestants or even, in order to escape expulsion, as Roman Catholics. As part of the County of Moers, Krefeld, thanks to the influence of the House of Orange, had a more liberal attitude and took in Mennonite refugees from Mönchengladbach as early as 1654[5].

There were repeated visits by Mennonite preachers and leading Quakers from England and the Netherlands, where they enjoyed religious freedom under the House of Orange, to the towns and cities on the Lower Rhine to meet with their brethren, to help consolidate young congregations and to do mission work in a liberal environment. At the Provincial Synod of Jülich in May 1680, the "spread of Quaker practices at Kaldenkirchen" was mentioned for the first time. And in early summer 1680, a Quaker visit in that town gave rise to tumultuous scenes, encouraged by both the Catholic priest and the Reformed minister. The missionaries were insulted, ridiculed and run out of town[6].

The discussion of Quaker practice at Kaldenkirchen at the Jülich Provincial Synod in 1680, the mention of sympathizers or followers, who were the only ones to listen to the Quaker missionaries in early summer[7], and the emigration plans among the folks of Kaldenkirchen, which started with the land purchase in Pennsylvania in March 1680, must all be seen together. In 1680, some people were expelled from Krefeld as well, among them the Quaker Hermann Isaaks op den Graeff, one of the thirteen emigrants, and Hendrik Jansen van Acken[8], son-in-law of Jan Strepers of Kaldenkirchen. They came back unmolested a few weeks later, however, probably helped by the influence of some Dutch friends.

In 1677, leading Quakers, William Penn, Keith and Furly had come to Germany and also visited the Lower Rhine region. One purpose of this visit was to do missionary work among groups with a similar religious outlook such as the Mennonites and the Labadists, the other to consolidate and organize Quakerism in the existing congregations[9]. It is fair to assume that already during this visit there were discussions on Quaker emigration to America. This assumption is founded not least on Penn's contacts to the Labadists[10]. "We are a family that live together in love – of one soul and spirit, entirely given up to serve the Lord," was the greeting of a leading Labadist to Penn on his visit to Wieuwerd, in the Dutch province of Frisia, the last Labadist bastion on the European continent. The affines will also have talked about the Labadists' intention to set up a kingdom of God in the New World. For as early as June 8, 1679, the former Reformed preacher Peter Schlüter, a native of Wesel[11], and the Dutchman Jasper Dankers left the group in

*Fig. 3 Cornelius Pronk (Amsterdam 1691-1759), Krefeld around 1730.
Ink, Municipal Archives, Krefeld.*

order to buy land in North America for a labadist settlement[12]. It took them a second trip, on which they embarked in Amsterdam on April 12, 1683, just weeks before the emigration of the thirteen families from the Lower Rhine, to find what they were looking for in the Maryland estate of Bohemia Manor.

Influenced by these ideas, the intending emigrants from the Lower Rhine gathered in Krefeld, even settled here for some time until their actual departure. The town thus became a bridgehead for early emigration from the Lower Rhine, especially so as Penn's treatise "Some Account of the Province of Pennsylvania, in America; ... Made publick for the Information of such as are or may be dis-posed to Transport themselves and Servants into those Parts" was published in London in 1681. Dutch[13] and German translations followed in Rotterdam and Amsterdam in the same year. The publication, also in 1681, of an "Information and Direction"[14] for intending emigrants by William Penn's land agent in Rotterdam, Benjamin Furly, brought the intermediary onto the scene who was keen to bring the information on the new settlement area to the largest possible audience in order to reach as many intending emigrants as possible. We can, therefore, assume that anyone interested in emigration on the Lower Rhine had quite extensive information on the departure and on Pennsylvania itself - to the extent that it had been explored at that time.

Although nine of the thirteen emigrants had settled in Krefeld by the middle of 1682[15], the attempt by local historians "to speak of an emigration from Krefeld"[16] can only be put down to extreme partiality toward their home town. It would be more correct to call Krefeld a gathering point at which all the lengthy preparations for emigration were made. The extent of such preparations becomes apparent from Johannes Herbergs' journal. As late as 1764, when the voyage across the Atlantic was already reasonably well organized, sixteen weeks passes between the packing of his goods in his home town and the day the ship actually put to sea bound for the New World.

An examination of Johannes Herbergs' journal shows that it was probably not written in one piece. Rather, the reader gets the impression that there was a draft on loose sheets which was then transferred to the book at a later stage. When Herbergs compares the speedy carriage ride from Harwich to London with the rides on the station waggon from the stop "King of Prussia" in Germantown, this inclusion of a later event indicates that the final version was written later. This impression is further strengthened by the fact that the description of the journey and of the country and its people make up one part, and the legal disputes are rendered in a second, separate part. For his description of "the country and its people" he relied not only on his own impressions but also on written sources. His enthusiasm for America is similar to that found in John Oldmixon's report on Pennsylvania[17], which, in turn, is based on a personal letter by William Penn to the latter. Herbergs even copies entire passages from Oldmixon, such as the explanation of the language of the Indians living at Philadelphia[18].

In order to keep the two blocks apart, the writer of the journal started his records once at the front end of the book and once from the back. The transcript does not follow this separation. The descriptions and events of both blocks have been arranged in chronological order, thus making it easier for the reader to follow the course of events.

Identifying the correct meaning of the numerous distorted English terms and names in the text was a major problem. Similarly, it was not always possible to fully clarify the names of German tradesmen, merchants and innkeepers in Philadelphia, since research on the history of early German settlement and every-day life in Pennsylvania is still relatively rare. This is also true of Philadelphia and even of Germantown, the first German settlement on Pennsylvania soil, which was founded by the thirteen emigrant families from the Lower Rhine together with the Frankfurt Company centered on Franz Daniel Pastorius.

In addition, the secret code used by Herbergs in some passages was transcribed and deciphered. It consists of putting the first letter of a word at its end and inserting an additional letter both at the beginning and the end.

We are particularly indebted to James Duffin of the Archives of the University of Pennsylvania in Philadelphia. His profound knowledge of the history of Philadelphia and Germantown helped to incorporate information on the acquisition and development of land by the Strepers family and their Pennsylvania descendants. In the same way it was possible to trace and recount the attempts of Johannes Herbergs and Peter Heinrich Strepers to recover "their" land with the help of the courts in Philadelphia and Bucks County from 1764 onward.

James Duffin pointed to the existence of large archival material at the Historical Society of Pennsylvania and the Philadelphia Library Company which allowed for a new and detailed look at the entire case. The correspondence between Jan Strepers' heirs on the Lower Rhine and the Pennsylvania relatives has survived surprisingly complete, albeit for the most part in English translations. It spans the period between 1683 and the mid-1730s. A large number of letters and notes from both parties also supply detailed proof of the legal dispute between Peter Heinrich Strepers and Johannes Herbergs and the new owners, supplementing the journal and extending to the time of Johannes Herbergs' death. In transcribing the journal, we did not attempt an exact reproduction to the letter. Its idiomatic idiosyncrasies, a combination of features from Lower Rhine Bergisch dialects, however, have been preserved. For better understanding, incomplete sentences were completed.

Up to approximately 1740, the early letters from Germantown and the Lower Rhine were mostly dated in the "old style", i.e. according to the Julian calendar, in the case of the Quaker letters without indication of day or month. For the sake of clarity, they have been converted to the Gregorian calendar.

Fig. 4 Johannes Herbergs' journal, 1764-66, privately owned.

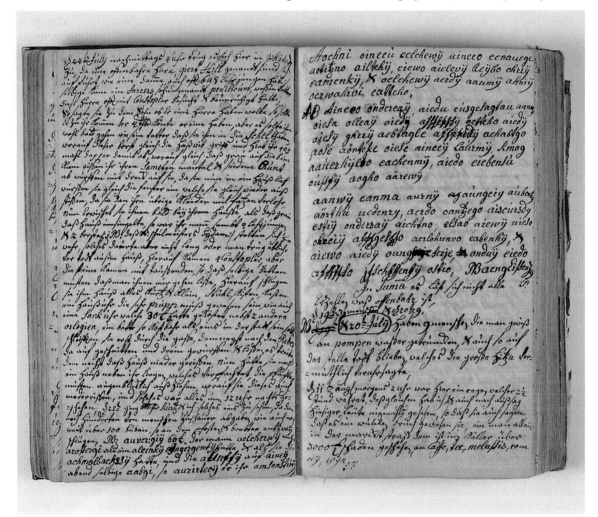

1 Today called Schwalmtal-Waldniel, in the district of Viersen, and Wuppertal-Ronsdorf.

2 viz. the Strepers family tree.

3 The Charter of Privileges, granted by William Penn, Esq; to the Inhabitants of Pennsylvania and Territories, in: The Acts of Assembly of the Province of Pennsylvania, Philadelphia, 1775, p. X.: "... I do hereby grant and declare, That no Person or Persons, inhabiting in this Province or Territories, who shall confess and acknowledge *One* Almighty GOD... shall be in any Case molested or prejudiced in his or their Person or Estate, because of his or their consciencious Persuasion or Practice..."

4 Marion Balderston, *James Claypoole's Letter Book. London and Philadelphia 1681-1684* (San Marino, California, 1967), p. 217. Guido Rotthoff, "Die Auswanderung von Krefeld nach Pennsylvanien im Jahre 1683", *Die Heimat*, LIII (Krefeld, 1982), 17.

5 Karl Rembert, *Die "Wiedertäufer" im Herzogtum Jülich, Studien zur Geschichte der Reformation, besonders am Niederrhein* (Berlin, 1899) p. 423 ff. Ekkehard Krumme, "Die Täufer in Gladbach", *Rheydter Jahrbuch für Geschichte, Kunst und Heimatkunde*, XII (Mönchengladbach, 1977), 9-58. Ekkehard Krumme, "Die Reformation und die Herausbildung evangelischer Gemeinden in Mönchengladbach im Zeitalter der Glaubensspaltung", *Loca Desiderata. Mönchengladbacher Stadtgeschichte*, II (Cologne, 1999), 370-389. Wilhelm Niepoth, "Evangelische im Kempener Raum", *Schriftenreihe des Landkreises Kempen-Krefeld*, VI (Kempen, 1958), 47 ff. Wolfgang Froese (ed.), *Sie kamen als Fremde. Die Mennoniten in Krefeld von den Anfängen bis zu Gegenwart* (Krefeld, 1995), p. 13.

6 Leo Peters, *Geschichte der Stadt Kaldenkirchen*, I (Kleve, 1998), p. 397 f.

7 Peters, p. 398.

8 Guido Rotthoff, "Die Auswanderung von Krefeld nach Pennsylvanien im Jahre 1683", *Die Heimat*, LIII (Krefeld, 1982), 13.

9 Friedrich Gorissen, "William Penn am Niederrhein", *Kalender für das Klever Land* (Kleve 1980), 195.

10 William Penn arrived with John Claus in Wieuwerd on July 12, 1677. See Trevor John Saxby, *The Quest for the New Jerusalem, Jean de Labadie and the Labadists, 1610-1744* (Dordrecht, 1987), p. 253.

11 Son of Henrich Schlüter and Adelheid Vorstmann, baptized at the Mathena Reformed Church at Wesel on February 18, 1646.

12 "Journal of a Voyage to New York", *Memoirs of the Long Island Historical Society* (Brooklyn, 1867), I.

13 William I. Hull, *William Penn and the Dutch Quaker Migration to Pennsylvania* (Swarthmore, 1935), p. 311.

14 Rotthoff, "Auswanderung von Krefeld", p. 15.

15 Charlotte Boecken, ""Dutch Quaker" aus Krefeld, die (Mit)Gründer Germantowns 1683?", *Die Heimat*, LIII (Krefeld, 1982), 27.

16 Wilhelm Niepoth, "Die Abstammung der 13 Auswanderer von Krefeld nach Pennsylvanien im Lichte niederrheinischer Quellen", *Die Heimat*, XXIV (Krefeld, 1953), 6.

17 Monsignore John Oldmixon, *Das Groß=Britannische Scepter in der Neuen Welt oder Politische und Geographische Beschreibung allen Engelländischen Plantagien, so wohl auf dem vesten Lande als denen in America gelegenen Insuln* (Hamburg, 1715).

18 Oldmixon, p. 223.

The Family of Jan Strepers

The Strepers family is to be found in Kaldenkirchen from the second half of the 16th century onward. The first known head of the family, Dirk auf den Striep, appears in the "Register of Incomes" of 1571. From the early seventeenth century onward, the Strepers family has been linked to the Reformed faith[1]. In a way, they can be called pioneers of this religion, since the first public sermon given by a reformed minister in Kaldenkirchen was held in Peter Strepers' house on August 20, 1609[2].

Jan Strepers was born around 1640 as the son of Leonhard Strepers and his wife Gertrud in Kaldenkirchen where he grew up together with his siblings Lambert, Wilhelm, Dierich and Gertrud. On May 12, 1669, Jan married Anna Doors or Theißen, daughter of Theiß Doors and his wife Agnes, in Kaldenkirchen[3]. Anna had been previously married to Henrich Kürlis from Waldniel. There were two children from this first marriage: Metgen (christened March 9, 1664) who married the Quaker Hendrik Jansen van Acken, and Jan (christened December 5, 1666) who died at the age of two.

Fig. 5 Tönis Kunders' house in Germantown.
Photography from the late 19th century.

Jan Strepers' brother Lambert married and moved to Heinsberg. Dierich left Kaldenkirchen as a young man. He was last heard of as being admitted to communion at the Willibrordi Church at Wesel on April 20, 1669 "on Maundy Thursday"[4]. Gertrud had been married to Arnold Simons since 1696. Jan's brother Wilhelm, born around 1644, went to Pennsylvania in Jan's place in 1683, in order to prepare parts of the property bought from William Penn for others who were to come later. In a letter dated August 18, 1685, Jan commissioned him to have sufficient land for his five families surveyed[5].

What five families could Jan Strepers have meant? Was he talking about his five under-age children Leonhard (christened March 2, 1670), Hendrik (christened July 24, 1672), Katharina (christened May 23, 1677), Anneken (christened July 16, 1679), Agnes (christened December 22, 1680) and, of course, Metgen Kürlis, his wife Anna's daughter from her first marriage to Henrich Kürlis? That is not very likely. More probably, Jan was thinking of families related by blood or by marriage in and around Kaldenkirchen who were prepared to settle in Pennsylvania or who had already moved there, such as his wife's brothers and sisters: Tönis Kunders[6] with Helene Doors, Peter Kürlis[7] with Elisabeth Doors, Leonhard Arets[8] with Agnes Doors, Reiner Doors or Theißen[9] with Margret Isaaks op den Graeff. All of the above Doors siblings, their spouses and Wilhelm Strepers emigrated to Germantown in 1683.

Whether Jan counted himself and his family in the five families or whether he included in that number Hermann Doors, who left Kaldenkirchen in 1684 to join the relatives in Germantown, remains uncertain. In any case, we may assume that in the initial years Jan definitely intended to move to Germantown, as becomes clear from his letters to his relatives there.

Rotthoff[10] assumes that no family ties existed with another 1683 emigrant, Johann Lucken. Lucken had not married Maria Doors, another of Jan Strepers' sisters–in–law, but Maria Gastes in Mönchengladbach. Maria Doors married Joachim Hüskes in the Reformed parish of Kaldenkirchen on April 8, 1674, and brought a child to be christened there in 1686.

As the last of the family, Paul Küsters, who had married Gertrud Doors in Kaldenkirchen on October 16, 1668, emigrated to Germantown with his family between 1691 and 1693. With Gertrud gone, all of the Theißen siblings except Anna Strepers and Maria Hüskes had left their home country[11].

Did Jan include his brother Wilhelm in this numbers game? James Logan and Richard Hill, soon to be part-owners of the Streper estate in Pennsylvania, had a rough outline drawn up of the later dispute over Jan's property from 1682 to 1727. A copy made by Judge C. Smyth is preserved at the Historical Society of Pennsylvania[12]. On the matter of the families sent to Pennsylvania by Jan Strepers, it tells us that he sent six families up to the year 1684 who where to settle and cultivate the land. "One of which was his Brother William Striepers Who was to Serve Jan Striepers three Years."[13] Thus, including Wilhelm Strepers with Tönis Kunders, Peter Kürlis, Leonhard Arets, Reiner Theißen and Hermann Theißen, six families would have left Germany between 1683 and 1684.

Jan certainly did not give preferential treatment to his brother Wilhelm, although the latter was supposed to be his most important contact in Pennsylvania. On the contrary, and surprisingly, Wilhelm was the only one among the fourteen relatives from Kaldenkirchen who was not given a lot in Germantown. He is recorded as a property owner in the first map of Germantown drawn up some years later by Pastorius and an assistant of his at the Frankfurt Company[14]. In this list of land owners, Wilhelm is recorded as successor of Johann Simons.

In the local literature about his home town[15], Wilhelm is repeatedly described as the husband who left his wife Beliken Tüffers and their five children behind in Kaldenkirchen and married again in the New World – a bigamist, in other words. If the person mentioned really was the same Wilhelm Strepers, the contract of marriage between Wilhelm and Maria Lucken dated July 29, 1685, and signed not only by Derick and Hermann op den Graeff, Tönis Kunders and Reiner Theißen – people thoroughly acquainted with Strepers family matters – but also by the Pietist and Quaker supporter Pastorius was a deliberate fraud. For this contract explicitly states that Wilhelm, a bachelor from Kaldenkirchen, intended to marry Maria Lucken[16]. This marriage contract made Wilhelm Strepers the owner of a property consisting of 200 acres of uncleared bush, one of the first fourteen lots assigned in Germantown. He, in turn, pledged himself to recognize Peter Simons, son of Johann Simons and Maria Lucken, as his own and to give him the same rights as any future children of his own. In a deed, made out on August 22, 1686, to Andres Souplis by Wilhelm Strepers with his wife Maria's consent, reference is made to a transfer of ownership of Johann Simons' property to Wilhelm Strepers[17].

If the Wilhelm Strepers who emigrated to America really was the husband of Beliken (Sibilla) Tüffers and not a person also named Wilhelm but coming from a different branch of the Kaldenkirchen Strepers, he would, indeed, have been of a loose character. One Wilhelm Strepers did marry Beliken Tüffers on August 19, 1663. Even before their first legitimate child was born, he is supposed to have had had an illegitimate son on February 22, 1664[18], whom he named Johannes. However, there is a confusion of names here. The Wilhelm Strepers in question, yet a third person of that name, was legally married to a Catholic. Johannes Strepers, therefore, was not the product of an extramarital relationship[19].

Wilhelm Strepers and Beliken Tüffers had five children: Peter (christened December 7, 1664), Dirk (christened August 22, 1666), Leonhard (christened July 8, 1668), Lyssken (christened January 25, 1670) and Jenneken (christened December 12, 1674). All of these Christian names had been common in the Strepers family since the late sixteenth century. All children were christened in the Reformed Church at Kaldenkirchen.

A letter from an unknown person from Krefeld to Gosen Cupers, clog maker in Kaldenkirchen, reports serious offences among the Baptist congregation here. The letter is undated but is seen in connection with a report from the Reformed minister Adolph Eylert of Kaldenkirchen to his fellow minister in Rheydt about a man of very limited means who had left his wife with five young children and had only returned to them after urgent written exhortation (possibly from Krefeld)[20].

Research links both reports to Wilhelm Strepers. If he really was identical with the man in question, his emigration to America would have to be seen almost as a family punishment. This would also explain Jan's behavior toward his brother whom he forced to work like a servant for three years before transferring the promised 100 acres to his name. By the same token, the remark in the bill of sale of 1696 that Wilhelm had renounced his parental inheritance by proxy but been indemnified for it (probably with the 100 acres in Pennsylvania) would be explained by the fact that the Strepers' who certainly did not enjoy the best of reputations in Kaldenkirchen because of their Mennonite and Quaker contacts did their utmost to get rid of their unpopular brother by sending him to the "North American wilderness" to start a new life there.

Against this background, it is hard to see Wilhelm Strepers as a religious refugee, although he joined the Quakers after he arrived in to Germantown. The widespread opinion that the first emigrants from Europe came to North America solely for religious reasons only is disproved by the laws passed in the young province of Pennsylvania by a General Assembly held at New Castle on October 14, 1700: "The LAW concerning Liberty of Conscience. An ACT against Riots, Rioters, riotious Sports, Plays and Games. An ACT against Adultery, Fornication, etc. An ACT against Rape or Ravishment. An ACT against Incest, Sodomy and Bestiality. An ACT against Bigamy. An ACT against Robbing and Stealing."[21]

If an act against bigamy was necessary in the very foundation phase of the province, this must have been a relatively common offence, due to the great distance from the home countries where the im-migrants' families had been left behind. This could mean that Wilhelm Strepers could, indeed, have lived in bigamy in Germantown.

This would be the only explanation for the Kaldenkirchen relatives' total silence on the fate of Wilhelm's wife and children in Germany. In spite of the many letters sent from Kaldenkirchen to Germantown, not a single mention is made of Wilhelm's first marriage or his children. If, indeed, Wilhelm was of such dubious character, it would be easier to understand his relationship with his brother Jan. In that case, the quarrels which existed at the very outset and which were passed on to the following two generations would appear in a different light. The focus, then, would not only be on the careless, not to say intentionally fraudulent, handling of someone else's property.

In the parish archives of the Roman Catholic church in Kaldenkirchen a Wilhelm Strepers is mentioned who must have come from a different Kaldenkirchen family and cannot have been Jan's brother. On December 2, 1681, there appeared before the pastor Aegidius Hinßen, the elders Jan Klincken, Matheiß Custers and Jan Lade, and Rutger Fleischawers, Peter Herman and Peter Kronenbroekers as jurors "the widow Beelgen Tuffers left behind by Wilhelm Strepers together with her brother-in-law Lienartgen Streepers and stated that her father-in-law Johann Striepers many years ago" had received 25 guilders from the local poor relief fund which debt had been passed on to Beelgen Tuffers, In recognition of this debt, she offered "all of her possessions" as well as one-and-a-half quarters of a morgen[22] of land located in the Heiderfeld between the lots inherited by Nieles Scherckens and Peter Striepers as security.[23]

This source makes it possible for the first time to determine what part of the family the Wilhelm Strepers who married Sibille Tüffers came from. Sibille Tüffers' father-in-law was called Jan Strepers. This could only be the Jan Strepers (senior) who was christened as a Catholic in Kaldenkirchen on May 24, 1623. His father, Leonhard Strepers (born around 1590), was the brother of Dierich Strepers (born around 1585), grandfather of the Jan Strepers who married Anna Doors. Until now,

Jan was only known to have had two children: Leonhard and Peter. Leonhard was Sibille Tüffers' brother-in-law who was mentioned in connection with her offer of security for the poor relief fund. Wilhelm Strepers, husband of Beliken Tüffers, who died before December 2, 1681, then would be a second cousin to the Wilhelm Strepers who went to America.

A family relationship between the emigrant Leonhard Arets and either Strepers or Theißen could not be proved from the church registers up to now. Jan Streper called Leonhard Arets his brother-in-law. Genealogists say that in the seventeenth century terms like brother, cousin, brother-in-law had a different meaning from today, especially when used in religious groups. On the other hand, degrees of kinship mentioned in the letters of the Strepers can in most cases be proved exactly. Only the term brother is frequently used synonymously with that of brother-in-law. In contract of sale dated July 17, 1696, Jan Strepers' siblings and brothers-in-law are listed. Leonhard Arets is not to be found among them. Hence, we must look for the brother-in-law Leonhard Arets either among the husbands of the sisters to Jan's wife Anna Doors or among the brothers-in-law of Anna's first husband Henrich Kürlis. Theiß Doors, father of the Theißen siblings, had married a woman named Agnes. Therefore, a daughter with the same Christian name would be quite likely. Since the Baptismal Register of the Reformed congregation of Kaldenkirchen only starts with the year 1663, it was not possible to identify a person given that name in baptism.

Following this survey of the ties between the family members, we will have to find out where the money to buy the 5,000 acres in Pennsylvania came from. The inheritance of the Strepers family in Kaldenkirchen was not large enough to pay the sum of £100 Sterling from it. On top of that, only a few years after buying the Pennsylvania property Jan Strepers contracted to purchase the inheritance from his parents Dierich and Gertrud Strepers. According to this contract, he bought his parents' property, i.e. the house, courtyard, barn, stables and garden located between the properties of Johann Ewalds and Wilhelm Janßen, a piece of land called the "fehn Camp", measuring roughly one and a half morgen and two small plots of uncleared land, from his co-heirs Lambert, Wilhelm, Dierich and Gertrud Strepers for the sum of 56 guilders which was shared between four heirs since Wilhelm had been indemnified by proxy for his share. It is possible that this deed of proxy, which was made out even before Wilhelm's departure for Pennsylvania, has something to do with the 100 acre lot Jan promised him in Germantown. This had been the subject of a contract concluded by the brothers in Rotterdam on May 3, 1683.[24]

After buying the Pennsylvania estate, the purchase of the parental property was a further investment that could not have been paid for by the yields of Jan Strepers' farm and his Kaldenkirchen business. Even if almost all of the members of Anna Doors' family decided to turn their backs on Kaldenkirchen and settle in the New World, this does not allow the conclusion that most of the funds came from them, as Anna Doors' share of the inheritance, as it were.

Although they are included in the church registers of the Reformed Church in Kaldenkirchen, the Doors family turned to the Mennonites at an early point in time. Theiß Doors, often also called Peters after his father according to Mennonite custom, father of Anna Doors, is mentioned in a list by the bailiff and steward of the district of Brüggen dated July 23, 1652, as a Baptist. The entry about him includes his occupation and property: "Theiß Dahrs, a shopkeeper, has a residential property with a small house and a vegetable garden. Also a quarter morgen of land and a quarter morgen of bush, altogether worth about 350 rix dollars."[25] Also listed is Reiner Doors, also a shopkeeper by trade with a property worth 200 rix dollars.

The difficulties suffered by Mennonites in the Duchy of Jülich in the second half of the seventeenth century, how they had to conceal or even entirely deny their faith, is shown by the problems Theiß Doors had to cope with from the authorities. On January 4, 1655, he was questioned in Brüggen Castle by the Kaldenkirchen priest and prior Gottfried Schirmer and Father Robert de Schapdriever. Because of his faith he had been expelled from Düsseldorf by order of the sovereign, but had not left the country. He was, therefore, to be sentenced to a fine of 100 gold guilders, and further residence in the country was excluded. In his defense, Theiß Doors pretended that his wife had been planning to convert to the Catholic faith for the last four years "provided she was not forced to go to Kevelaer straight away" – a place of pilgrimage dedicated to Our Lady and, for Catholics, a stronghold of the Counter Reformation in the seventeenth century. In order to demonstrate her intention to convert to Catholicism, they had given their youngest child a Catholic baptism[26]. Margaritha Doors was christened in Kaldenkirchen on January 4, 1655, the day of the proceedings at Brüggen Castle. This was too obvious an attempt to prove loyalty to the sovereign. Theiß Doors had to pay a heavy fine for his religion. He was lucky enough to escape being expelled from the country after all. Due to mediation of the Brandenburg government in Cleves, he was permitted to stay in the Duchy of Jülich.

The problems Theiß Doors and his wife experienced for their religious practice finally decided the next generation to emigrate to Pennsylvania with almost all their brothers and sisters. Only Maria and her husband Joachim Hüskes and Anna with her husband Jan Strepers stayed behind, although the latter had originally intended to leave and in spite of their enormous investment in the New World.

The lien levied on Theiß Doors' property means that the funds for buying the Strepers estate in Pennsylvania cannot possibly have come from this source. It is possible that the money came from the inheritance from Anna Doors' first husband, Henrich Kürlis. Besides, if the funds to finance the purchase had come from the Doors siblings, Jan Strepers would certainly not have been entered in the land register as the sole owner of the 5,000 acres. The possibility that the Strepers could have financed the land purchase from their own resources must be likewise excluded. If the family had had that kind of capital, Wilhelm Strepers would also have had the resources to buy land.

The question remains as to how Jan Strepers, a member of the Reformed Church, made contact with William Penn or, rather, with his land agent Benjamin Furly. The contact may have been established by members of the Doors family with their Mennonite and later certainly Quaker tendencies, or by his son-in-law, Hendrik Jansen van Acken, who married Metgen, the daughter of Jan's wife Anna from her first marriage. and who had contacts in the Netherlands. Hendrik Jansen van Acken is listed as a witness at the so-called Quaker marriage in Krefeld in 1681, along with members of the Doors family. On March 20, 1681, "there married at Krefeld the bachelor Derijck Isacks, a native of Krefeld, and Nolcken Vijten, spinster, born at Kempen." On the occasion of this wedding a document was drawn up and probably signed by all those present[27] who were members or sympathizers of the Krefeld Quaker community. Among these were Herman Doors, his sister-in-law Helene and his brother-in-law Leonhard Arets.

However, it is more likely that the guests were not predominantly members of the Krefeld Quaker congregation, but those close relatives that customarily were and still are invited to such festivities. This is where the question of who belonged to the family arises. On July 23, 1679, Abraham Isaaks op den Graeff, a brother of the bridegroom, had married Katharina Jansen (van Acken) from Mönchengladbach, possibly a sister of Hendrik Jansen van Acken, which would explain his invitation to the wedding. The bridegroom's mother, Margarete Peters, may have been a sister of Theiß Doors or Peters. This would make her sons, the op den Graeff brothers, relatives of Jan Strepers and Reiner Theißen, who always call them cousins in their letters.

Apart from Hermann and Helene Doors, Peter Kürlis and his wife Elisabeth Doors focussed on Krefeld at a an early stage (1681/1682). Whether they both became members of the Quaker community is unknown but probable, especially in view of the fact that the brother, Reiner Theißen, also joined the Quakers, at least after his arrival in Pennsylvania.

In 1680, the Quakers visited Kaldenkirchen, probably with the intent of spreading the faith. It is obvious that such attempts at missionary work were almost exclusively mediated and practised via local contacts because the reports from Kaldenkirchen, where some disputes were caused by the Quaker visit, also say that only those already interested beforehand could be reached.[28] The Quaker contacts with Kaldenkirchen were probably established through the Quaker community at Krefeld, that is to say mostly through the Doors family, Hendrik Jansen van Acken and the brothers op den Graeff.

On June 17, 1683, Jan Strepers made an agreement with the emigrant Johann Lenssen from Krefeld which gave the latter a lot of 50 acres of freehold land in Pennsylvania. In return, Jan Strepers was to receive an annual rent of one rix dollar and half a stuyver in Dutch currency. Apart from that, Jan Strepers gave Jan Lenssen a personal loan of 50 rix dollars for a term of eight years at an annual interest of six rix dollars. In addition, Jan Lenssen was to work for Jan Strepers twelve days a year for eight years. Lenssen, a weaver, was supposed to supply linen. In addition, being the astute businessman that he was, Jan Strepers lent Lenssen a loom with three combs for two years. In return, Lenssen was to teach weaving to Leonhard Strepers, Jan Strepers' thirteen-year-old son, within one year.

It can only be guessed whether Johann Lenssen was to give the loom to Leonhard Strepers after two years so he could then settle in Germantown and practise his trade there. But why would Jan have wanted his son to learn his trade in America although such an apprenticeship would have been much cheaper in the Lower Rhine region with its many weavers? Jan seems to have intended for his son to make his home in Germantown. The agreement ended with a clause subjecting Johann Lenssen to Pennsylvania jurisdiction in case he did not pay his dues.[29]

There have been repeated doubts as to whether Leonhard Strepers actually did arrive in Germantown. The agreement between Jan Strepers and Johann Lenssen, concluded just weeks before the latter's departure, seems to indicate that Leonhard traveled together with Lenssen. Otherwise an agreement made so close to departure does not make sense. The assumption that Leonhard did, indeed, go to Pennsylvania is supported by the following remark: "in Cpt. Jefferies' Shipp. Leonard Arrats & Agnistan his wife late of Crevelt near Rotterdam in Holland came in the C [Concord] of Lond. Wm. Jefferies commander arrived here the 6th of the mo./8 1683. Leonard Teison his Brother a freeman."[30] It is surprising that Leonhard Strepers, here called Theißen after his mother, on arrival in Pennsylvania was entered together with Leonhard Arets and his wife. It would have been more common for him as an apprentice to have become a member of Jan Lenssen's household for a year. If Leonhard traveled as a "member of the Arets family" we may conclude that Leonhard Strepers was a close relative of Leonhard Arets and his wife Agnes, Agnes then possibly being a Doors by birth and called Agnes after her mother. This is supported by the fact that Leonhard Arets, son of Arent Classen van Acken, was a cousin of Jan Strepers' son-in-law Hendrik Jansen van Acken.

It is not known when Leonhard Strepers returned to Kaldenkirchen. He seems to have gone back soon after his apprenticeship, however. There is no mention of him either in the correspondence between Jan and Wilhelm which began about a year after emigration or in the reports of Franz Daniel Pastorius on the Germantown residents. Leonhard Strepers died in Kaldenkirchen on August 19, 1725 at the age of 55 years. To this day, a slab in the outer wall of the Reformed Church of the town tells of his successful life as a merchant.

1 See the Strepers family tree.
2 Emil Becker, "Der Kaldenkirchener Kreis unter den 13 Auswandererfamilien von Krefeld nach Pennsylvanien aus dem Jahre 1683", *Heimatbuch des Kreises Viersen* (Viersen, 1983), p. 69.
3 Mennonites tended to take their father's Christian name as their family name (patronym).
4 Archives of the Protestant Congregation of Wesel: Admissions to communion Willibrord Church (Reformed), 1625-1764, p. 161.
5 Historical Society of Pennsylvania: Miscellaneous Papers, 1632-1764, Streper Papers, 1682-1772, Bucks Co., p. 198 (hereafter: HSP and page no.).
6 Tönis Kunders , b. around 1650 in Mönchengladbach, son of Coen Lenßen Heckers and his wife Anna, chris-

tened as a Mennonite on July 9, 1673 in Goch, married in Krefeld on May 31, 1677 in a reformed ceremony to Helene Theißen or Doors, b. around 1650 in Kaldenkirchen and christened as a Mennonite on May 20, 1670.
7 Peter Kürlis, christened September 9, 1652 in Waldniel in the Reformed parish of Goch, son of Johann Cürlitz, married to Mette Beckers on January 1, 1636, married Elisabeth Theißen on March 17, 1675 in the Reformed parish of Kaldenkirchen.
8 Leonhard Arets, b. in Mönchengladbach, son of Arnt Claßen von Aaken, first marriage to Katharina Kuhlen, married Agnes Theißen from Kaldenkirchen, see Arets/van Acken family tree.
9 Reiner Theißen, b. 1658/59 in Kaldenkirchen, probably married in Germantown to Margret Isaaks op

Fig. 6 Extract from the Register of "Poor Pensions". "Note of release" for the emigrant Wilhelm Strepers. Archives of the Catholic Parish of Kaldenkirchen, PA K 82-8a.

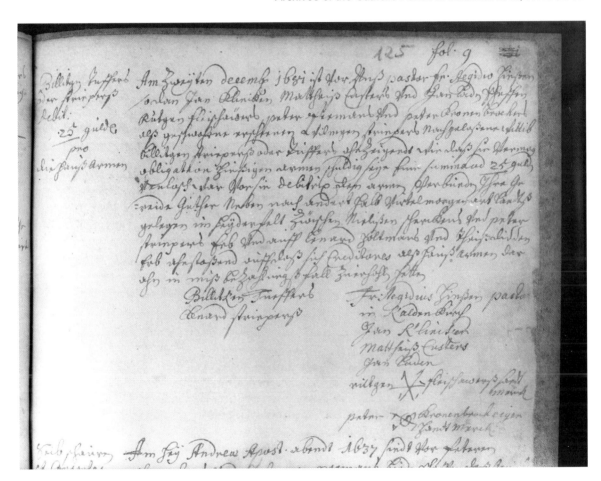

den Graeff, who had emigrated with her brothers Derick, Hermann and Abraham Isaaks op den Graeff in 1683. In several letters, Reiner Theißen calls the brothers Isaaks op den Graefff his brothers. Three of his children are given the names Isaak, Derick and Abraham in baptism. (cf. Becker, op.cit., p.18).

[10] Rotthoff, "Auswanderung von Krefeld", p. 18.

[11] Archives of the parish of Kaldenkirchen: 82-8a, fol. 72: On February 15, 1684 Paulus Cuesters and his wife Gertrud (Giertruetgen) as well as his mother Triencken Cuesters took a loan of 25 guilders from the Catholic Poor Relief. According to the same source (fol. 89), this loan was paid back in 1702 by Jan Dors or Streipers in the name of Paulus Custers (cf. op.cit., p. 20). Information from Dr. Leo Peters, Kaldenkirchen.

[12] HSP, p. 225.

[13] HSP, p. 225.

[14] James Duffin, "The First Map of Germantown", Germantown Crier (Germantown, 1992), XLIV,2,7.

[15] Peters, Kaldenkirchen, I, p. 399, ann. 240.

[16] Recorded in Pennsylvania Letter of Attorney Book. Information given by James Duffin.

[17] James Duffin, "Germantown Landowners III", Germantown Crier (Germantown, 1990) XVII,2,65.

[18] Becker, "Der Kaldenkirchener Kreis", p. 73.

[19] Baptismal Register, Roman Catholic Parish of Kaldenkirchen.

[20] Peters, Kaldenkirchen, I, p. 399.

[21] The Acts of Assembly. p.1.

[22] Historically a unit of square measurement, approx. 3,000 sp. yards. The term ("Morgen" = German for "morning") is derived from the area one could plough in one morning.

[23] Archives of the parish of Kaldenkirchen : 82-8a, fols. 67 and 9. Registry of the Poor pensions [p.116/1753] – Information given by Dr. Leo Peters, Kaldenkirchen.

[24] James Duffin, "Germantown Landowners III", Germantown Crier (Germantown, 1990) XVII,2,65.

[25] Peters, Kaldenkirchen, I, p. 395.

[26] Peters, Kaldenkirchen, I, p. 395 f.

[27] Hull, Quaker Migration, p. 422 ff.

[28] Peters, Kaldenkirchen, I, p. 397 ff.

[29] HSP, p. 195.

[30] Michael Tepper (ed.), Emigrants to Pennsylvania, 1641-1819. A Consolidation of Ship Passenger Lists from the Pennsylvania Magazine of History and Biography (Baltimore, 1975), p. 9.

Jan Strepers' Land Purchase

On March 9 and 10, 1682, Jan Strepers of Kaldenkirchen on the Lower Rhine bought 5,000 acres of land in Pennsylvania for himself and his heirs in perpetuity from William Penn, Esquire, of Worminghurst in Sussex through the agency of the Rotterdam merchant Benjamin Furly for the sum of £100 sterling with the obligation to pay an annual ground rent. On the same day as Strepers, the Amsterdam merchant Jacob Telner, who had already traveled to America between 1678 and 1681, and Dirk Sipman from Krefeld also bought 5,000 acres each. Strepers, Telner and Sipman belonged to the "First Purchasers", a group of 100 individuals who were allowed to buy a share of 5,000 acres of land each. The limit of the first 100 purchasers was reached on April 2, 1682.[1] On June 11, 1683, several other Krefeld residents, Govert Remkes

Fig. 7 Charter granted by Charles II, King of England, to William Penn, 1681. Detail. Pennsylvania State Archives.

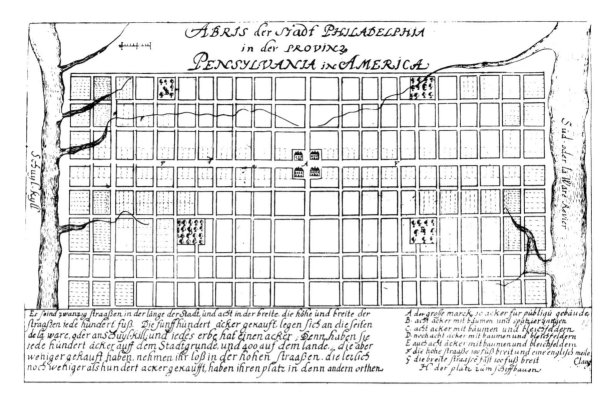

Fig. 8 Based on Thomas Holme, German Plan of the City of Philadelphia, in: Beschreibung der in America neu erfundenen Provinz Pensylvanien, Hamburg 1684. Augsburg University Library.

(corset maker), Leonhard Arets (linen weaver) and Jacob Isaaks van Bebber (baker) each bought 1,000 acres of land.[2] Between them, these six purchasers and the purchasers of the Frankfurt Company (Jacobus van de Walle, Gerhard van Mastricht, Johann Le Bruin, Dr. Thomas van Wylich – all born in Wesel – Johann Jacob Schütz, Daniel Behagel, Johannes Kemler, Balthasar Jawert, Johann Wilhelm Peterson)[3], called the "Hoch= Teutsche Compagnia"[4] by Franz Daniel Pastorius in his description of the Province of Pennsylvania, acquired the area in the German township for the establishment of Germantown. William Penn expected of both Sipman for the "Krefeld Landowners" and the Frankfurt Company that the buyers would see to it that families were quickly settled on their land in Pennsylvania.[5]

Under the contract with William Penn, Jan Strepers was allotted 50 acres in what was called the Liberty land, between Germantown and Philadelphia, to be divided into lots. He was also given the right to have 275 acres in Germantown surveyed for himself. The remainder of the 5,000 acres had not been assigned to any particular area. This was to be applied for on arrival in Pennsylvania and to be done by the public surveyor.[6] This means that with the purchase Jan Strepers had been given a deed which entitled him to have a certain acreage surveyed and transferred to his name, but that the selection of the actual area was to be made on the spot in Pennsylvania. As a First Purchaser, he was entitled – a gift from William Penn – to have an acre in the city of Philadelphia allotted to himself.

The deed of purchase for Jan Strepers no longer exists. The Board of Commissioners of Property in Philadelphia supervised William Penn's property and was also responsible for any subsequent sales. Furthermore, it monitored the regular payments of ground rent to the Proprietor of the province. A document issued by the Board dated April 15, 1707, shows the sale of part of Jan Strepers' original 5,000 acres to Leonhard Arets. It also quotes passages from the original contract of purchase:

"...AND WHEREAS by my like Indentures of Lease [and] Release, bearing date the Ninth [and] Tenth days of the month called March in the year of our Lord 1682 for the considera[t]ion therein men[t]ioned, I granted unto John Streipers of Kalkerchen in the County of Juliers in the borders of Germany, Merch[an]t, ffive thousand acres of land to be taken up in the s[ai]d province TO HOLD to him, his heirs [and] assigns forever UNDER the yearly Quitrent of one English shilling to be paid for every hundred acres thereof, that is to say two pounds tenn Shillings for the whole s[ai]d ffive thousand acres of which s[ai]d sum or yearly rent by one other Indenture, bearing date the ffirst day off Aprill in the year 1683 for the consideration therein mentioned, I Remised [and] Released to the s[ai]d John Streepers, his heirs [and] assigns forever the sum of two pounds five shillings to the End that the yearly Quitrent of ffive shillings onely [and] no more should remain payable for the s[ai]d ffive thousand acres forever."[7]

The form of a complete contract between William Penn and a buyer can be seen from an indentured letter[8] made out to Daniel Behagel, merchant in Frankfurt on the Main and a member of the Frankfurt Company. Like Jan Strepers, Daniel Behagel never set foot on American soil. The deed of sale

Fig. 9 J. Otto Schweitzer, Model of a monument to the Krefeld emigrants of 1683. Bronze, approx. 1914. Municipal Archives Krefeld.

to Daniel Behagel is the only one in German we know of. It is signed by William Penn. Judging from the style of writing, it may have been written by Franz Daniel Pastorius. The text of the part that still exists – the upper section was cut off and kept by the seller – mentions the transfer of the province of Pennsylvania to William Penn by Charles II.[9]

The German township, part of which was to become Germantown in 1683, had been reserved by William Penn from the outset for German settlement. When the settlers set foot on the land by the Delaware River in October 1683, they asked Franz Daniel Pastoríus to represent their interests and to negotiate the allotment of a continuous stretch of land in the river plain with William Penn. In the "Grund- und Lagerbuch" (Land Record Book) of the German township Pastorius described the first few years in the newly settled area.[10] He reports that the fourteen lots surveyed by Penn's Chief Surveyor, Thomas Fairman, on October 24, 1683, had already been distributed among the emigrants from the Lower Rhine by the following day.[11]

In that draw, Jan Strepers obtained Lot 1 on the east side of what was later to become Main Street, at the time of the foundation of Germantown still an Indian trail. In line with the requirement of William Penn, settlers were not allowed to establish themselves in scattered settlements or individual farms. From the outset, Germantown was to be laid out as a ribbon-built village, and this layout was assured by the draw of October 25, 1685. William Penn wanted his land to be settled in an orderly fashion and in accordance with his own ideas, and to support a viable political community that was to set its own laws and regulations, furthering peace and order in the community. Therefore, he gave Germantown a town charter on August 21, 1689, with all the ensuing rights and consequences. Franz Daniel Pastorius kept written records not only of this event but also of all the laws and regulations passed by the town council in the first few years.[12]

As early as April 1, 1683, William Penn released Jan Strepers from his annual rent of 45 shillings in return for a lump sum of £18 sterling. Generally, William Penn leased his land for one or more years

to the buyer and then formally released him from rent payments after this term had expired. This custom was adopted by the First Purchasers – including Jan Strepers. Merely an annual ground rent of five shillings remained for Jan to pay. On receipt of this amount, Strepers was issued with a plan of the city of Philadelphia to help him choose the acre of land that was Penn's gift.[13] As early as 1682, Penn had drawn up an ideal plan for the city of Philadelphia, his "city of brotherly love" and put all his ambition behind a speedy settlement of the area to be built up. For advertising purposes, his city plan was widely distributed and included annotations in English, Dutch and German (the latter two from 1684).

Jan Strepers bought his property without ever seeing it himself. When the thirteen families from the Lower Rhine with their heads Hermann Isaaks op den Graeff, Dirck Isaaks op den Graeff, Abraham Isaaks op den Graeff, Johann Lucken, Abraham Tunes, Johann Simons, Peter Kürlis, Reiner Theißen, Tönis Kunders, Johann Lenssen, Leonhard Arets and Johannes Bleickers sailed for America on July 28, 1683, only his brother Wilhelm was with them on board the Concord which, coming from London, landed at Philadelphia on October 6, 1683. Together with Jacob Telner and Dirck Sipman who, like him, stayed behind in Europe, Jan did accompany some of the emigrants as far as Rotterdam. Prior to the departure for London, the last business transactions were concluded.

Among them, one that was to create problems for the future was the agreement already mentioned between Jan Strepers and the linen weaver Johann Lenssen made out on June 17, 1683. Another was Jan's contract with his brother Wilhelm, dated May 3, 1683, which again and again played a part in the land disputes which were to follow. In return for three years' work in Pennsylvania, Wilhelm was to have 100 acres transferred to his name.[14]

Only a short time after the arrival in Pennsylvania, a lively trade with the newly acquired lots of land set in. Looking at the early distribution of land among the emigrants from the Lower Rhine, it is striking that most of them acquired only relatively

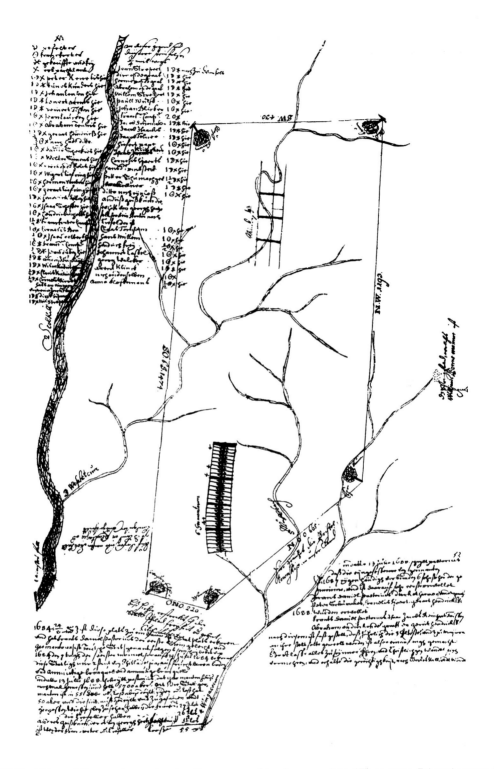

Fig. 10 First Map of Germantown showing the names of landowners, late 17th century. Privately owned.

small plots. Even Leonhard Arets, who had bought 1,000 acres, parted with half of his claim before departure. There seems to have been long-term planning behind the financial arrangements for emigration to Pennsylvania. Only the financially potent members of the group of religious refugees from the Lower Rhine or their sponsors acquired large tracts of land, in order to pass them on quickly in smaller shares to the less well-endowed members. The size of an average lot in the German township had obviously been set at 200 acres, as can be surmised from the frequent occurrence of that number. The fact that Dirck Sipman passed 2,000 of his 5,000 acres to the three op den Graeffs before departure certainly does not suggest that he bought the land for purposes of speculation. Neither can Strepers be called a speculator. After all, he originally intended to settle there himself, and he also wrote that his land was to serve as farm and building land for his "five families".

Against this background, Sipman and Strepers, along with the Amsterdam merchant Telner, appear as the main supporters and financial sponsors of emigration from the Lower Rhine. Is it idle speculation, then, to say that without Telner, Sipman and Strepers – together with the Frankfurt Com-pany – the purchase of a large continuous tract of land in the German township would never have been possible and, thus, the first German town on the American continent, Germantown, would not have been established?

In this context, the part played by Hendrik Jansen van Acken, husband of Jan Strepers stepdaughter Metgen Kürlis, who himself did not emigrate, is difficult to evaluate because of the scant source material relating to him. As a fervent follower of the Quakers and with the help of excellent contacts to his Dutch Quaker friends he seems to have been the driving force who made it possible for the thirteen families from the Lower Rhine to emigrate by winning wealthy investors. For him it was probably important to have helped to establish the Quaker settlement of Germantown in Pennsylvania. Although most of the emigrants had been baptized as Reformed Protestants in their home country, we may assume that they either directly or, like the members of the Theißen family, via the Mennonite faith, had already turned Quaker while still living on the Lower Rhine. In Germantown, in any case, except for Johann Lenssen, who remained a Reformed Protestant, all of the twelve other emigrant families professed the Quaker faith.

[1] Duffin, "Germantown Landowners I", p. 37.
[2] Samuel Whitaker Pennypacker, *The Settlement of Germantown Pennsylvania and the Beginning of German Emigration to North America* (Philadelphia, 1899), p. 2f. Rotthoff, "Auswanderung von Krefeld", p. 15.
[3] Deed of sale (February 24, 1701) between Daniel Falkner, Johannes Kelpius and Johannes Jawert as agents of the Frankfurt Company (seller) and John Ball (buyer). Property of the Rheinisches Freilichtmuseum.
[4] Franz Daniel Pastorius, *Umständige Geographische Beschreibung Der zu allerletzt erfundenen Provintz Pensylvaniae, In denen End=Gräntzen Americae In der West=Welt gelegen* (Frankfurt and Leipzig, 1700), p. 35.

[5] Pennypacker, *Settlement of Germantown*, p. 3.
[6] Collection of the Library Company of Philadelphia, Hill and Striepers Mss., Yi2, 7300½F, on deposit at the HSP (hereafter Lib.C. and Page no.).
[7] Krefeld Municipal Archives: Deed, Philadelphia, February 5, 1707. Property of the Savings Bank Foundation. For the full text refer to Appendix A.
[8] James Duffin, "Germantown Landowners I", *Germantown Crier* (Germantown, 1986/87) XXXIX, 2, 37: "Three major types of early deeds in Pennsylvania were Indentures, Deeds Poll, and Deeds of Lease and Release. The most common type was the Indenture 'a contract between two or more parties,' covering various types of conveyances beginning with the words 'This Indenture...' The term is derived from the

old English practice of cutting a sheet or parchment containing two copies of the deed—one for grantor and one for grantee - along an indented line through writing. The two deeds could then be fitted together to show that they were not forged."

9 Property of the Rheinisches Freilichtmuseum Kommern. For full text refer to Appendix B.

10 Grund- und Lager. Buch aller und jeden unbeweglichen Güter, geklärt, und ungeklärten Landes, in der gantzen German Township Durch Ordre Einer Daselbstigen Generalen Court - angefangen von Francisco Daniele Pastorio. Transcript by James Duffin: Unpublished Manuscript (Philadelphia, 1999). Excerpt from the text in App. C.

11 John F. Watson, *Annals of Philadelphia, and Pennsylvania in the Olden Time. Enlarged, with many Revisions and Additions, by Willis P. Hazard.* (Philadelphia, 1927), II, p. 18. James Duffin, "The First Map of Germantown", *Germantown Crier* (Germantown, 1992), XLIV, 9.

12 Gesetz, Ordnungen, und Statuta der Gemeind zu Germantown in denen daselbstigen Generalen, Raths- und Versamblungen von Zeit zu Zeit gemacht und verfertigt, p. 65 recto ff. Transcript by James Duffin: Unpublished Manuscript (Philadelphia, 1999). Excerpt from the text in App. D.

13 HSP, p. 227.

14 Duffin, "Landowners II", p. 67.

Fig. 11 Stained glass owned by Hermann op den Graeff (in 1637 mentioned as minister of the Mennonite Church at Krefeld). About 1630, manufactured according traditional Cologne glass painting of the 16th century. Privately owned.

The Land Dispute 1683-1715

One year after his arrival in Germantown, on October 22, 1683, Wilhelm Strepers wrote to his brother Jan that he was well and had already built a sizeable house with a cellar. Also, that he had had such a good harvest of grain, corn and buckwheat that he counted on having better supplies for the winter of 1684/85 than in the first after his arrival.[1] Since the group of thirteen families from the Lower Rhine had landed in Philadelphia in the fall of 1683, they had had to subsist on the provisions brought with them for the first few months, as it was too late in the year for planting, let alone for harvesting any crops. Hence, the new settlers suffered enormous hardship and deprivation during their first winter in Pennsylvania.

There had been an earlier letter, which does no longer exist, written on April 29, 1684, as can be seen from a reply from Jan Strepers dated August 18, 1685.[2] In his first letter, Wilhelm had asked Jan to send him some vital articles for daily use. Although the emigrants had been advised before their departure "to take butter and cheese, as well as clothing for two to three years, hardware for building, tools, ropes, English money or rix dollars, fishing nets and hunting rifles ....",[3] they could not take as much as they needed, due to lack of both space and money. Since the town of Philadelphia was no more than a year old, few goods were produced there at that time. No other places of production were nearby. Most goods had to be imported from Britain or other countries across the Atlantic or from the Caribbean. So, Jan sent a chest containing three loom combs, five shirts, and metal parts for a loom to Germantown, as Wilhelm had requested. In his letter of August 18, 1685, he asked whether the chest had arrived, since Wilhelm had not acknowledged receipt. In his first letter, Wilhelm seems to have asked for a year's pay that he had earned by clearing and preparing the Strepers' property. However, Jan reminded his brother that in his very first letter to him of October 13, 1684, he had already advised him to have a piece of cloth woven for him by Johann Lenssen, as the latter was bound by contract to do. This

Wilhelm could then sell for his profit. As far as he, Jan, knew, this had been done.

Jan also told Wilhelm that, according to his information, Dirck Sipman and others, like himself purchasers of 5,000 acres, had already had a piece of land in Germantown surveyed for themselves. He assumed that Wilhelm had already applied for and done the same in his name. And he reminded him that the land had to be large enough for his five families. This is the first mention of Wilhelm being sent to Pennsylvania as a "foreman" to prepare the nest, as it were. A later postscript added in a different handwriting (possibly the translator's) tells us who was meant by these families: "There went to Pennsylvania Jan Striepers bother Will[ia]m Striepers. Jan Striepers Wife's Brother Reiner Teissen & Herrman Teissen their Brothers in Law Thomas Conrats Leonart Arets & Paulus Custers."[4]

Since Dirck Sipman had not emigrated, Jan Strepers' information can only refer to lots that Sipman had sold, such as the 200 acres each to Jan Simons and Peter Kürlis. These were two of the fourteen lots which had been drawn for at the very beginning on October 25, 1683, in Franz Daniel Pastorius' dwelling. If, when speaking of the five families, Jan was referring to the Kaldenkirchen relatives already mentioned, it seems strange that Jan did not give them title to their own land and, thus, forced them to acquire lots of their own.

However, Jan also sounds an unusually friendly note in that part of his letter where he praises Wilhelm for having made such quick progress in clearing and cultivating Jan's land and building a house for him. In his letter of October 22nd, he does not refer to Wilhelm's second letter.

In October 1685, two years after arriving in Germantown, Wilhelm wrote to his brother, expressing his regrets that he had not heard from him. This letter and Jan's of August 18th of the same year seem to have crossed. Wilhelm was most surprised at his brother's silence because his three-year term of working his brother's land would run out in the near future. It was time to give him instructions as to how Jan's land was to be administered in future, since he, Wilhelm, intended to work his own land as soon as his term was over and to marry the Jan Simons' widow Maria, daughter of Wilhelm Lucken.

After his marriage and the end of his term as worker on his brother's land, he wanted to live on his own land. However, he promised not to leave the land he had cleared for Jan uncultivated, but to sow and work it until he had had a letter giving him further instructions. He finished by asking Jan to tell him where he could have those 100 acres surveyed that he was to have for his three years of toil.

There was another letter from Wilhelm Strepers, dated June 5, 1685, of unknown content, which is mentioned in Jan's reply of 1686 – there is no exact date. This letter had been personally delivered by a certain John Kipshoven. Since Jan mentions the name in his reply, we may assume that this person was well known to both brothers. In his reply Jan was slowly losing patience because his brother had not done what he had asked him to do. He insisted emphatically on being told who had woven his yarn, how many ells of cloth had been made, how wide the material was, and he wanted to know precisely how fine the comb had been in order to be able to judge the quality and, hence, the price of that material. He was expecting a report on the proceeds from the sale of the material. He also wanted Wilhelm, or somebody else, to write to him and tell him how many acres had meanwhile been surveyed and registered for him in Germantown. He urgently requested to ask also cousin Herman Isaak op den Graeff to help in finding out the location of the one acre in the city of Philadelphia. If there was any money needed for the transfer of the one acre in Philadelphia, that sum could be taken from the money for the material, just as had been agreed for the payment of surveying and transfer costs for his Germantown property.[5]

On February 25, 1687, William Markham and John Goodson, members of the Board of Property, issued a warrant on behalf of the Proprietor of the province for one acre of land to Jan Strepers, which was to be surveyed in a street in a favorable location in Philadelphia. This lot had already been promised to Jan Strepers by the Proprietor of the colony on July 25, 1686.[6] At long last, the efforts of Wilhelm and cousin Hermann Isaak op den Graeff had borne fruit. The warrant gave Jan the title to that acre, since a warrant was the order for the surveyor to make a precise survey for the purchaser of a property so far only vaguely described. In the case of Strepers, the order went to Captain Theodore Holmes, Chief Surveyor. As a next step, the purchaser was given a Return of Survey, a document on the survey which contained details of the property including the exact boundary lines of the lot or inheritance in question. After that, a Patent could be issued as deed of ownership but that was not required in the case of the First Purchasers.[7]

Jan Strepers' letters asking to have the survey, allotment and division into lots done the way he wanted became more and more demanding and insistent. At this stage, he had ceased to rely on his brother Wilhelm alone. On May 27, 1687, he wrote not only to his brother but also to the cousins Abraham and Hermann Isaak op den Graeff. He pleaded with them in the friendliest tones to have a lot of 200 or 100 acres in Germantown surveyed for him as fast as possible. The reason for this urgent request was, he wrote, that this was to be prepared for a family who was waiting for it as well as for a larger group of relatives in Pennsylvania, consisting of in-laws of the Theißen family. On that lot a house was to be built for him that nobody else was to move into. As soon as the desired lots had been surveyed and transferred, he intended to come to Pennsylvania. He was hoping that, in his absence, his cousins and his brother would put as much effort into his affairs as if they were their own.[8]

On April 13, 1688, Wilhelm reported that Jan's wish had been fulfilled, writing that two lots of altogether 200 acres had been allotted to Jan Strepers in Germantown and that Johann Lenssen had also been given 50 acres according to the agreement of June 16, 1683[9] between him and Jan Strepers. Wilhelm regretted not having received any information from Jan about the 100 acres that had been promised to him. For that reason, he had given the agreement between himself and Jan to Jan's brother-in-law Reiner Theißen and to the cousins op den Graeff to read. They had told him they could only interpret it to mean that he was entitled to 100 out of the 200 acres surveyed in Germantown. However, since they were supposed to represent Jan's interests, they could not take his side in the matter and had, therefore, referred him to the six elders of the Germantown community, who were to resolve the issue.

These decided in Wilhelm Strepers' favor: "According to this Agreement, we cannot find otherways, but what William Striepers must have from his brother Jan Striepers 100 Acres of Land, with a Town Lot, which Jan Striepers has in the Jurisdiction of Germantown."[10] Wilhelm closed his letter stating that Jan was left with a mere 100 acres in Germantown now that Jan Lenssen had been given 50 and he himself 100 acres. Besides, he wrote, he had added a list of expenses and income concerning both the three-year contract between them and the period in which he had no longer been in Jan's service.[11] Among other things, the list included what he had taken from the crops he had harvested for Jan and his own expenses in the course of looking after Jan's affairs in the years 1685 and 1686.[12]

Again and again, Jan's impending emigration is mentioned in letters exchanged between him and the Pennsylvania relatives. It has even been thought that Jan had actually gone to Pennsylvania between 1683 and 1700, because he did not appear at the baptisms of either his grandchildren or the children of close relatives.[13] However, this is mere speculation. In the well-documented correspondence of that time, there is nothing to indicate that Jan Strepers actually did travel to Germantown. In Reiner Theißen's letter of August 22, 1698, a possible move was mentioned when Theißen reported that he had by then cleared and ploughed 23 acres for Jan Strepers over six years. Jan now had to decide whether to come over and use the land himself. If not, could he send him a power of attorney to sell the land legally. This was particularly important in connection with the contract with Johann Lenssen, who declared that he was only willing to pay if shown a power of attorney.

In this letter Jan was reminded again that Wilhelm Strepers was still waiting in vain for a decision by his brother.[14] Therefore Wilhelm wrote to Jan again on September 5, 1698, saying that he had prepared his land for cultivation. He also informed Jan that Peter Kürlis and Tönis Kunders, both brothers-in-law of Wilhelm, had cleared the remaining land and fenced it in. Besides they had to keep the fences in good condition and to repair the trails on Jan's land all the time. The arable area now was about 24 acres with fences. Part of this was taken up by an orchard with 19 apple trees, all bearing fruit, which Wilhelm had planted while still in his brother's service.[15]

He stated that the friends Jan had installed to represent his interests had allowed him to take the 100 acres that were his due. However, since they did not have a power of attorney, the land could not be legally transferred to his name. Wilhelm urged Jan to give some person a power of attorney. He suggested either giving it to one of his brother's sons and to send him to Pennsylvania (this means that Leonhard, Jan Strepers' eldest son, cannot have been living in Germantown any more) or to authorize somebody in Pennsylvania to act as seller. Wilhelm excused his urgency with the fact that time was running out, quoting an English law under which land that had not been claimed within seven years reverted to the Proprietor of the province.[16]

If this interpretation of the law was correct, Wilhelm was right to fear the loss of the 100 acres promised to him. Neither in Jan's letters nor in any other correspondence from that time do we find an explanation of why Jan hesitated to make it possible for Wilhelm to obtain a warrant giving him the right to have the property that he had been promised in their contract surveyed as his own. Since Jan was always complaining that his property had not been allotted with the precision and the insistence that he had demanded and that his income from rent and the credit arrangement with Johann Lenssen was not collected and paid out to his satisfaction, he seems to have wanted to maintain a way of putting pressure on Wilhelm by his delaying tactics.

As far as the non-payment of annual rents was concerned, Wilhelm Strepers argued that neither he nor Johann Lenssen had failed to pay these out of malice. But there was nobody in Pennsylvania to collect such rent payments or to issue a receipt that would stand up in court. That was another reason for naming a trustee as quickly as possible.

Five more years passed without any progress on the matter. Possibly there were other letters which were irrelevant to the dispute. The stubbornness of the two brothers made a satisfactory result impossible, however. Jan continued to insist on being sent written confirmation showing that his claim to the 5,000 acres, the Liberty land and his one acre in Philadelphia had been realized and that the land had been surveyed, been recognized as his by deed and been entered in the land registers of Germantown and Philadelphia. Wilhelm, in turn, did not respond to this and delayed, assuming perhaps that his brother would come to settle in Pennsylvania in the near future and then look after his own affairs. He was waiting and begging more and more insistently for the 100 acres that Jan had promised him for specified services of land clearing, preparation, planting and house building to be finally transferred to him legally. By now, Jan Strepers had resisted this plea for thirteen years. Wilhelm's resistance to his brother's wishes may have been encouraged by the position he had meanwhile acquired in the community, although he had been the only one to arrive in Pennsylvania without a guaranteed land claim. The "General Court Book of the Corporation of Germantown"[17], begun on June 11, 1691, lists him as a member of various administrative bodies of Germantown. Having been given the less prominent position of "Fence surveyor" in 1691, from 1692 he was repeatedly elected one of the six committeemen. In this position, Wilhelm had a good overall knowledge of what happened in Germantown and, certainly, some influence as well, which strengthened his ambition and his self-confidence – especially in his dealings with his brother Jan.

The longer this conflict lasted, the less Jan seemed to trust in Wilhelm's correct administration of the land in Pennsylvania that Jan had entrusted to him. On May 13, 1698, fifteen years after the emigration of the thirteen settlers from the Lower Rhine, Jan Strepers gave "complete power of attorney" from the Krefeld district court to his brother-in-law Reiner Theißen and to Heinrich Sellen, naming both of them as trustees to administer "the inheritance and possessions situated in America in Pensilvania" in the best interest of the owners.[18]

The first task for brother-in-law Theißen and Sellen was to recover the title deeds to the 5,000 acres from Wilhelm, to start calculating as of that date the rent and interest payment accruing annually from the land sold and to collect them in Jan Strepers' name. Both trustees were also given a general power of attorney for selling all of the properties, with exception of the one acre of city property and the 50 acres in the Liberty land between Philadelphia and Germantown. Why Jan Strepers named Heinrich Sellen as his trustee in Pennsylvania is unknown. Possibly he was recommended to him by Franz Daniel Pastorius. The fact that Sellen, a resident of Kriesheim (German township), was present in Krefeld when the power of attorney was issued indicates that he was a well-traveled and experienced person by the standards of that time who had contacts and business interests spanning both continents.

Jan Strepers informed his brother, his brothers-in-law and Reiner Theißen, in particular, of the new situation. He reminded them of the frequent pleas by his Pennsylvania friends to send a legal representative to Pennsylvania to look after his land and financial affairs. He wrote to his relatives that for that reason he had named Reiner Theißen, brother of his wife Anna, and Heinrich Sellen as his legal representatives, by order of the Moers county court in Krefeld. After Sellen had consented before the court to accept that office, Jan Strepers assumed that his brother-in-law would also be willing to do so.

Jan Strepers informed Reiner Theißen and the other relatives that, according to the contract, his brother Wilhelm had to pay a ground rent of five shillings and Johann Lenssen one rix dollar and one stuyver in Dutch currency. As per his contract with William Furly, he asked the trustees to pay only one shilling to William Penn or his heirs. Reiner Theißen was also told that Jan Strepers had given a loan of 62 and a half rix dollars in Dutch currency to Johann Lenssen. On this amount, interest of seven and a half rix dollars annually had been payable for every year since Lenssen's arrival in Pennsylvania. Then there was the annual ground rent to be added to that sum, which meant that each year Johann Lenssen had to pay eight rix dollars and one stuyver in Dutch currency to Jan Strepers' representatives. Thus, in the fall of 1698, Lenssen, who had thus far been unwilling to pay, now had to pay 127 rix dollars and 32 and a half stuyvers to the trustees for 15 years. To complete the information given to his trustees, Jan had enclosed two copies of the contracts with his brother and Lenssen, certified by a notary together with his letter to Reiner Theißen.[19]

In case of the death of one trustee, in their power of attorney the couple Jan and Anna Strepers authorized the surviving one to appoint a second trustee of his own choice. Heinrich Sellen was aware of the delicate and difficult nature of the dispute with Wilhelm Strepers and Johann Lenssen in Germantown. Still, he consented to being a trustee. Initially, Reiner Theißen seems to have likewise exercised his power of attorney. However, being a close relative of Jan and Wilhelm, he was probably not keen to be drawn into the developing family conflict. And in view of the discord and strife already existing among the few settlers of Germantown, which was also deplored by Franz Daniel Pastorius in the introduction to his "Grund- und Lagerbuch", he certainly wanted to avoid further conflict. But perhaps it was only his annoyance over Jan Strepers' letter to Heinrich Sellen, accusing the two trustees of looking after the debtors better than after the creditors, that finally made him relinquish his office. During a court session in Germantown on March 4, 1700, he declared before the bailiff, three committeemen of the Germantown community and the surveyor that he relinquished the office entrusted to him by his brother-in-law Jan Strepers. Nevertheless, Reiner continued to look after Jan Strepers' property in the years to follow.

After Theißen's withdrawal, Sellen suggested Leonhard Arets, one of the thirteen "Krefeld emigrants" and also Jan Strepers' brother-in-law, who declared his consent to the court and was commissioned accordingly. The power of attorney for him was recorded in the "Grund- und Lagerbuch" of Germantown.[20] Whether there was any connection between the discord and strife and Theißen's decision to leave Germantown two years later to retire to his plantation at Abington, Montgomery County, is impossible to ascertain. Fact is that Reiner Theißen, who had held quite a number of important offices in the administration of Germantown, gave up his office of committeeman in midterm, and that a successor had to be elected on May 19, 1702.[21]

In his letter of July 13, 1698, to Johann Lenssen, Jan Strepers seems to have presented his account again to make sure. Quite cleverly he mentions the fact that it had been Johann Lenssen's wish to have trustees named to look after Jan Strepers' property and affairs in Pennsylvania. That was the reason why he, Jan, had named Heinrich Sellen and Reiner Theißen – at considerable expense. Jan now insisted that Lenssen pay all of the interest accumulated over 14 years, the ground rent and the loan, amounting to a total of 181 rix dollars and 32 stuyvers. He would be given a receipt for that amount which would henceforth release him from any and all obligations.[22]

By September 28, 1699, Jan Strepers still had not received any news from Heinrich Sellen, as he wrote angrily in a letter to him. But he did have worrying news from Germantown through other channels. For the two trustees Sellen and Theißen, he complained, were listening more to the debtors' arguments and did not do as he wished. Therefore, he made the point again that the vague claims of both his brother Wilhelm and Johann Lenssen were null and void and not founded in fact. He had to appoint Jan van Loeffenig and Matthias van Bebber as additional trustees along with Leonhard Arets, he wrote, to support Sellen in his efforts. Jan reminded Sellen again to present his bills to the two debtors. If these were not paid, he expected to be notified quickly. He implored his trustee not to sell a single square foot of land in Pennsylvania until he had given further instructions. Hoping that his trustees would now act in his interest, he promised them considerable rewards, without, however, naming any precise sum.[23]

If Wilhelm's concern that any land taken into possession had to be legally transferred within a certain number of years was founded in fact, Jan seems to have played for time and to deliberately have avoided giving his brother the 100 acres he had originally promised him for his work. But probably the real reason for Jan's procrastination was Wilhelm's reluctance to pay his annual interest and ground rent. Besides, he did not accept the bill of expenses Wilhelm had drawn up for the years 1685 and 1686.

On the same day (September 28, 1699), Jan Strepers wrote another letter to his "dear brothers" Reiner Theißen and Leonhard Arets expressing his pleasure at the fact that Jan van Loeffenig and Matthias van Bebber as well as Leonhard Arets had expressed their willingness to support Reiner Theißen in his trusteeship. Again, he put the greatest importance on the payment of Wilhelm Strepers' and Johann Lenssen's debts and asked to make sure that the gift from William Penn, that one acre in Philadelphia, was allotted to him in a good and appropriate location. It seems surprising that this was requested as late as September 1699, as the Secretary of the Board of Property with the help of Hermann Isaaks op den Graeff had already issued a warrant for this property on February 24, 1699.[24] It is possible that the lot had not yet been surveyed and transferred by September 28, 1699, or that Jan had not been notified of this and of his warrant. Arets and Theißen were also asked not to sell any land in Pennsylvania until they had further instructions and they, too, were told that the claims of brother Wilhelm and Jan Lenssen were totally unfounded.[25]

On September 23, 1700, the trustees Heinrich Sellen and Leonhard Arets in the presence of Hermann op den Graeff drew up a transfer deed for Johann Lenssen for the 50 acres agreed upon with Jan Strepers in Krefeld on June 17, 1683. Of these, 14¾ acres were to be in the inhabited part of Germantown, on the east side of Main Street. The remaining 35¼ acres were allotted in the so-called Side Land in the direction of Philadelphia. Johann Lenssen pledged – also on behalf of his heirs – to pay an annual ground rent of one rix dollars and one stuyver in Dutch currency to Jan Strepers and

his heirs on March 1st of each year.[26] Nevertheless, the dispute between Jan Strepers and Johann Lenssen on the purchase price continued, and the matter had to be decided by a court of arbitration on March 27, 1703. It ruled that Johann Lenssen was the owner of the 50 acres and had to pay £15 Pennsylvania silver to Jan Strepers' trustees before September 27, 1704. The payment of the annual ground rent remained unchanged.[27]

At a meeting of the Commissioners of Property on March 1, 1702, it was recorded that of the 5,000

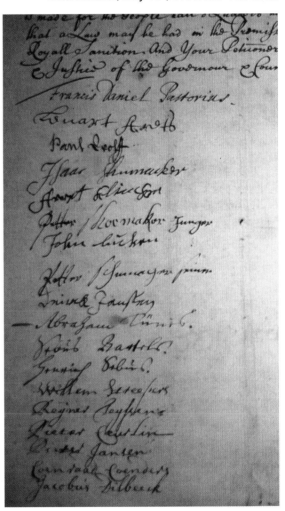

Fig. 12 Petition of the first German immigrants for naturalization, May 15th, 1706. HSP Am 3841.

acres originally bought by Jan Strepers, 50 acres had been allotted meanwhile in the Liberty land and another 275 in Germantown. 275 acres had been sold to Leonhard Arets, a sale which Jan Strepers did not know about at that time. All in all, the area claimed amounted to 600 acres.[28] Nevertheless, Leonhard Arets applied for a warrant for 4,675 acres to be surveyed on the Schuylkill River near the tract of land held by the Frankfurt Company. Following the application, such a warrant for 4,675 acres was issued on March 5, 1702 to Heinrich Sellen and Leonhard Arets in favor of Jan Strepers. The 275 acres bought by Leonhard Arets were transferred to his name on March 23, 1703, by Heinrich Sellen.[29] It seems a strange procedure that the trustee helped himself to a lot from the property he was supposed to be administering. On June 24, 1705, William Penn had a patent issued to the name of Jan Strepers confirming his ownership of 4,448 acres in Bucks County, i.e. less than the acreage originally applied for by Leonhard Arets.[30]

The patent corresponds neither to the acreage applied for by Leonhard Arets nor to the location originally chosen: an area on the Schuylkill River near the tract of land held by the Frankfurt Company. By contrast, the patent guaranteed an area of 4,448 acres in Bucks County bordering on the Delaware River, on the land of the London Company to the southwest, and on William Penn's property to the southeast. The location of this area can be precisely determined on the basis of further correspondence, of the entries in the journal and of the preparations for the court proceedings in Bucks County.

It is striking that an area was chosen deliberately that was not predominantly agricultural, as was originally intended in the application for the Schuylkill River area, but an area envisaged for "industrial" use. It was located in the catchment area of the Royal mines, and the patent included the transfer of mining rights without any obligation for annual or single payments to the owner. The question arises of whether Leonhard Arets, linen weaver from Germantown, could have had so much knowledge of the country that he could have subse-

quently asked to have the land surveyed not on the Schuylkill but on the Delaware River instead. This is doubtful. And it is even less likely that Jan Strepers could have known of the mineral deposits and have asked his trustees to have the Delaware area surveyed. If there had been any question of that, such an important consideration would certainly have been the subject of further correspondence.

There has been speculation in various publications that Jan Strepers spent some time in Pennsylvania. These are certainly based on his intention, expressed repeatedly, to emigrate to Pennsylvania. After all, he did have Wilhelm clear his land for later cultivation and even build a house for him, the location of which, Strepers Place, is still recalled in Johannes Herbergs' journal. From the well-documented correspondence between Jan and Wilhelm it is clear beyond doubt that Jan never took the step of traveling to Pennsylvania. We can only speculate as to his reasons. Had he lost interest in emigration after his wife Anna Doors had been buried in Kaldenkirchen on August 2, 1700? Did he not agree with the religious orientation of his brothers-in-law who had been brought up as Mennonites – at least those from the Theißen family – and had now joined the Quakers?

What influence did his eldest son Leonhard, who had been a linen weaver's apprentice with Johann Lenssen in Germantown, have on his decision? Leonhard will have told his father about the first few years in Pennsylvania, which must have been extremely hard for the new settlers. Did these descriptions make him give up his original plan? In 1700, Jan was at least 60 years old. Did he feel too old for the strenuous journey and, after the death of his wife, disinclined to make a new start in a strange country? Did the disputes with his debtors and the dissatisfaction with his trustees finally wear him down? In any case, it is certain that Jan Strepers did not visit Pennsylvania. And although more people from Kaldenkirchen whom he knew very well and to whom was related embarked on the voyage across the Atlantic after 1683, he never followed. Jan died in Kaldenkirchen on May 6, 1715 at about 11 in the morning.

1 HSP, p. 195, no. 3.
2 HSP, p.195, no. 4.
3 Rotthoff, "Auswanderung von Krefeld", p. 17.
4 HSP, p. 198, no. 5.
5 HSP, p. 197, no. 4.
6 Lib. C., p. 1.
7 Duffin, "Landowners I", p. 37.
8 HSP, p. 197, no. 6.
9 HSP, p. 195 ff.
10 HSP, p. 199, no. 7.
11 HSP, p. 199.
12 HSP, p. 200. For the full text, refer to App. E.
13 Becker, Der Kaldenkirchener Kreis, p. 72.
14 HSP, p. 200.
15 HSP, p. 200 ff, no. 10.
16 HSP, p. 201-202, no. 10.
17 The General Court Book of the Congregation of German-
    town or Raths Buch der Germantownischen Gemeinde
    angefangen den 2te tag des 4te Monats, Anno 1691.

    Transcript by James Duffin. Unpublished ms. (Philadel-
    phia, 1993).
18 Lib. C., p. 3a. For the full text of the document refer to pp. F.
19 HSP, p. 203 ff, no. 11.
20 Grund- und Lagerbuch of Germantown. Transcript by
    James Duffin. Unpublished manuscript, (Philadelphia,
    1993) p. 20.
21 Lib. C., p.3a; Grund- und Lagerbuch, p.50.
22 HSP, p. 204, no. 12.
23 HSP. p. 205, no. 13.
24 Lib. C., p.1.
25 HSP, p. 205 f., no. 14.
26 HSP, p. 183 ff.
27 Lib. C. p. 4.
28 Lib. C. p. 9.
29 Municipal Archives of Krefeld, Property of the Savings
    Bank Foundation.
30 HSP, p. 187 f. For the full text of the document refer
    to App. G.

Fig. 13 Peter Cooper, South East Prospect of the City of Philadelphia. Detail. Oil on canvas, approx. 1720. Library Company. Inv. No. 603.

The Dispute over Jan Strepers' Estate 1715-1726

Two months before his death, Jan Strepers had reinstated his brother Wilhelm as the trustee for his Pennsylvania properties. Since in the power of attorney, which was drawn up by both burgomasters of Kaldenkirchen, the division of the inheritance from Jan's and Wilhelm's parents was also mentioned, this document was to cause some irritation in the years to follow. Although Jan Strepers had taken over the Kaldenkirchen inheritance in a notarized "bill of sale" dated July 17, 1696, and Wilhelm had renounced his share on that occasion because he had already been compensated for it, both brother Wilhelm and the later buyers of the Strepers property in Pennsylvania occasionally – or as it suited them – interpreted this text as a transfer of title.

The transfer of Wilhelm's share of their parents' inheritance to Jan raises the question of whether the inheritance mentioned in the letter of sale of July 17, 1696, and acquired by Jan for 56 rix dollars was merely one part of the parental inheritance? Was the document perhaps referring to the maternal inheritance, the extent of which is not known? If so, was that property really valuable enough for Jan to swap it with Wilhelm? If the other siblings were still alive, the inheritance would have consisted of at least four equal shares. It is hardly conceivable that Jan would have exchanged the land in Pennsylvania, for which he had paid £100 32 years before for an insignificant piece of property in Kaldenkirchen. Or was he so worn down by the long dispute with his brother in America that he chose the less valuable share rather than have nothing at all? Reiner Theißen was the first to recognize the deed as a mere instrument for a trustee and to warn the Kaldenkirchen relatives of a possible misreading of it.

The text drawn up by the town clerk Johann Zielikens was signed neither by Jan nor by his heirs, but merely by the two burgomasters, Johann Franken and Hermann Mevissen, and by the town clerk.

Jan's heirs later concluded from this that no transfer of property could have taken place, since neither the lawful owner nor his direct heirs had signed the document,[1] a problem that was to lead to examinations by lawyers and litigation in the 1760s.

On July 17, 1715, Leonhard Strepers, Jan's eldest son, took a leading role for the first time in the family's dispute over Jan Strepers' estate in America. On that day he informed his uncle of his father's death in a letter that no longer exists. Wilhelm Strepers replied to this as late as August 20, 1716, offering his condolences on the death of his "beloved brother". But he quickly turned to business, writing that from his nephew's letter of the previous year he had gathered that both his brother and his heirs had made him trustee for the Pennsylvania property, as had also been agreed confidentially between Jan Strepers and Leonhard Arets, who had meanwhile passed away, in order to realize the best possible profit from it.[2] He promised to take care of the heirs' affairs with the help of Reiner Theißen, who, on November 23, 1715, had taken the place of the deceased Leonhard Arets, and assured them that there was no reason to distrust them. Wilhelm's letter shows clearly that he again considered himself the trustee for his brother's land, as he had been between 1683 and 1689 prior to his replacement by Heinrich Sellen and Reiner Theißen. He would have liked to involve Leonhard Arets as an advisor, but that had been prevented by the latter's death.

Unfortunately, Wilhelm wrote, Jan had given him and his heirs all rights of trusteeship to the Pennsylvania property, but since he did not have a legally valid power of attorney to prove this, neither he nor his heirs were able to sell the land, as they wanted to. As he could now see that Jan's heirs were also inclined to sell either the entire property or at least part of it, he needed them to send him a deed of transfer, signed by the burgomaster and the elders of Kaldenkirchen and bearing the seal of the court, This was to state that Jan Strepers and his heirs transferred the entire land bought in Pennsylvania and all the rights pertaining thereunto to his brother Wilhelm Strepers and his heirs in perpetuity. For unless that phrasing was used, no land could be sold in Pennsylvania. Was it a trick? Certainly. For such a far-reaching phrasing transferring Jan's entire property in Pennsylvania to Wilhelm would not have been necessary for a mere sale by a trustee. Thus, Wilhelm was trying to take advantage of his Kaldenkirchen relatives' ignorance and to fraudulently obtain the right to have a warrant issued and the land transferred to his name. This was indirect proof that the agreement concluded between himself and Jan in 1715 was worthless.

He was happy to answer the request by his second nephew, Hendrik Strepers, to put a value on the Pennsylvania estate. He had assessed it, together with their uncle Reiner Theißen and had arrived at a price of 2,062 guilders and 10 stuyvers in Dutch currency. If he succeeded in getting a higher price for it, the higher sum would, of course, be paid to the Kaldenkirchen relatives.

On August 31, 1716, obviously annoyed by Wilhelm Strepers' behavior, Reiner Theißen wrote to the brothers Leonhard and Hendrik Strepers and their sisters. His advice to them – which was certainly not in Wilhelm Strepers' interest – was to appoint new trustees as quickly as possible. The reason was that he distrusted Wilhelm Strepers, who in Leonhard Arets' very death chamber had urged him to assume the position of Jan Strepers' representative that he had had before, and this at a time when Jan had legally entrusted Wilhelm with his property in Pennsylvania. Wilhelm had given him a registered bond quoting the value of the property at 2,062 rix dollars and 10 stuyvers in Dutch currency. That was the sum that Wilhelm Strepers had mentioned in his letter to Leonhard Strepers as having been calculated with the help of Reiner Theißen, which was obviously not true. Reiner implored the siblings to name trustees, not only because of the difficulties caused by Wilhelm Strepers but also because of the still unfinished business with Johann Lenssen. If he finishes by saying that he was glad not to have agreed to Wilhelm Strepers' wish, we can conclude that he did not wish to be a party to such dubious proceedings.[3] Reiner Theißen chose his words carefully. After all, he was talking about close relatives. But his refusal to cooperate with Wilhelm Strepers as a trustee

for Jan Strepers' children was meant as a serious warning.

In the undertaking he gave to Reiner Theißen on August 23, 1716, Wilhelm pledged himself and his heirs to pay a total of £250 Pennsylvania silver to Jan Strepers and his heirs as soon as Jan Strepers' land was sold or to pay a fine of £500. Wilhelm seems to have equated the purchase price with the value of the land estimated by himself and (purportedly) Reiner Theißen at 2,062 Dutch guilders.

In his will dated October 18, 1717, Wilhelm Strepers bequeathed 250 acres to his stepson Peter Jansen (the son of his wife Maria from her first marriage), who already had possession of them. His son Leonhard Strepers was given another 250 acres adjacent to the aforementioned lot, as well as 50 acres in Krefeld, German Township. His son John Strepers received 50 acres in Sommerhausen along with the house and all its furnishings. His daughter Catherine Strepers was given the ownership of all those belongings she already had the use of, the value of which equaled her brothers' inheritance. John was supposed to administer the plantation on which William Strepers himself lived and to have the financial profit from it. In return, he had to pay for the living expenses of his mother, Maria Strepers, and to give her £9 Pennsylvania silver a year. At her death, the plantation was to be valued by independent experts and then bought for that sum by John Strepers. The sum was to be divided among the siblings, with John being entitled to take out £25 for himself before that division. Wilhelm's wife Maria was given the use of all of her husband's movable chattels, which were to be divided among her children only after her death. Leonhard Strepers was instructed to put 12 silver shillings at his mother's disposal every year. Finally, Wilhelm made his wife the sole executor. Johann Lucken, her brother, and Tönis Kunders were asked to assist her in this function.[4]

November 15, 1717, is given as the date of Wilhelm Strepers' death, although an inventory of his property had already been drawn up on November 8, 1717. Among other things, the inventory of the estate mentions that Jan Strepers still owed his brother £26 5s 4d. At the end of the inventory there is an almost cursory remark that the land that Jan Strepers had transferred to his late brother Wilhelm had a value of £250. That land Wilhelm also bequeathed to his children.[5]

It was this last remark in the inventory of the estate that made Wilhelm Strepers' heirs act quickly. They sought to sell the land fast that had fraudulently come into their possession. This is shown by a warrant issued by the Commissioners of Property, Richard Hill, Isaac Norris and James Logan, to the merchant Even Owen on April 29, 1718. The Commissioners noted that the one acre in the city of Philadelphia had been transferred from Jan Strepers' heirs to Even Owen. For this reason, Jacob Taylor, Chief Surveyor, was instructed to survey the property. The location of the acre in the city was given as "Mulberry Street or Sassafras Street on Delaware Side in ye said City".[6] With the Return of Survey, dated April 21, 1718, the patent on that acre was issued to Even Owen.[7] The deed confirmed that Jan Strepers had registered his land in Pennsylvania in his brother Wilhelm's name. This contract had been drawn up on March 4, 1715, in Jan Strepers' place of residence, Kaldenkirchen, by the burgomasters and elders of that city. The Board of Commissioners in Philadelphia obviously interpreted that document as a deed transferring the title, and it was officially entered as a deed at the Land Office. After Wilhelm Strepers' death, his sons Leonhard and John as his legal successors had sold the Philadelphia property to Even Owen, who was registered as its owner on April 12th and 14th. On receipt of the patent, Even Owen transferred the acre to the name of Richard Hill the very same day.

As Commissioner of Property, Richard Hill had probably been reluctant to buy the acre in the city of Philadelphia from Wilhelm Strepers' heirs directly. Since Even Owen made his new property over to Richard Hill the same day, he can only have served as front man for the latter, either because he owed Hill a favor or because he was paid to do so. At any rate, in buying the land Richard Hill took advantage of his position as Commissioner of Property, which meant that he knew about all land transactions made, to make a speculative purchase. The lot was in an extremely good location on what was then the edge of the built-up area. For a man in his position, it was easy to foresee the profit he would be able to realize within a very short period by buying this acre of the Strepers property.

About a year after Wilhelm Strepers' death, his widow Maria Lucken tried, for the second time apparently, to contact Jan Strepers' descendants in Kaldenkirchen. On October 2, 1718, she wrote to Leonhard and Hendrik Strepers and their sisters that she had already written a first letter and given it to John Kulp when he left for Germany. On his return, Kulp had told her that he had talked to the Kaldenkirchen relatives in person.

After the power of attorney issued by the burgomasters of Kaldenkirchen in 1715 had passed to Wilhelm's heirs with the ensuing expense and effort, she would do her utmost to keep down the cost of pursuing the matter. When Uncle Reiner Theißen had been asked for advice, he had scolded and even accused her of acting faithlessly. He had made a big fuss and caused quite a stir. However, she felt justified. She had a clear task set for her in the power of attorney. Nevertheless, she was being prevented from selling the land, and the whole enterprise cost more than was necessary. Because of these troubles, they were even obliged to have the land surveyed a second time, a very costly procedure in Pennsylvania. Further damage had been caused by Reiner Theißen, who had objected to the sale of part of the property because he thought it had been sold without power of attorney. Yet originally he had said to sell the land and even given detailed instructions. Why he was acting that way now she could not say. It was possible that he thought that she and her sons wanted to enrich themselves on someone else's property.

The situation with Reiner Theißen being what it was now, Maria and her sons Leonhard and John urged their cousins to decide whether they wanted to take the mandate to continue administering the land away from Wilhelm Strepers' heirs, a move which the latter would understand since they had nothing but trouble and expense with the sale.

However, if the Kaldenkirchen relatives still wanted them to proceed with selling the land, as had also been Jan Strepers' will with the consent of all his children, it would have to be possible according to English law under which so far they had no authorization. For that reason, they needed another power of attorney stating that they had the right to transfer land as hereditary property in perpetuity to the buyer. If this was granted, she wrote, they would pursue the matter to the best of their knowledge and ability. Maria Strepers and her two sons would be much happier if the matter were taken out of their hands since it brought them nothing but trouble, due not least to poor communication caused by the great distance between Germany and Pennsylvania.[8]

Jan Strepers had already distrusted his brother at a very early point in time. Was this why, after 1683, more close relatives, the brothers-in-law Hermann Theißen (1684) and Paulus Küsters (1691/92) sailed to America with their families in order to look into the situation? Why did Jan finally take the control of the Pennsylvania property away from his brother Wilhelm by giving a power of attorney to Heinrich Sellen and Reiner Theißen? The supposed exchange of the acquired and/or inherited land between Jan and Wilhelm Strepers seems to have been viewed with skepticism by Jan's heirs from the beginning. In any case, his children tried to make it appear null and void in the following years. Many letters were sent across the Atlantic and often left unanswered by the relatives in Germantown. Several times the heirs set out on the long and expensive journey to America in order to win back there land on the spot.

A first call to take back the land and to critically look into the actions of the relatives in Pennsylvania may have been contained in a letter from Reiner Theißen. On September 4, 1719, he wrote to Leonhard, Hendrik and Catharina Strepers in Kaldenkirchen and reminded them of his previous letter in which he had told them of Wilhelm's death and of his quarrel with Wilhelm caused by the latter's bad behavior. For when, after the death of brother Leonhard Arets, Wilhelm held the power of attorney issued by the burgomaster and the council of Kaldenkirchen in his hands, he acted as if all of Jan

Strepers' land were his own. That had caused him, Reiner Theißen, a lot of problems, as he had already described in detail in his last letter. And Wilhelm's sons had not behaved any better after their father's death. The land belonging to Jan Strepers heirs was at risk. That was why he was urging them a second time to send a well-founded power of attorney to him and his friend Caspar Hudts. He really would much prefer to keep out of the affair, as he had already written the previous year. But for the sake of friendship and justice he would work devotedly to do everything in his power.

As Reiner Theißen learned from a letter from Kaldenkirchen, such a power of attorney had been sent to Pennsylvania. When he had approached the Strepers on the subject, they had told him they had not received any. And strangely enough, they had only given him the letter addressed to him from Kaldenkirchen. He referred to his letter of the previous year, again asking his relatives to send the same power of attorney for the sale, signed by the burgomaster and the council, to him and Caspar Hudt. It would be best to send one of the Kaldenkirchen relatives to Germantown with the authorization to act in their name. Some action had to be taken, in any case, for at present the land was in the wrong person's hands.[9]

Four years after Jan's death, the first efforts at regaining the property in Pennsylvania started from the Lower Rhine. On December 15, 1719, Wilhelm Sieben, schoolmaster in Kaldenkirchen and husband of Jan's daughter Catharina Strepers, wrote to her cousins Leonhard and John and aunt Maria Strepers in Germantown. After a flowery introduction inquiring after the well-being of the American relatives, he quickly got to the point, appealing to the friendship and the close blood ties with the cousins and the aunt and explaining the difficulties in clarifying the property question caused by the great distance. He professed disappointment at the fact that, in spite of the power of attorney that had been "ceremoniously renewed" and been sent, as requested, by him and his relatives more than a year before, no news of progress in the property question had been received. Wilhelm Sieben refrained from actually saying that, to him, this delay in reaching an honest solution of the property problem was by itself an admission of dishonesty on the part of his Germantown relatives and that, instead of giving a straight answer, Maria Strepers and her sons merely announced their husband's or father's death.

Wilhelm Sieben asked to have future replies written by the same person that had already written Wilhelm Strepers' letters. Perhaps he was hoping that the writer, being familiar with events in Germantown, would unwittingly cause the relatives to give a more truthful account. Who might that person have been who handled Wilhelm's correspondence? Wilhelm was able to write. His signature is not that of an unpracticed hand but, rather, of an experienced writer. If that person was Franz Daniel Pastorius, which is likely, he could have been brought in by Wilhelm as an adviser. After all, as a lawyer and as "co-builder of Germantown", Pastorius was thoroughly familiar with matters of property and the legal problems connected with it.

Wilhelm Sieben took a sizeable risk by saying that the relatives in Kaldenkirchen were not mistrustful of those in Germantown and that they assumed the power of attorney and the transfer of rights would not be interpreted the wrong way. He stressed that from both Wilhelm Strepers letters and the replies it had become clear that Wilhelm and his heirs had pledged themselves to serve the interests of their Kaldenkirchen relatives.

Wilhelm Sieben's letter was found in the 1760s by Dr. Samuel Preston Moore, a counterpart of Peter Heinrich Strepers and Johannes Herbergs in the dispute over the return of the Strepers property. At the time, it was in the hands of William Strepers, a grandson of Wilhelm Strepers living in Chestnut Hill near Philadelphia. Ludwig Weiss, the lawyer of the German Society in Philadelphia, was among those present when the letter was discovered. On March 6, 1766, he translated it into English. A crucial passage confirming the claims of the Kaldenkirchen relatives ran as follows: "...thereto might be seriously considered purporting that our lands in that country might well be sold to advantage and in such manner that after sale being made thereof the consideration money could be transmitted to us either in coin or by bills of exchange and that at the sale thereof this precaution should be taken that the good and bad land is sold together..."[10]

So Wilhelm Strepers had been given clear instructions to sell, stipulating that the various properties were of different quality and that, therefore, the best land should not be sold first, to avoid the risk of being left with the poorer lands. These instructions from Jan Strepers' heirs made their claim to ownership clear. There is no indication that Wilhelm Strepers ever disputed that claim, although that did not prevent either him or his heirs from taking their own decisions on the spot in their own favor and ignoring the instructions and wishes of Jan Strepers' heirs.

Wilhelm Sieben made an offer to the relatives in Germantown. If these had any doubts as to the value of the parental property in Kaldenkirchen, the family there was willing to have the council value the property and also to furnish proof of the value of Lambert Strepers' inheritance which Jan Strepers had bought from his niece. This share was equal to the share that had been due to their father and uncle Wilhelm. By simply comparing the proportional value of the inheritance in Kaldenkirchen with the properties in Pennsylvania it would be easy to calculate credits and debits between the families. Thus, Sieben directly admitted that Wilhelm Strepers' heirs were entitled to some compensation. At the same time, he admonished his relatives to present an equally honest calculation of the value of the Pennsylvania property and its yields.[11]

Wilhelm Sieben expressed his annoyance at the fact that, although Wilhelm Strepers had chosen Reiner Theißen as his co-trustee after Leonhard Arets' death on November 3, 1715, with their consent, Theißen had not been informed on developments by the Germantown Strepers at all, that they in fact avoided speaking to him and had not even allowed him to read the power of attorney from Kaldenkirchen. Sieben made it quite clear that, despite the great distance, he also had other sources of information. His uncovering of the truth sounded like a call to his relatives to return to dealing fairly with each other since their lies had, in any case, been discovered.

At the end of his letter, Wilhelm Sieben again emphatically demanded information on the value of the properties after they had been cleared and prepared for cultivation. He expressly asked about the Germantown lot, the acre in the city of Philadelphia and the 50 acres in the Liberty land. That question again indicates that Wilhelm and his heirs in Germantown did as they pleased with Jan Strepers' property, without informing him or his heirs of their actions. The acre in Philadelphia, for instance, had been sold without their knowledge.[12]

This letter from Kaldenkirchen, which is dated December 15, 1719, also came into Reiner Theißen's hands. He had possibly been sent a copy, since the Strepers on the Lower Rhine no longer trusted the Pennsylvania Strepers. Reiner Theißen professed his understanding at the fact that Leonhard, Hendrik Strepers and their sisters were not pleased with the differences that had arisen between him and his nephews Leonhard and John Strepers in Pennsylvania as that could only harm their cause. He in turn asked for their understanding, writing that, indeed, he had no pleasure in reporting this. However, he defended his American nephews by explaining that the differences had not been caused by them but their father. This he had already written in an earlier letter which, however, had not reached the Kaldenkirchen relatives.

As has been already said, for safety's sake letters over such a long distance were given to travelers who either delivered them directly to the addressee or entrusted them to the mail in London, Amsterdam or Rotterdam. This was a relatively safe way to have letters delivered quickly and directly. The Pennsylvania Strepers occasionally mentioned, as did Reiner Theißen, that letters were sent together. On such occasions it could happen that unpleasant letters, such as those from or to Reiner Theißen, were intercepted by the Strepers of Germantown. Otherwise it is impossible to explain why letters that were sent to the same person at the same time by Theißen and the Germantown cousins were not also delivered together. This is how letters containing unfavorable reports about the overseas relatives could disappear.

Since Reiner Theißen had learned that his last letter had not arrived, he repeated what had happened after the death of Leonhard Arets, whom he also called an uncle of the Kaldenkirchen relatives.

After Leonhard Arets' death, Reiner Theißen took over the office of trustee as Arets had wished. However, he was soon to discover that he could not act with respect to the property since the power of attorney issued by Jan Strepers and his wife in his name in 1696 was no longer valid, as he had rejected it at the time. Subsequently, Leonhard Arets had been suggested by Heinrich Sellen and appointed in his place. Furthermore, meanwhile Wilhelm Strepers in the document issued in 1715 had been authorized to sell the land. That had been a reason for him not to get involved, which is why he handed over his authorization to sell and the letters concerning this property matter to Leonhard Arets' children. This authorization was then appropriated by Wilhelm Strepers, who did not inform or consult anybody. Since the Kaldenkirchen relatives had made it clear in their letters that they were going to accept Wilhelm as trustee only together with Reiner Theißen, Wilhelm had asked him to take Leonhard Arets' place. However, Wilhelm had soon come to regret this, since Reiner refused to go along with his dishonest dealings.

In the meantime, Reiner had learned that English people had acquired part of Jan Strepers' property and had it surveyed. Therefore, they themselves had had to commission a surveyor to do a new survey of the property, to mark it with stones and fence it in. John Strepers, Wilhelm's son, had inspected the land together with Reiner Theißen. It was a nice piece of land with a creek with enough water to drive a mill. John Strepers had shown great interest in it and had been willing to exchange it for another lot, but he, Reiner, had refused this and not given his consent.

When, some time later, they had been sitting together with Leonhard Arets' children over some accounts, John Strepers had again mentioned this exchange. Again he, Reiner, had objected and told him he did not have the right either to sell or exchange that land. Upon this, their uncle Wilhelm Strepers had said that the land in question was his own land and that he wanted to see the person who was going to take it away from him. That same evening, Wilhelm Strepers had gone to Philadelphia, had the power of attorney for the sale translated into English and the land entered into the register as his own.

A short time afterwards, he had again gone to Philadelphia to sell the lot in Philadelphia and also the 50 acres in the Liberty land near Philadelphia at a very low price, without telling or involving Reiner Theißen. So it was not true that no land had been sold, as Tönis Kunders had written to the Strepers in Kaldenkirchen. Kunders was a very devout man, and he certainly had not written such a thing out of malice but possibly because he had forgotten about the matter.

Reiner Theißen assumed his nephews and nieces in Kaldenkirchen could easily imagine how the land had been sold, if they knew that James Logan, William Penn's secretary, who had already acquired plenty of land, had bought that particular lot. With this remark, Reiner Theißen implied that the land had knowingly been sold, although James Logan, who should or could know both the laws of the country and the legal situation with respect to Jan Strepers' property, had evaded the law and acted improperly together with Wilhelm Strepers.

This assumption is supported by Reiner Theißen's next remarks. He wrote that the issue of the deed of sale had been delayed after he had made this wrongfulness known to others, explaining how Wilhelm had acted in the matter. Such brazenness had upset him, Reiner, so much that it had given him heart pains. He had also consulted with friends (probably Quakers) as to what could be done to prevent the matter from going any further or to bring it to a good end. There had been various discussions with Wilhelm as well as attempts to avoid any losses for Jan Strepers' children in Kaldenkirchen. But while these debates were still going on, Wilhelm had fallen ill and died. But Reiner Theißen did not want to leave unmentioned that, during a conversation in which he had appealed to his conscience, Wilhelm Strepers had said that he regretted the whole matter. He had probably had the wrong advisers.

After Wilhelm's death he had hoped to find his children easier to deal with since they knew exactly the legal situation with respect to the sale of the land. However, they had seemed even worse to him than their father. They did not even want to see him, and their mother had even agreed with them by invoking the old power of attorney for the sale according to which Jan Strepers' land was now theirs.

Some months later, he had heard that Wilhelm Strepers children were planning to sell all of the land. This had made him very angry since he feared they would half give it away without Jan Strepers' heirs ever seeing a stuyver. He had gone together with two witnesses to see them and had forbidden them to sell any of the land belonging to Jan Strepers' children until such time as the dispute over the authorization to do so, which had begun between himself and Wilhelm Strepers and which was now continuing with the latter's children, had been brought to a legally correct resolution.

Wilhelm Strepers' children also denied having received a notarized authorization from the Kaldenkirchen relatives. Instead, he had been shown a deed of sale, made out to Leonhard Strepers in Germantown. Reiner confessed that he had no great desire to continue the correspondence in this family matter. He declared they were all his friends, on both sides, and he regretted ever having gotten involved. From his letter they could now see how the matter stood. He would prefer to be released from all further obligations.

He had thought of a way to put an end to the entire conflict. He was wondering whether it would not be feasible to choose one or two of Jan Strepers' heirs to buy back the original property in Pennsylvania from Wilhelm Strepers' children by way of a notarized document. If they were willing to do this, it should be signed by all the heirs and sealed and then sent to the three uncles in Pennsylvania, that is to say to himself, Tönis Kunders and Peter Kürlis. And those two who were chosen by the family to be the purchasers should send a letter to these three, confirming that the three uncles could act as their authorized representatives.

All of the differences had their origin in Leonhard Arets' view that the land had been taken from the Kaldenkirchen relatives, in accordance with English law. This was not true. Their father, Jan Strepers, had unequivocally bought the land for himself and his heirs forever.

Reiner Theißen finished his letter by saying that if they agreed to this procedure they should obtain copies of the deeds of purchase with the sums paid by Wilhelm Strepers, so these purchase prices could be taken into account in making an offer. In the meantime, he would pay attention that no more land was sold.[13]

A letter from Reiner Theißen to Leonhard, eldest son of Jan Strepers, and his relatives, dated November 16, 1722, is the next to tell us of developments in the matter. He replies to a letter from Leonhard Strepers in Kaldenkirchen, dated October 31, 1721, the content of which is not known. Reiner confirmed that, on receiving that letter, he had contacted Maria Strepers and her son Leonhard, as he had been asked to do. He had not gone there by himself but, rather, accompanied by his brothers-in-law Tönis Kunders and Peter Kürlis. They had looked through every letter and not found any power of attorney except that given to Wilhelm Strepers and Reiner Theißen and their heirs. Leonhard Strepers had agreed to accept the power of attorney as successor to his father Wilhelm. Reiner and Leonhard had then consulted with each other and agreed to recognize Jan Strepers' land in Pennsylvania as belonging to his heirs in Germany. The authorization to sell served no purpose but to sell the land under trust and to send the proceeds to the heirs of Jan Strepers.

In his last letter of October 31, 1721, Leonhard Strepers in Kaldenkirchen had apparently again asked for a compilation of interest and ground rents. Reiner promised to follow this up and to send the requested list as soon as possible.[14]

In a letter dated April 9, 1723, Reiner Theißen sent to Leonhard Strepers of Kaldenkirchen and his relatives a copy of the mutual obligation between him and the American cousin Leonhard Strepers, as signed and sealed on December 31, 1722.[15]

In the accompanying letter Reiner Theißen wrote that it had not been easy to obtain, but that he had finally succeeded with the help of their uncle Tönis Kunders. He, in turn, had also issued such a letter of obligation to Leonhard Strepers, in order to exclude himself and his heirs from any claims against Jan Strepers' heirs. As was apparent from the document between himself and Leonhard Strepers, Griffith Jones, husband of Tönis Kunders youngest daughter, had meanwhile become a partner, since Leonhard Strepers was lame and, hence, very restricted in his activities.

Reiner Theißen made it clear in his letter that at that stage no land belonging to Jan Strepers' heirs had been sold with the exception of the 50 acres of Liberty land that Wilhelm Strepers had sold. However, he assumed that those 50 acres could also be recovered and bought back to the best advantage for Jan's heirs. He also mentioned the acre in the city of Philadelphia, the gift from William Penn to Jan Strepers, which had not been claimed until then. The documents on this had only recently come into his hands. Leonhard and his relatives could rest assured that he would look into that as well.

There followed a compilation of costs of additional surveys, sums that had been advanced by both Wilhelm Strepers (£10) and Griffith Jones (£4 11s 4d). On the other hand, Jan Lenssen still owed £8 13s 10d. The account was very short. If Leonhard and his relatives wanted a more detailed list this could only be done at considerable effort. Reiner Theißen concluded by explaining the exchange rate at the time, for better understanding. He wrote that £3 sterling were worth £4 in Pennsylvanian currency, and that £1 sterling was worth eleven Dutch guilders. Reiner implored the Kaldenkirchen relatives to finally tell him whether Leonhard Arets' children were to have the 275 acres for administering the Strepers' property or not. Together with Wilhelm Strepers he had calculated that Jan's heirs still owed Wilhelm 10 rix dollars.[16]

After this letter, there seems to have been no contact between the two families for about two years. In view of the fact that sometimes more than a year passed between a letter with a question and the letter of reply, it is understandable that the Kaldenkirchen relatives experienced a certain sense of despair.

On the one hand, however, the sons of Wilhelm Strepers continued to recognize the land of the late Jan Strepers as belonging to his heirs in Kaldenkirchen, as shown by a document dated January 18, 1725, according to which Leonhard Strepers, son of Wilhelm, together with Reiner Theißen from Abington and Griffith Jones acted as "trustees or agents for the children of John Strepers" and sold 4,448 acres out of the original 5,000 as well as the 50 acres of Liberty land and the one acre in Philadelphia to James Logan, William Penn's secretary. On the other hand, that same document states once again that on May 4, 1715, Jan Strepers – with the consent of his children Leonhard, Hendrik, Metgen, Catharina and Anneken – had transferred his land in Pennsylvania to his brother Wilhelm. From the very beginning, the Office of Records in Philadelphia had interpreted the document issued in Kaldenkirchen in 1715 to mean that Jan had transferred his property in Pennsylvania to Wilhelm and not just the rights to sell it on Jan's behalf. The irritations caused by the document from the burgomasters of Kaldenkirchen continued until the late 1780s when the writer of the journal, Johannes Herbergs, who had waged a bitter fight to regain the land, died in Philadelphia on July 13, 1789, on the eve of the outbreak of the French Revolution.

For the sale of the three lots, James Logan paid £200 sterling in English currency, to be given to Jan Strepers' heirs, and a further £75 in Pennsylvania currency directly to the three trustees. For this total sum, James Logan obtained the land as hereditary property. James Logan instructed John Askew, merchant in London, to pay the purchase sum to Jan Strepers' children, so that the transaction would be completed within eight months, making him the owner of the land. The document stated further that if one of the parties to the contract, James Logan or Jan Strepers' heirs, did not sign it, or if no payment was made, the (preliminary) contract concluded with the trustees would be null and void.[17] For the investigations later conducted by Peter Heinrich Strepers and Johannes Herbergs, this passage is of great importance, since they had to succeed in convincing the courts in Philadelphia and Bucks County that the contract had not been signed by all of the heirs and/or by some

who where not entitled to inherit, and was therefore invalid.

Several months later, on October 16, 1725, another agreement between Reiner Theißen, Leonhard Strepers, Griffith Jones and James Logan, signed and sealed by all of them (the seals were later removed), gave more concrete details of the sale of the land. The agreement stipulated that of Jan Strepers' original 5,000 acres, James Logan acquired approximately 4,420 or 4,440 acres plus 50 acres of Liberty land and the one acre in Philadelphia. For these, £200 sterling was to be paid to the heirs, plus another £75 in Pennsylvania currency in two installments of £35 and £40, respectively, on fixed dates. In return, Jan's heirs and Wilhelm's children were to issue letters certified by the courts and confirming that the transfer of property and the payments were legally valid.[18]

On April 10, 1728, Lawrence Alexander Grant and Richard Vile, sailors, affirmed by oath in front of Justice of the Peace Thomas Lawrence, that they had been present when the "heirs of Jan Strepers" signed the deed of sale in Amsterdam on July 21, 1726. A copy of the document was deposited in the Office for Recording Deeds of the City and County of Philadelphia on September 25, 1730.[19]

Since Leonhard Strepers had died in Kaldenkirchen on August 18, 1725, his brother-in-law Wilhelm Sieben seems to have continued the negotiations with the trustees in Pennsylvania. He probably also prepared the journey of those Kaldenkircheners who signed Logan's contract of purchase in Amsterdam. In Amsterdam he could be sure of the support of the van Acken relatives, with whom they certainly also stayed.

For the continuation of a smooth and legally correct transaction and for the general understanding of the reader, it is important to take a closer look at those persons described as heirs to Jan Strepers and his wife Ann, née Doors. In a list of June 26, 1726, which has been preserved in several different copies in English, the family ties are shown as precisely as was possible at the time.[20] The research done by Dr. Samuel Preston Moore, one of the later part-owners of the original Strepers property, gives an exact survey of who among the signatories of the contract with James Logan was entitled to inherit. This could have given clear evidence to the courts in Philadelphia and Bucks County as to who gave a valid signature and who did not. According to Moore's records[21], the children of the van Acken couple signed the contract. As Jan Strepers' grandchildren, they were entitled to inherit. Maria Sieben, wife of the late Leonhard Strepers, on the other hand, was not a direct heir. Her signature was invalid, as was that of Elisabeth Olmis, wife of the late Hendrik Strepers. His son, Hendrik, a grandson, appended a valid signature. Wilhelm Sieben, husband of the late Catharina Strepers, was not a direct descendant and, therefore, not entitled, nor was Lambert Moll, husband of the late Anna Strepers. With the exception of the van Acken children and of Hendrik Strepers, the majority of the signatories were merely related to Jan Strepers by marriage and not by blood. The document signed at Amsterdam was not legally valid because, firstly, some of those who signed it were not entitled heirs and, secondly, not all heirs (grandchildren) signed it. In addition, those who did not sign it had not issued a power of attorney to other entitled heirs. The legal opponent of Peter Heinrich Strepers and Johannes Herbergs in the mid-1760s, Samuel Preston Moore, was also confronted with the question of whether the signatures of those family members who were not direct descendants were legally valid in Germany or Holland. He instructed his advisers to investigate the matter from a legal point of view.

Although a contract of sale had been concluded between Jan Strepers' heirs – even if some of them were not his direct descendants – and James Logan, there seem to have been problems in connection with the transfer of the property to the buyer and the entry into the land register in his name. For only an May 15, 1727, a warrant was issued by the Commissioners of Property, listing the following facts: Reiner Theißen, Leonhard Strepers and Griffith Jones, as trustees of the heirs of Jan Strepers, First Purchaser of 5,000 acres of land in the Province of Pennsylvania, effected a sale to James Logan. 4,448 acres of the total of 5,000 had been allotted in Bucks County in 1703, as had been included in Jan Strepers' patent of 1705. Af-

ter the sale, the trustees noticed the following problems. Firstly, the Indians were claiming the land that had been allotted in Bucks County by William Penn's agents. Secondly, since Jan Strepers had not been naturalized in Pennsylvania (although this is always declared in the literature to have been the case), he was considered a foreigner and, as such, could not legally sell his land and his children's inheritance to a local citizen. Because of those difficulties, it was suggested that Jan Strepers' heirs renounce the property in Bucks County and the same number of acres be surveyed for the buyers in another location by the office of the Penn family, owners of the colony.

Since the buyers were James Logan and partners the suggestion was to survey the same number of acres in another location in Bucks County where they would be useful in setting up iron works. James Logan had already obtained the consent and approval of William Penn's heirs for such an enterprise. In line with these facts, James Logan was allotted 4,448 acres as hereditary property in the new township of Durham, Bucks County, to consolidate already existing properties, as it were. The warrant is signed by Richard, Hill, Isaac Norris and Thomas Griffiths. A copy of this warrant was issued on September 18, 1764, in the context of the legal dispute Strepers versus Moore.[22]

The fact that James Logan and his partner were given substitute lands in Bucks County located conveniently near the iron works he already operated shows the way in which Strepers' heirs and, indeed, Jan himself were deceived. As William Penn's secretary, James Logan naturally was quite familiar with the quality of the soils in the province of Pennsylvania. We may assume that he, who even after William Penn's death was on excellent terms with the proprietors, did everything in his power to exchange the area bought from Strepers' heirs against more valuable land in a location that he knew to have iron deposits in the immediate vicinity of his iron works. Likewise, the Indian claim to the original lot seems to have been a pretext, since the owners of the province had concluded detailed contracts with the Indians and did not allot any land to which Indians were entitled. And finally, the fact that Jan was not naturalized need not be considered an obstacle, either. In the contract between William Penn, Jan Strepers and others there is no clause to be found anywhere limiting the purchase, bequest or sale in any way. Therefore, we may rightly assume that the heirs far away on the Lower Rhine were quite insidiously "to be taken to the cleaners".

Against this background, the purchase price that James Logan had paid to the heirs at Amsterdam must be considered extremely low. As early as March 11, 1721, Leonhard Strepers paid £17 in Pennsylvania silver for 25 acres[23] in Germantown, and on May 13, 1729, Dirk op den Graeff sold to John Lewis of Philadelphia 95[24] acres in the township of Hanover for £90 in Pennsylvanian currency. It is, of course, impossible to compare the property sizes without knowing what the quality of the soil was or whether they were building, farming or forest land. Still, the payment of £200 sterling and £75 Pennsylvania for 5,000 acres plus 50 acres of Liberty land and the extremely valuable acre of Philadelphia property seems very low indeed. So this may safely be called a big fraud that was pulled over the Kaldenkirchen relatives.

What was Reiner Theißen's part in all of this? Reiner, who distrusted Wilhelm and later his heirs as well, as he had written in various letters to Jan's heirs in Kaldenkirchen. Why did he, who through his many and varied administrative functions in the Germantown community had a thorough knowledge of land prices, keep silent on such an outrageously low price? Was it resignation? Did he not have the courage to fight the machinations of his Germantown relatives? Was he only good at writing letters? Supposedly he had already admonished Wilhelm Strepers once and made him see the error of his ways before his death. Why was he keeping quiet now? Was it James Logan, secretary to William Penn and one of the most prominent and influential Quakers in Pennsylvania who intimidated him? Reiner Theißen was also a Quaker. Was this religious affiliation a reason why he was forbidden to speak or decided to keep silent himself? All of this is mere conjecture. But we are left with the impression that the Strepers of Kaldenkirchen were defrauded, intentionally and with the help of their own relatives in Pennsylvania.

On May 26, 1727, the Commissioners of Property, Richard Hill, Isaac Norris and Thomas Griffiths, issued a warrant in Philadelphia for the land purchase made by James Logan. This warrant recalled that the areas in question were 4,448 acres surveyed in the name of Jan Strepers in Bucks County and confirmed as his property by patent in 1705. Reiner Theißen, Leonhard Strepers and Griffith Jones had tried for years to sell the land for Jan and his heirs. This had not been possible since, for one thing, Jan died as a foreigner without having been naturalized, which had caused problems for the sale as hereditary freehold land. On the other hand, the Indians had registered their claim to the land, and, therefore, the only possibility had been to give it back to the Proprietor and to have the same acreage surveyed in another location, i.e. in Durham Township in Bucks County. James Logan was asked to submit the Return of Survey to the Commissioners as soon as the land was surveyed, after which the patent, the legal transfer of the property, could be issued to him.

1 Lib.C., p. 145. For the full text of the document see App. H.
2 HSP, p. 191.
3 HSP, p. 192, no. 15.
4 Lib.C., p. 6.
5 HSP, p. 193 ff.
6 Lib.C., p. 7.
7 Lib.C., p. 7.
8 HSP, p. 208, no. 7.
9 HSP, p. 207.
10 Lib.C., p. 11-12.
11 Lib. C,, p. 11-12.
12 Lib. C,, p. 11-12.
13 HSP, p. 209-212.
14 HSP, p. 213.
15 HSP, p. 213 f., see Appendix I.
16 HSP, p. 215.
17 Lib. C., p. 14.
18 HSP, p. 217.
19 HSP, p. 219-223, Municipal Archives Krefeld; Keussen Collection A 98. For the full text of the document refer to App. K.
20 Lib.C., p. 15-18. Metgen Kürlis, Anna Doors eldest daughter from her first marriage. She was born in 1664, died in 1719 and had six children with her husband Henrich Jansen van Acken, who died in 1715: Claus, Anna, Wilhelm, Agneta, Hendrik and Elisabeth. – Leonhard Strepers was the first son from Jan Strepers' marriage to Anna Doors. He was born in 1670 and died August 19, 1715. Leonhard married Maria Sieben, the sister of the Kaldenkirchen schoolmaster Wilhelm Sieben. They had five children, Anna, Elisabeth, Peter, Agnes and Katharina. The wife and all of the children were still living when the list of Jan Strepers' heirs was drawn up. Maria Sieben died on July 31, 1726 in Amsterdam, 10 days after the contract was signed. Heinrich Strepers was born in 1672. He died on July 26, 1724. he had to children with Elisabeth Olmis: Maria, Agnes and Hendrik. His wife and children were still living in 1726. – Catharina Strepers was born in 1677, she died on May 5, 1725. She had two children with Wilhelm Sieben, the schoolmaster: Peter and Adelheid, wife of Johannes Herbergs. Wilhelm Sieben and his children were still living in 1726. The latecomer Anna Strepers was born in 1786. She died on October 14, 1720. There were two children from her marriage to Lambert Moll: Anna and Johannes. The father and both children were still living in 1726.
21 Lib. C., p. 17.
22 HSP, p. 235.
23 Records in possession of the Rheinisches Freilichtmuseum Kommern.
24 Records in possession of the Rheinisches Freilichtmuseum Kommern.
25 HSP, p. 235.

The Dispute over Jan Strepers' Estate 1726-1764

On January 17, 1727[1], Wilhelm Sieben wrote a desperate letter to Hendrik van Acken in Amsterdam, telling him that after 18 years he was tired of taking care of the Strepers property matters. Since 1707, Wilhelm Sieben had been married to Catharina Strepers, one of Jan's daughters. Only a small number of letters from him to the Germantown relatives are known. That means that he became involved very intensively in the correspondence soon after his marriage by drafting letters for Leonhard Strepers of Kaldenkirchen – a task he was well qualified for as a schoolmaster – without, however, signing them himself. He mentioned that on the occasion of signing Logan's deed of sale in Amsterdam in 1726, brother-in-law Lambert Moll had agreed to continue the correspondence but had never done so.

The fact that Wilhelm Sieben in his letter again mentioned the handover of the Pennsylvania land does not allow the conclusion that in 1726 the family intentionally had the contract signed mostly by persons that were not entitled to inherit or that the contract was not fulfilled by James Logan. Rather, he seems to have been talking about some remaining lots that had not yet been sold.

Wilhelm Sieben coordinated his activities with the heirs in Germany and Holland. On May 11, 1728, he sent a letter addressed to Reiner Theißen with an accompanying letter to Hendrik van Acken asking the latter and his brothers Claas and Willem to read the letter and to make any corrections themselves that they felt might be necessary. This was certainly an attempt on his part to include the younger generation in the efforts to win back the Pennsylvania inheritance. On the other hand, the Amsterdam "bridgehead" also offered better contacts to speed up the mail to Philadelphia with the help of travelers to America via London. The letter to "Uncle" Reiner Theißen began by confirming the receipt of a letter in English, written by Griffith Jones and also signed by Theißen. In that letter they had

communicated the death of Leonhard Strepers, the last trustee of Jan's heirs in America.

In the letter to Reiner Theißen, an account was given about which lots were sold and which still remained. The heirs declared that 4,448 acres as well as 50 acres in the Liberty land had been transferred to James Logan. At the same time, they stated that 502 acres remained. In this context, the heirs in Kaldenkirchen and Amsterdam and the descendants of Metgen Jansen van Acken had several questions for the friends in Pennsylvania. Firstly, the heirs of Leonhard Arets wanted 275 acres for their efforts in connection with the administration of the Strepers estate in America without, however, specifying the details of their activity. This was incomprehensible, above all because the 275 acres were considered to be in lieu of the 10 rix dollars that Jan Strepers had owed to Leonhard Arets. From a letter written in 1687, Jan Strepers' heirs had understood that by then 200 acres in Germantown already cost as much as the entire 5,000 acres when Jan had bought them in 1682. Therefore, the deed for 275 acres made out by trustee Heinrich Sellen to Leonhard Arets was unacceptable. Secondly, they referred to the 100 acres which Jan had transferred to his brother Wilhelm for three years' work in Germantown. For this acreage an annual ground rent of five English shillings was payable but had never been paid. Thirdly, from the contract with Johann Lenssen both the ground rent and the interest on the loan, amounting to a total of 308 rix dollars and 31½ stuyvers still remained to be paid. Fourthly, they criticized the fact that both Hendrik and Leonhard Arets had appropriated 50 acres each. Wilhelm Sieben insisted on being told the grounds for this appropriation. According to the list submitted by the Germantown relatives, Jan Strepers' land had been distributed except for 27 acres which were of little value. Fifthly, they did not see the slightest necessity to pay Griffith Jones £10 since he had never been given power of attorney. They did remember Reiner Theißen's letter of April 9, 1723, in which he had told them that Griffith Jones would help him to administer the land since Uncle Leonhard Strepers had become lame. For such a short period of work, £10 was a distastefully large sum. Besides, they did not see why they should pay twice. If Leonhard Strepers was no longer able to act as trustee any more, then he could not be paid for doing so.

In a letter from Griffith Jones of November 20, 1727, he had promised that everything connected with the inheritance should be brought to conclusion by the trustees within the next two years and that the Kaldenkirchen heirs would then receive another £30 sterling. On behalf of the heirs, Wilhelm Sieben protested strongly against this offer: in his opinion, there were 308 Reichstaler and 31½ stuyvers from Jan Lenssen and £75 sterling from the sale to James Logan still to be paid.

A letter from Leonhard Streper written on September 5, 1727, met with no understanding at all. In it he told the Kaldenkirchen relatives that the family had drifted apart over the years, they did not know who was still alive and they had the impression that they had ceased to be friends altogether. Thereupon Wilhelm Sieben replied with much surprise that there had been letters from Germany every year reporting on everything. In view of a reaction like the present one from Leonhard Strepers, they had to doubt the "good harmony between the friends in Pennsylvania" and the relatives in Germany. Also, hearing that Anna Strepers, Leonhard's widow, was claiming a lot in Germantown for herself, they had the distinct impression that the relatives in Pennsylvania were taking advantage of the late Jan Strepers' estate as it suited them. The heirs in Germany, he wrote, did not intend to claim one pound sterling or one square foot more than was their due, and they expected the same attitude from the Pennsylvanian relatives.

Wilhelm Sieben's letters were written in a demanding tone. Although he repeatedly sounded a more conciliatory note on occasions, the overall tenor of his letters reflects an attempt to appeal to the American relatives' sense of honor. In a high moral tone, he reminded them repeatedly of the duty they had toward their God, and the question was asked more than once what, with so much dishonesty, the verdict would be at Judgement Day. Sieben could not have made his requests more insistent nor done more to deepen the rift between the families. It was an understandable reaction on the part of the Germantown relatives, whose family ties with

the Kaldenkirchen relatives had, after all, loosened over four decades, to pay no more heed to such demands. All the more, since they could be sure that criminal proceedings against them or collection of their debts was rendered impossible by the distance between the two continents. Wilhelm Sieben's letter was never answered. They played for time. And this tactic seems to have worked.

Wilhelm Sieben had already told Hendrik van Acken that he was tired of taking care of the matter of the inheritance. When no reaction came to his last letter, it seems that he asked Hendrik to take over the correspondence with the relatives in Germantown as an agent for the families in Germany. On June 10, 1729[2], therefore, Hendrik wrote for the first time to his "honored Uncle Reijner Tijssen". He thought it would be appropriate if members of the family from Germany or Holland came to Germantown in order finally to reach a conclusion of this matter of inheritance that would be satisfactory for all involved. This remark really should have sounded like a threat to the American relatives and made them do their utmost to come to an honest conclusion to the dispute. But apparently they did not consider Hendrik van Acken's words very important and, thus, did not take them seriously.

For some years, Hendrik van Acken did not seem to do very much in this matter. In a letter to his cousin Matthias Mickenschreiber, a merchant from Kaldenkirchen, who had married into the Strepers family, he complained that he had not had a reply from Elisabeth Olmis, Hendrik Strepers' widow, to a question regarding the Pennsylvania property in two years. In the meantime, he had also written to the friends in Germantown again and had been told that all of the land had been distributed between them in compensation for their efforts so far, and that, in addition, every trustee had been paid £10. The fact that the Germantown relatives had ceased to send letters indicated that they considered the matter closed. Now that the last uncles had passed away, nobody was left who was interested in taking care of the remaining land that was neglected and of little value.

Nevertheless, Hendrik van Acken advised that the remaining land should be secured by notary, even if they could not judge its condition and quality. Therefore, he suggested going to Pennsylvania himself. Although the land was now owned by so many different relatives, some of whom they did not even know, which made it more difficult to keep the remaining lots, he asked the relatives on the Lower Rhine to consider whether he should pursue the matter.[3]

Again it was a relative by marriage, Johann Christoph Ringel, husband of Elisabeth Strepers, one of Leonhard's daughters, who reacted to Hendrik van Acken's letter. From his letter of December 20, 1732, it became clear that his relatives had lost interest. After forty years, they had also lost faith in a peaceful and satisfying solution. They had been duped too often by the Germantown families. Quite cleverly, they instructed the young, and supposedly inexperienced, Hendrik van Acken, to buy their titles to the remaining lots in Pennsylvania, as Ringel wrote "... that I should write to their cousin whether he would not be willing to buy these properties for himself, and if he was inclined to buy said properties for himself they would leave them to him for a civil price ..."[4]. Hendrik van Acken replied to Ringel's letter as early as December 26, 1732. He was unable to quote the relatives on the Lower Rhine a price for the remaining land. He also asked them to consider the cost and risk he would incur traveling to Pennsylvania without even being sure of being able to conclude the matter in a satisfactory manner.[5]

Johann Christoph Ringel acknowledged receipt of the letter on January 30, 1733, and apologized for not having replied sooner. This had been due to Uncle Moll, who also had to be asked for his opinion. Ringel had to depart on a journey, but since cousin Mickenschreiber was informed concerning everything relating to the matter, he would contact Hendrik as soon as the family council had reached a decision.[6]

At the same time Peter Sieben, another Kaldenkirchen descendant of Jan Strepers, entered the scene after his father Wilhelm's death (buried May 1, 1729). He tried by every possible means to recover the Strepers property in Pennsylvania. He was also probably the one who, as the Ronsdorf schoolmaster, got Johannes Herbergs to move to

that town and finally persuaded him, together with the two merchants Matthias Mickenschreiber and Bernhardus Hollender, to travel across the Atlantic to recover the Strepers land. Through Peter Sieben's close contact with the religious group of the Ellerians in Ronsdorf, which at its peak had manifold contacts to the court of the Prince Elector of the Palatinate in Mannheim, to Frederick the Great, king of Prussia, and to the German ambassador at the English court, he had found enough support and courage to consider such a daring enterprise feasible. A number of important merchants from the Rhineland who were close to the Ellerians or followed their beliefs probably offered encouragement and support as well. To Herbergs, these contacts, of which he frequently boasts in his journal, seemed so significant that he ignored the problems he would be facing in Pennsylvania.

On April 11, 1733, Peter Sieben, who was still a schoolmaster in Kaldenkirchen like his father and had not moved to Ronsdorf at the time, wrote to Hendrik van Acken and thanked him for his letter to his mother-in-law. He informed the van Ackens in Amsterdam of his marriage to Anna Maria Knevels[7]. He had also heard from Matthias Mickenschreiber that Hendrik van Acken was planning to emigrate to Pennsylvania with his two sisters. The claims to the Pennsylvania property were not mentioned at all.[8]

On April 28, 1733, Hendrik van Acken replied to a no longer extant letter from Matthias Mickenschreiber dated April 28, 1733, that he did not understand why the friends from the Lower Rhine could not agree, a problem probably caused mainly by the objections of Lambert Moll. If Hendrik was to buy the remaining acres in Pennsylvania, he would need a notarized power of attorney from his friends for the purpose. This letter confirmed that the Philadelphia town lots had been sold, a fact that was later denied by Peter Heinrich Strepers and Johannes Herbergs. In the event of Hendrik's death, the power of attorney was to authorize his sisters, Agnes and Elisabeth, to bring the inheritance problem to a good end. Hendrik thought it best to have the power of attorney issued in Venlo, since the notary there had already been involved in the power of attorney for Reiner Theißen.[9]

On March 31, 1733, Hendrik van Acken wrote his next letter to Matthias Mickenschreiber and told the friends on the Lower Rhine that neither he nor his sisters were interested in buying the remaining land. He would rather give up his share of it than start a quarrel with the American relatives. Moreover, he had tried for a long time to obtain a power of attorney from the Kaldenkirchen relatives and from Lambert Moll, but had never received a reply. When he went to Pennsylvania with his two sisters, he would be very willing to take letters for the relatives over there. But he doubted whether this would help to bring the matter to a conclusion.[10]

Not long afterwards, Hendrik van Acken and his two sisters went to settle in Philadelphia. From a letter, dated May 31, 1735, from his brother Claas to Hendrik, who was now living opposite the Quaker meeting house on Second Street in Philadelphia, we gather that after his arrival Hendrik had succeeded, perhaps with the help of some Quaker friends, in obtaining more detailed knowledge about the "use" of the Strepers properties. For if Claas writes of "that princedom that our other friends [meaning the friends in Pennsylvania] took from us in such a wrongful and scandalous manner", he could hardly be talking about some few remaining acres which could still be surveyed, as is shown in Johannes Herbergs' journal, but must be referring to the entire former property of Jan Strepers. He also mentioned that the "general letter" had been sent by him to Kaldenkirchen. This was probably a letter from Hendrik van Acken from Philadelphia telling the relatives in Kaldenkirchen about his latest information on Jan Strepers' estate. Although they had been asked to give their views, unfortunately there had been no reply so far.[11]

In his letter to his brother Hendrik and his sisters Agnes and Elisabeth dated August 28, 1736, Claas again talks about Jan Strepers' land having been put to wrongful use and about the Kaldenkirchen relatives still being unable to agree on further steps. If Hendrik, who, before his departure, had distanced himself from any attempt to recover the Strepers' land, was now expecting a power of attorney from Germany again, he must have had some new information that made a recovery of the land seem possible.[12]

On December 18, 1736, Claas van Acken received another letter from his brother Hendrik, written on October 11th. Its content is unknown since Claas did not go into it in his reply of June 30, 1737. Instead, he told Hendrik that the friends in Kaldenkirchen had now written a power of attorney that, according to the experts on legal matters in England and Pennsylvania, was worthless since it had not been signed by all of the heirs nor issued by a court.[13] To correct that error, Matthias Mickenschreiber asked Claas van Acken on May 20, 1737, to send the invalid document back to save expense so that it could be then signed by all of the heirs.[14]

Although in several letters to the Kaldenkircheners Hendrik van Acken had specified precisely how they were to draw up the power of attorney for him, and although he had even given them the name of a notary in Venlo, the relatives ignored all of his advice. This is hard to understand. After all, there were experienced merchants among the Kaldenkirchen relatives who were used to international business transactions and who, therefore, should have been familiar with the correct way of drawing up a power of attorney for use overseas. Their long hesitation as well as the superficial way of dealing with the matter allow the conclusion that the Kaldenkircheners did not expect any success in the matter and, therefore, only reluctantly complied with the wishes of their young relatives, the van Ackens.

Initially, Hendrik van Acken does not seem to have had very good contact with his Pennsylvania relatives, as is shown by a letter from his brother Claas dated July 28, 1740, in which he tells his brother that Reiner Theißen had asked him in a letter of November 12, 1739 to send him a power of attorney at last, so he could bring the matter of the inheritance to a good end and sell the remaining land before he died.[15] Did Reiner not know about Hendrik's commission, or did Hendrik not trust Reiner because he suspected him of being in cahoots with the Strepers of the German Township? However, after Reiner's death in 1745, Hendrik was given the written documents about the dispute that Reiner had had in his keeping over the years.

In Claas van Acken's last letter of October 12, 1741, he again expresses his surprise at the fact that

Reiner Theißen had never approached Hendrik van Acken in Philadelphia about the land question. Without actually saying so, Claas obviously found this behavior suspicious, since he assumed that Reiner Theißen wanted to bypass Hendrik, who was familiar with the local situation, in order to have an easier time of it with the relatives far away.[16] After this letter, the correspondence between the relatives in Pennsylvania, Amsterdam and the Lower Rhine ceases.

Anthony Benezet, a Quaker sympathizer, who was head of a private school in Germantown from 1739 to 1742[17], was commissioned by Hendrik Strepers to make a legal study of the case for the heirs. The detailed assessment of events he wrote in 1744 or 1745 shows that at least the van Ackens kept trying to assert their rights in Pennsylvania.[18] In a letter to Richard Hill and Samuel Preston Moore, part-owners of the Strepers properties, dated February 18, 1746, James Logan also confirmed that Hendrik van Acken had urged him repeatedly and for years to give back Jan Strepers' land.[19] Certainly, the knowledge of the extremely low purchase price for the land played a part in these efforts. Benezet stated that the Kaldenkirchen relatives had only agreed to the ridiculous sum because they had been fully aware that the Pennsylvania relatives knew more about the land transactions and the rights pertaining to them and that they were at their mercy. In order not to be left completely empty-handed, they accepted a pittance for 4,448 acres in Bucks County, 50 acres of Liberty land and one acre in the city of Philadelphia. In December 1748, James Logan and his wife Sarah had the one acre in Philadelphia, Jan Strepers' former property, transferred to Richard Hill jr. and the physician Samuel Preston Moore (M.D.)[20]

It was only when Peter Heinrich Strepers and Johannes Herbergs appeared on the scene that a renewed attempt was made to recover the Strepers estate in its entirety. Johannes Herbergs seems to have been the driving force in that attempt. Certainly he had been animated to do so by his brother-in-law Peter Sieben, who had taken over the correspondence with the far away relatives in Pennsylvania from his father. Peter Sieben had been a resident and the schoolmaster of Ronsdorf since 1742. In 1743, Johannes Herbergs followed him there from Kaldenkirchen with his family. Since they were closely related – Peter and Herbergs' wife Adelgunde Sieben were brother and sister – it seems obvious that the brother had a hand in the move of his sister and brother-in-law.

The influence brought to bear by the Ellerians in Ronsdorf on the attempt to recover the Strepers land remains unclear. It is striking that after the early 1740s, there was no further contact made from Kaldenkirchen with the Germantown relatives. Since Herbergs and Strepers only asked Jan Strepers' descendants for reimbursement of their costs, as becomes clear from the journal, the Ellerians obviously had no investment in the undertaking. Various entries in his journal indicate that Johannes Herbergs was not a very religious person, anyway. Although he had a number of important functions among the Ellerians ("Scholarch"[21], city councilor), his affiliation with their church alone does not necessarily mean that he was to win the land back for Ellerian aims.

Before Peter Heinrich and Johannes Herbergs embarked for Pennsylvania, they had to be authorized by Jan Strepers' heirs, now in the second and third generation. To this end, Herbergs and Strepers obtained a general power of attorney that enabled them to take all necessary steps to recover all of Jan Strepers' properties, movable and unmovable, and to sell them locally. No specific instructions or limits were set down for this. The general power of attorney stated that Peter Heinrich Strepers and Johannes Herbergs were free in every decision. This was to facilitate the undertaking. If they had had to refer back to the heirs on the Rhine, the procedure would be drawn out too long. The power of attorney was issued on March, 1, 1764, by the Imperial Notary Wilhelm Hertel at Ronsdorf, place of residence of the Herbergs family and Peter Sieben.[22]

The same procedure was repeated on March 6, 1764, by the Imperial Notary Johann Gerhard Dellonge in Kaldenkirchen. Here Bernhard Hollender and his wife Agnes Strepers, Peter Hendrich Mickenschreiber and his wife Catharina Gertrud, née Thielen, Johannes Moll and his wife Gertrud Königs, Henricus Königs and his wife Anna Catharina Moll, Florens Petrus Dürselen, preacher in Vessem and Hoogeloon, and his wife Catharina, née Strepers, and Agnes Hüskes, née Strepers, with her sons Johann Leonhard, Gerhardus and Peter all signed the power of attorney.[23]

On March 19, 1764, Johann Christophel Ringels, together with his wife Elisabeth, one of Leonhard Strepers' daughters, and his children appeared before the notary Johann Gerhard Dellonge in Kaldenkirchen. His wife and his children, Johann Leonhard Ringels and his wife Maria Barbara Josepha, née Hiltzenberg, Maria Catharina, Anna Elisabeth, Magdalena and Johann Franciscus, gave a general power of attorney to their father to act in their joint interest together with Johannes Herbergs and Peter Heinrich Strepers in Pennsylvania.[24] Ringels seems to have decided on this step rather late. In the end, he did not travel after all. The reason for this is unknown. Possibly, a conflict developed between the families because he tried to force his collaboration on Johannes Herbergs and Peter Heinrich Strepers, who had been authorized by most of the Strepers family. The assumption of a conflict between the families is supported by the fact that Ringels did not contribute financially.

Equipped with their general power of attorney and with a document from the Kaldenkirchen ministers proving their family ties with Jan Strepers, Johannes Herbergs and Peter Heinrich Strepers embarked on their American adventure which was to occupy Peter Heinrich Strepers for several years, but Johannes Herbergs, on four journeys to America, for a quarter of a century.

The document certifying their descent and the confirmation of the title to the estate had been difficult to obtain for the Kaldenkirchen ministers since written sources were lacking. They had had to rely on statements of witnesses, on family records kept by Hendrik Strepers, Jan's son, and on dates they could find on grave stones. Their certificate does not mention any of these problems. Certainly, the ministers wanted to prevent any such details from causing unnecessary difficulties for Johannes Herbergs and Peter Heinrich Strepers in Pennsylvania.[25]

[1] Lib.C., p. 21.
[2] Lib.C., p. 22.
[3] Lib.C., p. 27.
[4] Lib.C., p. 27.
[5] Lib.C., p. 28.
[6] Lib.C., p. 29.
[7] Daughter of Johannes Knevels, preacher from Linnich. His son Johannes, a student of divinity, moved frequently in Ellerian circles at an early stage.
[8] Lib.C., p.30.
[9] Lib.C., p.31.
[10] Lib.C., p.32.
[11] Lib.C., p.33.
[12] Lib.C., p.34.
[13] Lib.C., p.109.
[14] Lib.C., p.36.
[15] Lib.C., p.110.
[16] Lib.C., p.111.
[17] Stephanie Grauman Wolf, *Urban Village, Population, Community, and Family Structure in Germantown, Pennsylvania, 1683-1800* (Guilford, Surrey 1976), p. 237.
[18] Lib.C., p. 117.
[19] Lib.C., p. 118.
[20] Lib.C., p. 121 ff.
[21] A scholarch was the school inspector of the congregation.
[22] HSP, p. 231.
[23] HSP, p. 231.
[24] HSP, p. 231.
[25] Kaldenkirchen church records, Protestant/Reformed congregation, p.77-81, HSP: Charles Morton Manuscripts, vol.1, p.6. Transcript by James Duffin, Philadelphia. For the full text refer to App. L.

Journal of Johannes Herbergs' Travels

This notebook belongs to Johann Herbergs of Ronsdorf, February 15, 1764

		Rhr[3]	Str[4]
Packed for Penselvania[1] 8 double dozen iron spindles per dozen total[2]			
44 St[5] per Rhr 7½ St		5	52
			44
	Rhr	6	36
5 dozen pans, for 179 pounds per 100 pounds total			
10 Rhr per Rhr 7½ St		17	57
		2	15
		20	12
½ dozen tailor's scissors assorted per dozen 5 Rhr		2	30
½ dozen common sugar tongs			48
½ dozen ditto with turned handles		1	
½ dozen fire tongs 7½ st apiece			45
½ dozen curling tongs/irons 11 st apiece		1	6
			46
total per Rhr 7½ st		6	55
	Rhr	33	43

Fig. 14 Extract from the Ordinance Survey Map of Ronsdorf of 1781, now lost. Surveyed by Johann Wynand Buschmann. HstA Düsseldorf, Map Collection No. HstA Düsseldorf, Map Collection No. 1490.

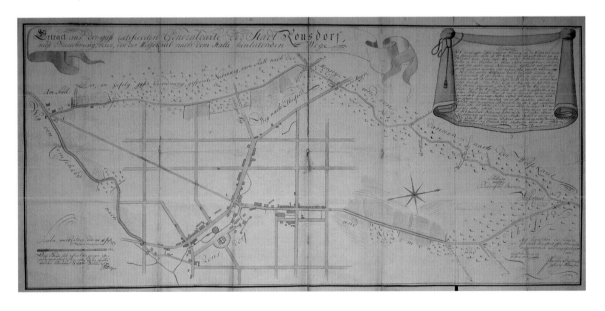

Carried over		33	55

Coffee grinders, common

No.0, ½ dozen, 19 st apiece		1	54
No.1, ½ dozen, 22 st apiece		2	12
No.2, ½ dozen at 25		2	30
No.3, ½ dozen at 28		2	48
No.4, ½ dozen at 32		3	12
No.5, ½ dozen at 37		3	42
No.6, ½ dozen at 43		4	18

Dutch

No.0, ½ dozen at 22		2	12
No.1, ½ dozen at 25		2	30
No.2, ½ dozen at 28		2	48
No.3, ½ dozen at 31		3	6
No.4, ½ dozen at 35		3	30
No.5, ½ dozen at 40		4	
No.6, ½ dozen at 46		4	36
per Rhr 7½ st freight		5	25
	Rhr	82	38

Carried over	Rhr	82	38

flatirons

One coal iron No.3 at	27 st		
1 ditto No. 1	18		
1 with rectangular bars			
No. 3	27		
1 No. 2 ditto	23		
1 ditto No. 1	18		
1 ditto ordinary	14		
1 English coal shuttle	60		
	3 7	3	7
per Rhr freight 7½			23½

6 dozen pieces of patterned ribbon 40 st apiece		48	
6 ditto 24 apiece		2	24
		136	32½

Description	Price		
Carried over		112	31½
½ dozen 2 punch pliers at	34 st	3	24
½ dozen ditto with colored necks	at 26 st	2	36
1½ dozen ordinary	at 15 st	4	30
2 dozen shovels, half polished, assorted	at 9 st	2	32
1½ dozen ordinary pliers	at 9 st	2	32
1½ dozen shovels, polished all over	at 10 st	3	
2 dozen ditto, black	at 7½ st	3	
1½ dozen baking irons[6]	at 7 st	2	6
freight per Rhr 7½ st		3	7
		140	23½

Description	Price		
Carried over		140	23½
300 drills, assorted, ordinary, per 100 pieces 45		2	15
100 ditto, fine		1	30
No. 2, ditto 49 pieces per 100 No.1 = 22½		1	22½
No. 2½ ditto 40 pieces		1	22½
No. 3 ditto 39 pieces		1	22½
No. 3½ ditto 29 pieces		1	22½
No. 4 ditto 24 pieces		1	22½
4 dozen sharp English chisels, assorted			
per dozen 30 st		2	
1 dozen No. 5, English		1	
2 dozen strips, sharp, assorted		1	
1 dozen English chisels, assorted		1	15
½ dozen No. 5 at		1	
1 dozen mortise chisels, assorted		1	10
½ dozen chamber locks with two latches at 40 st		4	
½ dozen with one latch at 30 st		3	
freight per Rhr 7½		3	7½
		168	33½

Two barrels sent franco to Mrs. Hartwichs[7],		
declared with coffee grinders and cake irons,		
total weight 660 pounds. Value 200 Fl.		
Marked IH. No. 1#, IH. No. 2.#. At customs		
had to give the chief officer 2 ducats	7	
consumed	13	30
Inspector	20	
double freight to Duisburg	9	52½
franco Rotterdam		

Sketch of a pothook

From the Lower Rhine via the Netherlands to England

1764, on March 4th, I started my journey with the Lord's help and blessing. On the same day I went by coach as far as Düsseldorf and on March 5th from Düsseldorf to Waldniel. The 6th, 7th, 8th and 9th of March I spent quietly at Waldniel. On March 10th and 11th I went to Millich[8] where at Ratheim[9] I saw a well which continuously boiled quite strongly, and if one threw a stone into it, it threw it back up straight away, and it is supposed to be bottomless. Where it comes out of the ground, the water is quite clean but it bubbles terribly. On March 12th and 13th, I was at Waldniel. On March 14th, I went to Breyell and Kaldenkirchen and back to Waldniel for cousin P[eter] H[einrich] Mickenschreiber's sake, as he wanted to negotiate with Königs. On March 16th, I went to the Hardt[10] and to Rheydt[11],

on the 17th to Waldniel, the 18th to Kaldenkirchen. On March 21st, cousin Strepers came back. He had spoken to the woman from Pennsylvania.

On March 22nd, we again went to Kaldenkirchen where cousin Strepers' throat went bad, so we had to interrupt our journey. On March 27th, we walked to the Meyerey[12], on the 28th to Vessem[13], from whence we departed for s'Hertogenbosch where the big church is quite beautiful to look at, with 168 pillars covered with sculptures, coats of arms and other things. On April 1st, we traveled from s'Hertogenbosch to Rotterdam. On April 2nd, we arrived at Rotterdam where I did not find my ironware but a letter from my wife that it had been sent from Duisburg on April 24th. Having heard from the boatmen from Arnhem that these goods would be delivered either to Amsterdam or to Dordrecht, I went to Amsterdam with cousin Strepers on April 3rd and arrived there on April 4th at half past six in

Fig. 15 Kaldenkirchen in 1764. Postcard based on a colored drawing. Archives of the District of Viersen.

Fig. 16 Wessem aan de Maas. View of the harbor. Photography 1992. Toon Driessens, Wessem.

the morning. There I inquired for the goods straight away, but the boatmen told me they had not yet loaded any ironware but another ship was expected tomorrow. So I am still in a great predicament.

[The following paragraph is crossed out to the bottom of the page:] Only on the afternoon of April 5th did I find out from another boatman that not only had my goods arrived but also been sent on to Rotterdam. So I took the barge to Rotterdam the same evening and found my goods there. But since cousin Strepers had traveled to The Hague and met cousin Johann Hollender there, I had a letter from them that evening that I had to be in Delft on April 7th to speak to cousin Hollender which also had the desired effect.

On April 8th, I went to The Hague, on the 9th back to Rotterdam, on the 10th to Hellevoetsluis[14], 8 hours from Rotterdam. On April 11th, we went on the packet boat. We had the wind against us. [End of the crossed-out section.]

Only on April 4th did I learn in Amsterdam that my goods had been sent from there to Rotterdam. After Mr. Quack had treated us with great honor and shown us through the entire city hall among which the armory deserves mention, where muskets for 22,000 men are always kept ready, to say nothing of all the Dutch and Spanish harnesses. At Blau Jan's[15], we saw one live and one dead lion, two porcupines, a white bear, a wolf, an ape, a long-tailed monkey, etc. But it was remarkable to see a sheep dog and a bitch play 6 pieces on a little flute and roll their eyes, and if one held something in front of their mouths the playing stopped, so without any doubt the air came through their mouths. But the penitentiary was pitiful to look at.

On April 5th, at 8 in the afternoon we went by barge to Gouda. From there we went to Rotterdam in the morning. On arrival I heard that my goods were there, but that cousin Hollender was in Delft. Since cousin Strepers wanted to go to The Hague and had to pass through Delft he met cousin Hollender there on April 6th. Upon which he wrote to me that I had to be at Delft on April 7th at 9 in the morning. This I did, and from there cousin Strepers traveled to The Hague in the afternoon and cousin Hollender and myself stayed until 9 in the morning of April 8th. Cousin Hollender traveled to Leiden and I to The Hague with cousin Hüsges, who had followed us to Delft. In The Hague we were then lodged at the Golden Hunter. At 3 in the afternoon, I met cousin Strepers with his cousin Deventer in the street as I was on my way to him, and he took us to his house straight away and treated us with great honor. Not only that he showed us around everywhere but he even succeeded in persuading the English ambassador[16] to give us a free pass. To whom we had to go on April 9th, at 10 in the morning as the clock struck, and he signed the free pass in person, telling us that he would not have done so had it not been for cousin Deventer. From there I departed for Rotterdam at 3 in the afternoon.

On the morning of April 10th, we went to see Mr. Johann Mickenschreiber where upon commendation[17] by cousin Hollender we could not only obtain a letter of recommendation but also draw 200 guilders in case we needed them. At 12 we sat down on the boat where we were lucky to meet a merchant from Amsterdam as well as two Austrian officers from Ireland who all spoke English. So, with a good wind we reached Brielle[18] between 3 and 4 o'clock, 6 hours from Rotterdam, and walked in 3 hours to Hellevoetsluis where we spent the night.

On April 11th at 3 in the afternoon we went aboard ship and had the wind against us. At 7 o'clock, cousin Strepers began to complain of feeling sick. But I was still quite well. At 8 o'clock after we had had some tea, I had to vomit, 6 to 8 times, but without trouble. But cousin Strepers held up well. Now there were about 20 of us on the ship, but none of them held up as well as we did, so the ship's crew said. Well, hearing that general vomiting it was as if the people had to vomit their hearts out of their bodies.

On April 12th, we really were on the raging open sea, so that we went up and down all the time, but that got a little better at 10 at night. On April 13th between 8 and 9 in the morning, we arrived safely in Harwich. After our bodies and clothes had been thoroughly inspected on board we were taken to shore in a bark. But our luggage was taken to the King's House[19], where we had to collect a paper upstairs and with that then go downstairs to where

our luggage was. When it had been handed over to us, we had to open everything up. Upon which everything was inspected very thoroughly, even the books were leafed through, the smallest piece of cloth looked into. They beat on the bottom of the suitcase I do not know how many times to find out if it was double. Luckily I had taken my things out of there in Rotterdam. So six of us took a coach at Harwich, at 12 English shillings each. For that money, we could each take 20 pounds of luggage. For anything above that, you had to pay 1 shilling per pound. Harwich is 72 English miles from London. We boarded the coach around noon. By then there were 18 of us outside in the front, at the back and on top of the coach. But since the four of us had contracted for the coach first we were among the six sitting inside. We had six good horses. Now, I have driven fast a number of times but never as fast as that save from the King of Prussia.[20]

Fig.17 Abraham Rademaker (1675-1735), Aent Niewe veer van Maaslandsluis te sien. Water color, 1730-1735. Historisch Museum Den Briel, Inv. No. 3723.

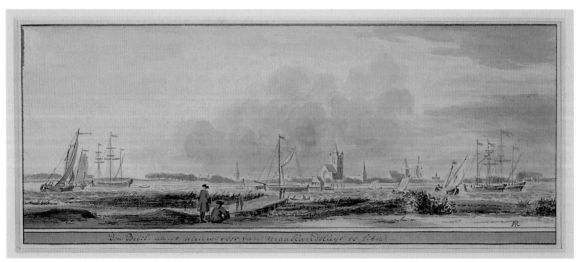

Fig.18 Ascribed to Christian Friedrich Fritzsch (1719-before 1774), Blaauw Jan's Menagerie, Amsterdam. Copperplate engraving, 1751. Amsterdam Historisch Museum, Inv. No. A29190.

[1] Pennsylvania. These goods, together with others were offered for sale on December 17, 1767: "To be sold, by Peter Heinrich Strepers, Living at the North East corner of Race and Fifth streets, A quantity of straw knives, spindles for wheels, chissels, planes, coffee mills, best and middling Mylander whetstones, best flints, German pruans, ozenbrigs linen, camel yarn of divers sorts and colours, small looking glasses, red chalk, and a small quantity of scythes; all which he will dispose of to merchants or shopkeepers, on the most reasonable terms" [Pennsylvania Gazette, December 17, 1767].

[2] The German is not quite clear here

[3] Rix dollars

[4] Stuyvers

[5] Stuyvers

[6] Predecessor of the waffle iron

[7] Probably a contact at Duisburg

[8] Part of the town of Hückelhoven in the district of Heinsberg; visit to the Moll and Königs family (see

Strepers and Königs family trees)

9 Hückelhoven-Ratheim. In the 16th century, Baptists had settled there. [Christian Hege and Christian Neff, *Mennonitisches Lexikon*, III (Karlsruhe, 1958), p. 429 f.].

10 Mönchengladbach-Hardt.

11 Mönchengladbach-Rheydt; residence of the Laufs family.

12 On, March 27, 1764, Herbergs and Strepers spent the night at Meijel in the Netherlands, v. p. 62. Alternatively, he could also be talking about the departure for 'sHertogenbosch in the Netherlands [Peters, *Kaldenkirchen*, I, p. 441, Report of the Protestant minister Eylert, Kaldenkirchen, 1682: ... "the third may cook a pound or take several on his neck and go to the meyerey of 's Hertogebosch to sell it."].

13 West of Eindhoven, Netherlands.

14 Voorne, Netherlands.

15 Blau Jan, an inn with a zoo and a collection of curiosities.

16 Sir Joseph Yorke, Baron Dover: b. 1724, d. 1792; 1760-1780 English ambassador in The Hague.

17 Recommendation from Johann Mickenschreiber, cousin of Peter Heinrich Mickenschreiber (v. Mickenschreiber family tree. Johann Mickenschreiber is godfather to Johannes Fredericus Mickenschreiber).

18 Province of South Holland, Netherlands.

19 Customs house.

20 This is already anticipating Herbergs' Pennsylvania experiences. Since 1761, there had been a coach link between the "King of Prussia" tavern in Germantown and the "George Inn" on Second Street in Philadelphia three times a week [Horace F. McCann, *History of Old Germantown*, p. 113].

London – Weeks of Waiting

On April 14[1], at 5 in the afternoon we were already in London. But that was where our misery really began, because we did not speak a word of English and they did not speak a word of German. So the two lieutenants[1] took us to an innkeeper who knew a little German, where we did not feel at all well on the first two days. We had been told so often that one had to be very careful in London. So we thought at first that we might have arrived at a dishonest place, but that turned out to be untrue. So on April 16th, we agreed with the innkeeper what we were to pay him per day – for our room, tea in the morning with bread and butter, some meat and a jug of beer at midday, bread and butter in the evening and another jug of beer. An English jug is about half a jug of ours. For both of us that came to 3 English shillings a day.

April 15th was a Sunday. So we went to the Low German church, hoping to meet Kenniß or Mumm there. But that was in vain. However, we did meet a person who accompanied us for more than half an hour. And he took us to a German inn where almost everybody was German, too, and where we would have liked to stay. But he[2] could not take us in.

On April 16th, we went to see those people who had been recommended to us, but we fared really

Fig. 19 William Marlow (1740-1813) Fresh Wharf, London Bridge. Oil on canvas. Museum of London, Inv. No. O. 4.

badly. No one whom we asked could understand us. When we showed them the address, one did not know it at all, another told us it was miles further on, a third that it was a mile back in the direction we had come from. Until we thought we would turn old and gray over it all.

But then we did find a man named Peter Stapel, who had been recommended to us by Mr. Mickenschreiber. Stapel is quite a good man who not only advised us in our business but also asked his office clerk, who is also a very friendly person, for help. He took us to other merchants, nota bene Quakers, who have chosen four of their number in London to watch over all Pennsylvania affairs. So we went there on April 19th at 11 in the morning. These people looked at our power of attorney and the family tree and said it was good. Now they were going to consider whether we should obtain a certificate from the London City Council that would be valid here in London, but which would cost £5 to £6 sterling. NB: this was done as desired on May 3rd. The Lord Mayor[3] not only signed it but also set the seal of the city underneath. The notary had to swear with his signature and seal that everything was translated correctly. In all this, Mr. Stapel's office clerk, called Mr. Mäilan, helped us.

One cannot describe all the treasures here in London. At the inns everywhere they have silver beer tankards to drink from. There are silver shops without number, and each shop has more silverware than two horses could pull away, not to mention of other valuable merchandise.

On April 18th, we went to London to see St. Paul's Cathedral Church (which might be counted among the wonders of the world) from bottom to top, which is 534 steps high. And walked around the top, too. We also carved our names there.

The two bridges over the Thames deserve to be mentioned and also the water art[4] which carries the water through the entire city into the houses. The number of people in the streets is indescribable, as many as on a good market day at home. The Exchange building is beautiful to look at, with all the Kings and Queens standing on it in marble as large as life. But the Amsterdam Exchange is superior to it in size.

Fig. 20 Bawles, The Inside View of the Royal Exchange London. Copperplate engraving, approx. 1750. Museum of London, Inv. No. A18026 9c.

Fig. 21 Dr. R. Williams, Scrapbook relating to the Tower of London, The Royal Armoury in the Tower of London.
Colored copperplate engraving. Published by Thos. Kelly, London, 1822.
Royal Armouries (The Board of Trustees of the Armouries, Inv. No. I.287).

The Tower is a very old and very strong, and also very large building, which we went to see on April 28th. Namely, first of all the armory, where 100 men could be armed straight away. With all sorts of different weapons, for sailors as well as for land soldiers. And the most interesting thing was that they were arranged in all sorts of patterns. Some pillars were hung around with pistols to look like a winding staircase. Other pillars were covered in spontoons all around. Along the walls (they were full of hunting knives, small pistols, knives as they are used on ships) there were all sorts of patterns, with thousands of brass[5], 2½ inches large or wide, 2½ feet long, in a rifle pattern, were also used on ships.

Now this one room was at least 180 feet long, 65 to 80 feet wide, about 15 feet high. And there was only a walkway around it. Otherwise, there was, so to speak, not a foot of vacant space from top to bottom. At the top, in front of the plaster there were

all sorts of muskets, and you could not see how they were attached. All in all, the armory at Amsterdam is just rubbish compared to this. Secondly, underneath this room there were the big guns with all of the equipment to transport them[6], of all different kinds. And there were also very valuable guns that they had taken from the Spanish and the French. Among other things a mortar big enough to throw a bomb of about 500 pounds and a gun about 20 shoes long and wide enough that once a man supposedly got a woman pregnant inside it. Thirdly, you can see there the Crown Jewels that are worn at the coronation of the king. First the crown, which has a stone of inestimable value set in it. One is worth £100,000 sterling and is an emerald, and there are diamonds and innumerable other stones. Next to it lie two swords, one the Sword of Justice and the other the Sword of Mercy. Then there are scepters, about 5 or 6, all very precious, and also 5 or 6 crowns that were worn by

Fig. 22 Thomas Rowlandson (1756-1827), The Line of Kings in the Tower of London.
From: "The Horse Armoury in the Tower". Pencil and ink, London 1800.
Royal Armouries (The Board of Trustees of the Armouries, Inv. No. I.45).

the Queens Elizabeth and Mary, the vessel out of which the princes are christened, item, out of which the King takes communion, the spurs worn by the King at his coronation etc. Fourthly, at the top you can see harnesses, suits of armor, helmets of different kinds. But there are life-sized effigies of all of the Kings of England from the very first onward, sitting there on horseback and made to look so lifelike that one would swear they were all alive, if one did not know better. That is worth seeing. Among others there was the harness worn by the great John of Gaunt himself, which looked terrible.

On April 25th, I saw the Queen[7] drive out. On April 30th, at 6 in the morning we went to Hyde Park where we arrived at 8 o'clock. Where the King[8] wanted to muster two dragoon regiments. At 10 the King arrived with Gramby and many other officers and

an escort of about 100. The King was sitting on a white horse and wearing a red coat and a hat with a gold trim. He is well built and seems to be of a rather merry disposition. The Queen's younger brother[9] arrived next in a carriage drawn by 16 horses. Immediately afterwards, the Queen arrived in a state coach, drawn by 6 dun-colored horses, also with an escort of 100 dragoons, very stately and moving quite slowly. So we walked up toward the King and the Queen as close as possible, so we could see them quite well. The Queen seems very young and short, otherwise she is not ugly. Laughed all the time that people were running toward her in big crowds to see her. Indeed, I think there were more than 40,000 spectators there.

Saint James[10] is an old building from the outside, large but not handsome. Now Westminster Cathedral, where the king is crowned, does deserve a mention. Though very old from the outside, inside it is decorated with far more than 100 marble statues, and the work and the marble itself are so fine that you can see your own image in it. There is nothing in Holland to match it.

We have been looking for a ship for a long time. First, we found one that was to leave for Philadelphia at the beginning of June. Next, a broker called Moeses told us about one for New York on May 20th or 25th at the latest. FOR NEW YORK, The Roebuck. And there was also written: Samuel Smith, Commander, Burthen 150 Tons, Carriage Guns, Men Answerable, A Prime Sailor, lying at Horslydown[11] and will depart with all Convenient Speed. The Commander to bespoke with daily on the Royal Exchange[12], and at the New York Coffee House in Sweetings Alley[13] at usual hours. Or, Josiah and James Boydell for the Commander to sail 25. May.

So we went by boat to the ship to see what it was like and we were treated to a punch and Philadelphia bread there. Then we made a contract with the captain. Since the best cabin had been booked entirely by a commissary for 100 guineas at his own expense, we had to talk him into taking us into the second cabin where the sailors are. Since six passengers had also already booked for this, the only thing we will get on the ship will be lunch and dinner together with the sailors, and water. So we have to bring bedding, tea and everything else we need ourselves, besides the 8 guineas everyone must pay the captain. So the voyage is going to cost us. Since London is very expensive and we have to wait so long here we made do as best we could. But I want to note just one thing here: a jug of beer, which is the cheapest beverage here, is about the size of half a measure at home. It costs about 8 stuyvers of our money. So one of our jugs is about 16 stuyvers.

The agreement we made here in London is 3 English shillings per day. And many people say that we have found quite a bargain. For that, we have a room with bed, chairs and a table. Between 9 and 10 in the morning we get tea with bread and butter, in the afternoon between 3 and 4 some meat and half a jug of beer like I have explained above, and at 10 in the evening bread and butter and a jug of beer. The beer is not enough, however, and we have to have an extra jug each in the middle of the day and in the evening. So we eat and drink for 3 English shillings and 8 pence, that is 1 rix dollar and 28 stuyvers in our money.

On May 5th, we went to Greenwich, 5 miles from London Bridge, where they have a house for invalids and people wounded at sea, built under King Charles the Second. So magnificent and so luxurious that it is worth seeing. It is entirely built of hewn stones. It lies right by the Thames. They say it is better than Saint James Palace where the king lives. Indeed, it is royal. Close to it there is a large garden with animals and we walked its length and width. There were so many deer in it that you could not even count them, and they were quite tame. We went there by boat down the Thames and walked back.

On May 8th, there was a public punishment executed on five soldiers at Saint James, where 3 spontoons had been set against each other. Their verdict was read out loud. Next each had to take off his shirt, one after the other. Then he was tied to the top of the spontoons with his hands. Then there were about 6 men with whips, and they each gave a certain number of lashes in the same place on his bare back until the blood flowed. Now I have never seen so many men with only one leg, or even without legs or arms, as I have seen here in London, by the hundreds.

Our life in London is as follows: in the morning, if we can sleep, we stay in bed until 8. Then we read until 10 o'clock when we are called to have tea. Well, there is bread and butter with the tea if we want. Then go we go straight back to our room which is two stories up and right at the back. There we read or write a bit, or we knit, until 1 o'clock. Then we dress and go to the Exchange, until just before 3. At half past three we go to the table. Then the innkeeper mumbles a few words into his beard like somebody saying in German "To your health!". That is all in the way of saying grace, before and after the meal. We have not yet seen anybody pray here.

Philadelphia.

Die Haupt Stadt in der Nord-Americanischen Provinz Pensylvanien
sie ist vom William Penn (dem Caroll II. König in Engelland
die ganze Provinz geschencket hatte) im Jahr 1682. zwischen
2. Schiffreichen Flüssen angelegt und deswegen Philadelphia genen-
net worde, weil die Einwohner in Brüderlicher Einigkeit daselbst lebe sollen.

Philadelphie.

La Ville Capitale de Pensylvanie Province Nord-Americaine,
William Penn, a qui Charles II. Roi d'Angleterre donna cette
Province entiere la planta en 1682 entre deux fleuves navi-
gables et l'apella Philadelphie, parceque les habitans y vi-
voient dans une Harmonie fraternelle.

Fig.23 Balthasar Friedrich Leizelt, "Vue de Philadelphia". Magic lantern picture. Really a representation of the Marine Hospital at Greenwich near London. Colored copperplate engraving, approx. 1776. Privately owned.

Then we get a piece of meat on the table, so raw that if you cut it sometimes the blood still runs out. Mostly there is a bit a of vegetable with it, namely whole heads of cabbage. They are just boiled in water and put next to the meat. Then you cut one of them into small pieces on your plate. And then you put a bit of sauce on top and eat it with the meat. And this is the way to do it: you take your knife in your right hand and your fork in your left. Then you cut off a piece of meat of the size you want to put into your mouth. Then you put some vegetable on the knife and smear it on the meat. And then put it into your mouth with your left hand. The meat is very fat here and the bread they have is only of one kind and even finer than our milk bread. But we got used to it. Often 20 to 25 people come here for dinner. But I have not seen a single one say grace before or after the meal. Then we go for a walk from 4 to 7 or 8. At half past 9 or 10 o'clock we eat some bread and butter or sometimes a piece of cold meat. At 11 o'clock we go to bed.

The English people love nobody but their own nation. But they like the Germans best, better than the Dutch. But the French they dislike so much that if they say the word "French" their exchange changes.

Now it is particularly good to see when the English start a fight with each other (which happens often), then they run toward each other straight away. Then they take off their clothes, off with the wig, off with the coat, off with the shirt. Only their breeches, their stockings and their shoes they keep on. And then they run at each other, they hit each other in the side, they grab each other around the neck as hard as they can. And when one has thrown the other to the ground three times they shake hands and kiss as if they were the best of friends. And all this happens with hundreds of people looking on.

Since here in London half an ounce of snuff is 3 stuyvers in our money and is not as good as ours by far we have given up taking snuff on May 6th. Smoking tobacco here is 44 stuyvers per pound in our money.

On May 13th, we saw the Queen's donkey[14] which is like a small mule in size. Also had ears like a donkey. Now this one had stripes in the middle of the front of its head, of a fresh reddish brown and white. In the middle of the front of its head those stripes were no wider than the back of a knife.

Behind the eyes they got wider and wider. Around the belly they were a good inch in width. At the end of the tail they were again as fine as a knife's edge. And all those stripes all around were so neat that you would say no painter could draw them like that. You could not have found one hair out of place. I also think that this donkey makes money every day (more than 10 guineas because there are so many spectators) although each only gives 3 halfpennies to the officer.

On May 16th, we went with Mr. Mäilan to see the Queen's elephant, an animal which seems most frightening. It is about 20 hands high and 6 to 7 shoes long. The trunk is about 1½ ells long and it can use it as conveniently as a man does his arm. It grabs the hay with it, shakes off enough to have the right quantity. And then it puts the hay into a hole below its neck. And all that is done so deftly that nothing falls to the ground. Head and neck are one piece. From the trunk which is about 3 to 4 inches thick at the bottom end the head widens towards the shoulder. It has small eyes, like a big

Fig. 24 North West View of the Tower of London.
Copperplate engraving based on a drawing by John Maurer (1713-1761), approx. 1750.
Museum of London, Inv. No. 7727.

calf. Instead of ears, it has large flaps of fur which it can flap loudly against its body. Its back is high in the middle, and the belly is no more than 1½ feet from the ground. The tail is like a cow's tail, has a lot of single hairs at the end, about half a finger long, and that is all the hair it has on its body. Its legs are very thick and one cannot see much of the joints. Its feet are just round thick runners, like a horse's foot. It is round in the front. Its hide looks a whitish blue and wrinkled, it is very ugly. It was tied with its left fore foot and also its left hind foot. But it never held its body still. Although its feet did not move it swayed its body forward and backward continuously, swinging about a foot and a half, and never stopped. It moved its trunk all the time, as high as the plastered ceiling.

The same day we went up the Thames out of London to a village where there was a house full of thousands of rare things, most of it animals from the sea, where I also saw two flying or winged fish. The animals were all stuffed, or dried, or they were hung in aquafortis.

On May 21st, our host demanded 3 shillings a week for our room. He said those had not been part of the agreement. But since we both had stated so explicitly, we moved that same day from [place name missing] to Tower Hill to Widow Stapelfeldt where we are to pay 3 shillings a week for our room. So now we keep house ourselves.

On May 27th, we went to the orphanage at the church[15] and listened to the singing, where about 400 children, both girls and boys, were sitting apart from each other in the most beautifully orderly fashion. The oldest were about 10 to 11 years old and the youngest 4 to 5, and they made such a varied music that even if they had done so for three hours the time would not have been too long, although the church was so full of people that you could hardly find a place to stand for the crowd. It lasted only a bit more than a quarter of an hour. The clothes the girls wore were all alike. And those of the boys were also all alike. And most of them were particularly beautiful children.

On May 29th, we went there and watched them work. The bigger girls spun on wheels of a new kind which had two wings, and they were spinning two separate lengths of yarns at the same time. The smaller girls were sewing. The bigger boys were all sitting in a row weaving linen. The middle boys were knitting purses and horsehair[16]. The smallest ones were all knitting stockings, and everything was very neat. Where they were sitting there were two wings of a building, each about 200 paces long. One was for the girls and the other for the boys. When they are 18 to 20 years old, they are married to each other and sent to the remote islands[17].

On May 30th, we bought a description of London. When we went along the streets on May 29th, we saw poor people sitting everywhere in the streets with gilded boughs or leaves of oak. And everybody going by bought some and pinned them to their chests. Indeed, even all the horses were thus decorated. The following day, Mr. Meilan told us the meaning of it, namely that King Charles the Second (whose father was beheaded) had had to flee on that day, and that he had spent three days hiding in the branches of an oak tree without food or water and had finally made a lucky escape. But 12 years later he was raised to the throne. And this King had had a lot of things made. There are five live-sized statues of him that we have seen, either hewn in marble or cast in copper.

On May 31st (on the day of the Ascension of Our Lord) at noon, about 150 orphans came walking, each holding a peeled willow branch about 7 or 8 feet long in his hand, with colored ribbons around their caps and screamed, beat their branches on certain spots and screamed loudly. Behind these children walked the priest, and behind him all the consistory, and they also had those white branches in their hands and cockades on their hats, although some were also carrying big sticks with large silver buttons on them. Now all this seemed very ridiculous, especially for somebody who did not know the meaning of it. The following day we learned what it had all been about. To wit: on all the land in London without exception ground rent must be paid to the churches. And every church asserts its claim to possession of its land on that day and in that manner. And there is such a noise among the children that it is quite astonishing.

Fig. 25 Elephant from the Royal Menagerie at the Tower. From: the Gentleman's Magazine for October. Copperplate engraving. London 1763. RFM.

After all of this was finished, around 1 to half past 1, several hundred boys aged between 12 and 16 assembled near the Tower. They had tied the afore-mentioned branches together in bundles of 6 to 8, so they were about 3 shoes long and as thick as a child's arm. Then they formed two groups which ran toward each another as if they were fighting a battle, and beat each other so heatedly as if they wanted to kill each other, and sometimes one party pushed the other back 100 to 200 steps. And that went on not only until the evening but was taken up again on June 1st at midday and lasted until the evening.

On June 1st, we saw the animals at the Tower[18] , 8 to 9 lions, one of which had sat there for 65 years, 5 tigers, one Philadelphia eagle etc. June 4th, that is today, is the King's birthday. This day I wrote home.

1   The two Austrian army officers.
2   The innkeeper.
3   Lord Mayor Sir William Stephenson.
4   Fresh water pipes.
5   Since the noun is missing it is impossible to say what kind of object Herbergs is talking about.
6   E.g. gun carriages.
7   Charlotte Sophie of Mecklenburg-Strelitz, b. May 19, 1744, d. November 17, 1818, married on September 8, 1761 to George William Frederick Guelph, Duke of Suffolk, b. June 4, 1738, d. January 28, 1820, crowned September 22, 1761, King George III of England.
8   George III, King of Great Britain and Ireland, Prince Elector of Hanover, King of Hanover from 1814, 1760-1829, b. June 4, 1738, in London, d. January 28, 1820, in Windsor.
9   George August of Mecklenburg-Strelitz, b. August 16, 1748, in Mirow, d. November 6, 1785, in Tyrnau/Hungary; Imperial Austrian Major General in Hungary.
10 Royal palace.
11 Horselydown, formerly a district of the City of London, today a street name. Horselydown Street runs roughly parallel to the access road to Tower Bridge on the right bank of the Thames.
12 Today between King William Street and Gracechurch Street.
13 Sweeting's Alley, street east of the Royal Exchange.
14 In Herbergs' time there was a menagerie at the Lion Tower, a part of the Tower of London.
15 The church and orphanage could not be identified.
16 Probably: from horsehair.
17 Outer Hebrides, Orkney Islands or Shetland Islands
18 Lion Tower, v. ann. 13.

Across the Atlantic

On June 5th, at 1 in the afternoon we boarded the ship, which then left straight away. But because of the tide we did not sail any further than Greenwich. On June 6th, we did not get far, either. On June 7th, we arrived at Gravesend. June 8th we spent at anchor. NB.

On June 9th, at half past 3 in the afternoon we left from Gravesend under a good wind. At 9 in the evening we lay at anchor. On June 10th, that was Whitsunday, at 3 in the morning the anchor was weighed. Under a strong wind we then got out into the open sea straight away, and where it was most dangerous there were signs made of big barrels floating on the sea. We took great care not to go there and had to throw out the plumb line all the time. And by less than 15 paces, we passed a ship that had gone down not long ago, and the mast was still about 20 feet above the water. At 3 in the afternoon we arrived at Deal where we lay at anchor until 10 in the morning of June 11th. We left there with the wind against us after Mr. Eling and his wife and 3 other passengers in the first cabin had come on board.

First of all I have to describe the ship. It has three masts and weighs 150 tons. There are altogether 34 people onboard. In the way of animals, there are 10 pigs, 8 sheep, 104 chickens, 48 ducks, 3 cats and 2 dogs. The first cabin sleeps 8 people, ours 24, but it is rare for all the sailors to be inside. Standing room is 4 feet long and a good 3 feet wide, and there is seating on chests all around. But when there are more than 10 or 12 inside, you have to lie down on your bed or you cannot stay. Besides, the first 5 or 6 days we suffered an amazing stench. Our food so far has been nothing but salted meat.

On the morning of June 12th, we saw innumerable sea hog[1] (we had a head wind that day) and afterwards we had rough weather. We had to tack a lot that day and did not make much headway.

On June 13th, we also had a head wind, and it was foggy. On June 14th, at 6 in the morning we lay at anchor because we had no wind at all. At 11 o'clock the anchor was weighed again but the wind was still bad. At 8 at night we were at anchor again. After having had a northwesterly wind at first, we now had a westerly wind and it blew right against us.

On June 15th, we had a good wind between 2 and 7 in the morning, and then little wind up to 12 o'clock. So we lay at anchor at the Isle of Wight[2]. Up to now, our food was salted beef that had been salted back in Carolina and was so salty you could hardly eat it. And the bread that was also baked in Philadelphia is also so hard that you can hardly chew it. The small beer that we brought with us is also finished now. Today we had bacon and peas for our midday meal for the first time, which tasted good.

On June 16th at 3 in the morning we had an easterly wind and were only lying by Portsmouth. This easterly lasted until a quarter past 1 in the afternoon June 11th when it suddenly changed to a southwesterly. From there we sailed into the open sea.

On June 17th, from 1 in the afternoon we had a southwesterly until half past 7 when such a dense fog came up that one could not see as far as a stone's throw. At 10 a very strong northerly came up which lasted until June 18th (we sailed 9½ miles in one hour) at 11 in the morning when it lessened a bit. It stayed northerly until June 19th at 1 in the morning.

On June 19th, at 2 in the morning such a strong easterly blew up that we made 6½ English miles in one hour. At 8 we had a big thunderstorm with lightning and rain (just like on land). It lasted until 11. All through the afternoon the good easterly kept up, so we made a continuous 5 to 5½ miles.

On June 20th, at 3 to 4 in the morning, we had a southerly, and that was not so strong. At 1 o'clock there was a southeasterly, which is the best wind you can have. It was very strong. We made 8½ English miles in one hour. That lasted until half past 11 at night when it turned a straight westerly.

From midnight on June 21st to 1 o'clock on June 22nd, we had a southwesterly wind, which then turned to the northwest, but it was so weak that we hardly moved for more than three hours on those two days. At 10 at night a west wind started blowing. We had west wind until 2 in the afternoon of June 23rd, straight from the west but so strong that our ship made 4½ miles an hour and the water was going across the bow. From 8 to about 11 or 12, the water raged incredibly. Indeed we sat on the ship and the water came over from one end of the ship to the other.

On June 24th, St. John's Day, I had a headache all day, so I did not get up from my bed until 2 in the afternoon. All that day until midday we had a northwesterly wind, then a southwesterly all of a sudden and then again a northwesterly at half past eleven. That night was the roughest we had had so far, and the ship was moving so much as if it was about to go down.

June 25th is the same as yesterday, but we are still going 4½ miles an hour. On June 26th, we still had the same wind but much rougher so the water came across the ship man-high. NB [in code language] cousin Strepers.

On June 27th, we have the same northwesterly, but rougher still, and the sailors tell us that no other storm could be compared to it. From 7 until 8 in the morning on June 28th it was so strong that all the sails were hauled in and most passengers were taken ill. So that if it had lasted much longer, they would all have had to lie down. Cousin Strepers was also feeling quite sick. And I had a strong headache from June 24th to 28th in the morning. At midday the wind died down a little (I felt much better from then on). We still have a wind from the west-north-west. We are making 5 miles an hour at present. Indeed the wind was so strong that water came over more than 18 shoes high.

But I cannot go on now without giving some picture of our cook. He is about 45 years old. Always has his mouth full of chewing tobacco and spits without looking where. His hands are full of warts as big as small hazelnuts. Indeed I think that if they were weighed they would be more than half a pound. He always goes about with his head bare, and without stockings. His has a piece of cloth tied in front,

dirtier than any cleaning rag could ever look. Our meat is rinsed and even cooked in the same dishes that the pigs are fed from and shit all over. And that meat was salted way back in Carolina and is too salty to eat anyway. Besides, the way the cook looks, even somebody who had not eaten for three days would not feel like eating, just from looking at him. The way we live here defies description.

At 4 in the morning of June 29th, we caught a northerly wind. So all the sails were hoisted, and we made 5 ½ miles straight away. In the evening, the cook had to wash himself. and then he was powdered and had to dance (NB The one with the scarlet coat). At midnight a southerly wind came up but just for 1 hour. NB

On June 30th, there was a northerly wind, and we made 6 miles. Around midday we saw land which we passed on our right. It is an island, called the Western Islands[3]. It measures 14 English miles all around. They grow a good wine there and make pottery. Belongs to Spain[4]. Is 843 miles from London. At 8 in the evening we were only 1 German mile[5] away from it. It is surprisingly high and mountainous.

On July 1st, we have a bad wind and make 3½ miles an hour. It is remarkable that the water of the ocean gives off such a shine or fire. Because if at night it is poured over the ship, the fire[6] runs across the ship. And in the sea you can often see it, too. At 3 o'clock again innumerable sea-hog showed themselves, which is a sign for a storm coming up.

Today we sailed past a spot where a ship went down that was supposed to measure the depth of the ocean. It had been full of ropes, one finger thick, with a heavy piece of lead attached. But when those ropes had been lowered into the water to their full length and had become so heavy on one side the ship capsized and sank without the ropes having struck bottom. Another remarkable thing is that where we are the days are much shorter. Because the sun comes up at 4:20 in the morning and goes down at 7:40. That in calm weather.

On July 2nd, we have a good wind but not much, so we only make 3 or 3½ miles. At 1 o'clock a big turtle came swimming up, at 4 another, smaller one. During the night we did not have any wind at all from midnight until half past 4 in the morning. On July 3rd, from 5 onwards we made 3½ miles again. Here we are right in the Sargasso Sea. Otherwise we had only very little wind. On July 4th, at 10 in the morning the wind died down so much that we did not have any wind at all and were dead in the water.

In this region there are fish that are very colorful, blue, black and silver, also small ones of about ¼ pound which swim around the ship in their hundreds, as well as a kind called shark. They are a kind that eat humans. Then a turtle came drifting close to the ship. For fear of those fish, no sailor was allowed to go into the water to swim after it. They put the boat to water but it had a leak. Right now the sea is completely calm.

Indeed, at 4 in the afternoon we saw a large number of sea-hog in the distance which then swam toward the ship until they were not even 4 paces away. There were far more than a hundred of them, and many of them leaping out of the water 6 or 8 feet high, so we could see them well. Then the captain shot at one of them, so they made off at such great speed that within a quarter of an hour they were at least 5 to 6 hours away from us. They continually turn in the water like a wheel so you can see them above the water. Afterwards, 3 sailors and the mate jumped into the sea and took a bath. Now they had a large dog, called Roebuck like our ship. He jumped after them three times and swam for such a long time that it was quite surprising.

On July 5th there was wind again, but west wind, so we had to tack. On July 6th, we also had a westerly wind so we did not get ahead at all. In the afternoon there was some southerly wind. We are making 2½ miles an hour.

Our ship is 82 feet long and 24 feet wide. It carries 150 tons, each ton 20 hundredweight, each hundredweight 112 pounds, that is 336,000 pounds altogether. Now the equipment weighs as much again as the cargo. Because one anchor weighs hundredweight and 14 pounds, another is some-what smaller and yet another smaller still. Now among the biggest merchantmen there are some carrying 800 tons.

On July 7th, we have little southerly wind. On July 8th, it was again so weak that we did not move ahead at all. The sea is so calm now that I have never before seen it like that. The sailors went for another swim. At 7 in the afternoon we got a northerly wind. Then we made 3½ miles. This afternoon there was a quarrel, so the captain closed the hatch.

On the morning of July 9th, we still had a good northerly wind, so we made 4 miles an hour. NB With the red coat, Paulus Mantel, and Mossis. At 1 in the afternoon, there was an easterly, and we are making 6½ miles an hour now. NB: Cousin Strepers.

On July 10th, we still have an easterly wind and are still making 6½ miles an hour. At noon we are still making 5 miles with the same wind. Today we saw many flying fish, indeed with hundreds of them in one swarm, like thrushes, ranging in size from ¼ pound to 2 to 3 shoes, flying above the water, often 100 to 300 pace. There were also a lot of plants[7] in the sea around here, all supposed to come from the island of Florida. The sea where we still are is called Western Ocean in English.

On July 11th, we still had an easterly but not a strong one, we are going at 3 ½ miles. At 10 in the morning, the captain of the warship caught a fish on the line, called a dolphin. There were two more swimming next to it which our captain caught with a harpoon. The first weighed about 15 pounds, the other two about 12 each.

On July 12th, we had a southeasterly wind, but not strong. Today I saw many of those plants, 3 to 4 rods[8] long and wide in one piece. At 5 in the afternoon, we had strong wind and made 6 miles.

On July 13th, we had a good southerly wind, so we made 7 miles. Now just before ¼ to 11, there was an unusual sight. Our captain called for everybody to come out of the cabin. I was just standing next to the captain. They all came up and watched the air drawing the water up from the sea in a strange shape that is called a water spout in English. This lasted about 6 minutes and looked as though there was a strong fire underneath and was drawn together like a large stream up into the beak. And the captains said they would not like to be in that spot now, it would pull the ship up with it.

NB Yesterday at midday we were supposed to be still 960 miles from New York. An English mile on land is supposed to be 5,000 feet and at sea 6,000 feet, and London is supposed to be 3,300 miles from New York.

On July 14th, we had a steady strong southwesterly wind, so we made 5 to 6 miles. On July 15th, we still had the same wind, but around midday it changed to the west and afterwards to the northwest. We went like that until 8 in the morning of July 16th and afterwards with a northwesterly wind. After that, we went along with a southerly wind and, therefore, did not make much headway. At 2 the wind had dropped altogether. At 4 in the afternoon, a fish came up called shark or man-eater in English. It was about 12 feet long and very thick. It hovered around the ship for about ½ hour, sometimes came up to the surface, too. It had 3 smaller fish swimming around it all the time. The captains did everything they could to catch it. Put a piece of beef, as well as a piece of pork weighing 5 pounds, on a hook that was about 1½ feet long and as thick as a finger. But the fish passed it quite close, so it was not hungry. Those fish, according to the sailors, stay with a ship for a long time, waiting for a dead man to be thrown overboard, to be there quickly and devour him. At 11 a slight southwesterly sprang up.

On July 17th, we still had a southwesterly but a bit stronger so we made 2½ miles but backwards so went backwards 38 miles. On July 18th, at 4 in the morning, we had a strong storm with rain until 8. Then the wind turned and blew directly from the west, and we had to sail south, so we did not get ahead at all.

On July 19th, the wind is very strong but straight from the west and as bad as it could be. We are heading straight south now, 16 miles backwards.

All 24 of us are crawling with lice so much that we can smash them on our bedclothes two at a time. At 10 at night we headed north until 6 in the morning of July 20th, then south again. Now the wind is not so strong any more, but still from the west. My snuff is all used up now. At noon the sun was directly above our heads, so we did not cast any shadow at all. On July 21st, there was a southwesterly and we made 3 miles. At 2 we saw well above 200 sea hog again. But they were all smaller than the ones before. Today, some people stole some fresh water, which is always kept under lock and key. At 3 a good southerly wind came up, so we made 6 miles at 8 and 7 miles at 12 o'clock.

At 8 in the morning on July 22nd, a large group of sea hog came swimming around and underneath the ship, and we could see them as clearly as if we had held them in our hands. They weighed between 60 or 70 and 100 pounds. From noon yesterday to noon today, we made 126 nautical miles. At 2 o'clock, a good 100 sea hog came up to the ship.

On July 23rd, there was a southerly wind, nice and strong. From noon yesterday to noon today, we made 158 miles. At 8 this morning, several sea hog could again be seen, and also flying fish. At noon we were close to Newfoundland. At 7, bad weather came up, and the wind began turning toward the west. By 12 it was coming almost straight from the west, so we made barely 3 miles. Today we saw a duck not far from the ship. Now, the distance to New York is said to be 1,050 English miles.

On July 24th, we had the wind right against us, and it was quite calm so the rudder was latched fast all afternoon and we did not advance at all. Today we measured the flow of the current.

On July 25th, it was still calm until 8 in the evening when the wind turned to the south, but it was very weak. So we are making less than a mile an hour. We now have the North Star to our left and the Dipper to our right and are sailing right between the two. Today at 3, we saw a ship in the distance.

On July 26th, we have a good wind but it is weak. Now we are close to Nova Scotia and on the other side Cape Breton Island, and here our snuff runs out [the line is crossed out after "here"].

On July 27th, the wind was a bit better. At 12, one of the white sea birds[9] was to be seen. Now there was also an inspection concerning the knives that had been stolen. On July 28th, we had the wind from southwest but not very strongly, so we made only 3 miles. We have had 8 days of very warm weather. At 3 we saw a three-master in the distance. NB illness Efferie. On July 29th, we had a good southerly wind and made 6 miles. At 10 o'clock we met a French ship. It had left from Guadeloupe 18 days ago. I also saw flying fish.

On July 30th at half past 4 in the morning a terrible storm blew up which lasted only 8 minutes. It came up so suddenly that not a sail had been lowered. The ship keeled to one side so much, you thought it was going to capsize. NB cousin Strepers. I was lying in the top boat on one side. At 8 we saw a white sea bird. Now we had storms like that throughout the day, but always hauled the sails in on time. At 6 we saw a two-master to the north, but far away. At 7 there was a strong storm lasting about 1 hour.

On July 31st, at half past 1 in the morning, a very strong storm blew up, and I was lying in the top boat (where I had slept the 9 previous nights) sleeping. But there was such a heavy rain that it ran under my body like a stream, so I went down. This morning at nine, another white bird could be seen, along with hundreds of flying fish. Now we had storms all through that day, so now we are heading straight south for that reason. At 5 we saw another ship toward the south. At 10 there was such a strong thunderstorm, followed by four more, with such thunder, lightning and wind that it was quite horrible. It lasted until after 12, and the sea looked like mountains of fire all that time.

On August 1st, at 3 in the morning there was an easterly wind. But it was so weak we did not make real headway. This morning we had a fish in our hands the captain had caught. Its weight would have been a good quarter of a pound. It had big fins and a horn at the top of its back, shaped like a half-moon. It was quite sharp at the tip and looked like the cock on a rifle. When it stood up it was so stiff one could not press it down. Just beneath it, though, there was a little spot where, if one pressed it, the tip receded and could not be seen any more. At 8 in the evening, a gentle easterly wind came up and grew so strong that by 10 we were making 6 miles. But at half past 1 on August 2nd, the wind turned to the west-southwest and grew so strong all through the day that the boats were tied to the ship with some additional thick ropes, so they would not be washed overboard by the waves going across the big ship. At 6 in the afternoon, a bird came to the ship that I had never seen before. It stayed around the ship for about ¼ hour. It whistled twice. Its shape – and also its color and its beak – were like that of a snipe, and it was about the same size. At 10 in the evening, it was so very rough that the waves washed across from one side of the ship to the other. The height of the waves now is unbelievable to anybody who has not seen it.

On August 3rd, the weather is with the same wind as yesterday, the wind is still as strong but mixed with rain. This lasted until 7 in the morning. After that it did not rain any more, only the wind continued. On August 4, at 5 in the morning, a north wind came up but was not very strong. At 7 we saw two ships toward the south. There are so many flying fish that they are no longer a novelty. Yesterday morning the sailors saw about 10 pairs of birds near the ship that looked like pigeons. At 4 in the afternoon we saw 3 ships to the south. At 8 there was no wind.

At half past 9, I saw a very big fish about 6 to 8 shoes long, coming up to the surface by the ship's stern with a very loud splash. And we were told it must be a shark. Upon which the captain threw the big hook, which is as thick as a finger and more than 1½ feet long, overboard with a piece of pork on it. And the fish was caught as soon as it had been thrown out. It was a small one, 5 ½ of my shoes in length, but it had an astonishing mouth and teeth. It was very fat, too. It probably weighed 150 to 160 pounds after the intestines had been taken out. It lived for about ½ hour afterwards. It had two flaps in front, as large as a goose's wing. Its tail looked similar. But one end was much longer than the other.

Fig. 27 Marcus Elieser Bloch, Queen trigger fish or Balistes Vetula. From: Bloch's Atlas. Naturgeschichte der Fische 1782-1795. Colored copperplate engraving.

It had 3 more of the same flaps on his back and rear end, but they were not as large. The remarkable thing was that there was another kind of fish attached to this one, which weighed about ½ pound. On its back toward the head it had a spot like a wooden disk with which it stuck so fast to the other fish that one could hardly pull it away. That fish is supposed to suck the big fish's blood, and its gills were in the wrong spot altogether. A remarkable fish indeed[10]. At half past 10, a wind blew up but with a strong rain. NB lever watch, shark, the log, ermine.

On August 5th, there was a southwesterly in the morning. This turned around completely at 7, so the ship turned around with it until it sailed west again. But the wind was not strong. At half past 6, we caught another man-eater or shark, a bit bigger than the last one. It probably weighed 170 to 180 pounds. It had a dolphin in its belly, weighing about 12 to 15 pounds, as well as three pieces of pork that it had been caught with. Again, there was a small fish of ¼ pound sucking its blood. At 10 o'clock we

caught two dolphins, one weighing about 15 pounds, the other 10 pounds. We had no wind during the night.

At half past 3 in the morning of August 6th, we had a southwesterly wind, it was middling good. At 3 in the afternoon, we saw a small boat to the north. But it was still a long way away. At 6 there was a heavy thunderstorm, followed by a second one, and that lasted until half past nine. I have rarely seen or heard such heavy thunderstorms. At 8 we got a strong southeasterly and made 9 miles an hour. But that did not last long.

I have eaten some shark's meat but it does not taste good. I have kept one of its front fins, a piece of its skin, and some bluish cartilage that is growing around its brain and is supposed to be good for a toothache, and some round bones from its back-bone.

I have also eaten some dolphin's meat. That tastes good. I have kept several bones from its backbone that look like beakers. Now our smoking tobacco is all gone. From the morning of August 7, such

Fig. 26 Marcus Elieser Bloch, Suckerfish. From: Bloch's Atlas. Naturgeschichte der Fische 1782-1795. Colored copperplate engraving.

strong southwesterlies came up that we had to tack, that the waves came across the ship who knows how many times, and that the sea was rougher than we had ever seen it. It is incredible how the ship is rolling now, from one side to the other, its bow up one moment, its stern the other. And the worst thing is that we do not know but we were supposed to see land yesterday or today. So now they say the captain is all confused and does not know whether to sail right or left.

On August 8th, we had a southwesterly. At 10 we saw a ship ahead of us which reached us at ¼ past 11, and our captain talked to it for ¼ hour. The ships sailed around each other 2 or 3 times without caring that the sea was raging cruelly.

Now I have noticed that in a stormy sea, one cannot see more than 4 hours away. The ships parted at half past 11, and at half past 12 we could no longer see the other ship. So my calculation is that the other ship made 3 hours and we made one. At 3 we saw two more ships but did not come close. At

half past 5 in the afternoon, we saw another water spout. But it was not as big as the first. We are supposed to be 90 hours from New York now. We had a bad wind.

On August 9th, at half past 12 in the morning we got a northeasterly but a weak one. Around noon we were making 4½ miles with that wind. Yesterday, near evening, a big bird like a lark came to the ship and sat in the boat. And it could almost be caught by hand, it was so tired. This morning from 9 onward until now we have had a three-master at our side that is heading for Maryland. Now at 6, the captains are talking to each other. That ship carries 140 felons who are all standing on deck right now. The ship comes from Bristol, and the felons are going to be sold, one for 7 years, the other for 12 years, according to their deserts. After that, they are allowed to return. That ship has been traveling for 11 weeks. At 6 we are making 8¼ miles with the same wind. The wind has kept up well. Now everything is full of sea hog as far as one can see, and here just around and under the ship they are coming together so close that the water is teeming and swarming with them. We have cast and shot for them who knows how often but in vain. In the distance one could see thousands of them all around.

At 4 on the morning of August 10th, we are still making 6 miles. Now a small sloop from Philadelphia passed our ship. At first, it did not want to reply but finally told us that it had left Philadelphia on Tuesday and was now 45 hours away from it. At 11 we came to a spot that was so full of fish that the water was solid. There were about 8 to 10 shoals, each shoal about 10 to 12 rods[11] long, and that kind of fish is called bluefish[12]. They are half the size of a herring.

At half past 11 in the morning of August 11th, one sailor, called Benjamin, much to our delight saw land for the first time. At 2 we headed straight east until 8 o'clock. But there was very little wind. We saw various kinds of land birds as well as wild duck.

Now everything is used up: tobacco, snuff, tea, sugar, brandy, so we will be in the same situation as Peter Cürlis.

Fig. 28 School of Archibald Robinson, View of New York from Le Jupiter of 74 Guns Lying at Anchor in the North River [Hudson]. Water color, 1794. Museum of the City of New York, Inv. No. 52.100.1.

August 12th. We are sailing due north with a northeasterly wind and have seen no land between 5 o'clock yesterday and now, at half past 11. But from now on, we will see it until we arrive in New York. At 5 in the morning on August 13th, I saw the first house, and there were green trees standing at the water's edge as if they had been planted everywhere. At 11 we got 2 pilots who are taking us to New York. At 5 everybody from the cabin was given pears, one each. At a quarter to ten at night, we anchored at New York. At 12 a fish swam by the ship, called a slobberer[13], a kind that is about 10 feet long. It blew water and gave a horrible roar. Also, it often came about two feet out of the water.

Abb. 29 View of the Entrance of New York Harbour from Najak, Fort Hamilton. Handzeichnung. Aus: Jaspar Dankers, Peter Sluyter, Journal of a Voyage to New York... in 1679-80. In: Memoirs of the Long Island Historical Society I, verlegt bei G. Hayward & Co., Brooklyn 1867.

1 Phoecaena communis Cuvier, a kind of porpoise.
2 For many years, Cowes on the Isle of Wight was the last stop before crossing the Atlantic.
3 Azores, a group of nine islands and some rocks.
4 Belonged to the Kingdom of Portugal.
5 7,420.44 meters = 4.21 English miles.
6 Herbergs is talking about marine phosphorescence, a phenomenon caused by the bioluminescence of a number of marine organisms, especially the flagellates Noctiluca miliaris and Ceratium tripos (unicellular organisms) occurring in large numbers, as well as certain medusas, pyrosomes etc. The chemical substances causing the luminescence are called luciferines. Information from Dr. Ulf Bleichle, Staatliches Museum für Naturkunde und Vorgeschichte, Oldenburg, Germany.
7 Sea weed of the Sargasso Sea (Sargassum).
8 The length of a rod differed from one place to another, both within Germany and between Germany and the American colonies, so that an exact definition is not possible. Herbergs could have been talking either of a Cologne rod, at 3.77 m, or an Aachen rod, at 4.51 m. [Rh. Wb. VII, col. 643].
9 Sea gull.
10 A suckerfish or shark sucker (Echeneiformes or Discocephali), an order of bony fish closely related to the perch family. In the Echeneiformes, the first dorsal fin has developed into a suction disk with lamellae with which they attach themselves to shark, tuna and other fish and clean the skin of their hosts of parasites – they are not bloodsuckers. The only suckerfish family are the Echinidae occurring in 8 different species in all tropical and temperate oceans. The most common species is Echineis saucrates, which grows up to 1 meter in length. The sucking organ of the shark sucker is ribbed on the surface. Information from Dr. Ulf Bleichle, Staatliches Museum für Naturkunde und Vorgeschichte, Oldenburg, Germany.
11 Rod, v. ann. 8.
12 Temnodon saltator, bluefish; a fish of a bluish color, common on the Atlantic coast of N. America.
13 Probably a whale.

From New York to Philadelphia

Here at New York the time is 4 hours and 20 minutes later than in London. Our passengers have the following names: Efferie, Stier, the captain's orderlies and Mr. Ellens' moor, English, Germans, Baltzer and wife, two sisters called Rennor from Heidelberg, Trippel from Switzerland, Caspar Metschelfeld from Seyden, sailors, Captain Smith, Mate Hodd, Second Mate Hemmelden[1], two Sams, 4 Scheckten[2], one Ben, 1 Henry, 1 Cäbenter[3], 1 Tellen[4], in the cabin Mr. Ellertz and his wife, two maids, the sea captain[5] and his cousin, a merchant in a red coat, NB.

At 8 in the morning on August 14th, they had us brought ashore in New York. New York is quite a pleasant place. The harbor goes almost all the way around the city because the city is surrounded by water on two sides and is located on the front tip. And everywhere there are places to land. We took lodgings at the house of a widow here whose husband had died 2 months before. His name was John George Cook, coffee merchant at the Royal Exchange. At 11 we had ourselves rowed across and met some Germans straight away. We asked them how far it was to Flatbush[6]. There were some from Mr. Rübel's congregation among them, and they made a big to-do about Mr. Rübel. One who lives right across the water took us into his house and made punch for us. Another who lives close to him drove us to his door with two horses. Mr.

Fig. 30 Based on George Heap, The East Prospect of the City of Philadelphia, in the Province of Pennsylvania. Copperplate engraving, The London Magazine for October 1761. RFM.

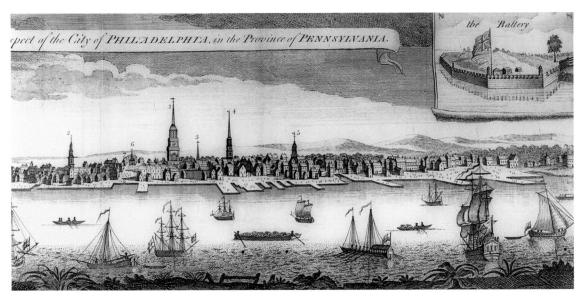

Rübel had visitors from New York just then and they were at table. We had to sit down with them and joined them for the meal. So he was right pleasant. We wanted to go back in the afternoon because it is no more than 4 miles from New York but we absolutely had to stay the night. He wrote out a recommendation for us and gave us some advice about how to tackle our business. He also asked me to give him the printed papers from Mr. Wülfing because he wanted to read them impartially. When I told him that I had those in New York, he said he would come and collect them this afternoon.

At 10 in the morning of August 15th, we went back to New York. The area is (very fertile), slightly hilly along the water's edge. We did not know most kinds of trees such as cedar, sassafras, a kind of nut tree and many others. They are all very yellow and very high. They have lot of peaches here in this country. And fish, as well as one kind like oysters but bigger and much better, are in great abundance. At low tide the oysters are there in such great quantity, so Mr. Rübel says, that the farmers have whole waggon loads of them in their cellars to sell.

They shoot 15 to 20 wild pigeon in one shot, and 8 to 10 snipe in one shot. To sum up, there is a lot of wild game. And everybody is allowed to hunt, both in Pennsylvania and in Long Island where Mr. Rübel lives.

Here in New York daylight comes 4 hours and 20 minutes later than in London. At 6 in the afternoon Mr. Rübel came to collect the books. He took us to see a man called Peter Remsen, a very clever man, whom we definitely should go and see on coming back.

The houses in this town are almost all made of brick. But the roofs are covered with cedar shin-

gles. Most houses in the country and the villages around the town have wooden walls all around and wooden roofs. The citadel[7] here is worth seeing, although there is no garrison in it any more, and it is falling into disrepair. But the big guns and batteries which can shoot across the water on both sides of Manhattan can be seen in great numbers. Here in New York, a third of the people are Indians or real blacks whom people buy for life and pay £80 to 100 for one. They also let them have children whom their owner then sells again. NB

At 1 o'clock on August 16, we traveled 30 miles from New York to Perth Amboy and ran aground half an hour away from Amboy. Then we had to shout and whistle for a long time until they came and picked us up in a small boat but we were never in any danger. At half past 8 we arrived here. There is only this one inn here. But I must say that I cannot remember ever having seen such an inn. All in all, there are 30 passengers big and small. We were seated at a table of six and waited on by two blacks. And all of the bedrooms at the inn were beautiful. Indeed I think they can take in 200 people here. At 10 o'clock the ship landed. There we handed our baggage to the waggoner.

On the morning of August 17th, we set out with 5 waggons, with 4 horses each and racing each other. Having left at half past 4, by 11 we had reached Cranbury, which is 20 miles. At 1 o'clock 10 people left Cranbury in one waggon, and at half past 7 we were already in Burlington, that is 30 miles. After [in Herbergs' secret code: we had eaten and cousin Strepers had joined in drinking punch and wine we had spent 20 shillings]. At 10 in the evening we went on the boat in Burlington and at 7 the following morning arrived at Philadelphia, where we first went to Mr. Ernst Kurtz, who is a very polite person in the European style. Not only did he urge us all day to have food and drink, he also found us lodgings and brought our luggage there.

---

[1] Probably: Hamilton.
[2] Perhaps: Jackson.
[3] Lebender (family name?).
[4] Probably: Dillon.

[5] No name given, probably Smith.
[6] On Long Island, now called Brooklyn.
[7] Battery Park at the southern tip of Manhattan.

SECOND STREET. North from Market St. th CHRIST CHURCH.
PHILADELPHIA.

Fig. 31 William Birch (1755-1834), Second Street North from Market Street with Christ Church. Colored copperplate engraving. Philadelphia 1799. Library Company, Inv. No. Sn15 (15c).

Philadelphia-Germantown-Bucks County

On August 18, 1764 – starting in the evening[1] – we contracted for our lodgings here in Philadelphia with Mr. Berenstecher, that is breakfast in the morning, lunch, dinner and bed for 12 shillings a week for each of us.

When we were discussing our business with Mr. Kurtz, where best to start, we decided to go first to the Registry Office and take copies from the Land Register. Now Mr. Kurtz told us that we could best learn about the whole business from Jan Janssen. But since he thought that the latter had some of our land in his possession and was a very greedy man who could never get enough land, he thought it would be better to keep very quiet.

Today a man from Germantown, called Valasch and originally from Krefeld, came to see Mr. Kurtz and told him there would be two men coming from Holland with claims in Germantown, and whether we were those men. Upon which he had replied that he did not know anything of our business. We came from Krefeld and had brought him a letter from his brother[2]. When we were sitting at table with Mr. Kurtz at lunch time, Christian Schneider came (and handed him a note), whom I still recognized straight away.

August 19th was a Sunday. So we did not do any work but went and had a look at the barracks[3] where the savages and the guns are.

On August 19th, we went into the barracks where about two-hundred savages live. Their language is said to be similar to Hebrew[4], one word serving the meaning of three, and of a very sweet and noble sound, accent and expression. Indeed no European language is supposed to be similar to it. "Anna" means mother, "issimus" brother, "netap" friend, "usqueoret" very good, "pane" bread, "metse" eat, "matta" not, "Mattáne hatta" I have not. They are a tall, strong, handsome people with long black hair and a brown skin and they wear unusual dress. They tie a blanket around their bodies, and large pieces of woolen cloth are tied around their legs. They make wooden spoons and bowls which they sell. They have thick pieces of wood, hollowed out for mortars to grind corn in, and make gruel, bread and many other foods from that.

According to people living here, the Indians are a people that can kill somebody in the most barbarous manner even if he has done them all the good in the world. I just want to write down one or two examples: in the present war, a savage had come to a man (who lived on the border) to buy a certain axe, called tomahawk. That man had treated him (the savage) well. Now that tomahawk had a certain sign on it, and therefore the savage did not like it. But the German assured him that they would do no harm. Upon which the following day, when he returned home after an hour's absence, he found his pregnant wife with her body cut open and his three children with their scalps taken, all dead in the house – and also the tomahawk that he had sold to the savage the previous day.

Otherwise they often kill people the following way, cut their bellies open, pull the intestines out and tie those to a tree and then make those people go around the tree by hitting them barbarously, until the intestines have been torn from their bellies altogether and they fall down. Not long ago, savages attacked a schoolmaster in his school with 9 children, 4 of whom they took away with them and 4 they killed together with the schoolmaster. The master was lying on the ground and holding the boys in his arms. And one boy was still alive until the following day and told what had happened. The master had pleaded for the children, they could do with him as they pleased. But it was in vain.

The illicit arrangements for marriage are rather remarkable. Just last week it happened in the house next to our lodgings that a man who had been away for 2 years and had left his wife, 2 daughters and a son behind returned to his old wife and brought a new one with him. But since they could not get along together for 12 days, the man had to leave again with his new wife.

Now some days ago, a special thing happened – not 10 houses away from our lodgings. 5½ years ago, when the war with the savages was still going

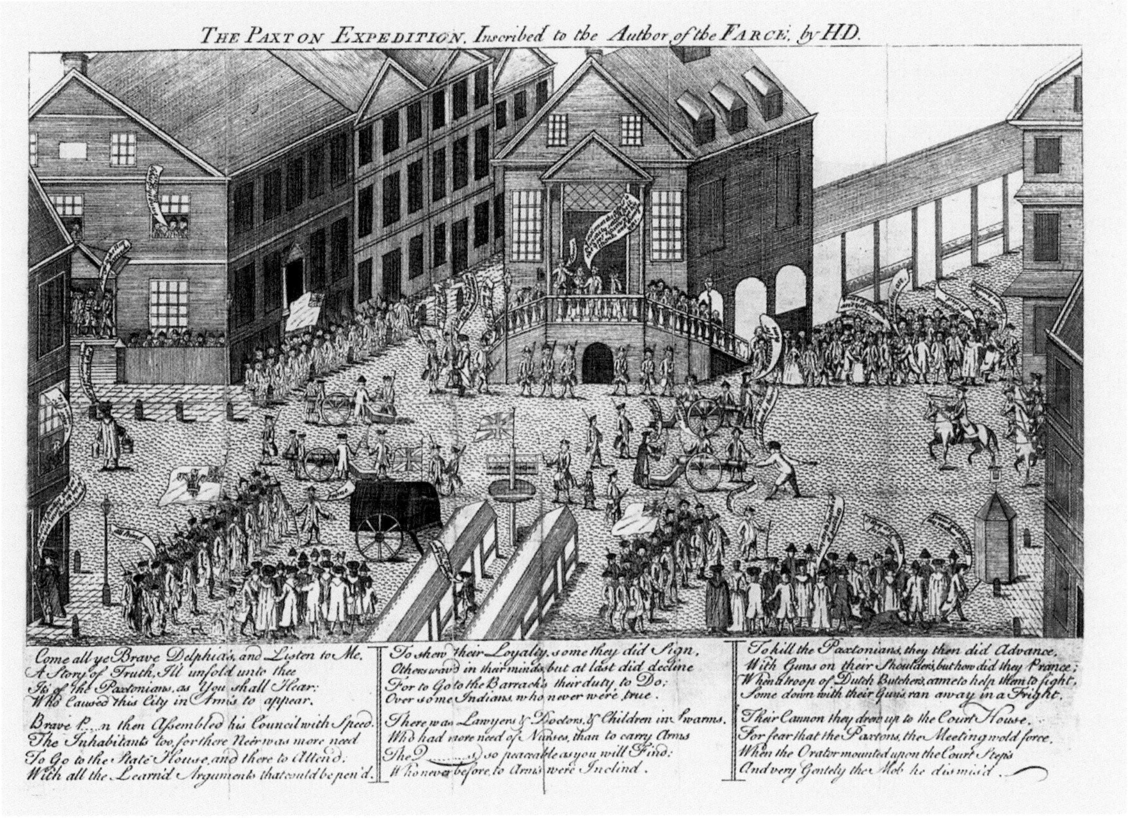
THE PAXTON EXPEDITION. Inscribed to the Author of the FARCE. by HD.
Come all ye Brave Delphia's, and Listen to Me,
A Story of Truth, I'll unfold unto thee
It's of the Paxtonians, as You shall Hear:
Who Caused this City in Arm's to appear.
Brave P....n then Assembled his Council with Speed.
The Inhabitants too, for there Neer was more need
To Go to the State House, and there to Attend:
With all the Learn'd Arguments that could be pen'd.
To shew their Loyalty, some they did Sign,
Others wav'd in their minds, but at last did decline
For to Go to the Barrack's their duty to Do:
Over some Indians who never were true.
There was Lawyers & Doctors, & Children in Swarms.
Who had more need of Nurses, than to carry Arms
The Q.......s so peaceable as you will Find:
Who never before, to Arms were Inclin'd.
To kill the Paxtonians, they then did Advance,
With Guns on their Shoulders, but how did they Prance;
When a troop of Dutch Butchers, came to help them to fight,
Some down with their Guns, ran away in a Fright.
Their Cannon they drew up to the Court House,
For fear that the Paxtons, the Meeting wold force,
When the Orator mounted upon the Court Steps
And very Gentely the Mob he dismis'd.

Fig. 32 Henry Dawson, The Paxton Expedition. Copperplate engraving/etching. 1764. Library Company, Inv. No. Cartoon [1764] Pax/795.F.20a, #1.

on, this man volunteered as a soldier, because they were recruiting so much here, with the consent of his wife. and he was a wealthy man. After he had been gone for half a year, the wife got married to another man (NB if somebody has a permit from the Governor, he can go and get married directly in the pub or wherever he wants). Now, five years later, the first husband comes back and finds the other one in his place with whom she has had 4 children in those five years. But the men agreed in the beginning that neither should sleep with her, and so they did for fourteen days. After which the first husband agreed with the second to pay him £200 to leave. And so the second had to leave, but without his children.

At 10 in the morning of August 20th, we went to the Registry Office with young Mr. Kurtz, where we had them look for the name of Johann Strepers. Finally we found the names of Jan and Leonhard Strepers[5] as having 100 acres in Springfield[6], and that James Logan bought 4,447 acres from Jan Strepers. We were told by the clerk to return the next day at 8 and he would look further. I paid 1 rix dollar.

Now we thought we should discuss matters with Christian Schneider, as he is a German lawyer, and this we did. He advised us to go to the Chief Surveyor, who kept all the records of all the land surveyed. But since he was not home, this had to be postponed.

Now Schneider and Kurtz mentioned a man named Ulrich, who was well-known in Germantown and who was then called. He was a very polite man who had already heard about our land a long time ago and told us where Jan Strepers had 100 acres. And also where the house was with the 25 acres. He advised us to talk to Mr. de Wies, who had kept the Registry for a long time and who should be most familiar with those old matters, just as he was familiar with the matter of James Logan, and who was a good and discreet man. So we went to his house but did not see him because he was out.

At 9 in the morning of August 21st, we went to see Mr. Luwig Weiss and presented our matter to him, upon which he made many comments. He also asked if Wilhelm Strepers still had the deed of sale in his possession and that the deed would still cause us a lot of problems. For example, the people who bought from him will tell us: How could we know that the deed was no good and that there was fraud behind it? We bought in good faith in that deed and we are going to keep what we bought. And according to the law here he would get away with that. Against which, we showed the letters no. 29 and 30 and how Uncle Reinhard Theißen had protested against the sale.

At 3 in the afternoon we presented our power of attorney and family tree to him. Upon which his advice was to stay away from Germantown for two more days. In the meantime, he was going to look everything up again, he also knew about a book and wanted to see if he could get hold of it, in which the oldest matters were recorded. But this was kept well hidden. He was very pleased with the map of Philadelphia. But he said there should also be a list indicating where our lots were. Did we not have that? Because he had seen several such maps and they always had a list attached of how the numbers of the lots were allotted. But he was very pleased that we had the map and he said he would do the best he could with it.

At 3 in the afternoon of August 22nd, Christian Schneider came with the news that Mr. Weiss had found the acre in town[7]. So we went to Mr. Weiss straight away. On the way there, we were approached by Mr. Ulrich who told us that the 50 acres had also been found, but we should not let Mr. Weiss know. When we arrived at his place, he told

us how he had found it. He had been to see the Chief Surveyor and looked up his records, and he had found no more than the acre in town, the 50 acres of Liberty land adjacent to Germantown, and the 4,448 acres bought by James Logan.

But we could still have the remaining 500 acres surveyed, because nobody was going to deny them to us. Upon which I replied that I was least worried about the land we owned in Germantown, Chestnut Hill etc. because we had enough documents to prove it and because we preferred 1 acre of our land to 3 out of the land that was still to be taken. Upon which he said every acre would cost £2.

Now Mr. Weiss started saying that he had the letter in his house that proved which acre in town had to be ours. But we were dealing with a very difficult man, because he was one of the most important men in town. And if the deed of sale given by Wilhelm Strepers was drawn up according to English law, we need not spend any money on it. This was his advice to us, because otherwise we would have to turn to Wilhelm Strepers' and Reinhard Theißen's children. And they had no money. Upon which we replied that if Wilhelm Strepers' deed of sale had been in accordance with English law, they would not have had to send a letter asking for another one. And that they had said in their letter that the deed was only valid for Wilhelm Strepers and his children. And secondly, that James Logan would not have paid any money to our parents or taken a receipt from them.

Upon which he said he could not say anything before he had seen the deed of sale. And he was going somewhere now to see whether he could get it. Perhaps he would get it. Perhaps he would not. Upon which we said that he should take the greatest care with our matter and that we would show our gratitude if he could find out. And that we were only going to accept a decision or judgement in writing, no matter what it said, because we wanted to tell him quite openly that we had to get a judgement here first. And if it should not turn out fair in accordance with legal practice here, then we only had to pass the matter on to the Prince Elector's Ambassador in London[8] who would then take care of the matter. Upon which he looked at the same spot

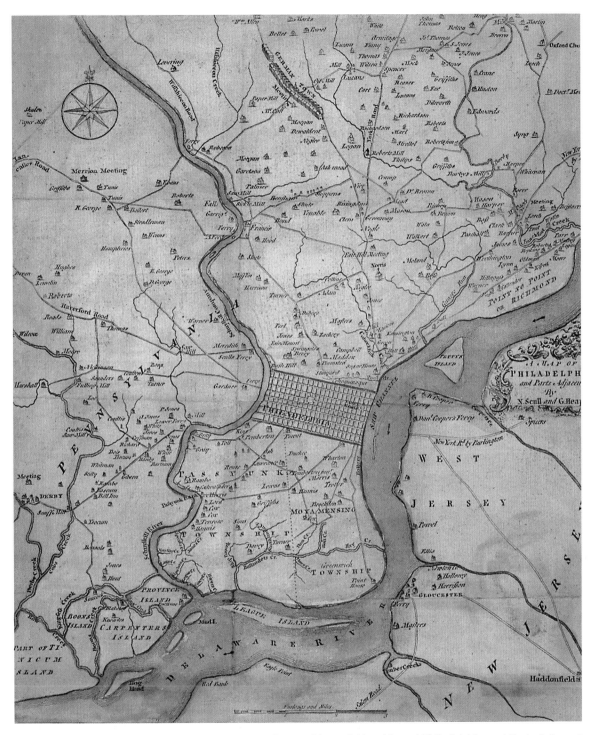

Fig. 33 Nicholas Scull and George Heap, A New Map of Philadelphia and Parts Adjacent. Colored copperplate engraving. From: Gentleman's Magazine for February, London 1777. RFM.

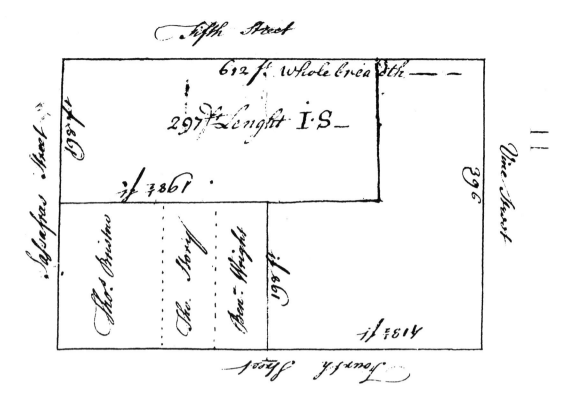

Fig. 34 Plan of the City Lot. Location of the Philadelphia acre. HSP, Strepers papers (1682-1772).

for a long time. Finally he said he could not do anything before he had seen the deed. And he was going to try to get it.

On August 23rd, we went twice to see Mr. Weiss but did not find him at home. On August 24th at 8 in the morning we did see him. We were given the copy of the deed but that was not at all to our liking. He, Mr. Weiss, also said that he did not want anything more to do with the matter because he could not do anything to help us. He showed me the deed of sale for the acre in town which said it was sold in the year 1718 [no precise date given[9]] and how many lots it was subdivided into. It was a very large sheet of parchment with a big seal on it. So the acre is here [sketch showing acre between Vine, Race, 4th and 5th Streets].

Now he wanted to obtain the copy of James Logan's deed of sale. He said the only thing we could do was to approach Wilhelm Strepers' children,

and if they took legal action against us, first of all we would have to find a guarantor, and second, it could take 7 or 8 years, like a lot of cases: So he would advise us not to take any risk and that the Governor had had 100 acres more than the 5,000 surveyed for us in Germantown and, thus, treated us honestly.

At 8 in the morning of August 26th, we went on the wagon to Germantown with Mr. Kurtz and walked from here to Chestnut Hill to cousin Wilhelm Strepers. When we introduced ourselves, both he and his wife[10] were slightly upset. But they urged us to stay for a meal, which we had ordered at an inn, however. Upon which he said he would like us to come back and go with him to his mother[11] who still knew about all the old matters. So we promised we would come back in a few days.

Over the meal we decided that the sooner this happened the better. We had the innkeeper tell him that we would be at his house at 8 the following morning. So we stayed in Germantown overnight.

On the morning of August 27th, we went to see a man whom Mr. Kurtz had said we should see called Jan Grothus whose father Hermen came from Bielefeld and who has been here for the last 50 years and lives only a mile to one side. We met him at a gentleman's named Schlöter, and they both seemed to be very good people. When asked about this and that, they could tell us about everything, but they also said that everything had been sold. And he, Schlotter, mentioned that he also had a piece of that land. But he assured us that he did not ask for any unlawful land, although he had paid for it honestly, and that it was not important to him. And they also warned us quite strongly against trusting anybody around here, whoever he might be, and if we had a year to spare it would be better. We replied we could not wait a year but possibly half a year. We should stay here quietly for a while and gradually find out what we could. He, Grothaus, said we should go to see his brother-in-law Wighard Miller. He still had letters in his possession from his father-in-law, who had been the first preacher in Germantown and written a lot, also about the first settlers in Germantown.

Fig. 35 Thomas Sully (1783-1872), James Logan.
Oil on canvas, 1831.
Library Company, Inv. No. 255.

So from there we went to Wilhelm Strepers, who gave us quite a friendly welcome. And he seems to be an honest man. He then told us that we could have the 50 acres on Chestnut Hill because a strange miller had those who would not part with them until somebody came who had a right to them. And that was the land that Herman Doors and an old woman had lived on. Yes, he said, old Logan had asked him to come about 7 or 8 years ago and had told him, "Do you know, if you are willing to sign a letter for me, I will give you another £100." But he had not wanted to go, and old Logan had died about half a year later[12].

After Wilhelm Strepers had found a horse for each of us, we rode to his mother who still lived 3 miles from him and was married to a man named Kerschner. When we talked to her about our matters, we met one of the most deceitful women I have ever known. She asked what we wanted in this country, after all, we knew quite well that everything had been sold to her father-in-law (she is Leonhard Arets' daughter and had been married to Wilhelm Strepers' son Jan first), as was shown in the deed of sale which we surely had a copy of. Yes, we said, we had received of copy of it, which was wrong, however, as we could prove sufficiently from letters from her late husband and his brother Leonhard Strepers. Upon which she said she still remembered well that Pastorius had translated the deed into English. But as Pastorius had died shortly afterwards[13], they had not been able to find the original. But what had been preserved in the Registry Office was considered the original now. Upon which we asked her whether she knew why that deed of sale existed, and that her father was the reason for the deed. I then showed her her father's letters about naturalization[14]. Besides, I said, she knew full well that Uncle Wilhelm's share of his father's inheritance amounted to no more than 12 rix dollar and all of this inheritance would not have been given in exchange for it.

To which she replied that all deeds of sale had been based on this one and that we would find it difficult to overturn everything, since James Logan had everything in his possession and he had also said that the deed was valid. Yes, and that Hendrik van Acken had tried the same thing as hard as he could without achieving anything.

So we asked if there was no land left at all save the 50 acres on Chestnut Hill. She said that there still was some money for us at Germantown, as well as several years' ground rent on 50 acres (because Uncle Wilhelm had sold 50 acres) and the other 50 acres should still be rendering about 5 shillings a year. But she did not know who was keeping the money for us.

On the morning of August 28th, we went from Germantown to Philadelphia. In the evening, cousin Wilhelm Strepers came to see us, as he had promised the day before. So we asked him for the name of the miller who had the land on Chestnut Hill, and whether he had a deed. He said, the miller's name was Joseph Mäerl and the only deed he had was the one he got from the people who had lived there, and that the miller had said, if anybody could give proof of it, he would give it up. Further, we asked him if he knew the Logans (these questions we asked to make him feel more secure because we knew they were together yesterday and today) and could he go to them on our behalf and ask them about the state of our affairs. He said he did not know them very well and that William, who had our land, was a very zealous man. But he was willing to go and see him. Now he wanted to tell us that he had gone to get a deed today from a [name omitted] and he had asked him whether there was still any land here for us. Upon which that man had replied that he believed there still was, but that Wilhelm Logan had the 50 acres. And that we would have a difficult time getting those back. Because the Logans would spend 7 years, and even £7,000 in court costs before they would give them up because Wilhelm was a very hot-headed man.

Now cousin Wilhelm Strepers said that his sister-in-law had paid money to Hendrik van Acken, and not just a little but a lot. But he did not know how

much. And he had also received money in Germantown because Reinhard Theißen and Hendrik van Acken had made her so afraid. But afterwards she had regretted it. He did not know either whether she had gotten a receipt for it. That same Hendrik van Acken had also tried this on his father[15], as he could still remember, who had not been so afraid but had asked him for his power of attorney, after that he had not bothered him any more. Cousin Strepers told us that some of our land was still held by strangers, something which he found difficult to bear.

From then on, every day we went from one to the other, for instance Christian Schneider, Mr. Weiss, Mr. Wenig, trying 2 or 3 times a day, but we rarely found anybody home or if we did they told us, you cannot do anything at the Registry Office at this hour, so you will have to wait until tomorrow.

On August 30th, we wrote home.

Riding a horse or driving a chaise is so common here, it is unbelievable. It does not stop from morning to night. And the horses are made to run all the time, even when they have a load. I once counted for precisely an hour how many horses came past our house. The net number was 124, and it went on like that all day.

On September 3rd, it was court day. At 5 in the afternoon, Mr. Weiss came and brought us the copy of Wilhelm Logan' deeds. While he was sitting with us, Wilhelm Strepers also approached us with two of his friends who had already been here in the morning and asked us to come and visit them, which we promised to do.

When Mr. Weiss wanted to show us with these copies that Logan could be perfectly certain concerning his purchase, which he repeated three times, we answered him that we would discuss this with Mr. Logan if we could speak to him. But we said that we did not want to know about any other deed of sale than the one that had been signed by our parents in Amsterdam, when they had received £200.

Then we went on to Peter Müller, where we wanted to have the deed translated, but he was not at

Fig. 36 William Birch (1755-1834), Back of the State House. Colored copperplate engraving, 1799.
Library Company. Inv. No. Sn22c/P.2276.50.

home. So we went back there at 8 in the evening. When he was called and we discussed the translation with him, I told him that the translation had to be exact and be certified with his signature and seal.

While we were talking, Mr. Weiss, who had been paying a visit to Müller, came downstairs. He looked rather upset (as though he was going to say, now he also sees that we are good friends). I told him straight away that I was there to have the deed translated. We are convinced that so far we have not met a single honest friend, so we have to be very careful (But I do not trust in anybody yet.).

September 3rd, 4th and 5th were court days and that is held publicly here. Because there was a lot going on during those days and the following as well, we could not have Logan's deed translated.

Court is held quite publicly here, and women and children, everybody who is curious, goes and listens. Very few written documents are shown in court, unless they are bills. When a lawyer speaks for his party, he stands up and behaves like a preacher, he holds his sermon for the highest judge, and when he has finished he sits down again. Then it his adversary's turn. And so they speak in turn until they have finished.

When I went back to Mr. Miller on September 8th to find out if the deed had been translated, for which reason I had already called 6 times, he was out again. But his wife showed me that it would soon be finished and said, her husband had told her that he had never translated anything that complicated in his life. He had had to go over it many times, had also called Mr. Weiss, who had also said that this was very difficult to translate. Right now, he had gone to see Mr. Weiss again. While we were talking, Mr. Miller came back. When I asked him whether the translation could not be done by tonight, he answered it could not possibly be finished before midday tomorrow because it was not easy to translate. Upon which he asked if we came from the Palatinate. I answered yes, but my cousin was residing half in Prussia[16], a question which Mr. Weiss had already asked me twice. Now I asked him what he thought of the deed.

He answered that it was such a strange deed, it was signed by the trustees. I do not know, and then he asked again whether we were both living in the Palatinate. I answered that my cousin's land was half on Prussian and half on Palatinate soil. But I was living 7 hours from Düsseldorf in the Duchy of Berg. Upon which he replied. "I do not know."

Since they kept asking about Prussia, we wrote a letter to the Prussian Privy Councilor, Resident and Superintendent of the Protestant congregations in Jülich and Berg[17], and gave it to several people to read, swearing them to silence, also told them that he had promised he would help us obtain what was rightfully ours, also through the Palatine ambassador in London. All the more so since the matter also concerned the Prussian Privy Councilor's brother-in-law[18].

On September 9th and 10th, we got the translation of James Logan's deed of sale. After we had read it we rejoiced because it refers mainly to Leonhard Strepers, Reinhard Theißen and Griffith Jones[19]. To my question if the deed was good, Mr. Miller only replied, "I do not know." Then he said, "If you had those 5,000 acres now, they would be worth £20,000." He also said that it had been so difficult to translate. When we had compared it and explained several things to him (such as the names of the burgo-

masters of Kaldenkirchen and Bracht[20] and also the Duchy of Jülich and Berg, he said he could translate nothing but what the original said. Since one can clearly see that the copy from Mr. Weiss does not correspond to the above names, it is all fraud.

At 9 in the morning of September 11th, I went to the Registry Office with Mr. Roos to obtain copies of all the deeds of lease or sale between Jan Strepers and Wilhelm Penn, which I duly found at the Registry Office and which consist of 4 originals. And I was given the promise that I would have copies of them the following Saturday. The registrar there started telling Mr. Roos straight away that somebody by the name of Logan wanted to have the land surveyed as soon as possible.

At half past 8 on September 12th, as we were having breakfast, young Mr. Kurtz brought us a letter which was the nicest one I have ever received in my life. Since Mr. Kurtz has done so much for us and liked my hunting knife so much, I gave it to him in exchange for an old one. Captain Sparks had brought it with him from London.

On September 12th, we went to Mr. Stelwagen and gave him Logan's deed to read, as well as the deed about the 5 shillings (this Mr. Stelwagen is one of the elders at the German Church). Upon which he told us that several years ago they had wanted to buy land from Dr. Samuel Preston Moor for a new church. Since the old church had become too small, they had intended to turn it into a schoolhouse. Since Logan had not been able to give them a valid deed, the sale had fallen through. And from what he heard now, this must be our acre.

Upon which he asked if I could leave Logan's deeds with him for a day or two, because they were having their synod now and he wanted to show it to them there tomorrow. And if they could help us to get what was rightfully ours, he was sure we would be amenable with respect to a site for their church, although they did not ask for it as a present but at a fair price. To which I replied that they would find us reasonable and be quite content with us.

On September 13th, at 9 in the morning, cousin Strepers left for Germantown. I told him to be careful with talking (especially with van Acken, who had waited for us here on September 11th from 4 to 6. And since we had just been out walking, he had left a note with his name at our lodging). But the cousin was somewhat annoyed. He said he was not going to visit anybody, NB patience. he came back after 4 days.

On September 14th, I spoke to Stelwagen and told him that I still wanted to wait a day or several before going to the lawyer. And we arranged to do that on Monday.

On September 15th, at 9 in the morning I went with Mr. Ross to Mr. Brockden and collected 5 deeds which had all been given to Jan Strepers by William Penn. I also had him look for any deeds that might exist about the acre in town. After he had looked in the house for about an hour, we went to the archives, where there were many deeds about it, but all warrants, at which he laughed very hard and said I would have to look for a good lawyer (as if to say, "With a good lawyer you should be able to resolve the matter") and it is a good thing that I am still alive. He is close to 80 years old and still reads without glasses. So I asked what the word warrant meant, and he said the deeds were not all that good.

Whereupon he said that I should go to the Surveyor General Lucken to get the copy about Jan Strepers' land and bring it to him, which I did straight away. But when I came back to him, he was not home. So I will take it to him on Monday.

On September 18th, we went to Mr. Brockden in the morning (at that time I was to be given 2 more copies, but they were not ready yet). So we had to wait until the following day. From there we went to the surveyor. There we asked for a copy of everything relating to Jan Strepers' land. He said he would give them to us, and they would be ready at 1 o'clock: When I came to collect them at 1, he had five of them, and I asked him if these were all. He answered, "Yes." After I had leafed through them for a bit, I asked him again if these were all, and he answered quite stupidly that there was one more concerning James Logan, and it would cost us too much to get a copy of it. Upon which I told

him, I had asked for all of them this morning. And I told him now to copy it and asked when I could collect it. He said, "At 4."

Now, when I went back at 4, two gentlemen had just gone in ahead of me and, I believe, were talking to him about our matter. For, as soon as I entered, they not only stopped talking but one went out (and when the surveyor told me I could go somewhere else for another ¼ of an hour) he went back in again.

While I was out of the house for a while, Mr. Ross arrived there looking for me. So the wife brought him a chair right away to sit down. And she told him she was related to us, for her grandfather's name was Reinhard Theißen. And the son said he knew a man who wanted to buy our land from us. When I came in, she introduced herself straight away. I had to promise to come back that evening with cousin Strepers, because then her husband would be home, too. And he spoke some German. She also offered us to have our lodgings and meals at her place. When we went to see her at 7, her husband was not home yet. She took us into a beautiful room, also wanted to give us some wine, which we accepted, and we promised to come back the following evening.

On September 20th, the miners arrived as well as Mr. Franz Caspar Hasenclever himself[21], and there was one from Schwartzenburg[22], an iron founder by trade. The other one was a certain N. Claeuser, from Burg[23], and they were so happy when we introduced ourselves as if we had been their brothers. We could not have been merrier. Now I also talked to Mr. Hasenclever about our matter. He promised to do as much for us as he could.

On September 20th, I went to cousin Lucken, who had forgotten to put his name under the copy. I had him sign it. When I arrived at his place there were two farmers with him. As soon as he saw me he winked to the farmers. They were asking him, as poor fellows, to come to the side with them. So he was standing by the house for several minutes and talked with them. But I could see enough to notice that he was not quite willing to promise to do what they were asking. Now I am quite con-

Fig. 37 Anon., Peter Hasenclever.
Oil on canvas (lost), late 18th century. Reproduction
from a glass negative. Deutsches Werkzeugmuseum
Remscheid, photography by M. Groß.

On the morning of September 23rd, we drove to Germantown, where I went to see cousin van Acken straight away to see if he had the bond. But he did not. So I went to Mr. Vanlaschet, who faithfully told us as much as he knew, among other things that the English Company had asked the King 4 years ago that it not only had to give notification of the land it had lost but also to sell it to the highest bidder, which had been done. Now Mr. Vanlaschet advised me to go and see a man called Winnert Neiss. He is a very old but important man. He had come to the country as a young child and still remembered many things about the old times. Now I asked him whether he had known Wilhelm Strepers. And he said quite well and he had been his uncle. He had married his mother's sister and had lived in this house (where he is living now). He showed me all the houses right across the road, just like on our plan of Germantown, from Reinhard Theißen's to Peter Kürlis' house, and he had also known Jan Strepers' house, but it had never been properly finished and fallen into decay in the end. And people had called it Strepers' place afterwards. Now the Lentzens had sold their land except for 10 acres, and 6 houses have been built on one side and 2 on the other.

On September 24th, we went to Peter Hasenclever, whom we met in New York[24], who treated us in a very friendly manner and told us to give him our names in writing, so he could speak to Mr. Ellen (who is among the highest-ranking men in the court in Philadelphia and is a business partner of Mr. Hasenclever's) on our behalf as if we were his brothers. So we wrote down our names and added a little note for him. In the afternoon and again in the evening Mr. Hasenclever came and had punch and tea with us at our lodgings. He told the whole story of his journey. Yes, he said, this transport had cost him more than 60,000 guilders altogether[25]. And now the miners were rebelling so they had to send out 2 constables this afternoon who threatened to put them in jail and told the innkeepers not to serve them any more. In the evening all the miners came and said they all wanted to go to the mine which is close to New York.

On September 24th, it was supreme court day. In the afternoon, a farmer from a farm behind Ger-

vinced that it had something to do with our matter. Because cousin Lucken knew well enough that I did not understand English and he would not have had to go to the side. But they thought I might understand a word. From there I went to Mr. Brockden to collect the deed for the acre. But he was not home.

That same morning, cousin van Acken had come to see us and we had talked to him about our matter. But we found that he did not know much about it. We said if he could help us to obtain Leonhard Strepers' bond that his uncle Hendrik van Acken had in his possession, after Reinhard Theißen had given it to him, we would show our appreciation [?]. In the afternoon two people came and asked us whether we wanted to sell any land, and I an-swered them that we had not got that far yet. Now [rest missing] mantown came to us and asked us whether we owned a property of 170 acres near N.[26]. We answered him that we did not know yet ourselves, what kind of land it was and why was he asking. He said he had bought it from his father-in-law, who could not give him a good deed for it. So he had thought he might ask us. I asked him whether he knew who his father-in-law had bought it from. He said, "No." And he stuck to that. His name was Hermanus Orius.

At 3 in the afternoon on September 25th, they held a horse race here (which happens every year) with £100 Sterling prize money. There were 5 horses, and none was allowed to be older than 4 years. The saddles were weighed, as were the men riding them. The riders wore blue silk waistcoats and wore small caps or had a kerchief wound around their heads. I have already seen many horses, but never any like these. But these are not only trained for this a whole year but also fed for it for a year. Now, there were posts put up in a circle 4 miles around, set at about 100 paces from each other. And they had to ride around those. I looked at the clock myself. After the start, they had gone around once in 4 minutes, and the second time which followed immediately afterwards, in 3¼ minutes.

So they rode 8 miles in 7¼ minutes. According our time measurement in Germany that means: 1 1/3 miles or 2 2/3 hours were ridden in 7¼ minutes. When these horses had been walked for ½ hour and the sweat had dried, two of them had to do another 2 rounds. But one little brown horse always won, which was always 25 to 30 paces ahead. Now there were innumerable spectators there, indeed if I had to guess, I would say about 15,000 people, and I think there were as many on horseback as on foot. This riding went on for 5 days. The other days they always made 4 miles in 4¼ minutes. On the first day the prize was £100, the second day £50 and the third day £25 sterling. These horses are trained and fed for this for a whole year, and none must be older than 4 years. They have legs and bodies like a doe and are so shiny that you could see you own reflection in them.

At 8 in the evening of September 25th, Mr. Kurtz sent for us and told us that Peter Müller had told him that a man called Peter Theißen was with him now who was his uncle. If we wanted to talk to him ourselves, we should go, because he wanted to leave again tomorrow.

So we went to Mr. Miller, greeted him and also cousin Theißen. When the latter asked us where we came from we said we had something for Peter Müller to write. Upon which he asked, "Where do you know me from?" So I said, it was my sense of family. Now he was a polite man of 68 years who had been present with his father Reinhard Theißen when the land was surveyed in 1703. He said to come and visit and stay with him for a month. So we could not yet visit all the Theißens. His brother still had £10 for us, his other brother also had a bond from Jonas for £10 and his third brother would transfer 30 acres on Chestnut Hill to us. So he said I should be at his house tomorrow morning at 6, and then he wanted to take me to Jones[27] and to Pol Kreppen.

On September 25th, we went to Jones. But we do not speak each other's language because they only spoke English among themselves. But I had to promise to come back again. So then we went to cousin Paul Krippner, who seems to be a very intelligent and clever man. He said, as far as the acre in town was concerned there was no hope of getting it, and James Logan was not to be trusted. But we had to take all we could now. Upon which I said, this seemed ridiculous to me, because we wanted everything that Jan Strepers had bought. To which he asked if we intended to maintain that. Oh yes, so he said, then come to me and I will help you with it.

So I left a copy of our documents with him, so he could see what was written in them. And we were to return tomorrow or the day after. So we said goodbye to cousin Theißen with the promise to come and visit soon. At 10 in the morning, Mr. Hasenclever came to say goodbye and told us to see his cousin[28] today because he had said he wanted to take us to Mr. Allen himself. And that he was going to New York with the miners now. But he would return in 14 days. Then he wanted to meet us and talk to us.

At 3 in the afternoon we went to Mr. Hasenclever, but did not find him at home. So we went and looked for him until we met him in the street. He approached us at once, telling us he had talked to Mr. Allen. He was going to come back in 14 days (because he had no time at all now) and then he wanted to do his best in our matter. When we were a stone's throw away, he beckoned me back and told me to come to his lodgings again between 6 and 7. So I went to him just after 6 and went with him straight into the inn. He took me up to his room at once, looked quickly at our documents and wrote a letter to the King's Counsel for me and told me he knew him well and the latter had to help him now just like he had helped him today. Because his ship had been stopped, and without the help of the King's Counsel that would have cost him £9,000.

Now he had written in his letter that we were from the Palatinate and countrymen of his. And whatever he did for us, he did for him. Now Mr. Allen had told him when he had called on him on our behalf that if we went to this lawyer (because he was the best) he could not advise us, he knew about it now, he wanted to do his best. Now we will see what the Good Lord will give in future.

At 10 in the morning of September 27th, I went to see cousin Paul Kripner. He told me again and again that we could not do anything against James Logan. Because the old man had been too cautious and because he knew everything through the writings of his brother-in-law Hendrik van Acken's papers. So I proved him wrong in every respect. Finally the only argument left to him was the letter that our parents had signed (namely the receipt)[29]. So I told him that our parents were unable to sell because they were a community of heirs.

Now I said I wanted to tell him the following but asked him to keep silent about it. I said, "My brother-in-law[30] has a brother-in-law[31] who is not only Privy Councilor to the King of Prussia but also Resident Superintendent of the Protestant congregation of Jülich and Berg." And the latter had instructed us to just obtain a written document about whether the people here were willing to give us our grandfather's inheritance in total or not. And it

did not matter to us if they wanted to give it to us or not, as long as we had that in writing. Then we would go to London and wait there until we had an answer as to what further steps to take. And that would show that the Pennsylvanians would have to be content with the judgement we would obtain there. Meanwhile his brother-in-law or brother of his present wife arrived – a very handsome man. He told him everything. Although it was in English, I could understand everything. After they had finished talking, they both got up and went out. But they wanted to keep me there for dinner at all costs.

At 7 in the morning of September 29th, we walked to Chestnut Hill again. Now we went to see Nice. He told us that his neighbors had come to him and asked him what we had said. He had answered them that we wanted to confiscate all the land. And they had told him we could not. But we were entitled to the quitrent from the beginning and we could have that. So I asked whether it was allowed to sell any of it, and whether, in addition to the interest from them we were not also entitled to the interest from the land. And he said he thought we were.

From there we went to cousin van Acken, who came with us. Then we came to the piece of land where the evil woman[32] used to live. The house had collapsed completely and there were only a few stones lying around. But there were the most beautiful apples there I have ever seen. And there were 80 to 90 trees. Now I went to the miller Mäerel, but he was not home. So I asked his wife to tell him when he came home that he need not look after the 17 acres of land any more.

From there we went to cousin Strepers, where we saw his mother, the widow Kerssener[33]. NB the evil woman. She asked at once how we were, So we said, "Well." Upon which she said straight away, "I do not know, children, what you want here. Have you been to see William Logan?" We said, no, we did not have anything to do with Logan. After we had seen Logan's deed of sale, we had realized that it referred to the three trustees[34]. Yes, she said, she had seen James Logan's documents and also our parents' signatures. Then I asked her whether she had seen any signature by a Strepers, and that several of them had still been alive at all times, and I could assert that here together with cousin Strepers. Whether our parents had not received any money in Holland? We said, yes, but we did not know whether that money came from a lease or from interest and principal from Jan Lentzen, and if they wanted to have that back, we could give it back to them.

While we were walking back with cousin van Acken to his house, Mäerel the miller stopped us near an inn on Chestnut Hill. So we talked to him and went inside. But he did not know any German. Then Judge de Wees joined us who spoke German well. So the miller said he should ask us whether our document was good. We said we could show him right then. That was not necessary, he said. Mäerel the miller said we could have the land. He did not want to give us any trouble. And the 33 acres were on the other side of the creek. Nobody had possession of them at the moment. We could have those, too. But nothing was grown on them. They were not worth much, either. [An undecipherable sentence in Herbergs' secret code follows].

October 1st here in Philadelphia is the day when the assembly men are elected (of whom there are 8). Now usually the old ones were just re-elected without any difficulties. But since the Quakers (who mostly make up this body, had taken to arms[35] on February 3, 1764, and thus according to their law) have done a great wrong, they have had to submit to the King's government, and a lot of pamphlets for and against this have been published. Now on this day there were two parties running against each other, namely one for freedom, which the Germans voted for. It was opposed by three former members of the Assembly (who had behaved well) who were Quakers. There were three Englishmen and two Germans. But the Quakers all voted for the old ones. Now one has to wonder and it would go too far to describe the great pains both parties took to get votes.[36]

That evening close to 6 o'clock, I was sitting outside the door with cousin Strepers and 4 others when a fireball came flying through the air, about as big as the crown of a hat and slowly went across above the houses. It looked as though it had fallen on the courthouse (where the ballot was being taken). I do not know if I have ever seen anything so terrible. This voting lasted from 8 o'clock on October 1st, all through the night to October 2nd, at 2 or 3 in the afternoon. And it seems as if there is going to be a big quarrel.

October 1st, Peter Theißen came to visit us and asked us to visit him in turn. Now in the afternoon of October 2nd, the results came out, and the Germans had carried the vote (namely the old freedom) against the Quakers (who wanted to be governed by the King of England). So now the Germans have three on the council, the English 3 and the Quakers 2.

Everybody says this is very promising for our matter and we could not have come here at a better time. Because now the Governor is very much against the Quakers (and William Logan[37] is a Quaker) and the land prices are also higher than ever before.

October 4th. Now the Quakers are threatening to overturn the election results but they will have difficulties doing so.

Going on horseback or driving chaises is so common here that I think there is no other place in the world like it. No apple, no jam, no milk, no chicken, no pig, no butter, nothing at all is brought into town unless on horseback. Indeed, no butcher drives just one cow or one sheep or other animals to be slaughtered, always at least two and on horseback. No cow is driven into the field without the driver being on horseback. Most people who drive a chaise ride next to it. On October 13th, a corpse came by in a wagon drawn by 4 horses, and there was a cortège of 18 people, all on horseback and not a single one on foot.

Among 1,000 people you will not find anyone walking even if they go only ½ hour from home, not even the poorest peasant. Cousin Wilhelm Strepers told us that a farmer who only had ½ hour to walk would rather walk for an hour to borrow a horse than walk that ½ hour. I may say that 1,500 horses come past here every day. But on Wednesdays and Saturdays, there is the market here. Then

Fig. 38 Henry Dawkins, *The Counter-Medly, being a proper Answer to all the Dunces of the Medly and their Abettors.* Copperplate engraving, 1764. Library Company, Inv. No. Cartoon 1765 Cou/968.F.1.

the riding and driving goes on from Tuesday and Friday evening, all night through, for the market. And the horses coming here on those days are so many you cannot count them. And what is more, even if a horse had only 3 legs it would have to go fast. No slave or serf, black or white, who is not on horseback, and most of them are women. And they all have saddles costing 20 to 24 rix dollars, even as much as £12. And they generally dress very expensively. The lowest women, maids for instance, wear blue silk shoes and velvet coats. No servant, no matter how low, even when pushing a cart full of manure, as soon as it rains he will wear his raglan. No maid will go across the street in the rain without wearing a long coat going down to her feet.

On October 4th, we went to see cousin Kripner, who is a brother-in-law of the nephews Claas and Hendrik van Acken and was married to their sister Elisabeth. He had all the letters from his brother-in-law Hendrik and offered to let us look through them and take everything that was useful for us. So we found many useful papers. Among others, two certified copies, one in German, one in English, both saying the same thing. So now we can prove that the word "for ever" was not in the deed of sale, as well as the fact that the deed is null and void. We also found the original of the bond of £500 that Leonhard Strepers gave to Reiner Theißen.

On October 5th, we went to Ludwig Weiss with these documents and let him read everything. I asked him what he thought of it now. He answered he could see well that we had been deceived, but who had deceived us? Not James Logan. Not Hyll either. The friends had deceived us. Whereupon I replied to him, no, nobody had deceived us because we were demanding all of our land back and with full justification.

If our friends had sold anything to Logan which they had not been authorized to sell, Logan could hold them liable. Whereupon he answered that Logan went by his and Wilhelm Strepers' deeds of sale. And we would see that we could expect to stay here for 3 or 4 years before judgement was given. He advised me, as he has often done, to start a weaver's shop here. I asked him if he was willing to try to represent our cause here for a certain sum, so a judgement was passed. It did not matter what the judgement was. So he said he had read through our papers in the last two days and asked nothing for doing so. And he was quite familiar with the matter. So I offered him a dollar. But he did not want to take it. So I put it on the table. Then he said he had a lot to write for William Logan and he knew that we had a hard man against us. But if we could get the original deed of sale and if it could be seen that even a single letter had been scratched off our whole case would be right.

Now we had been promised the 17 acres on Chestnut Hill, and I asked him how to go about this matter. He said we should sell them straight away. So I said, was it best to put them in the paper and to have them auctioned, or to sell them out of hand. No, he said. If you can sell it to the man who has it in his possession now, even getting one or several pounds sterling less for it, that would still be best. And give him a good deed. That way, you will get it in your possession, and that will be best for you.

On October 8th, we went to Germantown at six in the morning. On the way, we went to the spot where Mr. Weiss had told me our 50 acres of Liberty land were. That man had leased 3 acres from William Logan, and he had to pay £9 ground rent a year. From there, we went to Wilhelm Biden's widow, Johan Lentzen's daughter, and asked her what the situation was with respect to our land, whether they still had it all together.

Whereupon she asked what we meant by that. We said, after having introduced ourselves, that we wanted to settle up with them. So all of a sudden she lost her temper and went into a rage. Her father had paid everything up to the last penny before he died. And she had a good paper to prove that. And it was just knavery what we were trying to do. We said she should not say anything about knavery

Fig. 39 Johnson House, Germantown. Steel engraving, approx. 1900. GHS.

to us, or we would show her. For we had never had anything to do with knaves. And we were going to show her we were honest. Her two sons who were with her also tried to deceive us where they could. But that did not help.

From there we went to the house of Hendrik van Acken's niece. After she had told us through cousin Kripner that we should stay at her house if we were back in the area. But that women seems to be out of her mind with miserliness. From there, we went to Wilhelm van Acken. After we had had something to eat, we went to the man who had the lease of the 17 acres. But he had gone to town.

From there we walked all over the 50 acres, which have astonishing hills and valleys and also a nice creek running through. When we had almost reached the end, a man came up to us called Jan Jansen. We asked him, how far the land went that had been in Hermen Doors' possession. He said to come down with him to his house and he would show us. He had also bought 15 acres of it and wanted to show us his deed. And his house was partly on it. Now Reiner Theißen and Abraham Theißen had signed the deed (namely the deed made out to Wilhelm Strepers) for £14 2s 9d. This man had taken the 15 acres for £7 sterling (the sum Hermann doors was to give for 33 acres). The other £7 2s 9d were interest. Now Abraham Theißen thought if he gave me the £7 sterling, the remaining 18 acres would be his. It is all just fraud.

From there we went back to cousin van Acken and stayed the night.

On October 9th, we went 2 miles off the road to a paper miller, a man[38] aged 80 years, to ask him about old matters. He told us many things. He advised us to go and see a surveyor by the name of Lohman in Germantown, which we did. This man informed us quite readily and without charging us that Jan Strepers had 275 acres in the German township. He also gave us the plan on which the town lots were entered, which corresponded exactly to our plan. He seemed the most honest man we have met here so far. But he gave us the advice not to trust anybody much for the time being. And secondly, we should collect some documents

for evidence, because if our opponents saw that, they would be much more willing to negotiate. Otherwise, they would try to delay us by drawing out the court proceedings over 6 or 8 years. He wanted to try now to find out where Jan Strepers' land was located and tell us immediately.

On October 15th in the morning, I went to see Peter Miller. I wanted to go with him to the lawyer as we had agreed. When we were just by the door, Miller said I had to give the lawyer something. I answered yes, I knew that. So he said how much I wanted to give him. So I said 2 to 3 dollars, like others had told me. Upon which he replied in that case we did not even to go there. Because he knew that the lawyer would not accept those. So I asked him how much he suggested. He said, at less than £20 as these things go he would not go along. I said, "Stop. Do you make such a big thing out of it here? At home, this is easier than some cases worth 2 Louis d'Or. Because all we are trying to do is to get a judgement, and it does not even matter whether in the end it will be in our favor or against us. If only we can send an appeal to London. That is all." Upon which he said, I still should not give him less than £5. So I said, "Let us go back home until I have spoken to my cousin and we turned back."

So in the afternoon I went to see Paul Kripner, who had been to see me the previous day, and he asked me to tell him how things had gone with lawyer. So I told him what had happened. He said he wanted to go to the lawyer with me, and that Müller was downright rotten.

On October 15th, a corpse was driven past here, accompanied by 14 chaises and 22 mourners on horseback but not a single one on foot.

On October 16th, cousin Kripner came up to my room in the morning. He said he had thought the matter over. And since he knew the matter so well (and I told him as much as I could) he thought we should not go to anybody in town, no matter who. For they were all rotten. Instead, I should go straight to Germantown to Mr. Lehman and have our things or relevant documents translated, and then he would come with us to the lawyer.

Fig. 40 Christian Lehman House. Photography, First half of 20th century. GHS.

On October 17th, I went to Germantown, counting how many horses passed me on the way (which is two hours and I had walked it in 1½ hours). With chaises and wagons there were 135. And the saddles and chaises and carriages were so magnificent and expensive as if all these people were princes and princesses. The only thing missing on those equipages were silver horseshoes. The lowest farmers are wearing velvet breeches and camisols. And many farmers also have velvet coats.

Cousin Strepers had gone on a social visit to cousin Wilhelm Strepers on October 12th. He returned on October 18th.

On October 17th, I went to Germantown. Mr. Lehman had gone to Philadelphia. But since he returned in the evening, I had a long talk with him. But he said he wanted to think that night whether he wanted to accept us or not. Because for the time being, he knew, there was hatred from his neighbors because of our business. For another thing,

William Logan was also a good friend of his. Because everything the latter needed doing outside Philadelphia he had to do for him.

On October 18th at 7 in the morning, I went to see Lehman again to ask him what he had decided. And he told me that he was willing to help us with advice and writing, but it would be best for him and for us if we had his writings copied, so it would remain secret, which I promised. Then he read through our papers and drafted the first documents for the lawyer which I was to present. He said he would advise us to pay the lawyer four pistols[39]. He said, "You have kept so quiet here and thus frightened people here ten times more than if you had acted brutally."

On October 19th, we went to the King's Counsel with cousin Paul Kripner, but we did not find him at home. So we went back home. On October 20th, at half past 8 in the morning, we returned to see him and he took our case on. He also told us what we should have translated, namely the power of attorney of 1689 and our family tree. We gave those to Mr. Weiss at once and got them back on October 23rd.

On October 24th, Michel Schmit came to buy 35 acres on Chestnut Hill from us and we agreed on the sale. He got the land for £100 Pennsylvania money. But he came back on October 26th and told us that Mäerl, the miller, was planning to make trouble for us. So we went to Germantown on October 27th to have the land surveyed on October 28th. When we were about to start, Justice de Wees and Wighard Miller as the guardians for Mätters' four children, who are from a previous marriage, came and said they had to do so because the children had it in possession, so the latter would not find fault with them later, although they personally thought they would not gain anything from it. After that had been done and we had eaten and drunk well, this was lifted again.

On October 27th, NB I went to get money. On October 29th, cousin Kripner borrowed £25 sterling from Mr. Daniel Wiester. Now our money is all gone. And I do not know where we could get more from. Philadelphia, October 29, 1764.

On October 29th in the morning, I went to see cousin Paul Kripner and told him what had happened on Chestnut Hill and what did he think of it. He said, we had to take strong action against them because they could not prove any right whatsoever. If we did not, others might also try to present a semblance of a right and could cause us all the more trouble. And we should sue the miller through the lawyer, something that I also thought. But cousin Strepers insisted we should try it with good words only. NB

October 29th. I went from cousin Paul Kripner to Ludwig Weiss and asked him whether he wanted to accompany us to the lawyer the following day. He answered he would not like to do that at all. He would prefer if we took Peter Müller with us. So I asked him why he did not want to go to Miller. Then he told me why, and that was for the following reason (which he wanted to be kept secret, however). He had received £20 a year from Logan and £30 from Dr. Samuel Preston Moore. Now I

could easily imagine that that was not the proper thing to do at all. But he wished us luck because he could see that we had been deceived. But those who had done that were dead. If they were still alive, he would fight against it with all his strength. Then I asked for certain reasons NB whether they would be willing to come to an agreement, and if they were reasonable, I, for my part, would talk to them in more detail. So he said he would talk to both of them. But he could already imagine Logan's answer and that would be that he did not know why he should do us a favor. But Dr. Moore was a clever man. Logan was quite brutal, however.

In the evening I went to Mr. Ludwig Weiss again, and he told me that he had spoken to Dr. Samuel Preston Moore, who had said that, as far as he knew, his father-in-law had acted correctly in the matter. But Mr. Ludwig Weiss should come back to see him again. Now Weiss said he had done a rough estimate and had calculated that if we took our claim to court in full – since our grandfather had given £100 for it in 1683 – at 5 per cent per hundred, that would be £200 for 1702, and so forth until the present day the total would come to £1,600 sterling. If we would be satisfied with that? That was his own suggestion, however. Upon which I said, there had to be far more in it than that.

Because he did not like to go to the lawyer himself, he said he was going to give us good advice. We should get the copy in English from the Office of the letter of 1715 that James Logan bases his case on, and we should give that to the lawyer so he could see for himself. And we did so.

On November 1st, Brockden received 4s 6d for the English copy of 1715.

On November 3rd, we came to the house of the lawyer, who was out of town, however. On November 4th, cousin Strepers went to Chestnut Hill and returned on November 8th in the evening. On November 5th, Mr. Franz Caspar Hasenclever came to see me.

On November 5th, I went to the lawyer with cousin Paul Kripner. We went to his brother-in-law first (who seems to be a very clever man). He read through our papers and was very encouraging. When we came to the lawyer's, there were many people there. But he talked to us straight away. After he had read Reiner Theißen's power of attorney, he asked for our power of attorney, which I showed him directly. So he asked at once whether we had an eye-witness here who had seen how the papers were signed. Upon which we answered, "No." So he said in that case we had to leave the originals with him. As soon as he had the time he was going to see whether that would also be necessary. Upon which I left the originals with him – viz. our book of copies at the back – and there would still be enough time to take these to the Record Office. As far as the miller Joseph Mätters was concerned, we could sell him the land if it was not included in Logan's deed.

At 1 o'clock Justice de Wees came to me and said he had talked to cousin Strepers and that Mätters was going to come here on Wednesday to go to the lawyer then and make a contract. At 6 o'clock. Mr. Hasenclever came to me with a man named Hoffmann and asked me whether I had taken a lawyer. Upon which I replied yes. So he said that they had talked about our matter with the father [name not mentioned] of the man here with him and that he was somebody who worked only on land cases. And he was also admitted to almost every court for it. And he thought that we would not be wrong if we went to New York some time and talked to that man. Because he would tell us straight away how our case would be decided here and also in London.

Now Mr. Ross also knew this lawyer and he said that he was of great renown here. And that he was the most important man here at the court. Now Mr. Hasenclever said, if we had that man address the King's Counsel, we would probably win our case here. And that we would then not need to appeal to London. And his cousin would also come here soon, as well as the lawyer [no name mentioned] and then we could talk to both of them.

On November 6th in our neighborhood it happened that a big, strong, young man who, after he had had something to eat, had come home from his work as a day laborer at 11 at night on November

5th died all of a sudden. At 9 in the morning of November 6th, when the neighbors had not heard anything from him and went to look, they found him and two children dead in bed. And his wife could not speak at all and died at midday on November 7th. And they were all buried at 3 in the afternoon. A doctor had explained that this was caused by the smoke from the charcoal.[40]

At 10 in the morning of November 7th, I saw the miller Mätters ride past here with Wighard Miller. So I went to cousin Paul Kripner and with him to our lawyer straight away. We told him that the people were here now who wanted to buy the 17 acres and whether he had looked through our power of attorney (before he had asked if we had an eye-witness). So he said to let the people come to him which was as much as to say that our power of attorney was good.

On November 9th, cousin Kripner came to see us and suggested to us to open a weaver's shop here because it would be too costly for us to be here otherwise. And he knew of a partner for us, which we declined. We said if we started something like that we would do it on our own.

On November 9th, Mr. Franz Caspar Hasenclever came to see us and wanted to start the weaver's shop with us. He also offered to contribute £200. On November 10th, Mr. Hasenclever invited us for a glass of hock and a pipe of Dutch tobacco which tasted very good.

On November 10th, I wrote to my wife and on November 15th to my brother-in-law[41]. On September 6th, I wrote to my wife and on the 16th of the same month to Johann Gelissen, and on August 28th to Frau von der Euwen.

At 10 in the morning of November 10th, the miller Mätters called at our place and asked us to meet him at the King of Prussia[42], which we did, and where there was also the son of Jan Jansen who has 15 acres out of the 50 on Chestnut Hill. So the miller said he had been to see his lawyer Galwy, who had not been home, however, and he had his letter with him. Whether we could have it issued by Saturday. So we could then go with them to their lawyer and to ours. Upon which I replied, you can go by yourselves, between today and Wednesday, to both lawyers and find out. For we have decided that even if all of the lawyers here in Philadelphia decide against us, we will still take the case to court. And that had to happen on Wednesday because one of us would go to New York on Thursday and our case was also set to go to court that day. So they could now consider whether they wanted to have it before the law or not.

On November 12th, we agreed with Mr. Franz Caspar Hasenclever to have him as the third partner in the company. He contributed £25.

On November 14th, we went with cousin Kripner to the lawyer. The latter looked through our papers. But from the way he looked at them we could see that he had looked through them before. When we now asked him if our power of attorney was good, we got the answer that it was good for taking possession but not for selling because the widow had not ceded her rights to her children. Upon which we asked him if he saw a chance to force a judgement in 2 or 3 courts. He answered, not in 2, but in the 3rd. He asked us why we were in such a hurry. We answered that we would then appeal to London. Upon which he gave us back our papers at once, grew quite angry and opened the door for

Fig. 41 Hearth at the "King of Prussia" inn in Germantown, photography, late 19th century. GHS.

us. With that, we could go. But he said he would talk to Logan. Now we did not know what to think, why the man who had been so friendly toward us before now seemed so angry.

At 3 in the afternoon, cousin Strepers came to see us and asked whether we knew now who had Logan's land. We said no. "Then I will tell you", he said. "Mr. Allen has one quarter, the King's Counsel has one quarter, lawyer Galloway has one quarter and Mr. Turner has one quarter. And that is the truth," he said. "So now you are up against the biggest people here in Philadelphia." Upon which we said we were still not afraid.

Now we could see why he (the King's Counsel) sent us away so angrily, because he had a part in it himself. But we were surprised that he did not raise any other objection than that the widow had not ceded her rights to her children. So we could take the land into possession but could not give a valid deed. And if we wanted to appeal to London, did we know that we would have to raise bail. And where were we going to find the money for that. So I answered that Mr. Hasenclever would act as a guarantor for us. Upon which he said that he lived outside the county, so he could not be a guarantor.

In the evening Mr. Peter Hasenclever came to take leave because he was going to New York the following day. So I told him that I had suggested him as a guarantor. He said that was good. Upon which I told him, however, that the King's Counsel had rejected him because he did not reside in the county. So Mr. Hasenclever said if we went to see him again we should tell him that he would deposit a guarantee for us, even if it had to be £8,000. And that he was still owed £2,000 here in town which he could lay down right then. Whether he would not be satisfied with that? Now Mr. Hasenclever said: Do not aggravate anybody in this town, but one of you should come to New York with me. So we will try and help you wherever possible. Because here in Philadelphia they are just about all knaves and nobody can be trusted. Upon which we decided that cousin Strepers was to travel to New York the following Sunday. On November 17th, cousin Strepers went to Mr. Hasenclever again and he made us a present of 2 bottles of wine.

Fig. 42 Robert Feke (1724-1769), William Allen. Oil on canvas, approx. 1751. Independence National Historical Park, Philadelphia.

In the evening the miller Mätters came and asked us to give him time until the following Saturday because his lawyer was not in town. But he did not come to us on Saturday.

In the morning of November 18th, cousin Strepers went to New York. At 7 in the morning of November 18th, cousin Strepers went to New York and came back on December 8th in the evening.

On November 18th, at a quarter past 8 my nose started bleeding all by itself (on the right side), more strongly than it has ever bled in my life, as far as I can remember.

On November 19th, we took two rooms to start our weaver's shop. I started working on November 19th.

On November 19th, I met cousin Paul Kripner in the street on the way to our house. He told me that he was just coming from the King's Counsel and had told him in our name that we broke off with him. And that we would not come back to him. Upon which I asked him why he had done that, because, after all, the lawyer had told us he would speak to Logan. Upon which he said that cousin Strepers had told him how the lawyer also had a quarter of it. So he had thought it would be better for us if we stayed away from him altogether. Now I do not know whether he did that in good faith or out of knavery. Time will tell. Now he asked where cousin Strepers was. So I said, "To New York." At which he was very surprised and replied 3 to 4 times, "To New York." So he advised me to see to it that we got the 17 acres from the miller. As if to say, otherwise you may end up getting nothing at all.

On November 21st in the afternoon, the miller Mätters came to tell me that his lawyer was at home now, did I want to come with him. Then his lawyer was to come with us to our lawyer. And then we would see whether we would close the deal. I answered him, "We do not have a lawyer here any more. And ours told us that we could take possession of our land but could not sell it." I could not tell him any more before my cousin had returned from New York. If he wanted to call again in 8 days' time, he was welcome to do so. But I think we will bring it before the law. Upon which he mumbled some vicious remarks about possession and law and left in anger.

The same day, between day and evening, a man came to me and asked if somebody by the name of Strepers was living here. I said, yes, but that he was not here at the moment. He said that was a bother. I told him to tell me what he wanted from him because it was as good as talking to him. So he asked if I was together with him. I said yes. So he asked if we had land to sell here. I said that would only become clear after everything had been settled. We did claim land here, and when things had been settled we would also sell some of it. Upon which he said he wanted to buy all the land from us that we laid claim to before the case came to court. Whether we were willing to do that. Then

I should set a time whenever it suited me to talk about it. I said he had to see our papers first to know whether he could buy on that basis. So he said to set a time when he should call. Because he wanted to buy before the court. Then we would not have to deal with that either. So I asked him for his name. He replied, "Richard Stevens." He said he could come back the following afternoon between 2 and 3, and he wanted to do so.

In the morning of November 22nd, I went to cousin Paul Kripner and told him a little about this man and that he had promised to call on me that afternoon at 3. I asked him if he could also come this afternoon, as if by coincidence, because I could not talk to him completely freely [?]. So he said he would come.

Cousin Paul Kripner came at 3 and at 4 Mr. Stevens also arrived. He asked Kripner who he was. Kripner said that he was a distant relative of ours and that we had come here to look for land. Upon which he said he knew it well and if we wanted to sell our rights to him, he was willing to give the highest price and would also pay straight away. But he wanted to do that before the court and that would also be best for us. Then we would not have any more trouble and could leave whenever we wanted. And I should name a price for everything we had here. Upon which I answered him that since my cousin had gone to New York, on the one hand, I could not know what he agreed up there and, on the other, I would not do so anyway because I had to talk to him first and that he also had to look through our papers first and how much he thought he should give. Then he said again I should name a sum first. So I would see that he was reasonable and that he would give more than the others. Upon which I told him, let us wait until 8 days from today. Then, I thought, my cousin would be back. He was satisfied with that. And as soon as he had returned, we wanted to conclude the sale and he would pay us our money immediately. So then he would take over and we could go home.

Upon which cousin Kripner asked him who he was. So he said that he came from London and most of his friends were also in London. But his father[43] was a lawyer and living across the river in New

Jersey, and his brother[44] was a lawyer in New York. Then he wrote his name down for cousin Kripner and told me he wished for my sake that my cousin would come back soon, after cousin Kripner had told him about the matter with the King's Counsel.

Now he wanted to come back to me on Thursday to hear whether cousin Strepers had returned. He also asked Paul Kripner where he lived and said he would also call on him sometime, which I understood clearly. But he did not come back to me until now on Thursday.

On December 1st [rest missing]. On December 1st, the miller also came back to me to ask if cousin Strepers had returned. I said, "No." Upon which he left. On December 8th at 9 in the evening, cousin Strepers came back from New York, but had not spoken to any lawyer about our case, so we now have to wait until the next court day.

On December 19th, Mr. Stevens came back to us and said he had not been well for some time but was coming from his estate now and, as he was passing, wanted to call and hear if my cousin had come back. And if we were still thinking of selling. Upon which we answered as before, if we could get a fair price for it. Upon which he asked how much we wanted. So we said we would put that on paper and have it translated into English. Then we would give it to him in writing, which he liked very much, saying that we should not put a higher price on it than we really wanted to get. And that he would come back on the evening of December 21st.

On December 17th, cousin Strepers [rest missing]. On December 22nd in the morning, Mr. Stevens came back to us after we had given him our resolution in writing. And when he had read through it he said that at £3 sterling an acre we had put the price too high. Otherwise he did not say all that much against our demand. After he had read many of our letters he asked whether we did not have any warrants from the surveyor, and whether Logan still had our land in his possession, or if our properties were located somewhere else, and if we had talked to Logan. Upon which we showed him the warrants. Upon which he nodded his head

and said, Bucks County, that was good land there (to which I agreed readily NB). Now he said he had a partner, and when he had talked to him he would come back to us with more detail in 3 or 4 days.

On December 24th at 3 in the afternoon (just after cousin Strepers had gone to Germantown), Mr. Stevens called and told me his partner had just left town. But he had talked to him and they wanted to give us £4,000 sterling. If we were satisfied with that they would not only give us money and letters of exchange, to be drawn in London, but would also put up Mr. Hasenclever and others from this town as guarantors. But with the proviso that they wanted to have the next court day held first. Upon which I replied that we would not sell for that sum. And therefore we wanted to wait our time quietly, all the more because we had now entrusted the matter to a Royal Prussian Privy Councilor and Resident[45] and because I hoped firmly that, if we kept quiet, the matter would come to a quick end. Indeed, he said, we would see that we would get into a lot of trouble because it was split up among so many. For he knew our properties quite well, where they lay and who had them. Upon which I said that we claimed no other land than that in Bucks County that had been surveyed for our grandfather. So that we had no dealings with Logan but for the 50 acres of Liberty land. Upon which he said, "Listen, since I know this matter so well, if you leave a third to me I will give you £2,000, and that is more than you would get otherwise. And if you agree to this, I will tell you how we will go about it. We will go to New York quickly and quietly together with Mr. Hasenclever (who had also received 10,000 acres from them) and set it all down in writing." And then we should engage his father who is a lawyer in New Jersey and his brother, the King's Counsel in New Jersey, and another lawyer in New York. Then we should check our mail every 4 to 5 days. And then engage two lawyers from this town as well and then take possession of everything in one blow. Yes, he knew well that what he could not do nobody could do. I told him that on that basis the matter did not seem bad to me, I would inform my comrade of it when he came back and then talk to him in more detail. Upon which he asked when he should come back.

And I said I would come to collect him and the day was set to be December 27th.

December 26th, the weather is very changeable here, often it changes 3 or 4 times a day. It is very rare to remain the same for two days. So far, it has not been particularly cold, but the air is so subtle here, it cuts through everything. Xmas Day is celebrated in a number of ways here. Many and quite a few do not celebrate it at all. They work more than usual on that day. Many who call themselves by that name want to celebrate. They go hunting all day or dancing. Some leave their usual work and do something else, such as chopping wood etc. Others who celebrate it better than others, like we did, eat and drink expensively. But none of us went to church. Yes, our [rest missing]. Others also go to church.

Last night the weather was surprisingly stormy. And since the snow has been on the ground for 3 days, going by sleighs is more common than one can tell, and likewise the number of farmers coming to town every day with who knows how many hundreds of sleighs. Each is drawn by two horses. Most of the sleighs are of very expensive workmanship. They have carpets inside. And so they go whole nights just for the pleasure of it. And if one wants to rent a sleigh, one has to pay 5 shillings for every horse and 10 shillings for the sleigh.

On December 28th, Mr. Stevens called again. So we agreed with him not just by word but in writing to go to New York on December 30th and to conclude a binding agreement there. I wanted to take Mr. Rübel and Mr. Hasenclever with me. On the evening of December 29th, Mr. Stevens called and said he had to go to Amboy in the morning and would wait for me there on January 1st. On December 30th, there was no opportunity and in the evening Mr. Stevens sent someone to tell me that he would come and collect me if I wanted to come with him in his sleigh the following morning. Which I agreed to do. That day it was very cold.

On December 31st, we left at 10 in the morning. At half past 9, I got on the sleigh with Mr. Stevens, his wife and his sister-in-law and we went as far as Trenton, where we arrived at 1 o'clock and had

lunch [?] at the King of Prussia. At 2 we went from there to Princeton[46] which we reached at half past four. But the cold I suffered defies description. Even if I think of the winter of 1740, that does not seem anything compared to this one. More than a hundred times today I wished I was in Ronsdorf for 10 days, but, but. NB what happened in the night: NB in the evening many people felt an earthquake.

1765

On January 1st, we arrived at Amboy at 5 in the evening. On January 1st, we left at 9 in the morning and reached Brunswick at 2, and that is 28 miles. At 4 we left Brunswick and arrived here in Amboy at ¼ past 5. Today it was even about 3 degrees colder. Indeed, I often thought I would never get warm again. The wind is so subtle and penetrating here that nobody at home would believe it. Even if one is as warm as possible, within a quarter of an hour the cold has overwhelmed him to such a degree that he can hardly move or stir.

On January 2nd, Mr. Blomstäet called with three other gentlemen whom we had visited twice on the way. In the evening, Mr. Stevens came to take me to his father who then looked through our case very thoroughly. And the most important thing he wanted to know for our case was at what time Jan Strepers had died, and that we had to prove it. Besides I could not see anything in Mr. Stevens but that he stayed with his decision.

January 2nd I spent quietly at Amboy. In the evening, Mr. Stevens came to take me to his father-in-law. On January 3rd, we left Amboy in two sleighs which also carried Mr. Plumstead, his son and two other gentlemen. In the evening between 4 and 5 we finally reached New York. And Mr. Stevens asked me to come to a safe inn or to his brother's the following morning.

On January 4th, I went to the inn at 9 in the morning but Mr. Stevens had not been there yet. So I went to his brother's. Where I met Mr. Elliu, who left directly, however. And Mr. Stevens went with me straight to Mr. Rübel. Well, Mr. Rübel liked Mr. Stevens and Mr. Stevens liked Mr. Rübel, and the latter promised to come to New York the following morning.

See further down under January 5, 1765, which belongs here.

On January 4th at 11 in the morning, I went with Mr. Stevens to Mr. Rübel who gave us a friendly reception. In the evening we returned to New York.

[The following passages are put in brackets until the remark, "This belongs further down."] Then I agreed with Mr. Rübel that he should propose that, if he took a part, would it not be useful if they bought the whole property from us. Which he did. Mr. Stevens replied that he was going to talk to Plumstead who would also like to have ¼.

On January 5 at 8 in the morning, Mr. Rübel was already with me and left for Long Island again at 2 o'clock. As had been arranged, I met with Mr. Stevens [text missing]. We were to meet with Mr. Rübel at a certain house where I would find him, and he was going to show Mr. Stevens the contract, which everybody was then to sign. But at 10 o'clock, and also at 11 o'clock, we did not find Mr. Stevens there. So we went to the house where Mr. Peter Hasenclever lived, whom we also found there.

After I had told him about our matter and let him read the contract we had drawn up, he replied that, had he known earlier – and why had we not informed him of it earlier – he would have advised us differently. Indeed, he said, on the one hand we could not have found a better man to push the matter through, but on the other, not a worse person to deceive us. Because these people had almost put one over on the Governor. He said, "I cannot help it. If I see injustice like that, I have to tell the truth, and I know it to the last detail." I replied that things had not got that far yet and we could still be prudent if we only had good advisors.

I asked whether I might take the liberty, when Mr. Stevens showed the contract, to bring it to Mr. Hasenclever and show it to him, because I had reserved that possibility. Mr. Hasenclever said to do so because that was a matter of importance. And

he wanted to go with me to his lawyer, even if it cost me two pistols, so nothing prejudicial would be signed. Upon which we went to see Mr. Stevens' brother and, after we had sat there for ¼ hour, Mr. Stevens also arrived. And he was quite morose because the whole matter might fall through. He said he called on the lawyers here and they had told him unanimously that since Jan Strepers had not been naturalized the Proprietor would take everything back. But he wanted to go back to Plumstead again to find out whether the same rules applied in the Province[47] as they had here. And then he wanted to come to the house indicated to see us.

After ½ hour had passed, Mr. Stevens returned and said Plumstead had told him that things were different in Pennsylvania. And he wanted to have the contract finalized in English and also in German. And on Monday morning at 10 o'clock we wanted to go to Mr. Hasenclever to let him see. So Mr. Rübel said to him that he would also like to have 1/6 or 1/8 of it. And if they made a contract for a certain sum for all our rights so we could go home again. So Mr. Stevens said Mr. Plumstead thought it should be divided into four parts and he should have one of them. Upon which I replied that, if we could sell it all, we would not cede any of the 2/3.

Mr. Stevens said his brother would come to him for dinner that evening, and he would talk to him. And so we parted. Mr. Rübel went home (he said that if at all possible he would be back here on Monday morning) At 3 in the afternoon, I went to Mr. Hasenclever's lodgings. Since only Poolman was there by himself, I asked him to tell Mr. Hasenclever when he returned that I had heard he would have dinner with Mr. Stevens. And since our matters were bound to be talked about, he should act in a way that was best for us, and that I would call again on Monday morning.

This belongs further down [end of bracket]

Now I have forgotten to note. On January 3rd, we passed a place only 9 miles from New York where we had to cross the river. It is only just on Staten Island where we had lunch.

There was a woman there, about 35 years old. But I have never seen anything like her. And the gentlemen who were with me could not stop laughing about her. She was about [missing] tall and, as I estimated, at least 4 Brabant ells[48] around the waist. Since they all speak Dutch on Staten Island, I asked her if she knew how much she weighed. She said no. But if I had to give an estimate, and if my life depended on it, I would have estimated her at 350 pounds. Every time one looked at her one had to laugh.

On January 6th, outside my lodging so many wild duck came flying across the Hudson River that one could not count them. Indeed it looked like one big cloud. There may have been more than 10 to 12,000 of them. An hour later, about the same number came swimming, too. Yesterday and today it snowed all day. And the snow lies 4 foot deep. But where it was blown together it is more than 6 foot deep. It is still very cold now.

There is a lot of ice on the river so one cannot cross it without great danger. In New York there were many who wanted to cross. But they were not allowed to. – See opposite page.

Here I want to write down the days which were so extremely cold that I have never felt anything like it in Germany. December 30 and 31, 1764. January 1, 1765 as well as 3rd, 4th, 6[th,] 12th, 13th, 16th, 17th, 19th, 20th, 21st and February 2nd and 3rd it was so vehemently cold here that the river in New York (which is salt water) froze over, and that is not supposed to have happened as long as anyone can think. Quite generally, people say they cannot remember cold like this. In New York at the time I was there they paid up to 48 shillings for a klafter[49] of wood. In our money that would be 10 rix dollars. And now they say they are selling it for 16 rix dollars a klafter.

The Delaware froze solid on December 30th and stayed like that until February 16th. They roasted a whole ox on it, and many 1,000 spectators watched it.

On January 7th, at 9 in the morning, I went to Mr. Hasenclever to consult with him some more, and he seemed very loyal to me then. I told him I wanted

to go to see Mr. Stevens afterwards and that the contract should be written in the morning. Upon which Mr. Hasenclever said not to sign anything before I had given it to him to read. And he wanted to help us with our case. I should only remain firm and tell Mr. Stevens that Mr. Hasenclever had been recommended to me by a friend of his, and that I was not going to do anything without him.

Mr. Hasenclever said, "If you had spoken to me beforehand, I would have done my part for you. And I would have concluded the matter sooner than now. And you would not have been deceived. For I am allowed to write directly to King and Parliament. I am well-known there. Upon which I asked whether Mr. Hasenclever was willing to take one part. He said, "Yes." Upon which I said, then we could leave him part of our share. Upon which he said, "No, you go to Mr. Stevens now and ask him if he would be satisfied if we split it up in 4 parts. He 1 part, I 1 part, and you 2 parts. And then come back to me."

At 10 o'clock I went to Mr. Stevens, who went with me to a lawyer straight away who also spoke German and who was to write the contract. So I asked through the lawyer whether Mr. Stevens would agree to dividing it up into 4 parts and Mr. Hasenclever could also have one part. Upon which he said no, he was not going to give up any of his third part. So I said that we would give him some of our share. Then I asked Mr. Stevens if he wanted to walk to Mr. Hasenclever's with me. He said, "Yes," but I should call for him at 12 o'clock, and then he wanted to come with me. When he told the lawyer the content, I went to my lodgings.

At 12 o'clock, I went with Mr. Stevens to Mr. Hasenclever. So Mr. Hasenclever said that since he had been recommended to us, he would do his best. And if Mr. Stevens would cede a quarter to him. To which Mr. Stevens agreed at once. But he added that Mr. Plumstead would also like so much to have a share. Upon which Mr. Hasenclever said we want to have the contract made out for 4 parts. As soon as you come to Philadelphia, and if Mr. Plumstead was willing, they wanted to buy everything among the three of them. With that Mr. Stevens was completely content. As we went down, Mr. Hasenclever said to me to come back in ½ hour. Which I did. So he said we should not be in too much of a hurry to sell. Although it was a concern of his as well now. But he still wanted to work in our favor. We should not sign anything without telling him. And if we wanted to go home we should give him our papers. He wanted to grant us sufficient bail for them.

On January 8th, I went to Mr. Stevens 4 times and to Mr. Hasenclever 2 times. But the lawyer delayed from hour to hour. So that on that day nothing progressed. On January 9th in the morning, everything was supposed to be ready. So I went to Mr. Stevens at that time and he to the lawyer straight away. And I was to come to Mr. Hasenclever at 11 (now Mr. Rübel came to me again), which I did. But at 11 Mr. Stevens came and said it could not be ready before 4 in the afternoon, at which time we would meet at Mr. Hasenclever's.

On January 10th, the contract was finally ready and read out in the presence of Messrs. Rübel, Hasenclever and Stevens (in duplicate). Then they said if we signed this now, the matter would be settled and there was nothing prejudicial in it. Upon which I said, the gentlemen should not take offence but I would not sign anything, as I had said before, even from my own brother unless it was translated so I could see what I signed. And they would have to sign the German as well as the English for me. And if then after the translation it was like we had agreed I would sign straight away. Upon which Mr. Hasenclever said Mr. Pollmann should start on the translation immediately so we could have the matter out right the following morning. That midday Mr. Rübel went back home. In the evening I received the contract in German from Mr. Pollmann. After I had looked at it thoroughly, I resolved not to sign it as it was.

On January 11th at 9 in the morning, we met again at Mr. Hasenclever's. And I said that I would never sign the contract as it was. Upon which we debated for about an hour, And I finally said it would never happen. I would rather have our whole case come to nothing. So they finally did what I wanted, upon which Mr. Plumstead was called and the signing was done. I also received £50 in Pennsylvania

money from Mr. Hasenclever on the condition that, if they did not receive anything, we would have to return it. Otherwise £3,000 sterling would be deducted from the total.

On January 13th at 10 in the morning, we left New York and crossed the river in an astonishing cold. After two hours had passed and we had worked our way through the ice with great effort, we had finally crossed the Hudson River, which is about ¼ hour wide. At 9 in the evening, we arrived at Amboy, where Mr. Stevens stayed for 3 more days. The following day I had no possibility to get away. But on January 15th a sleigh arrived on which I could travel via Brunswick as far as Cranbury, where 4 of us hired a sleigh to Philadelphia. And there we arrived on January 17th at midday.

On February 1st, I stared weaving. On the 5th, I had finished what I wanted to do, namely salt-and-pepper cloth. But since the warp was finished I cut it off, and we put a finer one in.

February 23rd I will remember as much as I can. At 9 in the morning I suddenly had such heart pains which lasted about 5 or 6 minutes. If they had lasted for a long time I could not have stood it. I was in so much pain that I did not eat all day. In the evening I took some rhubarb[50], and now I feel better.

There is a note in the paper[51] that it has not been as cold as this winter in 40 years.

After Mr. Plumstead had come back to Philadelphia on February 2nd and cousin Strepers had also signed our contract in his presence, Mr. Stevens called on February 25th and told us he had spoken to Logan himself. And asked him on what he based his claim. Upon which he had replied, on his deed from the three trustees. And that, after all, Wilhelm Strepers had been given the land entirely in 1715. Upon which Mr. Stevens had asked him if he did not have a letter saying that the three trustees had given a pledge with a deadline of 8 months from Jan Strepers' heirs as was written in his deed. And would they have made such a pledge if everything had been transferred to Wilhelm Strepers in 1715. Upon which Logan had replied that he did not have any letter any more.

Now Mr. Stevens said he had also been to the Governor[52] and had talked to him. And the latter had told him that we must have an influential advocate in London. Because he had had letters from his father[53], the Proprietor. So I replied that during the time we had been to London there had been no Prussian ambassador there. Otherwise, if he had been there our matter here would not have been delayed for as long as it is now. Upon which he asked who our advocate was at the court of Prussia. So I told him that we had a Royal Prussian Privy Counselor and Resident and Superintendent of all of Jülich and Berg who was going to support our cause most strongly if we did not get our right here. Upon which he said it was good. He would engage Schu and Galloway for the next court and give them each £10. And Mr. Hasenclever should also bring 2 lawyers from New York and also his father-in-law[54]. And then we would see what this would happen.

On February 28th, cousin Strepers rode to Germantown with Mr. Stevens where Mr. Stevens had told about [?] cousin Peter Strepers through cousin Wilhelm Strepers when he had talked to William Logan. So he had told him that we must have an influential advocate in London. Because there had been a great gentleman who had talked to the King himself and upon which the king had sent two letters to the Proprietor that he should do us justice here speedily. Which the Proprietor here had written to his son, the Governor. Upon which cousin Wilhelm Strepers had gotten all confused.

On March 2nd, I went to Mr. Stevens together with Joseph Mätters and we agreed what the lawyers were to make of it[55]. After that it was to be sold.

Now Mr. Stevens said we should make sure to obtain the bond for £15 which Richard Hill had given to cousin Wilhelm Strepers and we should also find out where the original of 1715 was. For that reason, cousin Strepers went to Chestnut Hill today. He obtained the bond from Wilhelm Strepers. And it was the original.

On March 23rd and 24th, snow fell 3 to 4 feet deep twice in 24 hours, which has never happened here before in anybody's memory.

On April 9th, a race was held here. One horse belongs to lawyer Galloway here and the other comes from Long Island, 104 miles from here, which brought £1,000 sterling and won, ggggy.[56]

The first time they went around 4½ miles. That was in 6 minutes. The second time (although that was immediately afterwards) they ran in 5 minutes, and both rounds were won by the Long Islander. When the horses had rested for ¼ hour, they had to run for a second time (because it had been raining continuously the three days before, there was such a morass that the horses had to run with their legs halfway into the mud). When they were halfway around, the horse that had won the first time stumbled so that it was lame and lost. They went around twice in 13 minutes.

On March 27th in the morning, Mr. Stevens called and said to be at Mr. Aepply's at 7 in the evening and to bring two men with shovels. He wanted to be there at the same time with 4 men to fence in the two open spaces, because rails and posts and nails were already there. So we promised to be there at 7 in the evening. At 7 in the evening, we arrived at Aepply's house together. At half past 7, we began to put in holes for the posts quietly. And at 12 we were completely finished. And the two pieces of land were completely fenced in.

On March 28th at 6 in the morning, I was inside the fence and took possession. At 7 o'clock, cousin Strepers also arrived. And we both took turns at patrolling the two spaces. At 9 o'clock, ¼ hour after I had last patrolled both and found everything in order, Äpply's son came running in and said the fences had all been torn down. So cousin Strepers and I ran up quickly to Dr. Samuel Preston Moore and protested against his method. And we picked the rails right up again and wanted to nail them back on. Dr. Moore tore them off and we nailed them on. And the noise lasted a good while. Dr. Moore saw that there was no hope we would stop but instead kept at it although he told us more than 10 times not to nail any rail back on. So we kept nailing the rails back on merrily, right before his eyes. When he asked us for our names, we said, "Peter Heinrich Strepers and Johannes Herbergs." Which he wrote down and said I had rebelled

Fig. 43 Anon., Cliveden, Country Seat of Benjamin Chew. Drawing, First half of 19th century. GHS.

against him, in spite of about 60 witnesses. And so he left full of anger.

We kept on nailing as fast as we could, so the sweat ran off us. And when we were just nailing the last rail into place, Dr. Moore came up with a constable and arrested me. And he wanted to tear the fence down again straight away. But as Mr. Stevens came up at that moment, he took the hammer from my hand and told me to just stay standing on our land. He wanted to see who would tear off one single rail. Mr. Stevens and we as well stood inside the fence and Dr. Moore outside it. Then Mr. Stevens dared Moore to tear down a rail. And stood facing him, with the hammer in his hand. And Moore asked him why he meddled with this business. Mr. Stevens said he was taking our side and he should just dare and tear down a rail.

It was half past 11 now. After we had had two constables come to us so they would free us from the need to guard our fence so that it would not be torn down, I was led under arrest to the judge and that caused quite a stir. As we were brought before the judge, the man who had torn down the fence at once swore an oath that I had rebelled against Moore.

Upon which the judgement was passed at once that I had to put up £50 in bail or go to prison right then with the knaves and rogues. But as Mr. Stevens was there, he stood bail for me at once. And I had to pledge to appear in court the following Tuesday.

Afterwards we went straight back to our place. There was a carpenter there by the name of Schneck who offered to sell a finished wooden house (which was lying next to his own). It was 16 feet wide and 18 long. Mr. Stevens went to look at it straight away. And bought it, too, for [price missing], on condition that it had to be in place by the evening, closed on all sides and with the roof on it and ready to live in.

At 1 in the afternoon, the first cart of timber arrived on the site. At 7 in the evening, everything was ready and we could hang a pot of meat over the fire, with thousands of onlookers. Everybody said that never had a house been put up in such a short time, but rather 6 hours' time was unheard of. And yet everything was done quite well. But the best of it was this. Moore is just as popular here as Verhoeff is in Ronsdorf. And because the Quakers are forever trying to strangle the Germans, I cannot describe what joy there was among the Germans. And wherever a Quaker appeared he had to listen to all sorts of curse words and, indeed, how badly the Quakers had always treated the Germans.

Now the talk turned to how Moore had hired 200 sailors who were to pull everything down again by force in the night. When the Germans heard this, at once there were many more prepared to stay and help us than we wanted (because the house was so crowded with people that there was no room to stand). Outside was crowded. Äpply's house was crowded. And they all armed themselves with swords, hunting knives, sabers, cudgels and said now let the sailors come. Cousin Strepers and I meanwhile had a barrel of rum, beer and punch come for the crowd and had a whole pig of 65 pounds roasted which was ready and nicely roasted on March 28th at 2 in the morning and brought into the new house and eaten. And it went so fast you did not even find a bone of it afterwards. Now the people stayed with us until it was broad daylight and the danger over, although they had been taking turns all through the night to patrol all of Philadelphia. Now we had to live in fear for twice 24 hours. And if we kept up our cause during that time, then we were in possession (and under English law possession is set at 11 parts won with only 1 part remaining).

NB Pennington's house, which is next to ours, yields a rent of £160 sterling every year and is lived in by Mr. Benten who does a lot of trade by sea.

At 8 in the morning, again a constable came and said he had a warrant for Mr. Stevens. We now had our place permanently guarded by two constables. And we had to go with Mr. Stevens and Dr. Moore to the mayor. But because the mayor said the matter was too important to make a decision like that, he told us to come back to his house the following morning between 9 and 10, and each should bring a judge.

Now all of Philadelphia was astir. Indeed, women and children, I think there were few in the town that did not come and see, thousands of them coming and going and riding past all the time. Everybody said no house in Philadelphia had had so many

onlookers in all the time the town had been there. And all the talk, both among English and Germans, was about the knavish Quakers. Indeed if at home the same words had been spoken as here, the new buildings in Düsseldorf[56] would not have been big enough for one hundredth part of them. Indeed, we have many markets where not half as many people come together as came here. And there was a group of gentlemen standing together who said that the Germans had the reputation that they had to be in America seven years before they understood. And they thought these had not been here that long. Others said it seemed that the Germans wanted to get the upper hand here now.

Now there had been many that afternoon who had given a dollar to the town crier. And he had to ring his bell and announce that Dr. Moore had lost a red cow. Although he never had a red cow these 4 years. It was just for provocation.

At 1 o'clock we were told quietly, and by a constable himself, that Moore was running around trying to get constables. But they were all evading him. And they did not know what he was planning. Upon which another told me that Moore would come soon with the sheriff to throw us out of the house. Now I asked Stevens how we were to react to that. So he said if he came we should not say a word nor raise a hand. And when he led me out a bit by the arm, I should let myself be led a little bit. And when I then stood outside the door I should lock the door and above all take good care of the key. We just had to stay awake. At 5 we received word that Moore had sent to New Jersey (well, I had seen his servant ride past) for 150 negroes who were to wreck everything that night. Upon which who knows how many Germans came and offered again to stay with us. But we only accepted 20. But nothing of all that happened, but things stayed quiet.

From March 28th onward when I quarreled with Mr. Moore I had an unspeakable headache until April 8th (although I had 2 Spanish flies[57] applied. It did not help). And then the flow[58] suddenly shot into the small of my back so I could neither move nor stir unless with great pain. And that lasted until April 16th, but we still tried to look after our affairs as much as possible.

Fig. 44 William Birch (1755-1834), Goal in Walnut Street. Colored engraving, 1799.
Library Company, Inv. No. Sn24.

On March 30th at 10 in the morning, we went to the mayor with Mr. Stevens. Moore was there, too, with Justice Jones and 4 others. And Moore's servant and another swore an oath that I had rebelled against him. Upon which I then had to go and find witnesses. But when I came back with the witnesses the mayor said it was adjourned until court day.

On April 2nd, Mr. Stevens left for Amboy thinking he would be back on April 7th. He asked me to find out in the meantime in Germantown where the deeds had been made and when Wilhelm Strepers, Jan Strepers, Leonhard Strepers, Leonhard Arets, Henrich Zellen and Reiner Theißen had died. From Wilhelm Strepers I heard that his grandfather, Wilhelm Strepers, had died in 1717 and his father Jan Strepers in 1739.

On April 3rd I obtained the first land record from Jansen in Germantown about how they distributed all the land in Germantown from which I copied one thing and another. He offered that if I had more I wanted to copy I was free to do so. I also heard from Haas that the principal record that theirs had been copied from was in Johann Wüsters' hands.

On April 4th, Saur mentioned our taking possession in his paper.

On April 6th, Moore said he, Logan and two others wanted to spend £100,000 sterling on law suits.

On April 8th in the evening Mr. Stevens came back from Amboy. In the morning of April 9th, we called on him to hear what he had decided. So he said that he had taken possession in Bucks County also by leasing 175 acres to a German farmer for £4 and 10 shillings a year (which letter of lease we also signed then) but only for two years. And that he had posted a notice that on the following Tuesday, April 16th, every farmer had to present his deed and that we had to be there at that time, too. That place is 35 miles from here.

On April 11th, Mr. Stevens gave us a power of attorney in English which we were to look through and sign straight away. Now I had it translated immediately. But when we read it through we realized that if we signed, our hands would be so tied that we would not have any room to move nor stir. But we will take care.

On the morning of April 12th, Mr. Stevens called on us again and said that Moore and Logan were in the country now to get the sheriff and have our house torn down. So in the morning he had called on Benjamin Chew, but since the latter had had so many people around him he had not been able to talk to him much but that he had said they could not do that. He wanted to talk to him this afternoon and we should come to his place between 9 and 10 o'clock. Then he wanted to take us to Mr. Chew. We should also bring the power of attorney he had given us as well as all the principal originals. Upon which I told Mr. Stevens we would bring the copies but no originals. And we should find out when the land had been surveyed. If it had been more than 60 years ago, according to English law we would not get anything for it.

On April 15th, after we had entrusted the house to Mr. Ross, at 9 o'clock we rode with Mr. Stevens and Mr. Kurtz Junior, whom we took along for the language, to Bucks County to take possession there. At 6 in the evening, we had made 40 miles and still were 3 miles away from our land. Now Mr. Stevens had put up notices there a fortnight before that on April 16th, at 9 in the morning everybody living on the land that we were laying claim to should appear there.

Now the farmers had threatened both Stevens and us horribly. But when we arrived at half past 9 at the spot indicated where there were only two houses and a smithy, the farmers were also arriving. (I wanted to count them but could not because there were about 70 to 80 of them and they kept milling around each other. Now the farmers took us aside straight away and asked why we had taken up with such a knave, rogue, etc. Indeed

that fellow would send his own father and mother to the gallows if he could make a profit out of it. And if I wanted to go to him, I would hear that they would tell him so to his face. And we should take care. He would certainly deceive us. Upon which I said I thanked them for the warning. And we would be careful of him as much as possible. So they asked if it was true that we had given all the powers to him. I said, no, but we had let him have a share. But without us, he could do nothing.

Upon which they asked what our plans were now. I said, well, we wanted to read our title to them now, and after that had been done they should show their titles, too. And whoever could show the oldest and best title would certainly also win before the law. So most of them said that was right and they were dealing with honest Germans. If only you had not taken up with that knave. (NB Only I think that, had we not had the knave with us, they would have spoken to us differently.). Then we went into the house and Mr. Stevens read our deeds from the Proprietor out to them. When that had been done, the farmers made this objection and that, but without foundation, and we could disprove them. Now we thought the farmers would show their deeds as well but none appeared. Now I asked them how old their deeds were. So they said they were from the same year as ours. Upon which I asked them, if the Proprietor had made out two deeds for one piece of land at the same time. They said, no, rather Jan Strepers had sold it to Logan and Logan had given it back to the Proprietor and taken land in a different place. And so their deeds came from the Proprietor.

Now the farmers all rushed to Stevens so that he had to get on his horse and take off among a lot of bad words. When he had gone we wanted to see to our horses. Then the farmers had locked all our horses away and said they would like to talk to us once more. So they asked what our plans were if we won, and that we owed them a lot because they had paid for it. And if they had to cede it now, they would all be really ruined. Upon which I said in my opinion it would be best if they got together and discussed how much they hoped to give for each acre. And that way each could stay on his property. We did not want to be too hard on them.

Now one came up by the name of John Feer who had leased 175 acres of land for 2 years and wanted to get a letter of lease from us which we gave him straight away. Meanwhile the one who had had it before came up and said that if we sold it we should let him be next because he had had it in his possession. On April 17th, we rode to Dierich and Abraham Theißen. Abraham promised to get us a copy of the letter that had been made in Amsterdam.

On April 19th, 5 farmers from Bucks County came to us, asking us not to be too hard on them if we got the land, and they confessed that they had no paper, only improvement[59].

Now we have garden lettuce here and on April 23rd, we had asparagus. All of the cherry, peach and sassafras trees have been in full bloom since April 16th, indeed since April 14th and within two days everything was green and in bloom.

On April 27th, I rode with Mr. Kurtz to Chestnut Hill to hear from Delis Strepers whether he had the deed of sale which is supposed to have been made in Amsterdam. So he said straight away, "No." For on April 18th, Abraham Theißen and Johnson from Germantown had called and looked up all the papers. But the letter was not among them. He also let me look through all his papers. (So now we can see that Abraham Theißen is false and against us by consulting with Johnson.) Now Delis gave me a firm promise that he would get a copy for me from his sister-in-law of a letter which Logan had written 9 or 10 years ago. And he had promised them £100 each if they signed it. But they had not signed it.

On April 29th, it was the day for the Major Court to which I was bound for £50, as was Mr. Stevens himself. On that same day, I wrote down the names of the witnesses. On April 30th at 11, the court began. First the names of the jurymen (of whom there were 18) were read out. Then they all had to swear an oath. Among them, there were 6 Quakers who swore separately in their own way. Then all the constables, of whom there were about 20, who had to swear an oath about what they had seen or heard in the meantime (that was contrary to the laws). After that, the court was adjourned until the following morning at 10.

Now I needed an interpreter. But nobody wanted to do that for the reason, as they said openly, that they feared Mr. Moore would become their enemy.

May 1, 1765. This morning I went to Mr. Stevens and presented 12 witnesses to him whom I wanted to have summoned. He advised me against it until our case was called. Then there would still be time for it. And then I ran around again to find an interpreter, but in vain.

Now it was half past 9 (and at 10 the court was to start) that Mr. Noll sent for me (as I was just about to leave) to come to him straight away. Here were two gentlemen, just arrived from New Jersey. When I got there, Mr. Pollmann (as if in answer to a wish) was one of them, who promised me to get changed and come after me. Which he did.

In the morning, our case was not yet called. So we went together to our new house and had our meal brought there and ate inside together with Mr. Pollmann and young Mr. Kurtz. Afterwards, when it was 3 o'clock, we went with Mr. Stevens to the lawyers Dicenson and Thilmans with whom Mr. Stevens and Mr. Pollmann talked for a long time. And afterwards they said that no bill against us had been issued yet. As soon as it was issued, they would tell us. They also asked a lot of things.

At 6 in the afternoon, a bill against us was issued. After lawyer Tilghman had read it we went out together. Then Mr. Tilghman suggested straight away that we should wait until the next court session. But we said we would rather have it put through now. Upon which Mr. Stevens and Mr. Tilghman went to Dickinson who then came out with them. But he wanted to persuade us seriously to wait until the following court session. So we told them through Mr. Pollmann that we would rather lose now than win in 4 or 5 months time. Which, as Mr. Stevens said, seemed to have annoyed the lawyers very much. At 7 o'clock, Mr. Stevens came back and said if we risked £4 for each of the lawyers our case should go through. When cousin Strepers and I considered this that in 4 to 5 months we would eat for twice that sum, not to say anything about the lodging, we decided to do so.

On May 2ⁿᵈ, when we were back in court at 10 in the morning, both lawyers again recommended waiting for the following session. But we did as before. When Mr. Stevens gave them the money, we thought our case would progress (and NB now cousin Strepers was accused like myself). Now we were called to the front. Where, against all our ex-pectations, it was read out to us that we (Stevens, Strepers and myself) were bound over to the King for £200 sterling to reappear at the following court. And with that, we could leave. And Moore with all his witnesses was also bound for £20 to appear then.

On May 3ʳᵈ, I drove with Pollmann to Germantown and also took Mr. Christian Lehmann to Richard Jansen. And there we looked through the first land records. We found out about all of our land from them, except for 25 acres which we have not yet been able to find. And we stayed overnight with cousin Wilhelm Strepers. On May 4ᵗʰ, on the way back from Germantown Mr. Pollmann and I drove right against a tree. We fell out of the chaise. And I hurt myself very badly on my left arm and my right leg. It took a long time to get better, until July 24ᵗʰ, when it finally closed (namely the leg) and I suffered astonishing pain. It became a hole so deep that one could put a thumb inside, and it was all black from rotting flesh. It broke open again on August 10ᵗʰ, and healed over again on October 20ᵗʰ. 2 ligaments were cut away from it.

On May 4ᵗʰ, cousin Strepers followed us with Mr. Noll. Then we drove to Justice Eschschmit to ask him for his deed. But he was not home. So we asked his son to tell his father that as soon as he came to Philadelphia he should show us his deed as to how he came to have that land.

This is of all the most pleasant area I have seen here in Pennsylvania, apart from the fact that it is at some distance from the road.

On May 14ᵗʰ, I again rode with Mr. Stevens and Pollmann to Justice Ashmead and we also called on Mrs. Biddes and asked for her letter. The Biddes talked to us more nicely than before. But the Ashmeads were very hard to deal with. He has 27 acres of the Germantown land and says that his father

declares he bought it from Jan Strepers and he had good letters about that.

On May 16ᵗʰ, when it was the Day of the Ascension of Our Lord, cousin Strepers and I went to ask about the 50 acres Liberty land of the city of Philadelphia. And a man by the name of Kampman from Neviges, who makes woolen cloths for us, showed us some beautiful bushland. Concerning that bush, Logan had promised him through his driver, whom he had sent to him, to give him 20 shillings if he told him about any strange men who came and put up a fence around the bush and erected a house on it. Now we cannot but think that this must be our bush and the 50 acres of Liberty land.

That day Pollmann returned to New York. As we cannot be naturalized here for less than £40 to 50 sterling we asked him to find out if we could be naturalized in New York since he wants to be naturalized there himself. And he wanted to write us directly when the Assembly would be in session.

On May 21ˢᵗ, we had a letter from Mr. Pollmann that the New York Assembly would not sit before fall, but he wanted to be in Burlington[60] on May 27ᵗʰ and we should make sure that we were there too at that time. So we wanted to be naturalized there because the Assembly is sitting there now.

So we rode there on that day, 20 miles from here. When we arrived there, Mr. Stevens and his brother, who is a lawyer from New York and also an Assembly member, were also there. Now Mr. Stevens told us straight away this would of no use to us because a naturalization from New Jersey would not be accepted as valid in Philadelphia. But he had spoken to the King's Attorney that the latter would obtain naturalization for us for £5 sterling each.

On May 21ˢᵗ, Mr. Berenstecher set out, and the same morning the sheriff wrote down everything that was found up to May 22ⁿᵈ. It was more than £220 sterling and the auction only yielded £33 sterling. On May 22ⁿᵈ early in the morning, Mr. Berenstecher left. So now we have a new life style, doing our own housekeeping, but it is also a miserable life style.

On May 28th, we rode home again from Bristol[61].

On May 28th at 10 in the morning, Mr. Pollmann came after us and said we should dress at once and go to Burlington because he had had our names put in the file. But I asked Christian Schneider whether naturalization in New Jersey was also valid here. To which he said, "Oh yes, they make much more fuss about it here than in New Jersey, but somebody naturalized there is also naturalized here." Upon which we rode with him straight away and arrived in Burlington on May 30th at 9 in the morning. At 11 we were naturalized. Now all this including the travel expenses did not even cost us £12 sterling here.

On June 5th, I rode to Mr. Stevens to Bucks County because Bernhard Siegman wanted to buy 200 acres from us. On June 5th at 10 in the morning, I rode from here to Bucks County. Where I arrived wet to the skin at 8 o'clock. On June 6th, by 10 in the morning Siegman had not arrived. So we rode to Johann Nies (175 acres) We asked him whether he wanted to buy as well, otherwise we would have to have him summoned just like ... [name ommitted] who had 200 acres. He asked us what we were asking for an acre. So I said that those Germans who wanted to buy now were to have it for half the money, namely for £2 sterling an acre. But if it came before the court it would be twice as much. Now we met Bernhard Siegman with his brother and we agreed with him that he would call on us in a fortnight and finalize the sale.

On June 6th, we went back to Philadelphia. It is a distance of 40 miles. For Bernhard Siegman wanted to buy 200 acres.

Up to the beginning of May we did not have much heat here. But from May 24th to June 22nd, it was very hot and dry, so that although now and again there was a bit of a thunderstorm within 24 hours that was not visible any more. The dust here is so indescribable that often one can hardly breathe and the claps of thunder are so vehement here that one thinks it was striking right above one's head all the time. The houses shake afterwards as if there had been a strong earthquake. Also, the lightning often strikes.

Fig. 45 Old Germantown, drawings by Rudolf Cronau.
From: Die Gartenlaube, 1889.
Förderverein Auswanderermuseum Bremerhaven.

On July 14th, there was an indescribable heat here. The barometer was supposed to have reached 87 degrees at 11 o'clock. It had already been hot for a number of days before that, but not as hot as on that day. On July 19th and 20th, the heat is supposed to have been even greater, and according to many people who do not remember any heat like this in America, and if there had not been a wind the houses would have caught fire.

On June 7th in the morning, Mr. Stevens called and said he had tidings that were not good. For he had discovered in the Office that on the letter signed in Amsterdam there had been 11 signatures and we had to obtain the copy of Logan's deed to the Proprietor. And when we explained all the names to him he was quite content again.

Now we agreed with Stevens, because Moore and Logan had alarmed people everywhere, not just in town but also for 30 to 40 miles around, that we were claiming half of Frankfurt[62], half of Germantown and a quarter of the city of Philadelphia, that it would be good if we had a notice put in the paper about everything we were laying a claim to. And that in order to spoil their plans, if namely a jury saw that it was not so, the verdict would be more in accordance with what was right. On July 19th, we gave the above to the printer[63] to have it put in the paper.

We have tried four times now to find out about our Liberty land. We know roughly where it is but not exactly.

On June 12th, we sold 175 acres of land in Bucks County to Jan Feer at £2 an acre. We also gave him a deed but under the proviso that the surveyor should have preference.

On June 15th, I went with Stevens into the Office to cousin Lucken to find our Liberty land. Which was done. As soon as we had found it, I rode over there with Stevens and decided to have it fenced in the following week and also put a house on it. On June 18th in the morning cousin Strepers, Stevens and I went to Bucks County to contract for sale with many who only have an improvement. We also had a various newspapers with us where we had had our claim published.

On June 19th in the morning we met at Bernhard Siegman's. Where we had to have a long talk with the surveyor and were only held up for security reasons. But all in vain. At last, Fucks and Helbart arrived and wanted to make a contract with us. We insisted on 35 shillings per acre, which the two accepted. Upon which they agreed, namely apart from Johann Jürg Hellbat and Johann Jürg Fucks, Johann Küffer, Bernhard Siegman, Ludwig Lang and Johann Schumacher. These then complained very strongly that we were too hard on them. So Mr. Stevens then considered it good if we agreed to leave it to them for 30 shillings per acre. It would be better to make a sale now, but not later at that

price. Upon which they approached Mr. Stevens, asking him to wait with the transfer until the following week so they could talk to Pettersche[64]. To which Mr. Stevens said he wanted to come with them to Peters. So they asked why we were so hard on them. They wanted to give 25 shillings per acre. To which I said they should have the acre for 30 shillings under the condition that everything was signed that day. And if that did not happen, my word would not stand any longer than I was here now. And that I told them three times.

Upon this, they talked to Mr. Stevens for a long time. So Siegman, Helbart and Fucks came to me and said they had now finished with Mr. Stevens. He wanted to go with them to Peters Friday week. And they only had one last thing, that they wanted to pay in 4 installments. And I should promise them that, and then the purchase would be complete. They wanted to pay 30 shillings per acre when they had seen the deed to see if that was good.

Upon which I said if Mr. Stevens had agreed it with them that way, I would accept to have them pay in 4 installments. Only if they saw the deed and if one of them had anything against it, they would have to show it to us in writing, to which Siegman, Helbart and Fucks agreed. Upon which the purchase should be final.

On June 28th at 10 in the morning, the two Siegmans and Jan Lang called who had asked around everywhere the previous day. But they said that Peters was not at home and would not be back for 14 days. But this Jan Lang spoke very roughly and said, even if we gave him a good deed he would not pay one penny for it, or the matter had to be totally settled. Those three farmers then left without a word in spite of the fact that we had offered them a warrant deed.

On July 2nd, we went with Mr. Stevens to the lawyers Dickinson and Tilghman (because that was the first day of the Major Court). And they promised to bring our case up, but I was to bring my witnesses to Dickinson on June 3rd at 9 o'clock. Which was done.

On July 3rd at 9 in the morning, I took Mayer, Zengeisen, Hopkins and Plass to Dickinson. And they gave the lawyer the best testimony about me that could have been given. Now they had to appear before the court on July 4th at 10 in the morning. Now Mr. Stevens told us he had given Tilghman 40 shillings and we should also give Dickinson 40 shillings. Then our case would end well.

On the morning of July 4th on our way to the lawyer we met Mr. Stevens who said Mr. Tilghman had written him a note the night before saying that Dr. Moore wanted to present the case to 3 arbitrators. Whether we would be satisfied with that. And Dr. Moore wanted to get out of the case now. He was pretending that the land was the business of Morris, his cousin, and Hill, also his cousin. Upon which we replied, asking whether under English law Moore was allowed to tear down a fence when it was not his business. Upon which Mr. Stevens said he had talked about it with the lawyers and also wanted to talk with some good friends. The former had said we would do best to have the matter go to the arbitrators. Upon which we said we agreed to that but we thought that our case would be easy to solve through the law also since Dr. Moore had given in so much. After which we went to Dickinson. Now we gave him £2 telling him we did not need to contribute to the legal cost because this was for Mr. Stevens to pay by himself. But we gave him these so our case would be completed today and not adjourned again. To which he said about 4 times we should rely on it, it would not be adjourned. Then we went to the court at 10 o'clock, together with our witnesses and our interpreter. At 1 o'clock our case was brought up. And the lawyers, our two and the two for Dr. Moore babbled against each other for about ¾ of an hour. And the end of it was that Moore's lawyer had not finished because there had been three new actions brought against us. And so it had to be adjourned until the next court day, without us being bound for another £200.

Now Mr. Stevens told us that we were let off the £200 altogether because Dr. Moore had given up the case of rebellion he had brought against us altogether. And he had refused of his own accord to continue legal action [?]. As far as his brothers-in-law Hill and his son-in-law Morris were concern-ed he wanted to say [?] that the land was due them.

Fig. 46 Charles Wilson Peale (1741-1827), Robert Morris, approx. 1792. Oil on canvas. Independence National Historical Park, Philadelphia.

In the evening, our lawyer Tilghman had written a little note to Stevens saying that Moore's lawyer, Ross, had suggested to him that Moore wanted to settle with us out of court. Upon which Mr. Stevens suggested to us on July 5th that we should do so. To which we answered that our case against Moore was so well-known now that we would rather have it before the law. To which Mr. Stevens said that he feared if we refused that offer, Moore would put that in the newspaper just as we had done. So we decided to ask Moore if he would put it before the arbitrators, in which case 3, namely Mr. Allen, Mr. Stettman and Mr. [name omitted], the highest justices themselves as well as two lawyers and two men from New Jersey should be present. And this should be confirmed before the court by every-body, that these men's decision should be followed faithfully. Which was sent per memorandum to Mr.

Moore today at midday. But as he was not at home, we will have to wait for the answer.

If I think about it all and see the Divine Providence, I have to say, wonderful are His ways: firstly 1682, the deed of sale for the land in the Record Office, secondly 1689, the power of attorney NB ratification, thirdly 1702, Leonhart Arets' deed and which had not been sold yet in 1709, fourthly 1715, the power of attorney which was not signed by anybody, fifthly 1718, the second power of attorney which is very hard, but sixthly 1722, bonds by Leonhard Strepers and Reinhard Theißen and by Hill, seventhly 1724, that all of Jan Strepers' children had died that year, eighthly 1726, the deed made at Amsterdam and Logan's deed one year too early, ninethly, 1728, Hendrik van Acken's power of attorney which was not sent over, tenthly 1764 [in private code: that I was in such circumstances that I decided to travel and was not advised against it by my best friends, end of code] eleventhly that Hendrik van Acken was given all of the papers, both those received from Germany and those written here, by Reiner Theißen and that they had been kept by Paul Kripner, twelfthly that on October 4, 1764, we were offered by Paul Kripner to look these up and take with us what was useful. And we found better papers than we had and without which we could not have done anything. Yes, and when we had just taken those away with us, Abraham Theißen had come to him and wanted the papers back. He had been extremely upset to hear that we had them, thirteenthly [in code: that cousin Strepers did not hear], fourteenthly that Abraham Theißen's copy also fell into our hands. But to that there was no reply.

So cousin Strepers and I wrote a letter to Moore that he should declare within two days whether he wanted to put his words into practice, to hand it over to the arbitrators or not. After he had read the letter, he let us know that we would hear from him.

On July 14th, we dined with Kripner. And I asked him to let me have another look through the other papers which he allowed. For this I should come to him the following morning to have coffee with him, which I said I would do. On July 15th at 8 in he morning, I went to Kripner. When we had had our coffee and Kripner wanted to fetch the papers, Mr. Esquire Moore (sic!) came and said "Hadedu, Jan", and gave me his hand. I said "Hadedu, Mr. Moore" (and cousin Kripner was glad we were not looking through the papers yet). Moore now said that he was resolved firmly to take it to the arbitrators. And he wanted to hear when and in what way. So I told him that I wanted to talk it over with cousin Strepers and would let him know in 2 days' time when and in what way. But I gave him a firm promise to take it to the arbitrators.

So he asked whether we could not do this without lawyers if each takes 3 men with him. And then we could meet at his house or wherever we wanted. I told him we were planning to have 3 renowned men from the town and each could have a lawyer as well as a man from New Jersey. And the way we wanted it was that once the verdict had been given, it could not be overturned by any of the parties. He said he would be in favor of that but then we would have to wait until the next court day, and we would have to send him an eviction notice, and then the court would consider it.

But on the evening of August 20th, cousin Kripner said he feared that Moore was trying to take us in by a ruse, that he was maybe going to present letters from Logan and that the arbitrators would then grant him the lots. The same day we had an answering letter from Mr. Stevens in Amboy (whom we had written the above) that we should have no more dealings with Moore. For his father-in-law had advised him to settle the matter in court according to the law.

On July 24th in the afternoon, it happened here in Philadelphia that a public whore by the name of Giert Hill (who acts like a lady and often has 6 to 8 apprentices) caused a scandal. A minister's son came to her by the name of Penilicum[65] whose father had often come to this whore with the constables and harassed her. So she told the son if he wanted to have a whore, he should come to her. He could have one for 4 dollars. But he should be treated like his father that they would put him in the shell. Upon which this boy quickly took his horsewhip and gave her 4 or 5 neat lashes. At which the crowd became excited. They tore off her velvet coat and her silk coat, pelted her with dirt. When she then ran into a house, they broke the window. And those in the house pushed her out directly, and she lost her other clothes in tatters. Now she escaped from them into her house. When the crowd closed in around the house, her husband and 4 apprentices and 2 boys (1 NB the above schoolmaster's son-in-law) were there and fought back. But it did not take long before several were carried dead from the house. Then 4 constables arrived, but the stones came flying by the thousands, so that they had to plead to let them go again. Then they wrecked everything inside: chairs, tables, chests, a clock which must have been very nice, also a watch which had cost 30 shillings as well as two other timepieces. A bed as valuable as could be in this town they dragged through the street first, then to the river, then they ripped it open, threw it in the water and set it adrift. Next, the house was torn down. Now she had a second house next to her own, which was rented out. The tenants had to leave immediately, upon which they tore down that house as well. And all that was over by midnight.

On July 25th, Mr. Kurtz and I went there to have a look. There were still hundreds of people looking on as well as far more than 100 boys who broke the posts and planks. NB [in code: £60. The man who did not have larger than a little finger and when she had the smallpox and gave the ... one evening he cured her without pay.]

[Yet another one who kept precise records of how many came to see her and that the man kept locked up. AB, another said if she had all those she had had in her life she could build a wall around Tower Hill seven feet high. Even hearing the young boys talk, all their talk is about nothing else but how they lost their virginity [?] and how girls and how women are made NB Zengeisen. End of code] To sum it up, they are quite open about some things that cannot be told.

On July 19th there were 3 people NB and on July 20th, there were 9 people who had certainly drunk water from the pump and died on the spot, which was probably caused by the great heat. On August 11th at 2 in the morning, there was a rain here which lasted 2½ hours: I have never seen anything like it, and according to what people here say they also agree it was a deluge. One man alone, in Market Street, lost £3,000 worth of coffee, tea, molasses, rum, oil, wine etc. in his cellar.

On August 4th, we had gone on a pleasure ride on the river with Schmal, and from that time onward I had strong pains in my stomach. And on August 19th it happened that I had to empty my bowels, that I had to go 60 times in one day. And since the bloody flux is rife here, I was much afraid. On August 23rd it was extremely bad. Then I stopped it with milk bread fried in butter and nutmeg, after which it changed straight away.

On August 18th at 2 in the morning, a man in Race Street, an Irishman, murdered his wife. Then he dressed and laid her out properly, locked the door and made the coffin. When the neighbors looked through the keyhole they saw the woman laid out. This was reported to the authorities, upon which he was searched for by 4 constables who, however, could not find him. At 4 in the afternoon, he came with the coffin and laid his wife in it. Then the jury arrested him and pronounced a verdict and they declared him free. The same evening he put his wife on a cart and buried her. Everybody who had seen the woman, how she was bound by her arms that there were cuts 3 fingers deep, how she was beaten blue all over her body and how her neck was twisted, say publicly that she was murdered. But if the jury just says, "Not guilty", the man is free, (A jury consists of 6, also 12 or 24 men, and the latter is called Grand Jury).

On August 24th, when I heard that a ship with Germans[66] had arrived we went on board straight away. There was one from Remscheid on it by the name of [name ommitted] who came to me the same evening and told me then: [in code: That when he left Remscheid in May, they had had a big quarrel in Ronsdorf. Namely about the following matter:

Herr Wülffing had wanted the congregation to make a collection so he could continue to have his son study, which the congregation had refused to do. So Herr Wülffing had accused the A.G.H.R.[67] of sitting in a chair obtained by begging[68], and now they were quarreling wondrously. There may be something to this or not. It stays on my mind wherever I go, and I keep praying that the Lord in His mercy may preserve us from such temptation. End of code.]

On August 29th, Mr. Peter Hasenclever arrived here. And I complained about the poor progress of our affairs. He promised me straight away that before he left things should be put on a different footing. And he went to Mr. Allen on Chestnut Hill twice and discussed our affairs.

On the morning of September 4th, he sent for us to come and bring all our papers. When we arrived at his place, he had Supreme Justice Schmidt from New Jersey with him who was to look through them all. When I returned there 3 hours later at midday to tell him that Mr. Stevens had arrived, Mr. Hasenclever had young Allen, Dickinson and Supreme Justice Schmidt sitting with him and said Mr. Stevens should come to him immediately.

On September 5th at 10 in the morning, Mr. Hasenclever sent for us and said he had to leave that day but he had arranged our affairs in a way that they would proceed differently now because they had seen from our letter that everything was right. But he had also promised each of them £500 sterling if they brought the matter to a good end. At 5 in the afternoon, Mr. Stevens sent somebody to ask if we should take possession of the 50 acres of Liberty land. I had tell him that I would have requested that a long time ago. Upon which I went to see him myself. And they agreed which way it should be done. Then Mr. Schneck, a carpenter, was instructed to buy boards and timber that same evening and to contract for a wagoner to go at 3 tomorrow morning.

On September 6th at 8 in the morning [code: I hurt my "funny bone"] while unloading the boards from the cart, which was unusually painful.

[In code:] Now cousin Strepers did not want to have anything to do with all of this, stayed in bed, too, although I woke him four times, only arrived when the house was almost finished. [End of code]

On September 6th, I arose at 2 in the morning. But Mr. Schneck did not arrive until 4. Then we loaded the boards and beams onto a wagon with 4 horses and a cart with 3. Mr. Ross and I went ahead. I chose a spot where it should stand. At 7, the vehicles were also on the spot.

At ¼ past 7 Mr. Stevens also arrived. 25 minutes past 9 the house was finished, including the lock and everything on the door. At 11 o'clock Mr. Logan's driver came riding up and said we had built a house quickly there. We answered yes. Upon which he said he had to tell his master about this. We said he was free to do so. At half past 9, Mr. Stevens had left again.

At 4 in the afternoon, Mr. Logan sent Mr. Nübel to us who pretended to be not only overseer but also to have leased this bushland from a landlord who would arrive here from London within 10 to 12 days. Now he questioned us whether we wanted to leave the bushland straight away or not. We said, "No, but we are taking possession here in the name of Johann Strepers. And if your landlord thinks his right is better than ours, he can sue us." Upon which he, Nübel, said, "What do you think, if I burnt down your house?" Upon which we said, there was fire there and also inside the house. So he said we should take care that we did not burn too much young timber. Upon which we replied that that was our own business and we did not accept any reminder about it from him. So he said they had always paid great attention that not a single tree was felled. At which I said, we had heard that more than 10 ships had been built from the lower parts of the high trees as well as Logan's mill from this bushland (which Schneider had said 2 or 3 times in the presence of Nice, Kampmann and Ross). Then he said that was a lie. So I said how could that be a lie if quite close to this spot I could point out 15 to 20 stumps as well as the trees that were still lying there.

At half past 5, cousin Strepers and Ross went to town. And because a big thunderstorm came up, they stayed away and I was alone in the house all night. I did not hear or see anything.

On September 7th at 5 in the afternoon, the aforementioned Nübel came back again and said he ordered us again to leave the spot immediately.

Otherwise we would see what would come of it. To which we said we had told him before and it would not change. We were taking possession of Johann Strepers' 50 acres Liberty land.

At half past 5, Mr. Logan himself came riding up with his driver and asked if we had built a house here. We said, "Yes." He said, what would his brother[69] say when he came from England, who would arrive in 10 days, that we had built a house on his bushland without permission? To which we said, we were not carrying that bushland off. If his brother thought his right was better than ours it could be settled by the courts. To which he said, "Yes, I know well you think we should sue you. But you will see if we sue you. And my brother will not sue you either. And you had promised me, when you were at my house with Mr. Pollmann, to wait until my brother was here." To which we said, "Not so, Mr. Logan, but you told us you had word from your brother that he would be here in 6 weeks' time. And we were willing to wait those 6 weeks. But now we have waited 9 weeks." He said, "You would have done much better to have settled with Mr. Moore first. And if you had won that, then you would have won everything. But now you will be up against Moore, against us, against Mr. Allen, against Schippen, against the Chief Justice in Bucks County. And you must have a lot of money. And then you will be up against the Proprietor, too." We said as far as Mr. Moore was concerned, his deed had no connection with Mr. Logan's deed. And so the two could be started at the same time. And that if we were up against many now, we hoped we would be finished all the sooner. As far as the money was concerned, we did not need much here in the bushland. Yes, he said (Logan), Moore had two deeds, and if he is careful he will win with one. And you must not think you will be finished in 4 years. But I know well, you think there will still be London. But I know as much about the law in London as here. But I say you must have a lot of money. Mr. Hasenclever also presented money to the King's Counsel to continue your case. He told me so himself. And so you need not rely on that. And I have also heard that you promised Stevens a share of the land. But you did well to put it in the paper." We said, "We did not promise Stevens any land. And we only put our lands in the paper because there was talk everywhere that we were claiming all of Frankfurt, half of Germantown and who knows how much in New Jersey and just about half the town." Then Mr. Logan called Nübel to ask us again in his presence and in the presence of his driver and Nübel's brother-in-law, whether we would leave the bushland or not. But our answer remained as before that we maintained possession. Then Mr. Moore shook our hands and rode away with his driver. But when he had ridden a little way, he came back to us and asked us our names and whether we were both co-heirs, or whether we were trustees and whether we had a power of attorney from all of the other co-heirs. We told him our names, also that we were co-heirs and had the power of attorney from all of the other co-heirs. Upon which he said we should imagine he had come with one hundred men. But he firmly believed that cousin Strepers' father had signed. Upon which he rode off.

At half past 6, cousin Strepers left for Philadelphia. At 7 o'clock, Mr. Stevens came who had spoken to Logan on the way and rode back to Bucks County. Mr. Ross and I stayed in the house that night until September 8th at 11 in the morning, because after that time we had possession, and also went back to Philadelphia.

On September 8th, at 7 in the morning Mr. Kurtz brought a letter from my wife which she had written on May 6th to the new house in the bushland. To my great joy, I read that they were all still in good health. On September 10th, on my way to the Liberty house and bushland to see if everything was still in order I caught the young squirrel. On September 13th it died.

On September 10th, I went there[70] to see if everything was still in order. Then Peter Kampmann told me that on Sunday just about all of Germantown had been there. But they had not done anything to the house. On September 12th, I went there again. I found 11 people from Germantown in the bushland who wanted to collect wood and whom I chased out.

On September 16th, the crowd gave Franklin's portrait in a wig, as he always goes, a lashing by the turnpike and then burnt it near the old coffee house[71]. He is said to be the author of the Stamp Act[72].

On September 18th, we began to have our house in Philadelphia renovated in order to move in ourselves.

On September 18th, we had our house stripped and improved on the outside and also made ready on the inside. On September 25th, we moved into our own house and three of us live there now.

As we had not heard from Mr. Stevens for such a long time, I went to New York to see Mr. Hasenclever on October 9th to find out if he could do anything so we could go back to Germany.

I traveled to New York on October 10th. On October 12th, I arrived in New York where I heard that Mr. Hasenclever was planning to take a journey the following morning. I went to see him between 6 and 7 o'clock and had to have breakfast with him right away. And he decided at once to stay there another day. He wanted to talk to Mr. Dickinson on our behalf that day. So I went back to him on October 14th to hear what Mr. Dickinson had said. But he said he had not spoken to him. He said we had to decide to stay this winter at all cost because this was what he had agreed with Mr. Schmit. And we should see to it that now our case was continued quickly. Upon which I received a draft for £30 sterling in New York money from him and took my leave. Now he pretended he was going to Ringwood[73], but I heard from Mr. Jan Stevens that he had gone with Lord Sterle to Philadelphia. But I have not met him here in Philadelphia.

On October 14th, I started out for Flatbush. On October 15th, Mr. Rübel went hunting with me. He hit 9 snipe with one shot, and I 1 and the other time 2 with one shot. A miller whose house we stayed at told me that once he had shot 30 of the biggest snipe from inside the mill, in one shot, and they are half as big as the wood snipe in Germany whose beak is ¼ Cologne ell[74] long. Indeed, his servants often told him if he did not stop shooting snipe, duck and geese, they would feed them to the pigs. And his cousin had once hit 14 of the biggest black wild duck with one shot and his

neighbor once more than 100 wild pigeons with one shot and once 144 small snipe with one shot. NB there are 10 kinds of snipe here. And another neighbor once had taken 2 loaded rifles with him to the Know[75] and saw wild geese sitting there and he shot 8 sitting. And then with the other rifle 5. So there were 13 with two shots. Well, I must say I have never seen such a thing. Nobody bothers to fire a shot at 2 or 3 snipe.

When I left New York for Amboy on October 17th, it was just low tide, so the duck came flying down from above and close to our ship. I looked at my watch after they had flown about 30 minutes and they still continued for another 15 minutes solidly like a thick cloud, thousands and thousands of them.

Now Mr. Rübel wanted to go with me on October 16th in the morning to a spot where there are duck and geese in great numbers. But it rained all morning.

At the beginning of October, the geese come and stay all winter. But in the last days of October the snipe leave. Now many people here are suddenly dying of a stroke.

On October 24th, Logan from London had arrived here and sent his driver on October 27th to tell us that we should Expect to have to pay a lot of money, that his master was here now (but thanks be to God we are not afraid yet).

On October 29th, in the evening Mr. Stevens came back here. On October 30th, I went to see him and asked (as it the court had been in session again since the day before) whether nothing was progressing in our case. He answered that he wanted to go to Dickinson immediately and take out 6 to 7 warrants and send them to Bucks County and that our case should be continued quickly. He would tell us more toward evening.

That day at midday, a man from Bucks County by the name of Jan Jörg Kesser came. He wanted to buy about 200 acres of land and he would come back for new tidings in 4 weeks.

On October 29th, it was Majors Court. We urged our lawyers to obtain a verdict, also told them that

The FLYING MACHINE.

Fig. 47 The Flying Machine, Advertisement in the Pennsylvania Journal, April 16, 1767. Library Company.

if we did not get one we would travel home then and use other means. But Moore, Hill, two of them and a Morris through their lawyers managed to have us bound again for the Supreme Court. Each for [amount omitted].

Now the protests over the Stamp Act started, which was to begin on November 2nd.

On November 1st, we received 4 eviction notices from lawyer Tilghman, one to Nice, one to Helbart, one to Fucks and one to Mätters. They all had to be delivered that same day. So cousin Strepers rode to Bucks County with young Kurtz and I to Chestnut Hill. These eviction notices cost £7 sterling in lawyer fees alone and had to be delivered by 12 o'clock. Which was done, the last at 5 minutes to twelve.

On November 4th, Mr. Stevens came and told us he wanted to go to Burlington to see his father-in-law. So I asked him if it would not be good if we had the 50 acres of Liberty land surveyed and sold the mature wood. It seemed right to him and he wanted to go to the surveyor straight away.

On November 5th at 9 in the morning, Mr. Stevens called and said to get dressed straight away. He and the surveyor would ride on ahead. While we were surveying, Mr. Logan also came riding up. Now he wanted to talk to us. But since we did not have anyone with us who could speak both English and German, it was in vain. So he rode off himself and brought a woman and told us through her that his brother from London was here now. When he was not there, he looked after his affairs. But as he was here now, we should go to the latter and speak to him if we claimed any of that bushland. Upon which I told the woman to tell Mr. Logan that his brother could come to us just as well as we could go to him. And the bushland was ours. Upon which he, Logan, said he did not mean it that way and if we could come to an understanding and live in friendship, it would be better than going before the law. Upon which we promised we would come and see his brother.

On November 6th at 2 in the afternoon, we went with young Kurtz to the two Logans. There we were shown into a room and young Samuel Logan came in to us. Then we told him that his brother had said to us that it was not his business and that we would do best to talk to him. Upon which he said yes, that it had been bought by his late father and allotted to him. And that he would assert his right as well as he could, even if it should go to London. Upon which we said if that was the way he was talking, we did not have to say much here but he could do his best and so would we. Upon which cousin Strepers stood up at once and wanted to leave. So he quickly asked how we wanted it. So we said if he wanted to buy the 50 acres from us, he could take a man and so would we to have them valued. And he should have them at 1/3 less than their estimated value. Now he said if we should let it go to the arbitrators. We said, "No." If it should come before the arbitrators, he could seek his right and so would we. Upon which I asked him, what he would base his case on. He said on his deed. I asked if he did not know that his deed had been made 9 months before the agreement and what he thought of that. Upon which he was quite taken aback with surprise. So he asked if we had his deed. So we said yes, and where had we gotten it from, from Brockden's office. He asked whether the deed referred to the agreement. I said, "Yes." Upon which he said we would have done better to have finished the case against Moore first, then his case would also be finished because the deeds were quite the same. At which we told him of Moore's bond. And that we had heard that when Pennington had built his house, Mr. Logan was said to have given a deed to Moore as well. Upon which he said, "No." And he went and called his brother Wilhelm and asked him if Moore had received a deed from him about 4 or 5 years ago. And he also said, "No." But he said it very coldly and slowly. And William Logan then tried to blacken Mr. Stevens' name to us as that of a liar. Now William Logan asked cousin Strepers what his father's name had been. To which cousin H.P. Strepers said, "Peter". And he thought that he had signed, but that was wrong. He had already been 23 years old at the time. And as far as Hendrik was concerned, who had signed the deed, as far as we knew he had not been in Holland at that time. And that maybe his mother had signed for him. And that it says in the deed of sale, cousin Strepers said (which is written between the lines here for lack of space) could not stand up before the law here.

Yes, he said, he had 5 deeds. Then I said that none of them were any good. Upon which he said, "I can understand." Otherwise, they were quite friendly.

On November 7th, I went to the Liberty land to see if we should shift the house somewhere else. But since I found that it just stood on our land I left everything standing.

In the evening when I came home, cousin Strepers told me that Jan Feer's son had told him that Fucks wanted to come to us first. But all the others had agreed among themselves that they would rather go somewhere else than buy from us.

On November 12th, Mr. Stevens and I rode to Abraham Theißen to settle with him the matter of the 18½ acres he still has on Chestnut Hill, to show all the better that the trustees had not had any power of their own. He took us in in the friendliest possible way and said that he would call on us very soon to settle everything.

On November 18th, Mr. Stevens came to us and said he had talked to Sam Logan in the coffee house. And the latter had told him that cousin Strepers and I had promised him not to start anything with him before we had finished with Mr. Moore. Whether that was true. We said, no, rather we had promised him that, after we had consulted our lawyers, we would let him know first before we started something else. Upon which he, William Logan, asked whether we had engaged a lawyer against him. We said, "No." So we did not have to engage any against him. Now Mr. Stevens said we should call on him the following day at 10 in the morning not only to confront him with the above but also to tell him if he did not want to give the matter to the lawyers now, everybody was free to do what they could.

On November 19th, I went with Ross to see Logan. There I confronted him with what has been said above. Upon which he answered that the first was untrue, that he should have said such a thing to Stevens. And he only wished that Stevens would leave him alone in the coffee house, and in the latter matter we should give ourselves two days' time because he wanted to ask two good friends about it and then wanted to give us an answer.

The same day, cousin Kripner came to see us and said that that day a reputable man had announced his visit to him for this afternoon. And he was sure that he came to find out about our right.

On November 20th in the evening, we went to cousin Kripner. And he told us how the man had asked him about the grounds for our case and how he (Kripner) had also told him everything from the beginning in detail, both that the van Ackens did not have any legal right and that Henrich Strepers had not signed himself. And the man himself had said that the mother had signed for her son. Now Kripner said that this man was a very good friend of Moore's and Logan's but that he should also like to see that we obtained our right (I can only think that he is a Quaker preacher). Now the man had said that, after having been told the grounds of the matter like that, he had much better knowledge of the case than merely from what Moore and Logan told him. And we had enough justification to go before the law.

On November 23rd, I went again with Ross to Logan to hear an answer. Then he said that if we wanted to give it to the arbitrators with Moore and him at the same time, they wanted to take a lawyer each and everybody could do so. Upon which I answered that I agreed with him now to put it before the law with two lawyers. But as far as Moore was concerned, I had to consult our lawyers first. Upon which he said, the King's Counsel is your lawyer, is he not? I said, "Yes." So I should give him an answer in 2 days. I said we had another lawyer in New Jersey and that it would take 8 to 10 days. Now he said he wanted to talk again with Moore.

On December 3rd at 3 in the afternoon, the wife of Mr. Hoffmann who used to call himself Hadernach drowned.

On December 6th, I went with Ross to Logan and said that since we had heard in the meantime that Mr. Moore had told Pennington that he wanted it to go before the law, our lawyers had decided that we should not go with him to the arbitrators either.

So I asked him if he wanted to have it before the arbitrators, and if he did not, whether he would assure us that he would send us an eviction notice and that it would go before the court as soon as the law opened. If he did not do so, we would go and cut down the trees in the Liberty bush. Upon which he said he would talk to Moore and let us know the following morning.

On December 7th, Mr. Sam Logan called and said he had talked to Mr. Moore and that the latter wanted to bring it before the arbitrators together with him and that Moore should have said that to Pennington was strange. Upon which we said that our lawyers had advised us totally against doing anything with Moore. But we would present it to them again and give him an answer on Monday.

December 9th I wrote home.

On December 9th, I went with Ross to Mr. Stevens and we told him the above. And he said he thought the best would be to stop dealing with Moore altogether. What did I think? I said we also thought that, once we had finished with Logan, Moore's case would collapse by itself. He said that was so, and we should tell Logan only this: we were asking him for the last time if he alone wanted to bring it before the law and the arbitrators, if not, we would go to the bushland the following day with 20 wood cutters and would cut down all of the trees. When the above was told to Logan, he said that without Moore he would not let it go before the arbitrators, and if we wanted to go there with twenty men tomorrow, they would stop us with 40 men.

I went back to Stevens and told him that. Upon which he said that when he had talked to the lawyers, he would let us know. In the afternoon Stevens came and told us that when he had just been with the King's Counsel, both Logans had also arrived. So he had gone straight to Dickinson. And when he had arrived there, the latter had also told him that the two Logans had come and complained that we wanted to cut down the trees. He had said we had not been to see him yet. But he advised us to let it go before the arbitrators with Logan alone and not with Moore at the same time. From there he went to Tilghman, who gave the same advice as Dickinson.

From there he had gone back to the King's Counsel to hear what the Logans had done there. The latter told him they had asked him for advice. But he had said he neither could nor would advise them. Upon which they had said he was the Proprietor's Counsel. He had to advise them. To which he had replied that if the Proprietor's men came for advice, he would give it. But all three had thought it would be best not to cut down the trees the following day and just put up a fence all around instead.

On December 10th at 7 in the morning, I went toward the Liberty land. But I could not get more than one wood cutter who split rails all day. Now Logan had listened from afar if we were cutting down trees. But he did not come to us. On December 11th, we had 4 men to work on the fence. That morning cousin Strepers went with us and from there to Wilhelm Strepers.

On December 12th, Mr. Stevens called and said he had spoken to Pennington for a long time on the previous day. And the latter had asked him to talk to us and ask whether we would give him a deed. Then he would be willing to pay us £18 sterling a year from [omitted] on. And Stevens thought that would be good to break the ice. And he thought there would be many following that example. Now I told Stevens, I knew that Pennington wanted and had to sell his house now but could not. He would need a deed from us first[76]. And, therefore, he would still pay a bit more. And if he wanted to cede the lot behind ours and then pay £20 sterling a year, also for the previous years, we would agree. Which Mr. Stevens wanted to tell him.

On December 13th, Mr. Samuel Logan came to the 50 acres Liberty land with Mr. Naglee. By then we had fenced in one acre around the house, and had also built a fence around half the land. I walked toward them. Then Logan asked if we were cutting down the trees. I said yes, we were cutting down as much as we needed for the fence around our property. So he ordered the laborers to stop working. Upon which I ordered them to continue and that I would guarantee everything, or they

should ask Mr. Logan if he wanted to pay them. If they did not work, I was going to have other people come. All of which Naglee translated for him. Then they rode around the house and left.

On December 14th at 10 in the morning, when I arrived on the Liberty land, Samuel Logan, with Christian Lehman, Naglee as well as his driver and his servants, 14 in number, had not only torn down all of the fences but also demolished the house and loaded it on a wagon. Upon which I asked him at once why they had demolished our house and torn down our fence. To which Logan said the bushland was his. To which I said, "Not so, but it is ours and we have possession of it." And so I had to put the fence up again. And if Mr. Logan wanted anything from us, he could find us before the law. Upon which I started to put the fence up again. And as soon as I had put it up, Mr. Logan tore it down again. So Lehman said to me that this would not help us before the law and that I should leave everything lying until it came before the law (now I told Kampmann he should ride to Stevens as fast as he could). I told Christian Lehman I would get an answer from our lawyers. And if they thought it was good to put the fence up again, I would do so at once. Because I would not be pushed out of possession. To which Logan asked why we did not settle things with Moore. I answered him that Mr. Logan was well aware that there was no connection between Mr. Moore's case and his.

Now Lehman said we could well have peace and I should just leave everything lying until it came before the court and that would be the best for us. I said that I would do whatever my lawyers said. Logan said he was not angry with us but we did not have good advisors. If he had known earlier, he would have come to an agreement with us. To which I said I had no animosity toward Mr. Logan either. And what I wished him should also happen to me. And I could rightly say friend to the man and adversary in the matter. But his brother, and Moore, too, we had told them through Levis Weiss 1¼ years ago, before we had even spoken about the matter to anybody else. But we had had a dubious answer and indirectly been offered enough money to pay for our journey back to Germany. Logan said he did not know anything about

Fig. 48 James Smither (1741- after 1800), John Dickinson. Copperplate engraving, 1797. Library Company, Inv. No. P.9230.

that. Now Lehman said again I should promise I would leave everything lying, which he said about 10 times. But I answered him as before. Now Logan said if I rebuilt it, he would tear it down again. Upon which he gave order to the wagoners they should cart the fence away. And then they all left. Now I quickly put the fence back up that had stood around the house and made a fire.

At 2 o'clock Logan sent a cart with 3 men. They said they had orders from Logan to pull down the fence and cart it off. Upon which I went at them and dared them to have the courage to pull the fence down. So they said, then Logan would be back soon with others. I said they should tell Logan to come, it would take only half an hour for me to

have men there too. But they drove away and nobody returned. At 3 o'clock Mr. Stevens came and said we should just keep possession, that we should not stay away for 24 hours and should keep the fire burning.

In the evening I went to Stevens. Then he said that he had talked to our lawyers. Dickinson had advised us that it would be best for us to go home and submit a petition to the King, which was the best advice. And we should leave everything the way it was. He told the King's Counsel what Dickinson had said, The latter had jumped up and stamped on the floor with his foot and said we should not go home now. As soon as the court was in session again, he would get the Bucks County case through quickly. And, therefore, he had also told Peters to notify Logan to prepare for the trial. We would have to start proceedings against the Proprietor first. But he wanted to keep that short. And when that had been done, the Proprietor would be on our side and against Logan. Because the latter wanted a proper guideline. Now Mr. Stevens said people had to be hired, some 20 for Monday morning quite early, so we could put a log cabin there. I said I wanted to go there tomorrow and see how many people we could get and let him know.

On December 15th, I rode to the Liberty land. I found 16 men who promised to come. I told Stevens that, and he was quite pleased. [In code:] Now Stevens said cousin Strepers had to come as well. But he started a great fuss when I told him he had to come. He said he would not come. When the first possession had not been good, he should have known. Those who wanted to go could go. Indeed, from what I know about him now, I need great patience. That much I know I cannot have him go anywhere now. [End of code]

On December 16th, very early, I went to the Liberty land again. I found 12 laborers there, and they started cutting trees straight away until 10 o'clock when Mr. Stevens came up. He asked me if he should suggest to Logan to promise us that, in case the Bucks County trial went in our favor, we should have the 50 acres of Liberty land as well. If it did not, we would not dispute his right to the 50 acres of Liberty land, either. I said that since the law had been stopped now, it seemed best to me because Bucks County must go to court first. Now he said to stop everything here. He was going to see that he could speak to Logan. We had really already put the 4 heaviest logs up and had all the timber for the house ready.

On December 21st, Mr. Stevens told me to come to the English Coffee House[77] that evening. Then he wanted to submit Logan to some good questioning. And if he denied that he had said he would delay us for 3 years and his brother for 7 years through litigation, I would be there to hear. But as soon as Stevens entered, Logan left and was not seen any more all evening.

On December 31st it began to turn rather cold. Otherwise we had fairly warm weather, but on January 1, 1766, it was very cold until the 6th of the same month when the Delaware was frozen over.

On January 6th Mr. van Laschet called and told me that Naglee had said the King's Counsel had supposedly advised Logan to cart the house and the fence away. Have to find out about that.

On January 7th at 4 in the afternoon, our best friend here, Ernst Kurtz, passed away, and he was buried on the 9th. Upon which occasion, as he was the first to die from the German society, the entire society accompanied the corpse with two long poles hung with black ribbons, one carried at the beginning and one at the end of the funeral cortège. And that community numbered about 70 to 80 people. Upon which occasion Mr. Möllenberg had his text from Deuteronomy, Chapter 4, Verse 8-11[78]. But very simple. Oh, how I wish I was in Ronsdorf today, but patience, patience.

Here I will put some memories of how people up in Canistocken[79] bake their bread, of their household implements, as the doctor and Christian Lehman [?] have told us. NB [in code: Breyel earthenware hawkers[80]], down and low down. yes, yes, yes, etc. So the bread is baked like this: Several take flour one hour before a meal and mix it. And then it is pressed flat between both hands and then buried in the hot cinders. When the meal is done, the bread is always done as well.

Others who want to be somewhat cleaner use a board and the dough is slapped on to it. And then they spit in one hand and the spread the spittle over it. Then the dough is set against the fire. And when the meal is done, the bread has to be done as well.

For sleeping they do not have beds. Just four poles are rammed into the ground to look like this _/. Between these 4 people lie, 2 with their feet where the other two have their heads. And a carpet is spread over all of them. That is a good bed for travelling. There is no straw for a bed, nor do they have anything underneath them. Their children and the maids and servants always go to sleep in the corn. Whether it rains or not.

There is a fellow here who was captured by the savages more than 8 years ago and was returned in January 1765. So he ran around with the savages for 7 years. Now he is telling a lot about his adventures, among other things the savages had known that a bear had had cubs. So they had given him the choice between either chasing the bear from his cave or being killed by them. After long thought, since he had seen so often how terribly they treated people, he resolved to go into the cave, which was very narrow at the entrance. But a bit further in it was wide enough for him to walk through with his back bent. Now he had seen the bear with his two eyes shining like torches and he went around the bear as far away from him as he could. When he had gotten behind it, the bear slunk out of the cave without the slightest noise. Then the savages had killed it in front of the hole. Then he had to go back inside and bring the cubs out as well. And with that, it was alright.

On January 15th, Mr. Stevens called and said he had talked to lawyer Ogden in New Jersey. And if we wanted to leave a share to him. Because he had given him advice now and accepted it for our lawyer because he was such a clever man. And he would also come here during the Supreme Court. Upon which we said we would not cede any more shares. But our entire half we would sell for a fair price so we would be out of all this trouble all at once. Upon which he asked if we would leave it for the same price as his half. We said we would have to have a bit more for it. For, as he was well

Fig. 49   The London Coffee House, Southwest Corner of Front and High (Market) Streets. Photography, 1854.
Free Library of Philadelphia, Inv. No. O.P.E.P. #30.

aware, he had to bear the legal cost for his half all alone, so the other had to fetch more. He said we should think about it and he would give cousin Strepers £100 sterling so he would stay another year.

On January 26, 1766, the Delaware was free of ice again, and the weather was very pleasant and mild until February 13th.

On January 31st, Mr. Stevens called and said that since the Assembly was still sitting, we should get

naturalized a second time here. Because the naturalization in Burlington would be disputed here as invalid. Upon which he ran around for us everywhere and said we should come to him at 9 o'clock the following morning.

On February 1st at 5 o'clock, we went to Mr. Stevens. He had just gone to Mr. Allen. Well, we met in the street. So he went with us to Chief Judge Colman, who referred us to Mr. Schippen. He in turn referred us to Mr. Willing. When the latter had accepted the petition to submit it to the Assembly, we returned to Schippen who promised to go to Mr. Colman straight away. Which he did. And he brought his book with him in which all the names of all the people who had been naturalized were written down, which he treated like his Gospel that had to be kissed. Now he read us the oath in English and we had to repeat everything after him. And that oath took about ¼ of an hour. About which I had to laugh to myself because I could not repeat all the words properly, let alone understand them. So I was just watching out for the last word. And so everything went well. In the meantime we had to hold on to the book and to kiss it about three times. When that was done, we had to write our names into the book ourselves, and after we had pointed to our names with our fingers and said this is our own handwriting, Messrs. Coleman and Schippen attested it. The whole thing cost us 5 dollars. Then this act was over.

Now we have to go before the Assembly on February 3rd.

On February 4th, Mr. Weiss came to us and told us Mr. Hoffman sent his regards and asked us if we wanted to come to see him the following evening at a certain inn where he was going to have a separate room for us. We said we would.

On the evening of February 5th, Mr. Weiss came to fetch us and took us there. After we had been there a little while, Mr. Hoffmann arrived as well. And then he said that he was [in code: Hadernach], and he gave us a lovely treat and we had to promise to come and see him often. [in code:] that treat cost him £1 and two shillings.[End of code]

On February 13th cousin Strepers went hunting on Chestnut Hill and returned on February 21st.

On February 16th I went to see Mr. Stevens at 9 in the morning because he had returned from Brunswick the previous evening to hear what had happened with lawyer Ogden (because Stevens had called on him only for the sake of inducing him to buy the other half of our land). Then I heard from Mr. Stevens that Mr. Hasenclever intended to travel to London this coming March.

Now cousin Strepers had gone to Chestnut Hill on February 13th and had not yet returned. And I also wanted to talk to Mr. Hasenclever in person before he left. So I made up my mind at once and Mr. Hasenclever took the state boat[81] at noon.

When I arrived at Mr. Hasenclever he said yes, that had been his plans. But with the last packet boat he had received letters instructing him to stay another 4 months. Also he was supposed to travel to Canada first, and he might have to postpone his journey until late in the year[82].

Then I told him everything about our case and how it stood now and that we wished very much that he could be present in person at the next session of the Supreme Court on April 10th. Which he promised to do if it was at all possible. Now I heard the same thing from Mr. Hasenclever that Stevens had also told me, that Ogden was very ill. Only Hasenclever said, "If Stevens was a man with more influence and could push the matter through more forcefully, I would advise you not to sell. And since I have so much trouble[83] I cannot, or I would buy the rest from you." Now I told him that we were often short of money and if we approached Stevens for money, it was difficult to get anything from him, although he had ordered us recently to have the house made habitable. And when he came in a fortnight, he would pay for everything. And that we had paid as long as we had money, also that we had even borrowed money already, which we had then used for the £50 sterling. And when we approached him for money again, we received £6 twice. And that we had also urged him to sell several pieces that we did not need but could not see that he was doing anything in that respect. And that we could not help thinking that they were trying to make us tire of the whole thing because we had run out of money. And that we would give away the rest cheaply because we were tired of it all. To this Mr. Hasenclever said we should approach him one more time for money, and if he did not give us anything, then to write to him and he would send us letters of exchange. Upon which I took leave. And he asked me to give his regards to Mr. Allen and his family, and also if I should meet the King's Counsel, to give him his regards.

On February 16th I traveled to New York with W. Müller and N. Schreiner. At 7 in the evening, we arrived at Bordentown, a distance of 30 miles, having left Philadelphia at midday.

On February 17th at 10 in the morning, we sat down on the wagon, and it was very cold. At 7 we had reached Amboy, 40 miles distant. There the captain told us he was ready to sail at 8 the following morning. But just as he had held me up the previous time, so he held us up again, so that in the evening Schreiner almost came to blows with him. Upon which he promised to sail at midnight, but still it took until 5 in the morning before we actually left. And at 8 o'clock we arrived in New York.

Now we went straight away to see Mr. Stevens, the lawyer, whom I knew well and laid charge against the captain as well as the innkeeper (because he owns both the inn and the ferry). And Stevens promised to question both of them, which he did. And later we heard from others how the captain had talked about me as the one with the black wig, and wanted to know if I was strong. And on our return journey we found it much better, both the innkeeper's and the captain's behavior. Otherwise we had a rather pleasant journey. On February 26th, I returned from New York.

On February 26th I was back here in Philadelphia.

On February 27th I met Mr. Allen, who treated me very kindly, adding that I did not need to tell him anything at home because at home he did not listen. But come court day, he would take off his wig and open his eyes. Which I was happy to hear, since this is the only man who can help to bring our case to an end. Now the King's Counsel gave us a firm promise through Mr. Stevens that he would help to bring the Bucks County case to an end at the first court session, which will be on September 24th.

On March 9th there was a strong wind here, and on that day at the Capes[84] one ship from London and two from the West Indies went down. From the London ship only the first mate and one fine gentleman drowned.

On March 11, 1766, Mr. Stevens sent us a little note to come to his house immediately. Which we did. There was a gentlemen from Amboy by the name of Parcker there who said he wanted to buy our remaining half if we left it to him on the same conditions as Stevens and Hasenclever had theirs. Upon which we said that would not happen. [three quarters of line crossed out] then we would leave it. Upon which he said he would not do that. But we should bring somebody with us in the afternoon who could translate from English well. Then we wanted to see if we could reach an agreement.

In the afternoon we took Niclas Schreiner along (who is a good and trustworthy man). And we came very close since [three quarters of line crossed out] then from April 1st onward they should pay cousin Strepers (who declared his agreement to stay his until the matter was brought to an end) £100 sterling a year toward his cost of living without deducting this amount from the total later. They offered [one and three quarters of line crossed out], but if everything was won the £100 sterling should be deducted. And the £100 sterling should not be paid until the first trial had been held. Upon which we parted to give everybody time to consider.

On March 12th everybody stayed at home. In the evening Mr. Stevens came and copied several things from the Germantown records. I asked how Mr. Parker had decided. He said no different than what he had already said. And I said we would not decide differently than what we had said.

When cousin Strepers came home, I told him about this and asked if he wanted to go to see them the following morning to hear what they had decided, all the more because we can see and also are told by everybody what a big thing we will have. And in that way we can see that poison can be driven out by poison. Because they pretend that if it should come to trial they would bring 3 lawyers from New York in. And since one lawyer asks 100 pistols, one can easily imagine what will have to be done.

On March 13th, Vetter Strepers called on them. And since they remained so hard against him, he wanted to put them to a test and said if they wanted to pay £100 sterling now and also put £100 sterling into the pool they could deduct £100 sterling from the first payment and £100 sterling from the last. And so he wanted to live at our expense until the first trial. But Parker still said he did not want to do that.

When cousin Strepers told me this, I did not like it. So I went there with Mr. Schreiner and told Mr. Stevens that since I had heard from cousin Strepers, I could see that nothing would come of our agreement and that he, Mr. Stevens, would not hold it against us if we now concluded a purchase with somebody else. Upon which Mr. Stevens asked if cousin Strepers had not told me about his offer and did I accept it. I asked what cousin Strepers had said. So he said that if Mr. Parker paid £100 sterling now and another £100 sterling into the pool, we wanted to pay his expenses and that the first £100 sterling should be deducted from the first and the second from the last payment.

Upon which I said I had understood from cousin Strepers that they should give £100 sterling as a present now and the second £100 sterling which should go into the pool should be deducted from the first or the second payment. To which they both said that in that case they had misunderstood. To which I told them, regardless of whether we discussed the matter for a long or a short time, it would be no good, if they did not give us £100 as a present now and if cousin Strepers could not draw his £100 next New Year's Day, nothing would come of our agreement. Upon which they said, could we both come to them the following morning [quarter of a line crossed out] so we would see if we could conclude the agreement. Upon which Mr. Schreiner said that he had noticed from what they had said that they would not let it go. When I returned home, I told cousin Strepers the above. And that, if he was asked, he should stick to what I had said.

On March 14th, when we came to them they asked cousin Strepers straight away how he had meant it the previous day. So he told them the way we had agreed. Mr. Schreiner added that Mr. Strepers had been extremely surprised to hear how they had understood him. But, said Schreiners, they should decide quickly now. Because we had set down that the £100 had to be in sterling and that cousin Strepers had

to receive his £100 every year. Payments should start with September 25th and were to be made quarterly. Upon which they said they agreed and that we should sign the agreement the following morning.

On March 15th at 10 in the morning, after we had read out the agreements[85] and examined them as far as we had understood them, they were signed by the two parties and by Stevens and Schreiners as witnesses. And then we each wished each other luck. When this was over Stevens and Parker asked us if the matter could not be settled at all by the court, whether they could then bring it before the arbitrators. To which I replied we did not want to have it before the arbitrators at all because we reserved an appeal at any time. And if it should go against us, we would lodge our appeal in London straight away.

On March 16th two drowned men were found here near the town. On March 18th I received a letter from home from that London ship and on the 19th another from home through Mr. Peter Hasenclever which had gone via Carolina.

On March 22nd we went across the Schuylkill River and looked at the house of Blackbeard the pirate, in which house a lot of money is supposed to be buried, according to what the tenant said. And it is commonly said that the house is haunted. It is a beautiful house and the only one around here with a tiled roof. Both the bricks and the tiles are supposed to have been brought here from London. He was caught in 1718 and hanged.

Today, March 22nd, the meat of one of the oxen (of which there were two) which were lead through town on Wednesday, decorated with silk ribbons and guilded roses, in a procession with music was sold for 1 shilling a pound. It weighed 1,445 pounds, the other is supposed to have been even heavier. Today we bought 2 dozen plucked wild pigeons for a shilling, yesterday a farmer caught 84 dozen pigeons in one net, indeed they are so common at present that several wagons with four horses had loaded nothing but pigeons. Four years ago, they are said to have been so common here that not only the price for the meat (which was a shilling a pound then) went down to 4 pence but they also darkened the air with their flight, indeed they were sold for two coppers and a great many of them were spoiled.

On March 23rd and 24th we were invited by cousin Kripner. We also went with him to the meeting which was their Easter. That was 8 days before we celebrate Easter. The sects which exist here, as far as I know, without counting those I do not yet know are: Reformed, Lutherans, Catholics, Quakers, Presbyterians, the Count's people[86], Seven Days' People[87], Pietists, Beard People[88], Manists[89], Separatists, Bethlehemites[90] and Ephrata Cloister People[91], Jews, heathens, Atheists, all have total freedom and proclaim themselves openly.

On April 5, 1766, at the Capes 140 miles from Philadelphia a ship coming from London went down with 27 people on board with captain and mate. Nobody escaped but 4 single sailors. And a gentleman was on it who had received a large inheritance in London. And he also drowned with his wife and three children.

[1] Here begins the second part of the journal which reports only on the recovery of the 5,000 acres bought by Jan Strepers from William Penn in 1682.

[2] Possibly: Hermann von Laschet [Krefelder Archiv, NF 2, p. 64]. Only mention of the family name in the Krefeld fire cadastre of 1754.

[3] Philadelphia Barracks. Watson's Annals of Philadelphia and Pennsylvania, 1857, Chapter 57, The British Barracks, p. 7: These were built in the Northern Liberties soon after the defeat of Braddock's army... In the year 1764, the barracks were made a scene of great interest to all the citizens – there the Indians, who fled from the threats of the murderous Paxtang boys, sought their refuge under the protection of the Highlanders; while the approach of the latter was expected, the citizens ran there with their arms to defend them and to throw up intrenchments. Captain Loxley of the city artillery was in full army with his band. In time those Indians became afflicted with the smallpox, and turned their quarters into a very hospital, from which they buried upwards of fifty of their companions.

[4] The Mormons believe that the Indians are descendants of a Jewish tribe that emigrated during Old Testament times.

[5] Sons of Wilhelm Strepers.

[6] Springfied, Springfield Township, Montgomery Co.

[7] The acre was located between Vine and Race and Fourth and Fifth Streets.

[8] Franz Sigismund Count of Haslang auf Hohenkammer and Tistling, b. in Munich 1740, d. in Munich 1803; Minister Plenipotentiary of Palatine Bavaria to the Royal British Court at London [Chur-Pfälzischer Hoff- und Staats-Calender (Mannheim, 1762, 46 and 1766, 51); Hamberger/Meusel: Das gelehrte Teutschland (Lemgo, 17975), 3, 113; op.cit., Supplement II, (Lemgo, 18055), 11, 323].

[9] On February 28, 1718, a warrant was issued to Even Owen [Lib.C., p.8].

[10] William Streeper, son of John Strepers and Elisabeth Arets, married to Magdalene Castner, daughter of Georg Castner and granddaughter of Paul Castner (arrived in Germantown before 1690), left three sons and five daughters. Second marriage in 1744: Georg Kastner, see Küsters family tree.

[11] Elizabeth Arets, daughter of Leonhart Arets; on March

28, 1715, her marriage to John Strepers, son of Wilhelm Strepers and Maria Lucken is announced at a Meeting of Friends.

12 William Logan, d. October 31, 1751, Stenton, Pa.

13 Died between December 26, 1719, date of writing of will, and January 21, 1720, date when will was opened; contemporary witness William Bradford: "I think he must have died on December 27, 1719." [Arnim M. Brand, *Bau deinen Altar auf fremder Erde, die Deutschen in Amerika – 300 Jahre Germantown* (Stuttgart 1983) p. 101].

14 Jan Strepers had never been naturalized. In the opinion of his Germantown relatives, his land could not be sold for that reason.

15 John Strepers, see family trees of the 13 emigrant families/Strepers.

16 Peter Heinrich Strepers' property must have been located in the border area and partly on Palatine, partly on Prussian territory.

17 Johan Bolckhaus, stepson of Elias Eller, head of the Ellerian sect in Wuppertal.

18 Peter Sieben, schoolmaster from Ronsdorf, brother-in-law of Johann Bolckhaus.

19 Reiner Theißen and Leonhard Strepers were trustees of Jan Strepers' heirs, Griffith Jones was never nominated as a trustee. cf. p.50.

20 Heinrich Erkens and Hermann Pinner [Peters, Kaldenkirchen, vol. 1, p.174 ff.].

21 On September 19, 1764, the ship Polly and on September 20, 1764, the ship Sarah arrived in Philadelphia, carrying the tradesmen recruited by Franz Caspar Hasenclever and their families.

22 Possibly Schwarzenberg, in the Erzgebirge region of Saxony.

23 Probably Schloß Burg on the Wupper river.

24 This entry refers to a later date. This indicates that the journal was drafted on individual sheets and written down later.

25 Probably the transport of miners, foundry workers etc. from Germany to America.

26 The place is not named. It is probably Germantown, since Jan Strepers intended to have 250 acres there registered in his name.

27 Jones. Griffith Jones, son-in-law of Leonhart Arets.

28 Franz Caspar Hasenclever.

29 Deed of sale between James Logan and the heirs of Jan Strepers, Amsterdam, June 26, 1726.

30 Petrus Sieben, christened August 25, 1709 at the Reformed Church in Kaldenkirchen, schoolmaster in Kaldenkirchen and Ronsdorf, married Anna Maria Knevels on September 29, 1732 at the Reformed Church in Kaldenkirchen.

31 Johannes Bolckhaus, at the Reformed Church in Ronsdorf 1760 second marriage to Magdalena Wil-

helmine Knevel (Second Mother of Zion), sister of Anna Maria Knevels, married to Petrus Sieben on September 29, 1732 at the Reformed Church in Kaldenkirchen.

32 Elisabeth Arets.

33 Elisabeth Arets.

34 Reinhard Theißen, Leonhard Strepers and Griffith Jones.

35 "In February the famous march on Philadelphia occured...", Fogleman, *Hopeful Journey*, p. 143. On Wednesday, Dec. 14, 1763, the Paxton boys, numbering fiftyseven men, mounted and armed, came to Canestoga after riding all night. They surrounded the Indian huts and attacked them at day-break. Only six persons were found, and those, includ-ing the old chief, were murdered in cold blood in their beds. The fourteen who were absent were taken by the neighbors and lodged in Lancaster jail for safety. The Governor issued a proclamation ordering the offenders to be arrested. In defiance, the Paxton boys marched to Lancaster, broke into the jail, and murdered every one of the fourteen, not a hand being raised to defend them. (*Scharf and Westcott*, I, p. 241) - Other Indians, fearing further assault, sought refuge in Philadelphia, which in turn created indignition in the west. On January 3, 1764, settlers from the Lancaster County area united and on February 4, 1764, marched toward Philadelphia where armed citizens awaited them. - Cannon were sent to the barracks, a stockade thrown up there, and videttes sent out on the roads of approach. Next day was Sunday; defensive preparations were continued, a redoubt thrown up in the centre of the barracks parade-ground, and the gateways stockaded and loop-holed. At eleven o'clock that night an express came in with news of the mob's approach. Another arrived at two o'clock, and the alarm-bells began to ring. The people rushed out to obey the summons, and by sunrise on Monday the whole town was under arms. The old association artillery company mustered again and took charge of two cannon at the court-house. Business was sus-pended, shops did not open, the ferries were dis-mantled, and couriers charging back and forth along the streets kept up the excitement. (*Scharf and West-cott*, I, p. 242 n. I) - Accompanied by three others, Benjamin Franklin met the Paxton boys at Germantown, and there, through negotiations, a conflict was avoided." In: *Philadelphia: Three Centuries of American Art*.

36 William T. Parsons, *Pennsylvania Germans, a Persistant Minority* (Collegeville, 1985) p. 91: "If the Pennsylvania Dutch really cared for their own welfare, they would rather 'with a calm and wachtful Heart on Election-Day, ... vote for the true Friends of our old Fredom, namely Messers Isaac Norris, [John] Dickin-

son, [Richard] Harrison, [Henry] Keppele, &ca.' Clearly Sauer contributed to the major turnout of voters."

37 Logan, son of James Logan, secretary to William Penn.

38 Probably William Rittenhouse (1691-1774), son of Claes and grandson of Willem Rittenhouse. Information from James Duffin, Philadelphia.

39 Pistol: originally a Spanish gold coin, coined from the 16th century onwards. The value of a pistol varied in different European countries. In Germany, mainly the gold pieces of five talers were called pistols (Brockhaus, vol. 13,, p.165).

40 Miller, Peter: *Der Wöchentliche Philadelphische Staatsbote*, No. 148, Monday, November 12, 1764: "Last Tuesday morning, in this town in the house of a tawer by the name of Wilhelm Peterkop in Wood Street in the Northern Liberty a sad sight was seen. The man and both children were found dead in bed and the wife without speech. The coroner's inquest showed that their deaths were caused by suffocation from the vapors of a pot full of smoldering charcoal in a closed chamber. It seems as if they all had vomited or attempted to vomit. The wife died soon after, and they were all buried on Wednesday in the Lutheran cemetery in this town."

41 Probably Peter Sieben, schoolmaster in Ronsdorf.

42 King of Prussia Tavern, Fig. taken from Charles F. Jenkins, *The Guide Book To Historic Germantown* (Germantown, 1926), p. 83; p. 84: "Nos. 5516-5518-5520 Main Street cover the site of what, in Revolutionary times, was the King of Prussia Tavern. Its sign, which is still preserved, is said to have shown King Frederick on horseback and to have been painted by Gilbert Stuart while he was a temporary resident of Germantown. It was later painted over. In the rear there formerly stood a large barn which was used as a slaughter house by the British at the time of the Battle. The first stage coach with an awning was run from the King of Prussia to the George Inn, Second and Arch Streets, three times a week. About 1834 its use as tavern ceased. The doorway on the second floor, at the south end, which has been closed up, shows where at one time it had been connected with the next house below. Thomas Jefferson lived at this tavern for a considerable time during the month of November 1793, and on one occasion Alexander Hamilton and General Henry Knox dined with him here. – 'Andrew Weckeser begs leave to inform the publick, That he has opened a House of entertainment in Germantown, at the Sign of the King-of-Prussia, near John Jones's, Esp: where all Gentleman, Ladies, Travellers, &., may depend on the best usage. Their favors will be gratefully acknowledged by their humble Servant. Andrew Weckeser.' - Pennsylvania

Gazette, December 15th, 1757."

43 John Stevens (1682-1730), cf. Glossary of Names.

44 John Stevens (1716-1792), cf. Glossary of Names.

45 Johann Bolckhaus.

46 Princeton, New Jersey, north of Trenton in Mercer Co.- The carriage they traveled in was probably the Flying Machine since it served Princeton: "This is to give Notice to the Public, That the Flying Machine, kept by John Barnhill, in Elm Street, near Vine street, Philadelphia, and John Masherew, at the Blazing Star, performs the Journey from Philadelphia to New York in two Days, and from thence to Philadelphia in two days also; a Circumstance greatly to the Advantage of the Traveller, as there is no Water Carriage, and consequently nothing to impede the Journey. It has already been performed to the general Satisfaction of many genteel People. They set off from Philadelphia and New York on Mondays and Thursdays punctually at Sun Rise, and change their Passengers at Prince Town, and return to Philadelphia and New York the following Day: Passengers paying Ten Shillings to Prince Town, and Ten Shillings to Powles Hook, opposite New York, Ferriage free; and Three Pence each Mile any Distance between. Gentlemen and Ladies who are pleased to favour us with their Custom, may depend on due Attendance and civil Usage, by their Humble Servants [Pa. Ga., 26.06.1766].

47 Province of Pennsylvania.

48 Approximately 3 yards (1 Brabant ell = 69,5 cm).

49 A cubic measure for wood, approx. 3 1/3 m³.

50 Used for medicinal purposes, mostly as a laxative.

51 Either Peter Miller's *Der Wöchentliche Philadelphische Staatsbote* or Christopher Saur's *Pennsylvanische Berichte*.

52 John Penn, Deputy Governor 1763-1771.

53 Richard Penn, Proprietor together with Thomas Penn 1746-1771.

54 Richard Stevens' father-in-law.

55 I.e., the recovery of the land bought by Jan Strepers.

56 The barracks in the Extension, today the Karlstadt, which had been under construction since 1709 and were still being extended in the 1760s. – Information by Dr. Edmund Spohr, architect, Düsseldorf.

57 Muscae hispanicae, popular name of a species of the blister beetle family. A powdered preparation from it was used externally as a skin irritant.

58 (Wuppertal dialect:) A pain that manifests itself now in this spot and then in another, i.e. 'flows' from one to the other. [Rh. Wb., II, col. 687].

59 An improvement is a legal term from land law which means improving the land by such things as felling trees, putting up fences, building houses, etc. A crucial part of stating a claim to vacant land was to show that one had actually worked on it to make it better,

bring it into production from the wilderniss. The OED describes the word as follows: a. The turning of land to better account, the reclamation of waste or unoccupied land by inclosing and bringing it into cultivation (obs.); hence, in later use, cultivation and occupation of land; merged at length in sense 5. Now (as in N.Amer., N.Z.), the turning of farmland to better account by the erection of buildings, fences, etc. b. A piece of land improved or rendered more profitable by inclosure, cultivation, the erection of buildings, etc. (obs. exc. in U.S. dial.). Now (in N. Amer., N.Z.), the buildings, fences, etc., themselves. – Information from James Duffin, Philadelphia.

60 Burlington, New Jersey.

61 Bristol, Pa., is on the right bank of the Delaware opposite Burlington.

62 Frankford, today a northeastern part of Philadelphia.

63 Whereas a report has been spread, that we Peter Henderick Striepers, and John Harbergs, lay Claim to great Part of the North End of this City; to all Frankfort, and a Part of West New Jersey; which Report, her believe, has been spread with a Design to prejudice the Minds of the People against our Title and Claim; Therefore, to take off that Deception, we take this Method of declaring what we do claim, which is, Five Thousand Acres of Land in this Province, with its Privileges, purchased by our Grandfather John Striepers, of William Penn, Esq; deceased, late Proprietor of this Province, also Fifty Acres of Liberty Land, and one Acre in this City, as a free Gift of the said William Penn, Esq; to the said John Striepers; of which we find taken up on said Right as follows, viz. 4448 Acres in Bucks County, called Strieper, or the Dutch Tract, adjoining the London Company Lands in Tinicum Township; 275 Acres in New Providence Township, at a Place called the Trap; about 275 Acres in and about Germantown; also 50 Acres of Liberty Land, near Germantown, and three whole Lots in this City, lying in the Square between Fourth and Fifth streets, and Vine and Race streets. And whereas we can plainly make it appear that we, and those who have impowered us, are the true and lawful Heirs of the said John Striepers, wherefore we have come over on purpose to take Possession, and settle the aforesaid Estate; but as we are Strangers to the Laws of this Country, and unwilling to enter into Lawsuits, we offered to leave the Determination of our Title, and Matters in Controversy, to three or more Gentlemen, mutually chosen, which was refused; therefore we hope no Report will prevail in prejudice to our Title, and that if we are forced (contrary to our Inclinations) to bring Ejectments against those in Possession or otherwise, into the Law, we shall be esteemed and held excusable [Pa. Ga., 20.06.1765]. A later

advertisement tries to prevent the sale of part of the land in Bucks County: Whereas William Buckman, Sheriff of Bucks county, by an advertisement, in this Gazette, dated Newtown, Bucks county, July 30, 1768, offers to public sale, on the 30th of August instant, A certain tenement, plantation or tract of land, containing 175 acres, with a good log house and barn, and good meadow, bounded by the lands of James MacClaughlin, and others, lying and being in the township of Tenicum, late the property of Henry Preston;" This is to inform the public, that the said land never was the property of said Preston, and that William Buckman, the Sheriff, has no right to sell the same as such, but the sole right thereof is in me, as great grandson, and heir at law to John Strepers, late of Germany, to whom tract of land of near 5000 acres, of which this is a part, was originally patented; of which I think fit to give this public notice, that no man may plead ignorance thereof, and become a purchaser to his own wrong [Pa. Ga., 18.08.1768].

64 Probably William Peters, Secretary of Thomas Penn's Land Office, deposed in September 1765 for incompetence and corruption, Fogleman, *Hopeful Journeys* (Philadelphia, 1996), p. 145.

65 From Latin peniculus = brush, derived from penis; insulting name.

66 On August 26th, 1765, the ship Polly under Master Robert Porter, coming from Rotterdam via Cowes/ England, lands in Philadelphia [Strassburger-Hinke, I, p.704].

67 Johann Bolckhaus, Royal Prussian Privy Counsel, Resident and Superintendent of the Reformed Congregations of Jülich and Berg, Cleves and Mark.

68 cf. Goebel, III, p. 580.

69 William Logan, see Glossary of Names.

70 The house on the Liberty land.

71 Old English Coffee House, The London Coffee House, on the southwest corner of Front and Market Streets ["Historic Philadelphia, from the founding until the early nineteenth century". *Transactions of the American Philosophical Society,* XLIII, Part 1 (Philadelphia, 1953), p. 320 f.].

72 Stamp Act, passed on March 22, 1765 to cover the cost of the military forces stationed in the American colonies by putting a stamp tax on all documents and printed products of all kinds, playing cards and dice. In October 1765, the illegal Stamp Act Congress protested in New York: No taxation without representation.

73 Ringwood, Passaic County, NJ, iron and zinc deposits. P.H. was a manager there.

74 1 Cologne ell = 57,7 centimeters.

75 Possibly a distorted name of a tract of land.

76 The house stands on the acre in Philadelphia. Map

p. 94.

77 Old English Coffee House, an inn in Philadelphia.

78 Deuteronomy, Chapter 4, Verse 8-11:

8 And what nation is there so great, that hath structures and judgements so righteous as all this law, which I set before you this day?

9 Only take heed to thyself, and keep thy soul diligently. lest thou forget the things which thine eyes have seen, and lest they depart from thy heart all the days of thy life: but teach them to thy sons, and thy sons' sons;

10 Specially the day that thou stoodest before the LORD thy God in Horeb, when the LORD said unto me, Gather me the people together, and I will make them hear my words, that they may learn to fear me all the days that they shall live upon the earth, and that they may teach their children.

11 And ye came near and stood under the mountain; and the mountain burned with fire unto the midst of heaven, with darkness, clouds, and thick darkness.

79 Susquehanna region, land of the Conestoga Indians, Encyclopedia Americana, XII, p. 528, Conestoga Indians ... a once-numerous tribe of Iroquoian Indians, who lived along the lower Susquehanna River in Pennsylvania and Maryland and on the eastern bank of the Potomac River and Chesapeake Bay. In early colonial times the Conestoga were at war with the Mohawk and had nearly extermined them, but in 1675 they were overcome by other Iroquois tribes and later were forced to settle near the Oneida in New York. Eventually allowed to return to their old homeland in present-day Lancaster county, Pennsylvania, they declined rapidly, and in 1763 the remaining 20 individuals were massacred by white settlers. - The tribe was always friendly with the Dutch and Swedish settlers but remained a constant source of trouble to the English, with whom they carried on intermittent warfare. They made a treaty ceding some of their land to William Penn in 1701. The name of the tribe was derived from the Indian Kanastóge, meaning "at the place of the submerged pole." They were also known as Susquehanna Indians, from Susquehannock, a name applied to them by the neighboring Powhatan tribes. In early colonial accounts they are also often referred to as Minqua Indians [Frederick J. Dockstader, Museum of the American Indian, Heye Foundation, New York City].

80 The inhabitants of the village of Breyel on the Lower Rhine were well-known earthenware hawkers travelling up and down the country and carrying their wares in panniers on their backs. Especially noteworthy was their secret language.

81 The boat connecting New York and Philadelphia.

82 On December 22nd, 1766, Peter Hasenclever rejoined his family, who lived in Putney, six miles out of London. *Rheinische Lebensbilder* (Cologne, 1970), IV, p. 86.

83 Hasenclever had considerable problems with his English partners. *Rheinische Lebensbilder*, IV, p. 86.

84 Capes on the Delaware/ Atlantic: North Cape May, West Cape May, Cape May Point, Cape May.

85 *Die Heimat* (Krefeld, 1938), XVII, 318. Excerpt from the agreement: "1. to take possession peacefully of the tracts, pieces of land and leases in Pennsylvania that had been Jan Strepers' during his lifetime, 2. to take legal steps to recover the same, maintaining that all purchases of land had been done without the knowledge and consent of the legal heirs who had not transferred their rights to James Logan." v. App. K.

86 He is probably talking about the Moravian Brethren, founded by Count Nikolaus von Zinsendorf.

87 Alexander Mack's Brethren in Germantown. cf. William G. Willoughby, *Counting the Coast. The Life of Alexander Mack* (Elgin, Illinois, 1979).

88 Amish in Lancaster County.

89 Mennonites, 1764, cf. Aaron Fogleman, *Hopeful Journeys*.

90 Moravian Brethren, founded by Germans and Moravians on Christmas Eve 1741 in the presence of Count Nikolaus von Zinsendorf and his daughter Benigna, with establishments in Nazareth and Bethlehem, among others, today at Lititz. Lancaster County.

91 Ephrata Cloister, Lancaster County, Pa., founded by Conrad Beissel in 1732. The name Ephrata is first mentioned in a Hymn Book: "Ephrata in the Canestoge area, April 27, 1736." – cf. Everett Gordon Alderfer, *The Ephrata Commune. An Early American Counterculture* (Pittsburg, Pa. 1985).

Accounts

We received	£	s	d
April 14, 1765 from home			
600 guilders, that is in local money	91	3	9
one guinea at 34 shillings Pennsylvania currency			
on 27th from Messrs. Hasenclever und Stevens together	100		
on October 13th from Mr. Hasenclever			
£30 New York money, that is in local money	27	13	6
November 9th and 20th, December 14th and 16th from Mr. Stevens another	13	10	
March 15th received from Mr. Parker	165		
of these £165 spent			
to Ross and housekeeping			

Fig. 50 Green Tree Tavern, Steel engraving, approx. 1900. GHS.

	£	s	d		£	s	d
knitting wool	20	18	9				
my freight	17						
I for ship's provisions	6	17	4				
to W. Müller still to pay		18	7				
Cousin Strepers	25						
Cousin still to get another	74						
I for my own account	20	5	4				
I for letter of exchange of £40	165	0			397	7	3
on July 2nd still at Waldniel, due to me					40	7	3
					437	7	3

1764 expenses from board	£	s	d
from November 1st to May 20th, but since we owed two weeks' board together 216 days at 24 shillings every 7 days	37		6
1 gallon of rum and consumed with Mätters et Janssen		2	6
on 12th at the Schuylkill, at the little tree[1]		4	9
up to the 18th for tobacco, our laundry, paper		14	
on the 25th to the barber		12	
ditto that cousin van Acken ate with us and drinks, 1 tea pot, tobacco, 1 pound of sugar		14	9
up to December 16th tea cups, sugar, rum et tobacco		6	1
up to the 23rd when Mr. Stevens called		3	9
up to January 20, 1765, 1 gallon of rum and Mr. Hasenclever		8	6
1 gallon of rum and consumed with Mr. Hasenclever		13	7
up to February 10th and to cousin van Acken's wife:		10	8
2 gallons of rum and tobacco		8	
with Berenstecher across the river and nibbles		6	1
from March 2nd to 8th barber's wages		16	
up to March 31st paper. 1 sangaree[2]		4	6
one gallon of beer			6
on May 2nd consumed with Mr. Kurtz		1	
on May 8th 2 books of paper, pipes and tobacco		1	7½
on 14th each of us a hat at 32	3	4	
paid to Berenstecher for laundry up to the 19th	2		
on 21st tip to Bill		1	6
for butter, candles, tea and Mr. Ross		9	3
ditto one ham and one bread plate		11	9
sugar, eggs, bread		3	10
on 24th, meat, pepper, lettuce and milk		3	
on 25th meat, bread, beer and to Ross		18	1
on 31st from Mrs. Bärenstecher wood, glass		10	9
	9	9	0
	51	10	11½

	£	s	d
For household goods pan, pothook, pot 1 pillow, 1 blanket, 3 chairs, 1 tea kettle, 3 candlesticks	3	7	7

	£	s	d
from June 7th to 14th for housekeeping	1	4	11
on 15th, 2 hams 35 pounds at 7 pence a pound	1		
June, expenses from 17th to 23rd		19	1
from 24th to 30th		17	7½
July, from 1st to 7th		16	8
a tablecloth and a towel		6	9
up to July 14th	1	3	6
up to 21st	1		3½
up to 28th, including cleaning our room		19	5
up to August 4th including our laundry	1	14	6
up to August 11th	1	3	10
up to September 1st	3	12	5
up to September 8th and to the barber for ½ year	1	17	3
up to September 14th		14	9
up to 28th dito	2	3	9½
October up to 5th	1	7	7
up to den 19th	2	2	
up to October 26th with 1 purple cedar[3] and sawing wages for 2 carts of wood 12 s	2	13	
up to November 3rd	1	16	4
2 carts of wood at £4 8 s and up to last day of November	8	10	7
month of December	4	12	3
January 1766	3	16	4
month of February	2	14	7½
month of March including what was owed to Ross	7	14	6½
on the 13th paid W. Müller's bill		18	7
	14	12	0
	59	8	2½

	£	s	d
into our household with laundry, rent et	59	8	2½
other	51	10	11½
	110	19	2

1765	£	s	d
on June 7th paid to Mr. Stelwagen according to ticket for boards delivered	3	14	

	£	s	d
1765, on September 18th paid according to tickets everything spent on renovating our house, as well as on the fence of the Liberty land of the City of Philadelphia and what we received for it is listed under income	43	14	

	£	s	d
1764 spent on copying and travel			
on November 1st Brockden for the copy of 1715		4	6
our baggage from New York to Philadelphia		9	
postage for letters and a collection for poor Germans		10	

	£	s	d
on 27th Mr. Ehrenzeller for translating		3	9
from December 31st to January 17, 1765, when we made the contract with Messrs. Hasenclever und Stevens on			
copying and consumption	7	16	8
to Ehrenzeller again for translating		3	
Cousin Strepers consumed between New York and Philadelphia	4	4	1
four rides to Germantown, consumed	15	10	
on February 28th with Mr. Stevens to Germantown		7	6
2 more times to Germantown, consumed		6	6
NB Cousin Strepers £5 with Mr. Stevens and the two Kurtzes	9	6	
Cousin Strepers between Germantown and Philadelphia		10	
and on the 7th to Abington[4]		20	
up to April 3rd between Germantown and Philadelphia		14	6
on the 7th on taking possession		13	9
to the minister for the certificate[5] for naturalisation and 1 sangaree		9	6
on the 11th for postage and translating to Ehrenzeller		10	3½
on the 14th for a letter from home[6] and hiring horses		19	9
on the 15th when taking possession in Bucks County	6	12	9
on the 25th to Lehman for surveying and 1 sangaree	17		
on the April 27th to Delis Strepers		7	6
on the 30th to the court, consumption and the £6 we gave			
to the lawyers		6	16
on May 3rd and 4th with Mr. Pollmann and Mr. Lehman copied all of the deeds from the Germantown Land Records, total cost with consumption	2	14	3
	12	8	0
	37	15	7½

	£	s	d
On May 7th because Mr. Pollman refused payment for his efforts			
we invited him to Scheibler's together with Kurtz		14	
To witnesses in court		13	
on the 11th with Mr. Pollman between Frankfurt and Philadelphia		10	
on the 14th gone with Stevens and Pollman to Ashmead	7	6	
paid for hiring horses		10	
on the 17th for postage on a letter to Germany		4	
between the "Rising Sun"[7] and a lock on the fence		1	3
on the 19th and 21st between Weidman and for freight for the man who carted our house to its spot	1	5	
postage on the 21st		2	6
on the 26th we were naturalized in Burlington, total cost	9	2	10½
on June 1st postage for letters and consumption between Bucks County and Philadelphia and hiring horses up to the 7th	2	6	8½
on June 14th the copy of Logan's deed and consumption between Germantown and Philadelphia as well as to the surveyor	1	2	2
3 days consumption between Bucks County and Philadelphia and for hiring horses	2	15	
on July 4th to lawyer Dickinson	2		
on the 6th to Hinr. Miller for advertisement		12	

	£	s	d
ditto Brockden for Leonhard Arets' deed		8	6
postage for a letter from Germany		5	
on taking possession of the 50 acres of Liberty for food			
and drinks, et rum	3	4	
on October 9th I went to New York, transport and consumption	2		18
	29	1	6

	£	s	d
1766 on February 10th to New York, since we			
heard that Mr. Hasenclever wanted to go to England			
in 10 days, with transport and consumption	4	7	5
Cost of passage to Rotterdam	17		
from April 1st to 13th including what was taken from the ship	6	17	4
at Schils[8] und Newcastle[9] in England, consumed	1	7	9
transport to Middelburg 17 s sterling, makes	1	11	5
provisions on the ship on the way there		9	4
from Middelburg to Rotterdam transport and consumption	1	9	7
consumed at Rotterdam		18	9
from Rotterdam to home for transport and consumption and including the			
4 rix dollars 1/5 I had to give to the tobacco inspectors	3	19	3
	5	3	0
	38	0	10
that is in copying expenses	37	15	7½
travel expenses and lawyers	29	1	6
	104	16	11½

	£	s	d
our household, house rent, laundry, barber,			
brandy and other expenses	100	19	2
spent for the house	47	8	0
	253	4	1½

To be added to this cousin Strepers' expenses
from his own money

	sh	
copying expenses		
for the copy of Wilhelm Strepers' deed of sale	9	
including to Mr. Weiss for his efforts to check	16	
for the deed of James Logan without Mr. Weiss's efforts	12	
for translating to Mr. Peter Miller	20	
to the Registry Office for looking up papers one dollar	7½	
3 weeks' board	72	
paid for our deeds of sale 20 s 4=5	24	5
on September 15th for searching for the deeds on the one acre	5	
paid for that acre 10 s to the surveyor for a copy	4	6
on the 18th for another 7 copies	22	
one week's board	24	
Mr. Weiss	7½	
two weeks' board	48	

up to October 20th board, 3 weeks   72

on the 17th to Lehman £1 for the relevant documents

on the 18th to the King's Counsel £3

ditto to Weiss for the family tree et power of attorney

to Weiss for translating of power of attorney et family tree   20

From Caspar Michenfelder

If a wine gets moldy, take 2 to 3 new bricks straight from the oven or reheated, grate them small, add to the moldy wine and stir well. Let it stand until the taste is gone.

If a wine smells of sulfur

Take a warm, big loaf of bread, break it apart and place it on the spout of the barrel, and it will draw out the sulfur or the mould. But it has to be barley bread. Probatum est[10].

How to prevent wine from going moldy

Take crushed borax[11] and add it to the wine together with 3 handfuls of roasted or burned salt. This is added to 1 bucket of wine, then the barrel is closed tightly. When the wine is taken from the barrel after 8 days, it is good.

How to make a spoiled wine good again

Take wheat in proportion to the size of a bucket, put it in a small sack and hang it into the barrel of wine. When it is taken out after several days, everything will have been drawn into the sack.

How to give wine a nice color and sweet taste

Take a crushed sugarloaf and put in on the fire in a pan, let it melt and stir well so it does not burn. One can also pour a glass of wine into it first so it will melt better. When the sugar has melted, one has to be careful it does not boil over. Then take a wooden vessel and wet it with water. Then the molten sugar is poured into the vessel, and the sugar hardens. If you want to use it, take of it as much as seems good to you and melt it again with a little wine, then you can use it to your taste.

If you hang pure oat straw into a wine, the wine takes on a beautiful golden color.

How to help a wine when the yeast has gone down

To one ohm[12] of wine add 4 spoonfuls of roasted salt and a little tree oil, pour in hot into the spout, and the yeast will sink to the bottom.

How to help a tough wine

Add 6 pounds of chalk to one bucket, but the chalk must heated red-hot on a coal fire. Then 4 handfuls of salt are roasted, all this mixed together and put into the barrel like one puts a nice [word omitted] into it, stirred, poured over and put into the barrel and stirred. Probatum est.

How to revive a mat wine

To 2½ ohm of wine add 4 spoonfuls of salt. Roast the same over the fire until it turns brown. After taking it off the fire, put into the spout as hot as it can be. Then the wine will revive.

How to artfully enhance and sweeten a sour wine turned bad in a natural and uncomplicated manner

Take crushed raisins or sultanas without seeds boiled very gently in sufficient water for 4 hours. Squeeze the juice out well through a linen cloth, add quite a lot of sugar to sweeten and slowly and gently boil it to the thickness of syrup. Mix well with two measures of good wine and some good yeast of sweet white beer and pour this into a barrel of sour wine, place into a warm spot and the wine will turn to must. When this must has fermented you obtain the best wine from sour wine. Probatum est.

A recipe for making vinegar in 4 hours
First, take a quantity of turmeric and crush it small, add two albus'[13] worth of Bertram's wort[14], two albus' worth of saltpeter, 3 pounds of Spanish pepper, crushed small. Fill into a small bag, hang into the barrel which is only set at 5/4. Probatum est.

How to make a mother of vinegar[15]
Take bluepaper, smear it with sour dough and put into barrel [Rest missing].

How to make double aniseed brandy or Mannheim Water
First take a good schnapps, add to 6 quarters of schnapps about one quarter of filtrate (which is what runs off after the schnapps). 3 to 4 pounds of aniseed, NB alum[16] the size of a small egg and a little white cream of tartar, also add good spices according to taste. Put this together into a kettle. Then calculate how much brandy there will be and take the third part of fresh water and let it come to a boil. Then add 3 to 4 pounds of sugar depending on how sweet you want it. Then the whites of 4 eggs, before adding those, it must be boiling. But when the egg white is added, it has to boil and foam well, then to be strained through a cloth and left to cool. And then added to the brandy. Probatum est.

Concerning our workshop: 4 skeins, as they come from the spinners, they can be cut if they are double length. 2 courses of 16 schmitz[17], 21 courses done and the first 8 schmitz weighed 4 pounds.

Stoughtons Bitter
1 ounce gentian root[18], 1 ounce orange peel, 4 drams[19] cardamon seed, for every 5 drams at least ¼ ounce Peruvian bark[20], ½ ounce melissa, all crushed very small, leave standing for two weeks in 1 measure of good rubbing alcohol. Probatum.

A proven remedy if a person has an injury to his knee or other part of his body that begins to fester, take a handful of green rye, a handful of beet tops, and handful of myrrh, a handful of pastry flour, if lacking that, a small handful of crushed linseed oil, ½ measure of buttermilk and ½ measure of fresh water, cooked together well and put half of it in a cloth and apply as hot as one can stand. When it has cooled, apply the other half.

	Gl	St
another 6 penknives ½ crown 1 st	1	9
spent on my hat		11
2 penknives at 3 st		6
from Mr. Maylan for 1s new English money		11
one woolen cap, red		11
on May 18th 1 st to the poor and for 2 copper pieces 1 st		2
on the 19th string 2½ st 6 st cider		8½
3 corkscrews at 3 halfpennies is		4½
one pencil 1 st, on May 24th for 3 st cedar wood pencils		4
1 st for beer, ½ st poor money, 6 small spoons 2½ st		4
1 key ring 1 st, the description of London 1s		12

two punch I lost gambling in Philadelphia
see 1½ Pennsylvania 1s   10½
the other punch   10½

NB I forgot to include in the account what is due to me for the
carrier   5 Gl   5 St
for change from my own money   12
to Mrs. Conradts for laundry   1   4
                                                            Gl 7   1

The bill is in the back pocket of the book
for me another 3 measures of wine at Scheibler's at 1s
for me another jug of beer, another pot of beer at 8 st
sold another 6 pieces of ribbon   4   19
bought 1 piece of money 19 pence
the bet for a quart of wine like cousin Strepers said at   2   6
1 pound mustard seed   1
1 pair of gloves
had new soles put on my shoes and 3 Mont. 3 s 9d apiece   3   9
to Master Ross for his coat   7   6 pence
Lost gambling with Hasenclever 12 old pence, my trousers 2s
For what was bought for me separately and paid for out of my own pocket
paid in Fessem to the carrier out of my own money   5 Gl   5 St
still had   12
1 piece of ribbon, to wash   24
bought for myself the rings   7   1

                                                            Gl   St
From cousin Strepers   2   12
1 tobacco box   1   2
1 brush   4½
in Helvoet from an East Indiaman a pair of silver rings   2   5
For myself a pair of stockings   1   8
on April 17th from cousin Strepers a watch for 12 Rhr at   18
a penknife   6
a purse   5
small nuts 1½ st another st   2½
postage from Mr. Mickenschreiber   10
for beer 1 measure for my rings 1½ st   5½
now I deduct for myself 3 s   1   4
                                                           28   4½

Bought out of this for ½ st nuts 1 measure of beer, ½ st nuts
another measure of beer, in the coffee house above   7   1
3 st, to Jack 2½ st, 2 st to my Joe[21], ½ st nuts, for
poor money 3 st, 1 measure of beer, ½ st nuts, a pencil 2 st,
1 st nuts, nuts 1 st   21   3½

1764, on March 27th started the journey from Kaldenkirchen to Pennsylvania under God's blessing. Where cousin Strepers and myself consumed as follows [on the top left margin vertically: consumed as far as Waldniel 7 Rhr 23 st]

	Dutch Gl	St
and this we put on our account		
from cousin Symons[22] 8 ells of cloth at	2	2
at Blau Jan in Amsterdam	1	12
at the penitentiary in Amsterdam		6
in Delft in the church for tips		3
bought a new knapsack	12	
a grammar book in London	2	2
a comb		4
to a poor Saxon[23] 1s		11
at the Tower for seeing it	2	10
bought 1 1/32 ounce of silk 2s 5d	1	9
knitting needles		5
another one costs		4
small shirt buttons, for 4 pieces, silk thread 7		11
telescope	2	9½
black silk 10¼ st, whetting stone for razor 6 st		16¼
fishing rods 2 st		2½
seen the animals at the Tower	1	2

This was spent for the entire family

	Dutch Gl	St
On March 27th to Mr. Hambach for drawing up the family tree	2	15
for the poor		11
to Burgomasters Erckes and Pinnen for the seal	1	13
this we were paid by cousin Mickenschreiber	4	19

	Gl	St
spent in Meijel	1	14½
on the 28th the feast, each 4s	2	4
at midday in Eindhoven		9
on the 29th paid the fare to the carrier	5	5
at Fessem to the sexton and the maid		9½
in Boxtel paid for lunch	2	4
the fare to s'Hertogenbosch	2	10
the feast in s'Hertogenbosch	3	16
for white bread and cheese		7
freight for copper to Rotterdam	1	1
fare from s'Hertogenbosch to Rotterdam	1	12

	Gl	St
fare for the passage		4½
consumed in Rotterdam and in Gouda		3
2 cushions		4
a bottle of wine, a jug of beer and brandy on going		
to Amsterdam on the barge	1	7
the fare to Amsterdam including expenses for the Hunter[24]	1	18½
3 small glasses of brandy		6
consumed at the inn	3	3
on the barge two bottles of wine with Mr. Quack	1	8
I per[25] 2 cushions and fare	2	6

	Gl	St
coffee in Gouda		2
from Rotterdam to Delft		10½
on the 8th and the 9th consumed in The Hague	2	6
feast in Delft	4	8½
fare to Rotterdam		16
the feast in Rotterdam is	13	12
fare to Brielle	1	1
Freight for copper and portmanteau	12	
Copper and portmanteau to the inn		8
consumed		16
in Brielle for signing of the passport	1	4
freight from Brielle to Helvoet	2	12
from one inn to the other		8
consumed in Helvoet	4	18
the barge that took us to the packetboat	1	2
NB freight from Helvoet to Harwich makes 15 gl 10, which was compensated however by the passport		
the freight to the captain or the fare for the passage	16	2
to the porter who helped us	1	2
to take on board at Harwich	1	2
to have baggage inspected, and consumed at Harwich	2	13
to take our baggage to the coach		6
paid for fares 24s	14	4
for our baggage to London	4	15

	Gl	St
to the coachman at Colchester		12
consumed in Colchester	2	12
consumed in Witham	2	
consumed in Ingatestone	1	16
to the coachman		12
to the coachman in London		12
on March 31st we arrived in London		
baggage to our lodgings		12
one book of writing paper		12
on the 2nd for guide and interpreter	1	6
we have taken out in London	8	16

Description	Gl	St
on April 18th taken out for [omitted]		
but also paid for the watch from it		18
another	6	12
on April 21st paid one week's board	12	12
on the 26th in the evening Mr. Maylan called with		
whom we consumed 3s	1	16
on the 27th taken from the kitty 10s		6
on the 28th Mr. Maylan again with us		
out of which paid for the broker for the ship 5s		3
paid our board on the 29th	12	12
taken out another 10s		6
on the 29th Mr. Maylan called		
on the 2nd taken out another 10s		
of which lent to Mrs. Caunder[26] 1 and when she dined		
with us another 1		6
on May 5th taken out 10s		6
out of which paid 30 st postage on a letter we received on the 4th from Ronsdorf, Kaldenkirchen		
ditto Mr. Meilan called and we went to Greenwich,		
and treated him to a punch and for the drive and dinner 5s		
on the 6th paid to our host	12	12
on the 7th taken out 10s NB 30s		6
out of which bought 1 tea flask, 1 basket, 1 pound sugar, at 3s 2st, 1 pound tea at 9s, soap 6 st, consumed with Mr. Meylan who dined with us 12 st, 1 tea kettle, 4 drinking jugs, small pints[27], 1 hoop, 1 small pepper bottle, all made of tin, 5½s, laundry, costs 3s, another 3 bottles of		
English Bitter, for 3s silk		18
on the 13th paid to our host	12	12
taken out of the kitty another 20s		12
on the 16th treated Mr. Maylan 3s		
on the 17th treated Mr. Maylan again		
fishing rods, a mirror, NB 10s		
on the 20th board to the host	12	12
on the 21st, when the host demanded 3s a week for the room although this was included in the agreement,		
paid up to the 21st to the host 4s 10 st, Salmon for carrying 2s, consumed 1s 3 st, tobacco 2½s		
from the kitty another	3	12

Description	Gl	St
on the 22nd taken from the kitty for our own housekeeping	5	6
on the 24th from the kitty 10s		6
bought from this 2 pewter plates, 22d 1 butter dish, ¼ jug of gin, 1s, clay butter dish and a box with 4 bottles 4½s		

	Rhr	St
on 25th taken from the kitty 20s	12	
for brandy to Mrs. Conradts 2s		
for brandy to our hostess 2s		
another 4s for a whole bottle, to Peter Hendrik Strepers, 6s		
another 4s for a bottle of brandy		
on 25th another 10s	6	
lunch, Salm in the evening, back to cousin Strepers from		
the latter 1s 6d		
on the 28th another 5s	3	
room rent at 3s		
lunch		
on the 29th taken out the last 10s	6	
on the 30th eaten lunch and treated Mr. Maylan and		
gone to the ship		
received from Mr. Maylan 2 guineas at	25	4
lemons 26 st, a bed[28] for 29½s		
on June 1st honored Mr. Maylan with a glass of wine, a cheese		
at 30 st, 4 pounds of butter, 30 st		
paid to the captain for fares 16 guineas	201	12
straw for the bed, 10 st, 1 ham 7s 3d		
from Mr. Maylan 3 guineas	36	6
4 pounds of cheese, 1s 4d		
9 ½ pounds of sugar, 1 ounce of nutmeg, 2 pounds of green tea at 10s 3d		
2 pounds of liquorice and 1 pound of powdered sugar at 1s 10d		
1 bottle of brandy, 1 cedar wood pencil at 5s		
to Salmon first 4s, then another 2s which included the		
water carriage		
2 water jugs, 1 small funnel 1s 6d		
2 pairs of small cups 1d nails at 7d		
for lodgings and tips for the servant and the maid 6s 10½d,		
Gravesend		
Passage money 2s, for the man first to see land:		
Benjam. 2s,		
to Joh., who washed our laundry on the ship,		
for 1 pound of powdered mustard		
From New York to Philadelphia from the 18th to the 20th we consumed,		
boat, coach fare net 3 guineas	36	6
including the Rhr I gave to the registrar, at Scheibler's		
4½s to Mr. Weiss for his efforts and for money advanced 25s, on the		
26th for our lodgings 24s, at Scheibler's 7s, ditto to the washerwoman 11s		

Account of our travel expenses, both expenses and income

	Rhr	St
1764, March, 22nd. from cousin Bernhard Hollender in		
Dutch money	331 Gl	5 St
in addition	5	

Hendrich Königs		10
Widow Hüsges	2	10
Peter Hendrich Mickenschreiber	5	
F. P. Dürselen	8	15
	362	10

From cousin Bernhard				
Hollender in Delft another	210			
on order from cousin				
Hollender	231	0		
	803	10 St	535	40

letter of exchange Gl   600 Gl

1765, November, May 12th, 15th. received from H. D. Wüster
on a letter of exchange still to come £25 Pennsylvania money,
in exchange for £6 but when I counted it at home,
£1 15s was missing. So I went back to him
and told him. Then he replied he had received
it for £25. So I can be accused of not looking carefully enough. But it was paper. And it was impossible
for me to look so quickly. I am waiting for a ruling[29]

Income	Rhr	St
November 12th		
Daniel Wüster	100	
January 13. 1765, from Mr. Hasenclever in New York	200	
on April 26th, from Mr. Stevens	200	
on May 15th the letter of exchange from Germany from Hollender		
et Mickenschreiber, of 600 gl, that is £91 3s in local money		
9d per £ at 4 RhR	364	45
returned to Wüster out of that		
from Mr. Parker £165 sterling		

	Rhr	
1764, on March 4th consumed and spent on the journey to Philadelphia		
the coach 41 st, consumed 30, servant 4	1	15
consumed in Düsseldorf and for carrying		45
from Düsseldorf to Waldniel		52
from Waldniel sent a man to Düsseldorf twice,		
to fetch my things there	2	15
otherwise consumed between the Rur and elsewhere to March 27th	1	56
Rhr	7	3

Expenses	Rhr	St
1764, March 27th. in Meijel		
spent Dutch money	1Gl	14½ St
on the 28th in Asten[30]	2	4
Eindhoven		9

Description				
29th to Wilhem Janssen for fare	5	5		
in Vessem for tip		9½		
31st in Boxtel	2	4		
2nd the fare to s'Hertogenbosch	2	10		
consumed in s'Hertogenbosch	3	16		
for white bread on the boat		7		
the fare to Rotterdam	2	17½		
with copper et passage money	21	16½		
from Rotterdam to Gouda		3		
in Gouda consumed and barge	3	5½		
consumed in Amsterdam	3	9		
on the barge with Quack et				
fare to Gouda	3	14		
coffee in Gouda		2		
from Rotterdam to Delft		10½		
April 8th et 9th cloth for a portmanteau				
and knapsack	16	3		
consumed in The Hague	2	6		
consumed in Delft	4	8½		
fare to Rotterdam and Brielle				
and the feast and what we took with us	15	9		
copper, portmanteau to				
the inn and consumed	1	16		
signing of passport, fare to Helvoet	3	16		
the carriage to the inn		8		
consumed in Helvoet until the				
ship, including the barge	6	0		
Gl	67	4	44	48
			44	48
the fare from Helvoet to				
Harwich	16	2		
the servant and from board	2	4		
baggage inspection and				
consumed in Harwich	2	19		
the fare to London	18	19		
April 14th consumed in Colchester et				
coachman	3	4		
to London	5	0	32	16
	48	8		
for our baggage to our				
lodgings and 1 book of writing paper	1	4		
for guide and interpreter	1	6		
in London for various expenses	8	16		
spent another	6	12		
on the 21st paid for our board	12	12		
on the 26th Mr. Maylan called	1	16		
on the 28th to the ship's broker,				
who went there with us	6			

	Gl	St	Rhr	St
on the 29th paid for our board	12	12		
and for various expenses	6			
May 2nd paid for laundry and other	6			
on the 5th from the kitty, from which paid for incidentals	6			
on the 6th board and travelling equipage	36	12		
on the 13th up to the 20th 2 weeks' board and sundries	37	4		
on the 21st and 22nd board and room	8	18		
on the 24th up to the 27th for food and drink	24	0	117	4
	175	12	194	8

	Gl	St		Rhr	St
Carried over	175	12			
May 28th and 29th room rent and lunch	3				
June 1st invited Mr. Mayland for a glass of wine and for our meal and cheese and butter on board	31	6			
our fare to the captain	201	12			
for victuals taken on board	36	6			
to have our power of attorney translated and a legal question	54	4			
10th at Duyns[31] another brandy and on board for laundry and mustard	8	4			
August 14th, 16th, consumed in New York et fare	29	12½			
	539	16½		359	53
	67		4	44	48
	48	8		32	16
	655	9½		436	57

on the 20th at the registry		8s
at Scheibler's		4s
to Mr. Weiss for copies		25s
on the 26th our lodgings		24s
for laundry		11s
Copy of Wilhelm Strepers' deed of sale		9s
to Mr. Weiss for looking through		16s
Copy of Logan's deed		12s
on the 30th to Peter Miller for translating 20s		
for research in the registry		7½s
on September 10th, 3 weeks' board		72s
	208s	6p

Carried over	208	6
September		
Rent agreements and deed of sale that		
Jan Strepers received from William Penn,		
5 in number	24	5
on the 15th research for the 1 acre	5	
paid for copy of same	10	
to the surveyor for 1 copy	4	6
on the 18th, to the surveyor for 7 warrants	22	
October two weeks' board	48	
on the 20th three weeks' board	72	
on the 17th, to Lehman for the questions	20	
on the 18th, to the King's Counsel	60	
Translation of power of attorney	20	
August 29th, to cousin Strepers	50	
September 13th, to cousin Strepers another	20	
for copying	2	
from August 28th to October 29th, 8 times		
to Germantown for clarification,		
also having to spend on consuming with		
many people here in town		
in total	115	7
	682	

that is £3 sterling 2s

So up to October 29, 1764 we received
in total from cousin Hollender
and the other friends,

Hollender and Mickenschreiber	135	Gl St
cousins Königs and Moll	135	
niece Laufs[32] and cousin Dürselen	67	10
cousin Strepers	25	
	362	10

cousin Hollender in Delft			
advanced another		210	
letter of exchange to Peter Stapel		231	0
	Gl	803	10

see the bill of April 9, 1766
Now cousin Strepers out of his own
money advanced another · · · · · · · · · · · · 60
on April 27, 1765, cousin received
£4 Pennsylvania money

and I advanced at Vessem			
5 Gl 17 st, and of my ribbons et			
s		12	13½
	Gl	876	3½

on October 12th received from H. D. Wüster (should have been
£25, on counting turned out to be only £23 5s)
when I told him so, he replied he had received it like that,
returned on April 16th

expenses out of this as follows
April 14, 1765 a letter of exchange from home £52 sterling 17s
3d, on January 12th, from Mr. Hasenclever, and on April 27th
also from Mr. Stevens £50, together £100, on October 13th
from Mr. Hasenclever another £30 New York money, is
in Philadelphia money £27 13s 6d

Expenses

	s	d
on November 1, 1764		
paid to Brockden for the copy in English of Jan Strepers of 1715	4	6
1 bottle of rum 1s and with Müller	1	
et Janssen consumed at the King of Prussia	1	6
up to November 18th, that is 4 weeks' board	96	
on the 12th consumed on the Schuylkill	1	6
consumed at the little tree, ½ pound of tobacco and pipes	1	6
to put new soles on my shoes 3s, 3 small tubes 9d	5	9
cousin Strepers' boots 2s, cousin Strepers advanced another	1	
our baggage from New York to Philadelphia	7	6
from the boat to our lodgings	1	6
on the 10th 1 bottle of rum, on the 18th another bottle	2	
on the 18th a pound of tobacco and snuff	1	
paid for laundry. NB Märel, Scharss	10	
two books of paper, per book 6d at	1	
on the 23rd one week's board and 1 pint of rum	25	
NB otherwise 25s		
a letter to New York	2	6
on the 25th Mr. Hoffman and three others collected money for the		
poor Germans so they could get off the water[33], for which I gave	7	6
board up to December 1st and a bottle of rum	25	
to have the chimneys done	5	
on the 2nd sat with cousin van Acken and a punch	2	
on the 7th a jug for boiling water	3	
ditto paid to the barber	12	
¼ pound of tea, 1 pound of sugar, ½ pound of tobacco	3	9
on the 9th 1 week's board, 1 pint rum		
on the 6th again with cousin van Acken	239	
£ 12	6	6

		p
on December 11th 1 pint of rum, 3 pairs of small tea cups		
and for 2d tobacco at	2s	7p
on the 16th one week's board	24	
ditto 1 gallon of rum, 2 pounds of white sugar	3	6
on the 17th tobacco, snuff, matches, poor money	1	3

Description	£	s	p
on the 23rd one week's board		24	
for a punch when Mr. Stevens and 1 gallon of rum		2	6
to cousin Strepers			
on the 27th to Ehrenzeller for translating the contract		3	9
from October 31st, consumed at midday 3s 6d, at night 5s		8	6
1765, on January 1st consumed on the way to Amboy		5	4
on the 2nd and 3rd consumed in Amboy		13	10
on the 4th to New York and ferry money		2	7
on the 5th with Mr. Stevens to Flatbush and since I went with him			
I shared paying for the sleigh and a punch and the crossing		9	14
on the 13th in New York what was consumed together with Mr. Rübel and			
with Mr. Pollman		65	9
on the 13th, 14th and 15th consumed in Amboy		17	3
fare to Cranbury		2	6
on the 16th consumed in Cranbury		2	9
fare to Philadelphia		15	
midday and evening in Burlington		4	6
breakfast on the 17th		1	
Pollman for translating		7	6
		9	0
	7	16	8

Description	£	s	p
paid to Mr. Berenstecher from December 23rd to January 20th		63	
including 1 gallon of rum		1	
and for Mr. Hasenclever's food and drink with us paid to Mr.			
Bärenstecher		7	6
	14	10	4

Description	s	p
on March 2, 1765, cousin Strepers went to Germantown		
1 pound of sugar when cousins de Wies and van Acken	1	4
on the 2nd another 2 pounds of sugar	2	8
on the 3rd board	24	
on the 8th barber's wages	12	
on the 10th board	24	
ditto consumed at Scheibler's with the two Messrs. Kurtz	5	
on the 16th with Mr. Stevens, when he took the deeds with the men	4	6
on the 17th board	24	
ditto my black leather trousers 15s	15	
on the 18th at Mr. Apply's a sangaree et tea	2	
on the 20th I was bled	1	
ditto I a sangaree	1	6
for me rhubarb	1	6
snuff, pipes and a book of paper	2	6
on March 31st, board	25	
see above when cousin Strepers to Germantown on the 2nd	10	
and on the 7th taken on a ride to Abington	20	

on April 3rd I rode with Mr. Schreiner to Germantown
to find out where the deeds had been recorded, at Mrs. Magnets'

	£	s	d
1 pint of wine		2	6
on Chestnut Hill with cousin Wilhelm Strepers and Schreiner two sangarees		3	
with Jansen 1 gallon of wine, return		2	6
Hass took for one sangaree		3	
hiring horses		3	
a pencil at VanLaaschet's			6
	£9	10	6

		s	d
on the 7th board		24	
1 gallon of beer		6	
I to the collection		1	6
on the 17th on taking possession bought for the new house ¼ pound of tea, 1 loaf sugar, 3 pairs of rough tea cups and a basket		13	9
on the 9th ditto a sangaree		2	
on the 10th we wanted to get ourselves naturalized, had to have a certificate from the minister which is usually 1 dollar, but he wanted to take only 1 because we gave him a book of psalms for a present [...]		15	
ditto for a letter from New York and a glass of bitter water		2	2½
on the 11th to Ehrenzeller for translating the power of attorney which Mr. Stevens wanted to have us sign		7	6
on the 13th for paper		7	
on the 4th board		24	
ditto postage for a letter from home		13	9
ditto to Noll for hiring horses, 2 gallons of rum, one gallon of wine		6	
on the 15th we rode with Mr. Stevens and Mr. Kurtz, whom we took with us because of the language, to Bucks County, to take possession there as was done. There leased to a farmer 175 acres for 2 years, at £4 sterling, 10s Consumed in all during those 3 days including hiring horses	£6	12	9
on April 21st board		18	6
left as a deposit with Lehman		15	
on the 25th one sangaree		2	
on the 27th for me one pair of shoes at 8s 6d		8	6
	14	6	½

		s	d
on the 27th I rode to Delis Strepers to see a letter that was said to have 9 seals affixed to it, if it was the one signed in Amsterdam, consumed and hiring horses		7	6
on the 28 board		24	
on the 30th court, in the evening with the constable, Kurtz and Schreiner at Appely's 6 jugs of beer and tea		3	6
on the 1st given to our lawyers so the case could be concluded	£8		
ditto invited Mr. Pollman for lunch and Mr. Kurtz, because they did not only accompany us everywhere but also interpreted for us in court, bought them wine		7	6
to Porcket who was there for 2 half days as a witness and for loading 1 cart of stones		5	
on the 2nd for gin for Mr. Kurtz and ourselves		1	

on the 3rd and the 4th to Germantown, to copy at Janssen's
from the first court books where Wilhelm Strepers took his 100 acres,
which was indeed found out by Lehman and Pollman. Janssen said, I should
certainly give something to Lehman because he did not ask anything
for his trouble, paid to him

consumed at Mrs. Magnets' (for his trouble, paid to him)	7	6
consumed at Mrs. Magnets'	7	9
on the 4th when cousin Strepers came to see us another	11	6
at Hass' 5 sangarees, each ½ crown	12	6
hiring horses for 2 days with the chaise	15	
on the 5th board	24	0
£14	6	9

	s	d
on May 27th consumed at Scheibler's, Pollman, Kurtz and ourselves, because Pollman did not want anything for his troubles	7	6
ditto also paid what Mr. Kurtz and I had consumed at Scheibler's on April 27th	6	6
to John Plass who paid another man to work in his place for 3 days while he was a witness	13	
on May 8th ½ book of paper 1s, pipes and snuff	1	7½
ditto with Mr. Pollman 1 gallon of Madeira wine	2	6
on the 11th 1 gallon of rum, on the 12th to Frankfurt with Pollman	7	6
ditto board and for cousin van Acken and Mr. Pollman	25	
on the 14th with Mr. Pollman and Stevens to Germantown to Justice Eschschmit et Biddes, consumed	6	6
for me ½ yard of bandages for my arm at 6d and for schnapps 3d		3
for each of us a hat 64s at 32, for me a neckerchief of flowered cloth 56s at 4=6 at 2 yard		
paid to Noll for hiring horses and what was consumed	10	
Now Mr. Pollman did not want anything for his translating which would otherwise certainly have cost us £10		
on the 17th postage for letters to Germany	4	
had another chain and a lock put on the fence		9
at the "Rising Sun" a jug of beer	6	
paid for our laundry up to May 19th	40	
ditto board	24	
on May 19th at Weydman's, 6s	6	
on the 21st to the man who carted our house to the spot	12	
ditto Bärenstecher board for 2 days	7	
to Bill when he left as a tip	1	6
returned the £25 sterling to Daniel Wüster	500	
1 pound of butter and 1 pound of candles and one candle separately	1	9
¼ pound of tea, 1 jug of beer and to Mr. Ross 5s	7	6
£34	5	1½

Marked the barrels I H I H, No. 1#, No. 2#

	s	d
to Ehrenzeller for copying another	3	

1 gallon of rum and to Germantown 1 bowl of punch	2	6
between Germantown 1:1: and 2s	4	
1 gallon of rum and another gallon of rum	2	
on January 21, 1765 another gallon of rum	1	2
on the 25th when Mr. Hasenclever was there pipes and beer	1	3
on the 29th 1 gallon of rum and 1 sugarloaf	8	10
snuff		4
on the 26th one week's board	24	
and for van Acken eating with us	1	
on the 29th 1 gallon of rum, on February 1st 1 gallon	2	4
on the 3rd board anfd for cousin van Acken	3	
and his wife and children	24	
ditto one sangaree at Appelie's	2	
on the 4th 1 gallon of rum, on the 6th 1 gallon of rum	2	4
on the 10th board and on the 8th 1 gallon of rum	25	2
snuff		4
cousin Strepers consumed traveling to New York	84	1
on the 16th 2 gallons of rum and one week's board	24	7
consumed on 4 trips to Germantown	15	10
with Mr. Bärenstecher across the river	3	
to cousin Strepers	100	
For more small beer, poor money and snuff	2	9
on February 24th board	24	
on the 28th cousin Strepers rode to Germantown with Mr. Stevens	7	6
ditto snuff	6	4

£18 16 5

	Rhr	Str
1764, on February 15th sent to Pennsylvania as follow		
8 double dozens of iron spindles		
per dozen 53 St at	7	4
5 dozen cake pans, per 100 pounds 13 Rhr, that is 179 pounds	23	17
½ dozen tailor's scissors assorted	3	
½ dozen common sugar tongs		56½
½ dozen ditto with turned handles	1	12
½ dozen fire tongs	54	
½ dozen curling tongs/irons	1	19

Coffee grinders, common		
No.0, ½ dozen, 23 st apiece	2	18
No.1, ½ dozen, 26 st apiece	2	36
No.2, ½ dozen at 29	2	54
No.3, ½ dozen at 32	3	12
No.4, ½ dozen at 36	3	36
No.5, ½ dozen at 41	4	6
No.6, ½ dozen at 47	4	42

Dutch best quality coffee grinders		
No.0, ½ dozen at 27 st	2	42
No.1, ½ dozen, 30	3	

	Rhr	St
No.2, ½ dozen at 33	3	18
No.3, ½ dozen at 36	3	36
	73	42½

	Rhr	St
No.4, ½ dozen at 41 st	4	6
No.5, ½ dozen. 47	4	42
No.6, ½ dozen, 54	5	24
1 coal iron No.3		31
1 ditto No. 1		22
1 ditto with rectangular bars No. 3		31
1 ditto No. 2		27½
1 ditto No. 1		22
1 ditto ordinary		17½
1 English coal shuttle	1	12
6 dozen pieces of patterned ribbon 40 st apiece	48	
6 ditto 36 apiece	3	36
½ dozen 2 punch pliers at 40 st apiece	4	
½ dozen ditto with colored necks 30	3	
1½ dozen ordinary at 20 st	6	
2 dozen shovels, half polished, at 11 st	4	48
1½ dozen ordinary pliers at 11 st	3	18
1½ dozen polished all over at 12 st	3	36
2 dozen ditto, black, assorted at 10 st	4	
1½ dozen baking irons at 10½ st	2	34
Rhr	100	47

	Rhr	St
300 drills, assorted, ordinary, per 100 pieces 55	2	45
100 ditto, fine	1	50
No. 2, ditto 49 pieces per 100 No	1	40
No. 2½ ditto 40 pieces	1	40
No. 3 ditto	1	40
No. 3½ ditto	1	40
No. 4 ditto	1	40
4 dozen sharp English chisels, assorted per dozen 40 st	2	40
1 dozen No. 5, English	1	15
2 dozen strips, sharp, assorted	1	15
1 dozen English chisels, assorted	1	30
½ dozen ditto, No. 5	1	15
1 dozen mortise chisels, assorted	1	30
½ dozen chamber locks with two latches at 55 st	5	30
½ dozen with one latch at 40 st	4	
paid to the customs officer 3 ducats	10	30
to the inspector and consumed	13	50
double freight to Duisburg	9	52½
franco Rotterdam, per 100 gl import and the freight, that is at 300 gl	17	20
Rhr	83	22½

	Rhr	St
one hunting knife	3	30
4 ps. specimens[34]	4	
6 cat.[35]	1	48
Paid for barrels, straw and packing	3	20
	12	38
	73	42½
	100	47
	83	22½
	270	30

1766, on June 18th to Master Jacob Ziegenfus and Peter Schidt 8 dozen iron spindles, 2 dozen tailor's scissors, 7 dozen coffee grinders, 5 flatirons, 300 ordinary and 100 fine drills, No. 2, 2½, 3, 3½, 4 drills per 100 No. All this I sold for 104 gl 14 st. received this day [date omitted] with my thanks.

73	42½	104		210	
100	47	82		124	
83	22½	186	62	86	
258	52	3			
48					
210	52				

final total

From Master Trippel from Schaffhausen a recipe for stain at sea, August 8, 1764

A blue stain
¼ ounce indigo, ¼ ounce Arsenicum Rubonum[36], crush these two substances, each separately, into a powder, then mix them together well. Fill this into a glass bottle or a mortar and pour on it 1 ounce of concentrated oil of vitriol[37], rub it tiógether well until it has turned into a paste. Then keep it protected from the air in a jar with a glass stopper. Now if you want to use it, take warm water, as much or as little as you need and add of the blue color as strong as you want to have it.
To make a green stain, take the root terra menita[38], also crushed on stone. Add it to the blue and leave it for 2½ hours.

[Content of the pocket at the back of the book: 4 accounts]
[Sheet 1:]

What I paid from the kitty for my own, Johannes Herbergs', expenses

	Gl	St
Watch [?], cousin Strepers' silver rings	2	12
Amsterdam 1 box or tobacco box	1	2
also in Amsterdam a brush		4½
in Helvoet some silver rings from an East Indiaman	2	5
in London a pair of stockings	1	8
Cousin Strepers' watch 12 Rhr	16	10

one penknife 6 st, one purse		11
for small nuts in London		6
for postage for a letter from Mr. Mickenschreiber		10
for beer for four and another jug		14
to have my rings made		1½
at the coffee house for myself		3
to Jack for tips 2½ st, 2 St for having my shoes done		4½
for poor money 3 st, 1 pencil 2 st		5
6 penknives	1	9
spent on my hat		11
2 penknives 3 st apiece		6
from Mr. Meilan new money		11
a red woollen cap		11
2 pieces of copper money 1 st and 1 st to the poor		2
for fishing line 2½ st and ½ jug of cider		8½
3 corkscrews		4½ St
1 st pencil, 3 st cedarwood pencils		4
1 st for beer, ½ st for poor money		1½
6 small spoons, 1 key ring		3½
the description of London		11
two punch I lost with cousin Strepers at sea	1	1
	33	½

Now of what is shown on the right, half has to be added, that is	8	4
Now my brother-in-law's and my share of the		
traveling expenses	135	0
Rhr	176	5¼

Now the 20 guineas which Mr. Mickenschreiber
paid for me to Mr. Stapel
  20 – each at 11 gl 11 st
201
231 gl
231
176   5¼
Now my debit all this written down here, remains as my
credit gl 54 14¾

[Sheet 2:]

	s	d
on March 17th, for me a pair of black leather trousers at	15	
on the 21st bled	1	
ditto one sangaree at	1	6
for rhubarb	1	6
1 gallon of wine for sweating	2	
on the [omitted] to Kämly for 2 Spanish flies	2	
offering in church, I gave	1	6
on April 27th I bought a pair of shoes	8	6

I another gallon of wine with cousin Strepers, cost		1	
on May 14th 1½ yards of bandage 6d, for schnapps 3		9	
ditto two hats		64	
one flowered neckerchief at 2 yards		4	6
on June 1st I bought a squirrel for 2s and a cage for 5½		7	6
I 1½ yards of flowered material, cousin Strepers 1½ yards			
and Mr. Ross 2 yards flowered material		8	
on September 16th I had new soles put on my shoes		2	?
on October 8th a pair of stockings		4	6
on October 1st a pair of shoes 7s 6d, to the boy 3d		7	9
on January 11, 1766 a squirrel wheel		6	3
on March 31st I had a note put into the Germantown paper			
because of Mühlenberg		4	0
	7	3	3

[Sheet 3:]

		s	d
from September 2nd to 8th		13	3
ditto paid to the barber for ½ year		24	
on taking possession of the Liberty land for food, drink and wages		63	8½
from 9th to 14th		14	
from 15th to 21st		16	
from 22nd to 28th		27	9½
from 29th to October 5th including 10s postage		37	7
from 6the to 12th		20	11
from 12th to 19th		21	1
	11	19	1

on October 9th paid for fare to go to New York and back		15	5
consumed up to the 19th		42	7
from October 20th to 26th including one pearl cedar at 8s and sawing			
2 carts of wood 12s and laundry		53	
from 27th to November 3rd		36	4
all of November including the two carts of wood		70	7
	15	17	11
all of December not counting expenses on the			
Liberty land		92	3
all of January 1766		76	4
in February paid to Trautwein ½ year		24	
I consumed traveling to New York in 10 days		65	
otherwise spent that month		30	7½
all of March, including what was given back to Ross		154	6½
	46	6	½
the fare to New York another		22	5

[Sheet 3, inside left:]

		s	d
From April 1st to April 13th, including what I took			
with me on the ship		137	4

		£	s	d
my fare £17 sterling		340		
to Wilhelm Müller another			18	9
to Ross and pipes			10	8

To strip down our house, new roof, boards and ironware, with
wages for Andreas[39], the wood carver, amounts to a total of   £47   8
without what Stevens paid on top

[Sheet 3, inside right]
1766, April 9th what I bought for my own account as
well as what was given to me as presents by friends

	£	s	d
3 coconuts, 1 groat[40] apiece		1	
1 pair of wild pigeons			5
wheat for feed		1	
4 red birds called American nightingales	2		
1 cat's fur		1	

young Mr. Kurtz gave me a sea horse
preserved in spirit

[Sheet 4:]

	s	d
on May 21, 1765 1 bread, 8d, one ham, 13½ pounds at 7d at	8	8
for bowls, plates 1s 9d, 3 pounds of meat, 16d	3	1
on the 22nd postage for Mr. Hasenclever's letter about naturalization	2	6
1 pound of sugar, 1 bread		11
on the 23rd for hatching chickens: eggs and culture	2	6
2 loaves of bread, snuff	1	4
on the 24th, 2½ pounds of meat, 1s, lettuce and pepper	1	3
1 gallon of rum, 1 pound of powdered sugar and milk	1	9
on the 25th 2½ pounds of meat, 1s 3d, 1 bread and 1½ gallon of beer	2	7
6 eggs, 4d, 2d tobacco and to Mr. Ross 15s	15	6

on the 26th we rode to Burlington to be naturalized, something
they charge for £40 to 50 for each of us here in Philadelphia.
This cost us including what we consumed on two rides to Burlington and

	£	s	d
all other expenses, so spent in total	£ 9	2	10½

on the 30th at half past 11 we were naturalized.
on the 31st bought from Mrs. Bärenstecher wood, sand, a bottle and

	£	s	d
a glass for it		10	9
ditto a letter from Germany			6
on June 1st to June 7th consumed		27	5½
on the 5th and the 6th I to Bucks County, horse hire		7	
consumed with the horse		11	9

bought for ourselves through Schneider one pan, a pothook, a pot,
1 cushion, 1 blanket, 3 chairs, a tea kettle, 3 candlesticks,

	£	s	d
a table	3	7	7
	£17	8	

[Sheet 4, inside left:]

	£	s	d
on the 7th paid to Mr. Stelwagen for the boards according to paper	3	14	
from 7th to the 14th spent on the household		24	11
on the 14th the copy of Logan's deed		6	11
on the 15th 2 hams, 35 pounds at 7d a pound		20	
and on the 16th 8 pounds of veal and bread, also consumed on the way to Germantown and to the surveyor 3s for researching the Liberty land		15	3
from 17th to 23rd spent in total		19	1
horse hire and consumption on trip to Bucks County 3 days		55	
from June 24th to 30th consumed		17	7½
from July 1st to 7th consumed		16	8
on the 4th to lawyer Dickinson		40	
on the 6th to Henrich Miller for advertisement		12	
ditto to Brockden for Leonhard Arets' deed		8	6
a tablecloth and a towel at 4½ yards at 18d		6	9
up to the 14th consumed		23	6
from 15th to the 21st consumed		20	3½
to have our rooms cleaned		1	6
from July 22nd to 28th		17	11
postage for a letter from Germany		5	
to Catharina Kernen for laundry		7	6
from July 29th to August 4th		27	
from August 5th to 11th		23	10
from 12th to the 18th		24	
from 19th to the 25th		28	2
from 26th to September 1st		20	3
	£25	25	8

[Sheet 4, inside right:]

How to varnish over paintings
Cook glue from parchment barely thick enough to make it just stiff when it is cold. And paint over the painting twice. Then go over it twice with varnish. That is all.

Lacking parchment one can also use pig's bladder, cut small soaked in schnapps or brandy and then boiled. Paint over twice with this, as above. Learned from H. Lansche in Düsseldorf, on May 12, 1775.

[Sheet 4, 4th page:]
Without Eply's bill we paid for the new house £10 13s 7d

1 Green Tree Tavern, Germantown Avenue, built in 1748 by Daniel Pastorius [Ernest Howard Yardley, "Old Inns and Taverns of the Great Road", *Germantown Crier,* IV, 2, June 1952].

2 A drink made from wine, water and brandy sweetened and spiced, also a cold drink made from wine and lemonade or juice, derived from the Spanish word sangria.

3 The German is not quite clear here.

4 Abington, Montgomery Co.

5 Certificate to prove that he had taken communion.

6 Letters were often sent poste restante and then announced in the newspapers.

7 An inn halfway between Philadelphia and Germantown.

8 Chelsea or Chelmsford?

9 The Germanized name is Neu Castel (=new castle).

10 This is a proven remedy.

11 Sodium tetraborate.

12 An old fluid measure, varying between 159.8 liters (large ohm) and 95,71 liters (small ohm), depending on the region. Standardized to 150 liters in 1810 [Brockhaus, (Mannheim, 1991), XVI, p. 134].

13 Albus or white penny, a small silver coin minted in western Germany since 1366, first by Archbishop Bruno of Trier.

14 Radix Pyrethri Germanica, a medicinal plant.

15 Mother of vinegar: any substance soaked with vinegar, such as wood, wood shavings or the fungus acetobacter which covers the liquid turning into vinegar as a thin white film or collects at the bottom, can be used as a ferment for vinegar [Meyers Konversationslexikon, 6th edition, 1905-1913, XI, p. 365].

16 The German is not quite clear.

17 Schmitz: it is 5 (8) ells from one schmitz to the next, the daily output of a hand loom weaver; one schmitz is approximately 4 metres (13 feet); a "piece" = 8-12 schmitz [RHWb., vol. 7, col. 1500].

18 Radix gentiana.

19 Dram or drachm, an Apothecaries' weight equal to 1/8 ounce [Brockhaus, (Mannheim, 1988), V, p. 646].

20 Balsamum peruvianum, chinchona.

21 German not clear.

22 Probably: Petrus Simons, Kaldenkirchen, see Simons family tree.

23 Probably: Englishman (Anglo-Saxon).

24 The inn "The Golden Hunter".

25 Probably: Item per = ditto for.

26 Landlady in London.

27 As the German uses the diminutive form, possible a half pint jug.

28 Bedding or paillasse serving as a bed.

29 Probably by the court.

30 East of Eindhoven.

31 Probably Deal since the journal mentions anchoring there on June 10th.

32 Agneta Lauffs, née Strepers.

33 They could not get off the boat because they were unable to pay for the passage. The money owing was probably paid on November 29, 1764 [Strassburger/Hinke, 1, p.701]

34 Possibly: personal items, the German is not clear

35 Possibly: catalogues, here, books with tool samples

36 Red arsenic(II)-sulfide, mineral realgar, also known as ruby arsenic, red orpiment; the stain was probably used as a wood preservative. Information from Dr. chem. Manfred Schön, Zülpich.

37 German: Olium Vitrioli Consentratum = concentrated sulphuric acid. Information from Alexander Auer, pharmacist in Mechernich, Germany.

38 Terra Menita = yellow ginger or curcuma.

39 Possibly: Andreas Berenstecher or Andreas Borner.

40 An old English silver coin.

The Legal Dispute in Philadelphia and Bucks County

The entries in Johannes Herbergs' journal break off after April 5, 1766, without reporting any concrete success in the land case. The reader is told at the end that Peter Heinrich Strepers is to stay in Philadelphia until the legal action pending in the courts in Philadelphia and Bucks County has been decided. Johannes Herbergs, on the other hand, started on his homeward journey around April 13, 1766. His itinerary can only be pieced together from his accounts. In England he visited the cities of Chelsea and Newcastle. From England he sailed to Middelburg, and from there he went home via Rotterdam. It may be assumed that he met his relatives on the Lower Rhine to inform them on the status of the matter. But he will not have been able to give them much good news. The contracts concluded with Richard Stevens, Peter Hasenclever and James Parker were purely preliminary contracts which would only generate money if and when the court action was successful and the Strepers' lands recovered.

Johannes Herbergs and Peter Heinrich Strepers had prepared painstakingly for their journey to Pennsylvania, helped by their relatives on the Lower Rhine and from Ronsdorf. Any contemporaries that had connections to Pennsylvania or even knew the province themselves were contacted, for instance the "woman from Pennsylvania" to whom Peter Heinrich Strepers talked, and Hermann van Laschet in Krefeld, who gave them a letter for his brother Christian in Germantown.

The first visit in the New World was to Pastor Rübel on Long Island, who had been a minister in Philadelphia for several years and who certainly gave the two travelers good advice and names of contacts to further the undertaking. In Philadelphia the first person they approached was Ernst Kurtz, probably a former acquaintance of Pastor Rübel's and, in adition, being one of the first members of the German Society in Philadelphia, on close terms with the leaders of that organization, whose purpose was to help German immigrants and settlers with advice and support. However, Johannes Herbergs' and Peter Heinrich Strepers' experience with the representatives of this organization seems to indicate that the Society was established to further the interests of already established Germans rather than those of new arrivals.

Through their contacts with members of the German Society, Herbergs and Strepers deemed their "just cause" in the best of hands. Being unfamiliar with the legal customs of the province of Pennsylvania, the English laws and the web of relationships between German and English Pennsylvanians, however, they were soon forced to realize the many obstacles standing between them and the achievement of their goal of recovering Jan Strepers' land for his descendants.

At the very outset of their journey, adversaries in Ronsdorf had attempted to foil their plan of "taking the land back": Johannes Herbergs had yielded to the persuasive powers of his brother-in-law Peter Sieben, the Ronsdorf schoolmaster, and had left his home town Waldniel for Ronsdorf. There he had settled as a merchant and weaver, which was the occupation most frequent among the Ellerians. He soon gained access to the head of the Ellerians, Johannes Bolckhaus, probably again through the mediation of Peter Sieben. Under the protection of the head of the sect, Johannes Herbergs was elected to various influential positions in the community, which comprised both religious and secular responsibilities. He can certainly be counted among the members of Bolckhaus' inner circle.

A striking characteristic of the Ellerians was their recruitment of influential merchants. Their business sense formed a smooth alliance with their radical Pietist thinking. From their very establishment, they sought to present themselves as unique. The contents of the so-called "Shepherd's Purse"[1], which can be considered the book of minutes and membership roll of this chiliastic sect paint a terrible picture of its founder Elias Eller and his second wife Catharina vom Büchel. For example, the two called themselves the "founders of the new and magnificent kingdom of Christ". From their union was to come "the Governor to rule over God's people ... that unto him should be given the power over all flesh". Eller and his wife assured their brethren "that the kings of the earth would come and fall to their knees before them", and they were certain "that nobody understood the Holy Scriptures but they alone". Thus, it was only logical for them to conclude "that theirs was the kingdom in heaven and on earth". Referring to the Apocalypse and in analogy to names given to the Mother of God, Eller and Büchel call themselves "Elia the servant of God; the Right Hand of God; God's signet-ring; the Prince Zerubabel; Father of Zion" and "the Mother of Zion, the Mother of Jerusalem, the Mother Ewe of the Lambs; the Woman clothed in Sun; the abode of God among men; the Arch of the Covenant; the dove and beloved of Christ; the dove Copher; a chosen jewel". In the context of a sect with such an absolute leadership it is understandable that Herbergs blindly trusted Eller's successor Johannes Bolckhaus.

In his journal Johannes Herbergs presents himself as a purposeful businessman. His religious beliefs are a thing apart. Although during his stay in London, he complains that there is little or no prayer at meals – implying that he was quite zealous in his prayers – he also confesses freely to his diary that he, like many other inhabitants of Philadelphia, did not go to church at Christmas. Possibly he also indulged in the same leisure activities as most of them, hunting or dancing. Business, money was the focus of his attention, and money was what he pursued with an iron will, never shying away from any conflict arising in the course of the dispute with the new owners of the Strepers' properties, quite unlike his companion Peter Heinrich Strepers, who preferred to stay in bed when things got dangerous.

By the 1760s, the Ellerians, at times a breakaway group from the Reformed Church, that came together regularly in Ronsdorf for conventicles from which no information leaked to the outside world, as the members had pledged themselves to secrecy, had split up into three separate groups after a quarrel. Johannes Herbergs sided with the leader, Johannes Bolckhaus, hoping to obtain the latter's support for his case. His confidence in such support repeatedly figures in his journal when he threatens

his adversaries in Pennsylvania with Bolckhaus' power who, as Royal Prussian Privy Counselor and Resident and Superintendent of the Reformed congregations of Jülich, Cleves, Berg and Mark and through his brother Arnold, Regimental Physician in Berlin, seemingly enjoyed unlimited influence at the court of Frederick the Great of Prussia. Therefore, it is not surprising that Herbergs' adversaries in Ronsdorf, on hearing about his project, tried to put obstacles into his way.

As early as November 29, 1764, one of them, Lambert Verhoeff, wrote a letter in clumsy English to the head of the London department responsible for Pennsylvania affairs, telling him that Johannes Herbergs had set out for Philadelphia supposedly because of some dispute over an inheritance. What he really intended to do, though, was to make a collection. Verhoeff did not mention the precise purpose of this collection, but we may assume that it was supposed to strengthen Ellerian finances. He insinuated that, through contacts to emigrants from the Rhineland, a considerable sum was to be raised. For this purpose, Johannes Herbergs was carrying papers with him, all forged, which was not surprising in view of his dishonest character. It is more likely that Bolckhaus and his Ellerians were to share the profits if the journey was successful.

Verhoeff blatantly denounced Herbergs, implying a motive that is never mentioned in the journal. Herbergs' motives for his journey were always of a private nature. But Verhoeff aimed at inducing the Governor in Philadelphia to expel the supposed collector from the country.[2]

According to a note written by Richard Stevens on September 21, 1765,[3] Benjamin Franklin did, indeed, have this letter in his hands. Consequently, he was also involved in the matter. The influential Quaker families knew the channels through which they could obtain information about any person in Europe. Thus, Johannes Herbergs and Peter Heinrich Strepers were already scrutinized soon after their arrival in Philadelphia when they wanted to take possession of the land of their forebear. Isaac and Zachariah Hope, merchants in Rotterdam, on August 8, 1766, gave detailed information to Thomas Lamar, the brother-in-law of Samuel Preston

Moore about the families of both and their connection with Jan Strepers. The two merchants, both Quakers like Lamar, also referred to Verhoeff's information by saying that Herbergs was to be considered a leading figure in the sect, but they doubted that his accusations were founded. According to their knowledge, that reaction stemmed from a religious dispute, and that is historically correct. They showed that the Ellerians were suppressed both by Catholics and Protestants and that the most awful horror stories were told about the sect, which was already in decline. Since they, the Quakers, had been subjected to a similar contempt in their early years in England, they did not consider Verhoeff's letter to be of any consequence.[4]

The Hope brothers also believed that Strepers and Herbergs had been sent primarily by the merchants Mickenschreiber in Kaldenkirchen and Hollender in Waldniel, whom they thought to be descendants of Jan Strepers – the truth was that they had both married into the Strepers family – on the journey to Pennsylvania and that they were the real movers behind it, since they were also quite wealthy. It was from them that Herbergs and Strepers had received the necessary documents and letters of recommendation.

Ernst Kurtz seems to have been the only person in Philadelphia who honestly tried to help Strepers and Herbergs. Most of all, he told them where to find the documents that proved their claim to the estate. Thus, on the very first day they learned that Jan Janssen, whose family had immigrated to Germantown from the Wickrath area, knew best about the ownership situation and the origin of Germantown properties, since he was the largest landowner in Germantown. For the Janssen family kept private archives in which almost all land transfers were documented and also the first Germantown land records were kept. It is thought that, due to the stir caused by Strepers and Herbergs with their investigations in Germantown, these land records were incorporated into the Philadelphia records.[5]

But the two only slowly found out the names of the current owners of the Strepers land. James Logan, William Penn's secretary, had brought the

largest share into his possession, namely 4,448 acres in Bucks County which he knew to have iron ore deposits – something that Strepers and Herbergs obviously remained unaware of, since they assumed this property to have good farming soil. It was more difficult to locate the acre of Philadelphia property that had been William Penn's present to Jan Strepers, although that, too, had originally been bought by James Logan and subsequently been transferred to Richard Hill and Dr. Samuel Preston Moore in 1748. The 50 acres of Liberty land between Germantown and Philadelphia were by now the property of William Logan, one of James' sons.

Among the members of the German Society, it was mostly Ludwig Weiss who was again and again approached for help. However, well-meaning German settlers in Germantown warned Strepers and Herbergs against the intrigues of their German and English contacts who used every possible means to deceive them. Representatives of the German Society also tried to explain to them that the people from whom they were trying to recover the land were influential Quakers and that their claim might well be just but would probably still be impossible to win. Nevertheless, the two trusted the law, being probably more interested in court proceedings in London than in Philadelphia or Bucks County, since they considered their chances in London to be better because of the influence of the Ellerian leader Bolckhaus.

The visits to various relatives in and around Germantown did not help Strepers and Herbergs to get ahead with their investigations. They were received with open distrust. The remark that Hendrik van Acken had already tried to take possession of the Strepers estate in the 1740s was meant to give them a sense of uncertainty. By offering the prospect of some hitherto unsurveyed farm land and some accumulated ground rent, the relatives intended to keep them quiet.

Hendrik van Acken had done a good job. From Reiner Theißen, who died in 1745, he received all of the papers and letters that had been written in Germany and Pennsylvania on the Strepers case. After Hendrik van Acken's death (1753), his brother-in-law Paul Kripner had these documents in his keeping. He permitted Strepers and Herbergs to look through them and use everything they needed. He gave them every conceivable support, certainly also for the reason that after the death of his wife Elisabeth van Acken (buried on April 17, 1761) Kripner was not involved in the estate any more and, thus, not affected financially in any way.

Another way the two men tried to recover their inheritance was to approach the owners of the Strepers lots. These were craftsmen or farmers whom they offered deeds of sale on favorable terms. According to the legal usage of the time, they took possession of the land by fencing in their supposed property, quickly putting up a clapboard house on it and having a fire burn in the stove for 24 hours, thus seeking the legal conflict with the owners, who were now forced to institute legal proceedings for a return of the land. They also used this procedure themselves by filing suits against several farmers for return of the land.

Peter Hasenclever, a merchant originally from the Duchy of Berg and by then in the service of the English crown, commissioned to optimize the yield of the ironworks in the provinces of New York and New Jersey but also involved as a private investor, seems to have been the most honest helper of Strepers and Herbergs, although he also had a strong interest in obtaining parts of the Strepers land through a purchase on favorable terms. The contact was made through Franz Caspar Hasenclever, a cousin of Peter's who, on his behalf, recruited craftsmen from the Duchy of Berg and the Palatinate for his ironworks. Since Peter Hasenclever had his office in New York and was only temporarily in Philadelphia, several trips to New York were necessary to initiate the handover of the land.

The journal describes the influence Peter Hasenclever had on the Philadelphia judiciary. But even these contacts proved worthless. Apparently, all Quakers in influential positions had rallied against Herbergs and Strepers. On the one hand, this was certainly caused by the Quaker families' own financial interests in the properties they had bought from Wilhelm Strepers. On the other hand, the enmity between Germans and Quakers had grown to such a degree that neither party was prepared to negotiate fairly. What is more, Herbergs' comments on the Quakers were not conducive to a peaceful atmosphere for fair negotiations.

Things seemed to take a more positive turn when, in November 1764, Richard Stevens entered the picture and offered to buy the rights to the land. Initially they hesitated to give their consent, on the one hand because Peter Hasenclever had his own vested interest and warned them against Stevens, who was, indeed, a speculator, on the other because the price seemed too low. But on January 8, 1765, Peter Heinrich Strepers and Johannes Herbergs signed an agreement under which they transferred a quarter of the Strepers land to Richard Stevens, merchant from Philadelphia, and Peter Hasenclever respectively, provided it was pronounced to be theirs by a court.[6]

On March 15, 1766, a contract on the sale of the other half was finally signed. James Parker, a lawyer from Perth Amboy, had been induced by Richard Stevens to take this calculable risk.[7]

Under this contract, Peter Heinrich Strepers was to stay in America until the court case had been decided, with his living expenses to be advanced by the buyers. Herbergs left Philadelphia in order to make investigations in Germany for further material for the cousins to conclusively prove their legal claims.

When, due to liquidity problems, Peter Hasenclever sold his share of the Strepers land for £500 Pennsylvania, the £50 paid to Peter Heinrich Strepers and several sums he had advanced to Strepers and Herbergs to James Parker on March 11, 1769, Strepers was still in Philadelphia. From the deed of sale it is clear that the recovery of the entire Strepers land continued to be the aim: 4,448 acres in Bucks County, 275 acres in Germantown, 50 acres in Chestnut Hill, 75 acres in Trappe, now Montgomery Co., 50 acres in the Liberty land near Germantown and three or more lots in Philadelphia.[8]

On February 11, 1769, Richard Stevens gave an estimate of the value of the Strepers lands in a letter to the merchant Thomas Riche in Philadelphia, a business partner of Parker's.[9] The land in Germantown, on which twelve to fourteen houses had been built in the meantime, would be most difficult to recover, being the most valuable. If the entire property could be sold, Herbergs and Strepers were to receive £3,000 sterling. This sum would decrease if for certain areas no buyers were found. He estimated the value of the entire property at £30,000 Pennsylvania. Since Peter Hasenclever as an investor was familiar with land prices in Pennsylvania, we may assume that he, too, was mostly pursuing his own profit.

Two questions were important in the dispute between the parties: whether on March 4, 1715, Jan Strepers had authorized his brother Wilhelm through the Kaldenkirchen burgomasters and elders to do with the 5,000 acres in Pennsylvania as he thought fit and whether the property had been transferred to him in exchange for his share of his paternal inheritance. In this context Bernhard Hollender and Peter Heinrich Mickenschreiber, who were giving financial backing to the legal dispute, reacted to a letter from Philadelphia which had been instigated by Dr. Samuel Preston Moore. For he was particularly eager to compile material to defend his property. It was pointed out in that letter that beyond any doubt Jan had given complete powers to his brother Wilhelm as his agent. This view of things was hotly disputed by the merchants Mickenschreiber and Hollender.

In a letter written on November 17, 1764, in Mönchengladbach-Hardt to the notary Gerhard Delongue[10], whom they went to see later that day, Mickenschreiber and Hollender maintained that such a power of attorney as Jan Strepers had supposedly issued could never have been written in Kaldenkirchen but only in the court in Brüggen, which was responsible in that case. Therefore, the document was worthless. In addition, it had neither been signed by Jan Strepers nor by his heirs, which was most unusual. In the same letter of protest, the notary was requested to investigate the matter in Kaldenkirchen and Brüggen. On January 29, 1767, the bailiff Gottfried Casimir Bernardi issued a detailed statement in which he agreed with Mickenschreiber and Hollender.[11]

The lawyers in Pennsylvania, on the other hand, agreed with the views of the buyers in the colony who said it was true that the transfer of all rights to Wilhelm Strepers was not valid under English law. But since the power of attorney had been issued in a form that was legally valid according to German legal customs, it was also valid on American soil. Even James Parker seems to have agreed with this view, as he wrote in a letter to Johannes Herbergs on November 17, 1766.[12] The letter was addressed to Peter Sieben, Herbergs' brother-in-law, at the same time. Obviously, Parker assumed that Johannes Herbergs was traveling.

Nevertheless, Stevens, Parker and Hasenclever– just like their adversaries, above all the Moore and Logan families – tried to influence matters both through their contacts with influential lawyers and King's Counsels and through the Proprietor of the province himself. Hasenclever tried his luck with Thomas Penn by presenting himself as a successful businessman in American investments for the crown. In spite of this, Thomas Penn's answer, dated October 16, 1766, was not positive. He wrote that he was concerned to hear that the inhabitants who had bought parts of the Strepers property according to English law were now being driven off their land. He declared, also in his own interest, that the sale of the largest lot to James Logan had been completely lawful. If Jan Strepers' descendants wanted to register any claims, the courts in England would be the ones to turn to.[13] During his stay in London, Peter Hasenclever also reported to James Parker a conversation with Thomas Penn that took place on February 20, 1767. Hasenclever had tried to speak to Penn on behalf of Herbergs and Strepers but had to realize that, at least in the case of the Bucks County property, the exchange that had been made with Logan was irreversible.[14]

As Strepers' and Herbergs' adversary, Dr. Samuel Preston Moore pursued a twin strategy. On the one hand, he tried through middlemen to obtain every possible piece on information, also from Germany, to keep his share of the Philadelphia acre. On the other hand, he proposed as early as 1765 to have the matter settled through arbitrators to be nominated by the two parties to the conflict. That he was not interested in an amicable settlement becomes

Fig. 51 Philadelphia Calendar for the Year 1773, printed by Henrich Miller in Race Street. RFM.

clear from the payment to Catherine Strepers' sons in 1766, which was to satisfy potential claims by them to the Philadelphia acre.

The fact that the lawyer John Galloway, whom Richard Stevens wanted to recruit for his and Strepers' and Herbergs' purposes, also collaborated with Moore because he was also in possession of part of the Strepers estate becomes apparent from a letter to Moore dated February 7, 1766, as does the falseness of William Strepers Junior. Although he acted the loyal cousin, helping the two travelers, in reality he collaborated with the new owners and their lawyers behind their backs.[15] For on June 17, 1766, Moore certified having borrowed 29 papers in German from William Strepers, probably letters exchanged between Jan and Wilhelm Strepers and their families. These papers gave Moore complete knowledge of the true events, which showed that Strepers' and Herbergs' claim was justified. This knowledge he astutely used for his own ends, because he was now in a position to point out certain inconsistencies or matters needing clarification, and with this tactic he succeeded in considerably delaying the court case about the return of the property.[16]

Among these were the doubts cast on the family tree drawn up by the Reformed minister of Kaldenkirchen, Hamboch, for Jan Strepers' descendants. Herbergs was instructed to have this family tree certified by the Brüggen court, which was done on November 21, 1766. Of course, a translation of this certificate fell into Samuel Preston Moore's hands.[17]

One of the central questions for Parker was the issue of Wilhelm Strepers' paternal inheritance. To him, failure to furnish proof of its value and sale constituted a major disadvantage. The letter of sale of July 17, 1696, according to which Jan had bought the paternal inheritance and compensated his siblings equally for it, seems to have been unknown to him – and possibly also to Strepers and Herbergs.

James Parker enclosed a memorandum in his letter detailing the action that Herbergs was to take in Germany. As a first step, the genealogy for Peter Heinrich Strepers was to be drawn up anew and

sealed by the minister in Kaldenkirchen, and the testator had to be proved before the Lord Mayor of London who, in turn, had to set his seal to the certificate. This procedure was to be followed with the other pieces of evidence still to be furnished. The agreement between Jan and Wilhelm Strepers about the transfer of rights was to be declared null and void by the Brüggen court. The division of the paternal estate was to be looked into, especially the question of whether Wilhelm had received any payment when Jan Strepers took over the paternal property.

When Johannes Herbergs took the steps specified by James Parker, Franz Caspar Hasenclever and Johannes Andreas Borner were present and made a record of the proceedings to enable them to give correct statements before the courts in Pennsylvania.[18] They also questioned some citizens of the towns of Kaldenkirchen and Bracht who could give detailed information on the members of the Strepers family. They visited the cemetery of the Reformed congregation, saw the gravestone of Jan Strepers' son Leonhard, researched the family records and were present at the court session in Brüggen on March 28, 1768 – probably together with Johannes Herbergs – during which the family tree was certified to the full satisfaction of the Strepers clan and the agreement between Jan and Wilhelm Strepers was declared null and void.

Obviously Herbergs acted according to instructions. In a letter of February 1, 1769, to the lawyer John Stevens, Richard Stevens' brother, James Parker complained that he had never met a more stupid person than Johannes Herbergs, who returned to Europe to furnish extracts from the church records as evidence for births and marriages but then refrained from doing so because a lawyer in England deemed it unnecessary and the existing evidence sufficient – all this although Herbergs had been convinced of the contrary while he was in Pennsylvania. Parker professed himself sick of all these controversies which in the end proved to be so costly and uncertain.[19]

In the summer of 1769, Peter Heinrich Strepers also seems to have run out of patience. On August 8, 1769, James Parker told his partner

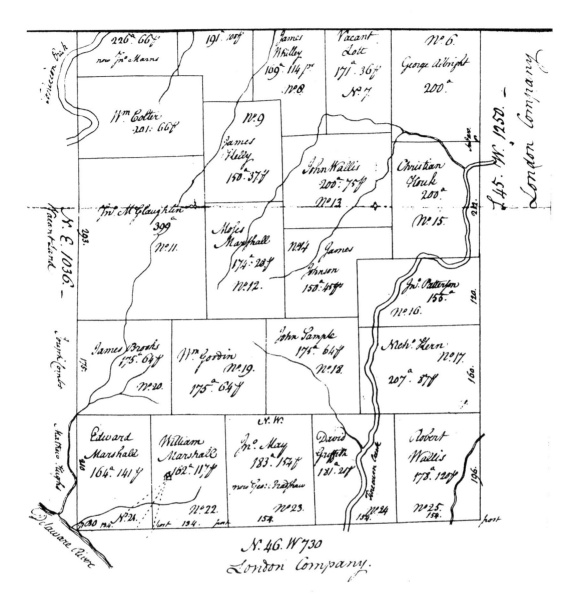

Fig. 52 Parts of Jan Strepers' land in Bucks County and their new owners.
HSP, Strepers papers (1682-1772).

Nicholas Waln in Philadelphia that Strepers was not prepared to stay in America more than another few months.[20] He asked Waln to implore the lawyers Dickinson and Tilghman to bring the Bucks County land case before the court immediately. Waln complied with Parker's wishes. He also named another witness who could testify to Peter Heinrich Strepers's identity, a friend of the latter from school in Kaldenkirchen who was living in Philadelphia.[21]

When, on top of it all, Strepers heard from Paul Kripner that now Samuel Preston Moore was prepared to settle the conflict amicably, he, who had been described by Herbergs as a coward, flew into a rage. He complained that that could have been done all these past five years, but that neither Moore nor the courts had been interested in dealing fairly. Although the matter had been dealt with in court so many times, no verdict had been given. Therefore, he had arranged with the Prussian and Palatine ambassador in London to submit a petition to the King and the Parliament to assert his rights.[22] In the letters from Strepers and Moore that followed – in part written by Moore's brother-in-law Hill – the adversaries blamed each other for the delays. Apparently both had been prepared to submit to the decision of the arbitrators. But one time they could not agree on the number of arbitrators to be nominated, another time not on their origin. Full of suspicion, Strepers had refused to have the case decided by men from Pennsylvania because he had probably ceased to trust anybody there.

On December 8, 1769, some months after having bought Peter Hasenclever's share in the Strepers estate, James Parker ceded half of his claim to Thomas Ritche, formerly of Philadelphia but by then a resident of Bucks County.[23] We may assume that, as in Hasenclever's case, a tight financial situation was the cause of this decision. Peter Heinrich Strepers was no longer mentioned in this contract. Whether he had already left Philadelphia cannot be ascertained. In any case, he did what he had threatened Moore with and submitted a petition to the King in London. However, we only know that he took this step at the end of 1771 or the beginning of 1772, because there was an

application to dismiss the case over the 50 acres of Liberty land belonging to James Logan. On January 23, 1775, the case was dismissed as applied for, since the plaintiff did not pursue the matter any further.

On April 29, 1772, James Parker wrote to Peter Heinrich Strepers in Germany telling him that he was annoyed that he had not known earlier about the early family papers that they had been given by Paul Kripner. For with the help of these documents, their adversaries had been able to anticipate each of their legal steps and play for time. He regretted that from now on Herbergs would be the only one responsible for taking decisions in the case in Philadelphia.[24] This may be an indication that Strepers left Philadelphia to return to Germany at the beginning of 1772. On June 29, 1777, forty years old by then, he married Maria Agneta Adriana Heijmans from Grambusch in the Reformed parish of Hückelhoven-Schwanenberg and probably a short time after the wedding moved to Issum, where their eldest daughter was born. With his return, Peter Heinrich Strepers lost interest in pursuing the case. He left any further steps to his cousin Johannes Herbergs.

One hundred years after his marriage, a descendant of his, Leberecht Lenssen from Mönchengladbach-Rheydt, recalled Peter Heinrich Strepers in the family chronicle[25] he began in March 1877. Here, Peter Heinrich is described as a handsome, very tall and slender man who could only escape the recruiting parties of Frederick the Great by hiding in a hollow in the ground for eight days. Because of the dampness there, he supposedly lost his hearing. According to the chronicle, even before his marriage Peter Heinrich had lived in Issum, where he ran a silk shop together with his partners Küppers and Leenderts. He met his wife in Kaldenkirchen, where she was employed in a shop. Peter Heinrich is said to have brought back some massive gold earrings from his journey to Philadelphia. The chronicler tells of a second journey to Philadelphia where Strepers supposedly bought 36 silver teaspoons for his daughter Cornelia Mechtildis. This is the only mention of a second American journey by Strepers. In contrast to the documented four journeys that Johannes Herbergs

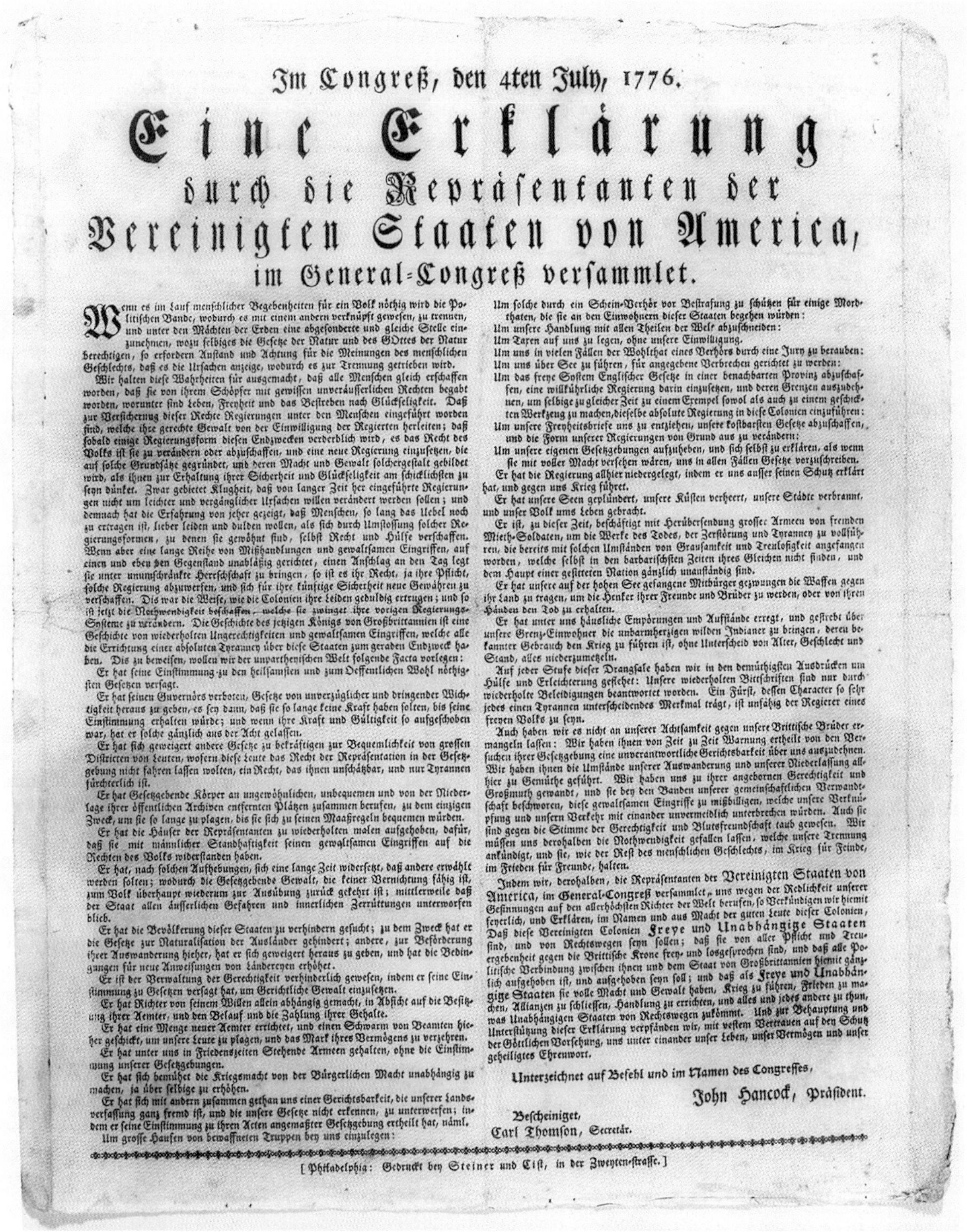

Im Congreß, den 4ten July, 1776.

Eine Erklärung

durch die Repräsentanten der

Vereinigten Staaten von America,

im General-Congreß versammlet.

Wenn es im Lauf menschlicher Begebenheiten für ein Volk nöthig wird die Politischen Bande, wodurch es mit einem andern verknüpft gewesen, zu trennen, und unter den Mächten der Erden eine abgesonderte und gleiche Stelle einzunehmen, wozu selbiges die Gesetze der Natur und des GOttes der Natur berechtigen, so erfordern Anstand und Achtung für die Meinungen des menschlichen Geschlechts, daß sie von ihren Ursachen anzeige, wodurch es zur Trennung getrieben wird.

Wir halten diese Wahrheiten für ausgemacht, daß alle Menschen gleich erschaffen worden, daß sie von ihrem Schöpfer mit gewissen unveräusserlichen Rechten begabt worden, worunter sind Leben, Freyheit und das Bestreben nach Glückseligkeit. Daß zur Versicherung dieser Rechte Regierungen unter den Menschen eingeführt worden sind, welche ihre gerechte Gewalt von der Einwilligung der Regierten herleiten; daß sobald einige Regierungsform diesen Endzwecken verderblich wird, es das Recht des Volks ist sie zu verändern oder abzuschaffen, und eine neue Regierung einzusetzen, die auf solche Grundsätze gegründet, und deren Macht und Gewalt solchergestalt gebildet wird, als ihnen zur Erhaltung ihrer Sicherheit und Glückseligkeit am schicklichsten zu seyn dünket. Zwar gebietet Klugheit, daß von langer Zeit her eingeführte Regierungen nicht um leichter und vergänglicher Ursachen willen verändert werden sollen; und demnach hat die Erfahrung von jeher gezeigt, daß Menschen, so lang das Uebel noch zu ertragen ist, lieber leiden und dulden wollen, als sich durch Umstoßung solcher Regierungsformen, zu denen sie gewöhnt sind, selbst Recht und Hülfe verschaffen. Wenn aber eine lange Reihe von Mißhandlungen und gewaltsamen Eingriffen, auf einen und eben den Gegenstand gerichtet, einen Anschlag an den Tag legt sie unter unumschränkte Herrschaft zu bringen, so ist es ihr Recht, ja ihre Pflicht, solche Regierung abzuwerfen, und sich für ihre künftige Sicherheit neue Gewähren zu verschaffen. Diß war die Weise, wie die Colonien ihre Leiden geduldig ertrugen; und so ist jetzt die Nothwendigkeit beschaffen, welche sie zwinget ihre vorigen Regierungs-Systeme zu verändern. Die Geschichte des jetzigen Königs von Großbrittannien ist eine Geschichte von wiederholten Ungerechtigkeiten und gewaltsamen Eingriffen, welche alle die Errichtung einer absoluten Tyranney über diese Staaten zum geraden Endzweck haben. Um dis zu beweisen, wollen wir der unpartheyischen Welt folgende Facta vorlegen:

Er hat seine Einstimmung zu den heilsamsten und zum Oeffentlichen Wohl nöthigsten Gesetzen versagt.

Er hat seinen Gouvernörs verboten, Gesetze von unverzüglicher und dringender Wichtigkeit heraus zu geben, es sey dann, daß sie so lange keine Kraft haben sollten, bis seine Einstimmung erhalten würde; und wenn ihre Kraft und Gültigkeit so aufgeschoben war, hat er solche gänzlich aus der Acht gelassen.

Er hat sich geweigert andere Gesetze zu bekräftigen zur Bequemlichkeit von grossen Districten von Leuten, wofern diese Leute das Recht der Repräsentation in der Gesetzgebung nicht fahren lassen wollten, ein Recht, das ihnen unschätzbar, und nur Tyrannen fürchterlich ist.

Er hat Gesetzgebende Körper an ungewöhnlichen, unbequemen und von der Niederlage ihrer öffentlichen Archiven entfernten Plätzen zusammen berufen, bis zu dem einzigen Zweck, sie so lange zu plagen, bis sie seinen Maaßregeln bequemen würden.

Er hat die Häuser der Repräsentanten zu wiederholten malen aufgehoben, dafür, daß sie mit männlicher Standhaftigkeit seinen gewaltsamen Eingriffen auf die Rechten des Volks widerstanden haben.

Er hat, nach solchen Aufhebungen, sich eine lange Zeit widersetzt, daß andere erwählt werden sollen; wodurch die Gesetzgebende Gewalt, die keiner Vernichtung fähig ist, zum Volk überhaupt wiederum zur Ausübung zurück gekehrt ist; mittlerweile daß der Staat allen äusserlichen Gefahren und innerlichen Zerrüttungen unterworfen blieb.

Er hat die Bevölkerung dieser Staaten zu verhindern gesucht; zu dem Zweck hat er die Gesetze zur Naturalisation der Ausländer gehindert; andere, zur Beförderung ihrer Auswanderung hieher, hat er sich geweigert heraus zu geben, und hat die Bedingungen für neue Anweisungen von Länderneyen erhöhet.

Es ist der Verwaltung der Gerechtigkeit verhinderlich gewesen, indem er seine Einstimmung zu Gesetzen versagt hat, um Gerichtliche Gewalt einzusetzen.

Er hat Richter von seinem Willen allein abhängig gemacht, in Absicht auf die Besitzung ihrer Aemter, und den Belauf und die Zahlung ihrer Gehalte.

Er hat eine Menge neuer Aemter errichtet, und einen Schwarm von Beamten hieher geschickt, um unsere Leute zu plagen, und das Mark ihres Vermögens zu verzehren.

Er hat unter uns in Friedenszeiten Stehende Armeen gehalten, ohne die Einstimmung unserer Gesetzgebungen.

Er hat sich bemühet die Kriegsmacht von der Bürgerlichen Macht unabhängig zu machen, ja über selbige zu erhöhen.

Er hat sich mit andern zusammen gethan uns einer Gerichtsbarkeit, die unserer Landsverfassung ganz fremd ist, und die unsere Gesetze nicht erkennen, zu unterwerfen; indem er seine Einstimmung zu ihren Acten angemaßter Gesetzgebung ertheilt hat, nämlich:

Um grosse Haufen von bewaffneten Truppen bey uns einzulegen:

Um solche durch ein Schein-Verhör vor Bestrafung zu schützen für einige Mordthaten, die sie an den Einwohnern dieser Staaten begehen würden:

Um unsere Handlung mit allen Theilen der Welt abzuschneiden:

Um Taxen auf uns zu legen, ohne unsere Einwilligung:

Um uns in vielen Fällen des Verhörs durch eine Jury zu berauben:

Um uns über See zu führen, für angegebene Verbrechen gerichtet zu werden:

Um das freye Systeme Englischer Gesetze in einer benachbarten Provinz abzuschaffen, eine willkührliche Regierung darin einzusetzen, und deren Grenzen auszudehnen, um selbige zu gleicher Zeit zu einem Exempel sowol als auch zu einem geschickten Werkzeug zu machen, diese absolute Regierung in die Colonien einzuführen:

Um unsere Freyheitsbriefe uns zu entziehen, unsere kostbarsten Gesetze abzuschaffen, und die Form unserer Regierungen von Grund aus zu verändern:

Um unsere eigenen Gesetzgebungen aufzuheben, und sich selbst zu erklären, als wenn sie mit voller Macht versehen wären, uns in allen Fällen Gesetze vorzuschreiben.

Er hat die Regierung allhier niedergelegt, indem er uns ausser seinen Schutz erklärt hat, und gegen uns Krieg führet.

Er hat unsere Seen geplündert, unsere Küsten verheert, unsere Städte verbrannt, und unser Volk ums Leben gebracht.

Er ist, zu dieser Zeit, beschäftigt mit Herübersendung grosser Armeen von fremden Mieth-Soldaten, um die Werke des Todes, der Zerstörung und Tyranney zu vollführen, die bereits mit solchen Umständen von Grausamkeit und Treulosigkeit angefangen worden, welche selbst in den barbarischten Zeiten ihres Gleichen nicht finden, und dem Haupt einer gesitteten Nation gänzlich unanständig sind.

Er hat unsere auf der hohen See gefangene Mitbürger gezwungen die Waffen gegen ihr Land zu tragen, um die Henker ihrer Freunde und Brüder zu werden, oder von ihren Händen den Tod zu erhalten.

Er hat unter uns häusliche Empörungen und Aufstände erregt, und gestrebt über unsere Grenz-Einwohner die unbarmherzigen wilden Indianer zu bringen, deren bekannter Gebrauch den Krieg zu führen ist, ohne Unterscheid von Alter, Geschlecht und Stand, alles niederzumetzeln.

Auf jeder Stufe dieser Drangsale haben wir in den demüthigsten Ausdrücken um Hülfe und Erleichterung gebeten: Unsere wiederholten Bittschriften sind nur durch wiederholte Beleidigungen beantwortet worden. Ein Fürst, dessen Character so sehr jedes einen Tyrannen unterscheidendes Merkmal trägt, ist unfähig der Regierer eines freyen Volks zu seyn.

Auch haben wir es nicht an unserer Achtsamkeit gegen unsere Brittische Brüder ermangeln lassen: Wir haben ihnen von Zeit zu Zeit Warnung ertheilt von den Versuchen ihrer Gesetzgebung, eine unverantwortliche Gerichtsbarkeit über uns auszudehnen. Wir haben ihnen die Umstände unserer Auswanderung und unserer Niederlassung allhier zu Gemüthe geführt. Wir haben an ihrer angebornen Gerechtigkeit und Großmuth gewandt, und sie bey den Banden unserer gemeinschaftlichen Verwandtschaft beschworen, diese gewaltsamen Eingriffe zu mißbilligen, welche unsere Verknüpfung und unsern Verkehr mit einander unvermeidlich unterbrechen würden. Auch sie sind gegen die Stimme der Gerechtigkeit und Blutsfreundschaft taub gewesen. Wir müssen uns derohalben die Nothwendigkeit gefallen lassen, welche unsere Trennung anfündigt, und sie, wie der Rest des menschlichen Geschlechts, im Krieg für Feinde, im Frieden für Freunde, halten.

Indem wir, derohalben, die Repräsentanten der Vereinigten Staaten von America, im General-Congreß versammlet, uns wegen der Redlichkeit unserer Gesinnungen auf den allerhöchsten Richter der Welt berufen, so erklären wir hiemit feyerlich, im Namen und aus Macht der guten Leute dieser Colonien, Daß diese Vereinigten Colonien Freye und Unabhängige Staaten sind, und von Rechtswegen seyn sollen; daß sie von aller Pflicht und Treuergebenheit gegen die Brittische Krone frey und losgesprochen sind, und daß alle politische Verbindung zwischen ihnen und dem Staat von Großbrittannien hiemit gänzlich aufgehoben ist, und aufgehoben seyn soll; und daß als Freye und Unabhängige Staaten sie volle Macht und Gewalt haben, Krieg zu führen, Frieden zu machen, Allianzen zu schliessen, Handlung zu errichten, und alles und jedes andere zu thun, was Unabhängigen Staaten von Rechtswegen zukömmt. Und zur Behauptung dieser Unterstützung dieser Erklärung verpfänden wir, mit festem Vertrauen auf den Schutz der Göttlichen Versehung, uns unter einander unser Leben, unser Vermögen und unser geheiligtes Ehrenwort.

Unterzeichnet auf Befehl und im Namen des Congresses,

John Hancock, Präsident.

Bescheiniget,
Carl Thomson, Secretär.

[Philadelphia: Gedruckt bey Steiner und Cist, in der Zweyten-straße.]

Fig. 53 First German print version of the Declaration of Independence of the United States of America of July 4, 1776. Printed by Steiner and Cist, Philadelphia. Deutsches Historisches Museum Berlin, Inv. No. 94/317.

took, there is no written evidence of such a second journey.

Herbergs continued energetically to pursue the return of the land. When in 1776 the Palatine Vice Chancellor Knapp wrote a report on the religious conflicts in Ronsdorf for the Mannheim court, he mentioned that Johannes Herbergs "had already traveled to Pennsylvania three times".[26] When, on Sunday, August 14, 1768, Johannes Herbergs sailed for the second time for Pennsylvania from London, he carried a letter of recommendation from the Secretary of State for the Colonies, Lord Hillsborough, to the Governor of Pennsylvania, obtained through the mediation of the Palatine ambassador at the British court, who acted on instructions from the Prince Elector Carl Theodore.[27] His third journey must have begun between 1772 and 1775. In 1776 he is back in Ronsdorf; on March 24, 1776 he is mentioned as a "Scholarch"[28]. Neither the minutes of the council in Ronsdorf nor the papers in the Library Company or the Historical Society in Philadelphia permit any conclusions as to the dates of the third journey.

After his wife had been buried in Ronsdorf on February 25, 1776, he stayed in the country for several years before being drawn again to Philadelphia. Since Herbergs appears before the court as early as April 1785, he must have arrived in Philadelphia at the end of 1784 or the beginning of 1785.[29] He was accompanied by Elias Werth from Ronsdorf, who was buried on June 17, 1785 in the cemetery of the First Reformed Church of Philadelphia.[30] In a letter written on September 26, 1785 in Philadelphia[31], Herbergs turned to Benjamin Franklin for help. He was now basing his hopes for obtaining his right on the new laws of independent America. But before Johannes Herbergs sailed for America for the fourth time, he again asked his Prince Elector for help. Surprisingly enough, this was actually given. An official of the Prince Elector mediated at a meeting with Franklin in Paris. Encouraged by this, Herbergs wrote a petition to Franklin who, in his journal, he had disparaged.

From a letter from Charles Moore, dated September 27, 1783, to his brother Samuel Preston, Herbergs' arrival after his fourth crossing can be dated in summer 1783.[32] Moore wrote that "Johannes Herbergs, the old stirrer" was back in the country. The Moore family was upset anew, for they had to fear that Herbergs wanted to take possession of the lots in Philadelphia. For that reason, Charles Moore had reacted quickly and contacted 83-year old Peter Tyson, Reiner's son, to look through all of the family papers again.[33] Another time the official records in Pennsylvania County were also combed through in order to find exonerating evidence to prove the rightfulness of the land transactions.

In 1788, both sides seemed to move closer to each other. There was the intention, after new court proceedings in October had not brought any decision[34], to finally settle the case with the help of arbitrators. Lists were drawn up and discarded again. The last list dates from April 10, 1789.[35] But a conclusion of the legal battle was never reached. In the Records of Deaths of the First Reformed Church of Philadelphia we find the following entry: "Buried 13 July 1789, Johannes Herbarg, poor, [paid] by Leonard Jacoby".[36] Jacoby was acting on behalf of the German Society of Pennsylvania. Johannes Herbergs had reached the age of 72 years. He had failed to fulfil his life's aim, the recovery of the Strepers land. He died impoverished. In the Register of Wills Office, the estate of Johannes Herbergs is recorded under Administration Estate No. 66. The minutes of the official recording are signed by Leonard Jacoby, Peter Heisseler [signed Peter Heisler] and William Vanpoole [signed Wm. Von Phull]. All of them were Philadelphia citizens. Leonard Jacoby who had been born in Krefeld and ran a shop for German and Dutch goods[37] was appointed executor of the estate. Johannes Herbergs' inventory contained:

1 Brown Cloath Coat & black Cotton			
Velvet Jacket & Britches	£ 1 15 -	2 Guns	1 5 -
1 Old Gray Coat 1 pear [pair] black briches		1 Portmantou	- 1 6
& One Jacket	- 10 -	1 Boxe with Schells	- 1 -
1 Strip Coat & breeches	- 15 -	3 Cases with empty Bottles	- 10 -
1 brown Great Coat	- 7 6	1 Deske & Drawers	- 7 6
1 paer Lether briches & d[it]o Jacket	- 10 -	16 large Saws	1 10 -
1 do Corelury Jacket & breches	- 7 6	2 small Saws	- 2 6
1 paer Satten breches & Jacket	- 5 -	3 Canes	- 7 6
2 paer Old briches	- 2 6	1 Tin funnell & 6 brushes	- 5 -
3 Linnen Jacket & 1 paer Drawers		2 Razon 1 Hohn, 2 Whetstones &	
& 1 paer breeches	- 7 6	two Razor Cases	- 5 -
7 paer [of] Stokings	- 2 6	Spring Lantz & Lances Sealing Waxe	
1 paer Lether Stokings	- 2 6	& Ruler	- 5 -
7 Stocks	- 2 -	8 Whips 3 Iron forks	- 1 6
9 blew Henkerchiefs	- 5 -	7 German books	1 - -
2 Cheek Sheets 2 Pillow Cases & 4 Towells	- 6 -	8 bundles Halters	- 10 -
1 Beaver & 2 Woll Hatts & Hatt boxe		1 Lott Mohear & Hatt bands	- 2 -
3 Periwicks	- 10 -	1 Lott Sundrees	- 3 9
2 paer Boats & 1 paer Shoes	1 - -	2 Doz Knee Garters	- 1 6
1 Silver Watch	3 - -	2 Doz Wheel Irons	- 10 -
1 paer Silver Shoe Buckles	- 10 -	½ Doz Snuffers	- 1 6
2 Silver Slock Buckels One paer Knee		One Lott of Sundrees	- 10 -
Buckles	- 12 6	One Lott of Hinges	- 5 -
1 Silver Tabel Spoon, 1 Tea Spoon,		One Lott of Thimbles & threat & Hair Pins	- 5 6
1 Tobacco Stopper, 3 Silver buttons sett	- 10 -	One paer Leather Stokings & 2 paer Shoes	- 3 -
1 Case with Knive & fork & Instruments	- 2 -	One Lott of Penn Knives	- 5 -
3 Paper Tobacco boxes 2 [bi?]nsckbeck		One Lott of Shumakers Aels & buttons	- 3 9
Stock buckels	- 2 6	One Lott of Seales	- 2 6
1 Pocket Compass	- 5 -	One Lott of Walfers	- 3 -
1 paer Plated Spors & 1 paer Iron	- 2 6	One Lott of Horn bottons Razors & Philes	- 4 -
2 Powder Horns & 3 Shot Pouches	- 2 6	One Lott Sundrees	- 2 6
1 boxe 2 Cork Screws 6 paer Specktakels	- 2 6	One Lott of Bruches beets Looks & bells	- 5 -
4 Duch Pips	- 2 6	One Lott of Kees, Looking Glasses Borrer	- 2 6
Tobacco boxe, & Tobacco	- 2 6	One Lott Colfin fumiture	- 15 -
1 Chest	- 5 -	One Lot of 25 Setts Casting Potts	- 15 -
2 Pewter Tea Potts & 2 Coffe Potts	- 4 -		
a Lott of Glass & Delft Ware	- 5 -	Philad[a] July 14th 1789. Philip Hall [in German], W[m]	
a Lott of Tin Ware	- 5 -	VonPhul, Philip Odenheimer, Sworn the 29th day of Sep-	
		tember 1789 Before Jno. Matthews D[t] Reg.	

1 Archive of the Reformed Church, Düsseldorf, AI IV b.
2 Lib. C.: p. 130.
3 Lib. C.: p. 136.
4 Lib. C.: p. 141.
5 Information from James Duffin.
6 HSP 247-53.
7 HSP 255; for the contract refer to App. M.
8 HSP 275, 276.
9 HSP
10 HSP 241-245.
11 Lib. C.: p. 145 and 156.
12 HSP 259.
13 Thomas Penn Letterbook, vol. 9, pp. 58-59.
14 NJHS, New Jersey Manuscripts, 1669-1840. Part III, No. 21.
15 Lib. C.: p. 137.
16 Lib. C.: p. 90.
17 HSP 265.
18 HSP 271.
19 Microfilm edition of the Stevens family papers in the New Jersey Historical Society, Roll 4, Frame 397.
20 HSP 277.
21 Lib. C.: p. 39, 40, 41, 42.
22 HSP 291.
23 HSP 279-281.
24 HSP 301.
25 Property of Margret Schopen, Mönchengladbach-Rheydt.
26 Nordrhein-Westfälisches HstA Düsseldorf: Jülich-Berg II, 1036, p. 352 r.
27 BayHSTA, Bavarian Embassy London 837.
28 School inspector.
29 Pennsylvania State Archives, record Group 33, Records of the Pennsylvania Supreme Court, Appearance and Continence Dockets, p. 225 (561).
30 Early Records of the First Reformed Church, p. 8.
31 American Philosophical Society, B/F 85, XXVII, fol. 37.
32 Lib. C.: p. 76.
33 Lib. C.: p. 76.
34 Lib. C.: p. 92.
35 Lib. C.: p. 97-102.
36 Sexton's Order Book, p. 2817; First Reformed Church of Philadelphia, Burial Records, p. 2570.
37 Seidensticker, Geschichte der Deutschen Gesellschaft, p. 500.

Appendix

Appendix A

William Penn, True [and] absolute proprietary [and] Governour in cheif of the province of pensilvania [and] Territorys thereunto, belonging To all to whom these presents shall come sendeth greeting. Whereas by my Indentures of, Lease [and] Release, bearing date the Tenth [and] Eleventh days of June in the year one thousand six hundred Eighty three for the consideration therein mentioned, I granted to Leonart Arretts then of Crevelt in the County of Meurs in the borders of Germany, Linnen Weaver (but now of Germantown in the s[ai]d province), the quantity of One thousand acres of land to be Laid out in the s[ai]d province, TO HOLD to him, his heirs [and] assigns forever UNDER the yearly Quitrent of One English shilling to be paid for every hundred acres there of (that is to say) Tenn shillings yearly for the whole forever, of which s[ai]d sum or yearly Rent by one other Indenture, bearing date the s[ai]d Eleventh day of June 1683 for the Consideration therein men[t]ioned, I Remised [and] Released to the s[ai]d Leonart Arets, his heirs [and] assigns the sum of Nine shillings to the End that only One shilling should remain payable to me as a yearly Quitrent for the s[ai]d One thousand acres forever of which s[ai]d One thousand acres the s[ai]d Leonart having taken up or disposed of the Quantity of seven hundred [and] seventy five acres, there remained to be taken up two hundred twenty five acres of the same. AND WHEREAS by my like Indentures of Lease [and] Release, bearing date the Ninth [and] Tenth days of the month called March in the year of our Lord 1682 for the considera[t]ion therein men[t]ioned, I granted unto John Streipers of Kalkerchen in the County of Juliers in the borders of Germany, Merch[an]t, ffive thousand acres of land to be taken up in the s[ai]d province TO HOLD to him, his heirs [and] assigrns forever UNDER the yearly Quitrent of one English shilling to be paid for every hundred acres thereof, that is to say two pounds tenn Shillings for the whole s[ai]d ffive thousand acres of which s[ai]d sum or yearly rent by one other Indenture, bearing date the ffirst day of Aprill in the year 1683 for the consideration therein mentioned, I Remised [and] Released to the s[ai]d John Streepers, his heirs [and] assigns forever the sum of two pounds five shillings to the End that the yearly Quitrent of ffive shillings onely [and] no more should remain payable for the s[ai]d ffive thousand acres forever. AND WHEREAS the s[ai]d John Streepers having Constituted Henry Sellen of Krisheim in the Germantownship [and] county of Philad[elphi]a in the s[ai]d province his to full Attorney by his Letter of Attorney, dated at Crevelt afore s[ai]d the Thirteenth day of May one thousand six hundred Ninty [and] Eight, proved at a court oil Record held at Germantown afore s[ai]d [and] there Recorded with full power to all altenate [!] [and] dispose of any of his, the s[ai]d John Streipers afore s[ai]d lands, As by the s[ai]d Recorded Letters, recourse being unto them, had in an more fully [and] at large appear. The s[ai]d Henry Sellen by value of all his powers [and] by his deed poll, tearing date the twenty third day of the ffirst month in the year 1702, did (for the considera[t]ion in the s[ai]d deed poll men[t]ioned) Grant [and] convey to the s[ai]d Leonart Arets the Quantity of two hundred seventy five acres as part of the [ai]d ffive thousand acres To HOLD to the s[ai]d Leanart Arets, his heirs [and] Assigns forever Which s[ai]d quantity of two hundred [and] seventy five acres being added to the above ment[i]oned two hundred twenty five acres, remaining untaken up of the s[ai]d Leonarts Own Originall purchase of One thousand acres, compleate the same ffive hundred acres. AND whereas by virtue of a warrant from my former com[m]ission[e]rs of prop[rie]ty, bearing date the Tenth day of November 1685, there was surveyed [and] laid out [and] also lately Resurveyed to the s[ai]d Leonart A certain Tract of land in the County of Philadelphia in the s[ai]d province Beginning at a post at a corner of my Mannor of Gilberts and Runing by the same land North Last five hundred [and] fourteen p[er]ches to a post then by Jacob Telnors land south Last One hundred ffifty six perches to a white Oak then by Edward Lanes land South West five hundred [and] fourteen p[er]ches to a black Oak Saptin then by s[ai]d Mannor of Gilberts North West One hundred fifty six perches to the place of Begining, containing five hundred acres which s[ai]d Tract the s[ai]d Leonart Requesting that I would Confirm to him by patent. KNOW WE that in Consideration of the Purchases afore s[ai]d [and] of the Quitrent therein after reserved [and] for other good Considerations me hereunto moving, I HAVE Given Granted, Released [and] Confirmed And by these presents forme my Heirs [and] Successors do give grant, Release [and] Confirm unto the s[ai]d Leonart Aretts, his heirs [and] Assigns forever All that the s[ai]d ffive hundred acres as the same is now sett forth bounded [and] Limitted as afore s[ai]d with all Meadows, Marshes, Pastures, Savannahs, Swamps, Cripples, Mines, Mineralls, Quarrys, Messuages, Houses, Buildings, Edifices, Gardens, Orchads, Woods, Underwoods, Timber [and] trees, Ways, Yards, Passages, Waters, Liberties, Com[m]odities, Advantages, Hereditam[en]ts, Improvem[en]ts [and] appurtenances, whatsoever to the s[ai]d ffive hundred acres of land or to any part or p[ar]cell thereof belonging or in anywise appertaining (three full [and] clear fifth parts of all Royall Mines ffree from all deductions [and] Reprisalls for digging [and] refining) of the same only Excepted [and] hereby reserved And also ffree Leave Right [and] Liberty to [and] for the s[ai]d Leonart Arrets, his heirs [and] assigns to Hawk, Hunt, ffish [and] ffowle in [and] upon the hereby granted land [and] premisses or upon any part there in TO HAVE [and] TO HOLD the s[ai]d ffive hundred acres of land [and] premisses hereby granted (Except before Excepted) with the appurten[an]ces unto the s[ai]d Leonart Arretts, his heirs [and] assigns To the only prop[rieta]rys [and] behoof of the s[ai]d Leonart Arretts, his heirs [and] assigns forever TO BE HOLDEN of me, my Heirs [and] successors prop[rieta]rys of Pensilvania As of our Mannor or reputed Mannor of Pringettsburg in the s[ai]d County of Philadelphia in free [and] com[m]on soccage by ffealty only in lieu of all other services VEILDING [and] payng therefore yearly from the first date of survey to me, my Heirs [and] successors at or upon the first day of the ffirst month (march) in every year forever thereafter at Philad[elphi]a One English silver six pence or value thereof in Coyn Currant to such p[er]son or p[er]sons as from time to time shall be appointed to Receive the same In Witness where of I have (by virtue of my Com[m]ission to my proprietary Deputies, bearing date the 28th day of October 1701) Caused my Great Seal of the   s[ai]d province to be hereunto affixed. Witness Edward Shippen, Griffith Owen, Thomas Story [and] James Logan, my s[ai]d Deputies or any three of them at the ffifth day of the second mo[nth] In the Sixth year of the Reign of our Soveraign Lady Ann, Queen of Great Brittain e[t] c[etera], the seven [and] twentieth of my Governm[en]t anno e[t] c[etera] Domini 1707 d[ei] g[ratia].

Appendix B
"Dieses ist ein Eingeschnittener Brieff gemacht auff den neunzehnten tagh deß von Jannewari, indem Jahr unssers Herrn Ein taußent [se]ckhundertzweyundt achtzich[8] und indem [Vier]undtdrytsichte Jahr der Regierungh Könighs Charles der Zweyte uber Engelandt Zwischen William Penn von Wurminghurst, inder graffschafft Sussex, Esquire, eines theyls, und Daniel Behagel handelsmann in francfurt ahm Mayn anderst theyls nach dem König [Carl] der andere durch einen offenen brief unter dern grossen siegel in Engelandt unter dem dato des tagh Marti indem dry und drytßigsten Jahr seiner Regierungh auß ursachgen wie darinnen vermelt an [obge]dachten William Penn seinen Erben und verordneten dem gantzen streich od[er] Theil des Landes in America mit allen denen darinen enthaltenen und darzu behörige Insullen ubergebben und zugestanden, wie daßelbe ostwarts gräntzet an dem delaware fluß, zwelff Meyllen von der Sta[t] [Neuw] Castlee etwaß gegen norden biß zu dem dry und fiertzigsten grade der Nord[breide] sich westwarts nach einem gezogennen [zireker]m zwölff meilen von gedachtem Neuwcasteel abgegen norden und westen von dem anfangh des viertzigsten grad der Nordtbreide und dann mit einer graden linie westwarts biß zu dem Grentzen, der obgemelde[ten] länge zu gleych mit unterschittl[ichen] grossen gewalt, vortrefflichkeit, Bottmäßigkeit herrschafft, fryheyt und befryungen, hat auch dabey solchem besachten streych landes, zu einer Landschafft und Herlichkeyt unter dem Nahmen Pensilvania gemachet, und in derselben eine neuwe anbauung od[er] anpffl]antzung zu bestättigen und noch ferner obbermelden William Penn seiner Erben und verordneten vollige macht und gewalt gegeben von Zeit zu Zeiten solche Stücke und Theile gedachter Landtschafft od[er] streichge Landes an die irrige an zu weißen zu vergebben zu verpachten, zu verlehnen, soo solche anzunehm [ ] illet und Er oder sie dieselbige richtig befinden entweder in einem einfächtigen lehen, oder nur auff Sie od[er] ihres Leibes Erben, oder auff Leben lang, oder gewisse Jahre in [erwehnten] William Penn seine Erben und verordneten gehalten zu sein, alß vonder herligkeit [wie ser] in [solchen] diensten, gebrauchen und ein kunfften, als besachten William Penn seine Erben und verordneten guttduncken wirdt, und nicht unmittelbar von dem König dessen Erben und nachkomen ungeachtet der verordnung: Quia Emptores terrarum soo inder regierungh König Eduward deß Ersten gemacht worden Nun dieses Eingeschnittene brief bezeuget, daß mehr gedachter William Penn, soo wol fohr [ ] als in ansehung der Summa von dryundtdrysich pfundt Seck Schillingh acht pheningh ₺ 33: 6: 8 [pfund] sterlingshs, soo schon vorgemelden Daniel Behageh[e]l zu handen zugestellet werden, deßen Empfangh auch gemelder William Penn hirmit bekennet, und dessenthalben auch wegen eines jedem Stück deßelben den gedachten Daniel Behaghel ihre verordnets und [verw]alten quittiret und loß zehlet mit dem nachfolgenden vorbehalt der renten [ ] dienstleystungen, hat an besagten Daniel Behaghel ubergebben zugestanden verhandelt verkaufft uberlassen und bestättiget, auch ubergiebet, stehet zu [ver]handelt verkaufft uberlasset bestatiget, durch diesem gegenwertig[en] brief in seinem wurklic[h]en besitz: [ ] durch krafft der verpachtun[g] [ ] deßelben an ihm vor ein gantzes iahr dur[ch] dem eingeschnittene br[ie]ff unter den dato des neghsten tages, von dem dato dieses gegenwertiges brieffs, und durch krafft der landtverordnung umb von dem gebrauch zu der besitzung uber zu bringen gemacht werden, und auch ihre Erben und ver[ord]neten dem volligen und rechtmässigen antheil und q[u]antitet der sechzehnhund[er]t seck und sechtzig und zweydritel 1666 2/3 Ackerlandes: ietwedder acker nach der abmessungh und rechnung der äcker [so] in und durch die indem dry und drytzighsten Jahre der Regierungh Königs Edua[rd] deß Ersten gemacht verordnung gedacht und angewiessen wirdt: in dem besachten Streichlandes, oder der Landtschafft Pensilvania gelegen und befindtlich daß die gedachte

sechzehnhundert secks undsechtzich und zweydritell an solchgem Örtern und theillen deß gedachten Streich oder der Lantschafft [ ] auf solche Ardt und weiße, und zu solchger Zeyten od[er] Zeit sollen gelösset und auß gesetzet werden, wie auch gewisse ubergebbunghen und verordnungen unter dem dato deß eylften July 1681 und von beiderseits, den besagten William Penn einestheils und den gedachten Daniel Behaghel und andern soo in gedachten Striech od[er] landschafft land angenomen anderntheils, bezeichnet gesiegelt und v[o]lzogen ist, sich mit einander, vergleichen festgesetzt und angewiesen worden, od[er] wird nach hiernechst zu bezeichnen zu siegeln und zu volzieren, durch die beyderseiderseyts theils vergleichen festgesetztet und angewiessen werden, und alsoo der gansche Estaldtrechttitull und Intres sein, daß gedachten William Penns wegen in und an den erwehnten zechzhenhundertdtseckund sechtzig und zweydritell Acker, und ietweders theil und stückleyn deßelben gantzen anden gedachten Daniel Behagel sowie Erben und verordneten vor Ewighlich zu ihrem gebrauche der gedachten Daniel Behagel ihre Erben und verordnete Ewigh gehalten zu seyn, solchges alß ein fryes und algemeyn lehnstuck von ihm den gedachten William Penn seine Erben und verordneten gleich von der gedachten herschafft und Winsor dafür jahrlichen andem gedachten William Penn seine Erben und verordneten dem Haupt und Erbzinß oder rent einen schillingh von einem jeden deß hundert aker der besachten sechzehn hunderdt seck und sechzich und zweydritell Ackers, an od[er] auf den Tagh d[e]ß Ersten Mertzens wegen und an Statt aller dinstleystunghen und geboten wie [auch] solchges sein möchten Ewigh abzustatten und erleggen, und der besachten William Penn vor sich und seine Erben und verordnets, verbindt undt vergleichet sich mit und gegen gedachten Daniel Behaghel seine Erben und verordneten auf diese volgende arth und weisse, daß ist zu sachgen daß der gedachten William Penn seine Erben und verordnet[en] ihre Erben und verordnet[en] sol und will [ ] und von solchger Zeit od[er] Zeiten als solche hirzu werden gesetz und an gewissen werden, in und durch solchge verordenungen und concessionen der bereits gemacht sein od[er] hernachger noch sollen gemacht werden sollen, nun die v[on ob]dachte zechzehnhunderdt seckundsechzich und zweydritel acker gantz klahr fry und leedigs zu machen alsoo daß sie konnen auggesetzet werden wie darinne sol gemeldet werden, und ein ieweders derselben von wegen und in ansehungh aller arten eines titulls od[er] anspruchs eines [indianers] od[er] eingesessenner, deß besachten Streychlandes od[er] solchem landschafft und alsoo daß besachten Daniel Behaghel seyne Erben und verordneten sollen und mögen these zechzehnhunderdt seckundzechzich und zwedritell Acker, und ein ieden stuck desselben ruich und friedlich besitzen und geniessen, vermö[gt] der wahre Intention und meynungh dieses gegenwartigen briefs ohnne die aller g[ering]hsten beunruingh od[er] hinderungh deß gedachten William Penn seine Erben und verordneten od[er] einigh andern persohn od[er] persohnen, wie sie auch sein mochten, die von od[er] durch ihn od[er] under ihm od[er] denselben od[er] einnigen derselben [einen] anspruch machgen oder machgen solten, und ferner daß er deß besachten William Penn seine erben und verordneten von Zeit zu Zeiten so[und will alle freunden und andere handlung und handlungen, sachge und sachgen vergebbungen und versichgerungen, wie solchge auch sein konte, daß sie durch und in [ ] desßelben Od[er] nach [ ] Intention solche ubergebungen undverordnungen die dergestalt gemacht seyn, od[er] noch sollen gemacht werden, thun machgen und volziehen wie [ ] fohr gedacht sol vergleichgen und angewiessen w[er]den Zu desse bessere beybringung vergebbung und versichgerungh der fohr ge[nann]ten Zechzehnhunderdt sech und sechtzig und zweydrittel ackers an ihm, den gedachten Daniel Behaghel sowie Erben Zu seinen und ihrer Erben Nutzen und letzlich [ ] und meynungh aller seytsparteyen [ ] gegenwärtigen zu desto besserer verwarungh und versicherungh des Titu[ll] [ ] forgedachten sechzehnhundertsekkundsechzich und zweydritel Ackers, und der ged[ac]hten Daniel Behaghel vergleichen versprechen und sagen zu [ ] [ ] verordnets, daß [ ] gedac[hte]n Daniel Behaghel nach solcher Zeit wann im [ ] gedachten Streichs landes oder landschafft [ ] ein gerin[g] und fest [ ] sollen und wollen machen und [der ver]fügungh thun damit dieser gegenwertige [unleserlich] deßelbigen indaß gemeldete Register auf soo eine art und weiße, alß [ ] sol verordnet und angewiesen [werden] [ ] gebracht und eingezeichnet werden.
(Unterschrift links)
auff die andere seyde stehet noch:
Sealed and deliveree by phillip fow ab Attorney for the within named William Penn by vertue of a legall Authority to hun by the said William G[ ]dit in the p[resent] of vs. Edward Groome, Tho:Coxe, Pill: Craske
(Siegel)
(Unterschrift rechts:) W[illia]m Penn.

Teil 2 (Über dem Text) soo en totden parrhemente ingeschneedenne brief van de afroop des st: van eyder hundert ackers - Dieser Eingeschnittene brief soo den 20tagh februwari indem vierunddrytsicht Jahr der Regierungh Carell des andere Königh uber Engeland etc. in dem Jahr deß Herrn 16[8]2 zwischen William Penn auff Wurminghurst inder Graffschafft Sussex Esquire eines theils und Daniel Behaghel von Francfordt an de Revier der Main kauffman

andertheils gemacht ist bezeuget nach dem William Penn durch seinen eingeschnittenne briefe, der verkauffungh und befryung | of Seale and Release | unte[r] dem datto des 28 und 29 tage Jannewari in Jahr des Herrn 1682 in ansehen wie darinne vermeldet ubergabe zustunde verhandelt verkaufft, uberliese und bestat getan gedachten Daniel Behaghel seine Erben und verordnedt vor Ewig das vollig[ ] und rechte antheil und quantitet der sechzehnhunderdtseck und sechtzich und zweydritel akers an des ietweder acker nach der abmessungh und rechnungh der Acker soo in und durch in dem dryund dryßichsten Jahre der Regierungh Konigh Edwardt deß Ersten gemacht ordnung gedacht und angewiesen wird in dem besachten Streichlandes od[er] der landtschafft Pensilvania in America gelegen und befindlich daß der gedachte sech[ze]hnhunderdtseckundsechzich und zweydrittel akers an solchen Örter und theilen des gedachaten Streichlandes oder der Landtschafft und auff solchge ardt und weise, und zu solcher Zeit oder Zeiten sollen gelösset und außgesetzet werden wie durch gewisse ubergebungen und verordnungen underden datto des 11. Jully 1681 und von beederseit den bes[ac]hten William Penn eines theils und den gedachten Daniel Behaghel und andern soo [gedac]hten Streich od[er] Landschafft Land angenomen, anderst theils ver gleichen gesetzt und angewies[e]n oder noch hiernechst zu bezeichnen zu siegellen und zu volziehn under und zwischen beyderseytstheiyllen wird verliehe[ ] und angewissen werden und auch d[er] gantze Estatrechttitull und Intrest [ ] gedachten William Penn wegen in und and[ern] [ ]wehnten sechzehnhunderdtseckundsechtzich und zvvey dritell akers [Streichung unleserlich] zu haben und zu behalten die gedachte sechzehnhunderdtseckund sechtzich und z[weydrittel] morgen od[er] aker und Jetwederes theyl und stücklein deßselben an Ihn den besachten Daniel Behaghel seine Erben und verordneten vor Ewigh zu seinen gebrauch deß gedachten Daniel behaghel seine Erben und verordneten vor Ewigh gehalten zu sein, solches alß eyn fryes und gemeinnes lehnst[üc]k von ihm den besachten William Penn seine Erben und verordneten gleich von der Her[r]schafft Windsor dafür Jährlichen an dem gedachten William Penn seine Erben und verordneten, der Haupt oder Erbzinß oder Rend einen schillingh von einen ieden der hunderdt ackers der besachten sechzehnhunderdt seck[und]zechzich und zweydritel ackers an od[er] auff den ersten tag deß mertzens, wegen und [ ] aller dinsstleystungen und gebotte wie auch solche sein möchten Ewigh abzusstatten und zu verlege. Nun diesser eingeschnittenne brieff bezeugeat, daß der besagte William Penn sowol fohr alß in ansehungh der s[um]ma von seck pfundt gangbare müntze in Engelandt so ihm vorgedachter Daniel Behaghel zu handen zu gestellet worden, deßen empfangh auch gemelden William Penn hirmit bekennet und deßenhalben auch wegen eines jedes Stücks deß selben dem gedachten Daniel Behaghel seine Erben und verordneten quittiret und loßzhallet und noch wegen vieler andern guten und [wich]tigen Considrationen so ihr in sonderheyt hier zu bewegen hadt nach gelaßen, befryet und loß gesprochen, und durch diesen gegenwertigen vor sich selbst seine Erben und verordneten löset[te] nach befryet und spricht loß Daniel Behaghel seine Erben und verordneten auf Ewigh, den Jahrlichgen Zins od[er] Rendt der summa von Zechzehn schillings soo ein antheyll ist deß fohrgedachten Jahrlichen Haupt od[er] Erbzinses oder rent auf einen schillingh von ietwedder hunderdt aker der besachte zechzehnhundertseck und zechtigh und zweydrittel [a]ker herkomen inden besachten William Penn: Erben und verordneten für Ewi[gh] statt und von wegen aller dienstleystungh gebotte und zinsen oder renten wie sie seyen und name halben mögten Zum Zeugnus dessen so haben die besaghte partyen unter diese gegenwartigen gegen einander ihr [H]änden und Siegel bey gefüget, so gegeben auff den Tag und Jahr erst oben beschrieben
(Unterschrift links)
auff die andere seyde deß parke[ ]te brief stehet noch
Sealed [et] Delivree by Benjamin [F]urly ab Attorney for the within named William Penn by vertue of a le[gal]l authority to hun by [the] s[ai]d W[illa]m given in the p[res]ente of John Makernes, Nathaniel Makernes, Tobias Ludwig Kolhans, Archibald Hope (Siegel) - (Unterschrift rechts:) W[illia]m Penn"

Appendix C

„Ansprach an die Nachkömmlingschaft, und Alle, die dieses Lager-Buch continuiren oder fortsetzen. Wehrte und Geliebte Nachkömlinge! Damit Ihr zu allen Zeiten wissen möget, von weme, wann, wie undt warumb die soge-nannte Germantownship sey angefangen worden; und also Eurer Vor-Eltern ursprung merckliche ungemächtigkeiten und wohlmeinendliche Intention Euck kürtzlich entdecket werde, habe ich allhier Vorredsweis was weniges darvon bey zu fügen, meiner Schuldigkeit zu seyn erachtet. Anfänglich nun Nachdem Carolus, dieses Nahmens der Zweyte, König von Engelland, durch sonderbahre Schickung des Allerhöchsten und aus erheblichen ursachen hiesige Lanschafft Pennsilvanien an Willjam Penn und seine Erben, krafft offenen brieffs de dato den 4.ten Marty 1680., übergeben und abgetretten hatte, sind nebenst andern auch einige Personen in Hoch- und Nieder Teutschland (:deren Nahmen in dem allgemeinen Patent oder Grundbrieff über diese Germantownship pag. 1.zu ersehen:) bewogen worden, in allem 43000. Acker lands in gemeldter Provinz Pennsilvanien von gedm Willjam Penn, vermittels Benjamin Furly, deßen gevollmächtigen zu Rotterdamm in Holland, an Sich zu kauffen, der zuverläßigen Absicht, bey damahligen schweren läufften sowohl selbst aus dem verwirrten Europa anhero (:als in ein zweytes Pellam:) zu entfliehen, wie nicht minder andere redliche und arbeitsame leut zu transportiren, umb allhier unter mehrerwehnten Willjam Penns verhoffentlich gerechten und liebreichen Regierung ein friedsam, still und Gottgefälliges Leben zu führen. Anno 1683. den 2.ten Monats (:Aprilis:) begab ich Frantz Daniel Pastorius mich (:gleich ein Vorläuffer vermuthlich vieler nachfolgenden ehrlichen lands leute:) auff den weg, und arrivirte den 20.ten des 6.ten Monats (:Augusti:) mit etlichen knechten und mägden[1] Gott lob! frisch und gesund zu Philadelphia. Bald darauff nembl. den 6.ten des 8.ten Monats (:Octobris:) kamen ebenfalls in besagtem Philad[elphi].[a] an Dirck= und Herman= und Abraham Isaacs op den Graeff, Lenert Arets, Tünes Kunders, Reinert Tisen, Willhelm Strepers, Jan Lenssen, Peter Kürlis, Jan Simens, Johannes Bleickers, Abrahan Tünes und Jan Lücken, mit dero respective Weibern, Kindern und gesind, zusammen 13. Familien. Da wir dann ungesäumt von Willjam Penn begehrten, daß er sämmtliche von obged[achte]n Hoch= und Nieder Teutschen erkauffte Land an einem stück, und zwar bey einem schiffbaren Strom, solte auslegen und abmeßen laßen. Dieweilen Er aber uns hierinnen nicht willfahren kunnte, sondern biß zu überkunfft mehrerer Hausgesinde eine Township unfern dem Philadelphischen Stattgebiet etliche meil oberhalb des Scullkill Falls, anpraesentirte, haben wir sothanen Landstrich besichtiget und demnach derselbe uns seiner hohen gebürg halber nicht anständig, von oftgem. Willjam Penn versucht, die Township lieber buschwarts ein auff ebenen grund zu zustehen; deßen Er wohl zufrieden, und darauff den 24en Octobris durch Thomas Fairman 14. losen oder Erbe abmeßen ließ, umb welche oberwehnte 13. Familien den 25.ten dito durch Zettul das los zogen, und sofort anfiengen Keller und Hütten zu machen, worinnen sie den Winter nicht sonder große beschwerligkeit zubrachten.

Den Ort nennten wir Germantown, welches der Teutschen item Brüder Statt bedeutet; Etliche gaben ihm den bey Nahmen Armen Town, sindemahl viel der vorgedn. ersten beginnere sich nicht einst auff etliche wochen, zu geschweigen Monaten, provisiren kunnten. Und mag weder genug beschrieben, noch von denen vermöglichern Nachkömmlingen geglaubt werden, in was Mangel und Armuth, anbey mit welch einer Christ[liche]n. Vergnüglichkeit und unermüdetem Fleiss diese German Township begunnen sey; da dann mehrgem[elte]n. Willjam Penns offtmaliger durchdringender Anmuthigung und würklichen assistenz nicht zu vergeßen; wie auch , daß, als Er nacher Engelland abgesegelt, gegen das Vorjahr einigen der Einwohner ir muth so gar entfallen, daß sie anders wohin verhausen wolten; welches doch auff der beständigern Zusprch unterblieben ist, und Sie anjetzo beederseits ursach haben, Gottes Vätterliche Güte und Vorsorg dankbarlich zu rühmen.

Anno 1684. den 20.[ten] u[nd]. folgende tag des 12.[ten] Monats (:Februar:) wurde von ged[achte]n. Thomas Fairman der umbkreiß der Germantownship, nemblich nach Innhalt des von Willjam Penn ertheilten, und ins general landmeßer Amt eingelieferten, warrants, 6000. ackers abgemeßen, kurtz darnach aber durch deßen ordre (:unerchtet [was] wir dagegen einwenden kunnten:) 1000. ackers darvon, langs der Scullkill seite, wieder abgeschnitten; wobey es also verblieben, biß Anno 1687. den 29. Decembris diese unsre Germantownship zum andern mahl von Thomas Fairman, und zwar mit accureter sorgfalt, gemeßen, und darinnen 5700. acker lands befunden worden, über welche wir das auff folgender Seite abcopirte Patent oder Grundbrieff genommen haben.

Ferner wurden zu selbiger Zeit allen und Jeden Einwohnern zu Germantown ihre gantze und halbe losen in richtiger Ordnung zugemeßen, wie aus dem Draught oder Abriss und gegenwärtigem buch, clärer erhellet; Nembl: 2750. ackers. Anno 1689. den 4.ten des 2.ten Monats (:Aprilis:) haben die Käuffer und Erbpachts leut denen die übrige 2950. ackers der Germantownship zubehören dieselbe durchs los unter sich in drey absonderliche Dorffschafften vertheilt; und Anno 1690. den 14.ten des XI.[ten] Monats (:Januar:) von Thomas Fairman die Durchschnitt dadurch thun laßen, den vordersten an Germantown anstoßenden Theil Krißheim; den Mittelsten (:von meiner geburts statt:) Sommerhausen; und den hindersten Crefeld benahmset; wie pag. 2 umbständlicher ausweiset.

Hierbey ist gelegentlich zu erinnern, daß Wir die Urheber dieses Wercks, wegen ermangelnder sattsamer experienz in solcherley sachen, vieles gethan haben, das Wir hernach theils selbst ändern, theils der Klügern Nachfahren Verbeßerung anbefehlen müßen. Dann in ansehung der beschwerlichen Ausrottung des holtzes etc. haben wir anfängl: die Erb oder Losen nur 7. ruthen breit ausgelegt; jedoch nachgehendts, da mit dergleichen harten arbeit waß beßer gewehren kunnten, dieselbe umb andere 7. ruthen und 4. fuß erweitert. Auch war unser ersteres Vornehmen, es bey 25 losen bewenden zu laßen, weßhalben wir dann vor dem sechsten Erb auff der West-seite (:als neben einer Zwerchstraß, und inmitten des Orts:) einen acker zum marck- und begräbniß platz, auch zu gemeinen Gebäuen vorbehalten haben. Dieweilen aber verschiedene, beedes gewesene Dienstboten und aus Teutschland überkommene, gern bey uns zu Germantown bleiben und wohnen wolten, vergrößerten wir die anzahl der losen auf 55. Ingleichen hatte unserer Intention nach die lange straß in einer geraden Nord West linj durch gantz Germantown lauffen und die Zwerchstraßen recht gegen einander über und von einerley Weite seyn sollen; welches doch die darzwischen fallende Sümpff und unbequemheiten; haubtsächl: aber die mit dem Volk anwachsende diversität der Sinnen und andere dergestaltige umbstände verhindert haben.

Zum beschluß mag ich wohl mit einem angehenckten NB. denen Nachkömmlingen zu wißen fügen, daß German Towns vornehmste eußerliche Auffnehmen (:wofern bereits so zu reden geziemet:) vom flax bau, spinnen und weben herrühre; und sonder Zweiffel durch dieses Kräutlein auch hinfüro die Armuth und Dürfftigkeit noch vieler curirt werden könne; weßhalben dann daßelbe mit gebührlichem Fleiß zu säen und wahr zu nehmen ist.

Hiermit nun abbrechende, wünsche ich von hertzen, daß die leider! schon all zu viel überthätige Zwietracht und Uneinigkeit aus der Germantowner hertzen und gemüthern gäntzlich vertilgt werde, sie sämmtlich aber, alte und Junge, große und kleine in wahrer Liebe zu Gott und ihrem Neben Menschen Fromm und Gerecht leben, gedultig leiden, selig steren, und so in die Ewige Ruh u. Herrligkeit eingehen mogen! Amen. Franz Daniel Pastorius."

[1]The America Joseph Wasey M^r from London Arrived 20th of 6th mo. 1683. - Jacob Shoemaker borne in ye Palatinate in Germany servant to Danel Pastorius & comp^a. In: Michael Tepper (Hrsg.): Emigrants to Pennsylvania, S. 17.

Appendix D

„... Demnach nun Willjam Penn Eigenthumsherr und Gouverneur über Pennsilvanien aus habender Macht vom König in Engelland, etc an Burgermeister, Schöfen und Deputirte der Gemeind zu Germantown Vermög eines absonderlichen Charters oder freyheit brieffs de dato den 12.ten des 6.ten Monats 1689. unter andern günstiglich erlaubt und zugestanden hat, daß Sie von Zeit zu Zeit in ihren generalen Rathsversamblungen so viele gute und billige Gesetz, Ordinanzien und Statuta, als zu heilsamer Regierung dieser gmeind und dero geschäfften nothwendig und ersprießlich zu seyn erachten machen und stabilisiren, sothanige behörlicher maßen in gang bringen und vollzihen; auch nach gefallen und erfordernder gelegenheit dieselbe verändern, wideruffen und neue Verfertigen mögen.

Als fügen wir, die jetzmalige erstere Burgermeister, Schöfen und Deputirte daselbst, allen und jeden burgern, Einwohnern und Untersaßen des Germantownischen Gebiets hiermit freundlich zuwißen, daß zu beförderung unsers noch Jungen, und erst vor wenig Jahren angefangenen Stattwesens und deßen Wohlfahrt, wie krafft der im gedachtem Charter an uns ertheilten gewalt bey Authorität des Königs und im nahmen Willjam Penns in etlichen Generalen Courten (:gehalten den 6.ten 15.ten und 22.ten tag des 6.ten Monats 1691:) folgende 38. gesetz und Ordnungen verfaßt - und anbey einhelliglich beschloßen haben, daß solche der Gemeind durch offentliche Vorlesung publicirt und bekannt gemacht werden sollen, damit sich so fort männiglich darnach richten, und niemand derselben unwißenheit zu bedeckung seines ungehorsam vorwenden könne. -

Gleich wie wir nun wolmeinentlich wünschen und gegehren, daß nebenst denjenigen, die hinfüro das Magistrats Ammt allhier bedienen werden, alle burger und untersäßen unsere Jurisdiction solche Gesetz und Statuta, so lang sie nicht geändert noch abgeschaft sind, mit grechtem Eyfer und Gewißenhalber folgleistung handhaben und unterhalten mögen; So müsen wir herentgegen die freveler und muthwillige Delinquenten ex Officio ernstlich warnen, und Einenjeden mit des heiligen Apostels worten also anreden: Wann du böses thut, so fürchte dich; dann die Obrigkeit trägt das Schwerd nicht vergebens: Sie ist Gottes dienerin, eine Rächerin zum Zorn, dem der böses thut.

Haubtsächlich und vor allen dingen nun sollen alle burger, Einwohner und Untersaß des Germantownischen Gebiets, oder welche sich sonst darinn befinden und auffhalten, die sonderbahre Providenz des Aller Höchsten, wie auch die gütige gelingigkeit unseres Königs und Gouverneurs, (:Vermittelst deren Einjeder sonder den geringsten Zwang oder überlast nach seinen besten Wißen und gewißen Gott unverhindert dienen und friedlicher als in meist den andern landen nun zur Zeit müglich ist, leben kan:) mit danckbarem hertzen erkennende, Sich vor allen Sünden und untugenden hüten, wordurch der große Gott himmels und der Erden beleidigt und erzürnt wird, als da sind: Fluchen und Schweren bey seinem heiligen Nahmen, lästerungen wider seine Göttliche Majestät, schandbare unzüchtige Reden, Schertz die den Christen nicht geziemen, würfel- karten und andere Spielen, lügen, falsche Zeugniß, Verleumbdungen, Pasquillen, Auffruhr, Fechten, Duelliren, todtschlag, brand, throh- Schmäh- und Schelt wort, absonderlich gegen Eltern, Obrigkeit, Meister und Frauen, Diebstahl raub, hurerey, Ehebruch, blut- und Sodomistische greueln, trunckenheit, verfälschung einiger handschrifften Siegel- Müntz- und Grentzscheidungen etc. wider welche und mehrere übelthaten bereits satt same Versehung in dißländischen Gesetzen unter empfindlichen Geld- und leibs straffen geschehen ist; wohin so wohl dißfalls, als auch die übrige darinn enthaltene Verordnungen betreffend, Jedermänniglich gewiesen: und Niemanden die Entschuldigung, daß Er der Englischen Sprach unkündig, gefolglich dergleichen gesetz nicht wiße, noch einigerley anderer Praetext und Ausred keines wegs befreyen wird.

Weiter sollen die vier nechst folgende fundamental articuln, welche die Urheber dieser Germantownship anfänglich zu mehrerm und schleinigern auffnehmen dieses Orts einträchtiglich fest gestellt haben zu allen zeiten unver-
brüchlich gehalten werden.

Nemblich:

1. Daß sowohl in Germantown, als denen darzu belangenden dorffschafften, alle Erg oder hofstett in richtiger
Ordnung und nach verfolg, sonder eines überzuschlagen, beedes auf der Ost und West seite biß ans Ende sollen
auffgenommen werden; Im fall aber beede Seiten gleich sind, so dann derjene, der ein Erb besetzen will, mit
denen, welchen das übrige land in sothaner dorffschafft zukommt, losen müße, wo Ihme anderst diese nicht
freywillig die wahl vergönnen und zustehen.

2. Daß, wo sich ihrer etliche Zugleich wollen niedersetzen, sie mit einander umb die Erbe, welche zuselbiger Zeit
auff zu nehmen sind, das los zihen sollen, es sey dann, daß Sie von selbst einem oder mehrern unter sich die
vorkiesung gestatten.

3. Daß, weilen Germantown Stattsweis angelegt ist, und Jedes gantze Erb 4; Ein halbes aber 2. acker begreifft,
kein Einwohner daselbst befugt seyn solle, sein wohnhaus sonder zuvor erhaltene bewilligung der gemeind, und
nun der generalen Court, außerhalb gedachten respective 4; oder 2. ackern zu bauen....

4. Daß, wofern auff eines oder des andern particulier land bequäme waßer plätz zu erbauung einigerley mühlen
gefunden werden, die gemeind freye macht soll haben, alldar selbst, oder durch Jemand anders sothane mühlen
auff zu richten; Jedoch daß sie den Eigener des lands vor solch stück nach wehrtierung unpartheyischer leut zu
frieden stellen müse. Im fall aber der Eigener selbst binnen Jahres frist eine mühl und gedachtem platz bauen will,
Ihme solcher nicht soll können abgetrungen werden.

Endlich sollen die übrige hiernachgestellte Gesetz und Statuta so land gültig seyn und bleiben, biß dieses Orts
obrigkeit in dero generalen Raths versamblungen, nach hernerm guth befinden, dieselbe entweder verändern,
oder gäntzlich abrogiren und auffheben wird, nemblich

5. Mag Niemand auff dem Seiten land, welches Er außer der Statt zu Completirunng seiner 50; oder 25. acker
besitzt, ein wohnhaus bauen, oder alldort eine haushaltung anrichten, wofern Er binnen Germantown keine
würckliche famili hat, bey straff von 25. [lb]

6. Die lange Straß durch die Statt oder Dorffschaften soll Einjeder vor seinem Erb so wohl von allen kleinen
baumstümpfen, (:knuysten:) als auch von wilden kraut gewächsen und andern unreinigkeiten zu aller Arbeit clar
und sauber halten; oder als Er in 8. tagen, nachdem es ihme von der wegmeistern ist anbefohlen worden, nicht
gehorsamt, 2. Schill[ing]. straff geben.

7. Von denen zwerchstraßen sollen nun vors erst nur zwey; nemblich die Schullkill und Mühlen straß eröfnet und
abgezäunet: und beede von dato an biß zu End des Octobers nechst künfftig durch gemeine frohndienst geclärt
werden. Die übrige vier mag derjene, der sie clar machen und besäen will, 6. Jahr land, nachdem Er solche
angenommen, oder noch annimmt, innhaben und gebrauchen, dafern Er nur unterdeßen 10. fuß breit zum fahrweg
liegen läßt.

8. Die bäum auf denen zwerch und Seiten straßen bis zu grentzlini sind vor die gemeind; und mag niemand
einigen darvon zu seinem privat gebrauch, bey straff von 5. lb.

9. Die eußere Zwerch Seiten sollen, solang keine zwischen zäun gemacht werden, von allen und Jeden, deren
land dardurch befreyet werd, zugleich nach Jedes proportion gezäunt und in gutem stand erhalten werden, auch
bey straff von 5. lb.

10. Mögen die Stacken an gedachten Zwerch und Seiten Zäunen biß zur zeit, da jede los deßelben Quartiers

absonderlich abgezäunt wird, anderthalb fuß in die Straß stehen; doch kommen dardurch solche 1½ fuß denen
Ecklosen nicht eigenthumlich zu, sondern verbleiben allzeit der gemeind und zur Straßen.

11. So Jemand einen Zwischen Zaun gemacht haben will, soll Er solches auff seine eigene kosten thun, und nicht
praetendiren, daß der nechste anstößer seinen theil daran tragen müße; Im fall aber dieser sich sothanig verfer-
tigten Zauns mit bedient, soll Er die helffte deßen, so Er genießt, an den, der ihn gemacht hat, verguthen..."

Appendix E

Ann° 1685
My Brother Jan Striepers -

		Debet	
		Shill	D
To 4 Weeks Board paid to my Wife when I was still in Your Service - - - - - - - - - - - - - - - - - 14		"	
To due for the half Year, that I should Work for myself & You to find me being		114	10
due for stockings		26	11
To a New Hat		12	
To 2 pair Leather Breeches		24	
To 2 Lesther Doublets		30	
To a panell Woolen Cloth Clothing, whereof the Eu cost 4 Guilders in Holland, I reckon		72	
To a panell of Serge Cloaths I reckon		30	
To Boxes & Hankercheifs I reckon		14	
To 22 Days Maintainance on Board		2	6
	RX 56 4	3	

[Marginalie] Ann° 1686 / 1686
My Brother Jan Striepers -

		Credit	
		Shill	De
Received of Brother Jan Striepers 13 Bush[el]ls cost 3 [...] the Bushell		39	
Rec[eive]d 14 Bushells [...] 3 Peck Rey cost the Bush [...] 3 [...]		44	3
Rec[eive]d 66 Pumpkins [...]		4	
D° 5 Bushells a 3 s		15	
D° 3 Peck of Beans is		4	
D° 4 Bushells & ½ Peck Rey is		12	4
D° 3 Bushells Furnips is		2	3
D° 10½ Bushells a 3 s		31	6
D° a Glass Bottle a 15 d is		1	6
D° 110 Trasses [...] a 1"ᵈ & [...]		9	2
Ditto 20 ------ a 1ᵈ		1	8
Ditto 2 Bushells a 3 s		6	
Ditto in Cash ------ 2 s 2½		2	2½
Ditto for House Rent		24	
Ditto for a Hog		21	
Ditto for 29 3/4 Ells Linnen a 2½ [...]		74	6
	RXʳ---48	4	5
Ballance due from my Brother Jan Striepers	7	5	10
	RX 56	4	3

[Wieder über beide Seiten geschrieben]
NB. 12 Stuyvers make one English Pensilvania Shilling, [...] [...] ditto Shilling
make one Rixdollar Pensylvania Value of Rixdollars Holland Rixdollars are 3 Pensylvania Stuyvers heavier than Pensylvania Rixdollars, the Word Penny Signifies a Pensylvania Stuyver, A Peck is the fourth part of a Bushell and five Bushells make one Creveld Malder.
I acknowledge the above Debet & Credits to be a true Copy of the Original
Signed Henrick Zellen.

Appendix F

"Wir Adolph Von Flodroff Schulteis der Statt und Graffschafft Maeurs auch der Statt und Herrlichkeiten Creivelt, Frimersheim p Johann Reiners und Johan Bruckmann beyde Scheffen des Statt und Landgerichts Creivelt thun Kundt und Zeugen mit diesem Offenen Gerichts Schein, daß für uns nach dieses Gerichts Gewohnheit persönlich erschienen ist Johan Stripers für sich und seine Hausfrau Anneken Thyßen, und hat an seinen Bruder Reinir Thyßen und Henrich Sellen, Welcher hiebey gegenwärtig dieses Stipulato angenommen hat, Vollkommene Vollmacht gegeben über ihre Erbgüter und Effecten so gelegen sind in America in Pensilvania, Allermaßen dann hiemit zu seinen, seiner Frauen und Erben Vollmächtiger in Optima Forma qualificiren thäte ognd^{te}. Reinir Thyßen und Henrich Sellen und Zwar dergestalt, daß sie Von Wilhelm Streypers des Johannes bruder die Kauffbrieffe von denen 5000 Ackers Abfordern, die Einnahm und Bezahlung der Jährlichen Pfachten bestermaßen beobachten, den Von denen Verpachteten als Verkaufften Landereyen aufkommende Gelder, Jährlichs richtige Rechnung machen, davon an niemand das geringste dan auff mehrgd^{tn}. Johan Strypers Speciale Ordre ausfolgen, und sonsten bey dieser Administration Schalten und Walten, so dann alles thun und Verrichten sollen, Was getreuen Vollmächtigern und Negotiorum gestoribus Zu Handeln und Zu beobachten obliegen thut, Und Wird denen Vollmächtigern hiemit gleichfals Vollkommene Macht gegeben, umb alle der Constituenten Erbgüther und Effecten (: Ausgenommen den einen Morgen so in der Statt Philadelphia, als auch die 50 Ackers so auf der Statt Grund gelegen :) - bestens und nach aller Möglichkeit und zu der Constituenten besten Nutzen Zu Verkauffen, jedoch mit diesem ausdrücklichen Vorbehalt, daß genet^{e}. Bevollmächtigte des Constituenten Ratification über solchen Kauff einzuholen sollen gehalten seyn; da auch Von diesen beyden Vollmächtigern einer mit Todt oder sonsten Abgehet, solle dem letztlebenden einen Andern Ehrlichen und frommen Coadministratorem Zu sich zu nehmen obliegen, gestalt er Johan Strypers hiebey Vor sich, seine Haußfrau und Erben handtastlich Versprochen, solches alles für genehm u. die Gevollmächtigte Schadloß zu halten, und denen jeden Vor die gethane Mühewaltung Zu Zulegen und Wiederfahren Zu lassen, Was in dergleichen Raison und discretion Verrichten. — Deß Macht und Gewalt geben den Strypers Erb und Guth bestehet dem Angeben nach in folgenden Stücken- In 5000 Acker Lands, und einen Acker in der Statt Philadelphia, und davon noch fünffzig Ackers auff der Statts grund, Welche fünffzig Acker dem Constituenten von William Pen als eine freye Gabe geschenckt worden darob das folgende Vorgezeiget und alhie de Verbo ad Verbum Inserirt ist, Ick hab geschreven aen myn Commissarius om ugt te Setten dat land in Pennsilvania dat Dirk Sipman, Jan Strepers, en Jacob Isaacs Sullen hebben voor haer Lott in de Stadt en on desselfs grondt, neffens welcke ick toe stae aen de beyde eerstgenoemde elck van haer in de Stadt Philadelphia in eenige bequaeme Straet en tot de daerde 1/3 eens Ackers, ende on de Stadts grond als een Vrye giffte elck van de twee eerstgenoemden ten minsten 50 Acker en 10. Acker aen de laetst genoemde, en daeren boven sal Dirck Sipman voor de 1000, die hy van Govert Rembkes gecoght heeft deselve Privilegie genieten als boven genoemd is, en off de gesonden boven gedagte Brief soude Verlooren komen te worden, Soo hebbe ick desen met myn eygen hand geteeckent den 15. der 5. / Maent 1686. en was onderteeckent W. Penn. Ferners soll denen Gevollmächtigte Zur nachricht dinen, daß Wilhelm Strypers, laut Contracts in Rotterdam den 23- 7 Monats in Erbpfacht habe 100 Ackers, Wovon er jährlichs gibt fünff Kopfstücke, und Jan Lenssen gleichfals Zu Erbpfacht, fünffzig Englische Ackers, Davon er jährlichs 1 . Rxthlr 112 str. dem Constituenten ausgeben muß, In Wahrheits Urkundt haben wir Schulteis und Scheffen unser Insiegelen ad Causas Angehangen. Also geschehen Crevelt den 13 t. May im Jahr 1698 Adolff Von Flodroff Schulteis und Secret."

Appendix G

"William Penn True and absolute Proprietary and Governeur in chiefe of the Province of Pensilvania and Territories thereunto belonging To all to whom these presents shall Come Sendet greeting Whereas by my Indentures of Lease and Release bearing Date the ninth and Tenth Days of March In the Year One thousand Six hundred and Eighty two I Granted to John Streiper of Crevelt in Germany Fife thousand acres of Land in this Province To Hold to him his heirs and assigns for ever under the Yearly Rent of One English Shilling vor every thousand Acres for ever as by the said Indentures Do at large appear and whereas by virtue of a Warrant from my Present Comissioners of Property Dated the three and twentieth Day of the Twelth Month in the year One Thousand Seven hundred and one There was laid out the twenty Sixth Day of the First Month March in the Year One thousand Seven hundred and three unto the said Striepers in Right of the said Purchase a certain Tract of Land Siituate in the County of Bucks in this Province Beginning at a Black / [...] by the River Dellaware [in] the Corner of [fehlt] Thence Northwest Six Hundred are lighty Six Perches to a white oak Then South west by the London Companies land One thousand One Hundred and Sixty Pearches to a Post Then by vacant Land South East three Hundred and twenty perches to a post. Then South East by Land appropriated to my own use three Hundred and Eighty two Perches to a white oak Then again by Land appropriated to my own use North East nine Hundred and forty Perches to the Beginning Containing Four thousand four hundred and forty eight acres Now at the Speciall Instance and Request of Leinert Aretts attorney for the said John Striepers that I would Confirm to the said John Striepers the said Four thousand four hundred and forty eight acres of Land by Patent Know Yee That for the Considerations in my said Indentures men[t]ion'd I Have Given Granted Release and Confirmed and by these presents for me my Heirs and Successors Do Give Grant Release and Confirm unto the said John Striepers his Heirs and Assigns for ever all that the said Four thousand four hundred and forty eight acres of Land (be it more or less) with all Mines Mineralls Quaries Meadows Marshes Swamps Cripples Woods Underwoods Timber and Trees Ways Waters Watercourses Liberties Proffitts Comodities Advantages Hereditaments and appurtenaries whatsoever to the said Four Four [sic] thousand Four hundred and forty eight acres (be it more or less) or to any Part or Parcell thereof belonging or in any wise appertaining and Lying within the Bounds and Limitts aforesaid (Three full and Clear Fifth parts of all Royall Mines Free from all Deductions and Reprizalls for digging and Refining of the Same only exceptet and hereby Reserved) and also Tree Leave Right and Liberty to and for the said John Striepers his heirs and assigns to Hawk Hunt Fish and Fowle in and upon the hereby granted Four thousand four hundred and forty eight acres of Land and [...]isses or upon any part or parcell thereof To have and to hold the said four tousand four hundred and forty Eight acres of Land (be it more or less) and premisses hereby granted (Except before Excepted) with their and every of their appurtenances to the said John Striepers his heirs and assigns To the only proper use and Behoofe of the saidjohn Striepers his heirs and assigns for everTo be Holden of me my heirs and Successors Proprietarys of Pensilvania as of our manner or reputed manner of Pensbury in the County of Bucks in Free and Com[m]on Soccage by fearly only in lieu of all other Services Yielding and Paying therefore Yearly tome my heirs and Successors (from the Date of Survey herein before men[t]ion'd) at or upon the first Day of the first Month March In every Yearfor everthereafter at Pensbury One English Silver Shilling for every thousand acres and so Proportionally or Value thereof in Coyn Currant to such Person or Persons as from time to time shall be appointed to receive the same In Witness whereof I Have By Virtue of my Com[m]ission to my Proprietary Deputies bearing Date the Eighth and twentieth Day of October in the Year One thousand Seven hundred and One Causd my Great Seal of the said Province to be hereunto affixed Witness Edward Shippen Griffith Owen Thomas Story andjames Logan my said Deputies or any three of them at Philadelphia the Twenty fourth Day of the fourth month call'djune in the fourth Year of the Reign of our Soveraign Lady Queen Ann over England eta, and the Five and twentieth of my Governement Anno Domini One thousand Seven hundred and Five Recorded / the 15.th 8.br 1706."

Appendix H
"Wir Johan francken, undt Herman mewißen beyde respce burgermeistern, und scheffen des fleckes undt Communität Kaldenkirchen Hertzogthumbß gülich Ambtes Brüggen Zeugen, undt Certificiren hiemit, waß gestalten auff heuth ahn untengemelten Dato Vor unß Persönlich Sistirt, Comparirt, undt erschienen der achtbahre Joen Strepers ubermitz, undt mit Zustandt deßen rechtmäßigen Erben, undt respce kinderen bnemtlich Leonard, Henrich sambt deren geschwestern Metgen Catharina, und Annecken Striepers Zu erkennen gebent, wie daß derhalb sich mit seinem auch respce bruder Wilhelm Striepers jetzo bey germantoin gelegen in America in die provintz pensilvanien über die ihnen beyden Von Ihren Elteren hieselbst Zu Kaldenkirchen hinterlaßenen Erbtheil, so bißher ohnZertheilt Verblieben, dermaßen Vereinbart, undt Vergliechen, daß Er Johan Strepers Vor ihm undt seinen Erben seines bruders Wilhelm hieselbst haben des Erb= undt antheil nunmehro eigenthümblich haben, undt Erblich besitzen sollen, hingegen Er Johan Strepers, undt deßen Erben seinem bruderen Wilhelm Strepers, auch deßen Erben die Von ihm in der provintz pensilvanien angekaufften Ländereyen, undt Erbschafften Mit allen, ein= undt Zubehör ap= und dependentien, wobey die brüderliche praetensionen, so Er wickelet [?] auff die alldaßige Erbschaft mit includirt, Hiemitten transportirt, undt obergeben haben, wie dan desfalß undt mit deßen Erben selbiges hiemitten realiter; undt würcklich Vor unß obenenten, respce bürgermeistern, undt Scheffen Obergebenen, undt transportiren, auch dan auff Ewig, undt Erblich Verziehen [?], undt plenarie renuntiren Thuen, Zur wahrer urkundt obiges, haben Wir gegenwertigen transport, undt Übergab neben unser eigen unterschrifft unseren gewöhnlichen gericht= und fleckes Einsiegel beygedrückt, undt befestiget so geschehen Kaldenkirchen d 4ten marty 1715. ist unterzeichnet Johs francken [ ]herman mewißen
In fidem premissorum hunc scripsi et subscripsi Johan Zielikens secretarius."

Appendix I
Know all Men by these Presents, that I Leonard Striepers of the County of Philadelphia in the Province of Pensylvania Yeoman, am held and firmly bound unto Reyner Teissen of the Same Place Yeoman in the Sum of Fivehundred

Pounds Law and Money [unleserlich] unto the said Rey-nerTeissen or his certain Attorney his Executors, Administrators or Assigns, to which payment well [...] to be made I bind myself, my Heirs, Executors, Administrators firmly by these Presents, Sealed with my Seal, Dated the one & thirtieth Day of December In the Year of Our Lord One thousand Seven hundred & twenty two - Whereas there are Several Lands in Pensylvania belonging to John Striepers, Brother of Willem Striepers, Father of the above Bound Leonard Striepers, Eldest Son & Heir at Law of his said Father Willem Striepers, who by a Late Power of Attorney or Instrument was Impower'd, to take up, and take Possession of the said Lands, and whereas the above named Reyner Teissen was designed and intended to have been equally concerned and interested in the Premises as it Since Appears, and as the said Lands are or ought to be in Equity, the Inheritance of the Heirs of John Striepers aforesaid. Now the Condition of this Obligation is such that if the said Leonard Striepers, his Heirs Executors Administrators and Assigns shall and do from time to time, and at all times for ever hereafter, permit & suffer and acknowledge & declare the said Reyner Teyssen, his Heirs Executors & Administrators to be equally concerned, entrusted and Interested in the Trust, Power& Lands aforesaid, with him the said Leonard Striepers and his Heirs and also if the Said Leonard Striepers & his Heirs in Conjunction with him the Said ReynerTeissen and his Heirs shall and do at any time or times, when thereunto Esquired Release the Land aforesaid unto the Heirs of John Striepers aforesaid without at any time or times hereafter, laying any Claim or title to any of the said Lands, but that the Heirs of the said John Striepers from time to time and at all times forever hereafter shall and Lawfully may quietly and Peacably have, hold, occupy Possess and enjoy all and Every the Lands aforesaid without any Molestation or Interruption from time the said Leonard Striepers his Heirs, Executors Administrators or Assigns, or from any other Person or Persons whom [...] I from [...] under him them or any of them or by his [unleserlich] their Means [...] Consent or Procurement; then this [...] obligation shall be void, and of Non Effect, but if any Default [...] happen to be made in part or in all Part & behalf of the said Leonard Striepers or his Heirs, contrary to the Tenor and true Interest and Meaning of this Same Obligation, then the Same shall stand, remain and be in full Power Force & Virtue. - Sealed & Delivered in the Presence of Leonard Striepers [...] Thönis Kunders Griffith Jones."

Appendix K

Jedermanniglich wann dieses zu Händen komt, geben, Claas, Annecke, Willem, Agneta / Hennrich und Elisabeth von Aaken, insgesamt Kinder von Metje Kenn / lings, einer Tochter von Jan Strepers seiner Frauen und Erben; Maria / Sieben weilen Wittwe von Leonard Strepers, Elizabetha Olmessen / weilen Wittwe von Hennrich Strepers & ihr Sohn Hennrich Streper / Wilhelmus Sieben Eheman und Erbe von der verstorbenen Catharina / Strepers, und Lambertus Mol, Eheman und Erbe von der verstorbenen / Anntje Strepers, als Kinder von Jan Strepers weilen von Kaldenkirchen / in dem Hertzogthum Gülesch auf den Gräntzen von Teutsch / land Kaufman, überlitten unseren Gruß zuvor. / Nachdem durch gewisse beweiß briefe von Vertrag und Ubertrag, ge / datirt 9 und 10 Martz 1682 gemacht oder erwähnet gemacht zu werden / zwischen William Penn weilen von Worminghurst in der Grafschaft / Sussex, Wassenträger [?] an der einen Seiten, und vorgemeltem Jan Strepers / an der anderen Seiten, Er gesagter William Penn aus betrachtung / darinnen gemeldet, zußtund überließ und bekräftigte an vorge / meltem Jan Strepers, seinen Erben &c: die Antheil und Größe von / fünf tausend Acker Land ~~zugeloohßen~~ die sollen zugelooßt, und / angetheilt werden an solchen Orten und Theilen von dem Landstri[ch] / [o]der Provintz von Pennsylvanien auf der Art und zu solcher Zeit und / Zeiten als wie man bey gewißen Clausulen in die beweiß und / Ubertrag gemeldet bestimmet hatte, um durch ihme gemel[tem] / Jan Strepers seine Erben und Assignatores, immerfort behalten zu we[r] / den, wie zu sehen ist durch herholte Beweiß Briefe (Indentures) / worauf uns beziehung. Und nachdem durch gewiße andere Beweiß / Briefe von Vertrag und Ubertrag, gedatirt 17 und 18 January dieses / Jahres gemacht zwischen Leonard Strepers, Sohn und rechtmäßiger / Erbe von Willem Strepers weilen von zu Germantown in der Graf / schaft Philad^a in der Provintz Pensylvanien Bürger, gestorben, Reynier / Tyson von Abington in gemelter Grafschaft Bürger, und Griffith Jones / zu d^o Germantown Bürger, vorgemelte Leonard, Reiner & Griffith in / Qualiteyt als Gevollmachtigte und Agenten der obengemelten Kinder / von dem verstorbenen Jan Strepers, der ein Bruder war von gesagtem Willem / an der einen Seiten, und James Logan, Kaufman zu Philad^a, an der an- / dern Seite. Sie [...] vorgem: Leonard Strepers, Reynier Tyson, und Gri[f-] / fith Jones, aus Betrachtung darinnen gemeldet, zustunden, überließen / und bekräftigten an geagtem James Logan die gantzen und gerechten An / theile und Größe von Vier Tausend Vier Hundert und Acht und Viertz[ig] / Acker Land, und fünfzig Acker frey Land (Theil von den 5 Tausend / Acker hierinnen zuvor gemeldet) und alle Stadt Lothen dazu gehorend / ein durch Ihme gemelten Jam^s Logan seine Erben und Assignatores immer- / fort behalten zu werden wie deutlich erhellet und dem jüngst her- / hohlten Beweißbriefe von Vertrag und Ubertrag worauf uns beziehen. / So sey jedermänniglich kund, daß vorgem: Claas, Antje, Willem, Agneta, Henn- / rich & Eliz^a van Aaken, alle

Kinder von Metje Kennling, die eine / Tochter war von Jan Strepers seiner Frauen und Erben, Maria Sieben / weilen Wittwe von Leonard Strepers, Eliz: Olmessen weilen Wittwe / von Hennrich Strepers, und ihr Sohn Hennrich Strepers, Wilhelmus Sie- / ben Ehemann und Erbe von der verstorbenen Catharina Strepers, und / Lambertus Mol Ehemann und Erbe von der verstorbenen Antje Stre- / pers, als Kinder und Erben von gesagtem Jan Strepers, sowohl für / und in Betrachtung einer Summa von Zweyhundert Pfund Sterling Geldt von Groß Brittanien, in dem jüngst citirtem Beweiß Brief / von Ubertrag erwähnet um bezahlt zu werden, wie auch wegen der / Summa von fünf Schillinge Pensylvanisch Courant Geldt Ihnen gleich / fals aus der Hand bezahlt durch vorgemelt: Jamˢ Logan an oder zu / vor dieses gezeichnet und übergeliefert wardt, den empfang, wessen / sie hierbey erkennen, und derhalben quitiren, und für ewig ent- / schlagen gem: Jamˢ Logan seine Erben und Assignatos aus kraft / dieses wie sie dan hiemit entlaßen, ihr recht abgestanden, und / übergetragen haben für ihnen und insgesamt Erben völlig wirck- / lich und ohne Vorbehalt, und noch Abstand thun an vorgem. James / Logan (nur in wirklichem Besitz seines Eigenthums sezzend) und an / seine Erben und Assignatos, die geamtlichen 4448 Acker Land, fünf- / zig Acer frey Landt und Stadt Loten [...] zugestanden / od: erwähnet zugestanden zu werden an gemelten Jamˢ Logan, wie / oben herholht, gesamtlich mit allem und jeglichen Rechten, Theilen / und was cum pertinentiis dazu gehören od: auf [...] Weise davon depen- / deren mag wie auch die reversiones und übrige Theile davon, gesamt / den gantzen Estat und Estaten, Recht, Titul, Belang, Theile, und / Theilen, Untertheil und Untertheilen, [...] und Forderung wie / genant; vorgem: Claas, Antje, Willem, Agneta, Hinnrich & Eliza- / beth van Aaken (und alle die andern personen schon zweymahl zuvor im / Texte mit Nahmen genant) für sich selbsten od: ihre Nachkömm- / lingen die öfters erwähnte 4448 Acker Land 50 Acker frey La[nd] / &c: haben mögten, und alle Acten, Schriften, und Beweißthümer dem [...] / gelehnt. Hiebey bey herhohlung zustehend, daß gem:. Jamˢ Logan di[e] / 4448 Acker Land &c: &c: halten und gebrauchen sol für sich, sei[ne] / Erben und Assignatos. So daß weder vorgem: Claas, Annecke, Willem, Agneta, Hendrik & Eliz: van Aaken &c: (wie öfters benahmet) / oder jemand von ihnen noch sie oder jemand von ihren Erben, oder einig a[n-] / der Person oder Personen ihrentwege niemand von sie oder in ihrem / Nahmen, Recht oder Statt soll oder will auf einigerley Art oder / Weise nach diesem [...], challengeren, od: forderung thun, auß / dem Gut, Recht, Titul, od: Intrese in od: von den Premises oder / einigen Theil oder Theilen davon dahingegen davon und von allem / und zugleichem Action, Recht, Gut, Titul, Belang, und forderung / von und in selbigem, oder einigen Theil oder Theilen dieselben gan[...] / lich sollen auf ewig ausgehalten, und bey diesen gegenwärtigen abge- / wiesen seyn. Zum Zeugniß we[...]n wir untergeschriebene / obenstehendes mit unsere Hand und Ziegel bekräftigen. [...] [21. Juny] / 1726 [...] / Claas van Aaken / Aneken van aaken / Willem van Aaken / Agneta van Aaken / Hendᵏ & Eliz. van Aaken / Maria Sieben / Eliz. Olmessen / Henricus Strepers / Wilhelmus Sieben / Lambertus Mol /

[...] / Erbgl Jan & Willem Strepers

„To all People to whom there presents shall Come Claus Annenke William Agneta Hendrick & Elizabeth van Acken, being all Children of Metje Kewrlings [Kürlis], who was a Daughter of John Strepers his Wife and Heir: Mary Sieben Late Wid: of Leonard Striepers Elizabeth Olmessen L Wid. of Hend[ri]k Strepers & her Son Hendrikus Strepers Wilhelmus Sieben Huband [sic] & Heir of Catherina Strepers deceased and Lambertus Moll the Heirs of John Strepers late of Kaldkirchen in the County of Guliers on the Borders of Germany Merchant deceased send Greeting whereas by & certain Indentials of Lease & Release bearing Date the ninth & tenth Days of March 1682 made or mentioned to be made between William Penn late of Worminghurst in the County of Sussex Esq. of the one part and the s[ai]d Jan Strepers of the other parts he the s[ai]d William Penn for the Consideration therein mentioned Did Grant Release & Confirm unto the s[ai]d John Strepers his Heirs & Assigns the Proportion & Quantity of five Thousand Acres of Land to be allowed & set out in such Places or Parts of the Track or Province of Pensylvania in such Manner and at such Time or Times as by certain Concessions or Constitutions in the same Indentials mentioned are appointed To hold to him the said John Strepers his Heirs & Assigns for Ever as by the same recited Indentures & Relation being thereunto had at large appears And Whereas by certain other Indenture of Lease & Release bearing Date the seventeenth & eighteenth Days of January last past made between Leonard Strepers, the Son & Heir at Law of William Strepers late of German Town in the County of Philadelphia in the Province of Pensylvania Yeoman dec[ease]d Riener Tyson [of] Abington in the said County Yeoman & Griffith Jones of Germantown afores[ai]d Yeoman the said Leonard Riener & Griffith being the Trustets or Agents for the afores[ai]d Children of the said John Strepers deceased who was the Brother of the s[ai]d William Of the one Part & James Logan of the City of Philadelphia in the s[ai]d Province Merch. of the other Part They the s[ai]d Leonard Striepers Riener Tyson and Griffith Jones for the Consideration therein mentioned did grant release and Confirm unto the said James Logan The full & just proportion & Quantity four Thousand four hundred & forty eight Acres of Land and fifty Acres of Liberty Land (part of the five Thousand herein before recited) and all City Lots thereunto belonging to hold to him the said James Logan his Heirs & Assigns for Ever as in and by the said last recited Indentures of Lease & Release Relation being thereunto had at large appears Now Know Ye that the s[ai]d Claus Anneke Willem Agneta Hend[ric]k & Elizabeth van Aaken being all Children of Metje Kewrlings whowas a Daughterof John Strepers his Wife & Heir Mary Sieben late Widow [of] Leonard Strepers Elizabeth Olmessen late Widow of Hendrick Strepers & her Son Hendrikus Strepers, Wilhelmus Siebens Husband & Heir of Catherina Strepers deceased Lambertus Moll Husband & Heir of Anneke Strepers deceased Children & Heir of the s[ai]d Jan Striepers as well for & in Consideration of the Sum of Two hundred Pounds Sterling Money of Great Britain in the said last recited Indenture of Release mentioned to be paid as of the Sum of five Shillings lawfull Money of Pensylvania to them in Hand also paid by the s[ai]d James Logan at or before the Seating & Delivery hereof the Receips whereof They do hereby Acknowledge & thereof do Acquit & for Ever Discharge the s[ai]d Jame Logan his Heirs & Assigns by these Presents Have remised released [...] Claimed & Confirmed And by these Presents Do for them & their Heirs respectively fully clearly & absolutely remise release & for ever [...] Claim & Confirm unto the s[ai]d James Logan in his actual Possession & Seiz in now being And to his Heirs & Assigns All those the s[ai]d Four Thousand four hundred and forty eight Acres of Land, fifty Acres of Liberty Land and City Lots afores[ai]d so granted or mentioned to be granted to the said James Logan as afore recited Together with all & singular the Rights Members & appurtenances whatsoever thereunto respectively belonging or in any wise appertaining and the Reversions & Remainders thereof and all & Every the Estate & Estates Rights Tit le & Interests Part & Parts Purpart & Purparts claim & Demand whatsoever of them the s[ai]d Claus Anneke Willem Agneta Hend[ric]k & Elizabeth Van Aaken being all Children of Metje Kewrlings who was a Daughter of John Strepers his Wife & Heir Mary Sieben late Wife of Leonard Strepers Elizabeth Olmessen late Wid[ow] of Hendrick Strepers & her Son Hendrick Strepers Wilhelmus Sieben Husband & Heir of Catharina Strepers deceased and Lambertus Mol Husband & Heir of Anneke & each of them of in & to the same Four Thousand four hundred & forty eight Acres of Land fifty Acres of Liberty Land & City Lots afores[ai]d. And all Deeds Writings and Evidences concerning the same to have / & to hold y.e said four Thousand fourhundred and forty eightAcres fifty Acres of Liberty Land & City Lots afores[ai]d & Premises with their Appurtenances unto the s[ai]d James Logan & his Heirs to the use of him the said James Logan his Heirs & Assigns for Ever so that neither they the said Claus Anneke Willem Agneta Hend[ric]k & Elizabeth Van Aaken being all Chidren of Metje Kewrlings who was a Daughter of John Strepers his Wife & Heir, Mary Sieben late Widow of Leonard Strepers Elizabeth Olmessen late Widow of Hend[ric]k Strepers & her Son Hendrekus Strepers Wilhelmus Sieben Husband & Heir of Catharina Strepers deceased and Lambertus Mol Husband & Heir of Anneke Strepers dec[ease]d or any of them nor their or any of their Heirs nor any other Person or Persons for them or any of them or in their or any of their Name or Names Rig[ht] orStead shall orwill by any Way or Means hereafter have Claim Challenge or Demand any Estate Right Title or Interests of in or to the Premises or any part or Parcel thereof But thereof & therefrom & of & from all & every Action Rights Estate Title Interest & Demand of in or to the same or any Part or Parcel thereof shall be utterly Excluded & for Ever Debared by these Presents In Witness whereof the s[ai]d [Blank in the Record]' have hereunto Set their Hands & Seals Dated the twenty first Day of July New Stile In the Year of our Lord One Thousand seven hundred & twenty six Claas Van Aaken (Seal) Aneken Van Aaken (Seal) Willem Van Aaken (Seal) Angeniet Van Aaken (Seal) Hendrik Van Aaken (Seal) Elizabeth Van Aaken (Seal) Marisa Sieben (Seal) Elisabeth Olmisse (Seal) Hendrikus Strepers (Seal) Wilhelmus Sieben (Seal) Lambertus Moll (Seal) Sealed And Delivered In the Presence of Us ... L. Lawrence Alexander Grant Rich[ar]d Vile § - §

Appendix L

HSP: Charles Morton Smith Manuscripts. Vol. 1, page 6, Historical Society of Pennsylvania; Transkription James Duffin, Philadelphia: „Nachdem von Seithen derer Erbgenahmen Jan Streepers bey uns Predigeren und Consistorialen der Evangelischen Gemeinde allhier zu Kaldenkirchen und Bracht behohrend angezeigt worden ist, wie dass nehmlich zur fortsetzung der in Penselvanien in America obhabender rechtsstreitigkeit Ihnen höchstnöthig wäre zu wissen wannehr Jan Streepers und dessen erben gestorben und begraben oder welche annoch am leben wären, mit bitt Ihnen darüber glaubhafften Extractum mitzutheilen, so haben wir in betracht dessen noch gar keine gestorbene im kirchenbuch bemercket stehen auff denen uns persönlich vorbracht gewor-dener dahier [?] wohnhafftigen fromme Ehrbahr= und glaubwürdigen alten leuthen benembtlich Died. van Hall Arnolden Cüsters und hedwigen Schmitz welche an eydes statt bezeuget haben, den Jan Streepers und dessen Kinder wohl gekent zu haben noch wohl zu wissen dass Jan Streepers im Jahr 1715 dessen Sohn Leon. Streepers im Jahr 1725 dessen Sohn Hin. Strepers im Jahr 1724 und Cath. Streepers im Jahr 1725 dahier zu Kaldenkirchen gestorben und begraben seyen, Ja Arn. Cüsters zeugt noch dabey sich wohl besinnen wie dass er bey der beerdigung des Jan Streepers mit auff unserem Kirchhoff gewesen, So also unter uns einhelliglich beschlossen und für gut befunden, dass nicht allein diese todesfälle des Jan Streepers und dessen Kinder also in behöhrender form gleich uns glaubhafft vorgebracht worden ist, sondern auch alle so man wüste und derer man sich nur erinnern kan wie auch alle welche uns künfftige nach des Herren anbethungswürdigen rathschluss zu sterben kommen von nun dem Kirchenbuch eingetragen, und dass denen Erbgenahmen von Jan Streepers der förmlicher bescheinigungs Extractus solle mitgetheilet werden, und zwarn um demehr annoch wohl in einem uns von obgem. Erbg. Streepers vorbracht gewordenem in folio bestehendem haussbuch des Hin. Streepers de dato Kaldenkirchen den 5 Aprilis 1686 angemerckt stehe dass im Jahr 1715 den 6 May nachmittags um 11 uhr der Jan Streepers dahier zu Kaldenkirchen gestorben und auch darauf begraben Nicht minder uns auch auss denen wahrhafft vorseynden alten denckmahlen als grabsteinen und dergleichen die richtigkeit der sachen constiere, worauff dan solchem noch im Jahr 1764, den 6 May denen obbenenten Erbg. der anverlangter Extractus allinger Sterbender auss der Streeperischer familie wie bräuchlich mitgetheilet worden ist.

"Wij onderschrevne Prediger, ouderligen, en Diackenen, van de gereformeerde gerneent tot Kaldenkerken, in den Lande van Gülick, op de frontieren van Duijtsland gelegen. Getuijgen en Certificeren hiermede hoe dat den Eersamen Jan Strepers alhier overleden in t jaer 1715 den 6 Maij- met Sijn wettige huijsvrouw Encken Dorsch getelt vier Echte Kinderqn, waerbij gestelt de Eentzige en wettige voordochter van voornoemde Ecken Dorsch, genaemt Metjen KOrlings, en also vijf rechtmatige Ergenamen van alle haere goederen soo met haer beijde hebben naergelaeten, welcke alle voorseijde vijf wettige Kinderen, en Erfgenamen in onse Reformeerde gerneinte nae uijtwijsen des kercken=Boecks alhier gedoopt sijn als volgt de Eerste een Dochter als vermeldt genaernt Metjen gedoopt den Negenden Meert 1664 getrouwt den 22: Xbr: 1682 met den Echtsaame hendrick Jansen Vanacken waar mede geteeld 6 kinderen met Naamen Claas Annecken Willem Anganita hendrik & Eelisabeth, soo is vooret= hendrik Jansse Van Aaken gestorven den 14 Xbr: 1715: En Voore= metje zijn huijs Vrouw 31: 8br: 1719: Naa laatende zijn gemelde Ses Kindere die Nogalen op dato in Amstrn in t seeven zijn De tweeden eene soon van voorheijden Jan Strepers genaemt Leonard gedoopt den 2 Meert 1670. getrouwt den 20 Maij 1698, met de Eerbare Jonge docther Maria Sijben, waermede getelt vijf kinderen met Namen, Annecken, Eleisabet, peter ageneess en Catharina, is voor: Leonard Strepers gestorven Ao: 1725 den 19 Agustus, naelaetende sijne voorseijde Huijsvrouw met de vijf gementioneerde Kinderen, soo met haere Moeder noch alle in t Leven. De derden van voorseijden Jan Strepers Kinderen eenen soon genamet Henderick gedoopt den 24 Julius 1672. Getrout d 4 october 1695. met de Eerbaere jonge dochter Eleisabeth olmis. Daernae gestorven Ao: 1724 den 26 Julijus. NaerLaetende sijne voorseijde huijsvrouw met Dreij Echte Kinderen genaemt Maria, Agneess, en Henricus welcke met haere voorsijde moeder noch alle in t Leven. De vierde eene Dochter van Voorno: jan Strepers genamet Catharina, gedoopt den 23 Maij 1677, daernae getrouwt den 21 September 1707, met den Eersamen Wilhelmus Sijben, Schoolmeester onser gereformeerde gemeinte alhier- is overleden den 5 Maij 1725, Naerlaetende haeren Voorseijden Mann Wilhelmus Sijben en twee Echte Kinderen, Genaemt Peter en Alitjen, welcke met haeren Vader beije noch in t Leven. De vijfde vaon voorseijde Jan Strepers Kinderen een dochter genaemt Annicken is gedoopt den 16 November 1686, getrout den 14 Spril 1716, met den Eersamen Lambertus Mool, en overleden, Ao: 1720 den 14 october naelatende haeren voornoemden man en twee Echte Kinderen, als een dochter geheeten Annicken, en een soon geheeten Johannes welcke met haeren voorseijden vader noch beijde Leven. overmits nu bovenstaende kinderen, en wettige Erfgenamen, van voornoemde Jan Strepers, en sijne hijsvrouw Encken Dorsch, van ons onderschrevene Consistorialen getuijgenisse der waerhijt behoorlicker wijse versocht, hebben wij sulz geensints verweijgen konnen maer nae waerhijt en Concientie Geerne willen mededeijlen om dies noodig sijne, sich op tijt en plaets daermede te konnen bedienen, daerom wij oock tot ojvconde van volle waerheijt en verseckeringe van alles, dit rechtmatig getuijgnisse met onse Christlicke Doopnamen, en Kercken Segel onderteijkent, soo geschiet tot Kaldenkerken in t Jaer onses Heeren Jesu Christi 1726 den 26 Junij Arnoldus Hambock Predicant van de gereformeerde gemaete tot Kaldenkerken Dirick heüskens ouderling tot Kalden Kercks hendrick höetz ouderling tot Kalden Kirchen giell hasen diacken tot Kalden Kirchen" [signed in German script] Jan Hasen diacken tot Kalden kirchen [signed in German script]

Kirchenbuch Kaldenkirchen, ev./ref. Gem., p. 77:
Nachdem von Seithen derer Erbgenahmen Jan Streepers bey uns Predigeren und Consistorialen der Evangeli-schen Gemeinde allhier zu Kaldenkirchen und Bracht behohrnd angezeigt worden ist, wie dass nehmlich zur fortsetzung der in Penselvanien in America obhabender rechtsstreitigkeit Ihnen höchstnöthig wäre zu wissen

wannehr Jan Streepers und dessen erben gestorben und begraben oder welche annoch am leben wären, mit bitt Ihnen darüber glaubhafften Extractum mitzutheilen, so haben wir in betracht dessen noch gar keine gestorbene im kirchenbuch bemercket stehen auff denen uns persönlich vorbracht gewordener dahier [?] wohnhafftigen fromme Ehrbahr= und glaubwürdigen alten leuthen benembtlich Died. van Hall Arnolden Cüsters und hedwigen Schmitz welche an eydes statt bezeuget haben, den Jan Streepers und dessen Kinder wohl gekent zu haben noch wohl zu wissen dass Jan Streepers im Jahr 1715 dessen Sohn Leon. Streepers im Jahr 1725 dessen Sohn Hin. Strepers im Jahr 1724 und Cath. Streepers im Jahr 1725 dahier zu Kaldenkirchen gestorben und begraben seyen, Ja Arn. Cüsters zeugt noch dabey sich wohl besinnen wie dass er bey der beerdigung des Jan Streepers mit auff unserem Kirchhoff gewesen, So also unter uns einhelliglich beschlossen und für gut befunden, dass nicht allein diese todesfälle des Jan Streepers und dessen Kinder also in behöhrender form gleich uns glaubhafft vorgebracht worden ist, sondern auch alle so man wüste und derer man sich nur erinneren kan wie auch alle welche uns künfftige nach des Herren anbethungswürdigen rathschluss zu sterben kommen von nun dem Kirchenbuch eingetragen, und dass denen Erbgenahmen von Jan Streepers der förmlicher bescheinigungs Extractus solle mitgetheilet werden, und zwarn um demehr annoch wohl in einem uns von obgem. Erbg. Streepers vorbracht gewordenem in folio bestehendem hausbuch des Hin. Streepers de dato Kaldenkirchen den 5 Aprilis 1686 angemerckt stehe dass im Jahr

p. 78:
1715 den 6 May nachmittags um 11 uhr der Jan Streepers dahier zu Kaldenkirchen gestorben und auch darauf begraben
Nicht minder uns auch auss denen wahrhafft vorseynden alten denckmahlen als grabsteinen und dergleichen die richtigkeit der sachen constiere, worauff dan solchem noch im Jahr 1764, den 6 May denen obbenenten Erbg. der anverlangter Extractus allinger Sterbender auss der Streeperischer familie wie bräuchlich mitgetheilet worden ist
1700 den 2 Aug. Ist Anna Doors Ehefrau von Jan Streepers begraben
1724 den 26 July Ist allhier Hin: Streepers begraben
1725 den 27 Ap. Ist Cath. Streepers allhier begraben
1725 den 22 Aug. Ist Leon. Streepers allhier begraben
1726 den 31 July Ist Maria Sieben Ehefrau von Leon. Streepers in Amsterdam gestorben und auch darauff begraben worden
1727 den 27 Oct. Ist Hinricus Streepers Jungman begraben
1729 den 1 May Ist Wilh. Sieben allhier begraben
1730 den 29 8bris Ist Elisabetha Olmis begraben
1741 den 14 Oct Ist Mathias Huskes zu Merschen begraben
1745 den 6 Feb. Ist Petrus Streepers allhier begraben

p. 79
1719 den 6 7bris Ist allhier begraben Joh. Küppers
1724 den 8 Dec. Ist allhier begraben Petrus Schuren
1726 den 27 Marty Ist allhier begraben Joh. in der Els
1728 den 2 November Ist allhier begraben Gerh. Hüsges
1733 den 14 Jan. Ist begraben Hermanus Hüsges Sohn von Gerh. Hüsges
1735 den 7 Feb. Ist allhier begraben Diedericus Symons
1734 den 10 7bris Ist begraben Died. am Haus
1736 den 2 Juny Ist allhier begraben Maria in der Els
1737 den 16. 9bris Ist allhier begraben Catharina Syben
1738 den 16 Octobris [?] Ist allhier begraben Cath. Küpers Haussfrau von der. [?] Weyers
1740 den 4 Ap. Ist allhier begraben Joh. Gerh. Küpers
1740 den 30 May Ist begraben Wilhelm in der Els
1742 den 18 8bris Ist allhier begraben Joh. Haasen
1744 den 10 Feb. Ist allhier begraben Maria Schuren
1745 den 28 Jan. Ist allhier begraben Gertruda Symons
1746 den 8 7bris Ist allhier begraben Maria Baums
1746 den 30 Nov. Ist allhier begraben Pet. Janssen
1746 den 18 Dec. Ist begraben Pet. Janssen Sohn von Joh. Janssen

1748 18 May Ist allhier begraben Gert Haasen
1750 den 25 May Ist allhier begraben Maria Aganeta Küpers
1750 den 7 Juny Ist allhier begraben Gertruda Haasen
1751 den 5 9bris synd allhier Died. und Anna Cath. Kinder von Pet. Symons
1751 den 10 Nov. Ist allhier begraben Maria Janssen Tochter von Joh. Janssen
1755 den 10 May Ist allhier begraben Jacobus Haasen
1756 den 4 Feb. Ist allhier begraben Anna Cath. Hüskes
1756 den 3 Marty Ist begraben Joh. in der Els
1756 den 10 Oct. Ist allhier begraben Marg. Lahr
1757 den 2 Juny Ist allhier begraben Sibilla Benson [?] Haussfrau von H. Dürselen und dass zwarn in unsere Kirche
1757 den 17 Dec. Ist allhier in unsere Kirche begraben Matthias Jacobus [Rest fehlt auf Kopie]

p. 80:
1757 den 24 Aug. Ist allhier begraben Catharina Küpers
1757 den 28 Dec. Ist in unsere Kirche begraben Herm. Mickenschreiber
1758 den 26 Feb. Ist begraben A. Maria Janssen Tochter von Hin. Janssen
1759 den 20 Marty Ist begraben Leon. Janssen Sohn von Joh. Janssen
1759 den 9 May Ist in unsere Kirche begraben Joh. Megdild Könings [?]
1761 den 26 Marty Ist auch in unsere Kirch begraben Chat. Odil. Gertruda
1761 den 14 Aug. Ist allhier begraben Cath. Haasen
1761 den 6 7bris Ist begraben Gertruda Haasen
1761 den 22 Octobris [?] Ist allhier begraben Joh. Died. Symons
1762 den 4 Marty Ist in unsere Kirche begraben Pet. Anton Pönsgen
1762 den 17 Nov. Ist in unsere Kirch begraben Matthias Mickenschreiber
1763 den 15 Juny Ist in unsere Kirche begraben Anna Maria Mickenschreiber
1763 den 12 July Ist in unsere Kirch begraben Anna Maria Streepers
1764 den 3 July Ist allhier begraben Elisabetha Wolter [?]
1765 den 28 Ap. Ist begraben Gert. in der Els
1765 den 15 July Ist begraben Sybilla Gert. Symons
1765 den 6 8bris Ist in unsere Kirche begraben Joh. Catharina Weyer
1765 den 19 Oct. Ist begraben Wilh. in der Els
1766 den 14 Marty Ist in unsere Kirche begraben Joh. Megdilda Cicilia Mickenschreiber
1766 den 26 [März?] Ist in unsere Kirche begraben Joh. Wilh. Pönsgen
1768 den 15 Marty Ist Pet. Hin. Frid. Strunck beerdigt
1768 den 4 Oct. Ist zu Bracht begraben Gerhardus Maubachs
1768 den 22 Dec. Ist allhier in unserer Kirchen begraben worden der HochEdele und Hochgelehrter Isaac Kuenen in der Rechten Doctor
1769 den 26 Feb. Ist allhier zu Kald. begraben Sophia Catharina Hüskes

p. 81:
1769 den 18 Juny Ist Catharina Schuren zu Bracht begraben
1770 den 2 Jan. Ist Cath. Hüskes zu Bracht begraben
1770 den 29 eod. [Jan.] Ist zu Bracht begraben Hinrichs Heuten und allhier Petrus Schmasen
1770 14 May Ist ein Kindt von Wilh. Pest allhier begraben

Appendix M
HSP 255: Original Agreement between Peter Hendrik Strepers and John Herbergs, of the one part, and James Parker, of the city of Perth Amboy, Middlesex Co., New Jersey, of the second part.
Articles of Agreement Indented made concluded and agreed upon the fifteenth day of March one thousand seven / hundred & sxty six Between Peter Hendrick Striepers late of / Germany but at present of Pensylvania Great Grandson of jan / Striepers late of Germany deceased andjohn Herbergs who is / intermarried with Hilladunda Seven daughter of Wilhelmus / Seven by Catharina Striepers a daughter of the said Jan Striepers / which said Peter Hendrick Striepers and John Herbergs as seized / in their own Right and as lawfully authorized by all others

- / Claiming under the said Jan Striepers are fully Impowered to / sell and convey all the Lands Tenements and Hereditaments / and Real Estate whereof the said Jan Striepers died seized in / Pensylvania of the first part and james Parker of the City of / Perth Amboy in the County of Middlesex & Province of New Jersey / of the second part as followeth Whereas the said jan Striepers died / seized of those four several tracts or Parcels of Land situate lying / and being in the Colony of Pensylvania Viz:1 of for thousand / four hundred & forty Eight acres of Land in Bucks County in the / Province of Pensylvania taken up for the said Jan Striepers and / Also of two hundred and seventy five acres of Land in the / German Town in Pensylvania aforsaid And also of fifty acres / of Land at Chestnut Hill near German Town aforsaid And Also of two Hundred & seventy five acres of Land in the Trap / near German Town aforsaid amounting in the whole to five / thousand and forty Eight acres of Land And also of fifty / acres of Liberty Land near German Town aforsaid And also / of three or more whole Lotts of Ground in the City of Philadelphia Now it is hereby concluded and agreed to and between the Partys to these / presents that the said James Parker shall and will frorn the / date of Use his best Endeavours to get Peaceable / Pohsehsion of the said several tracts of Land & Lotts of Ground / and Tenements thereon and if need be commence & prosecute / suits / For the Recovering the Pohsehsion thereof which suits shall be at his own proper Costs and charges and the said james Parker does for himself / his Heirs Executors Administrators and Ahsigns covenant Promise / and agree to and with the said Peter Hendrick Striepers &john / Herbergs their Heirs Executors Administrators and Ahsigns that / on his obtaining peacable pohsehsion of the four several Tracts / or parcells of Land or a Verdict orjudgement for the same and on / their the said Peter Hendrick Striepers and John Herbergs executing / to him the said James Parker such sufficient conveyance in the / Law as shall be advised by Council learned in the Law at the / proper Costs and charges of him the said iames Parker for / One Equal and individual Moyety or half part of the said four / several tracts or parcells of Lands shall and will pay or Cause / to be paid unto the said Peter Hendrick Striepers and John Herbergs / their Executors Administrators or Ahsigns the sum of seven - / Hundred & fifty pounds Sterling money of Great Britaun And / Farther that on his the said James Parker obtaining peacable / pohsehsion of the said several Lotts of Ground and of the said fifty / Acres of Liberty Land or Verdict orjudgement for the same / as aforsaid and on their the said Peter Hendrick Striepers and / john Herbergs, execitung to him the said james Parker such / sufficient Conveyance in the Law as shall be advised by / Council learned in the Law at the proper Cost and charge of / him the said james Parker for one Equal undivided / Moyety or half part of the said several Lotts of Ground with / the Mehsuages and dwelling houses thereon and of the sald Fifty / acres of Liberty Land and one half part of all such other Tracts or Lots / of Land in the said Colony of Pensylvania whereof the said jan Striepers died seized shall and will pay or cause to be paid / unto them the said Peter Hendrick Striepers and john Herbergs / their Heirs or Ahsigns the sum of two thousand two hundred / and fifty pounds Sterling money of Great Brittain And / the sald Peter Hendrick Striepers and john Herbergs for / And / And in Consideration of the several and Respective Sums of / Money to be paid as herein before is mentioned and agreed do / severally and respectively and for their several and Respective / Heirs and Ahsigns covenant promise and agree to and with the / said james Parker his Heirs Executors Administrators Ahsigns / by these presents in Manner and Form following that is to say / that they the said Peter Hendrick Striepers and John Herbergs and / all and everey other person and persons not at ever Reclaiming'or to / Claimany Right or title under them or Either of them or under / the said Jan Striepers or to the premihses herein before - / mentioned shall and will on his the said james Parker obtaining / such Pohsehsion Verdict orjudgement as aforsaid at the proper / Costs and Charges in the Law of him the said james Parker / his Heirs or Ahsigns well and truely and sufficiently in the Law / Convey and Ahsure or Cause or procure to be conveyed & ahsured / to the said james Parker his Heirs and Ahsigns or to such / Other person or persons as he shall constitute Elect nominate / or appoint one full and equal undivided Moyety or half / part of all the said Premihses with the Appurtenances & also / One Equal and undivided Moyety of all such other Tracts or / Lots of Land in the said Province of Pensylvania whereof he / the said jan Strievers died seized or Intituied unto by such deed or deeds Conveyance or Conveyances as shall be by Council / advised devised or Required And Whereas these is now due / and In arrear unto the legal Representatives of the said ja / Striepers unsiderable ground Rent and other Rents from the / Tenants holding the said tracts and lots of Land it is further agreed / and concluded between the partys to these presents that the said james / Parker shall be intituled unto One equal Moyety or half part / of the said Ground Rent & which shall be due and in arrear and other Rents now due and in arrear / for the said several tracts of Land & Lotts of Ground & Liberty / land at the time of Executing the said deeds or Conveyances for the same as aforsaid And it is further agreed by & between / the partys / The Partys aforsaid that the said Lots herein before mentioned / lying in the City of Philadelphia are to Contain as aforsaid & / If they are found hereafter by the aforsaid Partys to contain / Lehs Ground then the Partys of the second part are to pay only / In Proportion as they shall get Pohsehsion of the same and the / like is agreed in Respect to the said tracts of Land It is like= /

wise agreed that the said Peter Hendrick Striepers shall / Remain In the Province of Pensylvania to ahsist in the / Prosecuting such actions in the Law as now are hereafter / may be commenced in order to get Pohsehsion of the said several Lotts and tracts or parcells of Land as long as time as the said / james Parker shall think necehsary for which the said james / Parker agrees to pay to the said Peter Hendrick Striepers at the Rate of one Hundred pounds Current money of the Province / of Pensylvania p year from the twenty fifth day of / September now next to come untill which time the said / Peter Hendrick Striepers is to stay at his own Charge & Cost / without Receiving any Acknowledgement for the same / And for the true performance of all and Every the Covenants / Presents doth bind himself his Heirs Executors & Administrators / to the other Party his Executors administrators & Ahsigns in / the sum of six thousand pounds Sterling money of Great / Britain In Wittnehs Wehreof the Partys to these Pre= / sents have hereunto Interchangeably set their hands & seals / the day and year first above written / Sealed and Delivered the records (concluded / and in the first page & (dwelling houses) / in the second Page being first Interlined In the Presence of ------the words (and which shall be due and / in arrear) in the thirteenth line of the third page being likewise Interlinded / Peter Hendr Striepers / Johan: Herbergs / James Parker

Family Tree of the 13 Emigrant Families

Grammalogs and Abbreviations:

*	born	Z	Zeugen
~	christened	Twp.	Township
∞	married	Pa	Pennsylvania
†	died	Co.	County
±	buried	Mo. Mtg.	Monthly Meeting
p	parents		(monatliches Treffen der
f	father		Quäker)

Leonhard Arets

Leonhard Arets van Acken (see family tree Arets), *about 1652, emigrated to Pennsylvania in 1683, †03.11. 1715 Germantown (p: **Arent Classen van Acken**, *about 1632, ∞ 1st marriage about 1650 **Katharina Kuhlen**, *about 1630 Rheydt, †before mid-1665) ∞ **Agnes Doors** (see family tree Doors), christened:

1. Katharina Arets, *03.08.1684 Germantown, ∞ **Thomas Jones**

2. Margaret Arets, *27.11.1687 or 1688 Germantown, ∞ 27.06.1715 **Robert Thomas**

3. Elizabeth Arets, *16.06.1697 Germantown, will dated 07.09.1778, †1794, 07.08.1794 opening of the will, ∞ 1st marriage 28.03.1715 **John Streeper**, ~16.07.1688 Germantown, †1741 Germantown (J. Herbergs: 1739), p: **Wilhelm Strepers** ∞ **Marry Lucken**, christened:

> *1. Agnes Streeper*, ∞ **Garrett Dewees**, eldest son of **William Dewees**, survived by 4 sons and 1 daughter
>
> *2. William Streeper*, ∞ **Magdalene Castner** (daughter of **Georg Castner/Küsters** and granddaughter of **Paulus Küsters**), survived by 3 sons and 5 daughters, ∞ 2d marriage of **Magdalene Castner** 1744 **Georg Castner**

4. Sebella/Sibilla Leonhard (Arets), ∞ April 1710 Abington Mo. Mtg. *Anthony Klinken* (f: **Aret Klinken**, see family tree Klinken), *06.07.1688 Germantown

Johannes Bleikers / Priors

Jakob Priors, 1679 citizen of Krefeld, ∞ 27.10.1677 Krefeld/Ref. Church. **Katharina Classen**, Wickrath
Christian Preyers, 1679 citizen of Krefeld

I. Paul Priors, index of Mennonites 1621/22: Priors Paul, „gutes Erbe, handelt mit kleinem Garn und Leintuch", ∞ **N.N.**, christened: (index of Mennonites 1621/22, MG=Mönchengladbach): *2 sons:*

Peter Priors II. (?), Paulus Priors
II. Peter Priors, MG-Hardterbroich ∞ **Judith N.**, index of Mennonites 1654 MG-Hardterbroich: Priors Petter, wife Jutgen, 2 houses, linen dealer, christened (unsure): *Paulus Priors III.*

III. Paulus Priors, ∞ **Katharina N.**, index of Mennonites 1654: Priors Paulus, wife Treintgen, 6 children, tenant, weaver and bleacher, MG-Hardterbroich, christened: *Judith Priors IV.*, *1650/60

IV. Judith Priors, *1650/60, ∞ **Jan Blijkers/Blaker**, *about 1655 MG, emigrated to Pennsylvania in 1683, moved with family to Bucks Co. in 1702, christened Abington Mo. Mtg:

1. Gertsie Blijkers, *August 1677 Krefeld
2. Catharine Blijkers, †13.04.1703, ∞ 09.06.1702 Middletown Mo. Mtg. **Edmund Cowgill**, Newtown, *about 1667
3. Peter Blijkers V a., *Oct. 1683 on sea, aboard ship Concord
4. Paul Blijkers, *24.11.1685 Germantown, ∞ **Phebe Hibbs**, August 1715 Abington Mo. Mtg.
5. Samuel Blijkers V b., *21.02.1689 Germantown
6. Abraham Blijkers, *08.04.1699

V a. Peter Blijkers, *Oct. 1683 on sea, aboard ship Concord, ∞ 1st marriage 05.12.1708 Middletown Mo. Mtg. **Ruth Buckman**, (p: **William Buckman**, Newtown, ∞ **Sarah N.**), *22.04.1688 Bucks Co., †about 1750, christened: *John Blaker VI a.*, *about 1710, †15.05.1778

V b. Samuel Blijkers, *21.02.1689 Germantown, ∞ 1st marriage March 1721 Buckingham Mo. Mtg. **Sarah Smith** (p: **William Smith** ∞ **Catherine Croasdale**), *11.12.1689 Germantown, †1781, christened Wrightstown, Bucks Co.:

1. Peter Blaker VI b., *03.01.1722
2. Mary Blaker, *01.03.1723
3. Hannah Blaker, *19.05.1724
4. Lydia Blaker, *28.04.1726
5. Sarah Blaker, *23.12.1728
6. Judith Blaker, *30.10.1729
Samuel Blijkers ∞ 2d marriage 05.08.1765 Buckingham Twp., Bucks Co. **Catherine N.**, *about 1689 (1st marriage ∞ 1720 **N. Love**, christened: *Benjamin Love*)

VI a. John Blaker, *about 1710, ∞ 16.08.1735 **Catherine Williams**, christened:

> *1. Paul Blaker*
> *2. Peter Blaker VII.*, *1736
> *3. John Blaker*, *1739 Bucks Co.
> *4. Ruth Blaker*, *1740
> *5. Sarah Blaker*, *1744 Bucks Co., ∞ 21.04.1762 Wrightstown, Bucks Co. **James Hibbs** (p: **William**

Hibbs ∞ Ann Carter)

6. Phebe Blaker, *1746 Bucks Co., ∞ 12.12.1764 Wrightstown, Bucks Co. **Isaac Wiggens**

7. Catherine Blaker, *1748 Bucks Co.

8. Achilles Blaker, *1752, †19.11.1822, ∞ **Sarah Buckmann**, *22.11.1753, †10.09.1831

9. Mary Blaker, *1753 Bucks Co., ∞ 20.12.1775 Wrightstown, Bucks Co. **Joseph Hamilton**

Peter Blijkers ∞ 2d marriage 06.01.1757 **Mary Watson**

VI b. Peter Blaker, *03.01.1722, ∞ 1st marriage 13.01.1742 Christ Church Philadelphia **Agnes Ashbourn**, *about 1722, christened:

1. Jane Blaker, *26.12.1743, Bucks Co.

2. William G. Blaker, *30.03.1745 Bucks Co.

VII. Peter Blaker, *1736, ∞ 28.04.1763 Wrightstown, Bucks Co. **Sarah Hibbs** (p: **William Hibbs**, *1700, †1789, ∞ **Ann Carter**, *1701, †about 1801), *25.03.1733 Middletown, Bucks Co., christened:

1. John Blaker, *1765 Bucks Co., ∞ **N.N.**, christened: *Sarah, John, James Oliver, Mary Catherine, Susan, Matilda, Jane H., Harriet, Icey, Lucy Ellen, Fentond Blaker*

2. Ruth Blaker, *1767, Northampton Twp., Bucks Co.

3. Rachel Blaker, *1769, Northampton Twp., Bucks Co.

4. Joseph Blaker, *1771 Wrightstown, †before 1836 Cumberland Twp., Greene Co., Pa, ∞ **Catherine Clutter** (f: **Peter Clutter**), *about 1780, christened: *John* and *Ann Blaker*

5. Abraham Blaker, *1776 Wrightstown

6. Amos Blaker, *1778 Wrightstown

7. David Blaker, *1780 Wrightstown, †Feb. 1855 Greene Co., Pa, ∞ **Abigail N.**, christened: *John, N., David, Rebecca, Benjamin, Heaton Blaker*

Tönis Kunders

I. Thonis Comis, *1535 MG, represented the Mennonites of MG in 1591 at the „Conception of Cologne", ∞ **Sophia N.**, christened:
Gottschalk Comes II., *about 1565, †about 1652

II. Gottschalk Comes, *about 1565, ∞ **Sophia Viet/ Vitgen** (daughter of **Vit an de Heiden**), *about 1565/ 1571 MG-Venn, lived at MG-Obergeburth, christened:
Thones Comes III., *about 1596 MG, †1667 Goch

III. Thones Comes, *1596 MG, ∞ **Oelletgen N.**, *about 1603, index of Mennonites, MG 1654: 5 children, lived at MG-Obergeburth, christened:

1. Gottschalk Theunissen, *1625, †1667, ∞ **Helene Henrichs**, *1630, †1675

2. Anna Comes IV., *1632 MG-Alst, †20.04.1691

IV. Anna Comes, *1632 MG-Alst, †20.04.1691, ∞ **Konrad Lenßen Hecken** (F: **Lenz Hecken** ?), *about 1627, index of Mennonites, MG 1654: „**Coen Hecken Entgen** eheleuth" (married couple), christened:

1. Tönis (Anton) Kunders V., *about 1653 MG, ~09.07.1673 Goch/Menn. Church, 1679 citizen of Krefeld, emigrated to Pennsylvania in 1683, †1729 Westmont, Burlington Co., NJ, dyer and weaver
(unsure): *2. Gertrud Conrats* ∞ 24.06.1691 Krefeld/ Ref. Church **Arnold Küsters**, emigrated to Pennsylvania in 1691

V. Tönis (Anton) Kunders, *about 1653 MG, †1729 Westmont, Burlington Co., NJ, ∞ 31.05.1677 Krefeld/ Ref. Church. **Helene Doors** (see family tree Doors), *about 1650 Kaldenkirchen, christened:

1. Konrad Kunders, *27.07.1678 Krefeld, †10.03.1747 Germantown, ∞ 1st marriage 31.07.1704 **Anna Klinken** (f: **Aret Kinken**, see family trees Abraham Tunes/Klinken), ∞ 2d marriage 26.09.1721 Gwynedd Mo. Mtg. **Anne Burson**

2. Matthias Kunders, *04.02.1680 Krefeld, †02.04.1726 Germantown, ∞ 29.07.1706 **Barbara Tyson** (f: **Reiner Theißen**), christened:

> *1. Anthony Kunders*
>
> *2. Margaret Kunders*, *1709, ∞ 07.05.1736 Abington Mo. Mtg. **Jacob Shoemaker** (f: **George Shoemaker**, Cheltenham Twp.)
>
> *3. Cornelius Kunders*, *about 1712, †12.07.1770, ∞ 29.03.1732 Abington Mo. Mtg. **Priscilla Bolton**, †22.11.1765 (p: **Everard jr. Bolton** ∞ **Mary Naylor**), christened:
>
>> *1. Matthew Conrad*, *04.07.1733, ∞ 13.04.1760 Germantown Mtg. **Mary Roberts** (f: **Thomas Roberts**, †Bristol, Philadelphia Co.)
>>
>> *2. Mary Conrad*, *26.06.1735, ∞ 25.05.1762 Horsham Appointed Mtg. **Jacob Walton** (f: **Jeremiah Walton**, †Moreland)
>>
>> *3. Everard Conrad*, *21.01.1738, ∞ 18.06.1761 Abington Mtg. **Margaret Cadwalder** (f: **Isaac Cadwalder**, †Warminster, Bucks Co.)
>>
>> *4. Joseph Conrad*, *23.02.1742
>>
>> *5. Samuel Conrad* (twin), *13.11.1744, †20.11.1819, ∞ 06.11.1772 Horsham Mo. Mtg. **Hannah (Baker) Kenderdine**, widow of **Jacob Kenderdine**, christened:
>>
>>> *1. Sarah Conrad*, *21.08.1773, ∞ **George Webster**
>>>
>>> *2. Samuel Conrad*, *31.03.1775, †06.09.1775
>>>
>>> *3. Hannah Conrad*, *16.08.1776, †unmarried
>>>
>>> *4. Ruth Conrad*, *16.08.1778, ∞ 18.04.1802 **Isaac Parry**, her stepbrother (p: **Isaac Parry** ∞ **Grace N.**)
>>>
>>> *5. Samuel Conrad*, *04.07.1780, †18.11.

1827, ∞ 17.11.1807 Gwynedd Mo. Mtg. **Sarah Hallowell** (p: **William Hallowell** ∞ **Mary Roberts**), *17.03.1782, †14.07.1835, christened:

> 1. *Ascenath Conrad*, *08.09.1808, ∞ 11.11.1829 Upper Dublin Mtg. **Amos L. Lukens**
> 2. *Job Conrad*, *12.10.1810, ∞ 1836 **Ann Sill**
> 3. *Ephraim Conrad*, *11.04.1813
> 4. *Ruth Conrad*, *25.10.1815, ∞ 23.03. 1837 **Isaac Roberts** (p: **John Roberts** ∞ **Rachel Shoemaker**)
> 6. *Cornelius Conrad*, *19.04.1782, †06.07. 1782
> 7. *Cornelius Conrad*, *13.06.1783
> 8. *Priscilla Conrad*, *22.11.1785, ∞ **Jonathan Adamson**

6. *John Conrad* (twin), *13.11.1744
7. *Susanna Conrad*, *09.01.1750, ∞ 13.10.1773 Byberry Appointed Mtg. **Samuel Carver**, Byberry

4. *Magdalena Kunders*, ∞ **George Inglass**
5. *William Kunders*
6. *John Kunders*, ∞ 28.06.1748 Gwynedd Mo. Mtg. **Elizabeth Shoemaker** (f: **George Shoemaker**, Bucks Co.)
7. *Matthias Kunders*

3. *Jan Kunders*, 13.08.1681 Krefeld, †March 1765, ∞ 1st marriage 29.07.1706 **Alice Luken** (p: **Jan Lucken** ∞ **Maria Gastes**), ∞ 2d marriage **Elizabeth Denis**
4. *Anna Kunders*, *14.07.1684 Germantown, †02.05. 1752, ∞ 26.09.1715 **Leonhard Strepers**, *15.05. 1686 Germantown, †02.07.1727 Philadelphia (see family tree Wilhelm Strepers)
5. *Agnes Kunders*, *08.12.1686 Germantown, ∞ 26. 12.1709 **Samuel Powell**
6. *Hendrik Kunders*, *26.04.1689 Germantown, †12. 09.1758, ∞ 07.09.1710 Germantown Mo. Mtg. **Katharina Strepers** (p: **Wilhelm Strepers** ∞ **Marry Lucken**, see family tree Wilhelm Strepers). *Henry Cunrad, sixth son, had the same profession as his father, left 7 sons. Samuel, *1731 Philadelphia, †24. 04.1792 ebd., Henry's youngest son, called himself **Cunard**.*
7. *Elisabeth Kunders*, *08.05.1691 Germantown, †24. 03.1757, ∞ January 1710 **Griffith Jones**

Peter Kürlis

Peter Kürlis (see family tree Kürlis), Waldniel, moved to Krefeld in 1681/82, emigrated to Pennsylvania in 1683, ∞ 17.03.1675 Kaldenkirchen/Ref. Church **Elisabeth Doors**, *Kaldenkirchen, christened Kaldenkirchen/ Ref. Church:

1. *Mechtild Kürlis*, ~27.12.1675 (sp: Matthias Kürlis, Kaspar Hüskes, Anna Strepers)
2. *Johannes Kürlis*, ~03.02.1677 (sp: Jan Olmis, Anna Doors)
3. *Mechtild Kürlis*, ~27.08.1679 (sp: Reiner Doors, Katharina Brouwers, Mechtild Kürlis)
4. *Agnes Kürlis*, ~05.01.1681 (sp: Jan Strepers, Gertrud Doors)
5. *Mechtild Kürlis*, ~22.11.1682 Krefeld/Ref. Church
6. *Matthias Kürlis*, ~Germantown
7. *Peter Kürlis*, ~Germantown

Johann Lenssen/Lentzen

Johann Lenssen, *Mönchengladbach/Rheydt?, lived at Krefeld before marriage, †after Sept. 1731, ∞ banns 24. 11.1680 Krefeld/Ref. Church **Maria Peters Schmitz**, Mönchengladbach, baptized:

1. *Cathrine Lenssen*, ∞ William Biddis, bought Jan Strepers Land in Germantown in 1731
2. *Peter Lenssen*, †young
3. *Margaret Lenssen*, †young

Lucken

I. **Wilhelm Lucken**, *Rheindahlen, ∞ **N.N.**, christened:

II. **Jan Lucken**, *about 1595 Rheindahlen, †between 02.08.1636 and 05.08.1638, ∞ 1st marriage Rheindahlen **Boetzgen/Beatrix ther Meer** (f: **Mewis/Bartholomäus ther Meer** ∞ **Grechtgen/Margarete N.**), *about 1595 MG-Hoven, †before 14.02.1631, **Jan Lucken** ∞ 2d marriage after 04.11.1628 **Eva Hanssen** (p: **Heinrich Hanssen** ∞ **Katharina in der Sittardt**), christened in 1st marriage:

1. *Mevis Lucken*
2. *Wilhelm Jansen Lucken* III. a, *about 1620 Rheindahlen, †1694, chased away in 1652, lived at Wickrath till 1678, Rheydt till 1694
3. *Andreas Jansen Lucken*
4. *Tochter N.*, ∞ **Nikolaus Gerhardtz**
5. *Beatrix Lucken* III. b ∞ **Tonis Klinken**

III a. **Wilhelm Jansen Lucken**, *about 1620 Rheindahlen, ∞ 1649 Rheindahlen **Adelheid N.**, *about 1623 Rheindahlen, †after 09.02.1696 Krefeld, christened:

1. *Maria Wilhelmsen Lucken*, *1652 Rheindahlen, ∞ 1st marriage/banns 12.09.1679 Krefeld/Ref. Church **Jan Simons**, Mönchengladbach, 2d marriage 29.07.1685 marriage contract **Wilhelm Strepers** (see family tree Wilhelm Strepers), emigrated to Pennsylvania in 1683
2. *Boetzken/Beatrix Lucken*, *1654 Wickrath, ∞ about 1683 **Abraham Tunes/Klinken**, *between 1653 and 1669
3. *Johann Lucken* IV., *about 1655 Rheindahlen, †24.

03.1744 Germantown, emigrated to Pennsylvania in 1683
4. Giertgen Lucken, *1656 Wickrath, ∞ Rheydt/Ref. Church **Nelis Goertz**
5. Elisabeth Lucken, *about 1658, ±26.08.1714 Krefeld, ∞ Rheindahlen **Gerhard Huberts Loers**
(f: **Hupert Lohr**: 23.08.1638 index of Mennonites Rheindahlen; **Hubert Lohrenß**: 02.07.1652 index of Mennonites Rheindahlen), ±27.11.1711 Krefeld

III b. Beatrix Lucken ∞ 1644 **Thonis Klinken**, Klinken-Hof, MG-Bettrath, christened:
Abraham Tunis Klinken, emigrated to Pennsylvania in 1683

IV. Johann Lucken, *about 1655 Rheindahlen, 24.03. 1744 Germantown, ∞ 1683 **Maria Gastes**, emigrated to Pennsylvania in 1683, christened:
1. Elizabeth Luken, *28.09.1684, ∞ **Edward White**
2. Alice (Adelheid) Luken, *10.07.1686, †1726, ∞ 29.07.1706 Montgomery Co. **Jan Kunders** (p: **Tönis (Anton) Kunders** ∞ **Helene Doors**, see family tree Kunders), *03.08.1681, Krefeld, †March 1765, christened:
   Dennis Cunnard, ∞ 26.02.1732 Philadelphia Co. **Ann Knight** (f: **Isaac Knight**), christened:
   John Cunard/Conrad, *02.10.1735 Philadelphia Co., †24.09.1806, ∞ 02.05.1764 **Susannah Huntsman**, *March 1744, †29.10.1822, christened:
      Jonathan Cunard, *12.11.1776, †31.12.1846, ∞ about 1797 **Hannah Nixon** (p: **Samuel Nixon** ∞ **Susanna Roberts**), *27.01.1777, †about 1850, christened:
         John Nixon Conard, *about 1800, ∞ about 1823 **Rebecca Iredell**, *about 1798, †05.12. 1869
3. William Luken, *22.2.1688, †before 1741, ∞ 27.11. 1710 Abington Mo. Mtg. **Elizabeth Tyson** (p: **Reiner Theißen** ∞ **Margaret op den Graeff**), *07.10.1690 Germantown, ±18.02.1765 Germantown, christened:
   Elizabeth Lukens, *after 1716 Horsham or Upper Dublin, ∞ 1st marriage 16.01.1753 **Thomas Potts** (p: **John Potts** ∞ **Elizabeth McVeagh**), *about 1729, †29.07. 1776 perhaps Chelsea Forge, NJ, ∞ 2d marriage after 1776 **Dr. John Rockhill**
4. Sarah Luken, *19.09.1689
5. John Luken, *27.11.1691, ∞ 25.02.1712 **Margarete Custerd** (Küsters ?)
6. Maria Luken, *18.01.1694, †1772, ∞ 1712 **John Jarrett**, christened:
   1. Edward Jarrett
   2. Samuel Jarrett
   3. Philipp Jarrett
   4. Isaac Jarrett
   5. William Jarrett
   6. Sebastian Jarrett
   7. Mary Jarrett
   8. Elizabeth Jarrett
   9. Joan Jarrett
   10. Margaret Jarrett
   11. Sarah Jarrett
   12. John Jarrett
   13. Daniel Jarrett
7. Peter Luken, *30.03.1696 Abington Mtg., †22.09. 1741, ∞ 28.12.1719 Abington Mtg. **Gaynor Evans** (p: **Peter Evans** ∞ **Gaynor N.**), christened:
   Abrahm Lukens, *1722, †1800, ∞ 05.04.1745 **Rachel Iredell** (p: **Thomas Iredell** ∞ **Rebecca Williams**), christened:
      Seneca Lukens, *25.05.1751, †09.12.1829, ∞ 06.10.1777 **Sarah Quinby** (p: **Isaiah Quinby** ∞ **Rachel Warford**), christened:
         1. Tabitha Lukens, *24.10.1789, †04.02. 1882, ∞ 08.06.1807 **John Kirk**
         2. Isaiah Lukens, *1779, †1846
8. Hannah Luken, *25.07.1698, ∞ 30.07.1716 **Samuel Daniel Pastorius**
9. Matthias Luken, *13.10.1700, †1742, ∞ 27.06.1721 **Ann Johnson**
10. Abraham Luken, *16.09.1703, ∞ 27.04.1727 **Mary Maule**
11. Joseph Luken, *03.011.1705, ∞ 30.09.1728 **Susannah Maule**

op den Graeff

Herman Isaaks, Dirk Isaaks, Abraham Isaaks

I. Hermann op den Graeff, *26.11.1585 probably Aldekerk, 1605 citizen of Kempen, 1608 at Krefeld, †27. 12.1642 Krefeld, Mennonite minister, ∞ 16.08.1605 **Margarete Pletges**, *26.11.1588 Kempen, †07.01.1643 Krefeld (p: **Andreas Pletges**, †22.05.1608, ∞ 2d marriage 13.12.1584 **Adelheid Göbels** (f: **Syllis Göbels**, †15.03.1615 Krefeld), christened 18 children, 9 †young, 6 daughters married), christened:
1. Abraham op den Graeff, linen dealer at Krefeld, ∞ 1641 **Eva von der Leyen**, Radevormwald, christened:
   Hermann op den Graeff, †young
   two daughters ∞ Mennonites of Krefeld
2. Isaak op den Graeff II., *28.02.1616 Krefeld, †17.01.1669 Krefeld, ± 19.01.1669 Krefeld/Ref. Church

II. Isaak op den Graeff, *28.02.1616 Krefeld, ∞ **Margarete Peters** (probably **Doors**, f: **Peter Doors**, see family tree Doors); **Margarete Peters/op den Graeff** emigrated to Pennsylvania in 1683, †19.11.1683 Philadelphia, christened:
1. Hermann Isaaks op den Graeff, *1642 Krefeld, †1704/1708 Kent, Delaware, emigrated to Pennsylva-

nia in 1683, ∞ **Elisabeth/Debora van Bebber** (p: **Jakob Isaak van Bebber**, *about 1616 Mülheim/Ruhr, †about 1690 Germantown, ∞ **N.N.**, christened:

1. *Debora van Bebber*, *about 1648
2. *Isaak Jakobs van Bebber*, *about 1655 Krefeld
3. *Matthias van Bebber*, *about 1660 Krefeld
4. *Deborah/Elisabeth van Bebber*, *about 1665 Krefeld)

christened:

1. *Margarete op den Graeff* (?), *before 1680, ∞ 06.02.1697 **Peter Schumacher**
2. *Sytge/Syltge op den Graeff*, *about 1685 Germantown, ∞ **Jan Krey**, *about 1657 Kriegsheim/Palatine, †1719/20 Germantown, christened:
   Catherine Krey, ∞ **Christian Helderman**, *before 1715, †1800 Lower Salford, Montgomery Co., Pa

2. *Dirk Isacks op den Graeff*, *Krefeld, emigrated to Pennsylvania in 1683, ∞ 20.03.1681 Krefeld „Quaker marriage" **Petronella Vieten**, *Kampen/Kempen
3. *Abraham Isaaks op den Graeff*, *Krefeld, emigrated to Pennsylvania in 1683, ∞ 23.07.1679 Ref. Church **Katharina Jansen van Acken**, Mönchengladbach, christened:

1. *Annekin op den Graeff*, *after 1680, ∞ 06.04. 1709/10 **Harmon Dehaven**, *Mülheim/Ruhr, †1752 (p: **Evert ten Haven** ∞ **Elizabeth Shipbower**, christened: *Harmon (Hermann), Jacob, Gerhard*, *1687 Mülheim/Ruhr, †1746 Perkiomen, *Peter*, *between 1685 and 1687, Mülheim/Ruhr, †1768), christened:
   Jacob Dehaven, *before 1730 Lower Providence, Montgomery Co., Pa, †1761 Limerick, Montgomery Co.

2. *Jacob op de Graeff*, *after 1683 Germantown, ∞ **Anneken Dehaven**, *Mülheim/Ruhr
4. *Margrit Isaaks op den Graeff*, emigrated to Pennsylvania in 1683, ∞ **Reiner Theißen** (see family tree Doors)

Jan Simons

I. **Simon Janssen**, *Süsteren, ∞ **Katharina Wolters** (P: **Wolter Corst am Scheurendt**, MG-Eicken ∞ **Maria N.**, 1669 75 years, lived from 1654 at Krefeld), christened:
1. *Jan Simons II.*, emigrated to Pennsylvania in 1683, ∞ 1st banns 12.09.1679 Krefeld/Ref. Church **Maria Willemsen Lucken**, Mönchengladbach
2. *Wolter Simons*, †June/July 1734, unmarried, emigrated to Pennsylvania in 1684

II. **Jan Simons**, ∞ 12.11,1679 1st banns Krefeld/Ref. Church **Maria Willemsen Lucken** (p: **Wilhelm Jansen Lucken** ∞ **Adelheid N.**, see family tree Lucken), chris-

tened: *Peter Simons Jansen*, *30.11.1683 Krefeld, †1745, ∞ **Gertrud Neus** (p: **Jan Neus** ∞ 1682 Krefeld **Agnes Theißen/Schumacher**?, MG-Damm), christened:
1. *Agnes Jansen*, ∞ **Jacob Sauter/Souder**, 2. *Walter Jansen*, 3. *Mary Jansen*, ∞ **Phillip Markley**

Wilhelm Strepers

I. **Wilhelm Strepers** (see family tree Strepers), *about 1644 Kaldenkirchen, †1st week of November 1717 Germantown ∞ 29.07.1685 marriage contract **Maria Willemsen Lucken** (see family tree Lucken), *1652/54 (E: **Wilhelm Lucken** ∞ **Adelheid**) ∞ 1st marriage **Jan Simons**, Mönchengladbach, christened:
1. *Leonhard Strepers II a.*, *17.05.1686 Germantown, †02.05.1727 Philadelphia
2. *John Strepers II b.*, ~16.07.1688 Germantown, †1741 Germantown (J. Herbergs: 1739)
3. *Katharina Strepers*, *08.12.1690 Germantown, ∞ 07.09.1710 **Hendrik Kunders** (f: **Tönis (Anton) Kunders** ∞ **Helene Doors**, see family trees Doors and Kunders), *26.04.1689, †12.09.1758, *Germantown

II a. **Leonhard Strepers**, *15.05.1686, ~17.05.1686 Germantown, ∞ 29.09.1715 Abington Mtg. **Anna Kunders** (p: **Tönis Kunders** ∞ **Helene Doors**, see family trees Doors and Kunders), *14.07.1684 Germantown, †02.05.1752 christened Germantown:
1. *Dennis Strepers III a.*, *13.12.1715 Germantown, †25.07.1766 Philadelphia
2. *William Strepers III b.*, *15.12.1716, †20.06,1764, blacksmith
3. *Henry Strepers*, *about 1718
4. *Leonhard Strepers III c.*, *03.01.1719, †05.04.1796 Montogmery Co.
5. *Henry Strepers*, *1721 Germantown, †before 19.03. 1743 unmarried

II b. **John Strepers**, ~16.07.1688 Germantown, ∞ 28. 03.1715 Abington Mtg. **Elizabeth Arets** (f: **Leonhard Arets** ∞ **Agnes Doors**), *16.06.1697, †1794, christened:
1. *Wilhelm Strepers III d.*, *04.02.1719, †1773
2. *Agnes Strepers*, ∞ **Garrett Dewees**
Elizabeth Arets ∞ end 1742 Abington Mtg. 2d marriage **George Kastner**

III a. **Dennis Strepers**, *13.12.1715, ∞ about 1744 **Margaret N.**, christened:
1. *Henry Strepers IV.*, *28.08.1745, †04.02.1820 Germantown
2. *Dennis Strepers*, *10.03.1747 Germantown, †12.10. 1798 ∞ **Judith N.**, †10.10.1815
3. *Hannah Strepers*, *before 1749, †young

4. Hannah Strepers, *22.06.1750, ∞ 25.03.1769 **Elias Linkenhager**, *before 1746 Germantown
5. Leonhard Strepers, *before 1751, †young
6. Leonhard Strepers, *29.07.1753 Germantown, †1795 ∞ **Barbara N.**
7. William Strepers, *01.12.1755, †before 1766

III b. William Strepers, *15.12.1716, ∞ 1743 Abington Mtg. **Mary Dawes**, *16.04.1723, christened:
1. Abraham Strepers, *04.11.1747, †1792, ∞ about 1770 **Mary Deaves**
2. Mary Strepers, *14.07.1753
3. Ann Strepers

III c. Leonhard Strepers, *03.01.1719, †08.04.1796 ∞ 27.12.1744 Philadelphia 1st marriage **Rebecca Groothausen**, ∞after 1762 2d marriage **Margaret Righter** (p: **George Righter** ∞ **Elizabeth N.**), *12.05.1749, †05.10.1819, christened in 1st marriage:
1. John Strepers, *09.03.1745, †18.10.1817, ∞ 24.1.1771 Germantown **Deborah Levering**, *02.05.1749, †16.08.1777
2. Dennis Strepers, *1747, †1811, ∞ **Ann N.**
3. Sarah Strepers, ∞ **Johnson**
4. Elizabeth Strepers, *1753, †1833, ∞ 1st marriage 09. 07.1769 Philadelphia **Henry Cunard** (p: **Dennis Cunard** ∞ **Lydia Potts**), *17.05.1742, †1786, 2d marriage February 1793 **John Thomas** (p: **Evan Thomas** ∞ **Christiana Linderman**), *06.03.1765, †16.04.1841
5. Peter Strepers, *18.11.1754, †23.01.1820, ∞ 1st marriage 26.02.1788 Philadelphia Christ Church **Christiana Coxe**, ∞2d marriage **Anstina Rapp** ?, *18.06.1762, †28.01.1839 Germantown
christened in 2d marriage:
6. Ann Strepers, *04.05.1765, †March 1836, ∞ about 1790 **John Dull**
7. Leonhard Strepers, *30.01.1767, †young
8. Jacob Strepers, *04.06.1769, †28.02.1845, ∞ *Lydia Strepers*, *02.02.1765, †15.01.1837
9. Henry Strepers, *31.07.1771, †young
10. Rebecca Strepers, *29.05.1773, †24.06.1865, ∞ 1st marriage *James Harvey*, ∞ 2d marriage **John N.**
11. Daniel Strepers, *08.09.1775, †23.09.1803, ∞ **Elizabeth Hinkel** (p: **Peter Hinkel** ∞ **Elizabeth**), *12.05.1778, †08.02.1871
12. William Strepers, *09.09.1777, †22.02.1825, ∞ 1st marriage **Ann Wise**, †07.06.1806, ∞ 2d marriage **Elizabeth Carver**
13. Deborah Strepers, *30.12.1779, †24.08.1844, ∞ **William Yerkes**
14. George Strepers, *07.02.1782, †01.09.1864, ∞ 11.06.1807 Germantown **Elizabeth (Hinkel) Streeper**, *12.05.1778, †08.02.1871, widow of brother **Daniel Strepers**

15. Mary Strepers, *28.02.1784, †1852, ∞ 21.10. 1802 **Jonathan Jones**, *02.11.1781, †03.04.1857
16. Catherine Strepers, *19.03.1786, †03.05.1852, ∞ 11.03.1811 Philadelphia **James Monahan**, *01.11. 1778, †28.10.1841
17. Susanna Strepers, *25.09.1788, †12.03.1864, ∞ 21.06.1828 Plymouth Mtg. **Joseph Wilson**, Londongrove, †15.06.1835

III d. Wilhelm Strepers, *04.02.1719, †1773, ∞ 1744 Gwynedd Mtg. **Magdalene Castner**, *11.10.1724 (p: **George Kastner** ∞ **Mary**), christened:
1. Mary Strepers, *15.01.1745, †01.09.1835, ∞ 1st marriage **Anthony Hallman,** *08.11.1747, †13.12.1794, ∞ 2d marriage **N. Christy**
2. Elizabeth Strepers, *22.11.1747, †young
3. Agnes Strepers, *16.10.1748
4. Hannah Strepers, *19.10.1750, ∞ **John Piper**
5. John Strepers, *14.06.1753, †1790, ∞ **Barbara N.**
6. Sarah Strepers, *07.05.1755
7. George Strepers, *16.09.1757
8. William, †13.03.1828, ∞ **Lydia N.**, *02.02.1765
9. Magdalene Strepers, ∞ 19.11.1801 Philadelphia **Joseph Hinkel**
10. Lydia Strepers

IV. Henry Strepers, *28.08.1745, ∞ 28.11.1771 Springfield Twp., Pa, **Jane Hughes**, *1747 Plymouth, Pa, christened:
1. Henry Streeper V., *17.08.1777 Germantown, †07.02.1839 Philadelphia
2. Anna Streeper, *1780 Germantown, ∞ 06.05.1802 **Joseph Lehmann**, *about 1780
3. John Streeper, *1782 Germantown
4. Hannah Streeper, *1784 Germantown
5. Rebecca Streeper, *1786 Germantown

V. Henry Streeper, *17.08.1777 Germantown, ∞ 22.06. 1809 Philadelphia **Prudence Lear**, *05.01.1791 Philadelphia, †15.02.1822 Germantown, christened:
1. Wilkinson Streeper VI., *09.09.1809 Germantown, †16.01.1856 Salt Lake City
2. George Streeper, *05.09.1811, †24.06.1827
3. William Streeper, *08.09.1815 Germantown, †19.09.1864, ∞ **Mary Ann N.**
4. Wilhelmina Streeper, *17.02.1816
5. John Streeper, *10.05.1817 Germantown, ∞ **Rachel N.**
6. Elizabeth Prudence Streeper, *05.09.1820 Germantown, †25.04.1895

VI. Wilkinson Streeper, *09.09.1809 Germantown, ∞ 10.07.1834 **Matilda Wells**, christened:
1. Josephene Streeper, *06.05.1835, ∞ 25.03.1856 **Gorge Ogden Chase**, christened:

Kate Matilda, Josephine, Fanny Dean, Viola, Alice, Frank Leslie, Mary Ella, George Angel, John Wilkinson, David Nelson, Ethel, Leah, Valentine, Emma Eakle

2. *William Henry Streeper*, *01.08.1837, †04.10.1930 Centerville, Ut, ∞ 16.10.1867 Mary **Amelia Richards**, christened:

   William H. Streeper, *02.05.1869 Centerville, Ut
3. *Mary Catherine Streeper*, *02.05.1842 Philadelphia, †09.11.1911, ∞ 06.12.1862 Hugh **McSwein Dougall**
4. *George Wells Streeper*, *20.04.1844
5. *John Wilkinson Streeper*, *05.04.1846, ∞ 1870 **Polley Felshaw**, christened:

   John Wilkinson, *06.02.1872
6. *Matilda Streeper*, *21.09.1848
7. *Charles Augustus Streeper*, *25.11.1852, ∞ **Margaret Hargraves**

Reiner Theißen

Reiner Doors/Theißen (see family tree Doors), *1658/59 Kaldenkirchen, emigrated to Pennsylvania in 1683, †27.09.1745 in Abington, ∞ 1685 Germantown **Margret op den Graeff**, christened:

1. *Matthias Theißen*, *31.08.1686 Germantown, †April 1727, ∞ 29.01.1708 Abington Mo. Mtg. **Mary Potts** (f: **John Potts**, Haridless, Wales), *about 1688 Philadelphia, christened:

   1. *Margret Tyson*, *07.02.1708 Abington, †04.06. 1752 ebd., ±17.06.1752 ebd., ∞ 23.08.1729, Abington Mtg. **William Hallowell** (f: **Thomas Hallowell**, *06.03.1679 Hucknall, Nottingham, England, †14.02. 1734 Abington), *01.08.1707 Abington, †23.08.1794 ib.
   2. *Mary Tyson*, *25.03.1710, ∞ 18.10.1729 Abington Mtg. **Ellis Lewis**
   3. *Rynear Tyson*, *24.06.1711, ∞ 29.03.1739 Abington Mtg. **Grace Fletcher** (f: **Robert Fletcher**)
   4. *John Tyson*, *20.02.1713
   5. *Sarah Tyson*, *10.10.1714
   6. *Elizabeth Tyson*, *14.11.1716, †young
   7. *Isaac Tyson*, *20.10.1718, †08.09.1796, ∞ 26.03. 1748 Abington Mtg. **Esther Shoemaker** (f: **Isaac Shoemaker**, Cheltenham)
   8. *Matthew Tyson*, September 1720, †young
   9. *Martha Tyson*, *12.05.1722
   10. *Elizabeth Tyson*, *15.12.1723, ∞ 31.03.1742 Abington Mtg. **John Fitzwater** (f: **Thomas Fitzwater**)
   11. *Matthew Tyson*, *1725, †young
   12. *Matthew*, *14.03.1727, ∞ 01.05.1755 Horsham Mtg. **Mary Fitzwater**

Mary Potts ∞ 2d marriage 25.10.1732 **Thomas Fitzwater**

2. *Isaac Theißen*, *07.09.1688, ∞ 1st marriage 24.02. 1727 Abington Mo. Mtg. **Sarah Jenkins**, ∞ 2d marriage **Lydia N.**
3. *Elisabeth Theißen*, *07.10.1690 Germantown, ±18.02.1765 Germantown, ∞ 27.11.1710 Abington Mo. Mtg. **William Lucken** (f: **Jan Lucken**, see family tree Lucken)
4. *John Theißen*, *19.10.1692, ∞ 1st marriage 31.08. 1720 Abington Mo. Mtg. **Priscilla Nailer**, ∞ 2d marriage 01.03. 1764 Abington Mo. Mtg. **Sarah Lewis**, widow, Germantown
5. *Abraham Theißen*, *10.08.1694, ∞ 30.08.1721 Abington Mo. Mtg. **Mary Hallowell**
6. *Derrick Theißen*, *06.09.1696, ∞ 1st marriage 1727 Chester, N.J. Mtg. **Ann Hooten**, ∞ 2d marriage 24.02. 1738 Abington Mo. Mtg. **Susanna Thomas**
7. *Sarah Theißen*, *19.12.1698, ∞ 27.06.1722 Abington Mo. Mtg. **John Kirk**
8. *Peter Theißen*, *06.03.1700, ∞ 27.01.1727 Abington Mo. Mtg. **Mary Roberts**
9. *Henry Theißen*, *04.03.1702, ∞ **Ann Harker**

Abraham Tunes/Klinken

I. Tonis Klinken, *Mönchengladbach, ∞ 1644 **Beatrix Lucken**, Rheindahlen, christened:

1. *Abraham Tunes* **II a.**, emigrated to Pennsylvania in 1683
2. *Arnold Tunes* **II b.**, emigrated to Pennsylvania in 1684

II a. Abraham Tunes, *between 1653 and 1669, ∞ **Beatrix Lucken**, *between 1653 and 1669, christened Abington Mo. Mtg.:

1. *Elizabeth Tunes*, *12.05.1685 Germantown
2. *Katharina Tunes*, *26.01.1687 Germantown
3. *William Tunes*, *12.11.1688 Germantown, ∞ **Magdalena Levering**, *between 1678 and 1698 (p: **Wighard Levering**, *1648, †1745 Germantown, ∞ **Magdalena Boker**, *1648 Holland; p: **Rosier Levering**, *between 1605 and 1625, ∞ **Elizabeth van de Walle**, *between 1600 and 1625; p: **William Boker** ∞ **Sedonia Williams Braviers**, *Leiden/NL)
4. *Aeltje/Alice Tunes*, *mid-January 1692 Germantown, †1750/53, ∞ **Jacob Levering**, *21.01.1693 Roxborough Twp., Pa, brother of **Magdalena Levering**, christened:

   1. *Magdalena Levering*, *1716 Roxborough, ∞ Sept. 1740 **Samuel Showler**
   2. *Abarahm Levering*, *May 1717 Roxborough, †31. 10.1804, ∞ 14.11.1745 **Anna Thomas**
   3. *Wighard Levering*, *1719, †05.07.1782, ∞ **Elizabeth Sturges**
   4. *William Levering*, *1721, †07.11.1785, ∞ 16.05.

1751 **Margaret Lohrmann**
5. Jacob Levering, *1723, †before 1807
6. Anthony Levering, *1725, ∞ 12.12.1751 **Agnes Tunes**
7. Benjamin Levering, *15.09.1728, †25.02.1804, ∞ 02.04.1754 Roxborough **Catherine Righter**
8. Septimus Levering, *about 1731 Roxborough, †before1794 Loudon, Va, ∞ **Mary Thomas**, *1730, †16.06. 1794 Roxborough (f: **Griffith Thomas**)
5. Tunes/Anthony Tunis, *03.04.1694 Germantown, †1762 ib., ∞ 05.10.1718 **Mary Williams** (p: **John Williams** ∞ **Ellin Klinken**), *07.04.1697

II b. Arnold Tunes Klincken, †März 1708, ∞ **Niske/ Agnes N.**, christened Abington Mo. Mtg.:
1. Eleanor/Ellin Klinken, 24.08.1670 MG-Odenkirchen, ∞ 03.04.1696 Germantown **John Williams**, christened:

1. Mary Williams, *07.04.1697, ∞ 05.10.1718 Merion Mtg. **Anthony Tunis** (f: **Abraham Tunis**, Chestnut Hill)
2. Hannah Williams, *29.09.1702, ∞ 29.02.1728 Abington Mo. Mtg. **Lewis Roberts**
3. John Williams, *04.02.1705
4. Arret Williams, *13.12.1707/08
5. Anthony Williams, *03.01.1710/11, ∞ 28.12.1736 Abington Mo. Mtg. **Sarah Shoemaker**
6. Ann Williams, ∞ 07.08.1720 Merion Mtg. **Joseph Ambler**
2. Ann Klinken, 03.01.1684 MG-Zoppenbroich, ∞ 11.08.1704 Abington Mo. Mtg. **Cunard Cunrads** (f: **Tönis Kunders**, see family tree Kunders)
3. Anthony Klinken, *06.07.1688 Germantown, ∞ 24.02.1710 Abington Mo. Mtg. **Sebella Leonhard** (f: **Leonhard Arets**, see family tree Arets)

Family Trees

Family Tree Arets and van Acken

I. Class (von Acken) ∞ N. N., christened:

1. Jan Classen van Acken II a., *about 1630 Burtscheid/ Aachen, profession: 1654 wool-merchant and grocer at Mönchengladbach-city, as Mennonit chased away in 1654, found protection at 1685 Wickrath till 1685, moved to Rheydt, persecuted in 1694, thrown into dungeon, 1696 Krefeld citizen, ±14.12.1696 Krefeld

2. Arent Classen von Acken II a., Mennonite, *about 1633 Burtscheid/Aachen, ~Roman-Catholic, profession: about 1645 apprenticeship to a linen weaver at Rheydt, 1654 linen weaver at MG-Bungt, chased away, lived at Krefeld from 1654 to 1661, moved to Rheydt, chased away in 1694, 1694 Krefeld citizen with his four sons by name of Konrad, Peter, Wilhelm and Arnold, listed his damages caused by the action of the Palatine Electorate of 17.06. 1694, lost properties included (Krefeld, City Archive), †30.09.1712 Krefeld, ±03.10.1712 ib.

II a. Jan Claßen van Acken, *um 1630, ∞ 1st marriage about 1653 **Gertrud N.**, ∞ 2d marriage before 08.08. 1672 **Elisabeth Jansen Ravens** (p: **Jan Ravens** ∞ **N.N.**), ±05.02.1728 Krefeld/Ref. Church as widow van Aken; **Elisabeth Ravens** ∞ 16.01.1701 Krefeld/Ref. Church 2d marriage **Peter Bellen**,
christened in 1st marriage:

1. Marieken Jans van Acken, *about 1653, †before 06.08. 1708 Rotterdam, ∞ before 1687 **Leonhard Conradts**, *about 1650, ±31.08.1699 Krefeld/Ref. Church, christened:
   Gertrud Lenderts

2. Hendrik Jansen van Acken III a., *about 1655, ~10.04.1672 Goch/Menn. Church, lived at Krefeld since 1674, Krefeld citizen in 1689 with his sons by name of Claes and Henrich, †14.12.1715

3. Katharina Jansen van Acken, *about 1657 MG, ∞ 23. 07.1679 Krefeld/Ref. Church (probably banns) **Abraham Isaaks op den Graeff**,
christened in 2d marriage:

4. Gertrud Janssen van Acken, *about 1678, †18.02. 1755 Krefeld, ∞ 1st marriage 06.07.1698 Krefeld/Ref. Church **Leonhard Priors „von Creifeld"** (p: **Paulus Preyers** ∞ **Katharina N.**), †between 18.01.1706 and 22.12.1708, ∞ 2d marriage of **Gertrud van Acken** 02.03.1710 Krefeld/Ref. Church **Christian Henrichs von Dülken** (p: **Henrich von Dülken** ∞ **Maria ther Meer**), †07.03.1736

II b. Arent Classen van Acken, *about 1633, ∞ 1st marriage about 1650 **Katharina Kuhlen**, *about 1630 Rheydt, †before mid-1665 (p: **Leonhard Kuhlen**, Mennonite, ∞ **Margarete N.**), ∞ 2d marriage before 23.02.1666 **Maria Konradts Morians** (p: **Konrad Morians** ∞ **N.N.**), ~Goch, †13.01.1712 Krefeld, christened in 1st marriage:

1. Leonhard Arets van Acken III b., *about 1652, emigrated to Pennsylvania in 1683, †03.11.1715 Germantown

2. Nikolaus Arets van Acken, *about 1654, †05.08. 1730 Krefeld, ±08.08.1730 ib.

3. Jan Arentz van Acken III c., *05.03.1657 Krefeld, †06.01.1739 Krefeld, lived at Rheydt in a bakehouse about 30 years, 1694 Krefeld citizen

4. Maria Arents van Acken, *about 1664/65, ∞ 27.03. 1690 Goch/Menn. Church **Arnold van Vossen**, Arnold van Vossen emigrated to Pennsylvania
christened in 2d marriage:

5. Konrad Arents van Acken III d., *23.02.1666 Rheydt, †12.05.1725 Haarlem, ±Groote Kerk, profession: 1716 linen weaver at Krefeld

6. Peter Arents van Acken III e., *about 1667 Rheydt, †28.11.1751 Krefeld, ±30.11.1751 ib., profession: 1716 „Linnenreider" at Krefeld

7. Wilhelm Arents van Acken, *about 1669, unmarried

8. Katharina Arents van Acken, *about 1671, †15.03. 1747 Krefeld, ∞ 23.12.1691 Rheydt/Ref. Church **Matthäus te Kamp** Mönchengladbach, *about 1668, †04.08. 1755 Krefeld (p: **Jakob tho Kamp** ∞ **Katharina Joachims**)

9. Anna Arents van Acken, *about 1673, ±03.05.1734 Krefeld, ∞ 24.08.1698 Krefeld/Ref. Church **Wernerus Lenssen**, Wyck/Maastricht, †before 1712

10. Johanna Arents van Acken, *about 1675, †04.01. 1735 Viersen, ∞ 13.01.1704 Krefeld/Ref. Church **Jakob van Bekkerath** (p: **Jakob Heinrichs** ∞ **Katharina Vieten**), *1678 Rheydt, †18.08.1739 Viersen

12. Elisabeth Arents van Acken, *about 1677, †13.01. 1738, ±16.01.1738 Krefeld./Ref. Church

13. Margarete Arents van Acken, *about 1679, †21.05. 1757, unmarried

14. Arnold Arents van Acken, *Dec. 1680 Rheydt, ~1704 Krefeld/Menn. Church, †26.02.1740 Krefeld, ±01. 03.1740 ib., profession: 1716 linen weaver at Krefeld, ∞ banns 22.05.1709 Krefeld/Ref. Church **Katharina Jacobs von Beckerath** (p: **Jakob von Beckerath** ∞ **Katharina Vieten**), *about 1683, ±15.05.1741, childless

III a. Hendrik Jansen van Acken, *about 1655, ∞ 22.12.1682 Kaldenkirchen/Ref. Church **Mechtild Kürlis** (see family tree Doors), ~09.03.1664, Kaldenkirchen/ Ref. Church, †31.10.1719 Amsterdam, christened Krefeld:

1. *Claes van Acken*, *about 1686, ∞ **N.N.**, christened:
   1. *Jan van Acken*, *about 1725
   2. *Wilhelm van Acken*, *about 1730
   3. *Anna van Acken*, *about 1734
   4. *Margarete van Acken*, *about 1736
   5. *Hendrik van Acken*, *about 1738, †July 1741
   6. *Wilhelmine van Acken*, *about 1740, †July 1741
   7. *Elisabeth van Acken*, *about March 1741, †July 1741
2. *Henrich van Acken*, *about 1688, †after 1692
3. *Anneken van Acken*, *about 1690, ~13.04.1710 Krefeld/Menn. Church, †Amsterdam (?)
4. *Willem van Acken*, *about 1692, †between 14.12. 1766 und 07.06.1775, ∞ 26.05.1755 Philadelphia/First Ref. Church **Mary Gorgas** (p: **John Gorgas** jr. ∞ **Mary Walker**), *um 1736, †02.04.1832, christened:
   1. *Ann van Acken*, †1840, ∞ **George Wunder**, †06.11.1825
   2. *Susannah van Acken*, ∞ **N. Beck**
   3. *Margaret van Acken*, †26.06.1850, ∞ **Joseph Starne**
   4. *Paul van Acken*, ∞ **Elizabeth N.**, (Stepfather: **Conrad Ax**, †1804)
5. *Agneta van Acken*, *about 1694, †before 12.10.1741 Philadelphia
6. *Henrich van Acken*, *about 1697, †27.05.1753, ∞ 1st marriage 22.08.1745 Philadelphia Mo. Mtg. **Jane Goodson**, widow, ∞ 2d marriage 15.06.1748 Abington Mo. Mtg. **Rebecca Johnson (Jansen)**, Germantown
7. *Elisabeth van Acken*, *about 1699, ±17.04.1761, ∞ 07.11.1745 Philadelphia Mo. Mtg. **Paul Kripner**, †1776 Germantown, profession: merchant, ∞ 2d marriage 09. 11.1762 Philadelphia Mo. Mtg. **Susannah Head**, Philadelphia (f: **John Head**), †1793

III b. Leonhard Arets van Aaken, *about 1652, emigrated to Pennsylvania in 1683, †03.11.1715 Germantown, ∞ **Agnes Doors** (see family tree Doors), christened:
1. *Katharina Arets*, ∞ **Thomas Jones**, Abington
2. *Margaret Arets*, ∞ **Robert Thomas**, Olethgo, Abington Twp.
3. *Elizabeth Arets*, ∞ **John Strepers** (see family tree Wilhelm Strepers), Chestnut Hill

III c. Jan Arentz van Acken, *05.03.1657 Krefeld, ∞ **Margarete Davids/Veiten**, Rheydt (p: probably **Vit Dahmen** oder **Velbereiter** ∞ **Zilgen Peters Jentges**, f: probably **Peter Jentges** ∞ **Elisabeth N.**), christened:
1. *David Jansen van Acken*, *mid-1687 Krefeld, ~01.04.1708 Krefeld/Menn. Church, 1694 Krefeld citizen, †21.05.1756, profession: 1716 linen weaver at Krefeld, ∞ 09.07.1713 **Sophia Remkes** (p: **Johann Remkes** ∞ **Anna Abels**), *about 1689, ~20.03.1712 Krefeld/Menn. Church, †31.01.1740 Krefeld, ±01.02.1740 ib.
2. *Katharina Jansen van Acken*, ∞ **Johann Floh**

III d. Konrad Arents van Acken aus dem Rheidt, *23.02.1666 Rheydt, ∞ banns 13.11.1695 Krefeld/Ref. Church, ∞ 27.11.1695 **Sibille Bellen** or **Simons** (p: **Peter Bellen** ∞ **Beatrix ter Meer**, index of Mennonites MG 1654, lived at Hoven), *04.10.1668 Krefeld, †17. 07.1749, christened Krefeld/Menn. Church:
1. *Beatrix van Acken*, *09.09.1696, ~05.04.1716, †03.09.1759, banns 27.10.1715 Krefeld/Ref. Church, ∞ 17.11.1715 **Wilhelm Floh** (p: **Kornelius Floh** ∞ **Bilgen Peters**), *13.02.1689 Venlo, †15.07.1776, Krefeld/Menn. Church, profession: linen maker
2. *Maria van Acken*, *07.12.1698, ~02.04.1719, †14.10.1768, ∞ banns 25.05.1720 Krefeld/Ref. Church **Peter von der Leyen** (p: **Wilhelm von der Leyen** ∞ **Maria von Vorst**), *29.04.1697 Krefeld, ~25.03.1720 Krefeld/Menn. Church, †11.08.1742 Krefeld/Ref. Church, profession: silk maker
3. *Anna van Acken*, *23.11.1701 Krefeld, ~02.04.1724, †10.05.1756 Krefeld/Ref. Church, ∞ banns 14.05. 1724 Krefeld/Ref. Church **Johann Scheuten** (p: **Hermann Scheuten** ∞ **Margarete Bellen**), *22.09.1699 Krefeld, †21.08.1757 Krefeld
4. *Margareta van Acken*, *20.10.1705 Krefeld, ~14.04. 1726, †05.08.1779 Krefeld/Menn. Church, ±06.08.1779 Krefeld/Ref. Church, banns 10.08.1726 Krefeld/Ref. Church, ∞ 27.08.1726 Krefeld/Menn. Church **Friedrich von der Leyen** (p: **Wilhelm von der Leyen** ∞ **Maria von Vorst**), *um 1700, ~02.04.1730 Krefeld/Menn. Church, †23.11.1778 Krefeld/Menn. Church, title: councilor of commerce
5. *Katharina van Acken*, *26.07.1709, ~02.04.1730, †15.11.1787, banns 07.07.1738 Krefeld/Ref. Church, ∞ 23.07.1738 **Peter Schooren**, Aachen (f: **Gilles/Ägidius Schorn**), †14.06.1758
6. *Arnold van Acken*, *04.08.1712 Rotterdam, ~29.03. 1733 Krefeld/Menn. Church, banns 04.09. 1735 Krefeld/Ref. Church, ∞ 29.09.1735 Rotterdam **Marieken van Meurs** (p: **Albertus van Meurs** ∞ **Sibille Floh**), Rotterdam, *06.01.1709 Rotterdam, †18.03.1792 ib.

III e. Peter Arents van Acken, *about 1667 Rheydt, banns 22.06.1698 Krefeld/Ref. Church **Anna Davids** (p: **Vit Dahmen** or **Velbereiter** ∞ **Zilgen Peters Jentges**, f: **Peter Jentges** ?), *19.08.1674 castle of Rheydt, †14.03.1740 Krefeld, christened Krefeld:
1. *Tochter van Acken*, *about 1699, ±17.01.1729 Krefeld/Ref. Church
2. *Marieken van Acken*, *about April 1701, ~21.03.1723 Krefeld/Menn. Church †13.05.1769 Krefeld/Menn. Church, ±14.05.1769 Krefeld/Ref. Church
3. *Sibilla van Acken*, *about 1703/04, ~02.04.1724 Krefeld/Menn. Church, †07.03.1769 Krefeld, ±08.03.1769 Krefeld/Ref. Church, banns 22.06.1738 Krefeld/Ref. Church, ∞ 05.08.1738 Krefeld/Menn. Church **Abrahm**

Ewalts (p: **Leonhard Ewalts**, ∞ banns 31.08.1698 Krefeld/Ref. Church **Saen** (?) **Abrahams**), *1703, †30. or 31.08.1758 Krefeld

4. Elisabeth van Acken, *1707, ~14.04.1726 Krefeld/Menn. Church, †01.07.1748 Krefeld, 40 years, ∞ 16.01. 1742 **Arnold van Wyck** (f: **Lenß van Wyck** ?), *1701/02, ~14.04.1726 Krefeld/Menn. Church, †27.11.1751 Krefeld

5. Katharina van Acken, *about Dec. 1709, ~02.04. 1730 Krefeld/Menn. Church, †21.06.1769 Krefeld/Menn. Church, banns 20.09.1739 Krefeld/Menn. Church, ∞ 04. 10.1739 **Hermann Theißen** (p: **Theiß Ketels** ∞ **N.N.**), *14.02.1702, †08.02.1780 Krefeld/Menn. Church, ±09. 02.1780 Krefeld/Ref. Church

6. Arnold van Acken, *about 1713, ~03.04.1735 Krefeld/Menn. Church, †26.12.1781 Krefeld/Menn. Church (entry as well in the records of Goch/Menn. Church), banns 04.12.1746 Krefeld/menn. Gem., ∞ 21.12.1746 Goch/Menn. Church **Alida Reinermann**, Goch (p: **Hendrik Reyndermann** ∞ 08.08.1706 Goch/Menn. Church **Katharina Jansen von Aken**, *um 1677, ~16.05.1697 Goch/Menn. Church), *1713, †22.07.1779 Goch

Family Tree Brouwers
population record Kaldenkirchen 1624/26: Willem Breuers

Jan Brouwers, 1666 oath of allegiance, ∞ **Katharina van Solingen**, christened:

1. Katharina Brouwers ∞ **Johann de Wilde**, christened Kaldenkirchen/Ref. Church:

   Adelgunde de Wilde, ~08. ? 03.1669 (sp: Leonhard Küppers, Jan Brouwers, his daughter Katharina)

2. Dirk Brouwers, 1666 oath of allegiance, ∞ **N.N.**, christened Kaldenkirchen/Ref. Church:

   1. Agnes Brouwers, ~01.02.1665 (sp: Jan Huben, Katharina Brouwers, Katharina, Jan's daughter), †12. 03.1665

   2. Johannes Brouwers, ~29.12.1665 (sp: Jan Brouwers, Peter Kürlis, Johanna Huben)

Matthias Brouwers, 1666 oath of allegiance, ∞ **Peterken/Petronella N.**, christened Kaldenkirchen/Ref. Church:

1. Katharina Brouwers ∞ **Wilhelm Lappen**, 1666 oath of allegiance, christened Kaldenkirchen/Ref. Church:

   1. Katharina Lappen, ~27.12.1663 (sp: Hendrik Lappen, Adelgunde Brouwers, Matthias' Brouwers daughter, Katharina van Solingen, Jan Brouwers' wife)

   2. Wilhelm Lappen, ~07.02.1666 (sp: Matthias Brouwers, Christine Küppers, Jan Strepers' wife)

   3. Hendrik Lappen, ~26.11.1672 (sp: Hermann Lappen, Matthias Hanssen, Katharina Brouwers)

   4. Matthias Lappen, ~17.11.1675 (sp: Jan van Niel, Helene Schmitz, Rick van Schew, Sprockhövel)

2. Adelgunde Brouwers ∞ 26.11.1670 Kaldenkirchen/Ref. Church **Jan Schmasen**, Wickrathberg, christened Kaldenkirchen/Ref. Church:

   1. Peter Schmasen, ~11.10.1671 (sp: Wilhelm Lappen, Kornelius Zillissen, Maria Dürselen)

   2. Öletgen Schmasen, ~03.05.1674 (sp: Ruth van den Stillewater, Wickrathberg)

   3. Matthias Schmasen, ~28.06.1677 (sp: Hendrik Strucken, Lorenz Haasen)

   4. Petronella Schmasen, ~24.09.1679 (sp: Lorenz Haasen, Katharina Lappen)

   5. Maria Schmasen, ~09.03.1681 (sp: Jan Sieben, Gerrit van Leuen's wife, Gerrit Steppen's wife)

   6. Wilhelmus Schmasen, ~26.01.1685 (sp: Alexander de Boon, Katharina Brouwers)

   7. Maria Schmasen, ~04.09.1689 (sp: Johann van Well, Maria in de Betow)

Eleonore Brouwers ∞ **Jan Coenen**, christened Kaldenkirchen/Ref. Church:

1. Agnes Coenen, ~11.09.1667 (sp: Leonhard Strepers, Katharina (Brouwers), Peter Schrembges' wife, Eleonore Brouwers)

2. Wilhelm Coenen, ~06.02.1670 (sp: Wilhelm Lappen, Peter Sieben, Sibille Brouwers), †02.03.1670

3. Lambertus Coenen, ~10.02.1675 (sp: in lieu of Herr Johannes Sylius ?, minister at Amsterdam: Jan Brouwers, Johanna Coenen, Brüggen, Anna Strepers)

Katharina Brouwers ∞ **Peter Schrembges**, christened Kaldenkirchen/Ref. Church:

1. Tochter N. Schrembges, ~06.07.1670 (sp: Jan Schuren, Peterken (Petronella), Matthias Brouwers' wife)

Jan Coenen van Niel ∞ 1. Ehe **Eleonore Brouwers**, christened Kaldenkirchen/Ref. Church:

1. Katharina Coenen van Niel, ~22.05.1672 (sp: Lambertus Brouwers, Miss Maria Stephani)

Jan Coenen van Niel, widower ∞ 2d marriage Süchteln 03. 01.1675 Kaldenkirchen/Ref. Church **Katharina Middelbeck**, christened Kaldenkirchen/Ref. Church:

2. Ümmelken Coenen van Niel, ~08.11.1676 (sp: Hermann Middelbeck, Henrich Sieben, Johan Herzog)

Jan Coenen van Niel ∞ 3d marriage **Katharina Harmes**, christened Kaldenkirchen/Ref. Chruch:

3. Leonhard Coenen van Niel, ~06.03.1678 (sp: Gerhard Steppen, Jan Sieben, Catharina Silvig, Sittard)

Family Tree Coenen/Kuhnen

population record Kaldenkirchen 1624/26: Peter Köhnen
1666 oath of allegiance: Jan, Peter und Leonhard Coenen

Jan Coenen ∞ **Eleonore Brouwers**, christened Kaldenkirchen/Ref. Church:
1. *Agnes Coenen*, ~11.09.1667 (sp: Leonhard Strepers, Katharina (Brouwers), Peter Schrembges' wife, Eleonore Brouwers)
2. *Wilhelm Coenen*, ~06.02.1670 (sp: Wilhelm Lappen, Peter Sieben, Sibille Brouwers), †02.03.1670
3. *Lambertus Coenen*, ~10.02.1675 (sp: in lieu of Herr Johannes Sylius ?, minister at Amsterdam: Jan Brouwers, Johanna Coenen, Brüggen, Anna Strepers)

Jan Coenen, Witwer, ∞ 13.01.1675 Kaldenkirchen/Ref. Church **Elisabeth Küppers**, widow, christened Kaldenkirchen/Ref. Church:
Wendel Coenen, ~19.11.1677 (sp: Jan Baums, Peter Baums' son, Anna Bouten)

Claes Coenen ∞ **Katharina Laden**, christened Kaldenkirchen/Ref. Church:
Gertrud Coenen, ~14.09.1703 (sp: Gerhard Steppen, Goert Laden's wife Mechtild)

Family Tree Daems

population record Kaldenkirchen 1571: Peterken Dahmen, Johann Dahmen, Dierick Daem auf Heid
population record Kaldenkirchen 1624/26: Gotzen Dahmen, Johann Dahmen, Dierick Dahmen
list of the members of the Reformed Church of Venlo 1637: Lambert Daemen, Peter Daemen, Lambert Daemen's widow
1666 oath of allegiance: Andreas Dahmen, Henrich Daems

Jan Daems ∞ **Klara N.**, christened Bracht/Ref. Church:
1. *Maria Daems*, ~02.06.1664 (sp: Jan Reulen, Agnes, Hermannus Kats' wife, Katharina N.), †12.06.1664
2. *Johannes Daems*, ~17.05.1665 (sp: Matthias Thiefes ?, Maria Daems)
3. *Maria Daems*, ~18.09.1667 (sp: Gerhard Maubachs, Elisabeth, Jan Grieden's wife, Maria, Hermann Peters' wife)

Johannes Daems, widower, ∞ 04.10.1695 Kaldenkirchen/Ref. Church **Katharina Baums**, christened Kaldenkirchen/ref. Gem.:
1. *Henricus Daems*, ~15.06.1698 (sp: Rolf Daems, Maria Baums)
2. *Öemelken Daems*, ~06.02.1701 (sp: Kornelius Hoboken, Anna Schrörs)

Family Tree Doors/Theißen

population record Kaldenkirchen 1473/75: Peter an gen Daere
population record 1624/26: Ummel an gen Dohr, Goert Daers, Johan Dorsch, Dohrmann or Dorsch Haus

I. Tisken/Matthias an gen Door, *about 1550 Roman-Catholic, †19.03.1615 Kaldenkirchen, ∞ **N.N.**, christened **Peter an gen Door alias Küppers II.**, *about 1580 Roman-Catholic, †before 28.12.1638 Kaldenkirchen, profession: grocer

II. Peter an gen Door alias Küppers, *about 1580 Roman-Catholic, ∞ **Elisabeth Grieten**, Mennonite (index of Mennonites 28.12.1638: Lyßgen Daers), christened:
1. *Reiner Doors*, Mennonite (index of Mennonites 28.12.1638), ∞ **N.N.**, christened Kaldenkirchen/Ref. Church:
   Katharina Doors, ~29.10.1663, baptized as adult: „nae voorgaands bekenntnisse haars geloofs gedoopt" (Sp: Jan Strepers, Agnes Doors)
2. *Peter Doors*, ~09.12.1609
3. *Theis/Matthias Doors oder Peters III.*, ~18.09.1614 Kaldenkirchen Roman-Catholic, Mennonite (index of Mennonites 23.07.1652), 1666 oath of allegiance, profession: grocer
4. (unsure) *Margarete Doors/Peters*, ∞ **Isaak op den Graeff**? (see family tree op den Graeff), *28.02.1616 Krefeld

III. Theis/Matthias Doors oder Peters, ~18.09.1614 Kaldenkirchen Roman-Catholic, ∞ 1635-40 **Agnes N.**, *1616/18 Kaldenkirchen, since 1655 member of the Reformed Church at Kaldenkirchen, christened Kaldenkirchen:
1. *Anna Doors IV a.*, *about 1641 Kaldenkirchen, ±02.08.1700 Kaldenkirchen/Ref. Church
2. *Peter Doors*, *about 1643 Kaldenkirchen
3. *Gertrud Doors IV b.*, *about 1645 Kaldenkirchen, †28.02.1707/08
4. *Elisabeth Doors IV c.*, *about 1647 Kaldenkirchen
5. *Johanna Doors*, *about 1649 Kaldenkirchen
6. *Helene Doors IV d.*, *about 1650 Kaldenkirchen, ~20.05.1670 at Goch/Menn. Church
7. *Maria Doors IV e.*, *about 1653 Kaldenkirchen, †1742 Germantown
8. *Margaretha Doors*, ~04.01.1655 Kaldenkirchen/Roman-Catholic (sp: Arnold Küsters, Elisabeth Baums, Katharina Küsters)
9. *Agnes Doors* (?) *IV f.*, about 1657 Kaldenkirchen
10. *Reiner Doors III g.*, *1659 Kaldenkirchen, †27.09.1745 at Abington
11. *Hermann Doors*, ~16.09.1663 Kaldenkirchen/Ref. Church (sp: Margaretha Weyen, Peter Doors, Hendrik Doors), †14.10.1739 near Germantown as single, emigrated to Germantown in 1684

IV a. Anna Doors, *about 1641, ∞ 1st marriage about 1663 Kaldenkirchen/Ref. Church **Henrich Kürlis**, before Pentecost 1660 communicant at Waldniel, christened:
1. *Mechtild Kürlis*, ~09.03.1664, Kaldenkirchen/Ref. Church (sp: Peter Doors, Agnes Doors, Katharina Coenen), †31.10.1719 Amsterdam, ∞ 22.12.1682 Kaldenkirchen/Ref. Church **Hendrik Jansen van Acken** (p: **Jan Claßen van Acken** ∞ **Gertrud N.**, see family tree Arets/van Acken), lived at Krefeld since 1675, †14.12.1715 (baptisms see family trees Arets and van Acken)
2. *Jan Kürlis*, ~05.12.1666, †09.03.1669 (sp: Matthias Brouwers, Jan Hilkes, Sibille Brouwers)
Anna Doors ∞ 2d marriage 12.05.1669 Kaldenkirchen/Ref. Church **Jan Strepers** (see family tree Strepers), christened Kaldenkirchen/Ref. Church:
1. *Leonhard Strepers*, ~02.03.1670 (sp: Henrich Hoetmachers, Paulus Küsters, Gertrud Strepers), †19.08.1725 Kaldenkirchen, ±22.08.1725 ib.
2. *Hendrik Strepers*, ~24.07.1672 (sp: Matthias Kürlis, Gertrud Strepers), ±Kaldenkirchen 26.07.1724
3. *Katharina Strepers*, ~16.12.1674 (sp: Katharina Strepers, Joachim Hüskes), †young
4. *Katharina Strepers*, ~23.05.1677 (sp: Arnold Simons, Christina Schrörs, Helene Schmitz), ±Kaldenkirchen 27.04.1725
5. *Agneta (Agnes) Strepers*, ~16.07.1679 (sp: Jan Herzog, teacher of Solingen, Agnes Doors), †before 22.12.1680
6. *Agnes Strepers*, ~22.12.1680 (sp: Peter Kürlis, Gertrud Doors)
7. *Anneken (Anna) Strepers*, ~1686 Kaldenkirchen, †14.10.1720

IV b. Gertrud Doors, *about 1645 Kaldenkirchen, ∞ 16.10.1668 Kaldenkirchen/Ref. Church **Paulus Küsters** (see family tree Küsters), emigrated to Pennsylvania after 1691, christened Kaldenkirchen/Ref. Church:
1. *Arnold Küsters*, ~09.06.1669 (sp: Steven Steigh, Jan Strepers, Agnes, Matthias Küsters' wife)
2. *Johannes Küsters*, ~12.12.1670 (sp: Jan Hüskes, Agnes Doors)
3. *Matthias Küsters*, ~06.12.1671 (sp: Matthias Doors, Jan Olmis, Elisabeth Doors)
4. *Rainer Küsters*, ~02.12.1674 (sp: Agnes Doors, Joachim Hüskes, Elisabeth Doors)
5. *Elisabeth Küsters*
6. *Hermann Küsters*
7. *Katharina*, ~09.03.1687 Kaldenkirchen/Ref. Church (sp: Kornelius Huben, Katharina Hüskes)

IV c. Elisabeth Doors, *about 1647 Kaldenkirchen, ∞ 17.03.1675 ib. **Peter Kürlis** (see family tree Kürlis), Waldniel, moved to Krefeld in 1681/82 (?), emigrated to Pennsylvania in 1683, christened Kaldenkirchen/Ref. Church:

1. *Mechtild Kürlis*, ~27.12.1675 (sp: Matthias Kürlis, Kaspar Hüskes, Anna Strepers)
2. *Johannes Kürlis*, ~03.02.1677 (sp: Jan Olmis, Anna Doors)
3. *Mechtild Kürlis*, ~27.08.1679 (sp: Reiner Doors, Katharina Brouwers, Mechtild Kürlis)
4. *Agnes Kürlis*, ~05.01.1681 (sp: Jan Strepers ?, Gertrud Doors),
5. *Mechtild Kürlis*, ~22.11.1682 Krefeld/Ref. Church
6. *Matthias Kürlis*, ~Germantown
7. *Peter Kürlis*, ~Germantown

IV d. Helene Doors, *about 1650 Kaldenkirchen, ∞ 31.05.1677 Krefeld/ref. Gem.**Tönis (Anton) Kunders**, Mönchengladbach, *about 1653/55 ib., ~09.07.1673 at Goch/Menn. Church (p: **Konrad Lenßen Heckers** ∞ **Anna**), 1679 Krefeld citizen, emigrated to Pennsylvania in 1683, †1729 Germantown, profession: dyer and weaver, christened:
1. *Jan Kunders*, *03.08.1681, Krefeld, †März 1765
2. *Konrad Kunders*, *Krefeld, †1747 Germantown
3. *Matthias Kunders*, *Krefeld
4. *Anna Kunders*, *04.07.1684 Germantown, †02.05.1752
5. *Agnes Kunders*, *28.11.1686 Germantown
6. *Hendrik Kunders*, *16.12.1688 Germantown, †Sept. 1758, ∞ **Katharina Strepers** (p: **Wilhelm Strepers** ∞ **Marry Lucken**). *Henry Cunrad*, sixth son, had the same profession as his father, left 7 sons. *Samuel*, Henry's youngest son, called himself **Cunard**.
7. *Elisabeth Kunders*, *30.04.1691, †24.03.1757, ∞ before 1723 **Griffith Jones**

IV e. Maria Doors, *about 1660, ∞ 08.04.1674 Kaldenkirchen/Ref. Church **Joachim Hüskes** (see family tree Hüskes), christened Kaldenkirchen/Ref. Church:
1. *Ummelken Hüskes*, ~17.03.1675 (sp: Anton Hüskes, Agnes Doors)
2. *Jan Hüskes*, ~22.12.1675 (sp: Peter Kürlis, Kaspar Hüskes, Anna Strepers)
3. *Leonhard Hüskes*, ~21.02.1677 (sp: Jan Hüskes, Jan Strepers)
4. *Immelken Hüskes*, ~11.12.1678 (sp: Anton Hüskes, Agnes Doors)
5. *Leonhard Hüskes*, ~27.12.1679 (sp: Peter Doors of Leiden, Mechtild Hüskes)
6. *Matthias Hüskes*, ~02.03.1681 (sp: Leonhard Hillekens, Peter Sieben, Jan Olmis' wife)
7. *Agnes Hüskes*, ~30.05.1683 (sp: Peter Sieben, Hendrik Aertsen, Gertrud Doors)
8. *Matthias Hüskes*, ~10.02.1685 (sp: Arnold Simons, Katharina Bocks/Bücks)
9. *Elisabeth Hüskes*, ~25.07.1686 (sp: Christian Höts, Helena Strepers)

IV f. Agnes Doors ∞ **Leonhard Arets** (see family tree Arets), christened:

1. Katharina Arets, *03.08.1684, Germantown, ∞ **Thomas Jones**

2. Margaret Arets, *27.11.1687 or 1688 Germantown, ∞ 27.06.1715 marriage announced at the meeting of the Friends **Robert Thomas**

3. Elizabeth Arets, *16.06.1697 Germantown, will of 07.09.1778, †1794, 07.08.1794 opening of will, ∞ 1st marriage 28.03.1715 (marriage announced at the monthly meeting of the Friends) **John Streeper**, ~16. 07.1688 Germantown, †1741 Germantown (J. Herbergs: 1739, P: **Wilhelm Strepers** ∞ **Marry Lucken**), christened:

> *1. Agnes Streeper*, ∞ **Garrett Dewees**, eldest son of **William Dewees**, survived by 4 sons and 1 daughter
>
> *2. William Streeper*, ∞ **Magdalene Castner** (daughter of **Georg Castner/Küsters** and granddaughter of **Paulus Küsters**, survived by 3 sons and 5 daughters)

IV g. Reiner Doors/Theißen, *1659 Kaldenkirchen, emigrated to Pennsylvanien in 1683, ∞ 1685 Germantown **Margret op den Graeff**, christened in 1st marriage:

1. Matthias Theißen, *31.06.1686 Germantown, †April 1727, ∞ 29.01.1708 Abington Mo. Mtg. **Mary Potts** (f: **John Potts**, Haridless, Wales), *about 1688 Philadelphia, christened:

> *1. Margret Tyson*, *07.02.1708 Abington, †04.06.1752 ebd., ±17.06.1752 ebd., ∞ 23.08.1729, Abington Mtg. **William Hallowell** (f: **Thomas Hallowell**, Abington, *06.03.1679 Hucknall, Nottingham, England, †14.02.1734 Abington), *01.08.1707 Abington, †23.08.1794 ib.
>
> *2. Mary Tyson*, *25.03.1710, ∞ 18.10.1729 Abington Mtg. **Ellis Lewis**
>
> *3. Rynear Tyson*, *24.06.1711, ∞ 29.03.1739 Abington Mtg. **Grace Fletcher** (f: **Robert Fletcher**, †before marriage of daughter)
>
> *4. John Tyson*, *20.02.1713
>
> *5. Sarah Tyson*, *10.10.1714
>
> *6. Elizabeth Tyson*, *14.11.1716, †young before her father
>
> *7. Isaac Tyson*, *20.10.1718, †08.09.1796, ∞ 26.03.1748 Abington Mtg. **Esther Shoemaker** (F: **Isaac Shoemaker**, Cheltenham, †before marriage of daughter)
>
> *8. Matthew Tyson*, *September 1720, †young
>
> *9. Martha Tyson*, *12.05.1722
>
> *10. Elizabeth Tyson*, *15.12.1723, ∞ 31.03.1742 Abington Mtg. **John Fitzwater** (f: **Thomas Fitzwater**)
>
> *11. Matthew Tyson*, *1725, †young
>
> *12. Matthew*, *14.03.1727, ∞ 01.05.1755 Horsham Mtg. **Mary Fitzwater**, *24.12.1733 (p: **Thomas Fitzwater** ∞ **Martha N.**), christened:

>> *1. Martha Tyson*, *07.04.1756 Abington Mo. Mtg.
>>
>> *2. Mary Tyson*, *11.08.1757 Abington Mo. Mtg.
>>
>> *3. Grace Tyson*, †unmarried March/April 1809
>>
>> *4. Thomas Tyson*, lived 1809
>>
>> *5. Priscilla Tyson*, ∞ **N. Butler**
>>
>> *6. Elizabeth Tyson*, *about 1760, lived 1811, †before 1817, ∞ 1st marriage **Richard Roberts**, *Dec. 1722, †April 1794, ∞ 2d marriage about 1795 **William Edwards** (p: **William Edwards** ∞ **Meribah Gaskill**, Milford Twp., Bucks Co.), *18.04.1774, †21.03.1830

> **Mary Theißen/Potts** ∞ 2d marriage 25.10.1732 Abington Mtg. **Thomas Fitzwater**

2. Isaac Theißen, *07.09.1688, ∞ 1st marriage 24.02.1727 Abington Mo. Mtg. **Sarah Jenkins**, ∞ 2d marriage **Lydia N.**

3. Elisabeth Theißen, *07.10.1690 Germantown, ±18.02.1765 Germantown, ∞ 27.11.1710 Abington Mo. Mtg. **William Lucken** (f: **Jan Lucken**, see family tree Lucken), * 22.02.1688 Germantown, christened:

> **Elizabeth Lukens**, *after 1710 Horsham or Upper Dublin, ∞ 16.01.1759 **Thomas Potts** (p: **John Potts** ∞ **Elizabeth McVeagh**), *about 1729, †29.07.1776 probably Chelsea Forge, NJ

4. John Theißen, *19.10.1692, ∞ 1st marriage 31.08.1720 Abington Mo. Mtg. **Priscilla Nailer**, ∞ 2d marriage 01.03. 1764 Abington Mo. Mtg. **Sarah Lewis**, widow, Germantown

5. Abraham Theißen, *10.08.1694, ∞ 30.08.1721 Abington Mo. Mtg. **Mary Hallowell**

6. Derrick Theißen, *06.09.1696, ∞ 1st marriage 1727 Chester, N.J. Mtg. **Ann Hooten**, ∞ 2d marriage 24.02.1738 Abington Mo. Mtg. **Susanna Thomas**

7. Sarah Theißen, *19.12.1698, ∞ 27.06.1722 Abington Mo. Mtg. **John Kirk**

8. Peter Theißen, *06.03.1700, ∞ 27.01.1727 Abington Mo. Mtg. **Mary Roberts**

9. Henry Theißen, *04.03.1702, ∞ **Ann Harker**

Family Tree Dürselen

I. Albertus Dürselen, minister auf'm Höerschchen (Hörstgen, Kr. Moers), ∞ **Maria Magdalena Mickenschreiber**, ~25.04.1683 Wickrath, christened:

1. Agneta van Dürselen II a., *Odenkirchen, ~27.05.1707 Wickrath

2. Anna Katharina Dürselen, ∞ 08.11.1737 Kaldenkirchen/Ref. Church **Nikolaus Sempels** (p: **Johannes Sempels** ∞ **Isabella Aletta Grambusch**, †Brüggen)

3. Florens Petrus Dürselen, *Berggut Wickrath (Wickrathberg ?), ~06.10.1709, Wickrath, †Hoogeloon NL, profession: since 23.06.1738 vice-minister at Leende, 28.09.1740 assistant, since 1743 minister at Vessem

and Hoogeloon NL, Ref. Church, ∞ 22.11.1742 Kaldenkirchen/ref. Gem. **Katharina Strepers** (see family tree Strepers)
4. Friedrich Godhard Dürselen II b., ~19.03.1715 Hörstgen, Kr. Moers, ±20.03.1777 Kaldenkirchen/Ref. Church, profession: merchant at Kaldenkirchen

II a. Agneta van Dürselen, * Odenkirchen, ~27.05.1707, Wickrath, ∞ **Wilhelmus Schmasen**, *26.01.1685 Wickrath, †Dortrecht (p: **Jan Schmasen, Kaldenkirchen**, ∞ **Adelheid Brouwers**), christened:
1. Johannes Schmasen, ~17.12.1724 Kaldenkirchen/Ref. Church (sp: Peter Schmasen, Hermannus Theodorus Bachoven, Anna Katharina Weyenhorst, wife of the minister op t' Höerstgen, Agnes Köelkes, widow Mickenschreiber, Odenkirchen)
2. Friedrich Albert Schmasen, ~15.03.1726 Kaldenkirchen/Ref. Church (sp: Albertus van Dürselen, minister op 't Höerstgen, Matthias Mickenschreiber, Adelheid Schuren, widow Bachoven), †1811, ∞ **N.N.**, christened:
1.Carl Wilhelm Schmasen, ~09.08.1778, profession: mayor, ∞ **J.M.E. Schleicher**
3. Petrus Schmasen, ~18.05.1727 Kaldenkirchen/Ref. Church (sp: Meinert Dürselen, Hermannus Mickenschreiber, Bartina van der Horen)
4. Johann Friedrich Schmasen, ∞ **Cato Schmasen**, cousin, profession: merchant at Kaldenkirchen and Venlo, bought manor Altenhof/Kaldenkirchen

II b. Friedrich Gotthard Dürselen, ~19.03.1715 Hörstgen, Kr. Moers, ∞ 2d marriage (widower) 03.04.1753 Elberfeld **Anna Margareta Siebels** (p: **Abraham Siebel** ∞ **Maria Teschemacher** widow **Ochsen**, see family tree Siebel), ~18.01.1734, Elberfeld, †25.10.1819 Kaldenkirchen, christened Kaldenkirchen/Ref. Church:
1. Maria Catharina Dürselen, ~25.04.1756 (sp: Petrus Florens Dürselen, minister at Vessem, Maria Siebels, Katharina Sempels)
2. Wilhelmina Dürselen, ~22.09.1757 (sp: Abraham Siebels, Johanna Wilhelmina Wülfing), ∞ **Karl Friedrich Overbeck**, christened twins:
1. Anna Margaretha Overbeck, ~01.03.1780 Kaldenkirchen/Ref. Church (sp: Friedrich Albert Schmasen Margaretha Dürselen née Siebels)
2. Anna Karolina Overbeck, ~01.03.1780 Kaldenkirchen/Ref. Church (sp: Karl Overbeck, Agneta Lauffs née Strepers)
3. Friedrich Abraham Dürselen, ~14.10.1758 (sp: Johannes Peter Honsberg, Mrs Mickenschreiber, Rotterdam)
4. Friedrich Gotthard Dürselen, ~31.10.1761 (sp: Peter Hunsberg, Johann Schmasen, Mrs Mickenschreiber, Rotterdam, minister Laufs' wife, Rheydt)
5. Johanna Antonetta Dürselen, ~28.11.1762 (sp: Antonius Siebels, Maria Strepers, Johanna Elisabetha Ha-

chelbuch)
6. Wilhelmus Ludovicus Dürselen, ~01.04.1764 (sp: councilor of war Mr Plesman, widow Laufs née Mickenschreiber)
7. Franciscus Antonius Dürselen, ~28.07.1765 (sp: Anton Pönsgen, Düren, widow Orthmann, Elberfeld)
8. Karolus Friedericus Dürselen, ~08.03.1767 (sp: lieutenant colonel Samuel von Bathanay, Anna Gertrud Thielen)
9. Johanna Hermina Dürselen, ~17.04.1768 (sp: Johannes Hermannus Pönsgen, Ida Busch)
10. Anna Elisabetha Dürselen, ~10.12.1769 (sp: Friedrich Albert Schmasen, Peter Heinrich Mickenschreiber, Anna Mickenschreiber, Mrs Schmitzhuysen)

Family Tree In der Elst
population record Kaldenkirchen 1624/26: Tieß in der Elst, Johan in der Elst

I. Johan in der Elst (population record Kaldenkirchen 1624/26: Johan in der Elst)

II. Wilhelm in der Elst (?), 1666 oath of allegiance, ∞ **Adelgunde** (?) **N.**, christened:
1. Leonhard in der Elst III a.
2. Heinrich in der Elst III b.
3. Adelgunde in der Elst III c.
4. Johann in der Elst III d.

III a. Leonhard in der Elst, 1666 oath of allegiance, ∞ **Antonia N.**, christened Kaldenkirchen/Ref. Church:
1. Ummelken in der Elst, ~10.02.1664 (sp: Hendrik in der Elst, Bärbel, Jan Schremkes' wife)
2. Maria in der Elst, ~24.04.1667 (sp: Jan Schuren, Adelgunde in der Elst), ±02.06.1736 Kaldenkirchen/Ref. Church
3. Jenneken (Johanna) in der Elst, ~04.10.1671 (sp: Lambert Brouwers, Candidatus, Maria Stephani)

III b. Heinrich in der Elst ∞ 08.12.1669 Kaldenkirchen/Ref. Church **Gertrud Booms**, christened Kaldenkirchen/Ref. Church:
1. Maria in der Elst, ~28.09.1670 (sp: Wilhelm in der Elst, Sibilla Booms)
2. Peter in der Elst, ~20.08.1672 (sp: Peter Sieben, Katharina Booms)
3. Wilhelm in der Elst, ~09.06.1675 (sp: Jan in der Elst, Katharina Büdels) ∞ 02.02.1705 Kaldenkirchen/Ref. Church **Johanna in der Elst**, christened Kaldenkirchen/Ref. Church.:
> *Gertrud in der Elst* V., ~25.07.1706 (sp: Wilm Boums, Adelgunde in der Elst, Egtgen in der Elst)

III c. Adelgunde in der Elst Kaldenkirchen, ∞ 22.05. 1668 Bracht/Ref. Church **Peter Sieben**, Brüggen, christened Kaldenkirchen/Ref. Church:
1. Maria Sieben, ~24.01.1672 (sp: Wilhelm in der Elst, Katharina Nagels, Maria Schoeren, both from Brüggen)
2. Catharina Sieben, ~02.11.1674 (sp: D. Petrus Buschmann, minister at Schlicker-Ewick, Katharina Baenen)
3. Wilhelmus Sieben, ~27.06.1676 (sp: Johannes Graver, Brüggen, Maria Stephani, Slyck Ewigh)
4. Michael Sieben, ~11.12.1678 (sp: Jan Sieben, Jan in der Elst, Petronella Schuren)
5. Catharina Sieben, ~14.09.1680 (sp: Gerrit Steppen, Jungfrau Welters)
6. Michael Sieben, ~04.06.1684 (sp: Jan Sieben, Reiner Weerts, Elisabeth Schouren)
7. Elisabeth Sieben, ~21.08.1689 (sp: Hendrich Schuren, Agnes Sieben, Katharina in der Elst)

III d. Jan in der Elst, ±Kaldenkirchen/Ref. Church 27.03. 1726, ∞ 29.06.1686 Kaldenkirchen/Ref. Church **Katharina in der Elst**, christened Kaldenkirchen/Ref. Church:
1.Wilhelmus in der Elst, ~16.06.1686 (sp: Hendrik in der Elst, Antonius in der Elst)
2. Maria in der Elst, ~09.11.1687 (sp: Peter Sieben, Egtjen in der Elst)
3. Wilhelm in der Elst IV., ~20.04.1692 (sp: Hendrik Schuren, Antonius in der Elst)
4. Jan in der Elst, ~31.05.1696 (sp: Fisken Jutjens, Adelgunde Schuren [in der Elst ?], Peter Sieben's wife)

IV. Wilhelm in der Elst, ~20.04.1692 ∞ 03.11.1723 Kaldenkirchen/Ref. Church **Maria Schuren**, ±10.02. 1744, Kaldenkirchen/Ref. Church, christened Kaldenkirchen/Ref. Church:
1. Katharina in der Elst, ~27.01.1726 (sp: Hendrik Schuren, Katharina in der Elst)
2. Jenneken in der Elst, ~15.02.1728 (sp: Hendrik Schuren, Maria in der Elst, Gertrud Hasen)
3. Johanna in der Elst, ~23.08.1730 (sp: Dierich am Haus, Wilhelm Schuren, Maria in der Elst, Gertrud Hasen)

V. Gertrud in der Elst, ~25.07.1706, ∞ 22.11.1724 Kaldenkirchen/Ref. Church **Wilhelm Schouren**, christened Kaldenkirchen/Ref. Church:
1. Petrus in der Elst, ~10.02.1726 (sp: Wilm in der Elst, Dirk am Haus, Elisabeth Schouren)
2. Johanna in der Elst, ~15.04.1729 (sp: Wilhelm und Katharina in der Elst, Maria Schouren)
3. Peter in der Elst, ~19.10.1732 (sp: both Wilhelm in der Elst, Gertrud Schuren)
4. Henrich in der Elst, ~02.02.1738 (sp: missing)

Hendrik in der Elst ∞ **N.N.**, christened Kaldenkirchen/ Ref. Church:

1. Peter in der Elst, ~25.09.1686 (sp: Peter Sieben, Gert Steppen, Petronella Schuren)
2. Maria in der Elst, ~19.11.1691 (sp: Reiner Werts, Adelgunde Sieben née in der Elst, Öemelken Schuren)
3. Gertrud in der Elst, ~08.03.1694 (sp: Franz Hasen, Franz in der Elst)
4. Öemelken in der Elst, ~29.04.1696 (sp: Jan in der Elst, Maria Sieben in lieu of Meister Jan Schören an gen Brock, Elisabeth Werts)

Family Tree Franken

population record Kaldenkirchen 1624/26: Jan Voß or Peter Francken Gut, Johann Francken
1666 oath of allegiance: Coen Francken

Hendrik Francken, 1666 oath of allegiance, ∞ 03.07. 1663 Kaldenkirchen/Ref. Church **Margarete Lamberts van Düren** (f: **Lambert van Düren**, index of Mennonites 28.12.1638 and 23.07.1652), ~02.07.1663 Kaldenkirchen/Ref. Church (baptized as adult), christened Kaldenkirchen/Ref. Church:
Henrik Franken, ~20.11.1667 (sp: Jan Coenen, Jan Hilkes, Anna Doors, Henrich Kürlis' widow)

Family Tree Haus

1666 oath of allegiance, Kaldenkirchen: Tilman in gen Haus

Leonhard Haus ∞ **Margarete Fys/Hys**, christened Bracht/ Ref. Church:
1. Dirk Haus, ~26.03.1663 (sp: Jan ter Stegen, Geertgen Haus), ∞ 15.07.1709 Bracht/Ref. Church **Maria in der Elst**, christened Kaldenkirchen/Ref. Church:
   1. Eleonore Haus, ~12.07.1711 (sp: Hermann Haus, Egtgen in der Elst)
2. Peter Haus, ~15.05.1667 (sp: Margarete and Katharina, Jan Grieten's stepdaughters, Bracht)
3. Hermann Haus, ~06.10.1669 (sp: Peter Laden, Esther, Michael Hasen's wife, Adelheid Laden), ∞ 14.12. 1718 Bracht/Ref. Church **Barbara Hase**, Bracht, christened Bracht/Ref. Church:
   1. Leonhardus Haus, ~29.02.1720 (sp: Jakob Gebelen, Gertrud Haus)
   2. Elisabeth Haus, ~17.01.1723 (sp: Dirk Haus, Gertrud Hase)
4. Katharina Haus, ~26.06.1672 (sp: Wilhelm Hasen, Katharina Hefer ?)
5. Leonhard Haus, ~03.02.1675 (sp: Gört Laen, Adelheid Grieten)
6. Katharina Haus, ~23.03.1679 (sp: Dahm Hasen, Gertgen Haus)

Johann Haus ∞ **N.N.**, christened Bracht/Ref. Church:
1. Peter Haus, ~17.04.1689 (sp: Johanna Küppers, Adelgunde Tüffers)
2. Wilhelmus Haus, ~21.10.1691 (sp: Tilman Vos, Dirk Haus, Maria Pipers)
3. Gertrud Haus, ~24.01.1694 (sp: Niclaes ? Pipers, Agnes Laden, Gertrud Haus)
4. Magdalena Haus, ~11.12.1695 (sp: Peter Haus, Rudolphus Röelen, Adelgunde Lappen)

Leonhard Haus ∞ **Arnolda Haasen**, christened Bracht/Ref. Church:
1. Wilhelmus Haus, ~27.03.1757 (sp: Wilhelm Haasen, Katharina Feltges)
2. Hermannus Haus, ~21.03.1766 (sp: Franziscus Henricus Haasen, Johanna Schuren)

Leonhard Haus ∞ 14.02.1715 Bracht/Ref. Church **Hester Haasen**, christened Bracht/Ref. Church:
1. Katharina Haus, ~02.05.1717 (sp: Hermann Haus, Agnes Laden), ∞ 01.09.1740 Bracht/Ref. Church **Peter Voss** (p: **Tilman Gabriel Voss** ∞ **Hester Laden**), christened Bracht/Ref. Church:
 1. Hester Voss, ~21.05.1741 (sp: Jakob Steppen, Katharina Haasen, Leonhard Haus' wife)
 2. Margareta Voss, ~25.03.1744 (sp: Leonhard Haus, Margareta Voss)
 3. Anna Barbara Voss, ~16.01.1745 (sp: Godefriedus Voss, Elisabeth Haus)
 4. Anna Gertruda Voss, ~14.05.1748 (sp: Leonhard Haus, Margareta Coenen)
2. Margarete Haus, ~10.03.1720 (sp: Leonhard Hase, Gertrud Haus), ∞ 14.07.1743 Bracht/Ref. Church **Johannes Voss**, christened Bracht/Ref. Church:
 1. Hester Voss, ~24.06.1744 (sp: Gerhardus Voss, Katharina Haasen)
 2. Wilhelmus Tilmannus Voss, ~24.08.1745 (sp: Leonhard Haus, Margarete Voss)
 3. Anna Gertrud Voss, ~12.08.1747 (sp: Leonhard Haus, Katharina Haus)
 4. Jakobus Voss, ~10.08.1748 (sp: Leonhard Haus, Gertrud in der Elst)
 5. Anna Barbara Voss, ~14.09.1750 (sp: Henrich Maubachs, Elisabeth Haus)
 6. Maria Katharina Voss, ~20.01.1752 (sp: Henricus Heuten, Elisabeth Haus)
 7. Anna Elisabeth Voss, ~04.01.1754 (sp: Reinerus Haasen, Anneken Voss)
 8. Anna Gertrud Voss, ~10.07.1758 (sp: Diedericus Haasen, Katharina Haasen)
3. Leonhard Haus, ~30.08.1722 (sp: Dahm Hase, Petronella Werths), ∞ **Hester Haasen**, christened Bracht/Ref. Church:
 1. Hermannus Haus, ~19.08.1742 (sp: Dahm Ha-

sen, Gertrud Haasen)
 2. Anna Barbara Haus, ~02.07.1744 (sp: Reiner Haasen, Katharina Haasen)
Leonhard Haus, widower, ∞ 19.12.1724 Bracht/Ref. Church **Katharina Haasen**, christened Bracht/Ref. Church:
4. Leonhard Haus, ~23.09.1725 (sp: Arnold Tüffers, Maria in der Elst)
5. Elisabeth Haus, ~23.07.1730 (sp: Reiner and Gertrud Haasen, Peter Schuren's widow), ∞ 1751 Bracht/Ref. Church **Wilhelmus Haasen**, christened Bracht/Ref. Church:
 1. Barbara Haasen, ~04.06.1751 (sp: Leonhard Haus, Diederica Haasen)
6. Hester Haus, ~14.02.1732 (sp: Leonhard Haasen, Grietgen Haasen, Hester Laden), baptized by minister Schippers, Waldniel, ∞ **Wilhelm Haasen**, christened Bracht/Ref. Church:
 1. Theresia Haasen, ~30.04.1758 (sp: Leonhard Haus, Agneta Haasen)
 Wilhelm Hasen ∞ **Elisabeth Hausen**, christened Bracht/Ref. Church:
 2. Anna Gertruda Hasen, ~29.05.1761 (sp: Diedericus Schuren, Gertrud Haasen)
 3. Agneta Haasen, ~01.02.1766 (sp: Franz Henrich Haasen, Johanna Haasen)

Family Tree Herbergs
I. **Henrich in der Herberg**, Brüggen, ∞ **Maria** (?) **N.**, christened:
1. Gerhardt in der Herberg II, ~Brüggen (?)
2. Klara in der Herberg, ~ Brüggen (?), communicant 26.03.1655 Waldniel/Ref. Church, ∞ 10.01.1662 Waldniel/Ref. Church, **Johan Dams** (f: Henrich Dams)

II. **Gerhard in der Herberg**, * in Brüggen (?), ∞ 1st marriage 08.06. 1660 Waldniel/Ref. Church **Katharina Coenen** (f: Peter Coenen); ∞ 2d marriage **Gertrud Römckes** (?), christened Waldniel/Ref. Church:
1. Maria in der Herberg III a., ~20.03.1662 (?) Waldniel/Ref. Church, Good Friday 1678 communicant Waldniel/Ref. Church
2. Peter in der Herberg, ~08.10.1663
3. Helena in der Herberg, ~25.12.1665
4. Henrich in der Herberg, ~25.10.1668 (sp: Henrich in der Herberg, Herman Coenen, Katharina Buns, Konrad Buns, Hans Frach ?)
5. Johannes in der Herberg III b., ~27.10.1671 (sp: Matthias Langebrechts ?, Gertrud Coenen), communicant 1682
6. Katharina in der Herberg, ~12.08.1673 (sp: Adam Dahmen, Katharina Mols)

7. Henrich in der Herberg III c. (p: **Gerhard Herbergs** ∞ **Truitgen Römckes**, 2d marriage of **Gerhard Herbergs** (?), ~Pencost 1676 (sp: missing)

III a. Maria Herbergs, ~20.03.1662 (?), ∞ 06.02.1681 **Henrich gen Bruch** (p: **Gört gen Bruch** ∞ **Nölgen Cürlis**, †before marriage of son), christened: *Johannes gen Bruch*, ~01.06.1701 Waldniel/Ref. Church (sp: Johannes Herbergs, Tringen Köhnen)

III b. Johannes in der Herberg, ~27.10.1671, ∞ 04.11. 1705, Waldniel/Ref. Church **Maria Horn** (p: **Peter Horn** ∞ **Sibille ? Prollen**)

III c. Henrich in der Herberg, ~Pentecote 1676, ∞ 01.11.1707, Waldniel/Ref. Church **Maria Voß** (p: **Jan Voß** ∞ **Catharina Vetten**, see family tree Voß), christened Waldniel/Ref. Church:
1. Gerhard Herbergs, ~29.09.1708 (sp: Peter Herbergs, Jan Boßfeld, Anna Kehren),
2. Johannes Herbergs, ~25.05.1710 (sp: Johannes Grambusch, Johannes Herbergs, Katharina Voß), †before 08.11.1712
3. Johannes Herbergs, ~08.11.1712 (sp: Peter Voß, Maria Horn), †before 26.05.1717
4. Katharina Herbergs, ~29.04.1714 (sp: Gerhard Hermens, Hendrina Cronenberg, Maria Voß)
5. Hans Peter Herbergs, ~26.04.1716 (sp: Christian ? Essers, Sibille ?, Johan Voß's wife, minister at Maastricht, Franz Francken, Maria Neukirch)
6. Johannes Herbergs IV., *1717 Waldniel, ~26.05. 1717 (sp: Johannes Coenen, Gertrud Dahmen), ±13.07. 1789, Philadelphia/First Reformed Church, profession: 1774 ribbon maker and merchant, house owner, city councilor, school inspector 24.03. 1776, lived at Ronsdorf since 1743.

IV. Johannes Herbergs
* 1717, Waldniel
~ 26.05.1717, ∞ Kaldenkirchen/Ref. Church um 1737 **Adelgunde Sieben**, at her birth: Aeltjen (p: **Wilhelm Sieben** ∞ **Katharina Strepers**, see family tree Strepers), christened:
1. Heinrich Herbergs V a., *October 1738 Waldniel, confirmation 24.10.1755 Ronsdorf/Ref. Church, †13.03. 1814, ±15.03.1814 Ronsdorf, profession: weaver
2. Wilhelm Herbergs V b., *1742 Waldniel, confirmation 14.08.1761 Ronsdorf/Ref. Church, †03.12.1800 Ronsdorf, ±05.12.1800 ib.
3. Maria Herbergs, ~30.06.1745 Ronsdorf/Ref. Church (sp: Johannes Kaspar Bosselmann, Philippus Teschemacher, Anna Bolckhaus, Wilhelmina Schüller), confirmation 14.08.1761 Ronsdorf/Ref. Church, †25.10. 1820 Ronsdorf, ±25.10.1820 ib, unmarried

4. Johannes Herbergs, ~08.09.1746 Ronsdorf/Ref. Church (sp: Johannes Herbergs, Maria Magdalena Werth, Anna Maria Sieben), †08.09.1746 ib.
5. Daughter, still-burth, †24.02.1749 Ronsdorf
6. Anna Herbergs Vc., ~04.12.1750 Ronsdorf/ (sp: Anna Ellers, Katharina Gertrud Teschemachers, Johannes Schüller, Engelbert Werth)
7. Daughter, still-birth, †11.06.1753

Va. Heinrich Herbergs, *October 1738 Waldniel, ∞ 10.07.1759 Ronsdorf/Ref. Church **Katharina Elisabeth Sieben** (p: **Petrus Sieben** ∞ 28.09.1732 Kaldenkirchen/ Ref. Church **Anna Maria Knevels**, see family tree Sieben), *September 1734 Kaldenkirchen, confirmation 13.10.1751 Ronsdorf/Ref. Church, †11.07.1788 Ronsdorf, ±13.07.1788 ib., christened Ronsdorf/Ref. Church:
1. Elias Herbergs VIa., ~24.09.1760 (sp: Johann von [sic] Bolckhaus, Johannes Herbergs, Katharina Gertrud Weyermann, Anna Maria Sieben), †03.04.1823 Ronsdorf, ±06.04.1823 ebd., profession: merchant, shoestring maker at death
2. Timotheus Herbergs, ~25.03.1762 (sp: Johann Bolckhaus, Peter Sieben, Anna Wülffing, Adelgunde Herbergs)
3. Anna Herbergs VIb., ~09.06.1764 (sp: Magdalena Wilhelmina von Bolckhaus, Miss Maria Louisa Sieben, Philipp Weyermann, Wilhelm Herbergs)
4. Sara Herbergs VIc., ~09.04.1766 (sp: Adelgunde Herbergs, Sara Piepers, Peter Sieben, Peter Henrich Strepers [at this time in Philadelphia])
5. Johannes Herbergs, ~31.05.1768 (sp: Johann Bolckhaus, Johann Herbergs, Cäcilia Gertrud Meis, Johanna Margaretha Winckels), †02.09.1794 Ronsdorf
6. Sebulon Herbergs VI d., ~23.02.1770 (sp: Sebulon Schüller, Johann Wilhelm Beycken, Anna Maria Sieben, Miss Maria Herbergs), †06.11.1855 Ronsdorf, profession: revenue officer
7. Rahel Herbergs VIe., ~17.02.1774 (sp: Rahel Pieper, Miss Anna Herbergs, Hauptmann Johann Abraham Runckels, Daniel Sieben), †12.09.1853 Ronsdorf
8. Magdalena Wilhelmine bzw. Sulamith Herbergs VIf., ~01.09.1776 (sp: missing), †28.10.1813 Ronsdorf, ±30.10.1813 ib.
9. Child, still-birth, ~27.11.1778

Vb. Wilhelm Herbergs, *1742 Waldniel, ∞ 20.12.1773 Ronsdorf/Ref. Church (sp: Johannes Bolckhaus, captain Runckels, relatives and friends) **Anna Beycken**, *about 1750, †21.10.1802, widow at death, ±23. 10.1802 Ronsdorf/Ref. Church, christened Ronsdorf/Ref. Church:
1. Anna Herbergs, ~23.2.1775 (sp: Magdalena Wilhelmina Bolckhaus, Adelgunde Herbergs, Johannes Herbergs, Peter Sieben, teacher at Ronsdorf), ∞ 1st marriage 14.05.1801 Ronsdorf/Ref. Church (sp: Gerson

Wülfing, Samuel Clarenbach, Henrich Herberg) **Sebu-lon Clarenbach**, ∞ 2d marriage **Elias Dickmann**
2. Johannes Elias Herbergs, ~07.10.1778 (sp: Johannes Bolckhaus, Johannes Herbergs, Sara Pieper, Miss Maria Herbergs)
3. Sebulon Herbergs, ~04.02.1781 (sp: Sebulon Schüller, Johann Heinrich Bleckmann, Adelgunde, wife of minister Camphausen, Wermelskirchen, Miss Sara Beycken), †21.10.1786 Ronsdorf, ±24.10.1786 ib.
4. Debora Herbergs, ~15.06.1783, †05.04.1841 Ronsdorf, ∞ **Jonathan Hessebruck**
5. Eva Maria Herbergs, ~28.08.1785, †15.11.1838 Ronsdorf, ∞ **Josua Rauner**
6. Tochter, *18.05.1788, ~unbaptized, †18.05.1788, ±the same day Ronsdorf/Ref. Church
7. Johannes Sebulon Herbergs, ~02.01.1791 (sp: Sebulon Schüller, Johann Heinrich Bleckmann, Rahel Wülfings, Magdalena Wülfings), †10.04.1791, ±Ronsdorf/ref. Gem.

V c. Anna Herbergs, ~04.12.1750, ∞ 03.05.1783 Ronsdorf/Ref. Church (sp: Sebulon Schüller, Henrich Herbergs, Philipp Weyermann) **Johann Abraham Meis**, *about 1755 Ronsdorf, †18.04.1814 Ronsdorf, ±20.04.1814 ib., profession: ribbon maker, christened Ronsdorf/Ref. Church:
1. Johann Sebulon Meis, ~06.06.1784 (sp: Sebulon Schüller, Johannes Herbergs, Cäcilia Gertrud Meis, Witwe, Miss Maria Herbergs)
2. Anna Magdalena Meis, ~03.01.1787 (sp: Magdalena Wilhelmina Bolckhaus, Katharina Elisabeth Herbergs, Wilhelm Herbergs, Johannes Meis)
3. Johannes Elias Meis, ~27.09.1789 (sp: Petrus Coenen, minister, Elias Herbergs, Anna Herbergs, Anna Bleckmanns)
4. Eva Maria Meis, ~17.02.1793 (sp: Eva Maria Schüller, Jungfrau Maria Herbergs, judge Christophel Pieper, Johannes Rosenthal)

VI a. Elias Herbergs, ~24.09.1760, ∞ Neuwied 28.04.1793 **Christina Henrietta Friederica Bernhards**, †23.02.1807 Ronsdorf, ±25.02.1807 ib., christened Ronsdorf/Ref. Church:
1. Anna Magdalena Herbergs, ~11.05.1794 (sp: Eva Maria Schüller, Anna Meis, Heinrich Herberg, Wilhelm Herberg)
2. Eva Maria Herbergs, ~13.11.1796 (sp: Miss Maria Herberg, Anna Dreisbach, Johannes Klein, Abraham Meis), †21.09.1870 Ronsdorf, ∞ 29.04.1825 Ronsdorf **Johann Elias Godermann** (sp: Sebulon Herbergs, uncle, Anna Magdalena Herbergs, sister)
3. Johannes Herbergs, ~02.06.1799 (sp: Sebulon Schüller, Johannes Schatt, Miss Clara Bernhardt, Sara Spendik), †23.11.1803 Ronsdorf, ±24.11.1803 ib.

4. Anna Elisabeth Herbergs, ~23.02.1802 (sp: Miss Anna Schüller, Anna Elisabeth Sieben, Philipp Weyermann, Georg Hermann Pickardt)
5. Rahel Herbergs, *01.10.1804, ~08.10.1804 (sp: Maria Elisabeth Rosenthal, Sebulon Meis, David Wülfing)
6. Sohn, still-burth, †23.02.1807 Ronsdorf with his mother, ±25.02.1807 ib.

VI b. Anna Herbergs, ~09.06.1764, ∞ Ronsdorf/Ref. Church **Johann Christian Dreisbach**, ~Gemarke ?, christened Ronsdorf/Ref. Church:
1. Anna Henrietta Dreisbach, ~20.09.1795 (sp: Anna Meis, Christina Henrietta Friederica Herbergs, Daniel Sieben, Sebulon Herbergs)
2. Maria Henrietta Dreisbach, ~10.12.1797 (sp: Eva Maria Schüller, Maria Merkes, Johann Everhard Klein, David Wülfing)
3. Johann Sebulon Dreisbach, ~15.10.1800 (sp: Abraham Rosenthal, Elias Herbergs, Maria Louisa Schuchardt, Maria Herberg)

VI c. Sara Herbergs, ~09.04.1766, ∞ 03.05.1791 Ronsdorf/Ref. Church (sp: Abraham Rosenthal, Wilhelm Herbergs, Johann Abraham Meis) **Georg Hermann Pickardt**, ~Wingeshausen, christened Ronsdorf/Ref. Church:
1.Anna Magdalena Pickardt, ~25.11.1792 (sp: Eva Maria Schüller, Cäcilia Gertrud Meis, Johann Rosenthal, Heinrich Herbergs)
2. Johannes Elias Pickardt, ~11.05.1794 (sp: Sebulon Schüller, Elias Herbergs, Anna Maria Rosenthal, Maria Herbergs)
3. Anna Magdalena Pickardt, ~26.02.1797 (sp: Jungfrau Anna Magdalena Bleckmann, Anna Herbergs, Heinrich Rötzel, Christian Dreisbach)
4. Karolina Elisabeth Pickardt, ~17.03.1799 (sp: Maria Elisabeth Rosenthal, Karolina Kocher, Abraham Meis, Nikolaus Heser)
5. Johann Daniel Pickardt, ~01.01.1802 (sp: Johann Elias Clarenbach, Daniel Sieben, Anna Louisa Wülfing, Miss Anna Magdalena Weyermann)

VI d. Sebulon Herbergs, ~23.02.1770, ∞ Westhofen 12.08.1798 **Clara Josina Maria Osthoff**, christened Ronsdorf/Ref. Church:
1. Johann Karl Heinrich Herbergs **VII a.**, *21.08.1800
2. Anna Magdalena Herbergs, ~24.10.1802, †23.07.1805 Ronsdorf, ±24.07.1805 ib.
3. Elias Herbergs **VII b.**, *07.08.1805, ~11. 08.1805
4. Sebulon Wilhelm Herbergs, *1807, †18.12.1810 ib.
5. Debora Wilhelmina Herbergs, *02.11.1809, †18.07.1867 ib., ∞ 22.10.1839 Ronsdorf. **Peter Jacob Christians**, *13.11.1792
6. Anna Magdalena Herbergs, ~21.01.1812 (sp: Elias

Herbergs, merchant, Moritz Schorre), †09. 08.1815 ib.

7. *Friedrich Wilhelm Herbergs*, *11.05.1816, ∞ 24.11. 1847 Ronsdorf **Anna Catherina Herbertz**, *17.10. 1816

8. *Johanna Carolina Herbergs*, *19.05.1818, ∞ 05. 05.1840 Ronsdorf/Ref. Church **Gottlieb Stremmler**, *11.04.1814

9. *Helena Herbergs*, *28.02.1820

VI e. Rahel Herbergs, ~17.02.1774, ∞ Ronsdorf/Luth. Church 11.05.1800 **Johann Heinrich Schäfer**, profession: tailor, christened Ronsdorf/Ref. Church:

1. *Johann Hennrich Schäfer*

2. *Sebulon Schäfer*, *19.09.1805, ~20.09. 1805 (sp: Sebulon Schüller, Elias Herbergs, Johanna Katharina Pieper, Sara Pickardt)

VI f. Magdalena Wilhelmine or Sulamith Herbergs, ~ 01.09.1776, †28.10.1813 Ronsdorf, ±30.10.1813 ib., ∞ 17.04.1797 Ronsdorf/Ref. Church (sp: Gerson Wülfing, Johann Wilhelm Herberg) **David Wülfing**, administrator, christened Ronsdorf/Ref. Church:

1. *Anna Wilhelmina Wülfing*, ~17.08.1798 (sp: Anna Herberg, Miss Sara Wülfing, Miss Maria Herberg, Wilhelm Herberg)

2. *Peter Wülfing*, ~24.11.1800 (Z: Gerson Wülfing, Sebulon Clarenbach, Jungfrau Anna Herberg)

3. *Jonathan Wülfing*, *23.09.1803, ~28.09. 1803 (sp: Elias Herberg, merchant, Friedrich Hölterhoff, Schwelm, Rahel Wülfing, Anna Meis)

4. *Rahel Wülfing*, ~14.01.1806 (sp: Miss Friederica Hölterhoff, Schwelm, Eva Herberg, Eoban König, Noah Wülfing)

VII a. Johann Karl Heinrich Herbergs, *21.08.1800, ∞ 27.03.1823, Ronsdorf **Katharina Margareta Wilhelmina Thiemann**, christened Ronsdorf/Ref. Church:

1. *Wilhelmina Herbergs*, *28.06.1823 (sp: Sebulon Herbergs, grandfather), †16.10.1826 ib.

2. *Helena Herbergs*, *14.05.1825

3. *Wilhelmina Herbergs*, *07.08.1827, †25. 02.1828 ib.

4. *Maria Louise Herbergs*, *28.11.1828, †03. 09.1835 ib.

5. *Johann Karl Heinrich Herbergs*, *28.01.1831, ∞ 23.04.1861 Ronsdorf **Christiana Elise Gertrud Mahn**, *1835, christened Ronsdorf/Ref. Church:

   1. *Johann Karl Heinrich Herbergs*, *07.10.1861, †14.11.1861 ib.

   2. *Heinrich Karl Herbergs*, *03.06.1871

6. *Wilhelmina Herbergs*, *16.10.1833, ∞ 31.03.1862 Ronsdorf **Hermann Pees**, *1837

7. *Johanna Karolina Herbergs*, *23.11.1835, †26.09. 1836 ib.

8. *Marie Luise Herbergs*, *07.09.1837, ∞ 19.05.1859 Ronsdorf **Robert Eller** (f: **Johann Abraham Eller** ∞

Henriette Röder), *1833

9. *Johanna Herbergs*, *18.04.1840, ∞ 17.08.1867 Ronsdorf **Friedrich August Heyer**, *04.08.1841

10. *Hermann Peter Herbergs*, *12.04.1842, †24.12. 1842 ib.

11. *Bertha Herbergs*, *07.05.1844

VII b. Elias Herbergs, *07.08.1805 Ronsdorf, ~11.08. 1805 Ronsdorf/Ref. Church, profession: ribbon maker, ∞ **Maria Karolina Freyberger**, *1804/1805, christened Ronsdorf/Ref. Church:

1. *Reinhold Herbergs*, *21.11.1831, †19.02.1868 ib., profession: grocer, merchant, ∞ 31.01. 1855 Ronsdorf **Mathilda Alwine Winter**, christened Ronsdorf/Ref. Church:

   1. *Otto Herbergs*, *21.11.1855

   2. *Emil Herbergs*, *17.08.1857

   3. *Gustav Adolph Herbergs*, *17.01.1860

   4. *Victor Reinhold Herbergs*, *18.12.1861, †24.04.1863 ib.

   5. *Son*, still-birth, †10.05.1863

   6. *Klara Charlotte Herbergs*, *17.05.1865

   7. *Anna Mathilde Herbergs*, *15.10.1868

2. *Karoline Alwine Herbergs*, *02.12.1833

3. *Karolina Wilhelmine Herbergs*, *10.08.1835, †03. 11.1870 ib., ∞ **Heinrich Mühlinghaus**

4. *Maria Luise Herbergs*, *14.04.1837, ∞ 14.04.1862 Ronsdorf **Richard Stoodt**, *1836

5. *Sophia Augusta Herbergs*, *15.02.1839

6. *Friedrich Herbergs*, *07.12.1840 Ronsdorf, †27.09. 1862

7. *Ferdinand Herbergs*, *26.01.1843, †01.06.1864 Ronsdorf, profession: clerk

Family Tree Hilkes

population record Kaldenkirchen 1571: Johan Hilkens
population record Kaldenkirchen 1624/26: Johan Hilkens, Seib Hilkens, Gerardtgen Hilkes, Johan Hilkes
oath of allegiance 1666: Jan Hilkes, Leonhard Hilkes, Lambert Hilkes

Elisabeth Hilkens ∞ 02.09.1663 Kaldenkirchen/Ref. Church **Jan Coenen**, Waldniel, christened Kaldenkirchen/Ref. Church:

1. *Hendrik Coenen*, ~07.09.1664 (sp: Hendrik Bolten, Dirk in den Kamp, Katharina in den Kamp, Katharina Hilkes), †11.09.1664

2. *Hendrik Coenen*, ~13.10.1665 (sp: Leonhard Hilkes, Hendrik Hutmacher)

3. *Christine Coenen*, ~after 27.05. before 08.07.1668 (sp: Anton Hüskes, Eleonore Brouwers, Wendel Haasen/ Hansen ?)

4. *Dirk Coenen*, ~16.03.1670 (sp: Jan Hilkes, Henrich Haen, Sibille Tüffers)

5. Jakobus Coenen, ~23.01.1672 (sp: Peter Sieben, Dierixken Vincken)
6. Leonhard Coenen, ~09.02.1676 (sp: Leonhard Hilkes, Mechtild Küppers)

I. Leonhard Hilkes, 1666 oath of allegiance, ∞ **Christina Küppers**, christened Kaldenkirchen/Ref. Church:
1. Gertrud Hilkes, ~27. April (?) 1664 (sp: Matthias Küppers, Katharina Hilkes, Elisabeth Küppers)
2. Tochter N. Hilkes, ~05.12.1666 (sp: Anton Hüskes, Sibille Brouwers, Idt N.)
3. Jan Hilkes, ~24.02.1668 (sp: Jan Hilkes, Mechtild Schrembges), †07.06.1669
4. Adelgunde Hilkes, ~03.11.1669 (sp: Loy van Well, Elisabeth Küppers, Frau des Lorenz Hanssen)
5. Jan Hilkes, ~09.11.1670 (sp: Jan Strepers, Adelgunde Brouwers)
6. Peter Hilkes II., ~23.09.1672 (sp: Joachim Hüskes, Mechtild Schrembges)
7. Leonhard Hilkes, ~03.06.1674 (sp: Wilhelm Lappen, Christine Küppers, Arnold Simons)
8. Matthias Hilkes, ~07.03.1677 (sp: Peter Strepers, Katharina Küppers)
9. Helene Hilkes, ~01.03.1679 (sp: Gerhard Busen, Haren in Maas en Waal, Peter Huberts, Helene Strepers)

II. Peter Hilkens, ~23.09.1672, ∞ **Katharina Lensen**, christened Kaldenkirchen/Ref. Church:
1. Katharina Hilkens, ~26.09.1706 (sp: Matthias Lensen, Matthias Hilkens)
2. Johannes Hilkens, ~21.01.1708 (sp: Johannes Wildenraet, Johanna Schrembges)
3. Matthias Hilkens, ~06.10.1709 (sp: Dirk Lensen, Agnes Schrembges, Helene Hilkens)
4. Laurenz Hilkens, ~05.07.1711 (sp: Gerhard Hasen, Katharina Baums, Frau des Johannes Dahms)
5. Katharina Hilkens, ~18.07.1714 (sp: Johannes Dahms, widow Adelgunde Bachoven)
6. Petrus Hilkens, ~19.03.1717 (sp: Peter Küppers, Katharina Coenen)
7. Leonhard Hilkens, ~26.03.1719 (sp: Wilhelmus Lappen, Katharina Hasen)
8. Leonhard Hilkens, ~01.12.1721 (sp: Wilhelmus Küppers, Elisabeth Küppers)

Family Tree Hollender

I. Lebbert Hollender ∞ **N.N.**, christened:
1. Bernhard Hollender II., ~19.06.1622 Waldniel/Ref. Church (sp: his brother-in-law Peter Adams, his cousin Bernhard Hollender, Jen im Schro[...])
2. Johan Hollender (?) ∞ **N.N.**, christened:
  Peter Hollender, ~13.10.1652 Waldniel/Ref. Church
  Helene Hollender (?), Good Friday 1669 commu-

nicant, Waldniel/Ref. Church
II. Bernhard Hollender ∞ **Gertgen Knohren**, christened Waldniel/Ref. Church:
1. Adelheid Hollender, ~11.04.1652, Good Friday 1669 communicant, Waldniel/Ref. Church
2. Margarete Hollender, ~11.01.1654, Sunday before Pentecost 1673 communicant, ∞ 06.07.1688 Waldniel/Ref. Church **Wilhelm Hartmans** (E: **Hein Hartmans** ∞ **Jennichen Jaspers**, both †at son's marriage)
3. Peetz (Peter) Hollender, ~12.03.1659
4. Jan Hollender (?), *about 1664, Good Friday 1680 communicant, Waldniel/Ref. Church
5. Arnold Hollender III., ~08.06.1670 (sp: Peter Corstes, Paulus Schmits, Gladbach, Agatha Dienen)

III. Arnold Hollender, ~08.06.1670, ∞ 02.09.1702 Waldniel/ref. Gem. **Anna Engels** (p: **Konrad Engels** ∞ **Gertrud Wirtz**), christened Waldniel/Ref. Church:
1. Gertrud Hollender, ~06.02.1704 (sp: Jan Hollender, Gertrud Wirtz)
2. Bernhardus Hollender IV., ~20.06.1706 (sp: [...] Engels, Adelgunde Hollender), †18.09.1790 Waldniel, ±21.09.1790 ib., buried in church, profession: merchant
3. Konrad Hollender, ~29.09.1708 (sp: Peter Bosch, Elisabeth Engels)
4. Konrad Hollender, ~22.02.1711 (sp: Mattias Engels jr., Anna Dahmen)
5. Arnoldus (?) Hollender, ~28.01.1713 (sp: Gerhard Krämers, Gertrud Hollender)
6. Gertrud Hollender, ~21.12.1715 (sp: Johannes Herbergs, Margarete Neusen)
7. Gertrud Hollender, ~11.05.1717 (sp: Wilhelm Horn, Adelgunde Kessels)

IV. Bernhardus Hollender, ~20.06.1706, ∞ 1st marriage 06.06.1724 Kaldenkirchen/Ref. Church **Agnes Strepers,** (see family tree Strepers), christened Waldniel/Ref. Church:
1. Anna Elisabeth Hollender, ~24.02.1726 (sp: Arnold Hollender, Elisabeth Olmis)
2. Arnold Hollender V., profession: merchant
Bernhard Hollender ∞ 2d marriage 21.12.1784 dispensation Waldniel/ref. Gem. **Margareta Wolters**, *Rheydt/Ref. Church; **Margarete Wolters** ∞ 2d marriage 25.03.1792 Waldniel/Ref. Church **Martin Engels**, widower, Schwanenberg

V. Arnold Hollender ∞ 25.11.1755, Heinsberg/Ref. Church **Anna Gertrud Königs**, ~23. 08.1726 Heinsberg/Ref. Church (sp: Joh. Maximilian König, Gertrud von Linn, Ursula König), †03.12.1779 Waldniel, ±08.12.1779 ib., christened Waldniel/Ref. Church:
1. Petrus Henricus Hollender, ~19.05.1759 (sp: Peter Königs, Matthias Mickenschreiber, Agnes Hollender,

Anna Elisabeth Hamboch)
2. Bernardus Hollender, ~27.08.1762 (sp: Bernardus Hollender, Mrs Hollender in lieu of widow Maria Mickenschreiber née Strepers)
3. Petrus Henricus Hollender, ~23.05.1768 (sp: Jakobus Königs, Petrus Henricus Streper, Anna Gertrud Königs geb. Lüneschloss, Katharina Gertrud Mickenschreiber née Thielen)
4. Henrich Eberhard Hollender, ~06.11.1771 (sp: Bernhard Hollender, Anna Katharina Moll)
Arnoldus Hollender, ∞ 2d marriage 26.06.1780 Sittard **Katharina Judith Dorpmans**, †07.05.1798 Waldniel, ±09.05.1798 ib., christened Waldniel/Ref. Church:
5. Katharina Judith Hollender, ~09.08.1781 (sp: Bernhard Hollender, Catharina Judith Dorpmans, Sittard), †01.05.1782 Waldniel, ±03.05.1782
6. Katharina Judith Petronella Bernhardina Hollender, ~25.03.1783 (sp: Bernhard Hollender, Peter Hinrich Mickenschreiber, Kaldenkirchen, Katharina Judith Dorpmans, Sittard, Petronella Wyen, Meercamp)
7. Maria Katharina Hollender, ~20.03.1785 (sp: Jakobus Königs, Maria Dorpmans ?)

Family Tree Hüskes
record of members of the Reformed Church of Venlo 1637: Jan Hüskes
population record Kaldenkirchen 1571: Huiskens Hof
population record Kaldenkirchen 1624/26: op Hüskes
oath of allegiance 1666: Anton Hüskes

Jan Hüskes ∞ 1st marriage 08.05.1667 **Dirckxken (Diederica) Vincken** Kaldenkirchen/Ref. Church, christened:
1. Elisabeth Hüskes, ~25.09.1667 (sp: Jan Strepers, Miss Adelgunda Brouwers)
2. Eleonora Hüskes, ~14.04.1669 (sp: Paulus Küsters, Geertjen, Jan Olmis' wife, dyer)
3. Sibille Hüskes, ~08.02.1671 (sp: Anton Hüskes, Christine Küppers, widow Jan Strepers)
4. Sibille Hüskes, ~11. (?) 05.1672 (sp: Leonhard Hilkes, Christine Küppers)
Jan Hüskes, widower ∞ 2d marriage 15.04.1685 Kaldenkirchen/Ref. Church **Anna Lenens**, Venlo

I a. Kaspar Hüskes ∞ Kaldenkirchen/Ref. Church **Adelheid Dircks/Dierichs**, christened Kaldenkirchen/Ref. Church:
1. Jan Hüskes, ~11.12.1673 (sp: Jan Hüskes, Arnold Simons, Christine Küppers)
2. Gerhard Hüskes, ~22.03.1676 (sp: Jakob Aertsen, Maria Doors), ±02.11.1728 Kaldenkirchen/Ref. Church
3. Maria Hüskes, ~16.01.1678 (sp: Jan Strepers, Mechtild Hüskes)
4. Anton Hüskes, ~13.10.1680 (sp: Jan Olmis)

5. Petrus Hüskes, ~08.04.1684 (sp: Peter Sieben, Agnes op de Streep, Agnes Brouwers)
Kaspar Hüskes, Witwer ∞ 26.01.1696 Kaldenkirchen/ Ref. Church **Adelheid Stenden** (?), widow, Bracht

I b. Jan Hüskes ∞ Kaldenkirchen/Ref. Church **Katharina Bücks**, christened:
1. Dirk Hüskes II a., ~12.04.1676 (sp: Kaspar Hüskes, Arnold Simons, Maria Hüskes, Elisabeth Doors)
2. Gerhard Hüskes, ~22.05.1678 (sp: Leonhard Strepers, Mechtild Hüskes)
3. Ommelken Hüskes II b., ~15.05.1681 (sp: Joachim Hüskes, Katharina Kluten)
4. Elisabeth Hüskes II c., ~28.03.1684 (Sp: Christian Huts, Adelheid in der Elst)
5. Jan Hüskes II d., ~03.08.1687 (sp: Jakob Gebelen, Ömelken Bötels)

I c. Joachim Hüskes ∞ 08.04.1674 Kaldenkirchen/Ref. Church **Maria Doors** (see family tree Doors), christened Kaldenkirchen/Ref. Church:
1. Ummelken Hüskes, ~17.03.1675 (sp: Anton Hüskes, Agnes Doors)
2. Jan Hüskes, ~22.12.1675 (sp: Peter Kürlis, Kaspar Hüskes, Anna Strepers)
3. Leonhard Hüskes, ~21.02.1677 (sp: Jan Hüskes, Jan Strepers)
4. Immelken Hüskes II e., ~11.12.1678 (sp: Anton Hüskes, Agnes Doors)
5. Leonhard Hüskes, ~27.12.1679 (sp: Peter Doors, Leiden, Mechtild Hüskes)
6. Matthias Hüskes, ~02.03.1681 (sp: Leonhard Hillekens, Peter Sieben, Jan Olmis' wife)
7. Agnes Hüskes, ~30.05.1683 (sp: Peter Sieben, Hendrik Aertsen, Gertrud Doors)
8. Matthias Hüskes, ~10.02.1685 (sp: Arnold Simons, Katharina Bocks/Bücks)
9. Elisabeth Hüskes, ~25.07.1686 (sp: Christian Höts, Helena Strepers)

II a. Dirk Hüskes, ~12.04.1676, ∞ 17.10.1700 Kaldenkirchen/Ref. Church **Sophia Küppers** (see family tree Küppers) Kaldenkirchen/Ref. Church:
1. Matthias Hüskes III a., ~04.09.1701 (sp: Johan Hüskes, Katharina Küppers)
2. Gerhard Hüskes III b., ~23.09.1703 (sp: Peter Küppers, Oemeltjen Hüskes)
3. Leonhard Hüskes, ~16.09.1705 (sp: Peter Küppers, Katharina Box); **Leonhard Hüskes**, widower ∞ 04.09.1748 Kaldenkirchen/Ref. Church **Maria Drieser**
4. Mechtild Hüskes III c., ~Easter Monday 1707 (sp: Johannes Hüskes, Katharina Coenen)
5. Katharina Hüskes, ~15.03.1709 (sp: Arnold Tüffers, Elisabeth Hüskes)

II b. Ommelken Hüskes, ~15.05.1681, ∞ 03.02.1706 **Bartholomäus Maubachs**, Bracht, christened:
1. Gerhard Maubachs, ~30.07.1706 (sp: Johann Hüskes, Damian Hasen, Adelgunde Tüffers), ±04.10.1768 Bracht/Ref. Church.
2. Jan Maubachs, ~05.09.1707 (sp: Dirk Hüskes, Johanna Maubachs)
3. Jakob Maubachs, ~13.04.1709 (sp: Jakob Maubachs, Elisabeth Hüskes)
4. Sibille Maubachs, ~09.06.1710 (sp: Jakob Gebelen, Katharina Box/Bocks, Maria Baums)
5. Leonhard Maubachs, ~09.10.1712 (sp: Gerhard Hasen, Johannes Hüskes, Öeletjen Hasen)
6. Jakobus Maubachs, ~03.06.1714 (sp: Johann Hasen, Sophia Küppers)
7. Arnoldus Maubachs, ~15.11.1716 (sp: Michael Hasen, Gertrud Küppers)
8. Sibille Maubachs, ~19.11.1719 (sp: Jakob Gebelen, Hester Hasen)
9. Jakobus Maubachs, ~02.04.1725 (sp: Gerhard Hüskes, Mechtild Küppers)

II c. Elisabeth Hüskes, ~28.03.1684, ∞ 09.08.1733 Kaldenkirchen/Ref. Church **Henrich Schröers** (p: **Hermann Schröers ∞ Maria Baums**)
Henrich Schröers ∞ 2d marriage 23.06.1737 Kaldenkirchen/Ref. Church **Hester Maubachs** (p: **Jacob Maubachs ∞ Adelgunda Haasen†**, Bracht)

II d. Jan Hüskes, ~03.08.1687, ∞ 14.04.1716 Kaldenkirchen/Ref. Church **Gertrud Küpers**, ~27.12.1689 Kaldenkirchen/Ref. Church (sp: Leonhard Strepers, Mechtild Schremkes), christened Kaldenkirchen/Ref. Church:
1. Johannes Hüskes, ~23.08.1716 (sp: Peter Küppers, Katharina Hüskes), ∞ 15.03.1746 **Diederica Baums**
2. Leonhardus Hüskes, ~18.04.1718 (sp: Dirk Hüskes, Agnes Strepers), widower, ∞ 04.09.1748 **Maria Drieser**
3. Gerhardus Hüskes, ~28.01.1720 (sp: Matthias Küppers, Elisabeth Hüskes), ∞ 19.1.1742 Schwanenberg **Elisabeth Beckers**
4. Matthäus Hüskes, ~13.07.1721 (sp: Bartholomäus Maubachs, Elisabeth Küppers)
5. Katharina Hüskes **III d.**, ~23.04.1724 (sp: Matthias Hüskes, Helene Küppers), ±02.01.1770 Bracht/ref. Gem.
6. Mechtild Hüskes, ~15.09.1726 (sp: Peter Küppers, Mechtild Hüskes)
7. Sophia Hüskes **III e.**, ~05.12.1728 (sp: Jan Schröers, Anna Mickenschreiber, Frau des Gerhard Hüskes)
8. Diederich Hüskes, ~16.12.1731 (sp: Gerhard Hüskes, Mechtild Küppers)

II e. Immelken Hüskes, ~11.12.1678, ∞ 17.11.1700 Kaldenkirchen/ref. Gem. **Matthias Olmis**, christened:
1. Johannes Olmis, ~28.08.1701 (sp: Joachim Hüskes, Henrich Rahr, Krefeld, Elisabeth Olmis)
2. Maria Olmis, ~03.02.1704 (sp: Hendrik Strepers, Maria Doors)
3. Johannes Olmis, ~24.06.1708 (sp: Johann Hüskes, Elisabeth Olmis, Katharina Strepers)
4. Maria Olmis, ~10.04.1712 (sp: Wilhelmus Sieben, Elisabeth Hüskes)
5. Matthias Olmis, ~24.11.1717 (sp: Dirk Hüskes, Maria Sieben)

III a. Matthias Hüskes, ~04.09.1701, ∞ 25.01.1734 Kaldenkirchen/ Witwer **Agnes Strepers** (p: **Leonhard Strepers ∞ Maria Sieben**, see family tree Strepers), christened Kaldenkirchen/ Witwer:
1. Johann Leonhard Hüskes, ~31.10.1734 (sp: Peter Strepers, Peter David Katernberg, Elisabeth Strepers)
2. Diederich Hüskes, ~18.03.1736 (sp: Johann Christophorus Ringels, Mechtild Hüskes)
3. Gerhard Hüskes, ~02.03.1738 (sp: Matthias Mickenschreiber, Matthias Küppers, Mechtild Christina Kladders, Peter Strepers' wife)

III b. Gerhard Hüskes, ~23.09.1703, ∞ **Anna Mickenschreiber**, christened Kaldenkirchen/Ref. Church:
1. Sophia Katharina Hüskes **IV a.**, ~26.06.1729 (sp: Hermann Mickenschreiber, Diederich Hüskes, Agnes Köelkens, Mechtild Hüskes), ±26.02.1769 ib.
2. Hermannus Hüskes, ~17.09.1730 (sp: Peter David Katterberg, teacher at Kaldenkirchen, Matthias Hüskes, Maria und Agnes Mickenschreiber), ±14.01.1733 ib.
3. Anna Katharina Hüskes **IV b.**, ~16.07.1732 (sp: Daniel Laufs, minister at Eschweiler, Matthias Mickenschreiber, Maria Magdalena Mickenschreiber), ±04.02. 1756 ib.

III c. Mechtild Hüskes, ~25.04.1707, ∞ 04.06.1730 Kaldenkirchen/Ref. Church **Peter David Katterberg**, teacher at Kaldenkirchen (p: **Reinhard Andreas Katterberg**, teacher at Wickrathberg ∞ **Elisabeth Beckers**), christened Kaldenkirchen/Ref. Church:
1. Sophia Elisabeth Katterberg, ~25.12.1732 (sp: Matthias Hüskes, Elisabeth Katternberg)
2. Katharina Margaretha Katterberg, ~17.09.1734 (sp: Reinhard Andreas Katernberg, teacher at Wickrathberg, Anna Küpers called Mickenschreiber);
Peter David Katerberg ∞ 2d marriage Kaldenkirchen/ Ref. Church **Margarethe Catharina Seifferts**, christened:
3. Johanna Margareta Katerberg, ~06.02.1747 Kaldenkirchen/Ref. Church (sp: Petrus Weyer, Johanna Katharina Engelberts, Anna Hamboch née Moorrees)

III d. Katharina Hüskes, ~23.04.1724, ∞ 20.10.1749 Bracht **Leonhard Bolten**, christened Bracht/Ref. Church:
1. Gertrud Bolten, ~07.09.1750 (sp: Johannes Hüskes, Gertrud Haasen)

2. Elisabeth Bolten, ~17.06.1753 (sp: Wilhelm in der Elst)
3. Johannes Bolten, ~31.12.1754 (sp: Johannes Janssen, Sophia Hüskes)
4. Henricus Bolten, ~06.03.1758 (sp: Matthias Schröers, Diederica Baums)
5. Ida Bolten, ~02.10.1763 (sp: Gerhard Hüskes, Ida Bolten)

III e. Sophia Hüskes, ~05.12.1728, ∞ **Jakobus Maubachs** Kaldenkirchen/Ref. Church, christened Bracht/Ref. Church:
1. Gertrud Maubachs, ~10.08.1752 (sp: Gerhard Maubachs, Katharina Hüskes)
2. Jakobus Maubachs, ~22.12.1757 (sp: Jan Maubachs, Katharina Haasen)

IV a. Sophia Katharina Hüskes, ~26.06.1729, ∞ 18.01.1750 Kaldenkirchen **Johann Bergmann**, teacher, christened Kaldenkirchen/Ref. Church:
1. Maria Agneta Bergmann, ~between 29.11. and 31.12.1754 (sp: Matthias Küppers, Katharina Anna Hüskes)
2. Johannes Gerhardus Bergmann, ~11.09.1756 (sp: Johannes Laufs, minister at Rheydt, Engel Baums, Eva Mickenschreiber)
3. Gerhardus Bergmann, ~10.06.1761 (sp: Quirinus Quack, Anna Mickenschreiber, Katharina Lungen)
4. Johannes Petrus Bergmann, ~01.05.1763 (sp: Gerhardus Hüskes, Eva Mickenschreiber)
5. Anna Katharina Bergmann, ~14.04.1765 (sp: Peter Henrich Mickenschreiber, Anna Gertruda Bergmann, Katharina Margaretha Katerberg)

IV b. Anna Katharina Hüskes, ~16.07.1732, ∞ 10.07.1754 Kaldenkirchen/Ref. Church **Engel Baums**, christened Kaldenkirchen/Ref. Church:
1. Katharina Margaretha Baums, ~12.01.1755 (sp: Leonhardus Baums, Anna Mickenschreiber)

Family Tree Hutmacher
oath of allegiance 1666 Kaldenkirchen: Henrich Hutmacher

I. Hendrich Hutmacher ∞ **N. Coenen**, christened:
1. Hendrich Hutmacher II a.
2. Adelgunde Hutmacher
3. Barbara Hutmacher II b.

II a. Hendrich Hutmacher, oath of allegiance 1666, ∞ 04.03.1666 Kaldenkirchen/Ref. Church **Katharina Thomas**, Randerath, christened Kaldenkirchen/Ref. Church:
1. Geertgen Hutmacher, ~05.12.1666 (sp: Jan Coenen, Wendel in gen Kamp, Adelgunde Hutmacher)
2. Maria Hutmacher, ~10.03.1669 (sp: Jakob Janssen

Beck, Anna Doors, Henrich Kürlis' widow)
3. Sibille Hutmacher, ~11.10.1671 (sp: Jan Hüskes, Anna Doors)
4. Peter Hutmacher, ~19.12.1673 (sp: Hendrik Prollen, Heinken Boutten, Peter Kürlis, Agnes Doors)
5. Katharina Hutmacher, ~22.03.1676 (sp: Hendrik Bolten, Sibille Haenen)

II b. Barbara Hutmacher (alias Hendrichs, Hendrich's daughter) ∞ **Jakob Becks**, christened Kaldenkirchen/Ref. Church:
1. Gertrud Becks, ~23.08.1671 (sp: Henrich Hutmacher, Adelgunde his daughter, Katharina (Thomas ?), Henrich Hutmacher's wife)
2. Jenneken Becks, ~08.04.1674 (sp: Anna Bolten, Hendrik Hutmacher)
3. Hendricus Becks, ~20.06.1677 (sp: Hendrik Hutmacher, Sibille Hendrichsen alias Hutmacher ?)

Family Tree Knevels
Gerlach Knevels, ∞ **Sara**, christened:
Engelbert Knevels, ~13.03.1597 Elberfeld, ±17.10.1650 ib., profession: merchant; mayor 1630 und 1631, 1636, 1641 and 1642

Isaak Knevels, ~29.01.1651 Elberfeld/Ref. Church, ±1717 ib., profession: universities of Duisburg, Marburg, Leiden, minister at 1674 Leiden, 1679 at Linnich, 1697 at Soest

I. Werner Knevels, ~20.08.1645 Elberfeld/Ref. Church, ±11.11.1721 ib., profession: merchant (1703 grocer) and councilor, mayor 1687 und 1695, ∞ 10.11.1667 Elberfeld/Ref. Church **Elisabeth Springer (Sprenger)**, ~19.07.1643 ib., †before 22.03.1703 Elberfeld, christened Elberfeld/Ref. Church:
1. Isaak Knevels, ~08.05.1668, †23.04.1739 Solingen, profession: university of Duisburg, minister at Düren 1693-1704, at Solingen 1704-†1739
2. Anna Maria Knevels, ~05.01.1670 Elberfeld, ±08.07.1730 ebd., ∞ 1699 Elberfeld/Ref. Church **Johann Abraham auf der Heyden**, ~20.02.1658 Elberfeld, ±16.04.1716 ib., profession: merchant at Island zu Elberfeld
3. Johann Knevels II., *10.08.1672 Elberfeld, †1756 Linnich, profession: merchant; 1672 university of Duisburg, minister at Linnich 1698-1740, as successor of his uncle Isaak Knevels (since 1697 at Soest)

II. Johann Knevels, *10.08.1672 Elberfeld, ∞ Linnich (?) **Maria Elisabeth Thoma**, christened:
1. Sara Elisabeth Knevels, ∞ **Herman Adolph Jansen** (p: **Adolf Jansen**, Elberfeld, ∞ **Katharina Brügelmann**, Elberfeld), *1701 Elberfeld (?), †03.02.1747 Solingen,

profession: minister at Kirchherten 1725-28, at Kalden-kirchen 1728-31, at Homberg/Düsseldorf 1731-39, at Wülfrath 1739-42, at Solingen 1742-†1747, christened:
Johann Jacob Jansen, ~30.04.1730 Kaldenkirchen/Ref. Church (sp: Johannes Knevels, minister, Linnich, Elisabeth Thoma, Johann auf der Heyden, merchant, Elberfeld, Jakob de Weerth, merchant at Elberfeld)
Adolf Jansen, cousin of **Katharina Jansen,** *1670 Elberfeld, †1733 ebd., ±11.08.1733 ib., **Katharina Jansen** ∞ 1st marriage **Peter Bolckhaus,** †1709 Elberfeld, profession: ribbon maker, **Katharina Jansen** ∞ 2d marriage 12.11.1712 Elberfeld/Ref. Church **Elias Eller,** *30.06.1690 Elberfeld, ~14.07.1690 Elberfeld/Ref. Church, †16.05.1750, Ronsdorf, profession: merchant, founder of the sect of Zionites/Ellerians
Elias Eller ∞ 2d marriage 26.01.1734, Elberfeld/Ref. Church **Anna vom Büchel,** *1698, †1743, Ronsdorf, **Elias Eller** ∞ 3d marriage 15.09.1749, Ronsdorf/Ref. Church **Anna Gertrud Lucas,** widow **Bosselmann,** *1695 Elberfeld, ±27.07. 1763 Ronsdorf/Ref. Church
2. Anna Maria Knevels, ∞ 28.09.1732 Kaldenkirchen/rRef. Church **Petrus Sieben** (see family tree Sieben)
3. Magdalena Wilhelmine Knevels (2d Zions' mother of Ellerians, niece of minister Hermann Adolph Jansen, Kaldenkirchen) ∞ 1st marriage **Sebulon Schüller,** Köln, christened: 9 children, ∞ 2d marriage 1760 Ronsdorf/Ref. Church **Johannes Bolckhaus,** *1709 Elberfeld, †03.08. 1783 Ronsdorf, ±06.08.1783 ib.
4. Johann Werner Knevels, *Linnich (?), †ca. 1774 on St. John, Virgin Islands, profession: university of Leiden, moved to Ronsdorf in 1737, merchant; 1750 or later ref. minister of the Dutch colony of St. Jan/John.
5. Louisa Bernhardina Knevels, *Linnich, ∞☐Elberfeld **Peter Raukamp,** *1706 ebd., †1776, profession: merchant

Family Tree Königs

I. Eberhard Königs ∞ **Gertraud Linn,** christened: *Peter Königs* II., ~Millich

II. Peter Königs, ~Millich, †25.01.1767 Heinsberg, ∞ 10.10.1717, Heinsberg/Ref. Church **Katharina Dorpmans** (p: **Leonhard Dorpman** ∞ 1689 **Adelgunde Kamps,** Millich), ~12.12.1694, Heinsberg/Ref. Church, †01.04.1774 Heinsberg, christened Heinsberg/Ref. Church:
1. Eberhard Königs III a., ~27.06.1718 (sp: Eberhard Königs, Millich, N. Königs, Hünshoven, Adelgunde Kamps gen. Dorpmans) †20.12.1744 Heinsberg, profession: merchant
2. Bartholomäus Königs, ~26.11.1721 (sp: Ludwig Kreuter, Doverack, Gertrud Linn, Eberhard Königs' zu

Millich wife, Agneta Bolten), †young
3. Bartholomäus Königs, ~20.12.1722 (sp: Jakob Königs, Johann Beld, Sybilla Weydmans), ∞ 14.01.1759 Heinsberg/Ref. Church **Susanna Katharina Ens,** widow **Merkens**
4. Gerhard Sebastian Königs, ~19.11.1724, (sp: Bartholomäus Königs, Sebastian Cronenstein, Agnes Dorpmans)
5. Johanna Gertrud Königs III b., ~23.08.1726 (sp: Johannes Maximilian König, Gertrud von Linn, Ursula König), †03.12.1779 Waldniel, ±08.12.1779 Waldniel/Ref. Church
6. Jakob Wilhelm Königs, ~02.11.1728 (sp: Jakob König, Wilhelm Konzen, Cäcilia Dorpmans), †19.03. 1812, Heinsberg, ∞ 22.02.1756 Heinsberg/Ref. Church **Agnes Dycks,** widow
7. Adelgunda Ursula Wilhelmina Königs, ~04.04.1730 (sp: Mr Wilhelm Merkens, minister at Heinsberg, Adelgunde Kamp, Mechtild König called Janssen), Millich, †young
8. Adelgunda Ursula Wilhelmina Königs, ~04.04.1733 (sp: Bartholomäus König, Lambert Janssen, Gertrud Gelen called König, Gertrud Dycks called Merkens)
9. Johann Adolph Königs, ~18.09.1735 (sp: Mr Joh. Adolph Timmerman, Juris utriusque Dr., Düsseldorf, Mr Johann P. Grambusch, Juris utriusque Dr. at Hünshoven, Eberhard König, Brüggen, Katharina Judith Dorpmans called Ritzen, Sittard), †05.11.1813, Heinsberg, ∞ 02.06.1772 Heinsberg/Ref. Church **Barbara Merkens**
10. Adelgunda Ursula Königs, ~19.07.1739 (sp: Johann Tuyth, Katharina Bart. v. den Bruch called Dorpman)

III a. Eberhard Königs, ~27.06.1718, ∞ 20.12.1744, Heinsberg/Ref. Church **Anna Gertrud Lünenschloss** (p: **Rütger Lünenschloss** ∞ 06.08.1724 **Katharina Pfeiffers** 2d marriage, ~16.05.1696, daughter of **Katharina Strepers,** granddaughter of **Lambert Strepers,** see family tree Strepers), christened Heinsberg/Ref. Church:
1. Peter Rüdiger Königs, ~30.11.1747 (sp: Peter König, Rüdiger Lünenschloss, Adelgunde Dorpmann gen. Tuyth)
2. Johanna Katharina Wilhelmina Königs, ~17.08. 1749 (sp: Mr Johann Gotfried Meinard Wiedenfeld, minister at Heinsberg, Katharina Pfeiffer called Lünenschloß, Katharina Dorpmans called König)
3. Maria Gertrud Königs, ~24.10.1751 (sp: Gerhard König, Johanna Gertrud König, Maria Elisabeth Lünenschloß)
4. Johannes Wilhelm Königs, ~30.06.1754 (sp: Johann Peter Überfeld, Jacob Wilhelm König, Johann Wilhelm Lünenschloß, Anna Sibilla Wiedenfels née Lünenschloß, Juliane Tack)
5. Wilhelm Dionysius Königs, ~11.07.1756 (sp: Mr Dionysius Smithshuysen, Johann Wilhelm Lünen-

schloss, Lucia Katharina Lünenschloss)
6. *Maria Elisabeth Königs*, ~24.09.1758 (sp: Rüdiger
Lünenschloß, Rüdigers' son, Maria Anna Nonnenberg
called Pfeiffers, Gertrud Elisabeth Königs)

III b. Johanna Gertrud Königs, ~23. 08.1726 Heins-
berg/Ref. Church, ∞ 25.11.1755 Heinsberg/Ref. Church
Arnold Hollender, Waldniel (p: **Bernard Hollender** ∞
1st marriage **Agnes Strepers**, see family tree Hollender), ∞ 2d marriage Sittard **Katharina Judith Dorpmans**, christened:
Bernardus Hollender, ~27.08.1762 Waldniel/Ref.
Church (sp: Bernardus Hollender, Mrs Hollender in lieu of
widow Maria Mickenschreiber née Strepers), ∞ 18.04.
1794 Heinsberg/Ref. Church **Anna Maria Henrica Armand** (p: **Paul Armand** ∞ **Helena Schroer**, Maastricht)

Bernhardt Engels ∞ Hückelhoven/Ref. Church **Anna
Gertrud Königs**, christened:
Anna Elisabeth Engels, ~12.09.1773 Waldniel/Ref.
Church (sp: Konrad Engels, Waldniel, Gertrud Hollender
née Königs für Anna Katharina Moll, Millich), ∞ 26.04.
1795 Waldniel/Ref. Church **Maximilian Königs** (p: **Bartholomäus Königs** ∞ **Mechtilda Königs**, Millich)

Christian Henrich Essers ∞ Hückelhoven/Ref. Church
Isabella Königs, ~Hückelhoven/Ref. Church (?),
christened Waldniel/Ref. Church:
1. *Johannes Matthias*, ~24.09.1779 (sp: Johannes Peif-
fers, Keltzenberg, Petronella Essers), †young
2. *Anna Margaretha Essers*, ~21.10.1781 (sp: Johann
Wilhelm Schnetel, Magdalena Bohnen)
3. *Johann Henrich Essers*, ~ 23.01.1785 (sp: Johannes Langenberg, Süchteln, Miss Sibilla Lohein)
4. *Johannes Matthias Essers*, twin, ~16. 09.1787 (sp:
Johannes Rudolf Essers, Anna Königs, Hückelhoven)
5. *Margareta Elisabetha Essers*, twin, ~16. 09.1787
(sp: Henrich Königs, Margaretha Hollender née Wolters)
6. *Peter Konrad Essers*, ~10.03.1790 (sp: Franz
Henrich Essers, Anna Gertrud Engels)
7. *Katharina Aria Essers*, ~ 03.04.1794 (sp: Henrich
and Aria Schmits)

Johann Heinrich Königs (p: **Eberhard Königs** ∞
Anna Catharina Cox, Hückelhoven) ∞ 20.03.1782
Grambusch/Ref. Church Hückelhoven-Schwanenberg
Kunigunda Kremers (p: **Steffen Godfried Kremers** ∞
Maria Landmesser, Grambusch)

Family Tree Küppers
population record Kaldenkirchen 1571: Johann der Kuyper
population record 1624/26: Beel Kuypers
oath of allegiance 1666: Jan Küppers

I a. Matthias Küppers ∞ **Mechtild Schremkes**, christened Kaldenkirchen/Ref. Church:
1. *Peter Küppers* II a., ~06.04.1664 (sp: Gertrud
Schremkes, Leonhard Hilkens)
2. *Sophia Küppers* II b., ~25.03.1666 (sp: Kornelius
Booms, Katharina Brouwers, Peter Schremkes)
3. *Jan Küppers* II c., ~27.01.1669 (sp: Jan Hilkes, Elisabeth Küppers, Kornelius Booms' wife)
4. *Adelgunde Küppers*, ~06.03.1672 (sp: Leonhard
Hilkes, Christine Küppers)
5. *Peter Küppers junior* II d., ~03.05.1674 (sp: Lenz
Hanssen, Katharina Schremkes)

I b. Elisabeth Küppers ∞ 28.09.1665 Kaldenkirchen/
Ref. Church **Kornelius Booms**, christened Kaldenkir-
chen/Ref. Church:
Peter Booms, ~13.12.1665 (sp: Matthias Booms, Matthias Brouwers, Katharina Booms)

II a. Peter Küppers, ~06.04.1664, ∞ 08.08.1689 Kal-
denkirchen/Ref. Church **Agnes Strepers** (p: **Leonhard
Strepers der Junge**, ∞ **Helena Schmitz** ?), ~08.08.
1663 Kaldenkirchen/Ref. Church (see family tree Strepers), christened Kaldenkirchen/Ref. Church:
1. *Gertrud Küppers*, ~27.12.1689 (sp: Leonhard Strepers, Mechthild Schremkes), ∞ 14.04.1716 **Johannes
Hüskes** (see family tree Hüskes)
2. *Matthias Küppers*, ~08.04.1691 (sp: Dirk Küppers,
Katharina Küppers)
3. *Elisabeth Küppers*, ~31.01.1694 (sp: Johann Herzog, teacher at Solingen, Sophia Küppers), christened
Kaldenkirchen/Ref. Church:
      Elisabeth, ~29.06.1725, illegitimate (?) (sp: Johan-
      nes Hüskes, Mechtild Küppers)
4. *Dirk Küpers*, twin, ~28.10.1696 (sp: Peter Küppers,
Helene Strepers), †soon after birth
5. *Tochter N.N.*, twin, ~28.10.1696 (sp: Elisabeth Jansen, Katharina Küppers), †soon after birth
6. *Helena Küppers* III a., ~15.01.1698 (sp: Jan Küpers
and Johanna Schremkes, Fisken Lensen's wife)
7. *Mechtild Küppers* III b., ~29.01.1701 (sp: Tilmannus
Gabriel Voos, Katharina Booms)
8. *Eleonora Küppers* III c., ~04.03.1703 (sp: Wilhelm
Lappen, Maria Daems called Hüskes)
9. *Peter Küppers*, ~14.06.1705 (sp: Dirk Hüskes, Johanna Strepers)

II b. Sophia Küppers, ~25.03.1666, ∞ 17.10.1700 Kal-
denkirchen/Ref. Church **Dirk Hüskes**, christened Kal-

denkirchen/Ref. Church:

1. Matthias Hüskes, ~04.09.1701 (sp: Johann Hüskes, Katharina Küppers)

2. Gerhard Hüskes, ~23.09.1703 (sp: Peter Küppers, Oemeltgen Hüskes)

3. Leonhard Hüskes, ~19.09.1705 (sp: Peter Küppers, Katharina Box)

4. Mechtild Hüskes, ~25.04.1707 (sp: Johannes Hüskes, Katharina Coenen)

5. Katharina Hüskes, ~15.03.1709 (sp: Arnold Tüffers, Elisabeth Hüskes)

II c. Jan Küppers, ~27.01.1669, ∞ 12.01.1706 Kaldenkirchen/Ref. Church **Katharina Coenen**, christened Kaldenkirchen/Ref. Church:

1. Matthias Küppers III d., ~31.10.1706 (sp: Dirk Brouwers, Katharina Küppers)

2. Johannes Küppers, ~09.03.1708 (sp: Lambert Brouwers, Peter Küppers, Johanna Schremkes)

3. Johanna Küppers, ~24.04.1712 (sp: Dirk Hüskes, Agnes Schremkes, Agnes Brouwers)

4. Matthäus Küppers, ~24.03.1714 (sp: Wilhelm Schmasen, Gertrud Küppers)

II d. Peter Küppers, ~03.05.1674, ∞ 18.04.1700 Kaldenkirchen/Ref. Church **Johanna Strepers**, christened Kaldenkirchen/Ref. Church:

1. Wilhelmus Küppers, ~29.01.1701 (sp: Arnold Tüffers, Sibille Strepers)

2. Mechtild Küppers, ~23.13.1704 (sp: Dirk Hüskes, Agnes Strepers), unsure: ∞ 16.11.1732 **Henrich Bolten**, widower, christened Kaldenkirchen/Ref. Church:

   Magdalena Bolten, ~05.09.1740 (sp: Leonhard Bolten, Helena Küppers, Johann Schröers' wife); **Henrich Bolten**, widower ∞ 14.01.1742 Kaldenkirchen **Johanna Ewalds**, widow (Roman-Catholic)

3. Sibille Küppers, ~31.01.1706 (sp: Dirk Lensen, Katharina Coenen)

4. Gertrud Küppers, ~19.03.1709 (sp: Hendrik Bolten, Katharina Küppers)

III a. Helena Küpers, ~15.01.1698, ∞ 04.03.1725 Kaldenkirchen/Ref. Church **Jan Schröers**, christened:

1. Leonhard Schröers, ~05.01.1727 (sp: Jan Hasen, Maria Booms)

2. Maria Schröers, ~18.01.1728 (sp: Kornelius Schröers, Gertrud Küppers)

3. Johannes Schröers, ~23.01.1729 (sp: Peter Küppers, Katharina Baums)

4. Peter Schröers, ~26.03.1730 (sp: Hermannus Schröers, Elisabeth Küppers)

5. Maria Schröers, ~25.03.1732 (sp: Matthias Küppers, Margaretha Hoyer)

6. Agnes Schröers, ~17.01.1734 (sp: Henrich Schröers,

Eleonore Küppers)

7. Johannes Schröers, ~18.08.1737 (sp: Matthias Schröers, Gertrud Küppers, Johannes Hüskes' wife)

III b. Mechtild Küppers, ~29.01.1701, ∞ 15.10.1724 Kaldenkirchen/Ref. Church **Jan Hasen**, christened Kaldenkirchen/Ref. Church:

1. Petrus Hasen, ~07.09.1727 (sp: Hendrik Bolten, Hester Hasen)

2. Johanna Hasen, ~28.08.1729 (sp: Peter Küppers, Elisabeth Hasen)

3. Catharina Hasen, ~18.02.1731 (sp: Wilhelm Lappen, Katharina Coenen, Johann Küppers' widow)

4. Jacob Hasen, ~07.06.1733 (sp: Michael Hasen, Agnes Strepers, Frau des Peter Küppers), baptism by minister Laufs, ±10.05.1755 Kaldenkirchen/Ref. Church

5. Adelgunda Hasen, ~02.11.1738 (sp: missing)

6. Gertrud Hasen, ~23.10.1740 (sp: Bartholomäus Maubachs, Gertrud Küppers, Johannes Hüskes' wife), ±07. 06.1750 Kaldenkirchen/Ref. Church

7. Twins, ~29.08.1744, a) *Adamus Hasen*, b) *Wilhelmus Hasen* (sp: Michael Hasen, Matthias Küppers, Sibille Maubachs)

III c. Eleonora Küppers, ~04.03.1703, baptized:

Katharina Küppers, ~19.05.1726 Kaldenkirchen/ref. Gem., illegitimate (?), ∞ 24.09.1730 Kaldenkirchen/Ref. Church **Johannes Lappen** (E: **Wilhelm Lappen** ∞ **Maria Parollen**), christened Kaldenkirchen/Ref. Church:

1. Wilhelmus Lappen, ~25.10.1730 (sp: Peter Küppers, Maria Parollen)

2. Elisabeth Lappen, ~13.02.1732 (sp: Christian Lappen, Agneta Strepers)

3. Katharina Lappen, ~23.08.1733 (sp: Wilhelm Lappen, Gertrud Küppers)

4. Peter Lappen, ~13.02.1735 (sp: Matthias Küppers, Sibille Lappen called Maubachs)

5. Henricus Lappen, ~18.01.1737 (sp: Matthias Lappen, Helene Küppers)

6. Peter Lappen, ~05.01.1738 (sp: Peter Küppers, Matthias Lappen)

7. Henricus Lappen, ~11.10.1739 (sp: Henrich Bolten, Mrs Bachoven called Faber)

8. Agneta Lappen, ~08.09.1743 (sp: Johann Küppers, Johanna Streeraths)

III d. Matthias Küppers, ~31.10.1706 (sp: Dirk Brouwers, Katharina Küppers), ∞ 18.07.1734 Kaldenkirchen/ Ref. Church **Anna Mickenschreiber**, **Gerhard Hüskes'** widow, christened:

1. Maria Agnes Küppers, ~01.04.1735 Kaldenkirchen/ Ref. Church (sp: Josef Laufs, minister at Rheydt, Katharina Coenen, Agnes Hüskes called Strepers), ±25.05. 1750 Kaldenkirchen/Ref. Church

2. Johannes Gerhardus Küppers, ~01.07.1738 Kaldenkirchen/Ref. Church (sp: Florens Peter Dürselen, cand. theol., Peter Weyer, Maria Strepers, Matthias Mickenschreiber's wife, Margaretha Catharina Mickenschreiber, Odenkirchen), ±04.04.1740 Kaldenkirchen/Ref. Church

Family Tree Kürlis
oath of allegiance Kaldenkirchen 1666: Henrich Kürlis

I. Jan Kürlis ∞ **N.N.**, christened:
1. Heinrich Kürlis II a., †before marriage of daughter Maria
2. Peter Kürlis II b.,
3. Rolf Kürlis II c.

II a. Heinrich Kürlis, †before marriage of daughter Maria, ∞ **N.N.**, christened Waldniel/ref. Gem.:
1. Johan Kürlis III a.
unsure *2. Peter Kürlis*, ~17.11.1612 together with others, Waldniel/Ref. Church
unsure *3. Lenz Arnold Kürlis*, ~19.02.1617 (sp: Jan Scherrens ?, Katharina, Arnold Dahmens' daughter)
4. Peter Kürlis, ~08.08.1621 (sp: Jan Vruen ?, Franz the baker, Petronella, Arnold Dahmens' daughter)
5. Maria Kürlis III b., ~24.09.1622 (sp: Peter Adams, Matthias Wirtz)

II b. Peter Kürlis, ∞ **N.N.**, christened:
Tochter, ~26.04.1617 Waldniel/Ref. Church

II c. Rolf Kürlis ∞ **Mechtild Küppers**, christened:
1. Matthäus Kürlis III c., 09.05.1655 communicant, Waldniel/Ref. Church
2. Jan Kürlis III d.
3. Peter Kürlis III e.

III a. Johan Kürlis, ∞ 01.06.1636 Waldniel/Ref. Church **Mechtild Beckers**, christened Waldniel/Ref. Church:
1. Elisabeth Kürlis, before Easter 1659 communicant
2. Henrich Kürlis IV a., before Pentecost 1660 communicant
3. Margarete Kürlis, ~02.02.1651
4. Matthias Kürlis, Pentecost 1667 communicant
5. Petrus Kürlis IV b., ~29.09.1652, Good Friday 1669 communicant, moved to Krefeld in 1681/82, emigrated to Pennsylvania in 1683
6. Gertrud Kürlis, ~13.02.1656
Johann Kürlis, widower, ∞ 01.06.1663 Waldniel/Ref. Church **Sibylla Breuers** (?), ~Geilenkirchen (?) (f: **Abraham Breuers**, Geilenkirchen); **Sybille Breuers**, widow

of **Johan Kürlis** ∞ 2d marriage 18.07.1666 Waldniel/Ref. Church **Lenz Küppers**, widower

III b. Maria Kürlis, ~24.09.1622 Waldniel/Ref. Church, ∞ 14.06.1652 Waldniel/Ref. Church **Herman Wirtz** (f: **Matthias Wirtz**)

III c. Matthäus Kürlis, 09.05.1655 communicant, Waldniel/Ref. Church, ∞ **N.N.**, christened Waldniel/Ref. Church:
1. Rudolf Kürlis, ~23.03.1663
2. Mechtild Kürlis, ~11.05.1664
3. Maria Kürlis, ~01.08.1666
4. Rudolf Kürlis, ~28.10.1668 (sp: Peter Kürlis, Jan Kürlis, Löcken ? Kürlis, his brothers and sisters)
5. Henrich Kürlis, ~25.12.1671 (sp: Jan Hupertz, Elisabeth Sonnemans, Jan Kürlis' wife)

III d. Jan Kürlis, ∞ 14.01.1670, Waldniel/Ref. Church **Elisabeth Sonnemans**, 01.09.1658 communicant, Waldniel/Ref. Church (p: **Jacob Sonnemans** ∞ **Sybille Brauers**), christened Waldniel/Ref. Church:
1. Mechtild Kürlis, ~21.12.1670 (sp: Lenz Küppers, Katharina Küppers/widow Botsch auf Schom, Beth Schmälings von Doesberg)
2. Rudolf Kürlis IV c., ~07.08.1672 (sp: Peter Küppers, Matthias Horren, Katharina Dahmen ?, Mevrouw Kipshoven zum Ruderberg ?)
3. Elisabeth Kürlis, ~14.10.1673 (sp: Peter Kürlis, Katharina Ingenhoven, Bart im Kirspel Leut, Kaldenkirchen)
4. Katharina Kürlis, ~07.02.1677 (sp: Engelbert von Bucholtz, Lucken auffm Schum)
5. Sibille Kürlis, ~04.04.1679 (sp: Leonhard Breckels ?, Kleingladbach, Doctor of Laws, absent due to wartime, Helene Engels, Peter Kürlis' wife, in lieu of his cousin Matthäus Fetten)

III e. Peter Kürlis, ∞ 19.07.1677 Waldniel/Ref. Church **Helene Coenen**, widow of **N. Engels** ?), christened Waldniel/Ref. Church:
1. Mechtild Kürlis, ~24.07.1678 (sp: Jan Roelen in lieu of Henrich Coenen von Schwanenberg, Sybilla Brauers, Lenz Küppers' wife)
2. Mechtild Kürlis, ~01.10.1679 (sp: Johannes Heilger Engels, Matthäus Jöriskes, Katharina Coertges)
3. Rudolf Kürlis, ~01.01.1681 (sp: Adam Dahmen, Matthias Kürlis, Elisabeth Kürlis)

IV a. Henrich Kürlis, before Pentecost 1660 communicant, ∞ Kaldenkirchen/Ref. Church **Anna Doors** (p: **Matthias Doors** ∞ **Agnes N.**, see family tree Doors), christened Kaldenkirchen/Ref. Church:
1. Metgen Kürlis, ~09.03.1664 (sp: Peter Doors, Agnes Doors, Katharina Coenen), ∞ **Henderik Jansen van Acken**, lived at Krefeld since 1675, christened Kaldenkir-

chen/Ref. Church:
1. *Claes van Acken*
2. *Annecken van Acken*
3. *Willem van Acken*
4. *Agneta van Acken*
5. *Henrich van Acken*
6. *Elisabeth van Acken*
2. *Jan Kürlis*, ~05.12.1666, †09.03.1669

IV b. Petrus Kürlis, ~29.09.1652, emigrated to Pennsylvania in 1683, ∞ 17.03.1675, Kaldenkirchen/Ref. Church **Elisabeth Doors** Kaldenkirchen (p: **Matthias Doors** ∞ **Agnes N.**, see family tree Doors), christened among others Kaldenkirchen/Ref. Church:
1. *Mechtild Kürlis*, ~27.12.1675 (sp: Matthias Kürlis, Anna Doors, Gertrud Kürlis)
2. *Johannes Kürlis*, ~03.02.1677 (sp: Jan Olmis, Anna Doors)
3. *Mechtild Kürlis*, ~27.08.1679 (sp: Reiner Doors, Katharina Brouwers, Mechtild Kürlis)
4. *Agnes Kürlis*, ~05.01.1681 (sp: Jan Sieben, Gertrud Doors)
5. *Mechtild Kürlis*, ~22.11.1682, Krefeld/Ref. Church
6. *Martha Kürlis*, *about 1684 Philadelphia, †about 1716 Germantown, ∞ 20.08.1699 **Thomas Potts** (p: **Thomas Potts**, ~about 1658 Lianidloes, Wales, GB; p: **Thomas Potts**, ~about 1632, ∞ **Elizabeth N.**), christened:
   John Potts, *about 1710 Germantown, †06.06.1768 Pottstown, Montgomery Co., Pa, ∞ 11.04.1734 Coventry, Chester Co., Pa **Ruth Savage**, *about 1715, christened:
      Rebecca Grace Potts, *about 1755 Pottsgrove, †04.02.1797 Philadelphia, ∞ **Benjamin Duffield**
7. *Matthias Kürlis*, *Germantown

IV c. Rudolf Kürlis, ~07.08.1672, ∞ 02.11.1707, Waldniel/Ref. Church **Margarete Stümpges**, *at Rheydt (p: **Vit Stümpges** ∞ **Merken Drischer**, both from Rheydt), christened Waldniel/Ref. Church:
1. *Elisabeth Kürlis*, ~02.09.1708 (sp: Johann Kürlis, Christoffel Uphoven, Maria von den Drieß, N. Kürlis)
2. *David Kürlis Va.*, ~19.03.1710 (sp: Vit Stümpges, Michael Reiners, Mechtild Kürlis)
3. *Maria Kürlis*, ~22.05.1712 (sp: Dahm Drießen, Henrich D., Katharina Weydmans, Anna Stümpges)
4. *Johannes Kürlis V b.*, ~26.08.1714 (sp: Jan Neuenhaus, Anton Stümpges, Mechtild Kürlis)
5. *Sibilla Kürlis*, ~11.10.1716 (sp: Peter Stümpges, Maria Wirtz, Geertgen Bescheinen ?)
6. *Peter Kürlis V c.*
7. *Johan Wilhelm Kürlis*, ~05.12.1723 (sp: Arnold Hollender, Eva Köhnen)

V a. David Kürlis, ~19.03.1710, ∞ **Katharina Geuen**, christened:

1. *Rudolphus Kürlis VI a.*, ~01.01.1744 Waldniel/Ref. Church (sp: Mattheus Horn, Elisabeth Cürlis)
2. *Hermannus Kürlis VI b.*, ~27.09.1750, Waldniel/Ref. Church (sp: David Kürlis, Johannes Wirtz, Agneta Hermans)

V b. Johannes Kürlis, ~26.08.1714 ∞ **Elisabeth Essers**, christened Waldniel/Ref. Church:
Henricus Kürlis VI b., ~25.12.1743 (sp: David Kürlis, Katharina Geuen)

V c. Peter Kürlis ∞ **Gerdruth Hermans**, christened Waldniel/Ref. Church:
1. *Rudolphus Kürlis VI c.*, ~12.12.1745 (sp: Wilhelmus Hermans, Johannes Hermans, Gertrud Stümpges)
2. *Gertrud Kürlis*, ~21.11.1746 (sp: David Kürlis, Gertrud Hermans)
3. *Herman Kürlis VI d.*, ~11.02.1748 (sp: Matthias Hermans, Elisabeth Kürlis)
4. *Hermannus Kürlis*, ~25.07.1751 (sp: Johannes Kürlis, Sibilla Hermans)
5. *David Kürlis*, ~03.03.1753 (sp: Rudolphus Kürlis, Katharina Geuen)
6. *Abraham Kürlis*, ~05.02.1754 (sp: Abraham Moll, minister at Waldniel, Elisabeth Kürlis)
7. *Johannes Kürlis VI e.*, ~23.06.1757 (sp: Johannes Arnoldus Willer/Wyler, Maria Schmitz)

VI a. Rudolphus Kürlis, ~01.01.1744 Waldniel/Ref. Church, ∞ Waldniel/Ref. Church **Sibilla Kürlis**, christened Waldniel/Ref. Church:
1. *David Kürlis*, ~15.02.1781 (sp: Christian Bohnen, Gertrud Hermans)
2. *Peter Kürlis*, ~28.09.1782 (sp: Peter Kürlis, Sibilla Horn née Kürlis)
3. *Katharina Gertrud Kürlis*, ~13.10.1784 (sp: Rudolf Kürlis, Peters Sohn, Gertraud Hasten née Kürlis)
4. *Sibilla Gertrud Kürlis*, ~28.02.1787, addition obiit, died (sp: Hermann Kürlis, Maria Jansen née Kürlis, Margareta Hollender née Wolters)
5. *Sibilla Gertrud Kürlis*, ~31.05.1789 (sp: members of the consistorium)

VI b. Henricus Kürlis, ~25.12.1743 Waldniel/Ref. Church (sp: David Kürlis, Catharina Geuen), ∞ Süchteln/Ref. Church **Maria Margarete Traudin(g)/Traude**, ~Süchteln (?), christened Waldniel/Ref. Church:
1. *Johann Henrich Kürlis*, ~14.05.1772 (sp: Johann Kürlis, Margarete Essers)
2. *Magdalena Elisabeth Kürlis*, ~26.09.1773 (sp: Christian Essers, Magdalena Ophoven)
3. *Katharina Gertrud Kürlis*, ~08.10.1775 (sp: Maria Katharina Kürlis, Rudolf Langen)
4. *Rudolf Kürlis*, ~01.10.1777 (sp: Rudolf Kürlis, Maria Kürlis)

VI c. Rudolphus Kürlis, ~12.12.1745, ∞ Odenkirchen/Ref. Church **Sibilla Essers**, †before marriage of daughter Gertrud, christened Waldniel/Ref. Church:
1. Gertrudis Kürlis, ~12.04.1772 (sp: Hermann Essers, Gertrud Hermans, Odenkirchen, Hermann Essers, Odenkirchen, Gertrud Hermans, Waldniel), ∞ 08.07. 1798 Waldniel/Ref. Church **Winand Heimans** (p: **Petrus Heimans ∞ Cäcilia Greifenberg**, Lövenich)
2. Agnes Kürlis, ~28.01.1775 (sp: Gerhardus Schrey, Gertrud Kürlis)
3. Anna Elisabeth Kürlis, ~02. [?] 06.1778 (sp: Hermann Kürlis, Sophia Sieben)
4. Peter Kürlis, ~04.03.1781 (sp: Abraham Kürlis, Agnes Essers)
5. Agneta Kürlis, ~15.02.1784 (sp: Gerhard Schrey, Sibilla Kürlis)
Rudolf Kürlis, Witwer ∞ 23.06.1786 Waldniel/Ref. Church **Adriana Schmits**, *Kelzenberg

VI d. Hermannus Kürlis, ~25.07.1751 (sp: Johannes Kürlis, Sibilla Hermans), ∞ Waldniel/Ref. Church **Anna Katherina Holt**, christened Wadniel/Ref. Church:
1. Peter Kürlis, ~30.11.1786 (sp: Peter Kürlis)
2. Peter Henrich Kürlis, ~09.08.1789 (sp: missing)

VI e. Johannes Kürlis, ~23.06.1757, ∞ 30.11.1783, Waldniel/Ref. Church **Gerdrut Meinen**, ~Hückelhoven (p: **Johannes Meynen ∞ Margaretha Glaßer**)

Family Tree Küsters

population record Kaldenkirchen 1473/75: Jenniken Custer
population record Kaldenkirchen 1624/26: Custers Halffman, Lienard Küsters, der Custer
oath of allegiance 1666: Lambert Custers, Custers Lens

I. Ololus (?) **Küsters ∞ N.N.**, christened Kaldenkirchen/Roman-Catholic Church:
Reinhard Küsters **II.**

II. Reinhard Küsters ∞ 1598 N.N., *about 1542 Kaldenkirchen, †03.07.1616 Kaldenkirchen, christened Kaldenkirchen/Roman-Catholic Church:
Johannes Küsters **III.**, *1576, †08.04.1650

III. Johannes Küsters, *about 1576 Kaldenkirchen, †08.04.1650 Kaldenkirchen, ∞ **Walburgis N. Tieses**, christened Kaldenkirchen/Roman-Catholic Church:
1. Judith Küsters, *before 1609, ∞ 24.10.1621 **Hein Goetzen**
2. Mechtild Küsters, *before 1609, ∞ 17.02.1635 **Ruth (Rudolf ?) Lehens**
3. Hermanus Küsters, *about 1603, †07.04.1648, ∞ 1627 **Christina Tieses**

4. Arnold Küsters IV., *about 1606 Kaldenkirchen, †29.11. 1679 ib.
5. Lambertin Küsters, ~20.09.1609, ∞ 21.05.1633 **Itgen Benges**
6. Godefried Küsters, ~17.10.1613
7. Maria Küsters, ~21.04.1615, †23.09.1623
8. Reiner Küsters, *18.05.1618
9. Katharina Küsters, ~11.08.1619, †12.06.1635

IV. Arnold Küsters, *1606 Kaldenkirchen, †24.11.1679 Kaldenkirchen, ∞ 13.10.1629 Kaldenkirchen/Roman-Catholic Church **Katharina van Haren** (f: **Christoph van Haren**), *between 1606 und 1610, †24.01.1679 Kaldenkirchen, christened Kaldenkirchen/Roman-Catholic Church:
1. Maria Küsters, ~21.07.1630
2. Johannes Küsters, ~09.05.1632
3. Henrich Küsters, ~26.05.1635
4. Katharina Küsters, ~17.05.1637
5. Matthias Küsters, ~June 1640, ∞ 02.10.1661 **Cornelia N.**
6. Lambertus Küsters, ~07.09.1642, ∞ **Elske N.**
7. Paulus Küsters V., *1644, †18.07.1708 Germantown
8. N. Küsters, *about 1646
9. Luzia Küsters, ~14.02.1649, †31.03.1649

V. Paulus Küsters, *1644, ∞ 16.10.1668 Kaldenkirchen/Ref. Church **Gertrud Doors** (p: **Matthias Doors ∞ Agnes Hues/Hüskes** (?), see family tree Doors), Küsters emigrated to Germantown in 1691/93, christened:
1. Arnold Küsters VI a., ~09.06.1669 Kaldenkirchen/Ref. Church (sp: Stephan Steigh, Jan Strepers, Agnes, Matthias Küsters' wife), †Dec. 1739 Hannover Twp., Philadelphia Co., ±Manatawney Mennonite Cemetery
2. Johannes Küsters VI b., ~12.12.1670 Kaldenkirchen/Ref. Church (sp: Jan Hüskes, Agnes Doors), †before 11.10.1708 Germantown
3. Matthias Küsters, ~06.12.1671 Kaldenkirchen/Ref. Church (Matthias Doors, Jan Olmis, Elisabeth Doors), ∞ 06.11.1695 Krefeld/Ref. Church **Margaretha Hupps**, christened Krefeld/Ref. Church:
  1. Gerdruet Küsters, twin, ~10.12.1696 (sp: Paulus Custers, Theis Bosch, Gerdruet Dhors, Margaretha Hupps), ∞ 05.10.1717 Krefeld/Ref. Church **Peter Switzers**, Herdt
  2. Agnes Küsters, twin, ~10.12.1696 (sp: Margaretha Hupps, Margaretha Schmed, Anna Hollemans)
  3. Agnes Küsters, ~31.05.1699
  4. Anna Küsters, ~27.12.1718, ∞ 14.01.1742 Krefeld/Ref. Church **Henrich Schlims**
  5. Peter Küsters, ~05.02.1723
  6. Peter Küsters, ~30.06.1724, †09.07.1773 Krefeld, ∞ 04.04.1751 Krefeld/Ref. Church **Margaretha Schmitz**

4. *Rainer Küsters*, ~02.12.1674 Kaldenkirchen/Ref. Church (sp: Agnes Doors, Joachim Hüskes, Elisabeth Doors)
5. *Elisabeth Küsters*, not christened at Kaldenkirchen
6. *Anna Küsters*, ~26.12.1677 Kaldenkirchen/Ref. Church
7. *Hermann Streypers* [sic] *Küsters* **VI c.**, ~19.10.1681 Krefeld, †01.02.1760 Skippack, Montgomery Co.
8. *Katharina Küsters*, ~09.03.1687 Kaldenkirchen/Ref. Church (sp: Kornelius Huben, Katharina Hüskes)
9. *Eva Küsters* **VI d.**, †after 1748
10. *Margaret Küsters* **VI e.**, *about 1690

VI a. Arnold Küsters, ~09.06.1669 Kaldenkirchen, profession: mason, ∞ 1st marriage 24.06.1691 Krefeld/Ref. Church **Gertrud Conrats**, Krefeld, christened:
1. *Konrad Custer*, *1695, †1772 Rockinham Co, Va, ∞ 1st marriage **Susannah Adams** (p: **Richard Adams** ∞ **Gertien N.**), christened:
    1. *Charity Custer*
    2. *Arnold Custer*
    3. *Richard Custer*
    4. *William Custer*
    5. *Paul Custer*
    6. *Nicholas Custer*
    7. *Conrad Custer*
    8. *Joseph Custer*
∞ 2d marriage (?) **Margaret Morris**
2. *Katharine Custer*, *1700, ∞ **John Jenkins**
3. *George Custard*, ~1704 Germantown, †01.11.1755 (killed by Indians) Northhampton Co., Pa, ∞ 28.06.1731 **Mary Rhodes**, christened:
    1. *John Custer*
    2. *Rebecca Custer*
    3. *Samuel Custer*, ∞ **Catherine Jacob** (p: **George Jürgen Jacobs**, MG ∞ **Gertrud Priers** MG/Krefeld)
    4. *Mary Custer*
    5. *Hannah Custer*
    6. *George Custer*
    7. *Joseph Custer*
    8. *Martha Custer*
4. *Nicholas Custer*, *04.012.1706, †10.12.1784 Limerick Twp., Phildelphia Co., ∞ about 1732 **Susannah Margaretha Hoppin/Hoppe**
5. *Paul Custer*, *1710 Germantown, †10.11.1783, ∞ 1740 **Sarah Bell**, christened:
    1. *Jonathan Custer*
    2. *William Custer*
    3. *George Custer*
    4. *Nicholas Custer*
Arnold Küsters ∞ 2d marriage **Rebecca N.**, christened:
6. *Hannah Custer*, *about 1715
7. *Arnold Custer*, *1720, ∞ **Barbara N.**
8. *Dorothy Custer*, *1724, ∞ 08.02.1744 Philadelphia/First Presbyterian Church **Daniel Tool**

VI b. Johannes Küsters, ~12.10.1670 Kaldenkirchen, ∞ 30.08.1692 Abington Mo. Mtg. **Elizabeth Cassel**, christened:
1. *John Custer*, *19.08.1693 Bristol, †Febr. or March 1760 Philadelphia, ∞ 05.11.1717 **Elizabeth Hood**
2. *Margaret Custer*, *23.10.1694 Germantown, ∞ 1st marriage 07.03.1712 Abington Mo. Mtg. **John Lucken**, ∞ 2d marriage 07.04.1738 Abington Mo. Mtg. **Thomas Rose**
3. *Rynier Custer*, *05.08.1696 Germantown, †1770 Philadelphia Co., ∞ 11.04.1718 **Anne Hewitt**
4. *Mary Custer*, *01.03.1699/00, †24.04.1758 Bucks Co., Pa, ∞ April 1720 **William Michener** (p: **John Michener** ∞ **Sarah Moore**), christened:
    Mordecai Michener, ~30.05.1723 Plumpstead Twp. Bucks Co., Pa, †22.09.1795 Grove Mtg. House, Chester Co., Pa
5. *Hermanus Custer*, *13.01.1703, ∞ 1733 **Anne Large**
6. *Paul Custer*, *about 1706, †about 1745-50, ∞ 28.11.1730 **Ruth Kitchen**
7. *Peter Custer*, *about 1708, †14.05.1759 Hunterdon, N.J., ∞ 24.12.1733 **Ann Coar**
8. *Arnold Custer*
9. *Abagail Custer*
10. *Samuel Custer*
11. *Dorothy Custer*
12. *Charity Custer*

VI c. Hermann Streypers Küsters, ~19.10.1681 Krefeld, †01.02.1760 Skippack, Montgomery Co., ∞ 1706 **Isabella/Civilla Conrad** (V: **Peter Conrad**), †Feb. 1760 christened:
1. *Peter Custer* **VII a.**, *1709, †Oct. 1769 Worcester, Montgomery Co., Pa
2. *Gertrude Custer*, *1711, ∞ 1739 **Henry Umsted/Umstat**, †1788
3. *Margaret Custer*, *1713, ∞ 1735 **Geshart Bohrs**, *Holland, †01.05.1797 on sea
4. *Modlen Custer*, *1714, ∞ **Henry Tyson**
5. *John Custer* **VII b.**, *1715, †1794 Montgomery Co., Pa
6. *Rebecca Custer*, *1718, †1807, ∞ before 1748 **Henry Pennebacker/Pennebaker**
7. *Paul Custer* **VII c.**, *1720, †Febr. 1795 Montgomery Co., Pa, ∞ about 1759 **Gertrude Johnson**

VI d. Eva Custer ∞ 1713 **Godschalk Hermans Godschalk**
    E: **Jakob Godschalk**, *about 1666 Goch, ~07.04.1686 Goch/menn. Gem. (f: **Gottschalck Theunissen**, see family tree Kunders), ∞ 20.02.1689 **Adelheid Simons Hermans** (p: **Herman Davids** ∞ **Katharina Simons**), christened:
1. *Gottschalk Hermans Godschalk*, *1693 Goch, †before 26.09.1748 Towamencin Twp., Montgomery

Co., Pa, ∞ 1713 **Eva Custer**

2. John Hermans Godschalk, *1695 Goch, †Nov. 1759, ∞ **Dorothy Kolb**

3. Magdalena Hermans Godschalk, *1696 Goch, †before 1760 Pa, ∞ about 1720 **William Colley Nash**, *24.11.1694, †1760

4. Herman Hermans Godschalk, *1698 Goch, †1785 Doylestone, Bucks Co., Pa, ∞ about 1720 **Agnes Johnson** (p: **Klaus Johnson** ∞ **Katherine Conrad**)

5. Anna Hermans Godschalk, *1706 Goch, †1765, ∞ **Peter Conrad Custer** (p: **Herman Streypers Custer** ∞ **Isabella Cäcilia Conrads**) christened Towamencin Twp., Montgomery Co., Pa:

1. Jacob Godschalk, †1798, ∞ **Helena Shrager** (p: **Gerhard Shrager** ∞ **Janicken Hendriks**)

2. William Godschalk, †1781, ∞ **Gertrude Hunsicker**

3. Syken Godschalk, †vor 1769, ∞ **Goshen Shrager**, christened:

    1. Garrett Shrager
    2. Jacob Shrager
    3. Eva G. Shrager
    4. Margaret Shrager

4. Mary Godschalk, ∞ **John Johnson**, lived at Horsham Twp., Montgomery Co.

5. Catherine Godschalk, unmarried, lived at Towamencin Twp., Montgomery Co.

6. Margaret Godschalk, ∞ **Henry Cassel** (f: **Hupert Cassel**, Skippack)

7. Garrett Godschalk, †1769, ∞ **Edia Bohrs**, cousin

8. Janicken Godschalk, unmarried, lived at Towamencin Twp., Montgomery Co.

9. Magdalena Godschalk, ∞ **John Hendricks**

10. Gertrude Godschalk, ∞ **Matthias Hendricks**, lived Bucks Co.

11. John Godschalk, *22.07.1737, Pa, ∞ **Christiana Hendricks**

12. Anna Godschalk, *Pa, ∞ **Melchior Yoder**

13. Eva Godschalk, ∞ **Jacob Schwartz**, Bucks Co.

14. Peter Godschalk, ∞ **Levina Haldeman**

VI e. Margaret Küsters, *about 1690, ∞ about 1708 **Cornelius De Weese**, christened:

1. John/Johannes De Weese, ~29.05.1710 Skippack, lived at Heidelberg Twp., Berks Co.

2. Catrina De Weese, ~04.09.1711 Skippack

3. Garret De Weese, *about 1713, ∞ 1st marriage **Mary N.**, ∞ 2d marriage 26.12.1752 **Elizabeth Jones**, lived Robeson Twp, Berks Co.

4. William De Weese, ∞ 03.11.1743 **Rachel Huste**

5. Cornelius De Weese, ∞ **Margaret Richards**

6. Samuel De Weese, †1777, ∞ **Elizabeth N.**

VII a. Peter Custer, *1709, ∞ about 1728 **Anna Godschalk**, †28.09.1768

p: **Jakob Godschalk**, *1670 Goch, †May 1763, ∞ 20.02.1689 **Adelheid Simons Hermans** (p: **Herman Davids** ∞ **Katharina Simons**), *1667 Goch, †1709 christened:

1. Herman Custer **VIII a.**, *26.02.1728, †26.01.1800

2. Jacob Custer **VIII b.**, *14.10.1731, †14.12.1804 Skippack, Montgomery Co., Pa

3. Else Custer, *1733, ∞ **Balthasar Starne/Stern**

4. John Custer **VIII c.**, *1735 Worcester, Montgomery Co., Pa, †22.02.1794 Whitpane Twp., Montgomery Co.

5. Paul Custer **VIII d.**, *1738, †30.07.1800

VII b. John Custer, *1715, †1794 Montgomery Co., Pa, ∞ 1st marriage **Ester Johnson**, christened:

    Mary Custer, *09.10.1730, †1794 Chester Co., Pa, ∞ **Matthias Penneypacker**

∞ 2d marriage 09.08.1785 Montgomery Co. **Catharine Miller**

VII c. Paul Custer, *1720, ∞ 1759 **Gertrude Johnson**, christened:

1. John Custer, *01.06.1760, †22.10.1824, ∞ 1st marriage 04.04.1788 **Catherine Freed**, ∞ 2d marriage 27.09.1791 **Barbara Metz**

2. Benjamin Custer, *17.04.1763, †03.01.1832, ∞ **Maria Schneider**

3. Peter Custer, *1765, †1816

4. Elizabeth Custer, *1768

5. Sybella Custer, *1770

6. Magdalena Custer, *1772

7. Abraham Custer, *02.04.1774, †Dec. 1836, ∞ 24.12.1808 **Katharina Metz**, christened:

    1. Peter Custer
    2. Sybilla Custer
    3. Elizabeth Custer
    4. Magdalena/Helene Custer
    5. John Custer

8. Herman Custer, *1780

VIII a. Herman Custer, *26.02.1728, †26.01.1800, ∞ **Eva van Fossen**, christened:

1. Catherine Custer, *16.11.1756, †April 1840

2. Peter Custer, *04.11.1760, †1799

3. Anna Custer, *03.06.1762, †11.09.1839

4. Henry Custer, *03.09.1767, †08.08.1837

5. Levi Custer, *08.03.1770, †21.06.1845

6. Mary "Polly" Custer, *07.05.1772, †Aug. 1844

7. Cornelius Custer, *Nov. 1774, †08.07.1884

VIII b. Jacob Custer, *14.10.1731, †14.12.1804 Skippack, Montgomery Co., Pa, ∞ **Elizabeth van Fossen**, *14.06.1740, †19.11.1819

p: **Adam van Fossen**, *Worcester, Montgomery Co., Pa, †1771 ib., ∞ **Catherine N.**, †after 1765 Worcester, Montgomery C., Pa

    p: **Arnold van Vossen** ∞ 27.03.1690 Goch/Menn. Church *Maria Arents van Acken* (see family tree van Acken), *about 1664/65, moves to Goch 19.03.1690, christened (all children born between 1690 and 1720):
      1. Adam van Vossen
      2. Marieke van Vossen
      3. Cunard van Vossen, †before June 1777 Perkiomen Area, Pa, ∞ between 1711 and 1750 **Ankin Bon**
      4. John van Vossen, ∞ **Elizabeth Bon**
      5. Leonhard van Vossen
      6. Arnold van Vossen
baptized:
1. Peter Custer, *20.11.1761 Skippack, Montgomery Co., Pa, †27.04.1832, ∞ 1788 **Rebecca Vanderslice**, christened:
    1. Jacob Custer
    2. Elizabeth Custer
    3. Samuel Custer
    4. Anna Custer
    5. Anthony Custer
2. Samuel Custer, *1764, †01.11.1822
3. Joseph Custer, *1766, †10.09.1822
4. Catherine Custer, *1768
5. Mary Custer, *1770
6. Rebecca Custer, *1772
7. Anna Custer, *29.03.1775
8. Jacob Custer, *15.08.1778

VIII c. John Custer, *1735 Worcester, Montgomery Co., Pa, ∞ **Sarah N.**, christened:
1. John Custer, *1780, †1818
2. Paul Custer, *1784, †1832
3. Jacob Custer, *1786, †1832 Whitpane Twp., Montgomery Co., Pa
4. Jacob Custer?, *1787, †Sept. 1813 Philadelphia
5. Mary Custer, †1818
6. Rebecca Custer

VIII d. Paul Custer, *1738, †30.07.1800, ∞ **Elizabeth**, christened:
1. Mary "Polly" Custer, *1761
2. Anna Custer, *1763
3. John Custer, *1764, †27.12.1847 Montgomery Co., Pa
4. Susanna Custer, *1765, †1805
5. Elizabeth Custer, *1767, †18.10.1822 Derry Twp., Mifflin Co., Pa
6. Peter Custer, *02.02.1771, †24.07.1829
7. Jonas Custer, *20.01.1774, †07.12.1854 Montgomery Co., Pa
8. Sarah Custer, *1787 (?)

Family Tree Lenssen

population record Kaldenkirchen 1571: Sibille Lenssen
population record Kaldenkirchen 1624/26: Henrich Lenssen

Matthias Lenssen (f: **Lens Hanssen**?) ∞ 1st marriage **Katharina N.**, christened Kaldenkirchen/Ref. Church:
1. Peter Lenssen, ~09.02.1676 (sp: Henrich Bötels, Elisabeth Lenssen)
Matthias Lenssen, Witwer ∞ 2d marriage 31.03.1679 Kaldenkirchen/Ref. Church **Jenneken Schrembges**, christened Kaldenkirchen/Ref. Church:
2. Dirk Lenssen, ~29.05.1680 (sp: Lens Hansen, Dirk Bötels, Katharina Brouwers)
3. Katharina Lenssen, ~15.03.1682 (sp: Petronella Bötels, Lens Hanssen)
4. Jan Lenssen, ~03.03.1684 (sp: Peter Sieben, Mechtild Petermans)
5. Peter Lenssen, ~12.05.1686 (sp: Matthias Jütgens, Adelgunde Tüffers)
6. Matthias Lenssen, ~19.07.1688 (sp: Daem Hasen, Peter Küppers, Helene Strepers)
7. Leonhard Lenssen, ~19.03.1692 (sp: Jan Küppers, Gertrud Schrembges)
8. Elisabeth Lenssen, ~08.11.1699 (sp: Wilhelm Lappen, Katharina Coenen)

Family Tree Mickenschreiber

I. Matthias Mickenschreiber, Odenkirchen, ±17.11.1762, Kaldenkirchen/Ref. Church, ±in church, ∞ 15.11.1725 Kaldenkirchen/ref. Gem. **Anna Maria Strepers**, ~04.11.1696, †17.07.1763, ±in church, christened Kaldenkirchen/Ref. Church:

1. Maria Agnes Mickenschreiber, ~11.08.1726 (sp: Hermannus Mickenschreiber, Agnes Köeltgens, Elisabeth Olmis)
2. Anna Magdalena Mickenschreiber, ~11.01.1728 (sp: Bernhardus Hollender, Kunigunde Mickenschreiber)
3. Peter Hendrich Mickenschreiber II., *12.09.1730, ~17.09.1730 (sp: Johannes Quast, Agnes Strepers), †11.10.1788, ±15.10.1788 in church
4. Maria Elisabeth Mickenschreiber, ~16.12.1731 (sp: Peter Strepers, Elisabeth Olmis, Anna Mickenschreiber)
5. Hermanus Mickenschreiber, ~14.06.1734 Kaldenkirchen/Ref. Church (sp: Johann Laufs, minister at Rheydt, Peter Sieben, Elisabeth Strepers, Johannes Christoph Ringels' wife), ±28.12.1757 Kaldenkirchen/Ref. Church

II. Peter Hendrich Mickenschreiber, *12.09.1730, ∞ 1st marriage 26.06.1754 Hückelhoven **Johanna Mechtild Königs** (p: **Jakobus Königs**, minister ∞ **Odilia Eli-**

sabeth Heiymans, Otzenrath), Ratheim, †09.05. 1759, ±13.05.1759, ∞ 2d marriage 28.09.1759 Jülich **Gertruda Thelen** (p: **Wolradt Ludwig Thelen**, †23.08. 1771 Rheydt, ∞ **Katharina Gertrud Überfeld**, Kirchhoven), †16.07.1770 Kaldenkirchen, ∞ 3d marriage 02.03.1771 Sittard **Anna Gertrud Dorpmans** (p: **Johann Henrich Dorpmans**† ∞ **Katharina Judith Ritsen**) Sittard, *um 1742, †16.11.1820 Kaldenkirchen,
christened in 1st marriage:

1. Matthias Jakobus Mickenschreiber, *06.04.1755, ~Hückelhoven (sp: Matthias Mickenschreiber, Jakobus Königs, Maximilian Königs, brother-in-law Heinrich Krüder, Agneta Hollender née Strepers, Odilia Elisabeth Heymans our mother), †01.12.1756, ±Kirchhof Ratheim

2. Anna Maria Sybilla Mickenschreiber, *23.09.1757, ~27.09.1757 Ratheim (sp: Bernhard Hollender, brother-in-law Hoesch, minister at Voerde, Johannes Moll, my mother and my sister [sister-in-law] at Doveren and my aunt at Gronau), †15.06.1763 Kaldenkirchen
christened in 2d marriage Kaldenkirchen/Ref. Church:

3. Katharina Odilia Gertrud Mickenschreiber, *18. 07.1760, ~21.07.1760 (sp: father-in-law Wolrad Ludwig Thelen, mother-in-law, mother at Ratheim), †26. 03.1761 Kaldenkirchen

4. Johanna Mechtild Cäcilia Mickenschreiber, *11. 02.1762, ~14.02.1762 (sp: cousin Peter Henricus Strepers, sister-in-law Cäcilia Thielen, Jülich), †14.03.1766, Kaldenkirchen, ±18.03.1766

5. Anna Maria Agneta Katharina Mickenschreiber, *22.12.1764, ~27.12.1764, (sp: father-in-law Wolrad Ludwig Thelen, Jülich, aunt Betram, Jülich, my mother [mother-in-law])

6. Susanna Katharina Gertrud Mickenschreiber, *13. 02.1769, ~14.02.1769 at home (Z: brother-in-law Lenßen, Rheydt, sister-in-law Susanna Katharina Thelen, Michael Hollender, Waldniel), †19.03.1773
christened in 3d marriage:

7. Matthias Bernardus Mickenschreiber, *02.03. 1772, ~03.03.1772 (sp: uncle Bernardus Hollender, mother-in-law Katharina Judith Dorpmans née Ritsen), †16.05. 1773 Kaldenkirchen, ±18.05.1773

8. Johann Hendrich Mickenschreiber, *05.09.1773 (sp: brother-in-law Johan Henrich Thelen, brother-in-law Johan Henrich Dorpmans, sister Allegunda Lüneschloß née Dorpmans)

9. Johan Friedrich Mickenschreiber, *20.11.1774, ~27.11.1774 (sp: brother-in-law von Bergen, Friedrich Gotthardt Dürselen, sister-in-law Maria Katharina Dorpmans, Sittard), †12.12.1777, ±15.12.1777

10. Peter Arnoldus Mickenschreiber, *19.08.1776, ~28.08.1776 (sp: cousin Arnoldus Hollender, sister-in-law Katharina Judith Dorpmans)

11. Johannes Fredericus Mickenschreiber, *02.04. 1778, ~Kaldenkirchen (sp: cousin Johann Mickenschrei-ber, Rotterdam, sister-in-law Cäcilia Lenßen, Rheydt)

12. Michael Matthias Mickenschreiber, twin, *29.12. 1780, ~Kaldenkirchen (sp: Michael Lenßen, mother-in-law, Sittard)

13. Albertus Hermannus Mickenschreiber, twin, *29.12.1780, ~Kaldenkirchen (sp: Albertus Schmasen, niece Lauffs)

14. Johann Wilhelm Mickenschreiber, *05.09.1783, ~07.09.1783 (sp: minister Kohl, cousin Johann Wilhelm Lenßen, Rheydt, Miss Mayer, sister of cousin von de Berg, Henberg/Lenberg ?), †21.05.1784, ±23.05.1784

Family Tree Schuren

population record Kaldenkirchen 1473/75: Jennisken Schuyren, Lenart Schuyren
population record Kaldenkirchen 1624/26: Merrigh in der schueren, Dierich auff schoer, Klein Jan schouren, Peterman schuren, Schouren

Hendrik Schuren ∞ **N.N.**, christened Kaldenkirchen/ Ref. Church:

1. Wilhelm Schuren, ~02.02.1689 (sp: Jan in der Elst, Katharina Werts)

2. Katharina Schuren, ~03.12.1699 (p: **Henrik Schuren** ∞ **Elisabeth Schuren**), (sp: Wilhelm Sieben, Elisabeth Schuren)

Jan Schuren ∞ 30.05.1665 Kaldenkirchen/Ref. Church **Ummel Schrembges**, christened Kaldenkirchen/Ref. Church:

1. Frederick Schuren, ~09.04.1666 (sp: Stephan Weerts, Gertrud Goetzens, Peter Schuren's wife)

2. Jan Schuren, ~12.02.1668 (sp: Wilhelm in der Elst, Reiner Weerts, Gertrud Schrembges), †28.02.1668

3. Jan Schuren, ~20.01.1669 (sp: Matthias Küppers, Henrik Sieben, Gertrud, Peter Schuren's wife), †24.01. 1669

4. Elisabeth Schuren, ~05.03.1673 (sp: Gerhard Steppen, Adelgunde Sieben)

5. Frederick Schuren, ~25.01.1682 (sp: Leonhard Haasen, Petronella Schuren)

6. Matthias Schuren, twin with Johanna, ~02.04.1684 (sp: Jan Werts, Wilhelm Schrembges, Petronella Werts, Gertrud in der Elst)

7. Johanna Schuren, twin with Matthias, ~02.04.1684 (sp: Jan Werts, Wilhelm Schrembges, Petronella Werts, Gertrud in der Elst)

Family Tree Siebel

I. Reinhard Siebel, ~about 1590 Elberfeld/Ref. Church, ±01.02.1668 ib., profession: merchant at market Markt of Elberfeld, ∞ 1st marriage 11.01.1617 **Maria Müller**, ~25.07.1593 Elberfeld/Ref. Church, ±03.06.1628 ib., ∞ 2d marriage 1630, Elberfeld/Ref. Church **Anna vom Stiepel**, ~18.11.1607 Elberfeld/Ref. Church, ±16.07. 1686, christened:
Abraham Siebel II., ~1643 Elberfeld/Ref. Church, ±20. 07.1717 ib., profession: merchant, 1703 grocer, councilor at Elberfeld

II. Abraham Siebel, ~1643 Elberfeld/Ref. Church, ∞ 1st marriage 25.02.1669 Elberfeld/Ref. Church **Mechtild Braus** (p: **Anton Braus**, ~12.12.1621 Elberfeld/Ref. Church, ±15. 03.1674 ib., citizen of Elberfeld, ∞ 09.08. 1649 Elberfeld/Ref. Church **Anna Katharina von Dülcken**, ~01.06. 1625 Elberfeld/Ref. Church, ±01.04. 1675 ib.), ∞ 2d marriage **Anna Hochstrassen**, ±04.07. 1722,
christened in 1st marriage:
1. *Anton Siebel* III., ~15.01.1670, Elberfeld/Ref. Church, ±03.06.1721, profession: merchant and councilor at Elberfeld, 1716 mayor, ∞ 1691 Elberfeld/Ref. Church **Anna Margareta von Carnap**, ~11.10.1671 Elberfeld/Ref. Church, ±12.01.1736 ib., christened:
    Abraham Siebel IV., *20.09.1707 Elberfeld, ~28.09. 1707 Elberfeld/Ref. Church, †28.01.1777, Elberfeld, ±01.02.1777 ib., profession: merchant at Elberfeld; 1747-1771 several times coucilor, 1754 proposed as mayor, 1745, 55 and 65 mayor, 1746, 56 and 66 judge

IV. Abraham Siebel, *20.09.1707 Elberfeld, ∞ **Maria Elisabeth Teschemacher**, widow **Ochsen**, ~12.08. 1703 Elberfeld/Ref. Church, ±22.12.1768 ib. (p: **Johann Peter Teschemacher**, *1662 Elberfeld, ±15.02.1748 ib., profession: merchant and yarn bleacher at Mirke near Elberfeld, ∞ 20.03.1695 Elberfeld/Ref. Church **Anna Katharina von Carnap**, ~09.05.1663 Elberfeld/Ref. Church), christened:
1. *Anna Maria Siebel*, ~23.01.1732 Elberfeld/Ref. Church, †22.01.1790 Elberfeld, ±26.01.1790 ib.
2. *Anna Margareta Siebel*, ~18.01.1734 Elberfeld/Ref. Church, †25.10.1819 Kaldenkirchen, ∞ 03.04.1753 **Friedrich Gotthard Dürselen**, widower (see family tree Dürselen)
3. *Abraham Siebel*, ~15.01.1738 Elberfeld/Ref. Church
4. *Anton Siebel*, ~21.11.1740 Elberfeld/Ref. Church, †05.01.1775 Elberfeld, ±10.01.1775 ib.

Family Tree Sieben

I. Peter Sieben, Brüggen, ∞ 22.05.1668 Bracht/Ref. Church **Adelgunde in der Elst**, Kaldenkirchen, christened Kaldenkirchen/Ref. Church:
1. *Maria Sieben*, ~24.01.1672 (sp: Wilhelm in der Elst, Katharina Nagels, Maria Schuren, both of Brüggen)
2. *Katharina Sieben*, ~02.11.1674 (sp: D. Petrus Buschmann, minister at Schlicker-Ewick, Katharina Baenen, Brüggen)
3. *Wilhelmus Sieben* II., ~27.06.1676 (sp: Johannes Graver, Brüggen, Maria Stephani, Slyck Ewigh), ±01.05. 1729 Kaldenkirchen/Ref. Church, profession: teacher at Kaldenkirchen
4. *Michael Sieben*, ~11.12.1678 (sp: Jan Sieben, Jan in der Elst, Petronella Schuren)
5. *Katharina Sieben*, ~14.09.1680 (sp: Gerhard Steppen, Miss Welters), ±16.11.1737 Kaldenkirchen/Ref. Church
6. *Michael Sieben*, ~04.06.1684 (sp: Jan Sieben, Reiner Weerts, Elisabeth Schuren)
7. *Elisabeth Sieben*, ~21.08.1689 (sp: Hendrich Schuren, Agnes Sieben, Katharina in der Elst)

II. Wilhelmus Sieben, ~27.06.1676, ∞ 21.09.1707 Kaldenkirchen/Ref. Church **Katharina Strepers** (see family tree Strepers), christened Kaldenkirchen/Ref. Church:
1. *Petrus Sieben*, ~16.09.1708 (sp: Hendrik Strepers, Adelgunde in der Elst)
2. *Petrus Sieben* III., ~25.08.1709 (sp: Leonhard Strepers, Adelgunde in der Elst), †23.04.1775 Ronsdorf, profession: teacher at Kaldenkirchen; 1742 Ronsdorf
3. *Johannes Sieben*, ~16.11.1710 (sp: Hendricus Hamboch, minister, Hendrik in der Elst, Elisabeth Olmis), †before 05.02.1713
4. *Johannes Sieben*, ~05.02.1713 (sp: Dirk Simons, Anna Strepers)
5. *Henricus Sieben*, ~02.04.1714 (sp: Hendrik Strepers, Maria Strepers née Sieben)
6. *Henricus Sieben*, ~14.04.1715 (sp: Hendrik Strepers, Maria Strepers née Sieben)
7. *Johannes Sieben*, ~13.12.1716 (sp: Lambertus Moll, Katharina Sieben)
8. *Anna Maria Sieben*, ~19.03.1718 (sp: Lambertus Moll, Maria Strepers)
9. *Adelgunde Sieben*, ~07.05.1719 (sp: Jan Strepers, Anna Strepers), †23.02.1776 Ronsdorf, ±25.02.1776 ib., ∞ **Johannes Herbergs** (see family tree Herbergs), ~26.05.1717 Waldniel/Ref. Church (p: **Henrich in der Herberg** ∞ 01.11.1707 Waldniel/Ref. Church **Maria Voß**)

III. Petrus Sieben, ~25.08.1709, ∞ 28.09.1732 Kaldenkirchen/Ref. Church **Anna Maria Knevels** (p: **Jo-**

hann Knevels ∞ **Maria Elisabeth Thoma**, Linnich, see family tree Knevels), christened Kaldenkirchen/Ref. Church:

1. Johannes Wilhelmus Sieben, ~19.07.1733 (sp: Mr Johann Knevels, minister at Linnich, Peter Strepers, Sara Elisabeth Thoma, Katharina Sieben), ±21.05.1744 Ronsdorf/Ref. Church

2. Katharina Elisabeth Sieben, *25.09.1734, ~29.04. 1734 (sp: Mr Thoma, Auditeur at Venlo, Sara Elisabeth Janssen, minister Janssen's wife), confirmation 13.10. 1751 Ronsdorf/Ref. Church, †11.07.1788 Ronsdorf, ±13.07.1788 ib.

3. Maria Louisa Sieben, ~14.02.1736 (sp: Hermann Adolph Janssen, minister at Homberg, Miss Louisa Knevels, Maria Mickenschreiber), confirmation 20.05. 1753 Ronsdorf/Ref. Church

4. Tochter N., ~22.12.1737 (sp: Bernhard Hollender, Miss Wilhelmine Knevels, Adelgunda Sieben)

5. Johannes Sieben, ~02.11.1738 (sp: Johannes Schüller, merchant at Köln, Johannes Herbergs, Waldniel, Elisabeth Strepers), ±21.10.1748 Ronsdorf/Ref. Church

6. Daniel Sieben IV a., ~24.08.1741 (sp: Johann Werner Knevels, stud. theol., Linnich, Matthias Mickenschreiber, Agnes Hollender)

7. Elias Sieben, ~29.03.1743 Ronsdorf/Ref. Church (sp: Elias Eller, Daniel Schleyermacher, Anna Bolckhaus, Wilhelmina Schüller), ±15.09.1744 Ronsdorf

8. Elias Sieben, ~07.11.1744 Ronsdorf/Ref. Church (sp: Johannes Schüller, Peter Sieben), †09.11.1744 Ronsdorf, ±11.11.1744 ib.

9. Elias Sieben, ~30.10.1745 Ronsdorf/Ref. Church (sp: Elias Eller, Peter Wülfing, Maria Cholsmanns, Maria Christina Windgassen), ±23.02.1747 Ronsdorf

10. Sara Sieben IV b., ~10.05.1748 Ronsdorf/Ref. Church (sp: Sara Eller, Adelgunda Herbergs, Johannes Meis, Johannes Weyermann)

11. Elias Sieben, ~24.08.1750, Ronsdorf/Ref. Church (sp: Johann Bolckhaus, Johann Schüller, Cäcilia Gertrud Meis, Anna Margareta Kritter), confirmation 20.04. 1767 Ronsdorf/Ref. Church

12. Anna Sieben, ~11.05.1752 Ronsdorf/Ref. Church (sp: Anna Eller, Wilhelmina Magdalena Schüller, Henrich Rudenhaus, minister, Johann Arnold Herx)

13. Johannes Sieben, ~07.05.1754 Ronsdorf/Ref. Church (sp: Johannes Bolckhaus, Petrus Wülfing, Wilhelmine Magdalena Schüller, Maria Elisabeth Coenen), †09.05.1754 Ronsdorf

IV a. Daniel Sieben, ~24.08.1741 (sp: Johann Werner Knevels, stud. theol., Linnich, Matthias Mickenschreiber, Agnes Hollender), confirmation 21.06.1758 Ronsdorf/Ref. Church, †01.10.1829 Ronsdorf, ±04.10.1829 ib., profession: sexton, ∞ 04.05.1777 Ronsdorf/Ref. Church (sp: members of consistorium), **Anna Elisabeth Jäger**, *January 1749, †29.05.1814 Ronsdorf, ±31.05.1814 ib.,

profession: (at death) sexton, christened Ronsdorf/Ref. Church:

1. Magdalena Wilhelma Sieben, ~15.03.1778 (sp: Magdalena Wilhelmina Bolckhaus, Sara Spendick, Johann Christian Pieper, Johann Henrich Jäger)

2. Petrus Sieben, ~09.05.1779 (Z: Sebulon Schüller, Johann Herbergs, Katharina Elisabeth Herbergs, Maria Louisa Merckens aus Sittard)

3. Debora Sieben V., ~21.12.1780 (sp: Miss Debora Schüller, Maria Adelheid Halbach, Friedrich Pieper, Peter Jäger, Elberfeld)

4. Anna Sieben, ~30.09.1782 (sp: Anna Maria Rosenthal, Anna Katharina Hüttemanns, Philipp Weyermann, Johann Heinrich Bleckmann), †02.05.1786 Ronsdorf, ±04.05.1786 ib.

5. Johannes Wilhelmus Sieben, ~20.02.1785 (sp: Johannes Klophaus, Henrich Herbergs, Miss Maria Herbergs, Anna Herbergs)

6. Sara Sieben, ~01.04.1787 (sp: Cäcilia Gertrud Meis, Sara Piepers, Elias Herbergs)

7. Johann Joseph Sieben, ~14.06.1789 (sp: Joseph August Wülfing, Johannes Elias Bleckmann, Johanna Henrietta Ernst, Miss Sara Herbergs), †15.06.1791 Ronsdorf, ±17.06.1791 ib.

8. Johann Josua Sieben, ~06.04.1792 (Z: Josua Pieper, Johann Abraham Rosenthal, Jungfrau Maria Elisabeth Coenen, Jungfrau Anna Wilhelmina Piepers)

IV b. Sara Sieben, ~10.05.1748, confirmation 20.04. 1767 Ronsdorf/Ref. Church, †28.07.1825 Ronsdorf, ±31.07.1825 ib., ∞ 04.11.1775 Ronsdorf/Ref. Church (sp: Daniel Sieben, Jakob Spendick, Abraham Meis) **Johannes Spendick**, *about 1746, †23.06.1811 Ronsdorf, ±26.06.1811 ib., christened Ronsdorf/Ref. Church:

1. Magdalena Wilhelmina Spendick, ~07.08.1776 (sp: Magdalena Wilhelmina Bolckhaus née Knevels, Maria Margareta Spendick, Elias Spendick, Johannes Meis)

2. Johann Jacob Spendick, ~23.09.1777 (sp: Johannes Bolckhaus, Jakob Spendick, Anna Elisabetha Sieben, Katharina Elisabetha vom Kleef)

3. Sebulon Spendick, ~12.09.1779 (sp: Sebulon Schüller, Johann Herbergs, Sara Pieper, Elisabeth Herbergs)

4. Anna Spendick, ~22.09.1781 (sp: Cäcilia Gertrud Meis, Katharina Elisabeth Herbergs, Jakob Spendick)

5. Anna Debora Spendick, ~ 04.12.1782 (sp: Miss Debora Schüller, Anna Maria Spendick, Henrich Herbergs, Naphtali Spendick)

6. Anna Magdalena Spendick, ~17.04.1786 (sp: Anna Magdalena Bolckmanns, Anna Benninghoven, Enos Spendick, Elias Herbergs)

V. Debora Sieben, ~21.12.1780, ∞ 15.01.1804 Ronsdorf/Ref. Church (sp: Henrich Herberg, Johannes Spendick, Jakob Schnaut) **Johann Abraham Schnaut** (p:

Johann Henrich Schnaut ∞ Anna Margaretha Rensoh), *25.10.1779, profession: ribbon maker, christened Ronsdorf/Ref. Church:

1. Johann Abraham Schnaut, * 13.06.1804 Ronsdorf, ~17.06.1804 (sp: Daniel Sieben, Johann Jakob Schnaut, Wilhelmina Schnaut, Maria Katharina Jäger)

2. Henrich Wilhelm Schnaut, *30.12.1805 Ronsdorf, ~05.01.1806 (sp: Johann Henrich Schnaut, Johann Wilhelm Sieben, Anna Rauner, Anna Wilhelmina Monnhoff)

Family Tree Simons

population record Kaldenkirchen 1624/26: Lambert Simons, Jan Simons, Johann auf Simons Gut, Simons Halfmann, Lamert Simons, Lienard Simons, Jan Simons
oath of allegiance 1666: Johann Simons

I. Arnold Simons ∞ 18.01.1676 Kaldenkirchen/Ref. Church **Gertrud Strepers** (see family tree Strepers), christened:

1. Dirk Simons, ~20.12.1676 Kaldenkirchen/Ref. Church (sp: Lambert Strepers, Elisabeth Strepers), ±07.02.1735 Kaldenkirchen/Ref. Church

2. Katharina Simons II a., ~08.04.1678 Kaldenkirchen/Ref. Church (sp: Leonhard Strepers, Anna Doors)

3. Dirk Simons II b., ~04.02.1680 Kaldenkirchen/Ref. Church (sp: Wilhelm Strepers, Adelheid Simons)

4. Adelgunde Simons, ~22.04.1684 Kaldenkirchen/Ref. Church (sp: Peter Simons, Gertrud Olmis)

II a. Katharina Simons, ~08.04.1678, ∞ 17.05.1712 Kaldenkirchen/Ref. Church **Dirk Hansen**, christened:
1. Matthias Hansen, ~24.06.1714 Kaldenkirchen/Ref. Church (sp: Arnold Simons, Katharina Hansen)
2. Petrus Hansen, ~18.03.1718 Kaldenkirchen/Ref. Church (sp: Peter Hasen, Katharina Sieben)
3. Getrud Hansen, ~18.06.1723 Kaldenkirchen/Ref. Church (sp: Dirk Simons, Agnes Strepers)

II b. Dirk Simons, ~04.02.1680, ∞□ 10.11.1712, Kaldenkirchen/Ref. Church **Katharina Sieben**, christened:
1. Gertrud Simons, ~03.09.1713 (sp: Arnold Simons, Adelgunde Sieben, Katharina Simons), ±28.01.1745 ib.
2. Petrus Simons III a., ~03.11.1715 (sp: Wilhelmus Sieben, Elisabeth Olmis), †1770, profession: linen dealer
3. Michael Simons, ~08.01.1719 (sp: Leonhard Strepers, Elisabeth Schuren)
4. Alagunda Simons III b., ~05.10.1721 (sp: Hendrik Strepers, Maria Sieben)

III a. Petrus Simons, ~03.11.1715, ∞□17.01.1745 Wassenberg/Ref. Church **Anna Elisabeth Krüder**, christened Kaldenkirchen/Ref. Church:

1. Diederich Simons, ~26.08.1746 (sp: Daniel Krüder, Reiner Haasen, Alagunda Simons), ±05.09.1751 Kaldenkirchen/Ref. Church

2. Anna Katharina Simons, ~07.11.1749 (sp: Michael Simons, Agnes Strepers, Sibilla Nagels), ±05.09.1751 Kaldenkirchen/Ref. Church

3. Mechtilda Simons, ~25.12.1750 (sp: Daniel Camphausen, minister at Wermelskirchen, Anna Wiedenfeld, M. Agneta Grambusch)

4. Johann Daniel Simons, 08.06.1753 (sp: Matthias Lenzen, Elisabeth Nagels, Maria Strepers)

5. Peter Daniel Simons, ~23.09.1755 (sp: Daniel Krüder, Alagunda Simons)

6. Cäcilia Katharina Simons, ~15.04.1758 (sp: Michael Simons, Agneta Strepers)

7. Arnoldus Simons, ~17.06.1760 (sp: Diederich Schuren, Katharina Gilles), †1833, profession: owner of weaving mill, ∞ 1800 **Sibilla Elisabeth Poensgen**, *1770, †1850

8. Sibilla Gertruda Simons, ~24.02.1765 (sp: Hinricus Strepers, Sibilla Gilles), ±15.07.1765 Kaldenkirchen/Ref. Church

9. Diederich Rudolphus Simons, ~11.12.1768 (sp: Godefriedus Thoma, Barbara Gillesen née Frentz)

III b. Alagunda Simons, ~05.10.1721, ∞ 22.10.1747 Kaldenkirchen/Ref. Church **Daniel Camphausen**, minister at Waldniel (p: **Wilhelm ? Camphausen** ∞ **Sophia Blanckertz**), *about 1721, Wickrathberg, profession: university of Duisburg, minister at Waldniel 1743-53, Wermelskirchen 1753-1796, christened Waldniel/Ref. Church:

1. Wilhelmus Camphausen, ~23.02.1749 (sp: Ernst Camphausen, brother, Albert von Ingenhoven, Anna Elisabetha Krüder, sister-in-law)

2. Wilhelmus Diedericus Camphausen, ~15.09.1751 (sp: Sophia Blanckertz, minister Camphausen's mother, Agnes Strepers, Bernardus Hollender's wife), †04.08.1811 Wickrathberg, profession: university of Duisburg, minister at Erkrath 1772-73, Mettmann 1773-76, Haan 1776-77, Wickrathberg 1777-†1811

3. Peter Camphausen, *about 1753 Waldniel or Wermelskirchen, †21.04.1823, profession: minister at Mönchengladbach 1779-81, Kettwig 1781-†1823

4. Johann Daniel Camphausen, *1753 Wermelskirchen, †09.12.1813 Elberfeld, profession: merchant at Elberfeld; 1789 councilor, 1790-92 councilor, 1793 councilor, 1793 proposed as mayor, 22.08.1783 citizen of Elberfeld, ∞ 29.01.1788 Elberfeld/Ref. Church **Maria Charlotta Bergmann** (p: **Johann Caspar Bergmann** ∞ 1st marriage 22.08. 1749 Elberfeld/Ref. Church **Anna Maria Plücker**), ~20.12. 1769 Elberfeld/Ref. Church, †11.03.1818 Elberfeld

Family Tree Strepers

I. Dirk (Dietrich) auf den Striep (population record Kaldenkirchen 1571), *about 1530, ∞ **N.N.**, christened, Kaldenkirchen:
Peter auf den Striep II., *about 1560, population record Kaldenkirchen 1624/26; in Peter Strepers' house first meeting of members of Reformed Church of Kaldenkirchen in 1609

II. Peter auf den Striep, *about 1560, ∞ **N.N.**, christened:
1. Dietrich Strepers III a., *about 1585, population record Kaldenkirchen 1624/26, punished for baptism in Reformed Church in 1629 and 1630
2. Leonhard Strepers III b., *about 1590
3. Jan Strepers, *about 1593/95, population record Kaldenkirchen 1624/26, punished for baptism in Reformed Church in 1629 and 1630
unsure: *Zye (Elisabeth) Strepers, Gertrud Strepers*

III a. Dietrich Strepers, *about 1585, ∞ **N.N.**, christened:
Leonhard Strepers IV a., *about 1613

III b. Leonhard Strepers, *about 1590, ∞ **Lucia N.**, christened Kaldenkirchen/Roman-Catholic Church:
1. Jan Strepers IV b., ~24.05.1623
2. Eva Strepers, ~27.07.1625

IV a. Leonhard Strepers, *about 1613, oath of allegiance in 1666, ∞ **Gertrud Hutmacher** (?) (p: **Hendrich Hutmacher** ∞ **Gertrud** (?) **Coenen**), christened:
1. Jan Strepers V a., *about 1638/40, †06.05.1715 Kaldenkirchen, ±ib., profession: merchant, inn-keeper, 1680 consistorium member
2. Lambert Strepers V b., *about 1642, 28.05.1667 (25 years) admitted to the holy communion in Ref. Church of Heinsberg, †before March 1695
3. Wilhelm Strepers V c., *about 1644, †1st week of November 1717, Germantown, emigrated to Pennsylvania in 1683
4. Dietrich Strepers, 20.04.1669 (Easter eve) admitted to holy communion of Ref. Church of Wesel/Willibrordi-Church
5. Gertrud Strepers

IV b. Jan Strepers, ~24.05.1623 Kaldenkirchen/Roman-Catholic Church, ∞ **Christina Küppers** (see family tree Küppers), christened:
1. Leonhard Strepers junior V d.
2. Peter Strepers V e.
3. Wilhelm Strepers V f.
4. Elisabeth Strepers
5. Katharina Strepers (?)

V a. Jan Strepers, *about 1638/40, 1666 oath of allegiance, ∞ 12.05.1669 Kaldenkirchen/Ref. Church **Anna Doors** (p: **Matthias Doors/Peters**, see family tree Doors/Theißen), ±02.08.1700 Kaldenkirchen/Ref. Church
Anna Doors ∞ 1st marriage about 1663 **Heinrich Kürlis**, christened Kaldenkirchen/Ref. Church:
1. Mechtild Kürlis, ~09.03.1664 (sp: Peter Doors, Agnes Doors, Katharina Coenen), †31.10.1719, ∞ 22.12.1682 **Hendrik Jansen van Acken** (see family tree van Acken)
2. Jan Kürlis, ~05.12.1666, †09.03.1669 (sp: Matthias Brouwers, Jan Hilkes, Sibille Brouwers)
Anna Doors ∞ 2d marriage 12.05.1669 Kaldenkirchen/Ref. Church **Jan Strepers**, christened Kaldenkirchen/Ref. Church:
1. Leonhard Strepers VI a., ~02.03.1670 (sp: Henrich Hutmachers, Paulus Küsters, Gertrud Strepers), †19.08.1725 Kaldenkirchen, ±22.08.1725 ib.
2. Hendrik Strepers VI b., ~24.07.1672 (sp: Matthias Kürlis, Gertrud Strepers), ±26.07.1724 Kaldenkirchen
3. Katharina Strepers, ~16.12.1674 (Katharina Strepers, Joachim Hüskes), †young
4. Katharina Strepers VI c., ~23.05.1677 (sp: Arnold Simons, Christina Schrörs, Helene Schmitz), †24.04.1725 Kaldenkirchen
5. Agneta (Agnes) Strepers, ~16.07.1679 (sp: Jan Herzog, teacher at Solingen, Agnes Doors), †before 22.12.1680
6. Agnes Strepers, ~22.12.1680 (sp: Peter Kürlis, Gertrud Doors)
7. Anneken (Anna) Strepers VI d., ~16.11.1686 Kaldenkirchen, †14.10.1720

V b. Lambert Strepers, *about 1642, ∞ Heinsberg (?) **Lüttgen Bastians**, †11.09.1705 Heinsberg (f: **Bastian Willemsen**, tanner at Heinsberg, several times deakon of Ref. Church 1652-1665), christened Heinsberg/Ref. Church:
Katharina Strepers, †26.12.1742 Heinsberg, ±ebd. 29.12.1742, ∞ 1st marriage 19.06.1692 Heinsberg/ref. Gem **Johannes Pipers**, Brüggen, christened Heinsberg/Ref. Church:
1. Matthäus Pipers, *08.05.1693
2. Anna Maria Pipers, *25.03.1695
3. Katharina Pipers, *16.05.1696
4. Lambert Pipers, *09.10.1698
∞ 2d marriage 15.06.1704 Heinsberg/Ref. Church **Daniel Krüder**, christened Heinsberg/Ref. Church:
5. Mechtild Krüder, *13.03.1705, †21.05.1705
∞ 3d marriage 24.05.1706 Heinsberg/Ref. Church, **Lukas Überfeld**, Langenberg, †29.12.1745 Heinsberg, ±02.02.1745 ib., christened Heinsberg/Ref. Church:
6. Peter Überfeld, *06.03.1707
7. Katharina Gertrud Überfeld, *06.05.1708
8. Petrus Lambert Überfeld, *22.03.1716

V c. Wilhelm Strepers, *about 1644, ∞ **Maria Willemsen Lucken**, *1652/54 (p: **Wilhelm Lucken** ∞ **Adel-**

heid), ∞ 1st marriage **Jan Simons**, christened:
Peter Simons/Jansen, *30.11.1683 Krefeld, †1745, ∞
Gertrud Neus (p: **Jan Neus** ∞ 1682 Krefeld **Agnes Theißen/Schumacher** ?, Mönchengladbach-Damm; p: **Matthias Schumacher** ∞ **Margarete N.**),
christened 2d marriage:
1. Leonhard Strepers, ~17.05.1686 Germantown, †02.05.1727
2. John Strepers, ~16.07.1688 Germantown, †1741 Germantown (Johannes Herbergs: 1739)
3. Katharina Strepers, ~08.12.1690 Germantown

V d. Gertrud Strepers ∞ 18.01.1676 Kaldenkirchen/Ref. Church **Arnold Simons** (see family tree Simons), christened Kaldenkirchen/Ref. Church:
1. Dirk Simons, ~20.12.1676 (sp: Lambert Strepers, Elisabeth Strepers)
2. Katharina Simons, ~08.04.1678 (sp: Leonhard Strepers, Anna Doors)
3. Dirk Simons, ~04.02.1680 (sp: Wilhelm Strepers, Adelgunde Simons)
4. Adelgunda Simons, ~22.04.1684 (sp: Peter Simons, Gertrud Olmis)

V d. Leonhard Strepers, 1666 oath of allegiance, ∞ **Helena Schmitz** (?) (f: **Peter Schmitz** ?, 23.12.1660 Krefeld citizen), christened Kaldenkirchen/Ref. Church:
Agnes Strepers, ~08.08.1663 (sp: Matthias Küppers, Sibille Brouwers, Leonhard Janssen's wife), ∞ 08.08. 1689 Kaldenkirchen/Ref. Church **Peter Küppers** (see family tree Küppers)

V e. Peter Strepers, 1666 oath of allegiance, ∞ **Katharina Clouten**, christened Kaldenkirchen/Ref. Church:
1. Elisabeth Strepers, ~30.09.1663 (sp: Leonhard Strepers junior, Christina Küppers, Jan Strepers' wife)
2. Agnes Strepers, ~10.01.1666 (sp: Matthias Brouwers, Agnes Doors)
3. Jan Strepers, ~22.01.1668 (sp: Leonhard Küppers, Katharina van Solingen, Jan Brouwers' wife)
4. Tochter N.N., ~25.03.1670 (sp: Jan Strepers, Christine Küppers)
5. Christine Strepers, ~08.09.1674 (sp: Jakob von Wachtendonk, Gertrud Schuren)

V f. Wilhelm, 1666 oath of allegiance, ∞ 19.08.1663 Kaldenkirchen/Ref. Church **Sibille Tüffers** (probably p: **Wilhelm Tüffers** ∞ **Margarete Barhus**), christened Kaldenkirchen/Ref. Church:
1. Peter Strepers, ~07.12.1664 (sp: Jan Strepers, Margarete Barhus, Wilhelm Tüffers' wife)
2. Dirk Strepers, ~22.08.1666 (sp: Hendrik Kürlis, Helena, Leonhard Strepers' wife)
3. Leonhard Strepers, ~08.07.1668 (sp: Wilhelm

Tüffers, Katharina Clouten, Peter Strepers' wife)
4. Elisabeth Strepers **VI e.**, ~25.01.1670 (sp: Jan Strepers, Judith Tüffers)
5. Jenneken (Johanna) Strepers **VI f.**, ~16.12.1674 (sp: Dirk Tüffers, Katharina Lierezels ? of Goch)

VI a. Leonhard Strepers, ~02.03.1670, ∞ 20.05.1698 Kaldenkirchen/Ref. Church **Maria Sieben**, ~24.01.1672 (sp: Wilhelm in der Elst, Katharina Nagels, Maria Schuren, both of Brüggen), †31.07.1726, Amsterdam, ±ib., christened Kaldenkirchen/Ref. Church:
1. Anna Strepers, ~16.05.1701 (sp: Hendrik Strepers, Adelgunda Sieben), †autumn 1727
2. Elisabeth Strepers **VII a.**, ~18.11.1703 (sp: Peter Sieben, Katharina Strepers)
3. Peter Strepers **VII b.**, ~26.09.1705 (sp: Wilhelmus Sieben, Elisabeth Olmis), ±06.02.1745 Kaldenkirchen
4. Agnes Strepers, ~04.12.1707 (sp: Hendrik in der Elst, Anna Strepers)
5. Agnes Strepers **VII c.**, ~14.05.1711 (sp: Dirk Simons, Katharina Sieben)
6. Katharina Strepers **VII d.**, ~05.02.1713 (sp: Matthias Küsters, Katharina in der Elst)
7. Maria Strepers, ~10.05.1716 (sp: Lambertus Moll, Elisabeth Werts)

VI b. Hendrik Strepers, ~24.07.1672, ∞ 04.10.1695 Kaldenkirchen/Ref. Church **Elisabeth Olmis** (p: **Jan Olmis** ∞ **Maria**), ~02.06.1662 Krefeld, ±29.10.1730 ib., christened Kaldenkirchen/Ref. Church:
1.Anna Maria Strepers **VII e.**, ~04.11.1696 (sp: Leonhard Strepers), ±12.07.1763 Kaldenkirchen in church
2. Johannes Strepers, ~24.05.1699 (sp: Matthias Olmis, Ummelken Hüskes)
3. Agnes Strepers **VII f.**, ~12.09.1700 (sp: Joachim Hüskes, Gertrud Strepers)
4. Henricus Strepers, ~23.04.1702 (sp: Henricus Rahr, Krefeld, Maria Sieben), †27.10.1727, unmarried

VI c. Katharina Strepers, ~23.05.1677, ∞ 21.09.1707 Kaldenkirchen/Ref. Church **Wilhelmus Sieben** (see family tree Sieben), ~27.06.1676 Kaldenkirchen/Ref. Church, ±01.05.1729 ib., profession: teacher at Kaldenkirchen, christened Kaldenkirchen/Ref. Church:
1. Petrus Sieben, ~16.09.1708 (sp: Hendrik Strepers, Adelgunda in der Elst)
2. Petrus Sieben, ~25.08.1709, †23.04.1775
3. Johannes Sieben, ~16.11.1710 (sp: Henricus Hamboch, minister, Hendrik in der Elst, Elisabeth Olmis)
4. Johannes Sieben, ~05.02.1713 (sp: Dirk Simons, Anna Strepers), †young
5. Henricus Sieben, ~02.04.1714 (sp: Hendrik Strepers, Maria Strepers née Sieben)
6. Henricus Sieben, ~14.04.1715 (sp: Hendrik Strepers,

Maria Strepers née Sieben), †young
7. Johannes Sieben, ~13.12.1716 (sp: Lambertus Moll, Catharina Sieben), †young
8. Anna Maria Sieben, ~19.03.1718 (sp: Lambertus Moll, Maria Strepers), †young
9. Adelgunde Sieben, ~07.05.1719 (sp: Jan Strepers, Anna Strepers), †23.02.1776 Ronsdorf, ±25.02.1776 ib., ∞ **Johannes Herbergs** (see family tree Herbergs)

VI d. Anna Strepers, ~16.11.1686, ∞ 14.04.1716 Kaldenkirchen/Ref. Church **Lambert Moll**, Millich, †1749, christened Millich (?) /Ref. Church:
1. Anna Katharina Moll, ∞ **Henricus Königs**, christened:
   1. Peter Königs, Millich/Ref. Church, ∞ **Maria Eva Frings** (p: **Johann Wilhelm Frings** ∞ **Sibilla Simon**, Hünshoven)
   2. Matthäus Königs, Millich/Ref. Church, ∞ 02.08. 1780 Grambusch/Ref. Church Hückelhoven-Schwanenberg **Agnes Röhlen** (p: **Peter Röhlen** ∞ **Kunigunda Cremers** von den Hoff)
2. Johannes Moll ∞ **Gertrud Königs**, christened:
   Sibilla Agneta Moll, ∞ Schwanenberg/Ref. Church **Johann Maximilian Kremers**, christened:
      Sibilla Katharina Kremers, ~08.08.1786 Waldniel/Ref. Church (sp: Johann Moll, Franz Peter Kremers, Sibilla Königs, Schwanenberg, Frau Agneta von der Euen, Viersen)

VI e. Elisabeth Strepers, ~25.01.1670, ∞ 21.10.1692 Kaldenkirchen/Ref. Church **Jan van Rath**, Jüchen, christened Kaldenkirchen/Ref. Church:
1. Johannes van Rath, ~28.06.1693 (sp: Peter Strepers, Helena Strepers, Dirk Strepers)
2. Arnd van Rath, ~10.03.1697 (sp: Leonhard Strepers, Christine Strepers)
3. Dirk van Rath, ~19.02.1701 (sp: Joachim Hüskes, Petronella van der Horn, Umelken Hüskes), ∞ **Maria Katharina Spikers**, christened April 1734 **Sohn N.N.** (sp: Elisabeth Strepers, Jan Rath's wife, Johannes Christophorus Ringels)
4. Leonhard van Rath, ~27.12.1703 (sp: Peter Küppers, Elisabeth Strepers)
5. Katharina van Rath, ~28.11.1706 (sp: Dirk Simons, Maria Schmasen)
6. Sophia van Rath, ~25.08.1709 (sp: Hendrik Strepers, Anna Junkers)
7. Bartholomäus van Rath, ~11.12.1712 (sp: Bartholomäus Meyer or Moyer, Petronella Schmasen)

VI f. Johanna Strepers, ~16.12.1674, ∞ 18.04.1700 Kaldenkirchen/Ref. Church **Peter Küppers**, christened Kaldenkirchen/Ref. Church:
1. Wilhelmus Küppers, ~29.01.1701 (sp: Arnold Tüffers, Sibilla Strepers)

2. Mechtild Küppers, ~23.10.1704 (sp: Dirk Hüskes, Agnes Strepers)
3. Sibille Küppers, ~31.01.1706 (sp: Dirk Lensen, Katharina Conen)
4. Getrud Küppers, ~19.03.1709 (sp: Hendrik Bolten, Katharina Küppers)

VII a. Elisabeth Strepers, ~18.11.1703, ∞ 29.10.1730 Kaldenkirchen/Ref. Church **Johannes Christophorus Ringels**, Lennep (p: **Francisci Ringels** ∞ **Katharina Bergfeld**), christened Kaldenkirchen/Ref. Church:
1. Maria Katharina Ringels, ~26.08.1731 (sp: Franciscus Ringels, Katharina Bergfeld, Katharina Strepers)
2. Johann Leonhard Ringels, ~21.11.1732 (sp: Johann Jäger, Lennep, Peter Strepers, Katharina Sieben née Simons)
3. Maria Katharina Ringels, ~22.09.1734 (sp: Anton Wülfing and Katharina Ringels of Lennep, Agnes Hüskes called Strepers, Peter David Kadenberg, Elisabeth Strepers), ∞ 04.05.1760 Kaldenkirchen/Ref. Church, **Hinricus Jacobus Strunck**, Frankfurt, christened Kaldenkirchen/Ref. Church:
   1. Anna Elisabeth Strunck, ~13.05.1761 (sp: Jakob Strunck, Agneta Strepers)
   2. Johannes Hinricus Strunck, ~24.07.1763 (sp: Hinricus Strepers, Anna Elisabeth Krüder), ∞ **Maria Barbara Josepha Holtzenberg**
   3. Gerhardus Strunck, ~01.03.1769 (sp: Gerhardus Hüskes, Petrus Dürselen, minister at Vessem NL, Magdalena Ringels)
4. Anna Elisabeth Ringels, ~21.04.1736 (sp: Matthias Hüskes, Katharina Ringels, Maria Mickenschreiber), ∞ 23.04.1765 Bracht/Ref. Church **Johannes Klotz**
5. Magdalena Ringels, ~27.12.1737 (sp: Peter Sieben, Mechtild Kladders, Maria Magdalena Ringels)
6. Agneta Ringels, ~02.05.1739 (sp: Arnold Hollender, Agneta Hollender)
7. Johannes Franciscus Ringels, ~17.07.1740 (sp: Johan Ringel, Dehrendorf, Klara Wülfing, Lennep, Peter Simons)

VII b. Peter Strepers, ~26.09.1705, ∞ 25.01.1734, Kaldenkirchen/Ref. Church **Mechtild Christine Kladders**, Aldekerk (p: **Diedrich Kladders** ∞ **Gertrud Lapen**, †before marriage of daughter), christened Kaldenkirchen/Ref. Church:
1. Leonhard Diederich Strepers, ~12.12.1734 (sp: Diederich Kladders, Johannes Christophorus Ringels, Katharina Sieben née Simons)
2. Peter Henricus Strepers VIII., ~07.09.1736 (sp: Abraham Kladders, Aldekerk, Bernhard Hollender, Waldniel, Agnes Hüskes), 1764 journey to Philadelphia with Johannes Herbergs, †10.04.1781 Issum; 07.02.1768 sponsor at Philadelphia at baptism of Peter Henry Mueller (p:

William Mueller ∞ Susanna Maria), *05.02.1768, ~07.05.
1768 (sp: Peter Henry Stripers, Catherine Utrich)
3. Maria Strepers, ~21.03.1739 (sp: Christina Kladders,
Johannes Kladders, Katharina Strepers, Gertrud Simons)

VII c. Agnes Strepers, ~14.05.1711, ∞ 25.01.1734, Kal-
denkirchen/Ref. Church **Matthias Hüskes** (p: **Diederich
Hüskes ∞ Sophia Küppers**), ±14.10.1741 in Merschen
(Mersch/Jülich ?), christened Kaldenkirchen/Ref. Church:
1. Johann Leonhard Hüskes, ~31.10.1734 (sp: Peter
Strepers, Peter David Kadenberg, Elisabeth Strepers)
2. Diederich Hüskes, ~18.03.1736 (sp: Johannes
Christophorus Ringels, Mechtild Hüskes)
3. Gerhard Hüskes, ~02.03.1738 (sp: Matthias Mickenschreiber, Matthias Küppers, Mechtild Christina Kladders, Peter Strepers' wife)

VII d. Catharina Strepers, ~05.02.1713, ∞ 22.11.1742
Kaldenkirchen/Ref. Church **Florens Petrus Dürselen**
(p: **Albertus Dürselen**, minister zum Hörschgen ∞ **Maria Magdalena Mickenschreiber**, see family tree Dürselen), profession: minister at Vessem and Hoogeloon
NL, Ref. Church, christened Kaldenkirchen/Ref. Church:
Maria Dürselen ∞ Gerhard von der Kuhlen, Mülheim
a.d. Ruhr, christened Kaldenkirchen/Ref. Church:
    Peter Gerhard von der Kuhlen, profession: mer-
    chant at Kaldenkirchen

VII e. Anna Maria Strepers, ~04.11.1696, †17.07.1763
Kaldenkirchen, ∞ 15.11.1725 Kaldenkirchen/Ref.
Church **Matthias Mickenschreiber**, Odenkirchen, ±17.
11.1762, Kaldenkirchen/ref. Gem., christened Kaldenkir-
chen/Ref. Church:
1. Maria Agnes Mickenschreiber, ~11.08.1726 (sp:
Hermannus Mickenschreiber, Agnes Köeltgens, Elisabeth Olmis)
2. Anna Magdalena Mickenschreiber, ~11.01.1728
(sp: Bernhardus Hollender, Kunigunde Mickenschreiber)
3. Peter Hendrich Mickenschreiber, ~17.09.1730 (sp:
Johannes Quast, Agnes Strepers)
4. Maria Elisabeth Mickenschreiber, ~16.12.1731 (sp:
Peter Strepers, Elisabeth Olmis, Anna Mickenschreiber)
5. Hermanus Mickenschreiber, ~14.06.1734 (sp: Johann Laufs, minister at Rheydt, Peter Sieben, Elisabeth Strepers, Johannes Christoph Ringels' wife), ±28.
12.1757 Kaldenkirchen/Ref. Church

VII f. Agnes Strepers, ~12.09.1700, ∞ 06.06.1724 Kal-
denkirchen/Ref. Church **Bernhardus Hollender**, *20.06.
1706, Waldniel, †18.09.1790 (see family tree Hollender)

VIII. Peter Henricus Strepers, ~07.09.1736, ∞ 29.06.
1777 Grambusch/Ref. Church Hückelhoven-Schwanenberg **Maria Agneta Adriana Heijmans**

E: Georg Heinrich Heijmans, †16.12.1768
Hoven ∞ **Kornelia Wilhelmi**, *1716, †25.09.1782
Hoven, ±29.09.1782, christened:
1. Maria Agneta Adriana Heijmans
2. Johann Adolph Heijmans, †06.08.1772,
Hoven
3. Johanna Elisabeth Heijmans, *about 1745
†10.12.1827 Hoven, ∞ **Johann Wilhelm Rütger
Blancken**
4. Catherina Margaretha Heijmans, *about
1752, †20.07.1826 Hoven, ∞ 23.09.1783 Hoven
Johann Simon Büddingh
christened:
1. Kornelia Mechtilda Strepers, ~23.03.1780 Issum/
Ref. Church (sp: Abraham Kladders, Wilhelm Laufs), ∞
12.06.1803, Odenkirchen/Ref. Church **Johann Wilhelm
Lenssen**, christened:
    Sophia Henrietta Lenssen, *02.04.1804, ~07.04.
    1804 Odenkirchen/Ref. Church (sp: Sophia Lenssen,
    Kornelius Lenssen, Katherina Elisabeth Heimanns,
    Joh. Simon Büddingh)
Maria Agneta Adriana Heijmans ∞ 2d marriage
28.07.1782 Issum/Ref. Church **Diedrich Hausser**, Krefeld, christened:
2. Anna Maria Hausser, ~12.02.1783, Issum/Ref.
Church (sp: Diederich Hausser, Michael Hausser, Maria Schirges, Diederich Hausser's wife, Krefeld, Mrs
Blancken née Heimans), †18.04.1783 Issum

Family Tree Tüffers

population record Kaldenkirchen 1473/75: Tuffer
population record Kaldenkirchen 1571: Derick Tuffers
population record Kaldenkirchen 1624/26:

Nikolaus Tüffers ∞ **Elisabeth Jorissen**, christened
Kaldenkirchen/Ref. Church.:
1. Elisabeth Tüffers, ~20.04.1664 (sp: Hendrik Tüffers,
Geertgen Barhus, Anna Kürlis)
2. Margareta Tüffers, ~16.01.1667 (sp: Wilhelm Tüffers, Miss Katharina Ingenhaeff)

Henrich Tüffers (V: **Dirk Tüffers**, 1666 oath of allegiance), 1666 oath of allegiance ∞ 21.10.1666 **Geertgen
Heffen**, Süchteln, christened Kaldenkirchen/Ref. Church:
1. Peter Tüffers, ~06.11.1667 (sp: Dirk Tüffers, Jakob
Baums)
2. Petronella Tüffers, ~03.08.1670 (sp: Wilhelm Lappen, Geertgen, Wilhelm Tüffers' wife)
3. Hendrik Tüffers, ~16.04.1673 (sp: Wilhelm Strepers,
Adelgunde Tüffers)

Family Tree Voss

I. Peter Voss, ∞ **Adelgunde Dulcks**, Dülken, christened:
1. Herman Voss II a.
2. Johann Voss II b.

II a. Herman Voss, ∞ 07.06.1669, Waldniel/Ref. Church **Maria Joriskes** (p: **Wolter Joriskes** ∞ **Katharina Banten**), christened:
1. Peter Voss, ~08.03.1670 Waldniel/Ref. Church (sp: illegible)
2. Peter Voss, ~29.05.1672 Waldniel/Ref. Church, (sp: Jan Voss, Dülken, Libbertgen Ocken, Irmgard Siebmans, Jakob Voss' wife, Dülken)

II b. Johann Vos, ∞ 1st marriage 07.08.1674 Waldniel/Ref. Church **Katharina Fetten** (p: **Matthäus Fetten** ∞ **Maria Dahmen**), christened:
1. Peter Voss III., ~16.05.1675 Waldniel/Ref. Church (sp: Jan Kürlis von Brüggen, Jakob Voss, Dülken, Maria Hutmachers)
2. Maria Voss, ~25.04.1677 Waldniel/Ref. Church (sp: Herman Pauls, Maria Dahmen, Katharina Dienes, ∞ **Henrich in der Herberg** (see family tree Herbergs)
3. Adelgunde Voss, ~04.08.1680 Waldniel/Ref. Church (sp: Johannes Jonen in lieu of Johan Sieben of Brüggen, Irmgard Voss, Jacob Voss' wife, Dülken)
Jan Voss ∞ 2d marriage 23.09.1685 Waldniel/Ref. Church **Anna Kehren**, christened:
4. Henricus Voss, ~05.01.1687 Waldniel/Ref. Church (sp: Kehren ?, Jan Boßfelt, Arnold Voss), ∞ 16.11.1721 Waldniel/Ref. Church **Maria Dahmen** (p: **Lentz Dahmen** ∞ **Catharina Köhnen**)
5. Katharina Voss, ~09.01.1689 Waldniel/Ref. Church (sp: Matthäus Fetten, Margaretha Voss, Sophia Dahmen)
6. Henricus Voss, ~21.01.1691 Waldniel/Ref. Church (sp: Karl zu Weckers ?, Matthias Dahmen, Elisabeth Kehren), ∞ **Maria Dahmen**, christened:
   Johannes Voss, ~08.11.1722 Waldniel/Ref. Church (sp: Arnold Hollender, Maria Voss)
7. Wilhelmus Voss, ~26.08.1696 Waldniel/Ref. Church (sp: Peter Voss, Johann im Kamp, Mechtild Köllens)

III. Peter Voss, ~16.05.1674 Waldniel/Ref. Church ∞ **Maria Neukirchen**, christened Wadniel/Ref. Church:
1. Anna Katharina Voss, ~02.07.1702
2. Johannes Voss, ~14.03.1704 (sp: Peter Voss, Sibille Wilhelms)
3. Matthaeus Voss, ~19.07.1707 (sp: Johannes von Boven, Venlo, Gerhard Kremers, Anna Margareta, minister's wife of Gladbach, Adelgunde Voss)
4. Anna Voss, ~04.05.1710 (sp: Johann Konrad Hadernach Maria Geuen, Hendrich N.' wife)

Glossary of Names

van Acken, Agnes 55
   See Arets/van Acken family tree.
van Acken, Arents Classen 22
   See Arets/van Acken family tree.
van Acken, Claas 54, 56, 104
   See Arets/van Acken family tree.
van Acken, Elisabeth 55, 104, 179
   See Arets/van Acken family tree.
van Acken, Hendrik 53-56, 96, 102-104, 128, 178
   Son of Hendrik Jansen van Acken, see Arets/
   van Acken family tree.
van Acken, Hendrik Jansen, 12, 17, 21f., 30
   Married on March 9, 1774, at the Reformed
   Church in Kaldenkirchen to Metgen Kürlis,
   christened: Hendrik, Claas, Anneken, Wilhelm,
   Agneta and Elisabeth van Acken. Lived in Krefeld after 1675, corresponded with William Penn
   in 1688, was probably the son of Jan Claßen
   van Acken, who was expelled from Mönchengladbach 1654 because of his Mennonite faith,
   see Arets/van Acken family tree.
van Acken, Wilhelm, 53, 100, 103f., 106, 149,
   165f., 167f.
   See Arets/van Acken family tree.
Allen 130
   Son of William Allen (?).
Allen, William (1704-1780) 105f., 111, 127, 130f.,
   139f.
   Merchant and lawyer. Had considerable influence on politics and the judiciary in Pennsylvania. The building of the State House in Philadelphia was due to his initiative. In 1735 he held
   the office of Mayor, in 1741 that of City Judge.
   Between 1737 and 1759, he was active in various lower courts before becoming Supreme
   Justice of the Province of Pennsylvania. As a
   member of the Proprietors' Party, Allen was
   unable to bring his moderate political views to
   bear against those of Benjamin Franklin which
   were influenced by American nationalism. Therefore he resigned from his legal offices in 1774.
Andreas 173
   Occupation woodcarver, possibly the same as
   Berenstecher.
Aepply, Apply, v. Eppele
Arets, Elisabeth (1697-1794) 94f., 102

1st marriage to John Strepers, 2nd marriage to
N.Kerschner/Kerssener. She lived in German-
town. Mother of Wilhelm Strepers, a cousin of
P. H. Strepers.
Arets, Hendrik 53
   See Arets family tree.
Arets, Leonhard 17f., 20, 21f., 26-28, 30, 32,36,
   37, 41f., 44-46, 53, 95, 121, 128, 152, 174
   Emigrated from Krefeld to Pennsylvania in 1683.
   Burgomaster of Germantown 1691 and 1709,
   see Arets family tree.
Ashmead, William 124, 151, 167
   In the journal: Justice Eschmitt. Member of the
   Ashmead family from Germantown. In 1742
   Count Zinzendorf founded the first school of the
   Moravian Brothers in Pennsylvania in the house
   of the Ashmeads. After the Revolution, Ashmead
   began manufacturing the "Germantown Wa-
   gons".
Askew, John 49
   Merchant in London.
Auf dem Striep, Dirk 17
   See Strepers family tree.
Baltzer 87
   Baltzer and wife, passengers on the Roebuck.
Bärenstecher, Mrs. 173
   Wife of Andreas Bärenstecher (?).
Baynton, Peter 120
   Merchant and ship owner from Philadelphia.
   Around 1760 he ran a shop in Water Street to-
   gether with Wharton.
van Bebber, Jacob Isaacs 26
   Buys land from William Penn in 1682.
van Bebber, Matthias 36f.
   Agent of Jan Strepers.
Behagel, Daniel 26f.
   Member of the Frankfurt Company.
Benezet, Anthony 57
   Teacher in Germantown, Quaker.
Benjamin 84, 87, 159
   Sailor.
Benten, see Baynton
Berenstecher, Andreas 90, 124, 149, 165, 167f.
   Possibly: Andreas Berenstecher; landed in Phil-
   adelphia on September 16, 1751, on the ship
   Nancy from Rotterdam; innkeeper in Philadel-
   phia.
Bernardi, Gottfried Casimir 180
   Bailiff.

Biddes, see Biden

Biden, Catherine 105, 124, 167
Widow of Wilhelm Biden (William Biddis), daughter of Johann Lentzen.

Blackbeard 142
(d. 1718) English pirate, really: Edward Teach or Thatch. Plundered ships between the West Indies and the American coast.

Bleikers, Johannes 28
Emigrant in 1683, see Bleikers family tree.

Blomstäet, see Plumstead

Bolckhaus, Arnold 177
Regimental Surgeon in Berlin, opened the doors of the Ministry of Foreign Affairs (von Podewils) to achieve the nomination of Peter Wülfing as Councilor of the Consistory on April 3, 1749, and of Elias Eller to Privy Councilor and "Agent and Superintendent of all Protestant brethren in faith [in Berg] ..."

Bolckhaus, Johann (1709-1783) 98, 102, 113, 118, 129, 177f.
Stepson of Elias Eller, head of the Ellerian sect in Wuppertal-Ronsdorf. As such Royal Prussian Privy Councilor, Resident and Superintendent of the Reformed congregations in Jülich and Cleves, Berg and Mark.

Borner, Johannes Andreas 182
Witness at the signing of the contract.

Boydell, James and Josiah 71
Ship brokers in London.

Brockden, Charles 99f., 108, 134, 150, 152, 164, 174
Registrar of Documents for the City and County of Philadelphia.

vom Büchel, Anna (1698-1743) 176
Wife of Elias Eller, Ronsdorf.

Cäbenter 87
Sailor on the Roebuck.

Caunder/Conders, Mrs. 158f.
Landlady in London (?).

Charles II (1630-1685) 28, 71, 74
King of Great Britain and Ireland, King 1660-1685.

Chew, Benjamin (1722-1810) 118, 122
Lawyer. After studies in London and first activities in the legal profession, Chew was King's Counsel from 1755 to 1769. At the same time, he acted as City Judge in Philadelphia and was a member of the City Council. After retiring as King's Counsel he first went into private practice and later succeeded William Allen as Supreme Justice of the Province from 1774. With the Revolution, he lost all important functions.

Claeuser see Kläuser

Coleman 139f.
Probably "Senior Judge Coleman" or Esquire Coleman from Philadelphia.

Conradts 155
Mrs. Conradts did the laundry for Peter Heinrich Strepers and Johannes Herbergs.

Conrats, Thomas 32

Cook, George 87
Coffee merchant in New York.

Cupers, Gosen 19
Clog maker in Kaldenkirchen.

Cürlis see Kürlis

Custers, Matheiß 19
Elder in Kaldenkirchen.

Dankers, Jasper 12
Labadist.

Dellonge, Johann Gerhard 57, 180
Notary accredited at the Düsseldorf court.

De Shapdriever, Robert 20
Priest from Kaldenkirchen.

Deventer 63
Cousin of Peter Heinrich Strepers.

Dewees, William 92, 103, 108f., 165
Member of a prominent Germantown family of Dutch origin (De Wies) with the Anglicized name "Dewees" whose American roots were outside Germantown.

Dickinson, John (1732-1808) 123, 126f., 130, 132, 135, 137, 151, 174, 184
Politician and essayist. In his "Letters from a Farmer to the Inhabitants of the British Colonies" written in 1767 he denounced the British tax policy for the American colonies. Although initially in favor of a compromise with Britain, he later supported the Revolution. He served in the Revolutionary Army and wrote the first draft of the Articles of Confederation which established the United States of America initially as a loose confederation of states. He also played a major role in the discussion of the Federal Constitution of 1787. From 1781 to 1782 he was President of the State of Delaware, from 1782 to 1785 Governor of Pennsylvania.

Doors, Agnes 21
Wife of Theiß Doors, see Doors/Theißen family tree.

Doors, Anna 17f., 19f,. 35, 38, 49
See the Strepers and Theißen family trees.
Doors, Margaritha 21
See Doors/Theißen family tree.
Doors, Reiner, see Theißen, Reiner
Doors, Theiß 17, 20f.
See Doors/Theißen family tree.
Dürselen 12
Dürselen, Florens Petrus 58, 160, 163
Son of Albertus Dürselen, preacher in Hörstgen/
Moers and of Maria Magdalena Mickenschreiber,
see Dürselen family tree.
Ehrenzeller 151, 165, 167
Probably Jacob Ehrenzeller, naturalized on April
10, 1757; lived on Fourth Street in Philadelphia.
Efferie 81, 87
Passenger on the Roebuck.
Eling 77, 87
Mr. Eling.
Elizabeth I (1533-1603) 70
Queen of England, 1558-1603.
Ellen, see Allen
Eller, Elias (1690-1750) 176f.
Head of the Ellerian sect named after him, from
(Wuppertal-)Ronsdorf.
Ellertz, see Eling
Elliu, Allew (?) 114
Eppele 118, 120, 165f.
Probably innkeeper. A certain John George
Eppely was naturalized on April 10, 1760. Wil-
helm Apple, 29 years old, landed in Philadel-
phia on September 19, 1743, and took his oath
of allegiance as Wilhelm Apbel on September
20, 1743.
Erkens (Erckes, Erckens), Heinrich 156
1767-1772 Burgomaster of Kaldenkirchen.
Eschmitt, see Ashmead
von der Euwen, Agneta 109
Daughter of Sibilla Agneta Moll, married in the
Reformed Church of Schwanenberg to Johann
Maximilian Kremers, granddaughter of Johannes Moll and his wife Gertrud Königs and great-
granddaughter of Anna Strepers (christened July
16, 1679, married April 14, 1716, at the Reformed Church in Kaldenkirchen to Lambert Moll
of Millich, d. 1749).
Eylert, Adolph 19
Reformed Minister in Kaldenkirchen.
Fairman, Thomas 28

Chief Surveyor of William Penn.
Falasch, see Vanlaschet
Feer, John 123, 126, 134
Leases and buys land from Herbergs.
Filasch, see Vanlaschet
Fleischawers, Rutger 19
Juror in Kaldenkirchen.
Franken, Johann 41
Burgomaster of Kaldenkirchen.
Franklin, Benjamin (1706-1790) 131, 177, 168
Politician, scientist, author and printer. Through
the magazines he published, such as the *Penn-
sylvania Gazette* after 1729, Franklin had con-
siderable influence on the development of the
press in North America. From 1775 on, Franklin
actively supported the independence of the
North American colonies from the British mother
country. He was among the signatories of the
Declaration of Independence of 1776. From
1776 to 1785 he was Ambassador in Paris. Apart
from his political and publishing work, he was
also active in the sciences, among other things
he developed the lightning rod in 1752.
Frederick II (1712-1786) 55, 177, 184
King of Prussia, 1740-1786.
Fuchs, Fucks, Fox 126, 133f.
Also: Fuchs, Fucks, Johan Jürg.
Furley, Benjamin 11-13, 21, 25, 35
Rotterdam merchant and agent of William Penn.
Galloway, John 182
Galloway, Joseph (1731-1803) 109, 111, 118
Lawyer and Loyalist politician, member of the
Quaker Party. From 1756 to 1776 member of
the Pennsylvania Assembly, its President from
1766 to 1775. After Philadelphia had fallen to
the Continental Army of the American insurgents,
Galloway retired to England in 1778.
Gastes Maria 18
Wife of Johann Lucken, see Lucken family tree.
Gaunt, John of (1340-1399) 70
Fourth son of Edward III of England, Duke of
Lancaster. Never king himself, he was de facto
ruler of England after the death of the Prince of
Wales in his senile father's place and later for
his underage nephew Richard II. John of Gaunt
is considered the founder of the House of Lan-
caster.
Gelissen, Johann 109
Receives a letter from Herbergs.

George III of Hanover (1738-1820) 70f., 118, 137
King of England 1760-1820.

Goodson, John 33
Member of the Board of Property.

Granby, Marquess of[1] (1721-1770) 72
John Manners, Fourth Earl of Rutland, Baronet of Belvoir and Marquess of Granby. British military leader who fought on the continent in the Seven Years' War under Ferdinand of Brunswick/ Braunschweig.

Grant, Lawrence Alexander 49
Sailor, witness.

Griffith, Thomas 50
Signatory of James Logan's warrant.

Grothaus, Jan 95
Brother-in-law of Wighard Miller. Naturalized in Philadelphia Co. late in 1740. Member of the Church Council (elder) of the Lutheran congregation in Germantown 1762-1765. One of the spokesmen of the faction supported by H. M. Mühlenberg and the Lutheran ministry of Pennsylvania in the intra-church conflict that was taken to court (1762 ff.).

Grothaus, Herman 95
Father of Jan Grothaus. Inscription on the gravestone in the cemetery of St. Michael's Lutheran Church, Germantown: Harman Grothaus, born in the year 1670 and died 27th October.

Haas, Adam (1719-1781) 121, 166f.
Haas came to Germantown in 1748 and was naturalized in 1764. In 1761 he took over the "White Horse Tavern" on the road from Philadelphia to Germantown from John Theobaldt Endt. He was innkeeper there until his death in 1781.

Hadernach, Johann Konrad 135, 140
According to the journal later called himself Hoffmann; godfather at the christening of Anna Voss on May 4, 1710 at the Reformed Church at Waldniel (parents: Peter Voss, christened May 16, 1674 at the Reformed Church in Waldniel, married Maria Neukirchen, christened at the Reformed Church in Waldniel); probably related to Johannes Herbergs, see the Herbergs and Voss family trees.

Hamboch, Arnold 156, 182
(born around 1663) 1684-1728 minister at the Reformed Church in Kaldenkirchen. Wrote the family genealogy for Peter Heinrich Strepers on March 27, 1764.

Hartwichs 61
Mrs. Hartwichs, contact in Duisburg (?).

Hasenclever, Franz Caspar (1731-1780) 99, 101, 108-110, 179, 182
Merchant, cousin of Peter Hasenclever. In 1763/ 64 a major force in recruiting craftsmen from the Berg country for his cousin's ironworks in New Jersey. He traveled to North America in person in April 1764. In 1771 he was a member of the German Society in Philadelphia. Franz Caspar Hasenclever died in Philadelphia.

Hasenclever, Peter (1716-1793) 100, 101, 111, 113-118, 130-132, 141, 148f., 152, 155, 160, 164f., 168, 173, 176, 179f.
Merchant and entrepreneur. After several positions in the iron and textile industries which took him to various countries in western Europe, in 1763 he entered into cooperation with Andrew Seton and Charles Croft in London to promote, among other things, the production of iron in North America. Helped by his cousin Franz Caspar Hasenclever, Peter, who was born in Remscheid, succeeded in recruiting more than 500 people from the Berg country and the Palatinate for his new Jersey ironworks. After his American venture had gone bankrupt, Hasenclever returned to Germany in the 1770s and ran a textile manufacturing business in Silesia until his death.

Haslang, Franz Sigismund (1740-1803), 92, 98

Heijmans, Maria Agneta 184
Wife of Peter Heinrich Strepers, see Strepers family tree.

Heiseler, Peter 186
Citizen of Philadelphia, signatory of the inventory of Johannes Herbergs' estate.

Helbart, Jürg 126, 133
Owner of a part of Jan Strepers' land.

Hemmelten 87
Mate on the Roebuck.

Henry 87
Sailor on the Roebuck.

Herbergs, Johannes 11f., 14, 38, 45, 49f., 55, 57f., 176-180, 182, 184, 186
See Herbergs family tree.

Hermans, Peter 19
Juror in Kaldenkirchen.

Hertel, Johann Wilhelm 57
Notary accredited at the Düsseldorf court.

Hill, Giert 128
  Prostitute in Philadelphia. On July 29, 1765, "Der Wöchentliche Philadelphische Staatsbote" ran the following report: On Wednesday last, the bordello of famous Käte Hill, on Society Hill, was invaded by the self-righteous mob and all of her valuable belongings destroyed."

Hill, Richard (d. 1762) 18, 43, 50f., 57, 58, 104, 110, 118, 125, 127, 133, 178, 184
  Member of the reputable Hill family of Philadelphia. Married on February 2, 1720/21, to Deborah Moore (parents Mordechai Moore and his wife Deborah Lloyd), b. June 2, 1705, d. December 17, 1757, in Madeira. On June 26, 1749, Richard and Samuel Preston Moore sold a lot on Sassafras Street in Philadelphia to the local Reformed congregation for £150 sterling.

Hillsborough. Lord 186
  Secretary of State for the British colonies in North America.

Hinßen, Aegidius 19
  Rector of the Catholic congregation in Kaldenkirchen.

Hodd 87
  Mate on the Roebuck.

Hoffman, John William (d. 1775) 109, 164
  Having arrived in America in 1741, Hoffman was one of the founders of the German Society in Philadelphia and its first secretary (1764-1771). The sugar refiner was a well-regarded member of the Reformed Church on Race Street. His nephew was the merchant Leonhard Jacoby who, on behalf of the German Society, advanced the money for Johannes Herbergs' funeral.

Hollender 12

Hollender, Bernhardus (1706-1790) 55, 57, 159f., 163, 178, 180
  Merchant from Waldniel, see Hollender family tree.

Hollender, Johann 63
  See Hollender family tree.

Holmes, Theodore 33
  Chief Surveyor for Pennsylvania.

Hope, Isaac 177f.
  Merchant in Rotterdam.

Hope, Zachariah 177f.
  Merchant in Rotterdam.

Höpkins 126
  Court witness.

Hudt, Caspar 44

Hüsges, v. Hüskes

Hüskes, Gerhardus 58
  See Hüskes family tree.

Hüskes, Joachim 21
  See Hüskes family tree.

Hüskes, Johann Leonhard 58
  See Hüskes family tree.

Hüskes, Peter 58
  See Hüskes family tree.

Hüskes, cousin 63
  Possibly: 1. Johann Leonhard Hüskes, christened October 31, 1734; 2. Diederich Hüskes, christened March, 18, 1736, or 3. Gerhard Hüskes, christened March 2, 1738 (parents: Matthias Hüskes and his wife Agnes Strepers), see Strepers and Hüskes family tree.

Hyll see Hill

Isacks, Derijck 21
  Bridegroom at the so-called Quaker Wedding.

Jacoby, Leonhard 186
  Born in Krefeld, member of the German Society of Pennsylvania.

Jan van Gan, see Gaunt, John of

Jansen 164, 166

Jansen or Johnson, Jan (1709-1794) 90, 106, 121, 123, 149, 167, 178
  Largest landowner in Germantown, lived on the Wyck estate. Married to Agnes Klincken, six children. His father, Dirck Jansen, had emigrated from Wickrathberg to Pennsylvania before 1700.

Jansen, son of Jan Jansen 109
  In his will, Jan Jansen/John Johnson named three sons: Anthony, John and Joseph. Cf. Jansen, Jan.

Jansen, Peter 42
  Stepson of the emigrant Wilhelm Strepers.

Jansen, Richard 124

Jansen, Wilhelm 161

Jawert, Balthasar 26
  Member of the Frankfurt Company.

Jonas, see Jones

Jones 121
  Judge.

Jones, Griffith 48-51, 53f., 98, 101
  Son-in-law of Leonhart Arets.

Kämly 171
  Shopkeeper. Johannes Herbergs bought Spanish flies from him.

Kampman, Peter 124, 130f., 136

A certain Peter Kampmann landed in Philadelphia in 1752. A Wilhelm Kampmann, a Daniel Kampmann and a Johann Wilhelm Kampmann are listed in the church records of the Reformed congregation in Germantown in the 1760s.

Charles Theodore of Pfalz-Sulzbach (1724-1799) 186
Prince Elector of the Palatinate and Duke of Jülich-Berg since 1742.

Keith 12
Quaker, traveled with Penn to the Lower Rhine.

Kemler Johannes 26
Member of the Frankfurt Company.

Kenniß 67

Kernen, Catharina 174
Did the laundry for Johannes Herbergs.

Kerschner 95
Second husband of Elizabeth Arets (parents: Leonhard Arets and his wife Katharina Strepers); stepfather of Wilhelm Strepers, see Arets family tree.

Kesser, Jan Jürg 132
Landowner in Bucks Co.

Kipshoven, John 33
Takes a letter to Kaldenkirchen in 1686.

Kläuser, Peter 99
Probably identical with Peter Kläuser who in 1764 was reported to the Jülich-Berg government in Düsseldorf as wishing to move to New England and build workshops and ironworks there. The judge of the district of Bornefeld was instructed that emigration was forbidden and that Kläuser should be threatened with confiscation of his assets and imprisonment.

Klincken, Jan 19
Elder in Kaldenkirchen.

Knapp 186
Vice Chancellor of the Duchy of Berg.

Knevels, Anna Maria 55
See Knevels family tree.

Königs 12, 62, 160, 163
Possibly: Henricus Königs married Anna Katharina Moll (parents: Lambert Moll married to Anna Strepers, daughter of Jan Strepers on April 14, 1716), see Königs family tree.

Königs, Gertrud 57
See Königs family tree.

Königs, Henricus 57
See Königs family tree.

Kreppen, see Kripner

Kripner, Paul 101f., 104, 106-110, 112f., 128, 135, 143, 179, 184
Brother-in-law of Clas and Henrik van Acken; married their sister Elisabeth. Mentioned in 1764 in the list of Germantown inhabitants.

Kronenbroekers, Peter 19
Juror in Kaldenkirchen.

Küffer, Johann 126

Kulp, John 43
Took a letter to Kaldenkirchen.

Kunders, Thönis 18, 28, 34, 42, 47f.
1683 emigrant.

Kürlis, Henrich 17, 20f.
See Kürlis family tree.

Kürlis Metgen 17, 30, 49, 53
See van Acken and Strepers family trees.

Kürlis, Peter (b. 1652) 17f., 21, 28, 32, 34, 47f., 84, 100
Peter Kürlis from Waldniel was among the first emigrants in 1683 and was related to J. Herbergs and P.H. Strepers, see Kürlis and Doors family trees.

Kurtz, Ernst (1701-1766) 88, 90f., 94, 98, 101, 123, 129, 131, 138, 149, 151, 165, 176, 178
Contact between Johannes Herbergs and Kurtz was probably made on recommendation of Johann Caspar Rübel. Kurtz became a member of the German Society of Pennsylvania in 1765.

Kurtz, Peter 91, 98, 122f., 133, 151, 165-67, 173
Son of Ernst Kurtz.

Küsters, Paul 18, 32, 44
Brother-in-law of Jan Strepers, traveled to America in 1691/93.

Lade, Jan 19
Elder in Kaldenkirchen.

Lamar, Thomas 177f.
Brother-in-law of Samuel Preston Moore.

Lang, Jan 126

Lang, Ludwig 126

Lansche, H. 174
Painter (?) from Düsseldorf.

van Laschet see Laschet

Laschet, Christian van/von (b. around 1718) 90, 100, 138, 166, 176
Shopkeeper in Germantown. Arrived in Philadelphia in 1736 with his father Johann Jacob van Laschet and his brother Johann Peter.

Laschet, Hermann 90, 176

Lived in Krefeld.

Lauffs 12

Lauffs, Agneta 163
Niece of Johannes Herbergs, possibly: daughter of minister Johannes Lauffs from Rheydt, see Strepers family tree.

Lawrence, John 120
1765-1766 Mayor of Philadelphia.

Lawrence, Thomas 49
Justice of the Peace in Philadelphia.

Le Bruin, Johann 26
Member of the Frankfurt Company.

Lehmann, Christian (1714-1774) 106f., 124, 136, 138, 151, 153, 163, 166f.
Prominent member of a family from Saxony who joined the Moravian Brothers. Naturalized mid-April 1743, he refused to take the oath of allegiance for reasons of conscience. He lived in Germantown; owner of a gardener's shop, skilled cartographer and surveyor for Philadelphia County. A notary in later years, Lehman (like Christoph Scheibler) helped many German-speaking immigrants in drafting, translating, researching or transmitting wills, marriage certificates, deeds of transfer of house ownership as well as with the assertion of old legal titles. His knowledge and reliability earned him a good reputation and he was a respected—and for many Germans indispensable—authority on legal matters in the 1760s. In 1761 he surveyed land for the Germantown Lutheran congregation, and in the intra-church quarrel (1762ff.) he represented the faction supported by H.M. Mühlenberg and the Lutheran ministry.

Lenssen, Jan see Lentzen, Johann

Lenssen, Leberecht 184
Author of the Lenssen family chronicle 1877.

Lentzen, Johann 22, 28, 30, 32, 33-38, 42, 48, 53f., 100, 103
In June 1683 Lentzen and Jan Strepers concluded one of the first contracts of lease in Germantown. Jan Strepers leased 50 acres to Lentzen and lent him a linen loom with three combs for two years. In return, Lentzen was to teach the art of weaving to Strepers' son Leonhard. To this end, Leonhard was sworn to faithfully serve Lentzen by weaving. John Lentzen became "Fence surveyor" in 1704.

von Loeffening, Jan 36f.

Agent of Jan Strepers.

Löhman see Lehmann

Logan, James (1674-1751) 18, 43, 47, 49-50, 53f., 57, 91f., 94f., 98, 102, 108, 122, 125, 128, 131f., 152, 162, 174, 178, 180
Statesman and lawyer. James Logan came from a Scots family. In 1699 he became William Penn's secretary and in the same year sailed with him to the colony of Pennsylvania. As a confidant of the Penn family, he rose to the highest government and judiciary offices there. Among others, he held the office of Secretary of the Province, became Mayor of Philadelphia and was nominated Justice of the Supreme Court. Apart from his official duties, he was a successful investor in land and built up a large private library (Loganian Library). After retiring from public offices in 1747, he devoted himself to scientific and botanical studies.

Logan, James jun. (1728-1803) 101, 104f., 108, 133f.
James Logan's younger son, administrator of the Loganian Library.

Logan, Samuel 133-137

Logan, William (1718-1776) 96, 102f., 105, 107f., 111, 113, 117f., 121, 126, 131, 133-135, 137, 151, 178
James Logan's eldest son. Educated in England, he assumed various public offices in Pennsylvania. From 1747 until his death, he held a seat on the Pennsylvania Council. In 1756 he voted against declaring war against the Delaware Indians.

Lohman see Lehman

Lucken, Johann 18, 28, 42
1683 emigrant, see Lucken family tree.

Lucken, Maria 33, 42-44, 48
See Strepers family tree.

Lucken, Wilhelm 33
See Lucken family tree.

Lukens, John 99, 126
Quaker, member of a large and politically very active family who arrived in Pennsylvania with the first German emigrants to America in 1683, lead by Jan Lucken, and settled in Germantown.

Mackinet, Sarah (d. 1795) 165, 167
Sarah Shoemaker, landlady in Germantown. Daughter of Abraham Shoemaker and Amelia Levering. Her first marriage was to Daniel

Pastorius, Franz Daniel Pastorius' grandson. Her second husband was the saddler Daniel Mackinet, and her third marriage was to Andrew Heath. At her inn "Sadler's Arms", also called "Green Tree Tavern", the first meeting of the Germantown Assembly was held in 1760.

Mäerl see Matter

Magnets see Mackinet

Mailan, Maylan 68, 73f., 154, 158f., 161f., 171
Accountant in London.

Mantel, Paulus 79
Passenger on the Roebuck.

Mary Tudor (1516-1558) 70
Queen of England 1553-1558.

Markham, William 33
Member of the Board of Property.

van Mastricht, Gerhard 26
Member of the Frankfurt Company, born in Wesel.

Matter, Joseph 96, 102f., 108f., 111-113, 118, 133, 149, 164
Also: Joseph Matters; probably: Joseph Mather, miller.

Mayer 126
Court witness.

Mecklenburg-Strelitz, George August of (1748-1785) 70
Son of Duke Charles I of Mecklenburg-Strelitz, brother of the Queen of England Charlotte Sophie. George August was in the service of the Emperor of Austria in Hungary.

Mecklenburg-Strelitz, Charlotte Sophie of (1744-1785) 70
Queen of England, married to George III of Hanover since 1761.

Metschelfeld, Caspar 87, 153
Emigrated to America from Seyden/Seiden. On board of the Roebuck in 1764.

Mevissen, Hermann 41
Burgomaster of Kaldenkirchen.

Mickenschreiber 12

Mickenschreiber, Johann 63, 68
See Mickenschreiber family tree.

Mickenschreiber, Matthias 54-56
See Mickenschreiber family tree.

Mickenschreiber, Peter Heinrich (b.1730) 57, 62, 155f., 160, 163, 171, 178, 180
Merchant in Kaldenkirchen, third child of Matthias Mickenschreiber from Odenkirchen and his

wife Maria Strepers (daughter of Henrik Strepers and Elisabeth Olmis, granddaughter of Jan Strepers and Anna Doors, widowed Kürlis), see Mickenschreiber family tree.

Miller, Henrich (1702-1782) 151, 174
Printer in Philadelphia.

Miller, Peter (d. 1794) 96, 98, 101, 106, 108, 152, 162
Notary and lawyer. A native of Neu-Saarweden near Weilburg, he was Vice President of the German Society of Pennsylvania until 1772, then Justice of the Peace for the City and County of Philadelphia. For several years, he was the Registrar for German immigrants.

Miller, Wighard (1716/17-1795) 95, 108f.
Member of the Church Council of the Lutheran congregation in Germantown; possibly son-in-law of the Lutheran minister Anton Jacob Henkel. Wighard Miller is mentioned in 1768 as a landowner in Sommerhausen/Germantown.

Möllenberg see Mühlenberg

Moll 12

Moll, Anna Catharina 58
See Strepers family tree.

Moll, Johannes 57, 163
Cousin of Strepers and Herbergs, see Strepers family tree.

Moll, Lambert 50, 53, 55
See Strepers family tree.

Moore, Charles 186
Brother of Samuel Preston Moore.

Moore, Dr. Samuel Preston (1710-1785) 45, 49f., 57, 98, 108, 118-121, 123, 127f., 131, 133-136, 178, 180, 184, 186
A physician by training, Samuel Presten Moore held various public offices in Pennsylvania. For example, he was a member of the Loan Office, Treasurer of the Province 1754-1768 and Treasurer of the Pennsylvania Hospital in 1768/69.

Morris, Robert (1735-1806) 127, 133
Philadelphia, provided financial backing for the American Revolution.

Moeses 71
Ship broker in London.

Mossis 79
Probably Moses, ship's boy on the Roebuck 1764.

Mühlenberg, Heinrich Melchior (1711-1787) 138, 172

Lutheran minister from Einbeck and most prominent spiritual leader of German Lutherans in Pennsylvania in the 18th century. Founder of the German Lutheran Church in America.

Müller, Peter see Miller, Peter

Müller, W. 141, 149f., 164, 173
Possibly William Miller. Married Katherine, a christening registered in 1761 at the First Presbyterian Church/Philadelphia.

Mumm, Peter Arnold (d. 1797) 67
Came from the Mumm family of Solingen who played an important part in industry and provided several burgomasters. Mumm was engaged to Sarah Eller, daughter of Elias Eller from Ronsdorf. However, Sarah Eller was forced to marry a cousin.

Naglee see Neglee

Nägly see Neglee

Neglee/Negle/Negele/Negelie, John/Johannes 136, 138
Johannes Negelie landed in Philadelphia in 1738.

Neiss see Nice

Neuss see Nice

Nice/Neuss, Johann (d. 1794) 125, 130, 133
Probably a member of the Schwenckfelder religious group, the Nice family, originally called te Neues, emigrated to Pennsylvania from the Mönchengladbach area.

Nice/Neuss, Vinard 100, 102
Innkeeper in Germantown. Son of the Mennonite silversmith Jan de Neuss originally from Mönchengladbach.

Noll, Martin 104, 123f.
Innkeeper in Philadelphia. Naturalized in Philadelphia in mid-April 1761. 1765 member of the German Society of Pennsylvania.

Norris, Isaac 43, 51
Commissioner of Property.

Nübel 130f.
Mr. Nübel. One of the representatives of the faction supported by H. M. Mühlenberg and the Lutheran ministry of Pennsylvania in the intrachurch conflict that was taken to court (1762 ff.).

Ogden, David (?) 138, 140
Lawyer in New Jersey.

Oldmixon, John 14
Author of a report on Pennsylvania.

Olmis, Elisabeth 50, 54

See Strepers family tree.

op den Graeff, Abraham Isaaks 22, 28, 33
One of the 1683 emigrants, see op den Graeff family tree.

op den Graeff, Dirk Isaaks 18, 28, 33
One of the 1683 emigrants, see op den Graeff family tree.

op den Graeff, Hermann Isaaks 12, 18, 28, 33, 37
One of the 1683 emigrants, see op den Graeff family tree.

Orius, John Herman (?) 101
Really John Orrs, owner of part of the Strepers' tract in Bucks County.

Parker, James 141f., 148, 160, 179f., 182, 184
James Parker, lawyer in Perth Amboy.

Pastorius, Franciscus Daniel (1651-1719/1720) 14, 18, 22, 26, 28, 32, 35, 45, 95
Trained as a lawyer, belonged to Pietist circles in Frankfurt/Main from the 1760s on. He traveled to Pennsylvania in 1683, a few months before the Krefeld emigrant families, on instructions from the Frankfurt Company in order to prepare a settlement on the land bought from William Penn. Pastorius was one of the founders of Germantown and one of its first mayors. He was a member of the Assembly of Pennsylvania from 1687 to 1691 and head of the Quaker School in Philadelphia. Married to Anna Klostermann from Mülheim/Ruhr since 1688.

Penn, John (1729-1795) 118
Grandson of William Penn, son of Richard Penn. Governor of the colony of Pennsylvania 1763-1771 and 1773-1776.

Penn, Richard (1705-1771) 118, 131, 136
Son of William Penn. Proprietor of the colony of Pennsylvania, together with his brother Thomas.

Penn, Thomas 180
Son of William Penn.

Penn, William (1644-1718) 11-13, 17, 21, 25-28, 35, 37f., 47, 48f., 50, 98f., 118, 122, 125, 163, 178
Quaker and founder of Pennsylvania. From inherited debts of the English crown to his family, Penn bought land in North America. There he created a sanctuary-place of refuge for Quakers and other sects where they could not only acquire land on favorable terms but also were guaranteed freedom of worship. In 1682 he

founded Philadelphia. Penn was born in England and died there.

Pennington, Edward 120, 134f.
Merchant and sugar producer from Philadelphia. Around 1760 he built a large house at the northwest corner of Crown and Race Street.

Peters, William 126, 137
Probably William Peters, Secretary of Thomas Penn's Land Office, removed from office in 1765 because of incompetence and corruption.

Petersen, Johann Wilhelm 26
Member of the Frankfurt Company.

Pinner or **Pinnen**, Hermann 156
Burgomaster of Kaldenkirchen 1768-1773.

Plass 126, 167
Court witness.

Plumstead 114-117
In the journal: Mr. Bloemstäet. Council Member William Plumstead of Philadelphia died in 1765.

Pollmann, Johann Wilhelm 115, 117, 123f., 131, 151, 165-167
Pollmann, Peter Hasenclever's accountant.

Poolmann see Pollmann

Porcket 166
Court witness.

Quack 157, 161
Possibly Quirinus Quack.

Remkes, Govert 25
Manufacturer from Krefeld, bought land from William Penn in 1682.

Remsen, Peter 88
Merchant on Long Island.

Rennor 87
The Rennor sisters from Heidelberg, passengers on the Roebuck.

Ringels, Elisabeth 58
See Strepers family tree.

Ringels, Johann Christoph 56, 55, 58
See Strepers family tree.

Riche, Thomas 180, 184
Merchant from Philadelphia.

Ross, John or George 98f., 109, 122, 127, 130, 131, 134f., 148, 150, 155, 167, 172f.
Lawyer for S.P. Moore.

Rübel, Johann Caspar (1719-1797) 87f., 114f., 117, 132, 165, 176
A native of Solingen, Rübel was preacher at the German Church in Philadelphia, from 1756 to 1785 minister in Flatbush, Long Island. After his removal from office, he practiced as a naturopath.

Salmon 159
Ferryman (?).

Sauer/Saur, Christoph 121
1. (1693-1758) Christoph Saur the Elder came from Laasphe and founded a book printing shop in Germantown in 1738. Apart from the publication of a German newspaper and a German calendar, his most significant undertaking was the printing of the first Bible on the American continent in 1743. His Lutheran Bible appeared some years before the first English printings. Through his publishing activities, he became the voice of the Germans in Pennsylvania.
2. His son Christoph Saur the Younger (1721-1784) continued his father's work. Under his ownership, the printing shop became the biggest in the British North American colonies.

Scheckten 87
Sailor on the Roebuck.

Scheibler, Christoph 151, 159, 162, 165, 167
Innkeeper in Philadelphia.

Scherckens, Nieles 19
Owner of land in the Heiderfeld, Kaldenkirchen.

Schidt, Peter 170
Buys goods from Johannes Herbergs.

Schirmer, Gottfried 20
Minister in Kaldenkirchen.

Schlöter see Schlotter

Schlotter, Martin 95
Naturalized on April 10, 1765, member of the Church Council (Presiding Elder) of the Lutheran congregation in Germantown; member of the faction supported by H.M. Mühlenberg and the Lutheran ministry of Pennsylvania in the intrachurch conflict that was taken to court (1762 ff.).

Schlüter, Peter 12
Labadist, born in Wesel.

Schmal (?) 129

Schmidt, Michael 108
Possibly: Michael Schmidt married Barbara Kuenzli on August 20, 1754, at the Germantown Reformed Church of Pennsylvania.

Schmit 130, 132
Chief Justice from New Jersey.

Schneck 119, 130
Carpenter. Around the time of Herbergs' journal Johann Georg Schneck, David Schneck and

Jakob Schneck appear in Pennsylvanian sources.

Schneider, Christian 90f., 96, 125, 130, 173
Immigrated around 1754 at the latest, Schneider was naturalized in 1761. 1763 Inspector of the German Society of Pennsylvania. As a participant in the American Revolution, promoted to the rank of captain in 1776. From 1778 to 1781 he held the office of County Assessor for Philadelphia County.

Schons see Jones

Schreiner, Nikolaus 141f., 165f.
Immigrant from Saarbrücken, citizen of Philadelphia. Since 1760 married to Anna Maria Gampert.

Schu see Chew

Schumacher, Johann 126
Possibly: Johannes Schumacher and Elisabeth have Johann Conrad, born November 2, 1760, christened in Germantown.

Schütz, Johann Jacob 26
Member of the Frankfurt Company.

Sellen, Heinrich 35-37, 41, 44, 46, 53, 121
Heinrich Sellen arrived in Germantown from Krefeld between 1685 and 1690. Jan Strepers appointed him trustee for his land in Pennsylvania. Sellen was naturalized in 1709.

Sem 87
Sailor on the Roebuck.

Sengeissen, Ludwig 126, 129
Probably Ludwig Sengeissen from the Palatinate. Sworn to the Constitution in 1749.

Shippen, Dr. William (1729-1806) 131, 140
Lawyer. Member of an influential Presbyterian family in Philadelphia; began his professional career as an Admirality Court Judge in Philadelphia. In 1765 he was Secretary of the Pennsylvania Supreme Court. After the Revolution he held various judicial offices at the Philadelphia County Court and the Pennsylvania Supreme Court, where he became Chief Justice in 1799.

Sieben, Adelgunde 11, 57
See Herbergs and Strepers family trees.

Sieben, Maria 50
See Strepers family tree.

Sieben, Peter (1709-1775) 55-57, 98, 109, 176, 180
Schoolmaster in Kaldenkirchen and Ronsdorf, married on September 28, 1732, in the Reformed Church in Kaldenkirchen to Anna Maria Knevels; brother-in-law of Johannes Bolckhaus and Johannes Herbergs, whose wife Adelheid Sieben was Peter Sieben's youngest sister.

Sieben, Wilhelm 44f., 49f., 53-55
Schoolmaster in Kaldenkirchen, see Sieben family tree.

Siegman, Bernhard 125f.
Bernhard Siegman; landed with his father Johannes Sighman and his brothers Hans Georg and Johannes in Philadelphia in 1738.

Simons 156

Simons, Arnold 17
See Simons family tree.

Simons, Jan 18, 28, 32f.
One of the 1683 emigrants, see Jan Simons family tree.

Simons, Peter 18
Son of Jan Simons and Maria Lucken, see Jan Simons family tree.

Sipman, Dirk 25f., 28, 30, 32
Krefeld merchant, bought land from William Penn in 1682.

Smith, Samuel 71, 87
Captain of the Roebuck 1764.

Smyth, C. 18
Judge.

Souplis, Andreas 18
Lessee of Wilhelm Strepers in Pennsylvania in 1686.

Spark 98
Captain.

Stapel, Peter 68, 163, 171
Merchant in London.

Stapelfeldt 74
Landlady in London.

Stedman, Alexander 127
Lawyer in Philadelphia.

Stelwagen, Valentin 98, 150
In 1763 elder on the Church Council of the Reformed congregation in Germantown. In 1765 member of the German Society of Pennsylvania.

Stephenson, William 68, 182
In 1764 Mayor of London.

Sterle see Stirling

Stevens, John (approx. 1682-1730) 113, 182
Stevens arrived in New York at the age of 17. In 1714 he moved to Perth Amboy with his family.

Stevens, John (1716-1792) 113-115, 124, 132
Brother of Richard Stevens, merchant trading

with the West Indies and Madeira, moved to New York in April 1752. In 1751 for the first time member of the General Assembly of New Jersey in Perth Amboy, until 1762 member of the Lower House of the Assembly, in 1762 member of the Governor's Council until fall 1765, 1776-1782 Vice President of the Patriotic Council, 1782 member of the Continental Congress representing New Jersey, 1787 President of the New Jersey State Convention.

Stevens, Richard (1723-1802) 112-128, 130-142, 148f., 151, 160, 164-168, 173, 176f., 179f., 182
By his contemporaries, Stevens is described as short, red-haired and very lively. Frequently traveled the country on real estate business.

Stier 87
Passenger on the Roebuck.

Stillwaggon, John 174
Lived in the Northern Liberties next to Martin Noll. Mentioned on the occasion of a lottery for the extension of the Lutheran Church in Whitemarsh Twp.

Stirling 132
Lord Stirling, commander of a reserve division in Germantown during the War of Independence.

Streeper, Catherine 42, 182
See Wilhelm Strepers' family tree.

Streeper, Dennis/Delis 123, 151
See Wilhelm Strepers' family tree.

Streeper, Jan/John (1688-1741) 42-44, 46, 95, 121f.
Son of Wilhelm Strepers and Maria Lucken, see Wilhelm Strepers' family tree.

Streeper, Leonhard (1686—1727) 42-44, 46-49, 51, 53f., 121
Son of Wilhelm Strepers and Maria Lucken, see Wilhelm Strepers' family tree.

Streeper, Wilhelm (William) 45, 92, 94-96, 103, 107, 111, 118, 121, 124, 136, 166f., 182
Grandson of the emigrant Wilhelm Strepers, see Wilhelm Strepers' family tree.

Strepers, Agnes 17, 57
See Strepers family tree.

Strepers, Anna/Anneken 17, 49f.
See Strepers family tree.

Strepers, Catharina 17, 44, 49f., 53
Daughter of Jan Strepers, see Strepers family tree.

Strepers, Catharina 55
See Strepers family tree.

Strepers, Cornelia Mechtildis 184
Daughter of Peter Heinrich Strepers, see Strepers family tree.

Strepers, Dierich 17, 19f.
See Strepers family tree.

Strepers, Elisabeth 55
See Strepers family tree.

Strepers, Gertrud 17
See Strepers family tree.

Strepers, Hendrik 17, 42f., 46, 49, 134
Son of Jan Strepers, see Strepers family tree.

Strepers, Jan (1638/40-1715) 11f., 17-22, 25-28, 30, 32-38, 41-51, 53-58, 91f., 98-101, 106, 115, 117, 124, 128, 130f., 176, 178, 180, 182
See commentary on the journal and Strepers family tree.

Strepers, Lambert 17, 20, 45
See Strepers family tree.

Strepers, Leonhard (1670-1725) 17, 22, 34, 38, 41f., 46, 48-50, 53-55, 58, 91, 98, 100, 104, 121, 128, 182
Son of Jan Strepers, traveled as a teenager to Pennsylvania with the 13 emigrant families in 1683. Cf. also the contract with Jan Lentzen, who was to teach weaving to Leonhard; see Strepers family tree.

Strepers, Maria, see Lucken, Maria

Strepers, Peter 17
See Strepers family tree.

Strepers, Peter (1705-1725) 134
See Strepers family tree.

Strepers, Peter Heinrich (1736-1781) 11f., 14, 45, 49f., 55, 57f., 62-64, 98f., 107-109, 111-113, 117f., 120, 123, 126, 128, 130f., 133f., 136f., 139-142, 149, 151f., 155f., 159, 163-165, 168, 170-172, 176-180, 182, 184
Johannes Herbergs' traveling companion, see Strepers family tree.

Strepers, Wilhelm (approx. 1644-1717) 17, 20, 22, 28, 32-38, 41-49, 53, 92, 94f., 100, 106, 117, 121, 152, 162, 167, 179, 182
1683 emigrant; cf. commentary on the journal and Wilhelm Strepers' and Strepers family trees.

Taylor, Jacob 43
Chief Surveyor in Pennsylvania.

Tellen 87
Sailor on the Roebuck.

Telner, Jacob 25, 28, 30
Amsterdam merchant, bought land from William Penn in 1682.

Theißen, Abraham 106, 123, 128, 134
See Theißen family tree.

Theißen, Dierich (b.1696) 123
Son of Reiner Theißen, see Theißen family tree.

Theißen, Hermann (b.1663) 17f., 21, 32, 44, 95
Emigrated to Germantown in 1684. He was the brother of Reiner Theißen and Maria Doors, who married Jan Strepers in her second marriage. See Doors/Theißen family tree.

Theißen, Peter (b. 1700) 101, 103, 186
Son of Reiner Theißen; see Reiner Theißen's family tree.

Theißen, Reiner (1658/59-1745) 17f., 20f., 28, 32, 33, 35-37, 41f., 43-49, 51, 53, 55f., 92, 96, 98-101, 104, 106, 109, 121, 128, 178, 186
Brother of Anna Doors and brother-in-law of Jan Strepers. Emigrated to Pennsylvania in 1683. In 1692, 1693, 1694 and 1696 he was elected one of the four burgomasters of Germantown. Apart from holding public offices, he was also active in the Quaker congregation. In 1725 he was elected elder of the Abington Monthly Meeting.

Thielen, Catharina Gertrud 57
Wife of Peter Heinrich Mickenschreiber.

Tilghman, James 123, 126f., 133, 136, 184
Made Secretary of the Land Office of Thomas Penn in September 1765.

Trautwein, Johann Wilhelm 172
Landed in Philadelphia September 19, 1752, coming from Rotterdam.

Trippel 87
Passenger from Switzerland on the Roebuck 1764.

Tüffers, Beliken 18, 20
Wife of the Kaldenkirchen Wilhelm Strepers who did not emigrate.

Tunes, Abraham 28, 34
1683 emigrant.

Turner 111
Mr. Turner owned parts of Jan Strepers' land.

Ulrich 91
Probably Philip Ulrich, "Superintendent" of the German Society of Philadelphia. Arrived in Philadelphia on October 14, 1731 together with Christian Lehman, coming from Rotterdam.

Vanpoole/Van Phull, William 186
Citizen of Philadelphia, signatory of the inventory of Johannes Herbergs' estate.

Verhoeff, Lambert 177
From Ronsdorf, denounced Herbergs.

Verhoeff, Leonhard 119
Member of the Ronsdorf congregation, originally a captain from Amsterdam. From 1760 on, Verhoeff belonged to a section within the congregation that had split away from the line taken by Johann Bolckhaus, successor of Elias Eller.

Vijten, Nolcken 21
Bride at the so-called Quaker wedding.

Vile, Richard 49
Sailor, witness.

van de Walle, Jacobus 26
Member of the Frankfurt Company; originally from Wesel.

Waln, Nicholas 184
Lawyer in Philadelphia.

Weidman/Weydman 151, 167
Landlord of the "Rising Sun".

Weiss, Ludwig (1717-1796) 45, 92, 94, 96-98, 104f., 108, 136, 140, 152, 159, 162, 178
Member of the Moravian Brethren, immigrated in 1755; lawyer; member of the committee of the German Society of Philadelphia in 1764 and its president from 1775[?] to 1782, Justice of the Court of Common Pleas and Justice of the Peace for Philadelphia City in 1786, Justice of the Peace for Philadelphia County.

Wenig/Weniger, Adam 96
Possibly Adam Weniger. Arrived in Philadelphia on October 7, 1755.

Willing, Thomas 139
In 1764 Thomas Willing together with Benjamin Franklin, Benjamin Chew and Thomas Galloway stopped the Paxton Boys who had pursued the christianized Moravian Indians as far as Philadelphia. Mayor of Philadelphia, delegate at the Continental Congress and President of the First Bank of the United States.

Wiester see Wüster

Wistar see Wüster

Wülfing, Peter (1701-1776) 88, 129
Reformed minister in Ronsdorf (from 1745 until his removal from office in 1765). Publications: *Ronsdorffischer Catechismus zum Dienst der daselbstigen Jugend* (Düsseldorf, 1756); *Ronsdorfs gerechte Sache wider den General-Synod*

(Wülfing und Johannes Bolckhaus) (Düsseldorf, 1757); *Ronsdorffs silberne Trompeten oder Kirchenbuch*, (Mülheim am Rhein, 1761); *Ronsdorffs Music-Schul* (1762), *Ronsdorffs Göttliches ABC* (1761); *Grund-Glaubenslehre* (1761).

Wüster/Wistar, Daniel 108, 160, 164, 167
Family name anglicized to "Wister" or "Wistar": member of an old Quaker family from Philadelphia with a summer residence in Germantown and contacts and marriage connections to wealthy families of English origin in Philadelphia.

van Wylich, Dr. Thomas 26

Member of the Frankfurt Company, born in Wesel.

Yorke (1724-1792) 63
Sir Joseph Yorke, Baron Dover, English ambassador to The Hague 1760-1780.

Zellen see Sellen

Zengeissen see Sengeissen

Ziegenfuß, Jacob 170
Bought some of the goods Johannes Herbergs had brought from Ronsdorf

Zielikens, Johann 41
Town clerk in Kaldenkirchen

Index of Place Names

Further Reading

German and American Sources Related to Emigration

Glazier, Ira A.; Filby, P. William: Germans to America. Lists of Passengers Ariving at U.S. Ports, 56 Bände. Wilmington DE 1988.

Ham, Hermann van: Quellen zur rheinischen Auswandererforschung in den Staatsarchiven Koblenz und Düsseldorf. Rheinische Vierteljahrsblätter. 1936; 6:295-326.

Ders.: Quellen zur rheinischen Auswandererforschung in den Staatsarchiven Koblenz und Düsseldorf (Nachtrag). Rheinische Viertelsjahrsblätter. 1938; 8:315-332.

Holtmann, Antonius: Glazier/Filby, Germans to America, Bände 1-50 (1988-1996). Fallstricke für Genealogen. Genealogie. 1996; 45 (9/10): 274-280.

Ders.: Fallstricke und kein Ende: Band 54 von Glazier/Filby (Eds.), „Germans to America", Wilmington DE 1996. Ein Abgesang. Genealogie. 1997; 46 (3/4): 507-508.

Hönerlage, Regina; Kurfürst, Claudia; Wahl, Hans-Georg: Auswanderer aus dem Rheinland. Emigranten aus den Regierungsbezirken Aachen, Düsseldorf und Köln, 1816-1834. Düsseldorf 1997 (Veröffentlichungen der Staatlichen Archive des Landes Nordrhein-Westfalen, Reihe C: Quellen und Forschungen, Band 37) CD-ROM.

Landeshauptarchiv Koblenz: Bestand 403 - Inventar des Bestandes Oberpräsidium der Rheinprovinz, Teil 2. o. O., o. J., S. 1026-1028.

Schröder, Henning: Bibliographie zur rheinischen Auswandererforschung. Mitteilungen der Westdeutschen Gesellschaft für Familienkunde. 1985; 32, 33 (1, 4, 2): 17-19, 89-90, 33-37.

Strassburger, Ralph Beaver; Hinke, William John: Pennsylvania German Pioneers. A Publication of the Original Lists of Arrivals in the Port of Philadelphia from 1727 to 1808. Baltimore MD 1980.

Yoder, Don: Rhineland Emigrants. Lists of German Settlers in Colonial America. Baltimore MD 1981.

German Emigration to America
General Information

Bade, Klaus J. (Hg.): Deutsche im Ausland, Fremde in Deutschland. Migration in Geschichte und Gegenwart. München 1992.

Bickelmann, Hartmut: Deutsche Überseeauswanderung in der Weimarer Zeit. Wiesbaden 1980.

Brinck, Andreas: Die deutsche Auswanderungswelle in die britischen Kolonien Nordamerikas um die Mitte des 18 Jahrhunderts. Stuttgart 1993.

Helbich, Wolfgang J.: Alle Menschen sind dort gleich. Die deutsche Amerika-Auswanderung im 19. und 20. Jahrhundert. Düsseldorf 1988.

Hoerder, Dirk; Nagler, Jörg: People in Transit. German Migrations in Comparative Perspective, 1820-1930. Washington DC 1995 (Publications of the German Historical Institute).

Krohn, Heinrich: Und warum habt ihr denn Deutschland verlassen? 300 Jahre Auswanderung nach Amerika. Bergisch-Gladbach 1992.

Marschalck, Peter: Deutsche Überseewanderung im 19. Jahrhundert. Ein Beitrag zur soziologischen Theorie der Bevölkerung. Stuttgart 1973.

Assion, Peter (Hg.): Der große Aufbruch. Studien zur Amerikaauswanderung. Hessische Blätter für Volks- und Kulturforschung Nr. 17, Marburg 1985.

Emigration to America Related to Different Regions

Bartolosch, Thomas A.; Neutsch, Cornelius; Roth, Karl-Jürgen: Vom Westerwald nach Amerika. Auswanderung im 19. Jahrhundert. Hachenburg 1996.

Dies.: Siegerländer und Wittgensteiner in der Neuen Welt. Auswanderung im 18. und 19. Jahrhundert. Siegen 1999.

Becker, Emil: Der Kaldenkirchener Kreis unter den 13 Auswandererfamilien von Krefeld nach Pennsylvanien aus dem Jahre 1683. Heimatbuch Viersen 1983, S. 66-77.

Köppen, Ernst: Vom Rhein zum Delaware. Krefelder gründeten 1683 Germantown. Krefeld 1983.

Fertig, Georg: Lokales Leben, atlantische Welt: Die Entscheidung zur Auswanderung vom Rhein nach Nordamerika im 18. Jahrhundert. Osnabrück 2000.

Goebel, Klaus; Voigt, Günter: Die kleine, mühselige Welt des jungen Hermann Enters. Erinnerungen eines Amerika-Auswanderers an das frühindustrielle Wuppertal. 3. Auflage, Wuppertal 1979.

Macha, Jürgen: "...Ich will nich ueber Ammireka nicht stronsen...". Briefe von Eifel-Auswanderern als sprachhistorische Quelle. In: Nikolay-Panter; Janssen; Herborn (Hg.): Geschichtliche Landeskunde der Rheinlande. Köln 1994. S. 516-533.

Radmacher, Franz-Josef: Briefe aus Missouri. 1834-1836. Nachrichten eines Kundschafters der rheinischen Auswanderer. Meerbusch 2000.

Rotthoff, Guido: Die Auswanderung von Krefeld nach Pennsylvanien im Jahre 1683. Die Heimat. 53/ 1982.

Schmahl, Helmut: Verpflanzt, aber nicht entwurzelt. Die Auswanderung aus Hessen-Darmstadt (Provinz Rheinhessen) nach Wisconsin im 19. Jahrhundert. Frankfurt/ Main 2000.

Travels
General Information

Bausinger; Beyrer; Korff (Hg.): Reisekultur. Von der Pilgerfahrt zum modernen Tourismus. München 1991.

Gräf, Holger T.; Pröve, Ralf: Wege ins Ungewisse. Reisen in der frühen Neuzeit, 1500-1800. Frankfurt/ Main 1997.

Travels and Informations for Emigrants

Bretting, Agnes; Bickelmann, Hartmut: Auswanderungsagenturen und Auswanderungsvereine im 19. und 20. Jahrhundert. Stuttgart 1991.

Bromme, Traugott: Reisen durch die Vereinigten Staaten und Ober-Canada. Baltimore 1834.

De Haas, Carl: Nordamerika, Wisconsin, Calumet. Winke für Auswanderer. 2 Bde. Elberfeld u. Iserlohn 1848-49.

Duden, Gottfried: Bericht über eine Reise nach den westlichen Staaten Nordamerika's und einen mehrjährigen Aufenthalt am Missouri. 2. Auflage, Bonn 1834.

Görisch, Stephan W.: Information zwischen Werbung und Warnung. Die Rolle der Amerikaliteratur in der Auswanderung des 18. und 19. Jahrhunderts. Darmstadt 1991.

Immigration to America

Coan, Peter Morton: Ellis Island. Interviews. In Their Own Words. New York 1997.

Fogleman, Aaron Spencer: Hopeful Journeys. German Immigration, Settlement, and Political Culture in Colonial America, 1717-1775. Philadelphia 1996.

Gellinek, Christian: Those Damn' Dutch. The Beginning of German Immigration in North America during the Thirty Years War. Frankfurt/Main, New York 1996.

Grauman Wolf, Stephanie: As Various as Their Land. The Everyday Lives of Eighteenth Century Americans. New York 1993.

Helbich, Wolfgang J.; Kamphoefner, Walter D.; Sommer, Ulrike (Hg.): Briefe aus Amerika. Deutsche Auswanderer schreiben aus der Neuen Welt, 1830-1930. München 1988.

Moltmann, Günter; Bickelmann, Hartmut: Germans to America: 300 Years of Immigration, 1683 to 1983. Stuttgart 1982.

Reichmann, Eberhard; Rippley, La Vern J; Nagler, Jörg: Emigration and Settlement Patterns of German Communities in North America. Indianapolis IN 1995 (Max Kade German-American Center, Indiana University-Purdue University at Indianapolis and Indiana German Heritage Society, Inc. 8).

Totten, Christine M: Roots in the Rhineland: America's German Heritage in Three Hundred Years of Emigration, 1683-1983. New York 1983.

Trommler, Frank H./ McVeigh Joseph (Ed.): America and the Germans. An Assessment of a Three-Hundred-Year History. 2 Bände. Philadelphia 1985.

Pennsylvania - Philadelphia

Bolles, Albert S.: Pennsylvania - Province and State. A History From 1609 to 1790. Philadelphia 1899.

Pennypacker, Samuel Whitaker: Pennsylvania The Keystone. A Short History. Philadelphia 1914.

Ders.: The Settlement of Germantown Pennsylvania and the Beginning of German Emigration to North America. Philadelphia 1899.

Smith, Billy G.: Life in Early Philadelphia. Documents from the Revolutionary and Early National Periods. Philadelphia 1995.

Snyder, Martin P.: City of Independence. Viwes of Philadelphia Before 1800. New York 1975.

Watson, John F./ Hazard, Willis P.: Annals of Philadelphia and Pennsylvania in the Older Time. Philadelphia 1881.

Germans in Pennsylvania

Garvan, Beatrice B.; Hummel, Charles F.: The Pennsylvania Germans. A Celebration of their Arts 1683-1850. Philadelphia 1982.

Glatfelter, Charles H.: The Pennsylvania Germans. A Brief Account of their Influence on Pennsylvania. Camp Hill 1990 (Pennsylvania History Studies No. 20.).

Grauman Wolf, Stephanie: Urban Village. Population, Community, and Family Structure in Germantown, Pennsylvania, 1683-1800. Princeton 1976.

Hull, William: William Penn and the Dutch Quaker Migration to Pennsylvania. Swathmore 1935 (Reprint Baltimore 1990).

A. Gregg Roeber: Palatines, Liberty, and Property. German Lutherans in Colonial British America. Baltimore 1993.

Sachse, Julius Friedrich: The German Pietists of Provincial Pennsylvania. 3 Volumes, Philadelphia 1895-1900.

Splitter, Wolfgang: Pastors, People, Politics. German Lutherans in Pennsylvania 1740-1790. Trier 1998.

Strassburger, Ralph B.: Pennsylvania German Pioneers, 1727-1808, 3 Volumes. Norristown PA 1934.